ELEPEN
D0585378
INGHAM
DRAWN
ROM THE LIBRAR

BUREAU OF INTERNATIONAL RESEARCH
HARVARD UNIVERSITY AND RADCLIFFE COLLEGE

THE EXCHANGE OF MINORITIES
BULGARIA, GREECE AND TURKEY

·The M Co·

THE MACMILLAN COMPANY
NEW YORK · BOSTON · CHICAGO · DALLAS
ATLANTA · SAN FRANCISCO

MACMILLAN & CO., LIMITED
LONDON · BOMBAY · CALCUTTA
MELBOURNE

THE MACMILLAN COMPANY
OF CANADA, LIMITED
TORONTO

THE EXCHANGE OF MINORITIES BULGARIA, GREECE AND TURKEY

By

STEPHEN P. LADAS

NEW YORK

THE MACMILLAN COMPANY

1932

All rights reserved, including the right of reproduction in whole or in part in any form.

LC32008566
6001634714

Copyright, 1932,
By THE BUREAU OF INTERNATIONAL RESEARCH
HARVARD UNIVERSITY AND RADCLIFFE COLLEGE

The Bureau of International Research has aided the author in carrying on research and in publishing the results. The Bureau assumes no responsibility for the statements or views expressed.

Set up and printed. Published March, 1932.

V

Printed in the United States of America by
J. J. LITTLE AND IVES COMPANY, NEW YORK

TO
CHRISTINE LADAS

PREFACE

This volume prepared and published under the auspices of the Bureau of International Research of Harvard University and Radcliffe College is an attempt to describe and appraise the exchange of minority populations which has taken place from 1920 to 1930 in Bulgaria, Greece and Turkey. It is the result of a study carried out in the last four years in the course of which the author has twice visited the countries concerned collecting material and information and investigating the work performed by the Commissions set up under the Conventions entered into by the above countries and by the interested governments.

Although this volume went to press in September 1931, the author has not taken full account of developments after the end of 1930. At that time the Mixed Commissions constituted under the Greco-Bulgarian Convention of Neuilly and the Greco-Turkish Convention of Lausanne had nearly completed their labors. The Greek Refugee Settlement Commission was dissolved in December 1930. The Commissioner for the Settlement of Refugees in Bulgaria had almost completed his task.

The writer wishes to acknowledge his indebtedness to all who aided in his work: to Mr. Nicholas Politis, Minister of Greece at Paris, who suggested the writing of this book; to Mr. Charalampos Simopoulos, Minister of Greece at Washington, for his cooperation in supplying material; to Hazim Atif, Esq. of Istanbul for collecting for the writer valuable material on the settlement of Turkish emigrants in Turkey; to Colonel James de Reynier, Mr. G. Djoudjeff and Mr. Stéphane Gheorgopoulos, members of the Mixed Greco-Bulgarian Commission, for invaluable assistance in discussing problems with the writer and for supplying information and documents; to Mr. Karl Marius Widding, Señor Manuel Rivas Vicuña Sperlier, Mr. Kimon Diamantopoulos and Mr. Aristide Phocas, members of the Mixed Greco-Turkish Commission, for similar assistance; to Mr. A. A. Pallis, member of the Greek Refugee Settlement Commission, for placing his studies and statistics on the settlement of the refugees at the author's disposal. Thanks are also due to

Mr. Mamopoulos, legal counsellor, and Mr. Tatarakis, of the Greek delegation of the Greco-Turkish Mixed Commission, and to Mr. George Papadakis of the Greek delegation of the Mixed Greco-Bulgarian Commission for generous cooperation. Mr. Antonios Nicolopoulos of the General Consulate of Greece, at Istanbul, has been very helpful in supplying the writer with material. The writer is very grateful to Mme. André Papaioannou who was so kind as to send regularly to the writer the successive volumes of the Procés-Verbaux of the Mixed Greco-Bulgarian Commission and numerous other documents. Professor Eldon R. James, Labrarian, Harvard Law School, has assisted in the collection of material.

The writer owes thanks to Professors Manley Ottmer Hudson of the Harvard Law School and George Grafton Wilson of Harvard University for valuable suggestions and assistance. He wishes to thank Mr. Charles B. Eddy, Chairman of the Greek Refugee Settlement Commission who has been kind enough to read the chapter on the Settlement of the Greek Refugees and to make suggestions and criticism. In the writing of this book, the preparation of the manuscript and the revision of the proof, the writer has received invaluable assistance and unfailing encouragement from his wife to whom he wishes to acknowledge his deep gratitude. Mr. George W. Robinson of Harvard University is to be thanked for having checked the references and assisted in matters of form.

STEPHEN P. LADAS

October, 1931
New York City

CONTENTS

PART III

THE SETTLEMENT OF THE EMIGRANTS AND REFUGEES

APPENDICES

MAPS AND DIAGRAMS

THE EXCHANGE OF MINORITIES
BULGARIA, GREECE AND TURKEY

THE EXCHANGE OF MINORITIES BULGARIA, GREECE AND TURKEY

INTRODUCTION

§ 1. The Conventions for the exchange of national minorities. Among the changes brought about by the World War in the political geography of the globe, few are so arresting, both in their political significance and in their human aspect as the exchange of minority populations between Greece and Bulgaria and Greece and Turkey. In each of these countries there lived before the war a national minority, a part of the population akin in race, language, or religion to the neighboring State. During the war these minorities passed through many vicissitudes; at its termination upward of two million people belonging to them were exchanged. In other words, the Greek minority in Bulgaria and Turkey removed to Greece, while the Bulgarian and Turkish minorities in Greece joined their kin in Bulgaria and Turkey respectively.

This transfer of whole populations from the one country to the other as a result of war and by virtue of international agreements is unique, at least in modern times. History, indeed, gives many instances in the past when whole populations moved from one place to another, either to save themselves from extermination by victorious enemies or to be replaced by new settlers. The Assyrians, the Persians, the

Greeks, the Romans, and the Byzantines resorted to these transplantations of populations.[1] In modern history two famous cases of the exodus of minorities are the flight of nearly half a million French of the Reformed Church after the revocation of the Edict of Nantes (1685); and the expulsion of a similar number of Moriscoes from Spain (1609).

These uprootings of populations occurred in relatively unenlightened periods of history when respect for the rights of man was hardly recognized, either in international or in national law. The protection of religious, linguistic, or racial minorities, either by domestic law or by international agreements, does not really begin to take its modern form before the end of the eighteenth century. It gains a continually increasing consideration in the nineteenth century, and becomes a particularly thorny question in the Ottoman Empire and the Dual Monarchy.[2] With the breaking up of these two Empires at the end of the war, and the establishment of new states in their former territories, the protection of national minorities came to form the subject of special treaties, intended, in general, to protect the human and civil rights and liberties of the minorities included in such states.

Beside this protection, the treaties issuing from the Peace Conference have adopted in all cases of cession of territory a clause, already often used in the past, permitting a choice of national allegiance. Under this clause, the population of the ceded territory may either remain in that territory, in which case it is presumed to have accepted the nationality of the new state, or leave the country within a certain period. In both cases the persons concerned are allowed to retain their movable and immovable property wherever located. In theory this was thought to be liberal enough. In fact, however, national minorities inhabiting ceded territory were compelled to avail themselves of the option clauses and emigrate.[3]

[1] Professor Séfériades gives many examples from the history of these people in his lectures at The Hague on the Exchange of Populations, published in Académie de Droit International, *Recueil des Cours,* 1928, iv, chapter ii.

[2] *Op. cit.,* pp. 317 ff.

[3] Examples of such emigrations are found in Upper Silesia, Transylvania, Eupen and Malmédy, Danzig, etc.

Both these measures for the protection of minorities, namely special treaty provisions and option clauses, were adopted as concerns Bulgaria, Greece, and Turkey. The reasons why they were not considered sufficient in the case of these countries are considered hereinafter. Suffice it here to say that Bulgaria and Greece signed at Neuilly in 1919 a convention for the reciprocal and voluntary emigration of national minorities. This was intended to make it easier for the Bulgarian minority in Greece and the Greek minority in Bulgaria to exercise their right of leaving the country of origin and emigrating to the other country under conditions which would guarantee them the full value of the properties left behind. Former emigrants from the two countries belonging to the respective national minorities were included in the provisions of the Convention. On the other hand, Greece and Turkey signed at Lausanne in 1923 a Convention for the Compulsory Exchange of Greek and Turkish Populations. This convention was a result of the declaration of Turkey that it would refuse to allow the repatriation of over a million Greeks who were driven from or left Turkey between 1912 and 1922. Thus the convention served chiefly to register and confirm an accomplished fact, although it also permitted Greece to compel its Moslem population to emigrate to Turkey.

These two conventions confirmed or caused the uprooting of over two million people. This uprooting was accompanied by a great toll of human tragedy. An immense effort has been required to settle these people in the new territories in which they immigrated.

It is the purpose of this study in its first two parts to describe the origin, interpret the contents, and give an account of the execution of each of these two conventions, and also to describe the machinery under which the emigration and exchange were carried out between Greece and Bulgaria and Greece and Turkey. A third part is devoted to the settlement of the exchanged peoples in their new countries.

§ 2. The geographical and historical background. The exchange of minorities between Bulgaria, Greece, and Turkey derived its impulse from forces operating in the Near East through the latter part of the nineteenth century and the beginning of the twentieth. It was also the culmination and political liquidation of a series of migrating movements in the Balkans which began, for the most part, after the Balkan Wars. Before tracing this drama of the exchange of peoples to its double source, it is necessary to describe the physical setting in which it was enacted.

The present area of Greece and Bulgaria is a little less than 90,000 square miles, and their population is 11,800,000, or less than one-half of the area and population of Spain. On the other hand, Turkey in Europe today contains a little over 9000 square miles with barely a million inhabitants. Asiatic Turkey has an area of 285,000 square miles with about 12,000,000 inhabitants. In general, these are poor countries, with much sterile soil and an inadequate water supply. They suffer from terrible droughts in the summer months and from destructive winters. The name 'Balkans,' meaning 'mountainous' in Turkish, well expresses the aspect of the country. From the dawn of history the interior of the peninsula has been half-pastoral and half-agricultural, while always the coast has served as the outlet of the interior, and has been dotted by towns devoted to commerce and shipping. There is a natural economic relationship between the coast and the interior. In modern times, following the dependence of these Balkan countries on the West for raw materials and industrial products, new avenues of commerce have developed between the coast, the inland districts, and the adjoining territories. Thus economically these countries are naturally a unit, while politically they are divided.

The coast has been Greek for 2500 years by virtue of the Greek commercial and shipping settlements. The interior, beyond the Greek peninsula, has passed through many vicissitudes. Races have been superimposed and jumbled like geological strata. During the Byzantine period, Hellenism was diffused throughout the Empire and showed a capacity of absorbing the invading populations. However, the Greeks, before the end of the Byzantine Empire, had withdrawn for the most part from the rural districts of the interior and concentrated in the towns and on the coast. They retained in their hands to a considerable extent the administrative, ecclesiastical, and commercial positions; but they lost contact with the soil and the rural populations, especially in the regions of the Byzantine Empire which form today the territories of Serbia, Bulgaria, and Rumania.

When Constantinople fell before the Turks in 1453, and with it the remnant of the Byzantine Empire, the Turks had already annihilated, since the great battle of Kossovo (1389), all vestiges of independence of the South Slavs which had remained from the military empires of the Serbs and Bulgarians. The Greek Patriarch of Constantinople and the local Bishops were then invested with spiritual and, in some respects, judicial and administrative authority over all the Christian races in the Ottoman Empire. To all these races was applied the name 'Rûm' or Greek.

§ 3. The Ottoman Empire in the Nineteenth Century. The Ottoman Empire began to decline, very shortly after it had reached its zenith, because it failed to cultivate the intellectual and moral forces which make for the perpetual rejuvenation of states. But in its heyday it was served by a unique administrative system and an efficient military establishment which were manned in the main by Christian converts, thus contributing by a constant drain to the "maiming and warping of the subject peoples." The internal and external decay of the Empire was first disclosed by the Serb uprising and the revolts of the Pashas early in the nineteenth century, and particularly by the Greek War of Independence in 1821. The success of the Greeks in liberating a part of the Greek peninsula furthered the cause of the freedom of the subject races in the Balkans. Serbia, Montenegro, Rumania, and Bulgaria, the first three of which had preserved a certain measure of autonomy as tributary or semi-independent states, were separated from the Turkish Empire. The map on page 6 shows the gradual decline of the Empire by the emancipation of subject races.

In the latter part of the century the Balkan states, believing that the disintegration of the Empire was soon to be completed, prepared to claim their still subject kinsfolk for themselves at the time of its final dissolution. The Ottoman Empire was so far decayed that, left to itself, it probably would have disappeared long before the end of the nineteenth century. Its preservation into the twentieth century was due

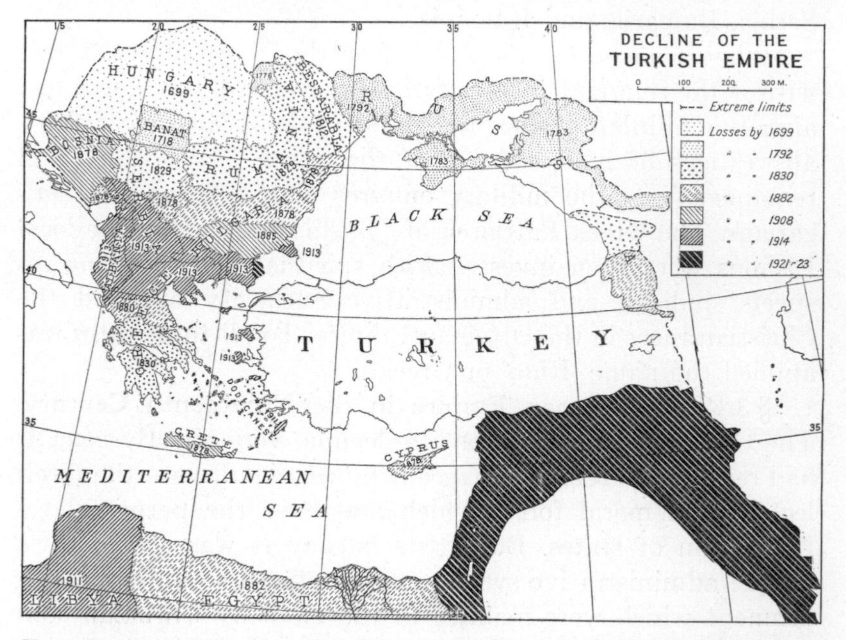

From Bowman, "The New World." Copyright, 1921 and 1928, by World Book Company, Publishers, Yonkers-on-Hudson, New York.

to the interwoven tangle of the conflicting interests of the great European powers. These interests are symbolically known to history as the *Drang nach Osten* of Austria-Hungary, the 'desire for warm waters' of Russia, the protection of the Suez Canal and the route to India of England, and the commercial and investment interests of France.

The Ottoman Empire might probably have owed a longer lease of life to these conflicting interests, had its rulers understood the necessity of satisfying the oppressed subject races by internal reform, and had they applied the processes of general education, development of communications, and free commercial intercourse to draw its peoples together. Such a rejuvenation and rebirth of the Empire was impossible under a government intellectually bankrupt and beyond hope of redemption. The Ottoman government preferred to repress the insurrections of the South Slavs in the beginning of the last quarter of the nineteenth century with terrible atrocities. All Europe was indignant, and Russia compelled the Empire, after crushing defeats, to sign the Treaty of San Stefano. This, though amended in the Congress of Berlin of 1878, had profound consequences.

§ 4. The conflicting claims. The Treaty of San Stefano revealed the plan for a Great Bulgaria, extending from the Black Sea on the east to the Aegean on the south, and as far west as Saloniki. The Bulgarians never forgot the grandiose prospect opened before their eyes. Their leaders, in an exalted nationalist spirit, saw in the Great Bulgaria of the Treaty of San Stefano the rebirth of the short-lived military Bulgarian Empires of Simeon (892-927), Samuel (993-1014), and Asen II (1218-40), which, exercising hardly more than a nominal authority, collapsed on the death of their military chiefs. The Treaty of San Stefano revealed the aspirations of Bulgaria, in which the Greeks and Serbs clearly perceived danger to their own claims. From this time began the struggle for supremacy between these peoples within the borders of the Turkish Empire.

The Bulgarians were first in the field. In 1885 the autonomous province of Eastern Rumelia was united with the principality of Bulgaria. 'Unredeemed Bulgaria' now expanded in the minds of the Bulgarians until it included the whole of Macedonia and the larger part of Thrace. The Bulgarians had succeeded in 1870 in obtaining from the Sublime Porte the establishment of a Bulgarian Exarchate at Constantinople, independent of the Greek Oecumenical Patriarchate. It was from this time that the name 'Bulgar' came to be distinguished from Greek in the Turkish Empire. In 1894 a new success was achieved, the consent of the Porte to the establishment of two Bulgarian Bishops in Macedonia. In 1895 a 'Supreme Macedo-Adrianopolitan Committee,' a precursor of the Macedonian Revolutionary Committee, was established at Sofia, and armed bands invaded Macedonia and Thrace. They were to supplement the work of peaceful penetration already entered upon by Bulgarian clergy, teachers, and other agents, to impress upon the uneducated and ignorant masses of Macedonian peasants that they were Bulgarians and that Bulgaria was to secure their freedom. In 1899 the Committee addressed a memorandum to the European Powers, calling upon them to assist in the creation of an autonomous Macedonia with its capital at Saloniki. It was expected that such an autonomous province would follow the destiny of the autonomous Eastern Rumelia and be annexed to Bulgaria at no distant time.

Serbs and Greeks awoke to the danger of the Bulgarian propaganda and designs. Soon both were conducting propaganda and had armed bands of their own in the field. They were, however, too late to undo the work that the Bulgarians had already accomplished. Serbia and Greece on the whole had no conflicting ambitions. The aspirations of the Greeks as to Macedonia did not extend to the northern and northeastern parts, where the Serbian hopes were centered. These parts of Macedonia, extending from Lake Ochrida in the west to Nevrokop and Tsoumaya in the east and to Petritch, Stromnitsa, and Monastir in the south, were inhabited, for the most part, by an ignorant South Slav population which had no national consciousness of any sort before the Bulgarian propaganda began its work. The question whether these Slavs are Bulgars or Serbs has been, and still is, a matter of bitter controversy. However, the Bulgars at least may assert that they were the first to awaken a national feeling among these people, and that this feeling was one of kinship with the Bulgarian nation.[4]

Even this did not satisfy the boundless aspirations of

[4] See on all this H. N. Brailsford, *Macedonia, its Races and their Future* (London, 1906); J. A. R. Marriott, *The Eastern Question: An Historical Study in European Diplomacy* (Oxford, 1917), pp. 362 ff.; Nevill Forbes and others, *The Balkans: A History of Bulgaria, Serbia, Greece, Roumania, and Turkey* (Oxford, 1915), 11. 407; G. F. Abbott, *The Tale of a Tour in Macedonia* (London, 1903), pp. 77 ff.; André Wurfbain, *L'échange Gréco-Bulgare des minorités ethniques* (Lausanne, 1930), pp. 22 ff.; Great Britain, Foreign Office, Historical Section, *Handbooks*, no. 21, Macedonia (London, 1920), pp. 13 ff.

Bulgarian nationalism. The vision of Great Bulgaria of the Treaty of San Stefano inspired larger claims, extending practically to the whole of Macedonia and Thrace. In this Bulgarian and Greek ambitions were in conflict. For a part of these provinces of the Turkish Empire Bulgarian claims were clearly untenable. This was the territory along the Aegean coast, which has been Greek from the dawn of history, and Eastern Thrace from the Maritza River to the Black Sea. There was also Southwestern Macedonia, along the Greek frontier south of Monastir and Florina, of whose inhabitants hardly any owned kinship to the Bulgarian people. In the rest of Thrace and Macedonia Greeks and Bulgarians were intermingled without any clear dividing line. Most of the towns were chiefly Greek; these were surrounded by rural districts purely Bulgar, purely Greek, or mixed. An ethnological map in colors would show patches and zones of Bulgars and Greeks inextricably interspersed.[5]

It is impossible to depend upon any so-called statistics or ethnological maps of these territories published prior to the World War. The Ottoman Empire had no reliable statistics. All other statistics or maps are either subject to bias or purely speculative. This much need be said here. Bulgaria, Serbia, and Greece each tended to exaggerate their claims. None had an overpowering claim on Macedonia or Thrace as a whole. From their smallness, their weakness, and their poverty, all hoped for as large territorial gains as possible to overcome these deficiencies, which compelled them to vegetate in a state of economic and cultural stagnation. Greece, in claiming the greatest part of Macedonia and Thrace, followed a national ideal and hope, that of reëstablishing a dominant Hellenism in the territories of the old Byzantine Empire. She refused to forget that until the middle of the nineteenth century the ecclesiastical unity of the Christians under the Greek Patriarch of Constantinople had been from the cultural point of view and in popular tradition predominantly Greek. Bulgaria, on the other hand, and, in a smaller

[5] An illustration is the city of Melnik in Northeastern Macedonia, which was wholly Greek, with a Greek culture of its own, in the midst of a rural population almost wholly Bulgarian.

measure, Serbia, had acquired their independence too easily with Russian help, and, moved by a rapid growth of national feeling and an excessive ambition, showed too little respect for the just claims of others, and a short-sighted view of political realities.

§ 5. The Balkan Wars. The more recent history is well remembered. In 1908 the Committee of Union and Progress, otherwise known as the Young Turks, effected a revolution in Turkey. Grossly mistaking the course which was necessary if the Empire was to be saved, they adopted as their keynote the 'Turkification of the Empire.' This brought matters to a head. An entente between the Balkan countries now appeared feasible despite failures in the past, and particularly in 1891, when the Greek statesman Tricoupis was unable to bring about an understanding with Stambuloff, prime minister of Bulgaria. The leaders of the Bulgarian, Greek, and Serbian national minorities in Turkey first joined hands at Constantinople, with the view of defending themselves against the efforts of the Young Turks for their extermination. Their example was shortly followed by the governments of the Balkan states. United by secret treaties of alliance, Montenegro, Serbia, Bulgaria, and Greece, one after the other, declared war upon Turkey, between October 8 and October 18, 1912. The resulting First Balkan War was short and decisive. When an armistice was declared on December 3, 1912, the Ottoman Empire had lost practically all its European territories except Constantinople.

The question of the division of the conquered territory brought on the Second Balkan War. Mr. Venizelos, the Greek Prime Minister, understood that, in view of their conflicting claims, Bulgaria and Greece could not possibly make an equitable and lasting division of Macedonia and Thrace without mutual concessions. He proposed to Bulgaria what was politically a very sound solution. Bulgaria was to receive all of Thrace proper. This included all the coastal section and the lower basin of the Maritza south of Adrianople, where Bulgarians were few and the population was Greek and Turkish. Venizelos thought that this territory would form a natural enlargement for Bulgaria, and would afford her an outlet to the Aegean through the railway which follows the course of the Maritza down to the port of Dedeagatch. On the other hand, Venizelos asked that Greece should have the territory adjacent to her borders, and consisting of the lower basins of the rivers Axios (Vardar) and Strymon (Struma). This included the coastal region of Macedonia, with Saloniki, which required for its economic life a certain extent of the interior occupied by a Bulgarian population. Venizelos believed that Bulgaria should consent to this concession, in return for the concession Greece was prepared to make in Thrace.

The Second Balkan War (1913), caused by the refusal of Bulgaria to accept the above solution, resulted, in general, in forcing upon Bulgaria the above division, with the exception that Greece kept the port of Kavala, which Venizelos wished to cede to Bulgaria. Venizelos had to yield on this point to the insistence of King Constantine and the General Staff of the Greek army, although he perceived clearly that it was politically unwise and dangerous to peace not to grant the town to Bulgaria. The changes brought about in the Balkan peninsula after the two Balkan Wars are shown on the map on page 12. The war rendered deeper the old national animosities and hatreds. The Bulgarian nation could not forget the humiliation of the defeat, and waited for an opportunity to take its revenge. The opportunity was given by the World War.

§ 6. The World War. During the course of this war Bulgaria succeeded in occupying all the territory to which she had aspired, and more. Her agreement of September, 1915, with the Central Powers promised to her part of Serbia proper, to which she had no rightful claim of any sort. It is well known that "the Bulgarian outrages upon Greeks and Serbs—men, women, and children—were among the most hideous of the war." [6] At the end of the war, Bulgaria emerged with a worse defeat and a greater humiliation than before. She lost Western Thrace to the Allied and Associated Powers, who later

[6] Isaiah Bowman, *The New World: Problems in Political Geography* (Yonkers, 1921), p. 302.

This could only be done by a slow process, beginning with the immediate application of adequate internal reform. The alternative solution, that of destroying or eradicating the minorities, had the merit of simplicity; in other respects it hardly requires discussion.

However, the new Turkish policy, begun early in 1914, was continued during the World War under conditions particularly favorable. The destruction of the Armenian race, especially in the outlying vilayets near the Russian frontier, is well known. A somewhat similar destiny befell the Greeks of Thrace and of the Aegean coast. The actual clearing away of this minority by the agencies of death did not reach the same extent as with the Armenian minority, since most of the Greeks were able to flee from the Turkish territory and seek refuge in Greece. The collapse of the Greek occupation of Smyrna and Western Asia Minor completed the catastrophe. The entire Greek population of the Aegean coast region followed the Greek army in its retreat. There are no accurate statistics of the Greek population in Turkey before 1914. In Eastern Thrace, including Constantinople, a total of at least 600,000 Greeks were living, one-half of whom were in Constantinople. The Greek population of Asia Minor was placed between 1,500,000 and 1,750,000. In the coastal section of Western Asia Minor, comprising the vilayets of Aidin and Broussa and the independent sandjaks of Ismid and Dardanelles, the Greeks probably exceeded one million. Another half-million lived in the Pontus, and the rest mainly in the vilayets of Sivas, Angora, Konia and Adana.[8] The Greek population, especially in Western Asia Minor, had increased largely during the preceding half-century, because of a high birth-rate and immigration from other parts of Turkey.

§ 7. **The course of migrations after the Balkan Wars.** Although before the Balkan Wars there were a number of group migratory movements between the Balkan countries, it

[8] Karl Dieterich, *Das Griechentum Kleinasiens* (Leipzig, 1915), p. 32. Mr. Pallis (in *Les Effets économiques et sociaux de la guerre en Grèce,* by A. Andréades et autres, p. 147) estimates the Greek population of Anatolia at 1,648,000. The figure of 1,600,000 is pretty generally accepted. Cf. Charles B. Eddy, *Greece and the Greek Refugees* (London, 1931), p. 251.

is the beginning of the First Balkan War in October, 1912, which really started a tide of national minorities, with waves of thousands of people, moving to and from the one country to the other in the Balkans. It has been found [9] that no less than seventeen migratory movements took place in Macedonia alone from 1912 to 1925. A great number of migrations also took place into and from Thrace and Asia Minor during the same period.

Chronologically these migrations may be described as follows. In 1912 a part of the Turkish population fled before the advancing armies of the allied Balkan states. Although no exact statistics exist, the number of these emigrants may be calculated as at least 100,000.[10] In 1913, as a consequence of the Second Balkan War, the following movements of populations took place: (*a*) 15,000 Bulgarians from Macedonia followed the Bulgarian army in its retreat before the advance of the Greek army; (*b*) 10,000 Greeks left the parts of Macedonia granted to Serbia and Bulgaria by the Treaty of Bucharest; (*c*) 70,000 Greeks were forced to emigrate from Western Thrace, which was then occupied by Bulgaria; (*d*) 48,570 Moslems emigrated to Turkey from Western Thrace under the terms of the Treaty of Peace of Constantinople of 1913, which will be considered hereafter; (*e*) 46,764 Bulgarians left Eastern Thrace and emigrated to Bulgarian Western Thrace under the same Treaty.

The migrations continued in 1914. The Young Turks decided now to put into effect their plan of ridding themselves of the national minorities and making of the Turkish Empire a homogeneous Turkish state. For the execution of this plan the Armenians must be exterminated and the Greeks must be driven from Turkey. The necessary complement of the plan was to persuade the Turkish minorities in the Balkan countries to emigrate to Turkey. A vigorous propaganda to this effect was carried on in the Balkan countries. As a result the following movements of population took place in 1914: (*a*)

[9] A. A. Pallis, *Statistical Study of the Racial Migrations in Macedonia and Thrace, 1912–1924* (in Greek) (Athens, 1925), p. 5.

[10] Mr. Pallis (*op. cit.*) calculates the Turks who left Greek Macedonia alone at this period as 10,000.

115,000 Greeks were expelled from Turkish Eastern Thrace and sought refuge in Greece; (*b*) 85,000 Greeks from the same region were deported to the interior of Asia Minor; (*c*) 150,000 Greeks were driven from the coast region of Western Anatolia and came to the shores of Greece; (*d*) 115,000 Moslems left Greece with the view of taking the place of the Greeks expelled from Turkey; (*e*) 135,000 Moslems emigrated from the other Balkan countries to Turkey as a result of the propaganda referred to above.[11]

During the World War the migratory movements were interrupted. However, the Bulgarian army, on the occupation of Greek Eastern Macedonia in 1916, deported to the interior of Bulgaria 36,000 Greeks. The Turkish government also continued the deportations of Greeks and Armenians to the interior of Anatolia.

Immediately after the Armistice, the migrations again began, being now mostly a return to their homes of populations deported and expelled. But not all of them returned. Of the 36,000 Greeks deported to Bulgaria from Eastern Macedonia only 17,000 came back, the rest having perished.[12] Many thousands were also missing from the Greeks of Eastern Thrace and the coast of Western Anatolia who returned from the interior of Asia Minor.[13] Even of those who had sought refuge in the country of their kinship many perished from privations. However, nearly all the surviving Greek refugees returned from Greece to Thrace and to the Anatolian coast districts. It is calculated that 51,000 Greeks returned to Western Thrace, 83,000 to Eastern Thrace, and about 100,000 to Asia Minor.

In 1919 and 1920 a new migratory current brought to the

[11] Official statistics of the Turkish Ministry of the Interior give the total number of Moslem emigrants after the Balkan Wars as 413,922. Deducting 113,922 as the Moslems who left the Balkan countries in 1912 before the advance of the allied Balkan armies, and 50,000 who emigrated from Western Thrace in 1913 under the terms of the Treaty of Constantinople, the total of emigrants in 1914 may be placed at approximately 250,000.

[12] See M. Ailianos, *The Work of the Greek Relief* (in Greek) (Athens, 1921), p. 58.

[13] Antoniades, *Le développement économique de la Thrace* (Athens, 1922), p. 223, cites official statistics showing that 49,721 out of the 84,799 Greeks deported from Eastern Thrace in 1914 returned there in 1918.

shores of Greece about 60,000 Greeks from Soviet Russia.[14] In the meantime the orderly reciprocal and voluntary emigration of Greeks from Bulgaria and Bulgarians from Greece began under the auspices of the Mixed Commission, created under the Convention of Neuilly, as will be seen below. But worse was still to come.[15]

In the fall of 1922 the Greco-Turkish War, a sequel of the World War caused by the occupation of Smyrna and Western Asia Minor by Greece, at the behest of the Allies, came to an abrupt end with the decisive victory of the Turks and the precipitate retreat of the Greek army. The Greek army was followed in its flight by the entire Greek population of the larger part of Western Asia Minor. The Greek population of Pontus also began to leave hurriedly. A little later, following the armistice of Mudania and before the Kemalist army occupied Constantinople and Eastern Thrace, the whole Greek and Armenian population of the latter region and a part of the population of Constantinople left their homes and sought refuge in Greece. Thus almost a million people were thrown upon the shores of Greece in the space of a few months. Following the Convention of Lausanne of 1923, the remaining Greeks in Turkey, excluding Constantinople, left the country under the auspices of the Mixed Commission, a total of over 150,000 persons. Under the same Convention the Moslems of Greece, with the exception of Western Thrace, who had always remained unmolested and content in the country, were compelled to leave for Turkey. They numbered about 400,000.

§ 8. The exchange of minorities as a solution of political problems in the Balkans. We have noted the conflicting claims of Bulgaria, Greece, and Turkey to territories inhabited by national minorities connected with ties of kinship to the

[14] These refugees were mainly from the Caucasian coast. Indeed, 47,091 came from Caucasus and 11,435 from other parts of Russia. After General Wrangel's defeat a number of Russians were transferred to Greece; 1200 of these settled in Saloniki.

[15] The figures given above are based on the statistics given by Mr. Pallis, foremost expert in the matter, in his *Statistical Study of the Racial Migrations in Macedonia and Thrace, 1912–1924* (in Greek) (Athens, 1925), and by Mr. Antoniades in *Le développement économique de la Thrace* (Athens, 1922), pp. 215, 217.

neighboring states, and the course of migrations and flights that carried great numbers from the territory of each state to those of the others. When peace was reëstablished in 1919 between Bulgaria and Greece and in 1923 between Greece and Turkey, there remained the problem of those who had emigrated from their country of origin and had left their properties behind. There was, further, the still larger problem of securing to the national minorities an adequate protection for life and property and other rights, with the view of obtaining political stability and peace in this part of the world. The exchange of minorities was resorted to as a solution to these two problems, as will be seen from the study of the origins both of the Convention of Neuilly of 1919 and of the Convention of Lausanne of 1923. This solution, however, was not first devised at the termination of the World War. The Conventions of Neuilly and Lausanne had their precursors in two pre-war agreements.

§ 9. The Turko-Bulgarian Convention of 1913. A Protocol annexed to the treaty of peace between Bulgaria and Turkey signed at Constantinople on September 16/29, 1913,[16] which terminated the war between the two countries that broke out while Bulgaria was engaged in war with its former allies, formulated for the first time the idea of an exchange of populations. This Protocol in sections A and B set forth the method of tracing the new frontier between the two countries, and in section C provided as follows:

Les deux Gouvernements sont d'accord pour faciliter l'échange facultatif mutuel des populations bulgare et musulmane de part et d'autre ainsi que de leurs propriétés dans une zône de 15 kilomètres au plus, le long de toute la frontière commune.

L'échange aura lieu par des villages entiers.

L'échange des propriétés rurales et urbaines aura lieu sous les auspices des deux Gouvernements et avec la participation des anciens des villages à échanger.

Des Commissions mixtes nominées par les deux Gouvernements procéderont à l'échange et à l'indemnisation, s'il y a lieu, de differ-

[16] See test in Martens, *Nouveau recueil général de traités,* 3d series, viii, pp. 85-86; and *British and Foreign State Papers,* cvii, pp. 713-714.

ences résultant de l'échange de biens entre villages et particuliers en question.

It was thus provided that the "authorized reciprocal exchange" of the Bulgarian and Moslem populations within fifteen kilometres of the entire common frontier should be facilitated by the two governments. The truth is that most of these people had already emigrated, and it was desired to confirm this situation by compelling the remaining inhabitants of Bulgarian and Moslem villages in Turkey and Bulgaria respectively to transfer their residence to the other side of the frontier.

A Mixed Commission, consisting of six Turkish and nine Bulgarian delegates, met at Adrianople on November 2/15, 1913, and signed a "Convention concerning the exchange of populations."[17] The first article of this Convention made it clear that what was intended was to confirm a *fait accompli.* Indeed, it was agreed that "the Bulgarian peasants of the districts of Kirk-Kilisse and Adrianople are to be settled in the Moslem villages of Thrace ceded to Bulgaria which have been abandoned by their inhabitants, since these districts are now occupied by the Moslem refugees who came from Thrace." It was also agreed that the Commission should proceed to the appraisal of the properties of the exchanged populations.

The Mixed Commission met again for the application of the Convention on May 10/23, 1914, and was presided over by Chukri Bey, Civil Inspector of the vilayet of Adrianople. It was decided to divide the Commission into two Sub-Commissions, of which one was to work in Turkey and the other in Bulgaria. On May 12/25 an agreement was made on the properties to be appraised. At the third meeting (May 14/27) a "violent discussion," as the Procès-Verbal states, was raised on the question of appraisal. This was concluded on May

[17] The text of this Convention, as well as of the Procès-Verbaux of the seven meetings of this Commission, referred to below, are found in Antoniades, *Le développement économique de la Thrace* (Athens, 1922), pp. 162, 171 ff.

This Convention was never ratified by the Bulgarian Chamber of Deputies, and is therefore denied any legal effect in Bulgaria. See Séfériades, *op. cit.,* p. 354.

17/30 with an agreement not to appraise pasture lands, forests, market places, and non-productive lands which were held by the emigrants in possession but not in ownership. The basis of appraisal was fixed at the meeting of May 20 as the prices appearing on the government fiscal registries.

It appears that the two Sub-Commissions of the Mixed Commission began work immediately in June and continued until October, 1914, when the entry of Turkey into the World War caused the discontinuance of the work. During this time the Commission completed the lists of Bulgarians and Moslems who were entitled to the benefits of the Convention and whose properties were to be appraised and liquidated. These lists show that 9714 Moslem families or 48,570 persons from the Bulgarian territory were 'exchanged' against 9472 Bulgarian families or 46,764 persons from Turkish Thrace.[18] The appraisal and liquidation of the properties of these persons were never carried out.

§ 10. The Greco-Turkish agreement of 1914. The Young Turkish government, having succeeded in making a convention with Bulgaria as to the exchange of minority populations, sought to reach a similar agreement with another of its neighbors. The occupation by Greece of the Aegean islands, some of which were dangerously close to the coast of Asia Minor, threatened, in the eyes of the Young Turks, the security of that coast, where more than a million unredeemed Greeks were living and prospering. The Greeks must be moved away and the coast peopled with Moslems. The Turkish government was well aware that the Greek government would never of its own will consent to receive these Greeks in exchange for the Moslems living in Greece. It decided, accordingly, to force the hand of the Greek government by expelling the Greeks from the Aegean coast regions or deporting them into the interior of Anatolia. The systematic carrying out of this plan began early in 1914. Within a few months

[18] When the Greek government during its occupation of Eastern Thrace in 1920 made a census of the population, the Bulgarians of this region numbered about 1000, which shows that the Bulgarian minority had emigrated practically in its entirety. See Pallis, *Statistical Study of Racial Migrations in Macedonia and Thrace, 1912–1924,* p. 21.

150,000 Greeks were forced to leave the western coast of Asia Minor and to seek refuge in Greece. Another 50,000 were deported to the interior of Anatolia. Vainly did the Greek government present repeated protests to the Sublime Porte. When the ground was thus prepared with a *fait accompli,* the Turkish Minister at Athens, Ghalib Kemaly Bey, expressed to the Greek Premier, Mr. Venizelos, "his personal opinion" that it would be a good idea to exchange the Greek rural population of the region of Smyrna against the Moslems of Macedonia. On May 5/18, 1914, the Turkish Minister followed up his suggestion with a letter, addressed to Mr. Venizelos, in which he stated that he had submitted his own idea of an exchange of populations to the Sublime Porte and had met with the latter's approval. He then proposed, in the name of his government, the exchange of populations suggested by him, and added that his government would desire a speedy adhesion to the idea on the part of the Greek government, in order to avoid the undesirable incidents which might occur by reason of the Moslem emigration in the vilayet of Smyrna. Four days later (May 9/22, 1914) Mr. Venizelos replied to the Turkish Minister, accepting the proposal of an exchange of populations, provided the free and spontaneous character of the emigration was secured and the properties of the emigrants were appraised and liquidated. He also proposed that the exchange be extended to Thrace.

A preliminary agreement appears to have been reached, on the basis of the above letter of Mr. Venizelos, in a note of the Greek Ministry of Foreign Affairs communicated on May 10/23, 1914, to Nedjib Bey, counsellor of the Turkish legation in Athens, and in subsequent communications between the two governments.[19] The points of agreement were the following:

1. The populations of the Greek villages in Thrace and in the vilayet of Smyrna, extending to the Straits, were to be

[19] Copy of the letter of May 5/18, 1914, from Ghalib Kemaly Bey; of Mr. Venizelos's letter of May 9/22, 1914; of the note communicated by the Greek government to Nedjib Bey on May 10/23, 1914, and of subsequent communications were kindly placed at the disposal of the writer by the Ministry of Foreign Affairs of Greece.

exchanged against the Moslem peasants of Macedonia and Epirus, simultaneously and on ascertaining their spontaneous desire to emigrate.

2. The exchange was to be carried out under the protection of the two governments, in accordance with a plan mutually agreed on, and under the control of a Mixed Commission which was to ascertain the spontaneous purpose of the people to emigrate.

3. The Mixed Commission in question, consisting of four members appointed by the two governments, was to appraise the movable and immovable property of the emigrants prior to their emigration. The Commission was to sit at Smyrna or at Saloniki. It could create Sub-Commissions.

4. Simultaneously with this work, a special Sub-Commission was to appraise the properties of Greeks of Thrace and Asia Minor who had already left their homes, as well as the properties of the Moslems of Macedonia and Epirus who had emigrated to Turkey.

5. The Mixed Commission was to include a neutral arbiter, to be appointed by a European state chosen by agreement between the two countries. This arbiter was to take no part in the discussions of the Mixed Commission; but he was to have power to settle finally all differences arising in it.

The Mixed Commission provided for in the above agreement between the two countries was established and met at the end of June, 1914, at Smyrna. Its first purpose was to draw up a convention concerning the following three points:

1. The conditions under which the voluntary emigration of Moslems and Greeks was to be secured.

2. The bases for the appraisal of the properties of former and new emigrants and for the payment of the balance by the one of the two governments which should finally be found debtor to the other on the general liquidation and compensation account.

3. The terms of the *compromis* or agreement for the arbitration of the differences that might arise.

The Commission held a number of meetings at Smyrna; but, making slow progress there, it transferred itself to Constantinople. Shortly thereafter, Turkey entered the war on the side of the Central Powers and the work of the Commission was suspended.

The Turko-Bulgarian Convention of 1913 and the stillborn Greco-Turkish Agreement of 1914 may be deemed the forerunners of the Convention of Neuilly of 1919 and the Convention of Lausanne of 1923.

PART FIRST

THE EXCHANGE OF MINORITIES BETWEEN GREECE AND BULGARIA

CHAPTER I

THE CONVENTION CONCERNING RECIPROCAL EMIGRATION OF 1919 AND SUBSEQUENT AGREEMENTS

§ 1. Origin of the Convention concerning reciprocal emigration of national minorities. Article 56, paragraph 2, of the Treaty of Peace between the Allied and Associated Powers and Bulgaria, signed at Neuilly-sur-Seine on November 27, 1919,[1] provided that "Bulgaria undertakes to recognize such provisions as the Principal Allied and Associated Powers may consider opportune with respect to the reciprocal and voluntary emigration of persons belonging to racial minorities." The Principal Allied and Associated Powers, in a decision issued on the same day, announced that they considered it "opportune that the reciprocal and voluntary emigration of the racial, religious, and linguistic minorities in Greece and Bulgaria should be regulated by a Convention concluded between these two Powers in the terms decided upon this day." Such a Convention was signed at Neuilly-sur-Seine on the

[1] This article is in part iii, Political Clauses, section iv, Protection of Minorities. The treaty was published separately, and may also be found in Carnegie Endowment for International Peace, *The Treaties of Peace, 1919–1923* (New York, 1924), and Martens, *Nouveau recueil général de traités*, 3e série, xii, pp. 323-423.

same day, November 27, 1919, by the Greek and Bulgarian plenipotentiaries.[2]

From this it appears clearly that the Convention concerning Reciprocal Emigration was, politically, a part of the settlement resulting from the Treaty of Neuilly. The origin and history of the drafting of this Convention is interesting enough to be described here. So far as the present writer knows, no such description has ever before been published. He has obtained his information from the perusal of the minutes of the "Committee on New States and for the Protection of the Rights of Minorities" of the Peace Conference of Paris, generously placed at his disposal by a member of this Committee.

While the Treaty concerning the Protection of Minorities in Greece[3] was being drafted by the above committee in July, 1919, Mr. Venizelos, the president of the Greek delegation at the Peace Conference, was advised to present "the views of the Greek delegation on the subject of the existence of these minorities and their organization as well as the provisions already taken or under consideration by the Greek government to insure the indispensable freedom and protection of these minorities." Mr. Venizelos, under date of July 31, assured the Committee of the readiness of Greece to sign such a treaty; and on August 9, 1919, he sent to the Committee a memorandum on the minorities. In fact, it appears that Greece was the only country which consented with readiness to sign a treaty concerning minorities, and the Committee took the step of communicating the draft to the Greek delegation for its observations.[4]

In the meantime, the Greek delegation communicated to the different delegations at the Conference certain clauses suggesting the establishment of a Mixed Commission to supervise the reciprocal emigration of Greeks residing in Bulgaria to Greece and of Bulgarians from Greece to Bulgaria. In this,

[2] See the text of the Convention in League of Nations, *Treaty Series*, i, pp. 68-72.

[3] Signed at Sèvres August 10, 1920. See Martens, *Nouveau recueil général de traités*, 3e série, xii, pp. 801-809; League of Nations, *Treaty Series*, xxviii, pp. 243-265.

[4] 35th, 42d, and 44th meetings of the Committee.

Mr. Venizelos was seeking to carry out a plan which seems to have occurred to him at least as early as 1915. In that year Mr. Venizelos sketched the idea of a reciprocal emigration between Greece and Bulgaria in his famous memorandum of January, 1915, to King Constantine, in which he urged the entry of Greece into the war on the side of the Allied Powers and against Turkey. Anxious that the coöperation of Bulgaria should be sought, he was ready, although reluctantly, to advise the sacrifice of Kavala to achieve this coöperation, in order to save Hellenism in Turkey and to insure the foundation of a real Great Greece, "comprising almost all the territories where Hellenism has exercised its action during its long history through the centuries." In this case, he added, Bulgaria would undertake to buy the properties of the inhabitants of the region of Kavala who might wish to emigrate to Greece; the Greek and Bulgarian populations on the opposite sides of the frontier would thus be exchanged, in order to achieve definitely a 'racial adjustment' which would permit at last the establishment of a true Balkan Confederation.[5]

Undoubtedly Mr. Venizelos felt that the peace negotiations afforded a good opportunity to achieve the 'racial adjustment' as a basis for the establishment of a real state of peace in that part of the Near East.

The Committee on New States considered on July 25, 1930, the clauses submitted by Mr. Venizelos.[6] It was agreed that it would be desirable not only to apply the principle of reciprocal emigration to Greece and Bulgaria, but to extend it to all the Balkan states. It was pointed out that there was no difficulty in this as regards Greece, Bulgaria, and Turkey, for Greece had herself proposed the principle and it could be imposed upon Bulgaria and Turkey. It would be desirable to include Serbia, but it could not be imposed on that country.

§ 2. **The drafting of the Convention.** A sub-committee appointed by the Committee on New States and consisting of Professor A. C. Coolidge (United States), Colonel Castoldi (Italy), and Mr. J. W. Headlam-Morley (Great Britain) pre-

[5] See Edouard Driault and Michel Lhéritier, *Histoire diplomatique de la Grèce de 1821 à nos jours* (Paris, 1925-26), v, p. 177.

[6] 37th and 38th meetings of the Committee.

pared a report on the clauses submitted by Mr. Venizelos. This was adopted by the Committee and incorporated in a letter addressed to the Council of Five.[7] Certain of the clauses proposed by Mr. Venizelos, relating to questions of reparations, were excluded by this report. The others, concerning emigration, were deemed useful and their adoption by the Council of Five was urged. The report recommended the extension of these clauses to all Balkan countries and to all inhabitants thereof and not merely to those of the transferred territories. The Committee concluded that, if extended in this way, the plan of reciprocal emigration "would do much to help a permanent settlement of the troubles which have so long affected the Balkans and be a valuable supplement to the clauses dealing with the protection of minorities." The Committee then suggested certain heads of agreement indicating the nature of the Convention as follows:

1. Greece, Serbia, Bulgaria, and Turkey agree that they will accord to all citizens within their territories the right to declare their desire to transfer their residence and remove to any one of the other states.

2. This right of option can be exercised at any period within two years from the coming into force of the treaty.

3. Those who under these clauses exercise this right of option shall have the free right to emigrate into the State which they choose without any form of hindrance or impediment and to take with them their movable property. The disposal of their immovable property will be controlled by the Commission to be appointed under the following clause.

4. There shall be established a Mixed Commission, to be appointed by the League for the purpose of supervising and facilitating the emigration and for dealing with the immovable property of the emigrants.

5. In order to facilitate this work, there shall be appointed sub-commissions, each of which will deal with the emigration between two countries; each of these sub-commissions shall consist of three members, one appointed by each of the interested countries, and the other, who shall be chairman, appointed from among its own members by the Central Commission.

[7] 38th meeting of the Committee.

6. The funds necessary for facilitating the emigration shall be advanced by the interested States to the Central Commission. The latter shall make such contributions as may be necessary from these funds to the individuals who exercise the right of option conferred upon them. They shall also advance to the emigrants the value of the immovable property, the ownership of which shall be transferred to the Commission. The latter shall arrange for the eventual sale.

The Committee then asked the Council of Five whether they would be permitted to adopt the procedure indicated, and, in particular, to enter into communication with Mr. Venizelos to ask whether he would agree to the proposed modification of his clauses; and, further, whether they would be permitted to lay this suggestion before the Serbian delegation.

On September 4 [8] the Supreme Council adopted a resolution accepting the report of the Committee and authorizing it to consult with Mr. Venizelos as to the best methods of putting his proposals into effect.

At the invitation of the President of the Committee, who communicated to Mr. Venizelos on September 10 the heads of agreement adopted by the Committee, the Greek delegation expressed its agreement with the modification suggested by the Committee; and on October 25 it submitted a draft treaty, of which the author appears to have been Mr. Politis. This was in the form of a convention between Greece, the Kingdom of the Serbs, Croats, and Slovenes, and Bulgaria for the recognition of the right of reciprocal emigration of racial minorities, and followed the general lines indicated by the Committee.[9]

[8] 43d and 49th meetings of the Committee.

[9] This draft, contained in the Minutes of the Committee on New States of the Paris Peace Conference, is published here for its historical interest and as forming the preparatory draft of the Convention which is to be interpreted in the following chapters.

DRAFT OF AGREEMENT ON BALKAN EMIGRATION SUBMITTED BY MR. POLITIS

Article 1

Greece, the kingdom of the Serbs, Croats, and Slovenes, and Bulgaria, in execution of article 56, paragraph 2, of the Treaty of Peace with Bulgaria, grant to all their nationals within their territories who belong to ethnic minorities the right to express their desire to emigrate.

Article 2

As for persons who, having already left their original residence, are already established in the State whose ethnic point of view they take, they shall have only the right to the liquidation of the property left by them in the abandoned country. This liquidation shall be carried out according to the provisions established hereafter.

Article 3

The Governments of the States above mentioned undertake to facilitate in every way the exercise of this right and to interpose no obstacles, directly or indirectly, to freedom of emigration; emigrants shall not be prevented under any pretext from carrying out their intention. Henceforth all laws and regulations whatsoever existing in each of these States which conflict with freedom of emigration shall be considered as null and void from the date of the coming into force of the present Treaty.

Any prosecution whatsoever, civil or criminal, on the part of the authorities of one of these countries against an emigrant shall not prevent his departure. However, in case of criminal prosecution of an emigrant the authorities of the prosecuting country shall deliver him to the authorities of the country where he is going in order that he may be tried.

It is understood that the existence of any process whatever pending before the courts, either civil or administrative, even interesting the Government (for example, claim for taxes, revenues, or fines, on any account, on the part of the Government or of the provincial, communal, or other authorities) shall not prevent the emigrant from leaving the country.

No obstacle shall be placed in the way of the exercise of the right of emigration even in the case of persons condemned for political acts or offences against the common law. Their declaration shall be made in writing to the Commission provided for below. Within thirty days from the date of their declaration the persons having thus expressed their wish to emigrate shall be delivered by the competent authorities of the country of their departure to those of the country of their destination. The individuals thus delivered shall be considered as definitively liberated from all prosecution or punishment if they have been condemned for political crimes. In the case of persons condemned for crimes at common law, the remainder of the sentence shall be served in the country of their destination.

Article 4

Emigrants shall be freed from all military obligations, previous or present, and their departure shall not be prevented on this account.

Article 5

The right of voluntary emigration may be exercised by any person over 18 years of age. It may be exercised within a period of four years from the going into force of the present Treaty by means of a declaration before the Mixed Commission provided for below or before its representatives. The choice of the husband carries with it that of the wife, the option of parents or guardians that of their children or wards aged less than 18 years.

Article 6

Those who emigrate will lose the nationality of the country which they abandon from the instant they leave it, and will acquire that of the country of their destination as soon as they establish themselves in its territory.

Article 7

Those who, in execution of these clauses, take advantage of the right of option shall have the right to carry with them, or to have transported, their movable property of any kind without any duty being imposed upon them on this account.

Likewise, in case the right of option is exercised by the members of a community which after their departure must be dissolved, the emigrants shall have the right to carry freely, or to have transported, all the movable property belonging to their communities, churches, convents, schools, hospitals, and establishments of any kind.

ARTICLE 8

So far as their immovable property is concerned, rural or urban, as well as that belonging to their communities, churches, convents, hospitals, and establishments of any kind, it shall be liquidated by a Commission conforming to the following provisions.

ARTICLE 9

From the date of the coming into force of the present Treaty, there shall be created a Mixed Commission, appointed by the League of Nations, or, in case of its failure to do so, by the principal Allied and Associated Powers, which shall have as its duty the supervision and facilitation of emigration, and the liquidation of the immovable property of emigrants.

Each of the Allied Powers interested shall have a member on this Commission.

ARTICLE 10

In order to facilitate this work, Sub-Commissions shall be appointed which shall deal with emigration between two countries, taking all measures suitable to assure the carrying out of the policy of emigration to the best interests of the emigrants. They shall fix the procedure of the declarations of emigration, and of the liquidation of the immovable property of emigrants.

Each of these Sub-Commissions shall have three members: one representative of each of the two States interested, and a third member chosen by the Central Commission among its own members. The latter shall be chairman of the Sub-Commission.

ARTICLE 11

The Commission shall take the necessary measures with a view to the sale of immovable property of which the ownership is transferred. They shall, in particular, estimate the value of immovable property by Mixed Commissions of experts, on which the persons interested shall be represented.

The difference in value of immovable property of emigrants shall be paid in to the Central Commission by the Government of the country of departure as soon as the former has notified it of the result of the estimate. One-fourth of this payment shall be made in the money of the country or its equivalent in francs, pounds sterling, or dollars, and three-fourths in short-term gold Treasury bonds in francs.

ARTICLE 12

The Commission shall advance to the emigrants the value of their immovable property determined as above.

ARTICLE 13

All civil or military pensions acquired by an emigrant at the date of the signature of the present Treaty shall be capitalized at the charge of the debtor Government, which must pay the amount to the Central Commission for the account of its owners.

ARTICLE 14

The Commission shall hold its first meeting within the shortest possible time after the going into force of the present agreement; it shall meet thereafter at such periods as it may consider proper, and as may be necessary with a view to the quickest possible accomplishment of its duties.

Its duties shall be terminated within six months after the expiration of the period of four years provided by Article 5 of the present Treaty.

ARTICLE 15

The funds necessary to facilitate emigration shall be advanced by the States interested to the Central Commission on the conditions fixed by it, and on its demand alone. The Central Commission shall make such redistribution as it may judge proper to the persons who exercise the right of option conferred on them.

ARTICLE 16

The expense of the support and operations of the Commission and its branches shall be borne by the Governments interested.

In the meantime, it appears, the Greek delegation were making an effort to have the Serbian delegation join in the proposed convention. This effort failed, as M. de Caligny, the French member of the Committee on New States, informed that body at its meeting of November 3, 1919. However, it was decided to send to the Serbian delegation the heads of agreement and to inquire whether they wished to participate. On November 8, 1919, hardly two days after the receipt of the communication, the Serbian delegation replied that they approved the ideas inspiring the draft, but did not believe either in the necessity or the advisability of the proposed clauses. Their view was that direct understandings between the two states interested would be more satisfactory. This view would have seemed reasonable enough, had it not been for the pretty obvious impossibility of bringing about any such understanding.

The Committee decided that it would be useless to continue by other means the effort to persuade the Serbians. The question then arose whether Bulgaria should be required to sign a convention with Greece alone. The Italian delegation expressed a negative opinion. The American delegation thought it might be well to put off the signature of such a convention until the question of Thrace was decided, as Thrace was one of the most important districts to which its provisions would apply. The British, French, and Japanese delegations considered that it would be desirable to require Bulgaria to sign the convention forthwith. It was pointed out that the convention would apply equally well to Thrace when its fate had been determined, and that the question of the adhesion of Turkey would be settled later, after the principle had been determined.

On the agreement by the Committee that Bulgaria should be given an opportunity of presenting her observations on the convention, the Italian delegation withdrew their objection. The American delegation did not insist on postponement. The Committee then proceeded in its 59th, 60th, and 61st meetings, of November 13, 15, and 17, to examine the draft convention proposed by the Greek delegation. Only minor alterations were made by the Committee in the above draft as prepared by Mr. Politis. The definite draft was officially accepted by the Greek delegation and then submitted to the Supreme Council.[10]

§ 3. Acceptance of the Convention by Bulgaria. While the draft convention was being prepared by the Greek delegation in October, this delegation suggested that it was necessary to insert an article in the Treaty of Peace with Bulgaria binding Bulgaria to accept provisions approved by the Allied and Associated Powers for reciprocal and voluntary emigration. At that time the inclusion of Serbia in the Convention was still contemplated as a possibility. This suggestion was accepted by the Committee, and it appears that the insertion of the provision which formed article 56, paragraph 2, of the Treaty of Neuilly was made at the last moment before the draft Treaty was delivered to the Bulgarian delegation for its observations.

On October 24, 1919, the Bulgarian delegation sent their observations on the provisions of articles 49 to 57 of the draft Peace Treaty, those concerning the Protection of Minorities. The delegation accepted all these provisions, called attention to the "pitiful state" of refugees in Bulgaria, and pointed out that "it is of pressing importance to settle the problem of emigration, from which Bulgaria suffers so much." "For if the discontent of these refugees is further increased by a final refusal to permit them to return to their homes, this would constitute a constant obstacle to the calming of popular discontent."

The Committee on New States, in considering the above remarks,[11] found that among these refugees there were political agitators, whose return to the districts transferred to neighbor states would be undesirable. It was thought that it would not be just to impose on the Serb-Croat-Slovene State or on Greece the obligation of receiving an indefinite number of persons of possible active Bulgarian sympathies simply on

[10] It was first intended that the Convention should be signed also by the Allied and Associated Powers. Subsequently, on the suggestion of the Drafting Committee, the approval of the Allied and Associated Powers was put in the preamble of the Convention.

[11] 54th meeting of the Committee, October 28, 1919.

the ground of their previous residence in districts previously, or by the present Treaty, ceded to Serbia or to Greece.

When the definite draft Convention was adopted by the Committee on New States on November 17, and was to be submitted to the Supreme Council, the question arose whether it ought to be submitted to the Bulgarian delegation for its observations. The Committee agreed with the view of the American delegation that the impracticability of extending the Convention to other Balkan States might well cause the Bulgarian delegation to object that the provisions of the Convention were not 'reciprocal' in the spirit of article 56, paragraph 2, of the Peace Treaty, as they only concerned Bulgarian minorities in Greece and Greek minorities in Bulgaria, while they made no provision for the large Bulgarian minorities in Serbia and Dobrudja. In view of this fact, and because the proposed convention might appear to be an aggravation of the Treaty of Peace and go beyond the terms of article 56, there was felt to be a moral obligation to submit the draft convention to the Bulgarian delegation.

On November 19, the Supreme Council approved a report of the Committee on New States incorporating the draft convention, and decided to submit the draft to the Bulgarian delegation. This was done on the same day, and on November 23 a reply was received from the Bulgarian delegation.[12] Four days later the Peace Treaty and the Convention were signed at Neuilly.

The reply of the Bulgarian delegation stated that they approved entirely the provisions of the Convention and noted "with the greatest satisfaction that the draft was based upon entire reciprocity between the two States interested," and "hastened to adopt its provisions all the more willingly because the composition and functions of the Mixed Commission were of such a nature as to inspire in it the greatest confidence." A fuller acceptance of the Convention cannot be conceived.

The Bulgarian reply asked only two questions with regard to the draft Convention. First, whether the taxes due to the

[12] 62d meeting of the Committee on New States, November 24, 1919.

state were to be paid by the emigrants. Secondly, the following question: "The Bulgarian Delegation understands that by virtue of Art. 11, par. 2, and by application of the rules of reciprocity, the excess in value of the immovable property liquidated shall be paid to the State interested and that particularly it shall not be retained on account of the unilateral application, with regard only to Bulgaria, of Art. 177 (*b*) and (*h*) of the Peace Treaty. However, the conditions necessary for its applications are completely lacking in this case, otherwise the reciprocity, by which the draft Convention is inspired, would be vain and the financial situation of Bulgaria would have to support new charges, difficult at present to foresee."

The Committee decided on November 24, in examining the reply, to answer that the Bulgarian interpretation was correct. This point is to be kept in mind. It is considered in a subsequent chapter.[13]

From the above, the following conclusions are to be drawn. First, the idea of a reciprocal emigration of national minorities between Greece and Bulgaria originated with Mr. Venizelos; secondly, the Convention respecting Reciprocal Emigration was conceived as a supplement to the provisions of the treaties for the protection of minorities; thirdly, the Bulgarian government welcomed the Convention with satisfaction; and, lastly, the Convention was so drawn as to insure full reciprocity between the two countries. In this all honor is due to the statesmen who drafted the Convention not on the basis of taking advantage of a defeated Bulgaria but of promoting and securing peace in the Balkans.

§ 4. Protection of national minorities by treaties. The Convention concerning Reciprocal Emigration between Greece and Bulgaria, the history of which is described above, attempted to solve the problem of Greek and Bulgarian minorities in the two countries in a more radical way than the provisions for the protection of minorities of the Treaty of Neuilly and of the Treaty concerning the Protection of Minorities in Greece, signed at Sèvres, August 10, 1920.

[13] See Chapter XV, The Payments.

Under the provisions of the Treaty of Neuilly, part iii, section iv, Bulgaria undertook to assure full and complete protection of life and liberty to all inhabitants of Bulgaria without distinction of birth, nationality, language, race, or religion (article 50). Further, the Treaty provided (articles 51-55) for equality before the law and enjoyment of equal civil and political rights for all Bulgarian nationals; for the free use of any language in private affairs; and for the right of racial, religious, or linguistic minorities to establish and maintain charitable, religious, social, and educational institutions in Bulgaria.

Greece, on the other hand, under the Minorities Treaty of 1920 undertook similar obligations. In addition, she promised (article 3) to permit Bulgarian nationals habitually resident in territories transferred to Greece by treaties subsequent to January 1, 1913, to choose Bulgarian nationality. Persons thus choosing were to transfer their place of residence to Bulgaria within twelve months. They were entitled, however, to retain their immovable property in Greece.

This provision seems quite extraordinary when it is compared with the Convention concerning Reciprocal Emigration of 1919, which was a specific attempt to encourage emigration and to liquidate the properties of emigrants so that they should retain no link with the country which they left. By permitting members of the Bulgarian minority in Greece to choose Bulgarian nationality and quit the Greek territory and yet retain their properties in Greece, the Minorities Treaty encouraged irreconcilable Bulgarians to refuse to take advantage of the Convention respecting Reciprocal Emigration and to retain the hope that some day the territory in question would again become Bulgarian.

In addition to this, article 4 of the Treaty concerning the Protection of Minorities in Greece recognized as Greek nationals persons of Bulgarian nationality, born in the territories transferred to Greece from parents habitually resident therein, even though such persons at the time of the coming into effect of the treaty were not habitually resident in Greece. In other words, all refugees in Bulgaria born in Macedonia and Thrace under the above conditions were free to return to Greece and remain there. This, again, was in conflict with the whole purpose of the Convention, that of clearing up the inextricable intermingling of the two racial elements in these territories and establishing a racial homogeneity therein.

This strange conflict between the two Conventions is only explained by the fact that the above provisions were typical of all the treaties concerning the protection of minorities drawn up by the Peace Conference, and by the further fact that when the Convention respecting Reciprocal Emigration was being drafted the Minorities Treaty was already prepared. Yet this treaty was not signed until several months later, and it is a great puzzle that the conflict with the provisions of the Convention of 1919 was not corrected.

Be this as it may, it must be recalled that in 1919, when the treaties concerning the protection of minorities were being prepared, great hopes were placed in the efficacy of their provisions. The hostility which they met from some of the states, as Jugoslavia, Rumania, and Poland, served only to enhance these hopes. It was a mark of great perspicacity on the part of the sponsors of the idea of the Convention respecting Reciprocal Emigration to realize that something more than treaty provisions for the protection of minorities was necessary if it was desired to eradicate the causes of racial antagonism between Greece and Bulgaria.

§ 5. Contents of the Convention concerning Reciprocal Emigration. The Convention concerning Reciprocal Emigration was intended to encourage reciprocal voluntary emigration of the national minorities of the two countries. Its first article declared that the Contracting Parties recognized the right of those of their subjects belonging to racial, religious, or linguistic minorities to emigrate freely to their respective territories. The signatory states undertook to facilitate, by all the means at their disposal, the exercise of that right, and to place no restriction on the right of emigration, except in the case of a person definitely sentenced for an infraction of ordinary law (articles 2 and 3).

The voluntary character of the emigration is particularly emphasized. The agreement was primarily not for carrying out the emigration, but for recognizing *the right* of national minorities to emigrate and for facilitating the exercise of such right. At the same time no provision was made against compelling national minorities to emigrate. The emphasis is put on securing the exercise of the right; it was agreed "not to place directly or indirectly any restriction on the right of emigration, notwithstanding laws or regulations to the contrary."

Since the Convention set up a machinery for facilitating and supervising the emigration, it was provided that persons desirous of obtaining the advantages of the Convention should exercise the right of emigration within a period of two years [14] from the constitution of the Mixed Commission, by means of a declaration before the Commission or its representatives. The emigrants were to lose the nationality of the country which they left and acquire that of the country of destination (articles 4 and 5).

For the purpose of facilitating the exercise of the right of emigration and removing any obstacle thereto, the Convention contained provisions calculated to guard against pecuniary injury to the emigrants. The latter could take away their movable property, enjoying for this purpose exemption from custom duties in both countries. On the other hand, their immovable property was to be liquidated by a Mixed Commission, according to a procedure to be determined by it, and was to be paid for by the Commission from funds placed at its disposal by the two governments (articles 6, 7, and 10).

Within three months from the entry into force of the Convention, a Mixed Commission was to be constituted, composed of a member appointed by each of the signatory states concerned, and of an equal number of members of another nationality, appointed by the Council of the League of Nations.

[14] The draft prepared by the Greek delegation and submitted to the Committee on New States provided for a period of four years. In this it showed a closer grasp on realities. As will be seen, the period of two years had to be lengthened to four. See *infra,* p. 91.

One of the latter members was to be the President of the Commission.

The Commission was to decide by a majority vote, the President having a casting vote in case of a tie. The powers of the Commission were to be these: To supervise and facilitate the voluntary emigration; to liquidate the immovable property of the emigrants; to fix the conditions of emigration and of liquidation of real property; and, in general, to take the measures rendered necessary by the execution of the Convention, and to decide all questions to which the Convention might give rise (articles 8 and 9).

In view of the lack of provisions in the Convention with regard to the bases of appraisal and liquidation of estates of emigrants, it is clear that the discretionary powers of the Commission were large. The two governments were to turn over to the Commission, for transmission to the rightful parties, the value of the real properties liquidated, which were to remain the properties of the said governments. The expenses for the maintenance and working of the Commission and its agencies were to be borne by the governments concerned in proportions to be determined by the Commission (articles 10, 11, and 13).

The Convention had a political purpose, namely, to clear up an atmosphere heavy with national animosities and historical enmities. It was meant not only to facilitate the emigration of dissatisfied minorities, but also to compose difficulties created in the past. The Commission was, accordingly, given the additional authority to liquidate properties left by Bulgarians or Greeks who, prior to the coming into force of the Convention, had already emigrated to the country to which they belonged by race, religion, or language (article 12). This provision had been contained in the draft prepared by the Greek delegation.

§ 6. Ratification and application of the Convention. The Convention was ratified by both countries. The exchange of ratifications took place at Paris on August 9, 1920.[15] According-

[15] League of Nations, *Treaty Series,* i, p. 68.

ing to its final provisions, the Convention was to be ratified and to come into effect at the same time that the Treaty of Neuilly should be ratified and enter into force as between Greece and Bulgaria. The Treaty of Neuilly went into effect on August 9, 1920. This date, then, is that on which the Convention concerning Reciprocal Emigration became effective.

The Convention did not become applicable in Thrace immediately. This province, which Bulgaria by the Treaty of Neuilly had ceded to the Principal Allied and Associated Powers, was ceded to Greece by the Principal Allied and Associated Powers by the Treaty concerning Thrace, signed at Sèvres on August 10, 1920, but not ratified until August 6, 1924, long after the Conference of Lausanne.[16] Article 3 provided that "the provisions of the Convention concluded on November 27, 1919, between Greece and Bulgaria, relating to reciprocal emigration, will apply *ipso facto* to the territories referred to in Article 1." The Treaty of Lausanne of July 24, 1923, ratified on the same date as the treaty last named, confirmed the cession of Western Thrace to Greece and defined the boundary between it and the territories possessed by Turkey. The Mixed Commission, taking note of a declaration of the Greek member, affirmed that the application of the Convention in Thrace began on October 26, 1923.[17]

The Convention, composed of sixteen articles, was not an entirely satisfactory document. It left far too many questions to be determined by the Mixed Commission. It bears the earmarks of hasty preparation. Most of its provisions refer to the right of emigration itself and few deal with the property interests. Such important questions as that of the properties of communities; the definition and delimitation of the persons who had already emigrated from the two countries; the bases of appraisal of properties; the payments under the Convention, etc., were either left undetermined or merely outlined. These questions came up again and again in the deliberations of the Commission, often raised insurmountable difficulties,

[16] For the text of the Treaty, see League of Nations, *Treaty Series*, xxviii, pp. 226-242. The ratification by Greece was deposited February 11, 1924.

[17] See Commission Mixte Grèco-Bulgare, Procès-Verbaux, viii, 156th meet., October 26, 1923, p. 1014.

and caused excessive delays in the completion and termination of the work of the Commission.

§ 7. **The Rules for the execution of the Convention.** In view of this character of the Convention, other documents were subsequently necessary to supplement it. The Rules on the Reciprocal and Voluntary Emigration of Greek and Bulgarian Minorities were worked out in 1922 by the Mixed Commission. They were meant to determine the rules to be followed by the Commission in facilitating and supervising the emigration of minorities, the liquidation of properties, and the duties and rights of emigrants.

The Commission adopted the Rules on March 6, 1922; and on the same date it communicated them to the two interested governments, with the request that they take the necessary measures for rendering the Rules effective in their respective territories.[18] The two governments approved the Rules and published them in their respective official journals. They also took the legislative and administrative measures required for the application of the Rules in their entirety. As the application of these measures was subject in each country to the condition of reciprocity, the Mixed Commission on November 11, 1922,[19] declared that such reciprocity existed, and decided to proceed forthwith with the application of the Rules.[20]

§ 8. **Contents of the Rules.** The Rules, composed of seventy-six articles, were divided into two parts. The first section of the first part dealt with general questions. It was provided that freedom of emigration and the exercise of the other rights arising under the Convention were to be secured through the Mixed Commission and its agents. Such agents were to be the Sub-Commissions and such others as the Commission was to appoint. The Sub-Commissions were to decide

[18] Procès-Verbaux, v, 96th meet., p. 662, and 99th meet., pp. 676-678.

[19] Procès-Verbaux, vi, 115th meet., pp. 785-786. The rules were approved and published in the Official Journal in Bulgaria June 28, 1922, and in Greece September 1, 1922. The laws were published in Bulgaria May 1, 1922, and Greece June 2/15, and August 11/24, 1922.

[20] The Rules were amended in many respects by subsequent decisions of the Commission, for which no explicit approval of the governments was required.

in the first instance, in conformity with the Rules and the instructions received from the Mixed Commission, all questions relating to concrete cases of emigration of persons belonging to the minorities and domiciled in their district. Article 5 provided also that the Sub-Commissions should make a first appraisal of the real property that new and former emigrants desired to have liquidated by the Mixed Commission. The *procès-verbaux* of such appraisals were to be submitted to the Commission, which would determine finally the amount to be paid.[21] Article 6 laid down the rule that all decisions of the Sub-Commissions were to be subject to revision by the Mixed Commission in case of appeal or at the initiative of the Commission. This rule later suffered many qualifications.

Section II of the first part dealt with the conditions required for admission to the benefits of the Convention; Section III with the rights and obligations of persons admitted to such benefits. Such persons were distinguished as future emigrants and persons who had already emigrated. A third class was constituted by the communities (*communautés*). These were regarded by the Rules as juristic persons, and the same criteria of race, language, and religion were applied to them as to physical persons. All this part of the Rules was modified by subsequent decisions of the Commission, as will be seen in following chapters.

The Rules further determined the conditions and facilities of emigration, and defined the property which the emigrants could take with them and that which could be liquidated by the Commission or sold by the emigrants themselves. The Rules also specified that the basis of appraisal of real estate should be "the actual value at the time of liquidation," and that payments should be made partly in cash and partly in government bonds. Special provisions were made for persons who had already emigrated and for the restitution to them of property confiscated or subjected to restrictions during their absence from the country.

The second part of the Rules dealt with questions of pro-

[21] This simple method of appraisal proved, as might have been expected, impracticable. The actual methods in which various kinds of properties were appraised are described in following chapters.

cedure, relating to the declaration of emigration; the proof of membership in a racial, religious, or linguistic minority; the application for liquidation; the establishment of the property rights of applicants; the appraisal of properties, and so forth.

The Rules were hardly adequate for the proper execution of the Convention. After more than a year from the time of the constitution of the Commission had been allowed to go by without any serious work, the actual drawing up of the Rules was hurriedly completed in less than two months. The result was a defective document, which had to be completed, corrected, and modified by a great number of subsequent decisions of the Commission. The various decisions of the Commission completing or modifying the Rules will be referred to below as the various questions are considered.

§ 9. **The Plan of Payment.** At the same time with its work on the Rules, the Mixed Commission began to draw up the Plan of Payment. The Plan was adopted December 8, 1922,[22] and approved by the two governments. Its purpose was to establish the rules according to which payments were to be made by the Greek and Bulgarian governments to emigrants, and to regulate the transfer of funds from the one country to the other. The two governments were to advance to the Mixed Commission the funds necessary for the payment of the value of the liquidated property, which was to remain the property of the two governments. The Plan established the rule that ten per cent of the appraisal of the real estates of emigrants was to be paid in cash by the country in which such estates were to be left. The remaining ninety per cent of the appraisal was to be paid in public bonds, bearing interest, of the state to which the emigrants transferred themselves. Each government, in this respect, was put in the other's place for the payment of ninety per cent of the appraisal. The Plan was based on the assumption that the liquidation of the real estates of emigrants would be made before their departure from their country of origin. In fact, the situation developed otherwise. A great number of emigrants left their country of

[22] It was subsequently amended on September 28 and October 26, 1923.

origin, in order to establish themselves in the country to which in race, religion, or language they were akin, before the liquidation of their property was completed.

Accordingly the Commission, on August 14, 1926,[23] adopted a new Plan to adapt the payments to the new conditions. This new Plan, not being approved by either of the two governments, never went into effect. The other provisions of the Plan of 1922 dealt with the general organization of payments, the cash payments and the mechanism of the payments in bonds, the liquidation accounts between the two governments, the regulation of the debts between them and between the National Banks of the two countries, and, lastly, the guarantees given by each government for the bonds.

§ 10. The Caphandaris-Molloff Agreement. With the termination of the work of liquidation by the Mixed Commission, the subject of payments assumed a great importance and caused continuous friction between the two governments and the Commission. The question of adequate guarantees to be given by each country for the bonds delivered to emigrants and of the amortization of such bonds as well as the question of settlement of accounts between the two countries formed the subjects of long negotiations between the Mixed Commission, the Financial Committee of the League of Nations, and the governments concerned. These resulted finally in an agreement, known as the Caphandaris-Molloff Agreement from the names of the Ministers of Finance of the two countries, who negotiated and signed it at Geneva on December 9, 1927, with the coöperation of the Financial Committee of the League of Nations and the advice and assent of the President of the Commission. This Agreement was meant to take the place of article 9, paragraphs 2, 3, and 4, and articles 11-19 of the Plan of Payment of December 8, 1922. It was ratified by the Bulgarian government on April 3, 1928, and by the Greek government on December 9, 1928. The ratifications were deposited at the Secretariat of the League of Nations on February 22 and March 8, 1929, respectively. This Agreement is considered in Chapter XV.

[23] Procès-Verbaux, xv, 279th meet., pp. 1788-89.

CHAPTER II

THE MIXED COMMISSION: ITS AGENCIES AND THEIR WORK

§ 11. Constitution of the Mixed Commission. According to article 8 of the Convention concerning Reciprocal Emigration of November 27, 1919, the Mixed Commission was to be created within three months from the entry into force of the Convention. As the Convention came into force August 9, 1920, the Commission should have been constituted by November 9, 1920. As a matter of fact it was not constituted until December 18, 1920, at which date its members met at Geneva and exchanged their full powers. The Commission decided that this date should be considered as that of its constitution.[1] For the appointment of the two neutral members of the Commission the intervention of the Council of the League of Nations was necessary, according to article 8 of the Convention.

[1] See League of Nations, Document C. 442. M. 319. 1921. I.

The Council decided on September 20, 1920, upon two neutral members of the Mixed Commission, whose names do not appear in the *Procès-Verbal* of the Session of the Council. The Chairman was requested, in consultation with the Secretary-General, to take the steps required to make the appointments final. On October 20,[2] the Council was informed by the Greek member, Mr. Demetrius Caclamanos, that one of the two members invited to sit on the Commission had agreed to sit and the other had refused. M. Paul Hymans, the Belgian Member of the Council, was asked to find a substitute. It would seem that Commandant Marcel de Roover of Belgium was this second choice, in place, perhaps, of the Swiss judge Thélin. Lieutenant-Colonel A. C. Corfe, from New Zealand, was the other neutral member appointed to the Commission. Colonel Corfe acted as President for the first six months from the constitution of the Commission. Mr. G. Tsorbazoglou, resident minister, and Mr. Vladimir Robeff were the members appointed by the Greek and Bulgarian governments respectively.

The Convention provided (article 8) that the Chairman of the Commission should be chosen from the two neutral members, but it was not specified who was to appoint him. The choice of the President, as the Rapporteur to the Council of the League, M. Léon Bourgeois, noted, was of special importance; according to article 9 of the Convention he had the casting vote in case of an equal division. The Council recommended that the two members appointed by it should act as President in turn, each for six months, and that the first President should be chosen by lot at the first meeting of the Commission.

On March 23, 1926, Major de Roover requested to be relieved of his duties, and M. James de Reynier, of Switzerland, was appointed in his place as of June 15, 1926.[3]

§ 12. Duties of the Commission. The Commission was granted very large powers by the Convention. It had, in the

[2] League of Nations, Council, *Procès-Verbal of the Tenth Session,* p. 9.

[3] See League of Nations, *Official Journal,* August, 1926, p. 1069; Commission Mixte, Procès-Verbaux, xiv, 268th meet., p. 1727.

first place, to make sure of the voluntary character of the emigration, to see that it was properly carried out, and that no pecuniary damage was suffered by the emigrants. It was to determine whether and in what cases the members of communities dissolved by reason of the emigration should have the power to take away freely the movable property belonging to such communities. It was to proceed to the appraisal of immovable property; to determine the procedure of liquidation; to receive funds from the two governments and to make payments to individual emigrants; and, in general, to take all measures required for the execution of the Convention. The Commission was to serve, so to speak, as an intermediary agency between the governments and the emigrants, and to see that the latter should receive no pecuniary damage by reason of their emigration. It was endowed with functions of a legislative, administrative, and judiciary character, as will be seen later in this chapter. Its work involved many delicate legal questions, such as the determination of the bases of appraisal of properties, the status of communities of emigrant minorities and their properties, the interpretation of the tangled provisions of the land law in regions formerly under Turkish rule, and so on.

§ 13. Qualifications of the members of the Commission. Under these conditions it would seem evident that the neutral members appointed to the Commission should have been persons not only absolutely impartial and disinterested, but also possessed of great ability in handling complex situations, and of the legal training and judicial attitude necessary for deciding tangled legal questions.

Originally, the name of M. Thélin, a Swiss Federal Judge, was put before the Council of the League of Nations for membership in the Commission. This would have been a happy choice. It is probable that he declined and that Commandant Marcel de Roover was the second choice. With regard to the second neutral member of the Commission, it was stated by M. Léon Bourgeois, then President of the Council, that it would be advisable to reserve the seat for a national of one of the British Dominions, "which had not yet had an opportunity of participating in the work of the League." [4] Without reflecting on the appointee from New Zealand, one may doubt whether the institution of Mixed Commissions should serve as an opportunity for nationals of various countries to learn to participate in the work of the League. Certainly, the confidence in international institutions is severely damaged when the appointees are not qualified by the training and experience needed for the work they are called upon to execute.

In the case of the Mixed Commission, the neutral members, besides possessing the above-stated qualifications, needed to be persons of prestige and authority, with ability to deal with such imponderable elements as differences of national psychology and modes of thought, and a working experience with financial questions, questions of value and price, assessment of damages, etc. Nor could their ignorance or inability in these respects be wholly supplied by advice given by various experts. For it was of the utmost importance that their authority and prestige in the eyes of the members representing the two countries should be of a high level, if an efficient Commission was to be set up. In the countries where the Commission was to function only personal prestige and authority could be victorious against the antagonistic spirit of the national members.

The writer has ascertained from his study of the *Procès-Verbaux* of the Mixed Commission, as well as from personal observation and information gathered at Geneva, Sofia, and Athens, that the neutral members of the Mixed Commission lacked the qualifications most necessary for this work. Colonel A. C. Corfe, of New Zealand, was the member appointed with the desire of giving to this Dominion "an opportunity of participating in the work of the League." He would be a perfect member of a Commission for delimitation of boundaries, but it is doubtful whether he had any place in a Commission having to deal with economic and legal questions. His reports to the Commission disclose that he never really appreciated the

[4] See League of Nations, Council, *Procès-Verbal of the Ninth Session*, p. 5.

extent of its work, and he had no ability, or made no significant effort, to speed up the work. In some quarters there existed doubt of his entire impartiality.[5]

Commandant de Roover, from Belgium, gave to the work of the Commission the benefits of a keen intelligence and an enormous activity. Indeed, his was a devastating activity to such an extent that it annoyed one of the two governments, which brought about a request from M. de Roover to be relieved from his duties. M. de Roover's ability manifested itself in drawing perfect theoretical plans for the work of the Commission which could not possibly be executed in reality. He withdrew from the Commission before the main work of liquidation began.

His successor, M. James de Reynier, of Switzerland, was former Chairman of the Danzig Harbor and Waterways Board; former member of the Committee of Experts for the delimitation of the Port of Danzig for the purposes of the Polish Postal Service; and former Provisional Records Commissioner for the Saar Basin plebiscite. His impartiality and fairness were never doubted. He was very industrious, and imbued with the desire of completing the work of the Commission. His mind remained always alert and resourceful. But his reports to the Commission show that his expectations and conclusions were divorced from reality, The work of liquidation remained somewhat outside his comprehension. He was not possessed of legal training.

Similar remarks may be made with respect to the members appointed by each of the two governments concerned. The Bulgarian member, Mr. Vladimir Robeff, was replaced on July 22, 1925, by Mr. G. Djoudjeff who remained continuously in service from that time. The original Greek member, Mr. G. Tsorbazoglou, was replaced successively by Messrs. P. Metaxas (August 8, 1924, to February 21, 1925), Colocotroni (to May 1, 1925), Joannes Papas (to February 3, 1926), C. Xanthopoulos (to May 5, 1926), S. Gheorgopoulos (to January 18, 1929), and G. Exintaris. The common criticism to be

[5] See, for instance, his action in bringing about a modification of the rate of conversion of buildings, and the discussions in the Commission, *infra*, §§ 191-193.

made against these members is that they were all diplomats primarily and not lawyers or practical men. The frequent change in the person of the Greek representative has not permitted continuity and unity in the preparation of his work or in his position and views. Mr. S. Gheorgopoulos has been undoubtedly the outstanding national member of the Commission. It was due to his industry and practical mind that the Commission completed the most of its work during the two and a half years of his service on the Commission.[6] But, strangely and needlessly he too often antagonized the neutral members of the Commission; this caused a slowing up of the work, ill feelings, and a spirit of opposition to his proposals even though they were sound.

In general, and especially in the first part of the life of the Commission, an antagonistic spirit prevailed between the national members. Each took a different view on many points, not always very essential, and showed a determination to abide by his view, forgetful of the advantages of a speedy termination of the work of the Commission.

§ 14. **Juridical and political status of the Commission.** The intervention of the Council of the League was necessary only for the appointment of the two neutral members of the Commission. When the question of the nomination of these members came up before the Council of the League, it was clearly understood that "the responsibility of the Council was limited to the appointment of the Commissioners, and that it was not required to interfere with the general activities of the Commission," and that "these [members] shall act under the control and the responsibility of the High Contracting Powers," [7] viz., Greece and Bulgaria. This was not, however, the original feeling of the two members nominated by the Council of the League, who took upon themselves, quite unwarrantedly, the title of "delegates of the League of Nations," and considered themselves entitled to report to the Secretary-

[6] See his comprehensive reports from tours of inspection and action on his proposals. Commission Mixte, Procès-Verbaux, xxi, 360th meeting, August 18, 1927, annex i; xxii, 371st meeting, October 6, 1927, p. 1.

[7] See League of Nations, Council, *Procès-Verbal of the Ninth Session,* pp. 5, 121; and cf. League of Nations, *Official Journal,* October, 1920, pp 410-413.

General on the work of the Commission. This was given up later, at the instance, it is believed, of the Greek member, Mr. Gheorgopoulos.[8]

The understanding of the Council of the League was that the neutral members were to act under the authority and on behalf of the countries concerned. This meant, of course, the joint authority of the two countries. But what did this 'authority' signify, and how was it different from the authority exercised by each of the two governments over its own appointees?

This question came up often at the meetings of the Commission. Three different positions seem to have been supported. The Greek position was that the neutral members of the Commission were merely high functionaries of the two governments, deriving their authority and their powers solely from the confidence of the said governments. According to this view, the two neutral members did not differ from the other two members of the Commission, except in that they were appointed by the Council of the League and that they assumed in turn the Presidency of the Commission. The Bulgarian position was that the four members of the Commission should be considered as four arbitral judges, of whom two were interested in the questions decided, while the two others should give a disinterested opinion. The neutral members of the Commission seemed to hold the view that they were two arbiters deciding questions between two parties, the members representing the two governments.

None of these three views seemed to fit with the provisions of the Convention which defined the powers of the Commission. Indeed, article 9 of the Convention, besides enumerating in the first two paragraphs some of the functions to be exercised by the Commission, provided, in the third paragraph, that "in general, the Mixed Commission shall have full powers to take the measures rendered necessary by the

[8] See League of Nations, Document C. 442. M. 319. 1921. I; Commission Mixte, Procès-Verbaux, viii, August 30, 1923, p. 981. See also Procès-Verbaux until December 15, 1925 (xiii, 249th meeting) where the neutral members are designated as "Delegates of the League of Nations." For some time after December 21, 1925, they are designated as "Members appointed by the Council of the League of Nations," and later merely as "neutral members."

execution of the present Convention and to decide all questions to which this Convention may give rise." If this provision be considered in connection with that of article 15, that "the High Contracting Parties undertake to make in their respective legislation the modifications necessary to secure the execution of the present Convention," it will be seen that the Mixed Commission as a body was given practically unlimited powers, so far as the execution of the Convention was concerned. The Commission had the power to interpret the Convention, to fix the conditions of emigration and of liquidation of real property, and to take all necessary measures. The two governments were bound to make the required payments, to put no obstacles in the way of emigration under the Convention, and to modify their laws when necessary to secure the execution of the Convention. It might be said [9] that the internal sovereignty of the two governments was limited with regard to the matters dealt with by the Convention, for which the jurisdiction of the Mixed Commission was paramount.

To this position of the Mixed Commission under the Convention accords the provision of the fourth paragraph of article 9, that the decisions of the Commission should be taken by a majority vote, the Chairman's vote being decisive in case of tie. In view of the fact that only a neutral member of the Commission could hold the office of Chairman, it follows that the votes of the two neutral members in the Mixed Commission could decide all questions. Under these conditions, it would be futile to argue that these two members were "under the authority and joint control of the two governments." These terms, as used in the report of M. Bourgeois, could have no legal connotation and must be taken only in a general political sense. This, indeed, is consistent with the fact that the Mixed Commission and its agents were to be maintained, under the provision of article 13, by funds provided by the two governments. The governments, then, could presumably kill the Mixed Commission by ceasing to defray the expenses of its maintenance. The further political significance of the terms "authority and joint control of the two

[9] See on this point André Wurfbain, *L'échange Grèco-Bulgare des minorités ethniques* (Lausanne, 1930), pp. 56 ff.

governments" is that a neutral member losing the confidence of one of these governments could be made to resign from the Commission.

However, for all practical purposes, it should be understood that the Mixed Commission was free from the control of the two governments, and that this was so by reason of the fact that the national members, each of whom presumably acted in accordance with instructions from his government, formed the minority in the Mixed Commission as against the two neutral members.

In practice, the action of the Mixed Commission conformed to the above theory of its juridical and political status. Indeed, the Commission, according to the position of the neutral members stated above, would have the right to take decisions even though one of the national members should be absent. A motion, however, by the President to have the Commission take a decision to that effect was not insisted upon against the objection of the national members. On the other hand, the consequence of the acceptance of the Greek position would be that the Commission could not decide anything against the combined votes of the two national members, which expressed the agreement of the two governments. In fact the practice was that, inasmuch as the two neutral members had a preponderance of votes over those of the Greek and Bulgarian members, the Commission took many decisions by the vote of the neutral members.[10] It is well that it did. In very numerous instances the work of the Commission would have remained at a standstill if the opposition of the two national members could have prevented the taking of a decision. This was the fate of the Mixed Commission for the Exchange of Greek and Turkish Populations, the neutral members of which did not constitute a majority.[11]

§ 15. Interference of the Council of the League. The original disinclination of the Council of the League to interfere with the general activities of the Mixed Commission was

[10] See, for instance, Procès-Verbaux, xvi, 302d meet.; xvii, 327th meet.; xix, 345th meet., p. 2; xx, 353d meet., p. 15; xxi, 356th meet., p. 8. At this last meeting the Commission decided to increase the number of functionaries against the objections of the Greek and Bulgarian members that the budgets of their countries could not support any additional burden.

[11] See *infra*, § 239.

overcome at a later time, in consequence of the serious frontier incidents between Greece and Bulgaria in October, 1925. The Commission of Inquiry appointed to investigate these incidents submitted to the Council of the League two political recommendations which were adopted by the Council on December 14, 1925.[12] They called for the hastening of the liquidation of emigrants' properties and for the extension of the time-limit for the deposit of applications for the liquidation of properties of Bulgarian refugees in Bulgaria who came from Greece. Reports on the carrying out of these recommendations were sent to the Secretariat of the League and submitted to the Council until September, 1927. At that time,[13] the Council thought that it no longer need occupy itself with the activities of the Commission. At the same time, however, it requested the Financial Committee of the League to give advice on any technical aspects of the financial side of the liquidation to the President of the Commission whenever he should wish to consult them. This opened a new avenue for the intervention of the Council. The neutral members of the Commission availed themselves generously of this opportunity of bringing to bear upon the two governments the influence of the League. As will be seen, this influence was continuously exercised thenceforth.[14]

The neutral members of the Commission, however, took so much advantage of the authorization given by the Council to consult the Financial Committee that on one occasion their trip to Geneva was regarded as calculated to put undue pressure upon the Greek government. Steps taken by the Greek government and the Financial Committee compelled the neutral member, Colonel Corfe, to renounce his trip to Geneva, and obliged the President, who had started for Geneva, to continue his voyage to Paris and London, where a rendezvous was arranged for him by the President of the Financial Committee.[15]

[12] League of Nations, *Official Journal*, February, 1926, pp. 172-175. See also *infra*, p. 92.
[13] *Ibid.*, October, 1927, p. 1112.
[14] See *infra*, § 209.
[15] Procès-Verbaux, xxxii, 469th meet., January 14, 1928, p. 2.

§ 16. **Substitutes for members of the Commission.** No provision was made in the Convention for appointing substitutes for the members of the Commission, either those appointed by the two governments or those nominated by the Council of the League. The Council thought it proper that the right should be given to the members whom it appointed to nominate substitutes in case of their absence, and that they should inform the Secretary-General of the League by telegram of such nomination. Later the Mixed Commission decided, on December 20, 1920, that the Greek and Bulgarian members must be represented by substitutes designated by them whenever they were prevented from attending a meeting.[16] In case no such substitute was designated, the Mixed Commission decided (against a proposition of the President to the effect that the Commission should not be prevented from holding meetings and taking decisions) that a protest should be addressed by the President to the governments concerned.[17] The neutral members of the Commission were on several occasions represented by Secretaries of the Commission, or by a President of a Sub-Commission.[18] But when a neutral member was unable to attend the meetings by reason of sickness, the Commission decided that it would hold meetings and take decisions by majority vote of its three other members. Each of the latter, however, would have the right to oppose the taking of any decision unless the sick neutral member should be consulted and should express his opinion by a representative.[19]

§ 17. **Place of meeting of the Commission.** The Commission met for the first time at Geneva on December 18, 1920.

16 Procès-Verbaux, i, 2d meet., p. 6.

17 Procès-Verbaux, xv, 271st meet., July 7, 1926, pp. 1743-45.

18 On the departure of the President of the Commission, de Reynier, to Geneva, in September, 1927, a President of a Sub-Commission was asked by him to take his place at the meeting of the Commission. This was in accordance with the view taken by the Council of the League. But M. de Reynier did not notify the Greek and Bulgarian members of the substitution. For this reason the Greek member refused to attend the Meetings of September 14 and 15. These two meetings were then held as extraordinary meetings and not as meetings of the Mixed Commission and dealt only with an urgent question. The Commission met again on September 22, when M. de Reynier returned from Geneva. Procès-Verbaux, xxii, 3d and 4th extraordinary meetings.

19 Procès-Verbaux, ix, 171st meet., February 6, 1924, pp. 1076, 1077.

From this date until January 26, 1921, it held at Geneva twenty-seven meetings in an effort to arrive at an interpretation of the Convention. At the end of January it proceeded to Sofia and in March to Athens,[20] where it remained until December 9, 1922, when it suspended its meetings, to resume them on February 5, 1923, at Sofia.[21] In the meantime the Sub-Commissions began the preparatory work in Bulgaria and Macedonia and the Commission thought it advisable to be near the centres of emigration and liquidation. But on November 7, 1924, it accepted the proposal of the Greek government and decided to transfer its seat to Athens.[22] It returned again to Sofia on October 1, 1926,[23] where it sat continuously, with the exception of brief visits to Saloniki and Geneva, until March 15, 1929. At that time the seat of the Commission was again transferred to Athens.[24]

§ 18. Decisions of the Commission. The Commission, as stated above, could take decisions by a majority vote. As a matter of fact, most of the decisions taken by the Commission were reached in this way. Few unanimous decisions were arrived at, and these mainly in matters of small importance. In the beginning of the work of the Commission there was a tendency to seek unanimous decisions. This was, however, later abandoned.

At an early date [25] the Commission decided that as a rule it would not change its prior decisions and would not reconsider a question which had been previously decided by a unanimous or majority vote. In exceptional cases the following procedure was followed. A member of the Commission who desired to reopen the discussion on a certain question and to set aside a decision taken thereon, was to prepare a memorandum setting forth his proposal and the reasons for it. A copy of the memorandum was to be delivered to the President

[20] See League of Nations, Document C. 442. M. 319. 1921. I.
[21] Procès-Verbaux, vi, 128th meet., pp. 829-830.
[22] Procès-Verbaux, xi, 208th meet., p. 1297.
[23] Procès-Verbaux, xv, 277th meet., pp. 1777-78.
[24] Procès-Verbaux, xxxi, 460th meet., November 23, 1928, p. 13. To March, 1929, the Commission had sat for 56 months at Sofia and for 39 months in Greece.
[25] Procès-Verbaux, i, 11th meet., January 4, 1921, p. 49.

and to each of the members of the Commission. At the first meeting of the Commission following the lapse of three days from the delivery of the above memorandum, the President was to put to vote the question of reopening the discussion according to the request made. In case three-quarters of the votes were in favor of the request, it was to be accepted.

This procedure, adopted at a time when the Commission indulged in theoretical discussions and plans, has been rarely followed in the course of the work of the Commission. Whenever the revision of a decision has been in question, it has been placed on the agenda by common agreement of all the members.[26]

§ 19. Correspondence with the two Governments. At an early meeting the Commission decided to correspond directly with the Greek and Bulgarian governments, especially on questions which required the execution of certain measures from such governments or their officials. All such official correspondence of the Commission was signed by the President and the Secretary-General of the Commission, and copies were delivered to the Greek and Bulgarian members of the Commission.[27] Later, the President was authorized by the Commission to intrust the neutral member with the signature of all documents binding the Mixed Commission.[28] The two governments rarely replied to the Commission. Important communications on its part often remained without answer or even acknowledgment of receipt. The neutral members of the Commission resented with good reason this attitude of the governments.[29]

§ 20. Immunities and privileges of the Commission and its agents. Before it left Geneva, the Commission, considering that it was indispensable for its proper functioning that its four members, their substitutes, and the Secretary-General of the Commission should enjoy diplomatic immunities, including the use of telegraphic cipher, decided to ask, through

[26] Procès-Verbaux, xxii, 365th meet., September 1, 1927, pp. 1, 4.
[27] Procès-Verbaux, i, 2d meet., December 21, 1920, p. 8.
[28] Procès-Verbaux, xv, 273d meet., July 24, 1926, p. 1759.
[29] See, for instance, Procès-Verbaux, xxvi, 410th meet., April 9, 1928, pp. 17, 18; xxx, 440th meet., September 28, 1928, p. 1.

its President, the two governments concerned to grant such immunities.[30] The governments complied with the request. In 1923 the Commission asked the same immunities for the Presidents of its Sub-Commissions, who were neutrals.[31] The two governments were also asked to grant free passage on the trains in Bulgaria and Greece to the members and secretaries of the Commission and Sub-Commissions,[32] and to exempt from all personal direct tax all the functionaries and employees of the Mixed Commission and of its agents.[33] The Bulgarian government replied to the last request that it could only exempt from taxes the Greek and neutral members of the Sub-Commissions in Bulgaria. The Greek government exempted the neutral and Bulgarian members and also the Bulgarian employees of the Sub-Commissions.[34] Later the Commission took a decision, against the combined vote of the Greek and Bulgarian members, to consider as exempt from any personal tax its functionaries and employees and those of its agencies in both countries.[35] But although this decision was communicated to the two governments, it appears to have been of no effect in Bulgaria.[36]

§ 21. The three periods of the work of the Commission. The work of the Commission may be divided into three periods: the preparatory period; the supervision of emigration; and the work of liquidation of the properties of emigrants. The preparatory stage began with the constitution of the Commission on December 18, 1920, and continued until the end of 1922. In waste of time it stood preëminent. More than a year was lost in discussions on the interpretation of two

[30] Procès-Verbaux, i, 5th meet., December 23, 1920, p. 17.
[31] Procès-Verbaux, vii, 133d meet., March 13, 1923, p. 857.
[32] Procès-Verbaux, vi, 110th meet., p. 764.
[33] Procès-Verbaux, xiii, 248th meet., December 15, 1925, p. 1578. The question was again called to the attention of the two governments on September 16, 1926 (xv, p. 1870).
[34] Procès-Verbaux, xvi, 307th meet., December 10, 1926, p. 2044.
[35] Procès-Verbaux, xxvi, 409th meet., April 4, 1928, p. 2.
[36] Procès-Verbaux, xxx, 441st meet., October 2, 1928, p. 2.
In April, 1930, the Commission contemplated the deduction of the amount of taxes paid by such employees from the funds placed at its disposal by the Bulgarian government. The application of this measure was postponed for some time to give time to the Bulgarian government to execute the above decision of the Commission. See Procès-Verbaux, xxxix, 545th meet., April 16, 1930, p. 2.

articles of the Convention. It was only at the end of this time that the Commission undertook the working out of the Rules of Emigration and Liquidation.[37] For another half-year the Commission waited for the abrogation of all exceptional laws and measures taken by the two countries concerned against the property of persons who had emigrated in the past. The Convention (article 15) provided that "the High Contracting Parties undertake to make in their respective legislation the modifications necessary to secure the execution of the present Convention." But certainly such modifications were not a condition precedent to the beginning of the execution of the Convention. The work of drawing up the Rules, collecting declarations of emigration, and taking measures for the liquidation of real property could start and go on while the legislative modifications were being prepared in the two countries.[38]

Then for three months more, December, 1922, to February, 1923, the Commission discontinued its meetings—an interruption in no way justified, which once more delayed the beginning of the main work of the Commission.

In the second period, the Commission performed a more or less political work, a sort of plebiscite, by attempting to secure the free exercise of the right of emigration of members of national minorities. In this the Commission was only partly successful, as will be seen. This work mostly ended by the close of 1924, when, after successive extensions, the period for filing declarations of emigration expired.

The third period, from January, 1925, on, is that of the liquidation of the properties of emigrants, and comprises the

[37] The working out was decided upon January 11, 1922, and the Rules were prepared by March 3, 1922. Procès-Verbaux, iv, 75th meet., p. 515; v, 95th meet., p. 656.

[38] Bulgaria had promulgated the law of July 27, 1921, which was deemed sufficient for the application of the Convention; she "need not be called upon to take any other legislative measures for this purpose." As for Greece, a decision of the Commission, pointing out the measures which should be taken, was communicated to the Greek government, and there was "every reason to believe that it would shortly be carried into effect." See Report of the Commission to the Council of the League, League of Nations, Document C. 442. M. 219. 1921. I, p. 7.

From July 27 to November 7, 1922, no meeting of the Commission was held. See Procès-Verbaux, vi, pp. 770, 773.

most important work of the Commission. This includes the economic and legal phases of the work; the Commission acted very much like a tribunal, on the basis of elaborate and complicated machinery and procedure, which will be described in following chapters.

§ 22. Personnel of the Commission. For the fulfilment of its duties the Commission needed various agents and instrumentalities. In the first three years its work was not very complicated. It was only at the end of 1922 that it began collecting declarations of emigration. During this period, besides the Secretariat with its services of translations and archives, the Commission had created only two Sub-Commissions. With the beginning of 1925, when the work of the Commission became more complicated, and such questions as survey of properties, establishment of property rights, appraisal, liquidation, and payment formed the main business of the Commission, not only was the number of Sub-Commissions increased, but other expert personnel was placed at its disposal, and agencies of coördination of the various parts of the work were created.

In close connection with the Commission, a Reporting Committee was established, consisting of a Greek and a Bulgarian representative and of the neutral member of the Commission who was not its President for the time, to relieve the Commission of matters of detail. Also two neutral technical advisers were attached to the Commission: an expert agronomist, Mr. Fluck, and an expert architect, Mr. Savoie. Their functions were to give their opinion on technical questions asked by the Mixed Commission; to supervise from the technical point of view the work of the lower agencies of the Commission; and to give their opinion on objections against the decisions of those agencies.[39]

§ 23. Sub-Commissions and Centres. The first agencies of the Commission to be established and the most important were the Sub-Commissions. Early in 1921 it was decided that

[39] Procès-Verbaux, xv, 278th meet., p. 1781; 279th meet., p. 1791; 295th meet., p. 1904; xviii, 336th meet., April 15, 1927.

each Sub-Commission was to be composed of a neutral President, a Greek and a Bulgarian member, and a Secretary without right of vote. All were to be appointed by the Commission. The Greek and Bulgarian members of the Commission proposed their respective candidates for members of the Sub-Commissions. The Commission had the power to dismiss the Greek and Bulgarian members of Sub-Commissions on the proposal of the respective members of the Commission, or directly in case of grave omission in their duties.[40] Originally two Sub-Commissions were established, on July 7, 1922, one in Greece and one in Bulgaria.[41] In February, 1924, a second Sub-Commission was established in Bulgaria, and in March and September of the same year second and third Sub-Commissions in Greece, with a view of speeding up the work of liquidation of real property.[42] Third and fourth Sub-Commissions were established in Bulgaria on May 16, 1925. At the same time the Sub-Commissions in Greece were increased to seven, the first, third, fourth, fifth, and sixth working in Macedonia, and the second and seventh in Thrace.[43] Lastly, in July, 1925, it was decided to increase the Sub-Commissions in Bulgaria to six and those in Greece to twelve.[44]

In order to secure the connection between the Sub-Commissions in Greece (Macedonia and Thrace) and the Hellenic authorities and a spirit of unity among the Sub-Commissions, a delegate of the Mixed Commission, Mr. Saunders, was stationed at Saloniki. He was assisted by the members of the First Sub-Commission, who formed, with him, the "delegation of the Mixed Commission in Saloniki."

In July, 1926, Directors in the Centres of Sofia, Saloniki, and Comotini (Thrace) were appointed. These were: M. Godineau, President of the First Sub-Commission in Greece,

[40] Procès-Verbaux, i, 22d meet., January 20, 1921, p. 103.
[41] Procès-Verbaux, vi, 109th meet., p. 761. The Commissions began their work on November 15, 1922, *ibid.*, p. 781.
The Sub-Commission in Greece was enlarged on December 15, 1923 (*ibid.*, viii, p. 1043) by a Vice-President, a second Greek and a second Bulgarian member, and another Secretary.
[42] Procès-Verbaux, ix, 174th and 195th meet., pp. 1085, 1091, 1189.
[43] Procès-Verbaux, xii, 230th meet., p. 1427.
[44] Procès-Verbaux, xii, 234th meet., p. 1469.

at Saloniki; Mr. Nicol, President of the Second and Seventh Sub-Commissions in Greece, at Comotini; and Mr. Saulus, President of the First Sub-Commission in Bulgaria, at Sofia. To these were soon added representatives of the Greek and Bulgarian members of the Commission.[45]

§ 24. **Their duties and functions.** The duties and functions of these various agencies of the Mixed Commission were as follows:

In the first year, the two or three Sub-Commissions that were established dealt with all questions referring to concrete cases of emigration of members of the minorities in their respective districts. They delivered to such persons passes, certificates of exemption from customs duties, permits for travel at a reduced price or gratuitously, etc. They also effected a provisional appraisal of the real estate which emigrants desired to have liquidated through the agency of the Commission. When the emigration was completed and the questions of establishment of rights and of appraisal of real property became the main business of the Sub-Commissions, their number was successively increased. By the summer of 1928 eleven local Sub-Commissions were engaged effectively in the establishment of rights and appraisal of properties in the various districts in Bulgaria and Greece.[46] Three central Sub-Commissions were working in the three centres of emigration and liquidation: one in Sofia, one in Saloniki, and a third in Comotini in Thrace.

The local Sub-Commissions received from the Presidents of the central Sub-Commissions the files of liquidation as well as the drafts of land survey, reports of experts, etc. The actual work of establishment of rights and appraisal of real estate by the local Sub-Commissions is described below. When this work was completed the files were returned to the Presidents of the central Sub-Commissions.

The relations of the local Sub-Commissions with the state authorities were limited to correspondence with the local authorities for the details of procedure, not involving questions

[45] Procès-Verbaux, xv, 272d meet., p. 1753; 278th meet., p. 1783.
[46] Procès-Verbaux, xv, 272d meet., p. 1753.

of principle or political difficulties. For such questions the local Sub-Commissions reported to the Presidents of the central Sub-Commissions.

The central Sub-Commissions dealt with questions of emigration of members of minorities and also with questions referred to them by the local Sub-Commissions. Questions involving the intervention of the superior civil or military authorities, questions of interpretation of the Rules of Emigration and Liquidation and of instructions of the Mixed Commission, or technical questions relative to liquidation, were referred to the delegate of the Mixed Commission or to the Mixed Commission. The central Sub-Commissions were responsible to the Mixed Commission for the whole work of liquidation in their respective territories. They directed the service of land surveyors and of architect experts, distributed the work among the local Sub-Commissions, and secured the coördination of the work of the above services, of the appraisal teams, and of the local Sub-Commissions, so that the last-named could obtain in due time the plans of land survey and the reports of experts necessary for enabling them to take decisions of appraisal.

The Presidents of the central Sub-Commissions centralized the decisions of establishment of rights and the decisions of appraisal of the local Sub-Commissions; they caused the files to be completed; and they added their remarks on any part of the file, including the decisions of the local Sub-Commissions.

The delegate of the Mixed Commission in Saloniki was the link of connection between the Sub-Commissions and the Hellenic authorities, and secured unity in the interpretation of the Rules of Emigration and Liquidation and the instructions. He was assisted by the two members of the central First Sub-Commission in Greece, who constituted with him the delegation of the Mixed Commission in Saloniki. The delegation acted as an intermediary between the Mixed Commission and the Sub-Commissions for all questions involving the intervention of the superior civil or military authorities and for questions of interpretation of the Rules and the instructions of the Commission which were not relative to questions of administration or liquidation.[47]

The Centres in Sofia, Saloniki, and Comotini attended to the coördination of the work and movements of the Sub-Commissions, land surveyors, appraisal teams, expert architects, to the calling together of the delegations of emigrants, to the organization of the distribution and receipt of files, the reckoning and verification, the organization of counter-surveys (in case of appeal), and the transmission of the files to the Mixed Commission.

The representatives of the Greek and Bulgarian members of the Commission at the three Centres, Sofia, Saloniki, and Comotini, were appointed for the purpose of using their influence on the interested persons for the speedy constitution and the coming together at the fixed dates of the delegations of emigrants convened by the Directors and of taking all useful measures to this end.

Two reserve members, Greek and Bulgarian, were attached to the Mixed Commission for the purpose of replacing without delay any member of the Sub-Commissions who might be temporarily incapacitated. At other times these members were at the disposal of the Mixed Commission.[48]

The Sub-Commissions were an adequate agency for the carrying out of the emigration of the minorities and dealing with the questions arising therefrom. But for the problem of liquidation of properties their members did not possess the requirements necessary for surveying, examining, and appraising the various kinds of real estate. Accordingly, various expert agents were employed for these matters: land surveyors, architects, agronomists, foresters, engineers, etc.

§ 25. Other agents of the Commission. The first class of experts appointed by the Mixed Commission were the land surveyors. Their function was to measure the exact area of rural estates under liquidation, since Greece and the new provinces of Bulgaria possessed no government survey of lands and the areas stated by the interested parties were

[47] Procès-Verbaux, xii, 230th meet., May 16, 1925, pp. 1427-33.
[48] Procès-Verbaux, xv, 236th and 248th meet., pp. 1482, 1578.

always inexact or exaggerated. By the summer of 1925 eighteen parties of land surveyors had been organized in Macedonia.[49] A chief of the service of land surveying, of a neutral nationality, was appointed in July, 1925.[50] In the following summer the formation of two parties of land surveyors for Bulgaria was authorized by the Commission.[51] The services of land surveying were under the orders and responsibility of three Directors in the three Centres: Sofia, Saloniki, and Comotini.

The next class of experts comprised the staffs of agronomists. These attended to the appraisal of rural estates on the basis of a tariff of lands which is dealt with below. Each staff numbered three agronomists: a Greek, a Bulgarian, and a neutral President. Decisions were taken by the President, the Greek and Bulgarian experts giving only their opinion.

The first staff was created early in 1925 in Greece, and a second for Bulgaria in May, 1925.[52] A third was constituted in July, 1926. They were placed from the summer of 1926 under the immediate direction of the central Sub-Commissions.[53]

A staff of forester experts made the appraisal of forests. Its composition and procedure were similar to those of the staffs of agronomists.

Expert architects had charge of the appraisal of buildings and building lands on the basis of a tariff of prices considered below. Their findings were communicated to the members of the Sub-Commissions, who sent their technical advisers to the spot. Only in Thrace the appraisal of buildings and building lands was made by a staff of two architects, a Greek and a Bulgarian. It was thought that by the collaboration of representatives of the two countries the work would be speeded up and simplified.[54]

The data for each individual file and the file of each village were gathered by the compiling services of the three Centres,

[49] Procès-Verbaux, xii, 236th meet., p. 1482.
[50] *Ibid.*
[51] Procès-Verbaux, xiii, 262d meet., p. 1688.
[52] Procès-Verbaux, xi, 216th meet., p. 1325; xii, p. 1399; xv, p. 1746.
[53] Procès-Verbaux, xiv, 266th meet., p. 1713.
[54] Procès-Verbaux, xv, 292d meet., p. 1881.

working under neutral chiefs. When fully made up, the files were examined by teams of Greek and Bulgarian checkers, who scrutinized them with a view of detecting errors or mistakes.[55]

§ 26. Decisions of agents of the Commission. The Sub-Commissions took decisions by majority vote. The staffs for appraisal decided by the vote of the President, the Greek and Bulgarian members having only a right to give their opinion.[56]

In case of the absence or inability to attend of a member of a Sub-Commission or staff, the President of the Sub-Commission or staff applied to the President of the central Sub-Commission. The latter, in agreement with the member representing the interested country, sent the reserve member, or, if he was not available, a functionary of the Mixed Commission of the same nationality. If, within four days from the date of request, the substitute was not sent, the Sub-Commission or staff might deal validly with any question that its President should consider necessary to place on the agenda.[57]

Similarly, in case of the absence or incapacity of a representative at the Centre, the Director might request of the Mixed Commission, by wire, the appointment of a temporary substitute. If, within three days from the receipt of the telegram and its communication to the interested member of the Mixed Commission, a substitute was not designated, the Director of the Centre might deal validly with any question on which regularly the opinion of the representative would be asked.[58]

§ 27. Network formed by this organization. The network constituted by these various agencies of the Mixed Commission may be seen in the table on the following page.

§ 28. Inefficiency of the agents. All these agents of the Mixed Commission acted in accordance with the Rules of Emigration and Liquidation and the numerous decisions and instructions of the Commission, which in many respects modi-

[55] Procès-Verbaux, xv, 282d meet., August 20, 1926, p. 1807; xvi, 302d meet., November 20, 1926.

[56] Procès-Verbaux, xv, 278th meet., August 10, 1926, p. 1783; xiii, 250th meet., p. 1590.

[57] Procès-Verbaux, xv, 271st meet., July 21, 1926, p. 1745.

[58] Procès-Verbaux, xviii, 332d meet., April 2, 1927, p. 2299.

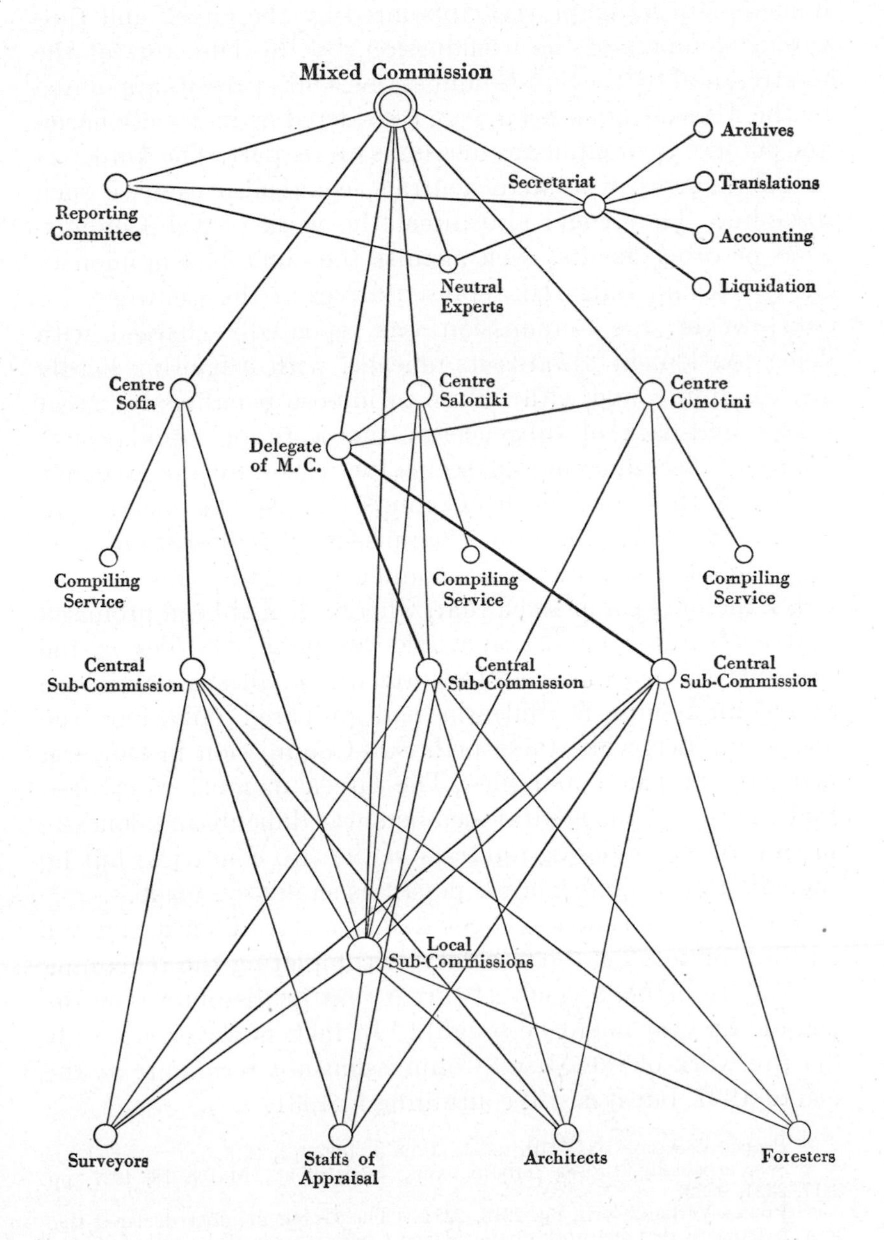

Mixed Commission
Archives
Secretariat
Translations
Reporting
Committee
Accounting
Neutral
Experts
Liquidation
Centre
Sofia
Centre
Saloniki
Centre
Comotini
Delegate
of M. C.
Compiling
Service
Compiling
Service
Compiling
Service
Central
Sub-Commission
Central
Sub-Commission
Central
Sub-Commission
Local
Sub-Commissions
Surveyors
Staffs of
Appraisal
Architects
Foresters

fied and supplemented the Rules. They were surrounded by numerous other employees appointed by the Greek and Bulgarian members of the Commission, by the Directors of the Centres, and by the Sub-Commissions. Only persons appointed by the Mixed Commission were considered as its functionaries and subject to disciplinary measures on its part. The Directors of the Centres, who were neutrals, could also exercise such discipline. They could also direct the work of Sub-Commissions or other agents, even against the combined opinion of the Greek and Bulgarian representatives at the Centre.[59]

However, the Commission was repeatedly charged with being too lenient towards its officials, with exercising hardly any discipline, and with failure to impose penalties for great delays and lack of diligence in the work of liquidation.[60] Laxity of discipline, indeed, seems the reason for the excessive delays in the work of the Commission. At the meeting of March 18, 1927, when the Commission was discussing once more the plan of work for the coming spring and summer, the Greek member complained that, whereas it had been promised that each Sub-Commission would complete 900 files in the previous three months at the rate of ten files a day, three Sub-Commissions in Bulgaria had prepared only half the above number, while the fourth Sub-Commission in Bulgaria had only prepared four files. The Greek member recognized that the rôle of the neutral members was difficult and delicate, in view of the opposing interests of the two countries; but he thought that a provision for penalties should be made.

At the same time the Greek member attempted to impress on the Commission the necessity of completing the remaining work by resorting to a covert threat that its dissolution by the end of the year might be sought.[61] In fact, however, not only did the work of the Mixed Commission not terminate at the end of 1927, but it is still continuing in 1931.

[59] Procès-Verbaux, xix, 345th meet., June 4, 1927, pp. 2, 5.

[60] See, especially, Procès-Verbaux, xvii, 327th meet., March 18, 1927, pp. 2217, 2221, 2222.

[61] Procès-Verbaux, xvii, pp. 2218, 2221: "The Greek member declared that he is persuaded that the work of the Mixed Commission will be terminated at the end of the year, basing his opinion on other data than those possessed by the Commission."

Moreover, when the Mixed Commission, at its meeting of May 14, 1927, asked the Directors of the Centres to furnish lists of functionaries who, in their opinion, had not the qualifications required for the positions occupied by them, the Greek and Bulgarian members refused to consent to the removal of such persons without a previous report from the Presidents of the Sub-Commissions on the persons whose removal was requested by the Directors.[62] The danger of imposition and arbitrariness on the part of the latter might exist, of course, but it was hardly reasonable to expect other than favorable reports from the Presidents on their colleagues in the Sub-Commissions.

The fact is that the neutral members of the Commission, moved by a curious *esprit de corps,* always protected the neutral agents and employees, while the national members had a tendency to defend the employees of their own nationality, provided these were stanch supporters of national interests.

§ 29. General scheme of the work. The general scheme of the work of the Commission, based upon the above-described organization, was as follows:

First, the Sub-Commissions, and, on appeal, the Mixed Commission, decided whether an applicant was qualified to avail himself of the Convention. His emigration was facilitated in the way described in Chapter IV.

In case he desired to dispose of his real property himself, he was allowed to do so within a certain period. Persons who had already emigrated were allowed to take possession of property that they had left in their country of origin and dispose of it in the same way as new emigrants. This is considered in Chapter V.

At the expiration of the period referred to above, the Commission, *ex officio,* or on the application for liquidation of new or former emigrants, undertook to liquidate the real property. For this purpose, the Sub-Commissions first verified the existence of property and property rights; then the land surveyors

[62] Procès-Verbaux, xx, 353d meet., p. 15. Also Procès-Verbaux, xxiii, 377th meet., p. 19.

measured the land claimed by emigrants; next, the various agencies of appraisal made an appraisal of the property. These various stages of the work are dealt with in Chapters VI to XII. The various items gathered with respect to the property of each applicant were compiled, verified, and audited by the appropriate services at the three Centres, Sofia, Saloniki, and Comotini, and, assembled for each village, were submitted to the Reporting Committee and the Mixed Commission for final decision. This part of the work is described in Chapters XIII and XIV. The liquidation price was paid to the interested person and the accounts between the two governments were regulated as considered in Chapter XV.

At the end of 1929, when the work of establishment of property rights, of surveying, and of appraisal was nearly completed, it was decided to concentrate all the services of the Commission operating in Macedonia and Bulgaria at Athens, where the Commission was sitting. This concentration was effected on May 1, 1930. It was thought that by this concentration a fusion would be brought about between the various services previously existing in Bulgaria and Greece, and between them and the Secretariat of the Mixed Commission. After the concentration the various services of the Mixed Commission were grouped as follows: (1) A Directorate of the agencies of the Commission, something like the old Directorate of the Centres; (2) a Service of File-Compiling common for both countries; (3) a Sub-Commission common for both countries; and (4) a Delegation of the Mixed Commission at Sofia.[63]

[63] Procès-Verbaux, xxxix, 540th meet., April 2, 1930, p. 18.

CHAPTER III

ADMISSION TO THE BENEFITS OF THE CONVENTION

§ 30. The three conditions. The Convention concerning Reciprocal Emigration between Greece and Bulgaria was not a general convention for emigration. Its advantages could be claimed by certain classes of persons, the reciprocal emigration of which was considered as likely to be favorable to the permanence of peace and the improvement of the relations between the two countries. In order that this result should be achieved, it was desirable that the reciprocal emigration should be effected and terminated within a brief period of years. Further, new emigrants as well as former emigrants, in order to enjoy the benefits of the Convention, should manifest their intention in a prescribed way. The Convention provided for all these things and the Rules adopted by the Commission contained detailed regulations. Thus, admission of a person to the benefits of the Convention was subject to three conditions: that such person was within the class of persons defined in the Convention as entitled to its benefits; that action was taken within the time-limit fixed in the Convention; and that a declaration of emigration and application for liquidation were duly filed with the Mixed Commission.

I. Persons Entitled to the Benefits of the Convention

§ 31. **(a) New emigrants.** By article 1 of the Convention Bulgaria and Greece recognized the right of those of their subjects who belonged to racial, religious, or linguistic minorities to emigrate freely within their respective territories. To these new emigrants, the Convention through the provisions of article 12 added the former emigrants, and the Mixed Commission added as a third category the communities dissolved by reason of the emigration of their members. Each of these categories will be considered hereafter.

With regard, first, to new emigrants, or persons wishing to emigrate from the territory of the one country to that of the other after the entering into effect of the Convention, they could claim the advantages of the Convention (1) if they were nationals of the country from which they emigrated; (2) if they belonged to the Greek or Bulgarian racial, religious, or linguistic minority; (3) if they were above eighteen years of age; and (4) if they desired to emigrate from the territory of the country of which they were nationals to the country to which they were nationally akin.[1]

§ 32. **Subjects of the country of emigration.** The first requirement was not satisfied by persons who were not subjects of the country of emigration. Thus, Bulgarian nationals established in Greece, or Greek nationals established in Bulgaria, wishing to emigrate to Bulgaria and Greece respectively, were denied the benefits of the Convention.[2] This rule was inter-

[1] Convention, articles 1 and 4; Rules, article 7, par. (a).

[2] See, for instance, the case of Athanase Semerdjis: Procès-Verbaux, vii, 132d meet., March 10, 1923, p. 846.

preted by the Commission as not excluding women belonging to the Greek or Bulgarian minority who would have been entitled to claim under the Convention but for their change of nationality by marriage. Such women were given the right to claim the advantages of the Convention for their own property, and this right was also recognized in favor of their heirs in the descending line.[3] This decision was clearly opposed to the text of the Convention. It would, perhaps, be in accordance with its spirit if it concerned only women released from their husbands by death, divorce or separation.

§ 33. Members of national minority. The second requirement was correctly interpreted by the Commission to mean that any one of the three criteria of race, religion, or language might justify a claim under the Convention. In other words, a person could file a declaration of emigration and an application for the liquidation of his real property if he was akin to the country to which he desired to immigrate either by race, by religion, or by language. Moreover, it was decided that whenever a doubt should subsist in the Commission or its agents as to whether a person was akin by his race, religion, or language to the people of a country, this doubt should be resolved in favor of the person in question.[4] This decision was in agreement with the Convention. It tended to secure the right to emigrate of all persons proving to a certain degree their kinship to the people of the country of immigration. It is to be noted, indeed, that although, theoretically, these objective criteria seem preferable to the subjective criterion which was really important, namely, the national consciousness and aspiration of each person, they were extremely difficult of application in the countries concerned. In both Greece and Bulgaria the tests of race and language were of small help in this respect. There has been for many centuries such an intermingling of races in Northern Macedonia and Thrace and in Bulgaria that the distinction of Greek and Bulgarian by race, considered as a biological term, is often difficult. On the other hand, by the force of intensive propaganda and especially as

[3] Procès-Verbaux, viii, 154th meet., September 28, 1923, p. 1006.
[4] Procès-Verbaux, i, 7th meet., December 27, 1920, p. 23.

a result of the illiteracy of the people living in small villages, many members of racial minorities spoke the language of the prevailing majority, which was imposed upon them or was easier to learn. The test of religion or church affiliation was perhaps the least subject to difficulties. In this corner of Europe the conceptions of nation and religion were often interwoven. The church of Bulgaria was separated in 1870 from the Greek Oecumenical Patriarchate of Constantinople. It was therefore declared 'schismatic,' and a sharp division arose between those belonging to the Greek Orthodox church, recognizing as its head the Oecumenical Patriarch of Constantinople, and the followers of the Bulgarian Orthodox church, recognizing as its head the Bulgarian Exarch.

An interesting case, illustrating the importance of this division, was that of Thodor Nicoloff of the village of Hascovo in Bulgaria. He claimed in his declaration of emigration that he had 'the Greek consciousness' and that he wished to live in Greece. His claim to be admitted to the benefit of the Convention was opposed by the Bulgarian member on the ground that he was attached to the Bulgarian nationality by both blood and language. The Greek member supported his claim on the ground that he had celebrated his marriage with a Greek woman and had christened his children in the Greek church, and that in view of the fact that religion is confused with national consciousness by Greeks and Bulgarians, this was the best proof that Nicoloff had ceased to have a 'Bulgarian consciousness' and belonged to the Greek minority. The Commission thought that a doubt existed as to the religion of the applicant, of which he should have the benefit.[5]

Another case illustrating the application of the criteria is that of the people who had emigrated from Madritza, a village near Ortakeuy and Adrianople.[6] Most of the inhabitants of that village, at its occupation by the Bulgarian army in 1913, emigrated to Greece. It was shown that their language and race were Albanian, while their religious affiliation was with the Greek Oecumenical Patriarchate. The Commission, taking

[5] Procès-Verbaux, xv, 279th meet., August 10, 1926.
[6] Procès-Verbaux, xxi, 303rd meet., August 26, 1927, pp. 8-22.

into consideration the fact that their declarations of emigration manifested their desire to be nationally attached to Greece, that they had no longer the power to recover the lands they left in Bulgaria, which had already been distributed in part to refugees, and that the spirit of the Convention was to facilitate the movement of minorities towards the country to which they were akin by at least one of the three ties, race, religion, and language, admitted these persons to the benefits of the Convention. The case was certainly on the border line, and one might, theoretically, agree with the view of the Bulgarians that the Madritzans were in no way members of the Greek minority in Bulgaria. But the Commission was moved by the consideration that these people had left their lands in Bulgaria, and that these lands had been distributed to Bulgarian refugees. They themselves were established in Greece and wished to remain there. Their admission to the benefits of the Convention was an equitable solution.

§ 34. **Above eighteen years of age.** The third requirement was stated in article 4 of the Convention. The right of voluntary emigration belonged only to persons over eighteen years of age. The limitation is explained by the seriousness of the act embodied in the declaration of intention to emigrate. The Commission interpreted liberally this provision so as to include married men below eighteen years of age who, by reason of the marriage, were emancipated from parental control.[7] The declaration of intention to emigrate on the part of the husband implied that of the wife; the declaration of the parents or guardians implied that of their children or wards under eighteen years of age (article 4 of the Convention). Children above eighteen years of age were required to file a declaration of emigration distinct from that of their parents. Guardians could file declarations of intention to emigrate in behalf of their wards, even when they themselves had not the right to claim the advantages of the Convention (Rules, article 8).

§ 35. **Emigrating to the country to which they were akin.** The fourth requirement, that the emigration should be made

[7] Procès-Verbaux, viii, 152d meet., September 20, 1923, p. 995.

from the country of which the would-be emigrants were nationals to the country to which they were akin, is clear from the whole scope of the Convention. It was intended to accomplish, indeed, a voluntary exchange of populations, and not to furnish a convenient system of emigration and liquidation of property to members of minorities leaving the country in which they were established in order to go anywhere they desired. Two decisions of the Commission show, indeed, a certain flexibility in the application of this requirement. A decision of March 3, 1923,[8] granted the advantages of the Convention to persons residing in a country other than the country of origin or the country of kinship, who had preserved the nationality of the country of origin (Bulgarian, Greek, or Turkish) or adopted the nationality of the country of kinship (Greek or Bulgarian) to the exclusion of any other nationality. Thus, Greek nationals, belonging to the Bulgarian minority in Greece, and established in the United States of America, could apply for the liquidation of their property by the Mixed Commission. No question of emigration arose in respect to these persons, but their application for liquidation implied their intention to be considered as emigrating to Bulgaria, their country of kinship.

Another decision of the Commission [9] approved a decision of the Sub-Commission in Bulgaria allowing the advantages of the Convention to persons emigrating from Western Thrace under the régime of inter-allied occupation. During this time the Convention was not applied to Western Thrace, which was not considered part of the Hellenic territory. But when finally this province became Greek, on the coming into force of the Treaty of Lausanne, the Convention was applied retroactively to members of the Bulgarian minority who had emigrated from Thrace.

§ 36. **(b) Former emigrants.** The definition of the second category of persons entitled to the benefits of the Convention gave much trouble to the Commission. The reason was the inadequacy of the text of the Convention. Article 12 provided:

[8] Procès-Verbaux, vii, 131st meet., p. 839.
[9] Procès-Verbaux, ix, 188th meet., June 2, 1924, p. 1139.

Persons who before the entry into force of the present Convention have left the territory of one of the contracting States and have already established themselves in the territory of the State to which they belong by race, religion, or language, shall have a right to the value of the property left by them in the country which they have left, such value to be that resulting from the liquidation which will be made of the property by the Mixed Commission.

This article raised many questions, the most important of which was that in connection with the word 'before' of its first sentence. How far back did that period prior to the coming into effect of the Convention extend? The general purpose of the article is clear. The advantages of the Convention, that is, the liquidation of the property left in the country of origin and the payment for the same, should inure not only to new emigrants, to persons wishing to emigrate after the coming into effect of the Convention, but also to those unfortunate refugees who, either voluntarily or fearing danger to their lives and safety, had already emigrated to the country to which they were nationally akin. Several tens of thousands of Greeks from Bulgaria and Bulgarians from Macedonia and Thrace had, long before the Convention concerning Reciprocal Emigration was entered into, left their homes to take refuge in the country to the people of which they were akin by race, religion, or language. These refugees often left their property behind them and such property was seized or confiscated by the respective governments. Article 12 was intended to redress this injustice and enable them to have such property recovered and liquidated by the Commission. A similar treatment was to be afforded to such refugees as to new emigrants, since the same causes of political disturbances, national animosities, and dissatisfaction with territorial settlements impelled both classes of persons to unite themselves with their conationals or coreligionists and to make their new home in another country.

§ 37. Having emigrated after December 18, 1900. Since the Convention did not fix the date in the past which should delimit this class of former emigrants who were entitled to apply for the liquidation of their property, the Mixed Commission undertook to supply it, by virtue of the general power of interpretation given by the provision of article 9 that "the Mixed Commission shall have full powers . . . to decide all questions to which this Convention may give rise." This provision, however, in no way empowered the Commission to complete the provisions of the Convention and add thereto something that was not provided for. It is very doubtful whether the provision of article 12 was meant to apply to any other persons than those who had left the territory of one of the contracting countries in order to seek refuge or settle in that of the other as a result of the World War and the political disturbances incident thereto. The Convention was a document connected with the Treaty of Neuilly and was meant to deal with the effects of the same war. Any further extension of the period to which the provisions of article 12 were to be applied lacked all solid foundation. If a longer period had been intended by the parties to the Convention, it would have been expressly provided for, as was done in the Convention of Lausanne concerning the Exchange of Greek and Turkish Populations of January 30, 1923.[10]

However, the Commission thought otherwise. Seeking to ascertain and follow the spirit of the Convention, it gave full consideration to the actual situation in the Balkans, and, in particular, in the territories occupied at the beginning of the twentieth century by Turkey and Bulgaria and from 1913 by Greece and Bulgaria.[11] It saw a succession of political events

[10] Article 3 of that Convention, for the similar case of persons who had already left the respective territories of the two countries, sets the limit as October 18, 1912, the day of the beginning of the war between Greece and Turkey. See the text of the Convention, League of Nations, *Treaty Series*, xxxii, pp. 76-87.

[11] See the memorandum submitted by the neutral member of the Commission with the agreement of its President (Procès-Verbaux, ii, 48th meet., July 11, 1921, pp. 239 ff.). It is there said:

"Un ensemble de territoires Balcaniques était, en 1900, reparti en trois Etats: Turquie, Grèce, et Bulgarie. Sur cet ensemble de territoires vivaient, pêle-mêle, des Bulgares, des Grecs, et des Turcs, habitant chacun sa propriété.

"Une succession d'événements politiques et de guerre ont tout bouleversé.

"Des frontières se sont plusieurs fois déplacées; des migrations d'individus ou de groupes d'individus se sont effectuées en tous sens, certains d'entre eux cessent d'être propriétaires, d'autres le restant. Puis, après toute cette ébullition, le calme revient avec la signature des Traités qui ont mis fin à la guerre mondiale.

"De nouvelles frontières sont tracées qui partagent cet ensemble de terri-

during these years and in those territories, in consequence of which the boundaries of the states were repeatedly modified, giving rise to several migrations of racial minorities and to the abandonment, seizure, and confiscation of properties. It was the feeling of the Commission that all injustices done to such minorities ought to be and might be redressed, since the Convention fixed no limit in the past to which this remedial activity of the Commission might extend.

In this view the Commission was encouraged by its members representing the two countries concerned. The Bulgarian member requested that the period of retroactive effect should be the same for both countries, and should be sufficient to include the great movements of population between Greece and Bulgaria. He eventually suggested that the period should go as far back as 1903.[12] The Greek member, more closely concerned with the interpretation of article 12, shifted his position several times. He first suggested that only movements of population between the signing of the Convention and its coming into effect should be taken into consideration. Later he wished to include all migration which had taken place during the World War. Then he proposed that different periods should be adopted with respect to the various territories of each country, coinciding with the date on which each territory was placed under the sovereignty of the country. And, finally, this last proposal was so modified as to make the various

toires en Bulgarie et Grèce. Mais il se fait qu'au moment de cette stabilisation, de nombreux individus se trouvent d'un côté de la frontière—celui où les ont appellés leurs affinités ethniques, linguistiques ou confessionnelles, tandis que leurs propriétés (celles dont ils sont encore propriétaires, nous ne parlons de rien d'autre)—tandis que leurs propriétés, dis-je, sont de l'autre côté de cette frontière.

"C'est ici qu'intervient la Convention et son article 12 avec, non seulement un louable sentiment humanitaire, mais encore un grand sens pratique.

"Elle dit pour chacun d'eux; laissons cet homme où ses affinités l'ont porté et, puisqu'il possède une propriété de l'autre côté de la frontière, pour simplifier tout, s'il le désire, le pays, sur le territoire duquel est située cette propriété va la lui racheter, à sa valeur actuelle.

"Il n'est en rien, nous ne saurions assez le répéter, question de responsabilités engagés par des Gouvernements successifs, et, de même, le détail des déplacements effectués par chaque individu, comme la date de ces déplacements sont sans importance.

"C'est une situation réelle, présente, que l'on dénoue par un simple marché dans lequel les deux éléments sont tous deux réels aussi: la propriété d'une part, le payement de l'autre."

[12] Procès-Verbaux, ii, 29th meet., February 21, 1921, pp. 122 ff.

periods coincide with the time each territory was occupied militarily by each of the two countries. The Greek member then declared that he preferred the fixing of the period earlier than the beginning of the World War; and he eventually went so far as to desire its extension as far back as 1906, when many Greeks left Bulgarian territory and sought refuge in Greece.[13]

The Commission, to which an excellent memorandum was submitted by its neutral member, M. de Roover, thought that the fixing of the period at twenty years before the coming into force of the Convention would be the most equitable solution. This included the limits suggested by the members representing the two governments and was a period generally admitted in the law as causing prescription of real property rights. Accordingly the Commission declared that "article 12 is applicable to persons who, besides fulfilling the other specific conditions, have emigrated in the course of the twenty years last preceding the coming into force of the Convention, namely, between December 18, 1900, and December 18, 1920." [14] In this last part of the decision the Commission erred. The Convention, according to its final provisions, was to enter into force at the same time that the Treaty of Neuilly came into effect as between Greece and Bulgaria. The Convention was ratified August 9, 1920. The Treaty of Neuilly entered into effect August 9, 1920. This date, then, was that on which the Convention came into force. The date of December 18, 1920, erroneously stated by the Commission, was that of the constitution of the Commission.[15]

§ 38. Other requirements for former emigrants. The former emigrants, besides proving that they had emigrated

[13] Procès-Verbaux, i, 18th meet., January 13, 1921, pp. 80, 83; ii, 32d meet., February 28, 1921, p. 143; 37th meet., April 4, 1921, p. 162; 43rd meet., April 25, 1921, pp. 193, 194; 44th meet., April 28, 1921, p. 211; 45th meet., May 3, 1921, p. 218.

The Greeks who were driven out from Bulgaria in 1906 and found refuge in Greece are placed at 37,500. See Charles B. Eddy, *Greece and the Greek Refugees* (London, 1931), p. 45.

[14] Procès-Verbaux, ii, 48th meet., July 11, 1921, pp. 239 ff.

[15] A provision of the Rules (art. 7, note ii) prescribed that whenever a doubt should exist as to whether the date of emigration of a person was before or after December 18, 1900, but this person could prove satisfactorily that he had the disposal of his property after December 18, 1900, such person obtained the benefit of the doubt.

after December 18, 1900, were required to qualify by certain other conditions in order to be able to claim the advantages of the Convention. The provision of article 12 referred, generally, to 'persons.' This might mean any person, or certain classes of persons not defined in this provision, as their delimitation was implied from other stipulations of the Convention. The word 'persons,' indeed, was to be interpreted in connection with the whole purpose of article 12, which, as we have seen, was meant to redress certain injustices suffered by people who had emigrated in consequence of the political disturbances of the past years. It should also not be forgotten that this was a Convention between Greece and Bulgaria for the reciprocal emigration of their nationals. The word 'persons' should, therefore, be taken in the light of the provisions of the Convention defining the emigrants.

As we have seen, the new emigrants were to satisfy four requirements.[16] The first, that they should be nationals of the country from which they emigrated, would seem to be applicable to the former emigrants, with, however, one qualification. Certain parts of the territories of the two countries in which migration of populations took place, belonged, prior to 1912 or 1919, to Turkey, and the former emigrants had the Turkish nationality. The Commission decided, accordingly, that persons who belonged previously to the Greek or Bulgarian racial minority might claim the advantages of the Convention, if at the time they left their country of origin they were nationals of that country.[17] Thus, persons who had left Macedonia or Thrace when these provinces were parts of the Turkish Empire, and who had possessed the Turkish nationality, were included in the stipulation of article 12. Later, the Rules (article 7 (b) 3) added the qualification that these persons were entitled to the advantages of the Convention if they, since their emigration, either had preserved their old allegiance or had acquired the nationality of the country to which they emigrated, Greece or Bulgaria, to the exclusion of any other nationality.

[16] See *supra,* p. 76.
[17] Procès-Verbaux, iii, 57th meet., August 3, 1921, pp. 362, 364.

The second requirement for emigrants, that they should belong to the Greek or Bulgarian racial, religious, or linguistic minority, was assuredly applicable to former emigrants. It was so expressly provided by the Rules (article 7 (b) 2).

The third requirement, that emigrants should be above eighteen years of age, was clearly inapplicable to persons who had emigrated in the course of the twenty years preceding the coming into effect of the Convention. The Convention could control the future, not the past. The migration of populations to which article 12 referred had nothing in common with the orderly, free, and supervised new emigration that the other provisions of the Convention were dealing with.

The last requirement, that the emigrants on leaving their country of origin should go to the country of their racial, religious, or linguistic kinship, was also applicable to former emigrants, but needed to be qualified in view of the period of the past twenty years to which article 12 referred. This requirement was, accordingly, set down in the Rules (article 7 (b)) as follows: "the persons who had left the territories now under Greek or Bulgarian sovereignty in order to establish themselves in the territories now under Bulgarian or Greek sovereignty." Persons, however, whose emigration at the time it was made fulfilled this requirement, but who were now established in a third country, could still claim the advantages of the Convention if they still preserved the nationality of the country of origin or had acquired that of the country of their kinship.[18]

§ 39. Constructive emigration. A provision of the Rules (article 7, remark 1), completed later by a decision of the Mixed Commission,[19] dealt with the case of members of national minorities who, between December 18, 1900, and December 18, 1920, were domiciled in a place within the Turkish Empire and owned at the same time real property located in one or several other places in the Turkish Empire. If the place where these persons were domiciled and the place where their property was located had ceased to belong to the

[18] Procès-Verbaux, vii, 131st meet., March 3, 1923, p. 839.
[19] Procès-Verbaux, viii, 155th meet., October 2, 1923, p. 1011.

same country, they might claim, in respect to the recovery and liquidation of such property, the same rights as if they were effectively domiciled in the place where any such property was located. Thus, a member of the Bulgarian racial minority domiciled in 1912 in Eastern Thrace and having real estate in Western Thrace before his emigration to Bulgaria, was considered as domiciled in Western Thrace and therefore as a former emigrant, now that Eastern Thrace formed part of Turkey and Western Thrace was under the Greek sovereignty. The decision of the Commission above referred to declared that this provision was still applicable even though such persons had acquired the property in question after their emigration, on condition that the acquisition had taken place while the Turkish sovereignty existed in the place where the property was located, or that the acquisition was made by gift or transfer before December 18, 1920, or by succession at any date.

Persons belonging to the respective Greek or Bulgarian minority who had left their country of origin after December 18, 1920, or who were leaving that country without filing declaration of emigration in order to go to the country of their kinship, were assimilated, in respect to the rights to their property, to emigrants.

§ 40. **(c) Communities.** The two categories of persons considered above are individuals only. In general it was impracticable to make the provisions of the Convention include also juristic persons. Such provisions as those referring to membership in a racial, religious, or linguistic minority, to the age of emigrants, to the loss of nationality, to the removal of obstacles to departure, etc., clearly indicate the intent of the Convention to restrict the provisions of the Convention to individuals.

There was one entity, however, besides individuals which was expressly referred to by the Convention. This was the community (*communauté*). The second paragraph of article 6 read as follows:

Similarly, in cases where the right of emigration is exercised by members of communities (including churches, convents, schools, hospitals, or foundations of any kind whatever) which on this account shall have to be dissolved, the Mixed Commission provided for in Article 8 shall determine whether and in what circumstances such members shall have the option of freely taking with them or having transported the movable property belonging to the communities.

Article 7 of the Convention provided for the liquidation by the Mixed Commission of "real property, rural or urban, belonging to voluntary emigrants or to the communities to which Article 6 refers."

Article 12, which referred to past emigrations, spoke only of 'persons,' and it was difficult to make this word apply to communities. The latter were contrasted to emigrants in article 7 ("voluntary emigrants or communities") and formed the subject of a separate paragraph in article 6. Yet the Mixed Commission, pursuing its task of completing the Convention, interpreted the word 'persons' as including 'juristic persons' (*personnes morales*), in accordance with the view of the Greek member of the Commission, to which the Bulgarian member, at first opposed, acceded later.[20] This decision was doubly unfortunate. It interpreted the word 'persons' generally as including 'juristic persons,' which is inadmissible in view of all the provisions of the Convention above referred to. What, of course, was in the mind of the members of the Commission was to include the communities in the word 'persons' of article 12 so as to permit the liquidation of properties of communities whose members had emigrated prior to the coming into force of the Convention. The second mistake is that 'communities' were considered at the time by the Mixed Commission as juristic persons, the Greek member agreeing with the Bulgarian member in this at the time, although he subsequently took another and what is believed to be the sound position.

The question of the nature of the communities referred to in the Convention, the confused discussions in the Mixed Commission on this matter, and the Advisory Opinion of the Permanent Court of International Justice on communities,

[20] Procès-Verbaux, ii, 48th meet., July 11, 1921, p. 239.

are considered in Chapter VII. Here it is sufficient to say that it would be hardly possible to make of the 'communities' a special category of entities entitled to the benefits of the Convention. Article 7 simply provided for the liquidation of properties of communities, while article 6 spoke of the right of *members* of communities dissolved by the emigration to take away the movable property belonging to the communities. As will be seen in another place, the distribution of the property of the communities seemed merely an additional pecuniary advantage enjoyed by the emigrants.

In view of the fact that the Mixed Commission decided, or assumed, that communities were juristic persons; and for the purpose, on the one hand, of determining the question of the removal of the movable property of communities by the emigrating members, and, on the other hand, of proceeding to the liquidation of real properties of communities; for these reasons the Rules concerning Reciprocal and Voluntary Emigration adopted by the Commission, and a number of subsequent decisions undertook to define the procedure for dealing with claims concerning property of communities.

The Rules, indeed, placed the communities in a third category, additional to the former and to the new emigrants, as admitted to the benefits of the Convention. The application for liquidation in the case of communities was filed by the council of the emigrating community or by the member of the Commission representing the country to which the community was racially akin.

The Bulgarian member urged that the administrative communes were also to be considered as included in the term communities, and therefore entitled to the benefits of the Convention, whenever they were deemed to be dissolved by reason of the emigration of the inhabitants. This view was strongly opposed by the Greek member. The neutral members sought and received advice from the Legal Section of the Secretariat of the League of Nations on this point, following which they sided with the Greek member, and a decision was taken on December 3, 1926,[21] excluding communes from

[21] Procès-Verbaux, xvi, 304th meet., pp. 2017-18.

the application of the Convention. This decision was sound. Not only do inhabitants of communes not own the special property of the commune, but the existence of the commune, the cell of the state organization, is independent of that of individuals, and of their emigration.

According to the Rules, communities, in order to be entitled to the benefits of the Convention, should satisfy the conditions of emigration and nationality required of former and new emigrants.[22] The provision of 'constructive emigration' above referred to [23] was contained in the Rules without restriction to individuals. The question of its application to communities was presented in an important case, that of the convent farm or metochy of Rosino or Rogen, near Melnik in Bulgaria.

This convent farm belonged to the Greek convent of Iveron in Mount Athos. That convent, represented by the Superiors Daniel and Ambrosios, filed, in 1923, for the convent farm of Rogen in Bulgaria, a declaration of emigration and an application for liquidation. The Commission decided that the provision for constructive emigration of the Rules, article 7, remark 1, applied not only to individuals but also to juristic persons (*personnes morales*).[24] As has been explained above, this provision of the Rules provided that persons who were domiciled in a certain part of the Turkish territory between 1900 and 1920, and at the same time owned property in another part of such territory, were to be deemed as domiciled in the latter for the purposes of claiming the advantages of the Convention concerning Reciprocal Emigration.

II. Period within Which the Convention Could Be Availed of

§ 41. Provisions of the Convention and extensions by the Commission. Article 4 of the Convention respecting Reciprocal Emigration provided that the right of voluntary emigration might be exercised during a period of two years

[22] See *supra*, pp. 77, 84.
[23] See *supra*, p. 86.
[24] Procès-Verbaux, xxiii, 385th meet., November 24, 1927, p. 8.

from the date of constitution of the Mixed Commission, by means of a declaration before its representatives. The Commission having been constituted December 18, 1920, the period in question should terminate December 18, 1922. However, the great waste of time by the Mixed Commission in the first year of its existence and its inability to determine the rules of emigration and liquidation at an early date, coupled with the continuing state of war between Greece and Turkey and the uncertainty in regard to Thrace, caused the extension of the period to October 15, 1923, by a decision of the Commission, acquiesced in by the two governments.[25] The period was again extended successively to May 1, 1924, August 31, 1924, and December 31, 1924.[26] Within this period the declaration of emigration, as well as the application for liquidation, referred to below, were to be filed.

§ 42. Further extension in favor of Bulgarian refugees. A special extension of the time-limit for depositing declarations of emigration and applications for liquidation was granted in September, 1926, to Bulgarian refugees from Greece. On September 1, 1926, the Commission had registered 28,547 declarations by Bulgarians emigrating from Greece, covering about 77,248 persons. The declarations were made by 18,708 new emigrants (52,549 persons) and 9839 former emigrants (24,699 persons). The above special time-limit was to expire December 15, 1926.[27] This extension was given in accordance with the resolution of December 14, 1925, of the Council of the League of Nations, adopting the political recommendations of the Report of the Commission of Inquiry, which, under the chairmanship of Horace Rumbold, had been appointed to investigate the incidents of October, 1925, upon the Greco-Bulgarian frontier.[28]

[25] The decision of the Commission of June 29, 1922 (Procès-Verbaux, vi, 108th meet.), was communicated to the two governments. The Greek and Bulgarian members declared at a subsequent meeting of the Commission (Procès-Verbaux, vi, 112th meet.) that their respective governments acquiesced in such extension of the period.

[26] Procès-Verbaux, viii, 151st meet., September 4, 1923, p. 991; 165th meet., January 9, 1924, p. 1053; ix, 195th meet., September 2, 1924, p. 1187; xi, 200th meet., October 11, 1924, p. 1242.

[27] Procès-Verbaux, xv, 276th meet., August 3, 1926, p. 1771; xvi, 302d meet., November 20, 1926, p. 1973.

[28] League of Nations, *Official Journal,* February, 1926, pp. 172-175.

The political recommendations of this Commission were two: that the work of liquidation of properties of the emigrants should be hastened; and that the time-limit for the filing of applications of liquidation of Bulgarian refugees should be extended. The latter recommendation was based on the following considerations:

During the last fifty years, as a result of successive wars, drastic alterations of frontiers have involved frequent changes of nationality for the inhabitants of the districts in question, with the usual train of attendant misfortunes, resulting in many cases in sudden mass emigrations. These populations . . . which are comparatively backward, have been worked upon by contradictory propaganda, which has led them to mistrust one another and to seek to do each other injury. Today the respective populations of Bulgaria and Greece have become comparatively homogeneous, but at the price of unquestionable sufferings. These sufferings have implanted feelings of hatred, which cannot be expected to disappear quickly in view of the fact that the means at the disposal of the Governments are unfortunately too limited to allow them to devise and execute measures of relief and remedies on the large scale required. . . .

There are in Bulgaria a considerable number of refugees of Bulgarian race, who came from Greece at different periods and have been unwilling to avail themselves of the Convention on Voluntary Emigration . . . although they were entitled to do so. On the other hand, these refugees claim the rights conferred by the Treaty between the Principal Allied Powers and Greece concerning the treatment of minorities, signed at Sèvres on August 10th, 1920. According to Articles 3 and 4 of this treaty, natives of districts now incorporated in Greece have the right to return there even if they left these districts many years ago, and in any case they are entitled to retain their real property in these districts. The number of these persons at present in Bulgaria is considerable. Most of them have left property in Greece, for which they have received no compensation, and, under the pressure of circumstances, the Greek government has employed this land to settle the Greek refugees from Turkey. To oust these refugees now in order to permit of the return of the former owners would be impossible, nor would such a proceeding be desirable, for its consequences would be to recreate in Greece minorities which events have caused to disappear. . . .

If these Bulgarians are to be asked to give up a right, it is only just that they should be compensated for the value of the property they left behind them. The value of this property will undoubtedly be very difficult to estimate in view of the considerable period which has elapsed since the departure of most of the owners. In the interests of reconciliation between the two nations the Greek Government should, nevertheless, display special good-will in this respect. The Commission considers that these problems could be solved either by extending in favor of the persons in question the time-limit provided for making a declaration of emigration under the Convention for Voluntary Emigration, or by the signature of a special protocol between the two Governments.

In this way the Bulgarians who did not see fit to avail themselves of the right, which has now lapsed, of emigrating under the Convention might be led to renounce their Greek nationality, receiving in return for the rights conferred on them by the Minorities Treaty the value of their property calculated on a liberal scale. The Macedonian Revolutionary Committee's influence would decrease as it found fewer and fewer grievances and sufferings to exploit amongst the refugees in Bulgaria. The Greek population near the frontiers would have less to fear from 'comitadjis' and from the rancor of the Bulgarian population whose place they have taken.

On the initiative of the Greek member of the Mixed Commission, the Commission extended the time-limit for the deposit of declarations of emigration and applications for liquidation by Bulgarian refugees from Macedonia and Thrace for a further period of three months. The Council, to which a report on this matter was presented at its session of September, 1926, adopted a resolution expressing its satisfaction and its desire to be kept informed by the two governments of the progress achieved in this important work.[29]

This wish of the Council was fulfilled, the two governments and the Commission addressing letters to the Secretary-General, which were submitted to the Council at its session of December, 1926. It was shown that the first political recommendation of the Rumbold Commission was being complied with, although with a certain slowness. The second recommendation met with much less success in its applica-

[29] League of Nations, *Official Journal*, October, 1926, pp. 1246, 1395-98.

tion. Although the time-limit for depositing applications for liquidation of Bulgarian refugees in Bulgaria coming from Greece was extended as above, the number of applications received until December 3, twelve days short of the expiration of the extension, was 2943, affecting only some 9000 individuals. Sir Austen Chamberlain, as Rapporteur to the Council,[30] pointed out that the Council had been led to expect a very much larger number, and could not but feel grave concern at the small result achieved. He made it clear that the Council, which had accepted the assurances given by the representative of Bulgaria, looked to the Bulgarian government to announce a much more satisfactory result when the subject was next considered. The Greek government, in its letter of December 6 submitted to the Council, called attention to the fact that the President of the Mixed Commission stated, at a meeting of the Commission on November 5, 1926, that not only some of the persons concerned, but even certain of the Bulgarian prefects were unaware that an extension of the time-limit had been granted. Clearly, no serious effort had been made by the Bulgarian government to induce persons entitled to the benefits of the Convention to avail themselves thereof, and the influence of the Macedonian Revolutionary Committee was allowed to prevail over these persons. No campaign of publicity on a large scale was undertaken. Merely the extension of the period was published in the Bulgarian *Official Gazette* of August 26, read only by judges, lawyers, and public authorities. At the next session of the Council, on March 11, 1927,[31] it was reported that the final number of declarations received until the expiration of the period on December 15, 1926, was a little over 4000, affecting some 13,000 persons. Sir Austen Chamberlain confessed that the result was disappointing.

§ 43. Late admission to the benefits of the Convention. By a decision of February 6, 1925, the Commission allowed the Sub-Commissions to admit to the benefit of the Convention in exceptional cases persons who, for special reasons,

[30] League of Nations, *Official Journal,* February, 1927, pp. 153-155, 234-237.
[31] League of Nations, *Official Journal,* April, 1927, pp. 396-397.

failed to file their declaration of emigration before December 31, 1924.[32] Such special reasons were considered to be, in particular: illiteracy; residence abroad and return to the country of origin after the expiration of the period; coming of age after December 31, 1924; recent death of husband and ignorance of the husband's failure to file declaration; erroneous filing of the declaration with the Greco-Turkish Commission instead of with the Greco-Bulgarian; difficulties encountered in regard to establishing membership in a minority, etc.[33] A decision of the Commission also authorized the acceptance of declarations of emigration after December 31, 1924, by persons whose property rights were established on shares of estates liquidated by the Mixed Commission, in so far as such persons possessed the other requirements for claiming under the Convention and their shares had not already been liquidated.[34]

By two decisions of the Commission taken on January 30, 1928,[35] no late declaration of emigration or application for liquidation was to be accepted in the future for no reason whatsoever. Only such late declarations as were already registered at one of the Centres could be examined as to their merits and be accepted in case of special reasons.[36] Exception was made for declarations of emigration of owners of shares of property liquidated by the Mixed Commission, considered in the preceding paragraph. These could be filed within fifteen days after the communication of the lists to the interested member of the Mixed Commission.

[32] Procès-Verbaux, xi, 223d meet., p. 1381. Whenever special reasons did not exist, the Commission refused to accept late declarations. Thus, the joint filing of declarations of emigration of the inhabitants of the village Efrem (Urumkeuy) after December 31, 1924, could not be justified by any special reasons and was refused. Procès-Verbaux, xii, 229th meet., p. 1416).

[33] Such decisions authorizing acceptance of late declarations appear in Procès-Verbaux, xv, 290th meet.; xvi, 302d meet.; xix, 348th meet.; xx, 355th meet. (1927); xxvi, 406th meet. (1928).

[34] Procès-Verbaux, xvii, 322d meet., February 12, 1927, p. 2158; xix, 348th meet., June 17, 1927, p. 6.

[35] Procès-Verbaux, xxiv, 398th meet., pp. 6, 9.

[36] Even when such reasons were lacking, the Commission accepted late declarations of emigration, when the interested persons were determined to emigrate in any case, and the liquidation of their properties did not present difficulties. See, for instance, Procès-Verbaux, xxxi, 453d meet., November 6, 1928, pp. 1, 6.

§ 44. Period for filing declarations of communities. The Commission, as has been stated above,[37] had decided that communities form a distinct category of persons entitled to the benefits of the Convention. The Rules had provided that declarations of emigration of communities dissolved by reason of the emigration of their members could be filed by the members, by the councils of the communities, or by the interested national member of the Mixed Commission. It was felt that difficulties might be experienced in the timely filing of such declarations, in view especially of the fact that the members might be separated and settled in different localities in their new country. For this reason communities were considered as entitled by special reasons to be admitted after the period for ordinary declarations had expired. The ultimate time-limit was April 1, 1927.[38]

III. Applications by Emigrants

§ 45. The declaration of emigration. Article 4 of the Convention required the filing of a declaration by the persons wishing to avail themselves of the Convention. The Rules provided that this 'declaration of emigration' was to be filed with the Mixed Commission or one of its Sub-Commissions. This formal act was so framed as to state the definitive decision of the emigrant to leave the country of origin in order to emigrate and settle in the country to which he was nationally akin. It constituted 'a solemn and irrevocable act.' The former emigrants filed with the Mixed Commission or its representatives, a declaration stating their desire to avail themselves of the Convention. Persons who had left their country of origin after December 18, 1920, or were leaving without filing a declaration of emigration, were assimilated to new emigrants and had to fulfil the formalities required for the latter.[39] The form of the declaration was defined by the Rules (article 33); blank forms were supplied to persons applying therefor. They contained a questionnaire in three languages, French,

[37] See *supra,* p. 88.
[38] Procès-Verbaux, xv, 286th meet., xvii, 323d meet.
[39] Procès-Verbaux, vii, 131st meet., March 3, 1923, p. 840.

Bulgarian, and Greek, and could be filled in any of these languages. Until the constitution of the Sub-Commissions the declarations were sent to the Mixed Commission.

§ 46. **Certificate of membership in a minority.** The declaration of emigration by new and former emigrants was accompanied with a certificate of membership in the Greek or Bulgarian racial minority. The form of this certificate was also determined by the Rules (article 34). It was delivered gratuitously to the applicant by the mayor of the township of his domicile. In case the township authority refused to deliver such a certificate, the applicant appealed to the Sub-Commission of his district. After an inquiry, the latter might release the applicant from the obligation of presenting the above certificate.

§ 47. **Application for liquidation of property.** The emigrant who desired to have his real property liquidated by the Mixed Commission filed an 'application for liquidation' according to a specified form. This application might be filed at the same time with the declaration of emigration or at a subsequent time.[40] More than one application might be filed if they concerned different properties. This application was not a condition precedent to liquidation by the Commission, as will be seen.[41] The Sub-Commissions were empowered to liquidate *ex officio* property, the liquidation of which was not applied for till the date of their visit to the village where such property was situated.

§ 48. **Revocation of declaration.** The declaration of emigration was considered to be irrevocable by the Rules.[42] However, the Commission allowed the Sub-Commissions to accept revocations of declarations of emigration which might be presented to them and to classify them according to the reasons invoked for such revocation.[43]

[40] Rules, article 37.
[41] See *infra*, pp. 152-153.
[42] Rules, article 8, par. 4. By exception, declarations filed prior to the publication by the Commission through the press of the modes of payment and modes of valuation of property under liquidation might be revoked within two months from such publication.
[43] Procès-Verbaux, xi, 200th meet., October 11 and 13, 1924, p. 1252; 205th meet., October 16, 1924, p. 1274.

Later the Commission refused to accept revocations by emigrants, on the ground that their properties were occupied before liquidation,[44] and authorized the Sub-Commission to admit revocations already made, on condition (*a*) that there was no objection on the part of the authorities of the country of origin concerning the undesirability of the interested person, and (*b*) that such person was not owner of real property which was occupied definitively by refugees, and (*c*) that such person had not applied for the liquidation of immovable property which the competent authority declared was specifically destined to the settlement of a specified category of former emigrants.[45] The final date for filing revocations of declaration of emigration was fixed at July 28, 1925.[46] But even after that date applications for revocation of declarations of emigration were admitted in exceptional cases.[47]

§ 49. **Declarations for absent persons.** A special procedure was followed for the liquidation of shares of real estate recognized as owned by absent persons who filed no declaration of emigration. Such a case was, for instance, presented by sisters owning shares in real estate, who thought that the declaration of emigration and application for liquidation filed by their brothers was sufficient for the liquidation of the whole estate. The Sub-Commissions sent to the Mixed Commission distinct lists for each village of absent persons who filed no declaration, indicating the name of such persons, their share, etc. These lists were transmitted to the interested national member of the Mixed Commission and such member entered into communication with the persons in question. An informal declaration of these persons that they desired to avail themselves of the Convention, or, in its absence, a declaration to this effect by the above member of the Mixed Commission,

[44] Procès-Verbaux, xii, 229th meet.. May 15, 1925, p. 1416.
[45] Procès-Verbaux, xii, 235th meet., July 28, 1925, p. 1471.
[46] Procès-Verbaux, xii, 242d meet., October 9, 1925.
[47] For instance, the applicant was of Greek origin and his emigration to Bulgaria would take him away from the country of his national kinship (Procès-Verbaux, xxiv, 398th meet., January 30, 1928); the applicant was engaged to a Greek man and her property was not occupied by refugees (*ibid.*); the applicant was the wife of an emigrant and her husband had died after the filing of the declaration of emigration (xxvi, 412th meet., April 26, 1928).

was equivalent to filing a regular declaration of emigration and application for liquidation.[48]

§ 50. **Declarations of communities.** The property of communities dissolved by reason of the emigration of their members could, if movable, be taken away by the members of such communities; if immovable, it was to be liquidated by the Mixed Commission. The members themselves, the council of the community, or the interested national member of the Mixed Commission were empowered to file a declaration of emigration of the community, according to a decision of the Commission which did not prejudge the ultimate determination of the question of communities. This decision was only preliminary and tended to facilitate the initiation of the liquidation of the community properties.

Convents raised the question as to the persons who should declare their intention to emigrate or their desire to avail themselves of the Convention. It would seem that the dissolution of a convent community is caused, under the Convention, by the emigration of the monks. They should, therefore, declare their intention to emigrate and apply for the liquidation of the property of the convent. But a certain sort of convents, or convent farms, called metochies, were not independent institutions or foundations, but were dependencies of other convents. In such a case the departure of the representatives of the mother convent who resided in such a metochy did not seem to be an emigration of a community.

This question arose with the declaration of emigration and application for liquidation of the metochy of Rogen in Bulgaria, referred to above. There was disagreement between the Greek and Bulgarian members as to whether this metochy formed an independent community or was a dependency of the convent of Iveron on Mount Athos.[49] The departure of the representatives of this convent from the metochy would not cause a dissolution of a community, and would not, in itself, occasion the liquidation of its property by the Mixed Commission.

[48] Procès-Verbaux, xxi, 359th meet., August 12, 1927, pp. 2-5.
[49] Procès-Verbaux, xxii, 370th meet., pp. 1 ff. and annexes.

The Greek position was that the liquidation of the convent farm or metochy of Rogen could be claimed on either of two grounds. First, because by the departure of the monks of that metochy from Bulgaria there was a case of dissolution of a community. That the convent farm or metochy of Rogen formed an independent entity was shown by the Greek member by various decisions of Turkish tribunals before 1912, recognizing ownership or granting title to that metochy and not to the convent of Iveron. Secondly, because the convent of Iveron could claim under the provision for constructive emigration of the Rules, article 7, remark I. The Bulgarian member denied the independent personality of the metochy of Rogen, but presented no proofs except the fact that it was called a metochy and not a convent. As a dependency of the convent of Iveron it could not file a declaration of emigration and application for liquidation under the Convention. Also the Bulgarian member denied that article 7, remark I, of the Rules could be applicable to the convent of Iveron, on the grounds, (1) that the provision in question concerned only individuals; (2) that the declaration filed in 1923 did not show on its face that the rules governing the convents of Mount Athos had been complied with, with respect to making and filing such application; and (3) that the property of the metochy of Rogen did not belong to the convent of Iveron but to the Oecumenical Patriarchate, which could not claim under the Convention, the Patriarch being a Turkish subject. As has been seen above, the Commission decided in 1927 that the provisions for constructive emigration of article 7, remark I, of the Rules applied not only to individuals but also to juristic persons (*personnes morales*). In regard to the regularity and authoritativeness of the declaration on behalf of the convent of Iveron, the neutral members of the Commission noted [50] that, in case the Commission should deem it necessary, it might write to the convent of Iveron and be informed whether it confirmed the declaration signed by the Superiors Ambrosios and Daniel in 1923. The contention in regard to the property rights is considered below.[51]

[50] Procès-Verbaux, xxiii, 374th meet., p. 14.

[51] See *infra,* § 113.

CHAPTER IV

THE MIGRATION

§ 51. The twofold action of the Commission. Article 2 of the Convention concerning Reciprocal Emigration provided that the Contracting countries undertook to facilitate by all the means at their disposal the exercise of the right referred to in article 1, namely, the right of those of their subjects who belonged to racial, religious, or linguistic minorities to emigrate freely to their respective territories. The same article stipulated that the Parties undertook to place no restriction on the right of such emigration, directly or indirectly, notwithstanding laws or regulations to the contrary, which in this respect should be deemed to be without effect. Further, article 9 provided that the Mixed Commission should have the duties of supervising and facilitating the voluntary emigration and of fixing the conditions of emigration. Lastly, accord-

UNIVERSITY COLLEGE LIBRARY NOTTINGHAM

ing to article 11, funds should be advanced to the Mixed Commission by the states concerned with a view to facilitating emigration and under conditions fixed by the Commission.

The effect of these stipulations of the Convention and its general spirit defined clearly the work which the Commission was called upon to execute with respect to emigration. Persons wishing to avail themselves of the Convention were to emigrate of their own will and free act. The duty of the Commission was to supervise and facilitate this voluntary emigration. This called for a twofold action on the part of the Commission: first, to grant to candidates for emigration all facilities provided by the Convention; and, secondly, to insure the freedom and voluntary character of the emigration.

The unfolding of the action of the Convention in each of these respects is described below.

§ 52. **Preliminary measures.** Even before the adoption of the Rules of Emigration and Liquidation in January, 1921, the Mixed Commission published an announcement to the national minorities in Greece and Bulgaria of the constitution of the Commission in accordance with the Convention, and of its determination, under the shield of the League of Nations, to secure the rights of the new and former emigrants in a broad and humanitarian spirit and to grant them the proper facilities.[1] This was not unnecessary, in view of the suspicion and misconceptions prevailing in the minorities of the two countries. At the same time, the Commission decided to notify the two governments of the movements of emigrants from the one country to the other and to inquire as to the nature and extent of facilities which the governments intended to afford to emigrants. The two governments were asked to keep the Commission constantly informed of the facilities of settlement, immediate or ultimate, temporary or permanent, which they were able to grant to emigrants.[2] The Rules, which were adopted March 6, 1922, laid down the conditions of emigration and the rights and obligations of emi-

[1] Procès-Verbaux, ii, 32d meet., January 28, 1921, p. 139.
[2] Procès-Verbaux, i, 12th and 16th meet., January 6, 11, 1921, pp. 51 ff., 67 ff.

grants. They were, however, in many respects amended by subsequent decisions of the Convention.

The intention of emigration was manifested by the declaration of emigration. This, with the certificate of membership in a minority, and the application for liquidation, in case the emigrant left in the country of origin real property to be liquidated by the Mixed Commission, constituted the file of the emigrant.

§ 53. Period within which candidates for emigration should leave. The Rules provided (articles 11 and 20) that candidates for emigration who did not own any real property should leave the country of origin within three months from the date of registration of their declaration of emigration. However, if they were members of a family or household that possessed real property and lived under the same roof, they were allowed to stay until the date of departure of the members of the family who owned real property.[3]

Persons owning real property should leave the country within three months from the registration of the sale of such property, in case the sale was made directly by them, or from the liquidation of the property by the Commission. A decision of the Commission made it clear that no candidate for emigration was to be deprived of his property before he had received the price, either in cash or in bonds presenting all desirable guarantees; and that the Commission would urge no one to emigrate, before it was assured that he would receive in due time the value of the property of which he had requested the liquidation.[4] This decision, however, was modified later, and emigrants were required to leave the country of origin within three months from notification of the liquidation of their property. The notification was made by the competent local authorities, in accordance with the lists communicated to them by the Directors of the Centres.[5]

[3] Procès-Verbaux, xii, 235th meet., July 28, 1925. Exceptions were made in the case of prisoners set free with the view of their emigration, and of soldiers discharged at the request of the Sub-Commission, whose sojourn in the country of origin could not exceed one year from the date of their exemption from military service.

[4] Procès-Verbaux, iv, 75th meet., January 11, 1922. See also Rules, article 20.

[5] Procès-Verbaux, xxxi, 454th meet., November 7, 1928, p. 5.

§ 54. Insuring the freedom and voluntary character of the emigration. The free exercise of the right of emigration provided for in the Convention could be endangered in two ways: by measures taken or influence exercised in the two countries for the purpose of compelling persons belonging to the minorities concerned to leave their country of origin; or by 'boycotting' the Commission and prevailing upon persons wishing to emigrate to remain in the country of origin.

§ 55. Opposition of the Macedonian Revolutionary Organization. The second danger existed by reason of the activities of the so-called Macedonian Revolutionary Organization. From the beginning this organization brought pressure to bear upon the Bulgarian minority in Greece as well as upon the Bulgarians who had already emigrated from Greece with the purpose of dissuading them from availing themselves of the Convention and deciding for emigration.[6] This is easily explained when it is recalled that, for two-score years prior to the coming into force of the Convention, this organization had made an enormous effort to secure Bulgarian supremacy in Macedonia and Thrace. All this black and bloody propaganda was to come to naught if the Bulgarians of Macedonia and Thrace were to decide for emigration and go to Bulgaria.

This explains the fact that for some years after the constitution of the Commission no desire was manifested by the Bulgarian minority in Greece to emigrate to Bulgaria. The Commission, indeed, began collecting declarations of emigration only in November, 1922, almost two years after its constitution. During this time, oral or written petitions were addressed to the Commission stating the desire for emigration. The Greek minority in Bulgaria, attracted for various reasons to the country of its national affinities, manifested a willingness to emigrate to Greece. Among these reasons may be mentioned the feeling of patriotism, the expectation of being allotted rich lands in Eastern Macedonia and Thrace vacated

[6] See Memorandum on the Mission and Work of the Mixed Commission on Greco-Bulgarian Emigration, May, 1929, p. 6. This memorandum was prepared by the neutral members of the Commission for submission to the Secretariat of the League of Nations. A copy was kindly furnished the present writer by M. de Reynier, President of the Commission.

by the Turks, and the desire to save their properties from the expropriation carried out under the social legislation of the Bulgarian agrarian government of Stambulinsky.[7]

§ 56. Consequences of the Greek disaster in Asia Minor. Under these conditions it appeared very doubtful whether emigration of any significance to the two countries would take place. Indeed, by June, 1923, or more than six months after the collection of declarations of emigration began, the Commission had registered only 197 declarations of Greek families in Bulgaria and 166 of Bulgarian families in Greece. But the situation changed radically from the end of the year 1922, with the swarming of refugees from Asia Minor and Eastern Thrace into Greece, and with the threat of an impending war on the frontier of Western Thrace. The consequences of these events to the minorities in Greece and Bulgaria were the following.

In the beginning of 1923, for military reasons and to insure the security of the railway line from Gumuljina to Dedeagach, the Bulgarian inhabitants of villages along the railway were deported to the Greek islands and Thessaly. 1500 to 2000 families appear to have been deported in this way. They were brought back only in the fall of 1923, after the signing of the Treaty of Lausanne with Turkey, when the possibility of war on the Maritza vanished.

This deportation frightened the Bulgarian peasants, and many, to avoid being deported, escaped to Bulgaria, either with the authorization of the Greek authorities or by secretly passing the frontier. The deported population, on their return to their villages, found their homes and lands occupied by refugees and could hope for nothing better than to be allowed to emigrate to Bulgaria.

On the other hand, the influx of the Greek refugees and the resulting abundance of manual workers in Macedonia and Thrace rendered the situation precarious to Bulgarian farm workers. This factor, too, acted as a stimulus to emigration.

In the meantime, the Greek government proceeded with

[7] See Constatations des Membres de la Commission Mixte relatives à la situation des Emigrants en Grèce et en Bulgarie (annexed to the above memorandum), March, 1925, p. 7.

the settlement of more than a million refugees from Asia Minor and Eastern Thrace. This would have been an immense task for any government. For Greece, impoverished by a state of war that had lasted nearly ten years, it was a work that could not be accomplished unless the burden was supported by all the native population. The villages and towns in Macedonia and Thrace, whether inhabited by Greeks or Bulgarians, must absorb the refugees. Houses there must be to receive them, lands to be distributed to them. The newcomers must be aided by the natives or perish.

The Bulgarian government asserted that the Bulgarian minority was made to bear a greater share of the burden of the settlement of the refugees than the Greek population. The neutral members of the Commission, who investigated in the early part of 1925 the condition of the minorities in the two countries,[8] were unable to express an opinion on this point, as no general impression could be gathered.

§ 57. Settlement of the Greek refugees. The fact is that the parts of Greece where refugees were settled were mainly Macedonia, Thrace, Thessaly, and the Islands. Only in the first two of these districts was there a Bulgarian minority established. Western Macedonia did not lend itself to an extensive settlement of refugees. It was, in general, densely populated. It had not been a theatre of war operations. Almost all the available land was occupied. The soil is poor and mostly arid. There were small but compact Bulgarian communities in the northern part of this region. They did not suffer anything from settlement of refugees.

On the contrary, in Central and Eastern Macedonia and Western Thrace there were many conditions making for extensive settlement of refugees. The country was largely depopulated as a result of military operations during the Balkan wars and the World War. Large numbers of Turks had been obliged to leave the country prior to the Treaty of Peace and afterwards as a result of the Convention for Compulsory Exchange of Populations. The land is rich. There were great areas of uncultivated soil which could be put into

[8] *Ibid.*, p. 13.

use with the aid of productive works, such as drainage and irrigation.

The great mass of the rural refugees swarmed into these regions. Many of them were settled in the houses and on the lands of villages abandoned by Turkish or Bulgarian emigrants. Others were placed in the homes and were allotted the lands of natives, whether Greeks, Moslems or Bulgarians. As was to be expected, the Greek refugees settled among Bulgarians regarded the latter as undesirable foreigners. Notwithstanding the orders of Greek authorities, conflicts arose, and the Bulgarian minority suffered from the unfriendly attitude of the newcomers.

In the meantime, various bands of Bulgarian brigands passed the Greek frontier and spread disorder and insecurity in these regions. The Greek authorities, assuming that these were set on foot by the Macedonian Revolutionary Organization, were, rightly or wrongly, apprehensive of the aid that these bands might find among the members of the Bulgarian minority. The latter, therefore, suffered from the suspicions and vexations of the police.

The outcome of all these factors was that a general desire for emigration was aroused among the Bulgarians of Macedonia and Thrace. Accordingly, while the number of declarations for emigration of Bulgarian families from Greece, notwithstanding the influx of refugees, had risen only to 166 for the months between November, 1922, and July 1, 1923, it rose abruptly during the succeeding months, being 288 family applications in July and 349 in August. The Bulgarian minority of Western Macedonia, however, showed no change of attitude, and has remained in Greece.

§ 58. Counter-effects on the Greek minority in Bulgaria. The above-described situation in Greece had its counter-effects on the Greek minority in Bulgaria. In the beginning, to the people belonging to this minority, the proposition to leave their homes and their agricultural or business establishments in Bulgaria and seek to reconstruct a new life in a Greece swarming with refugees was by no means attractive. The Commission began collecting declarations of emigration in November, 1922, at about the time the refugees from Asia Minor and Eastern Thrace had reached Greece. From that time until June 1, 1923, the Commission had received but 197 declarations of emigration of Greek families from Bulgaria.

In the meantime, Bulgarian refugees from Thrace, having escaped deportation to Thessaly and the Islands, arrived in Bulgaria. When the Bulgarian government took no measures for their settlement, they overran the Greek villages in the neighborhood of Philippopolis. The feelings of these Bulgarian refugees toward the native Greeks in Bulgaria were anything but friendly.

Besides, the settlement of the refugees in Greece determined, as was said above, the Bulgarian minority to leave Eastern Macedonia and Thrace. Inasmuch as the Bulgarian government did not create an administrative agency for the settlement of these emigrants, they were left pretty much to their own resources and quickly descended upon the Greek villages in Southern Bulgaria. They manifested to the inhabitants of these villages an extreme hostility and forced them to leave and emigrate to Greece. The Sub-Commissions intervened on several occasions, without much success, for the protection of these Greeks.

As a general result, practically all the Greeks from Bulgaria had to leave and emigrate to Greece. As compared with the above number of declarations of emigration to June, 1923, there was a sudden increase in the following months, for instance, to 365 for the month of July, and 313 for August.

§ 59. Intervention of the Mixed Commission. While these events were taking place, the Mixed Commission made efforts to ameliorate the tragic position of the minorities in the two countries and to insure in the utmost possible measure the voluntary character of the emigration. In the autumn of 1923 it worked out a programme of assistance to be rendered to Bulgarian Thracians returned from deportation who found their lands and homes occupied by refugees. This programme was accepted and applied by the Greek government.[9]

[9] *Ibid.*, p. 12. Live-stock, foodstuffs, and money were distributed to Bulgarians. See also Procès-Verbaux, viii, 160th meet.; ix, 186th meet. and annex to 185th meet.

After agreement between the Greek and Bulgarian governments, the Convention was declared applicable from October 26, 1923, to Thrace, which had been excluded until that time, as not forming part of Greece.[10] The President of the Sub-Commission in Greece was ordered immediately to Thrace to begin the application of the Convention. He there arranged for the immediate departure to Bulgaria of isolated Bulgarians whom nothing retained in Thrace and who desired to go away, and also of Bulgarian women and children whose heads of families were already beyond the Greco-Bulgarian frontier. No formal declaration of emigration and certificate of membership in a minority or compliance with other formalities provided by the Rules was required. The delivery of passes under such conditions in no way prejudiced the carrying out of the regular procedure at a later time. At the same time the President of this Sub-Commission coöperated with the Governors of Macedonia and Thrace and the local authorities for the reëstablishment of the conditions which would permit the free determination necessary for voluntary emigration.

The Mixed Commission transferred its seat to Saloniki, and for some time (November 22, 1923—May 17, 1924) concentrated in its own hands the issue of passes to emigrants and former emigrants leaving Thrace or returning to Thrace,[11] the Sub-Commissions issuing passes only in certain specified cases.[12]

The Commission also intervened both in Bulgaria and in Greece to insure that the burden of the settlement of refugees should be borne equally by the Bulgarian and Greek native populations. Through its Sub-Commissions it endeavored to prevent any further settlement of refugees in lands and homes of prospective emigrants, and then intervened to distribute the refugees in the best possible way, so that they might be grouped together in a certain number of houses, and to place the soil at the disposal of candidates for emigration who wished to cultivate it, or of refugees, in case the prospective emigrants did not plan to cultivate the land before their

[10] Procès-Verbaux, viii, 156th meet., October 26, 1923.
[11] Procès-Verbaux, viii, 160th meet.; ix, 186th meet.
[12] Procès-Verbaux, ix, 180th and 184th meet.

departure.[13] Later the Commission called upon the two governments to prohibit the dispossession of prospective emigrants before the harvesting or vintage of their cultivated lands, and to insure to them the liberty to harvest these lands, notwithstanding the granting of them to refugees. The Commission also decided to indemnify the prospective emigrants who should be unable to harvest the produce of their lands.[14]

§ 60. Suspending acceptance of declarations. Certain events spread alarm and terror in some localities among members of minorities, and resulted in a desire of emigrating in great masses and great haste. Outstanding in this respect are the events in Tarlis in Greece, which made necessary a direct investigation by the Mixed Commission,[15] and in Stanimaka in Bulgaria for which a special investigation was also made.[16]

In view of these incidents, the Commission took up the question of how far declarations of emigration made in the time of excitement and fright should be considered irrevocable, as article 8, paragraph 3, of the Rules provided.[17] On July 31, 1924,[18] the President of the Mixed Commission, as an administrative measure, telegraphed to the Sub-Commissions to refuse acceptance of declarations of emigration when they were suspected of being made under the influence of fright, and to accept those declarations only which were recommended by the representative of the country into which the emigrants intended to immigrate. Thus for three months acceptance of declarations was suspended.

At this time, the Geneva Protocols for the protection of Minorities in Bulgaria and Greece intervened. Their history is as follows.

§ 61. Geneva Protocols for the protection of minorities. A proposal was submitted to the Council by Mr. Politis, representative of Greece, and Mr. Kalfoff, representative of

[13] See the conclusions of the investigation in Procès-Verbaux, ix, 194th meet., August 16, 1924, p. 1167.
[14] Procès-Verbaux, xi, 210th meet., November 12, 1924, p. 1306; 222d meet., February 3, 1925, p. 1371; 228th meet., May 2, 1925, p. 1411.
[15] Procès-Verbaux, xii, 228th meet., May 2, 1925, p. 1411.
[16] Procès-Verbaux, ix, 196th meet., September 6, 1924, pp. 1196, 1199.
[17] Procès-Verbaux, ix, 192d meet., July 30, 1924, pp. 1151, 1155.
[18] Procès-Verbaux, ix, 193d meet., July 31, 1924, pp. 1161-64, 1185.

Bulgaria, and adopted on September 29, 1924.[19] Each of the two governments being desirous of insuring equal treatment to persons belonging to the Bulgarian minority in Greece, and to the Greek minority in Bulgaria, in accordance with the terms of the Treaty of Neuilly of November 27, 1919, and the Treaty of Minorities of August 10, 1920, came forward with the proposal of appointing the two neutral members of the Mixed Commission, Colonel Corfe and Major de Roover, as special representatives of the League of Nations, to assist the two governments in their efforts to achieve the protection of minorities, during the term of their appointment to the Commission. They were to act as an advisory body for Greek and Bulgarian minority questions. For this purpose they were to undertake an inquiry on the spot into the needs of persons belonging to the minorities, especially in the matter of education and religious worship, and were to submit to each government reports on the measures to be taken. They were to be at liberty to collect any information which might seem to them desirable or helpful in their work. The Bulgarian and Greek representatives on the Commission were to assist them.

Colonel Corfe and Major de Roover were also to be entitled to receive individual or collective petitions from persons belonging to the two minorities, to give their opinion on such petitions and to forward it to the representatives of the two countries on the Commission. The latter were to endeavor to settle the matter on the spot or send the opinion to the government and inform the two neutrals of the decision thereon. A report to the Secretary-General of the League was to be submitted by Colonel Corfe and Major de Roover every six months on their work in connection with this scheme. Before the expiration of their term of office on the Mixed Commission, each government would come to an agreement with the League as to the measures to be taken to insure the continued protection of the two minorities in accordance with the spirit of the above scheme.

The proposal of each government, after approval by the

[19] League of Nations, Document C. 533. 1924. I (*Official Journal,* October, 1924, pp. 1349-51, 1599-1600).

Council, constituted a distinct Protocol, which was signed by the representative of the government making the proposal, the President of the Council, and the Secretary-General. The final clause provided also that the stipulations of the Protocol were to come into force as soon as they had been approved by the Council.

The two Protocols for the protection of minorities were of great importance. Here were two governments coming before the Council and proposing to appoint the two neutral members of the Commission as their technical advisers to help them to perform their full duty in protecting the minorities. As Professor Gilbert Murray, Rapporteur to the Council, remarked, he could not regard this action without profound emotion. "The particular problem with which they have to deal is one of the bitterest in Europe; there have been, in the past, few race antagonisms like that between Greek and Bulgar; and doubtless it has of late been made even more intractable by the acute sufferings through which both peoples have passed."

However, on February 3, 1925, the Greek National Assembly unanimously adopted a resolution rejecting the Protocol signed at Geneva on September 29, 1924, on the ground that it was at variance with the Treaty of Minorities, that it instituted a procedure inconsistent with the principle that the provisions relating to minorities preclude any interference in the internal affairs of the state, and that the Protocol, so far from insuring a period of peace, was a source of conflicts and continual friction. The first two grounds could hardly be supported. The report of the President to the Council of the League on March 13,[20] proposed rightly that these two contentions in the Greek note should be rectified in a reply which the Secretariat should be requested to prepare.

The Council expressed its deep regret at having proceeded to sign, through its President, an instrument which it felt justified in regarding as a contract between itself and the

[20] The resolution of the Greek National Assembly was communicated to the Secretary-General, and it was asked by the Greek government that the question be placed on the agenda of the next session of the Council. See League of Nations, *Official Journal,* April, 1925, pp. 478, 482, 577.

government of Greece. It appeared, however, that Mr. Politis, who signed the Protocol, was not authorized to append to it the final clause, by the inclusion of which it was withdrawn from the parliamentary sanction required by the constitution of Greece in the case of any international instrument of this nature. Mr. Venizelos told the Council that Mr. Politis, although his good faith was not in doubt, had made a political mistake in signing the Protocol, ignoring the realities of political life. He thought also that the Greek National Assembly had done a great service to the Council by rejecting the Protocol. The position of the two neutrals acting as special representatives of the League of Nations, in a position to interfere every day in the internal administration of the country, would have had the result that one part of the population would be placed in a privileged situation vis-à-vis the other parts, for, after having exhausted all the means of recourse allowed by law to all the citizens, it would possess the additional right of recourse every day to an international authority for purposes of revising the legal acts of the authorities of the country. Such a situation would be likely to exasperate feelings and bring on civil war.

Mr. Venizelos, in presenting the position of Greece before the Council of the League, acted on the instructions of a government in the hands or under the influence of military men. This does not mean that he would have expressed himself in favor of the Protocols had he acted on his own responsibility, but he would perhaps have suggested an alternative. The Protocols were unacceptable in their form for several reasons. They purported to provide for a reciprocal situation in Bulgaria and Greece. However, at the time, most of the Greeks in Bulgaria had emigrated or declared their intention to emigrate to Greece, and there were indications that practically no Greeks would remain in Bulgaria. Consequently the Protocol signed by the Bulgarian government for the protection of the Greek minority in Bulgaria was illusory. This seemed to lend justification to the criticism of Mr. Politis made by Mr. Venizelos, that he ignored the realities of political life. Further, the natural tendency of the Protocols would have been to discourage emigration, since under them minorities were to enjoy as full international protection as possible, and therefore the Protocols tended to nullify the Convention concerning Reciprocal Emigration and its whole purpose. From this point of view it would appear that the political recommendations of the Rumbold Committee of Inquiry in 1926,[21] namely, that an extension of time be granted to Bulgarian refugees to file declarations of emigration, grasped the realities of the situation much more adequately than the Protocols. From another point of view the Protocols were objectionable, since they appointed the neutral members of the Commission to hear petitions on the part of minorities, render opinions, etc. These members had given no proof of qualifications to act in this most delicate task, and there was no desire on the part of Greece to intrust them with it.

Subsequently, the Greek government advised the Council of the measures taken or to be taken for the Slav-speaking minority in Greece, and this communication was considered satisfactory by the Council.[22]

§ 62. Effects of the Protocols on the Convention. The adoption of the Protocol, before its rejection by the Greek National Assembly, raised the question of the revocable character of declarations of emigration. At the meeting of the Commission on October 1, 1924,[23] the Bulgarian member argued that the Protocol of Minorities had intervened, and that many Bulgarians regretted their declarations of emigration, expecting a new era for the minorities. He thought that such persons should not be considered as finally bound to emigrate, as this would be cruel and unjust. The Greek member thought that the Protocol of Minorities simply charged the Commission with the application of the clauses already existing in the Treaty of Neuilly and the Treaty concerning the Protection of Minorities in Greece, and that, consequently, no legal change has come about in the situation. Neither had any actual change occurred which should cause the abolition

[21] See *supra*, p. 92.
[22] League of Nations, *Official Journal,* July, 1925, pp. 876-877, 950-952.
[23] Procès-Verbaux, xi, 200th meet., pp. 1246-52.

of the irrevocable character of the declaration of emigration.

The Commission had already suspended for three months, in July, 1924, the acceptance of declarations of emigration. The neutral members of the Commission were of the opinion that although the Rules established the principle that declarations should be irrevocable, it was the intent of the Commission to allow revocation in concrete cases when very serious reasons were invoked. Instructions to this effect were sent to the Sub-Commissions.[24]

§ 63. Emigration of persons prosecuted for criminal acts. Article 3 of the Convention provided that no obstacle should be placed in the way of the departure of a voluntary emigrant for any reason whatever, save in case of a final sentence to imprisonment for an infraction of ordinary law. In case of a sentence which was not yet final, or of penal proceedings under ordinary law against an emigrant, he was handed over to the authorities of the country to which he was going by the authorities of the prosecuting country with a view to his trial. In interpreting this provision, the Commission decided [25] that a final sentence for an infraction of ordinary law but not to imprisonment, a final sentence for a political infraction, or penal proceedings for such an infraction could form no obstacle to the departure of emigrants.[26]

The Commission undertook to determine the mode according to which such persons were to emigrate. Thus, it decided that persons sentenced for an infraction of ordinary law but not to imprisonment and otherwise qualified to emigrate should be delivered, with the judgment concerning them, at the frontier to the authorities of the other country, which might act according to the instructions of their government. As regards prospective emigrants under a sentence or penal proceedings for a political crime, they might, at the option of the country which detained them, be set free with the view of

[24] See on this *supra,* § 48.

[25] Procès-Verbaux, vi, 116th meet., November 14, 1922, p. 792.

[26] According to the interpretation admitted by the Commission, sentences to imprisonment for an infraction of ordinary law constituted an obstacle to emigration only if they became final before the date of declaration of emigration. See Procès-Verbaux, xiv, 267th meet., June 12, 1926, p. 1723.

their emigration, or be delivered at the frontier to the authorities of the other country.

The Commission also took into consideration the fact that, so long as the state of war or of siege continued, the immediate departure of persons under a sentence or penal prosecution for a political as well as for an ordinary crime might constitute a danger to the security of the state, and it decided that the application of article 3 of the Convention might be suspended temporarily, at the request of the respective governments, in respect of certain persons.[27]

§ 64. Facilitating the emigration. The other action of the Commission, besides that of insuring the freedom and voluntary character of emigration, consisted in the measures taken to facilitate the emigration of the two minorities. This the Commission sought to accomplish by the grant of passes (*feuilles de route*), having the force of regular passports, by facilities of transportation, exemption from customs duties for the export and import of movable property of emigrants, and by protective measures with respect to the requisition and transportation of movable property.[28]

§ 65. The granting of passes. Passes were granted by the Sub-Commissions to candidates for emigration presenting a certificate of the fiscal authorities indicating that their taxes [29] were paid.[30] No such certificate was required from indigent

[27] Procès-Verbaux, vi, 116th and 117th meet., November 14, 15, 1922. Political prisoners were allowed to arrange their affairs in the country of origin before their emigration; they were not permitted to return to such country later, save by special consent of the authorities (vii, 131st meet., March 3, 1923).

[28] All documents issued to emigrants by public authorities or to be used before the Commission and its agencies were exempted from taxes or fees, including the stamp. Exception was made for purely judicial acts issued by the Courts. See Procès-Verbaux, iv, 72d meet., January 3, 1923, p. 478.

[29] The claims of a private order of the state against candidates for emigration were not assimilated to taxes, and could not, therefore, justify a refusal of a certificate of payment of taxes for the issue of passes to emigrants, although the state might resort to judicial seizure of the movable property of emigrants. This rule was applied in respect to the so-called *Demir Basch;* or claims of the state for the price of seed. See Procès-Verbaux, xi, 207th meet., November 4, 1924, p. 1293.

[30] Special provisions were made for securing the National Bank of Greece and the National and Agricultural Banks of Bulgaria, to which candidates for emigration might be indebted. In general, whenever the payment of such debts as well as of the taxes could be secured through the real property under liquidation by the Commission, passes were granted for journeys of emigrants. Procès-Verbaux, xi, 201st meet., October 18, 1924, p. 1260.

persons, if they presented a certificate of their township vouching for their indigence.[31] A person who filed an application for liquidation of real property could in no case be deemed an indigent.[32]

Passes were also granted to prospective emigrants who wished to visit the country of immigration for the purpose of choosing an estate or of preparing for settlement, on presentation of a certificate from the police authorities to the effect that no objection to such journey existed; also to former emigrants who filed a declaration of emigration and wished to return to the country which they had left in order to care for their families and their affairs. The granting of passes to the latter class was conditional upon favorable information as to the person concerned from the authorities of both countries (Rules, article 24).[33] Later this facility was granted also to persons who, not having filed a declaration of emigration, desired to make such a visit in order to decide whether they would file such a declaration.[34]

After their definitive emigration, the emigrants might return to the country of origin, being given the same usage in such case as former emigrants. Whenever, however, they were summed for the purpose of appraisal of their property, the presentation of the letter of summons to the Sub-Commission served as warrant for the delivery of the pass.[35] The

[31] By a decision of March 15, 1923, the Commission allowed the Sub-Commissions to dispense with such certificates of indigence, when they could not be easily obtained and the indigence of the applicant was proved by other means. Procès-Verbaux, vii, 134th meet., March 15, 1923.

[32] The decision referred to in the previous note allowed exceptions in this case too.

[33] This information might be dispensed with by the Sub-Commission, in case the member of the Sub-Commission representing the country to which the former emigrant wished to go consented immediately to the delivery of the pass. Otherwise, the Sub-Commission or the member in question might ask the diplomatic, consular, or police authorities whether any objections to the journey of the applicant existed. If no reply was received within thirty days from the date of such inquiry, it was presumed that no objection existed. Procès-Verbaux, vii, 132d meet., March 10, 1923. The Commission decided that objection on the part of the authorities of a country on the sole ground that the former emigrant was unknown to them would not prevent the issuing of a pass. The Greek authorities seem to have objected on this ground to many former emigrants. Procès-Verbaux, xi, 222d meet., February 3, 1925.

[34] Procès-Verbaux, vii, 138th meet., March 28, 1923.

[35] Procès-Verbaux, xi, 222d meet., February 3, 1925.

former emigrants of the villages which were visited by the Sub-Commissions for the purpose of liquidation of properties were also summoned, and passes were granted to them in due time by the Sub-Commissions.[36]

§ 66. Facilities for transportation. At the first, free transportation by railway was granted to indigent emigrants and members of their families and also for fifty kilogrammes of luggage per person (Rules, article 13). By a subsequent decision of the Commission,[37] the railway fares on the trains of the Greek and Bulgarian states were reduced by 50% for persons emigrating under the Convention. This reduction extended to the members of their families and to their movable property. The same reduction might be granted by the Sub-Commissions to emigrants wishing to visit the country of immigration for the reasons considered above, in case the applicants were of limited means and the trip was deemed necessary. This decision was carried out by the two governments. It seems, however, that the use of passes and certificates of reduction of railway fares gave room to abuses.[38] In view of the fact that many landed emigrants left their country of origin before the liquidation of their property, and that some of them were without any resources at the time of emigration, the Sub-Commissions were authorized to give such persons privileges similar to those granted indigents in regard to free railway transportation.[39]

§ 67. Exemption from customs duties. The emigrants were free to take with them or to have transported their movable property of any kind. No export or import duty could be levied on such property. Likewise the former emigrants had the right to seek out and have transported, free from custom duties, the movable property which they had left in their country of origin. The certificates of exemption from customs for new and former emigrants were issued by the Sub-Commissions.[40]

[36] Procès-Verbaux, xiv, 266th meet., June 10, 1926.
[37] Procès-Verbaux, vii, 135th meet., March 16, 1923.
[38] Procès-Verbaux, xi, 200th meet., October 11, 13, 1924, p. 1256.
[39] Procès-Verbaux, xii, 230th meet., May 14, 1925, p. 1434.
[40] Convention, article 6; Rules, articles 14, 26; decision of the Commission, September 6, 1924 (Procès-Verbaux, ix, 196th meet., p. 1200).

The food for the maintenance of the family of the emigrant cultivator until the next harvest, and also the seed which he might need for his planting and sowing, enjoyed the exemption from custom duties and the reduced railway tariff.

On the other hand, merchandise, and in general all products which the emigrant had meant for sale, were regarded as business property and were excluded from the exemption from custom duties and the reduced tariff (Rules, article 14).

§ 68. **Taking away movable property.** Movable property, within the meaning of article 6 of the Convention, was deemed to include the house furniture; household utensils, clothes, and effects; implements of husbandry and tools of trades and professions; and the live-stock and flocks usually kept by an emigrant.[41]

The existence of movable property and the question whether a certain property was movable and could be carried away by the emigrants were sometimes examined by the local Sub-Commissions. No serious difficulties seem to have arisen on these points. Testimonial evidence was admitted in such cases.[42]

In view of the provision of article 6 concerning the movable property of communities, the Mixed Commission decided [43] that in case of emigration of all the members of a community, such members might take with them the movable property of the community, in so far as it could be removed without injury to the immovable property. In case of partial emigration, the movable property could not be taken away pending the determination of the whole question of communities.

§ 69. **Requisition of movable property.** In certain cases movable property of candidates for emigration as well as of other inhabitants of the country, in particular, live-stock and cereals, was subjected to requisition by the military or civil

[41] Special measures were taken for preventing frauds in the exemption from custom duties of live-stock transported by emigrants. The Sub-Commissions exercised the necessary control in granting certificates of exemption with inventories of live-stock. See Procès-Verbaux, xi, 213th meet., November 19, 1924, p. 1313.

[42] Procès-Verbaux, xxxii, 468th meet., December 22, 1928, pp. 19, 22.

[43] Procès-Verbaux, xii, 235th meet., July 28, 1925, p. 1480.

authorities. The Commission considered that, inasmuch as the Convention provided that the emigrants had the right to take away or have transported their movable property of any kind, requisitions of their movable property were contrary to the Convention. And, whenever such property was requisitioned without being paid for, there resulted a claim of the emigrants against the state which could not be classed with the claims arising from the liquidation of immovable property. It was accordingly decided that the chattel property specified in article 14 of the Rules could not be subjected to requisition, and that all requisitions, past or future, on goods not included in article 14 of the Rules should be paid for to the emigrants before their departure.[44]

§ 70. **Recovery of seized movable property.** Article 27 of the Rules provided, in connection with the right of former emigrants to look for and take away or have transported the movable property which they had left in the country of emigration, that movable property which had been confiscated or seized for reasons other than those of ordinary law, and which was still in the hands of the authorities, should be delivered to them, and that no fee for storage or for other cause could be demanded of them. For goods which had been sold or used by the authorities after October 4, 1920, and for which there existed written evidence, the claimants were reimbursed by the Mixed Commission; if they had been sold, at the price received by the treasury; if they had been used, at a price determined by the Mixed Commission. A decision of the Commission made it clear that the provisions of the Rules for reimbursement for the goods of emigrants used by the authorities applied also to goods wasted or destroyed, and that such waste or destruction could be proved by any means of evidence.[45]

§ 71. **Change of nationality of emigrants.** According to article 5 of the Convention, "emigrants shall lose the nationality of the country which they leave the moment they quit

[44] Procès-Verbaux, vii, 133d meet., March 13, 1923; ix, 190th meet., July 26, 1924.

[45] Procès-Verbaux, xi, 206th meet., November 1, 1924, p. 1285. Greece and Bulgaria passed laws in order to carry out these provisions. *Ibid.*

it and shall acquire that of the country of destination from the moment of their arrival there." It would seem that the passage of the frontier between the two countries was the definite act which caused the loss of the one nationality and the acquisition of the other. The stipulation of this article was self-executing, and no municipal law was required to carry it into effect.

§ 72. Statistics of emigration under the Convention. Migrations of minorities between Greece and Bulgaria had their chief beginnings during and after the Balkan Wars. Even before that time there had been a notable exodus of Greeks from the Bulgarian Black Sea coast and the Maritza valley, as a result of an anti-Greek movement in those regions in 1906. This movement was occasioned by the antagonism between Greeks and Bulgarians in Macedonia. Following many atrocities against them, the Greek inhabitants of towns and larger villages in the regions of Burgas, Kavakli, and Philippopolis sought refuge in Greece and were settled by the Greek government in the district of Volos in Thessaly. These refugees numbered about 35,000. There remained at the time of the Balkan Wars in Bulgaria some 45,000 Greeks.

During the Balkan Wars no change seems to have occurred in this old Greek population in Bulgaria. When, as a result of these wars, Bulgaria first occupied Eastern Macedonia and Western Thrace, there were migrations of the Greeks of these sections to Greek Macedonia, while many Bulgarians left Greek Macedonia. At the conclusion of the Balkan Wars some of the emigrants returned to their homes, but the larger part settled in the country of their kinship. It would appear that 60,000 Bulgarians had thus definitively emigrated from Greek Macedonia, and 80,000 Greeks from Bulgarian Macedonia and from Western Thrace, which remained Bulgarian in 1914.

During the World War, when the Bulgarian armies advanced in 1916 for the occupation of Eastern Macedonia, the majority of the Greeks of this section fled before the advancing Bulgarians. Most of the Greeks who remained were deported to Bulgaria, and it would seem that few of them escaped death. When, in 1918, Eastern Macedonia and Western Thrace were occupied by the Greeks and the Allies, the emigrant Greek population returned to their homes. At the same time, however, a number of the Greeks in Old Bulgaria emigrated to Greece, being wearied by the vexations and difficulties of the previous decade. Especially did this apply to Greeks living near the Greco-Bulgarian boundary. The outcome, therefore, of all these migrations of Greeks from Bulgaria was that only a little over 30,000 Greeks remained in Bulgaria.

It appears from the statistics of the Mixed Commission that practically all of the Greeks in Bulgaria declared their intention to emigrate and left the Bulgarian territory in the years 1923 to 1928. Indeed, in all, 46,000 Greeks availed themselves of the Convention. Of these 16,000 were former emigrants, who had left the Bulgarian territory prior to the coming into effect of the Convention. At the present time, only a few hundred Greeks remain in Bulgaria.

The migrations of Bulgarians from the territories forming until 1912 part of the Turkish Empire and subsequently acquired by Greece date as far back as 1902 and 1903, when the Turks undertook to repress by atrocities the revolutionary movements among Bulgarian peasants instigated by the Macedonian Revolutionary Committee. From that time to the Balkan Wars a number of Bulgarians who were threatened with prosecution at the hands of Turks emigrated to Bulgaria. But these migrations were slight compared with those which followed the Balkan Wars, and later the advance of the Greek and Allied armies near the end of the World War. It is impossible to determine with accuracy the numbers of these emigrants. Probably the figure of 70,000 would be near the truth. The Greek census of 1920 showed that there remained at the time in Greek Macedonia and Thrace a total of 139,000 Bulgarians.

According to the figures of the Mixed Commission, the Bulgarians who availed themselves of the Convention numbered, with their families, 92,000 persons. Of these, 39,000 had left Greece prior to the coming into effect of the Convention. This shows that not all of the Bulgarian former emigrants sought the benefits of the Convention. At least 30,000 'boycotted' the Convention, clearly under the influence of the Macedonian Revolutionary Committee. It may be that many of them were rural workers and had no property left in Macedonia and Thrace of which they could seek the liquidation. But it would appear from the proposal made at the present time (July, 1931) by the Bulgarian government, that the Commission should accept 6000 late declarations of former emigrants in Bulgaria, that a great number of them left properties in Greece.

In addition to the 39,000 former emigrants, a total of 53,000 new Bulgarian emigrants left Greece after 1923. These are only part of the 139,000 Bulgarians who lived in Greece in 1920. The Greek census of 1928 gives the number of Bulgarians in Greece as 82,000. Of the Bulgarians remaining in Greece the greater number are found in the northern part of Western and Central Macedonia, far from the Greco-Bulgarian boundary. They form compact Bulgarian villages in the regions of Florina, Kastoria, Enotia, Ghumendza, and Edessa; the remainder are scattered in small numbers in the regions of Sidirocastro, Seres, Drama, and Zichni, in Eastern Macedonia. There are no Bulgarians left in Western Thrace.

CHAPTER V

DISPOSAL OF IMMOVABLE PROPERTY BY EMIGRANTS

§ 73. Right recognized by the Commission. Article 7 of the Convention provided that "real property, rural or urban, belonging to voluntary emigrants or to the communities . . . shall be liquidated . . . by the Mixed Commission." And article 12, concerning the former emigrants, stipulated that they "shall have a right to the value of the property left by them . . . such value to be that resulting from the liquidation which will be made of the property by the Mixed Commission." It would seem that the Convention expected that all real property of new and former emigrants was to be liquidated by the Commission. However, the Rules provided for two kinds of disposition of real property: direct disposition by the new and former emigrants themselves or by their agents within a specified period; and liquidation by the Mixed Commission in case no such disposition was made, or in case an application for liquidation by the Commission was filed.

The right to dispose of their property was brought to the knowledge of the members of minorities at a very early time.[1] It belonged to persons who filed a declaration of emigration

[1] Procès-Verbaux, i, 12th and 16th meet., January 6, 11, 1921.

and it could be exercised regardless of the general prohibitions of transfer of real property existing in the countries concerned (Rules, article 15).[2] Although no precise statistics exist on the direct sales by emigrants of their immovable properties, the writer was informed by the members of the Commission that only in rare cases did such sales take place.

§ 74. Time-limit for direct disposal. The time-limit within which direct sales could be made was originally fixed at August 31, 1924, but provision was made for granting extensions. Later, the Commission decided that the final date on which candidates for emigration could dispose of their property was, for each locality, the date which the competent Sub-Commission should fix for its visit for the work of appraisal of properties under liquidation.[3] Notice of this date was sent one month in advance by the Sub-Commission to the mayor of the village and was advertised on bulletin boards in the offices of all the Sub-Commissions.[4]

In the case of urban property, even though the owner had applied for its liquidation by the Mixed Commission, it might be sold until the above-mentioned date. In the case of rural property, if the owner had applied for its liquidation by the Mixed Commission, it might be sold by him only on special authorization by the competent Sub-Commission, given by a unanimous vote.[5]

§ 75. Limitations of the right. Whenever an application for liquidation by the Commission was made, a permission to the applicant to sell his real property directly was not granted if it exposed creditors to certain risks. The authorization to

[2] Laws were passed in the two countries to permit such sales by emigrants as an exception to the existing prohibitions. See Procès-Verbaux, viii, 154th meet., September 28, 1923, p. 1004.

[3] Procès-Verbaux, ix, 189th meet., July 16, 1924, p. 1140.

[4] Rules, article 42.

In case on the date fixed by the Sub-Commission a sale was under negotiation and certain formalities were yet to be complied with, the Sub-Commission allowed a further period, but it also proceeded to gather the factors of appraisal of the property in question, so that it could appraise it later, in case of the unsuccessful termination of the negotiations for sale.

[5] Procès-Verbaux, xii, 229th and 235th meet., pp. 1149, 1474. By an exception late sales were allowed provided the property was not yet liquidated, the interested person proved his ownership, and no occupation by refugees had taken place. *Ibid.*, xvi, 302d meet., p. 1981; xvii, 316th meet., p. 2114; 320th meet., p. 2141; xviii, 333rd meet., p. 2309; 334th meet., April 12, 1927, p. 18.

sell was communicated to creditors whose names appeared in the file of the applicant and to the fiscal authorities, so that they could take steps for the security of their claims.[6]

The settlement of refugees in the rural and urban property of prospective emigrants caused certain limitations to the absolute power of disposal of such property by emigrants. Whenever rural or urban property had not been occupied by refugees, the above rules prevailed. In the case of urban houses in which refugees had been settled, the prospective emigrant could apply for the evacuation of his house with a view to its direct sale, on condition, however, that he had not applied for the liquidation of such house. Rural property occupied by refugees could not be sold directly by an emigrant. A sale of urban or rural property begun before occupation by the refugees could not be stopped by that fact.[7] It has already been seen [8] that the Commission took special measures to prevent unjust treatment of emigrants by reason of the settlement of refugees.

§ 76. Extent of the right. The direct disposal of real estate by emigrants included not only sale, but also exchange of properties between persons emigrating reciprocally from the two countries. In this case they were required to make a deed of sale in each of the countries before the competent authorities.[9] Emigrants were also free to rent their real property until the time of liquidation.[10]

It is evident from the above statements that the Commission aimed to encourage the direct disposal of real property of emigrants until the last possible minute. This was sound policy. The owner was encouraged to dispose of his property if he found it to his interest to do so. Yet he was not compelled to a forced sale when, under the conditions of emigration, property was depreciated in price. A further aid was the exemption of sales of emigrants' property from all

[6] See the case of Tachtadji, Procès-Verbaux, xxviii, 427th meet., July 11, 1928, p. 20.
[7] Procès-Verbaux, xii, 229th and 235th meet., pp. 1149, 1474.
[8] *Supra,* p. 108.
[9] Procès-Verbaux, xi, 200th meet., October 11, 13, 1924, p. 1253.
[10] Procès-Verbaux, xi, 207th meet., November 4, 1924, p. 1294.

taxes and registration fees.[11] In case the sale was made before the filing of a declaration of emigration, but with a view to such emigration, it was exempted from taxation if the competent Sub-Commission decided that the sale was preparatory to the emigration.[12]

§ 77. Properties of former emigrants. Whatever is said above on the power of emigrants to dispose directly of their property applies both to new and former emigrants. (Rules, article 28.) Something, however, was necessary to place the latter in the same position as new emigrants. The property that they had left in the country of origin on their emigration had often been subjected to exceptional legal and administrative measures: seizure, sequestration, confiscation, etc. They could not dispose of such property unless all such exceptional laws and measures were abrogated or revoked. These measures had been taken by the two governments on their own territory, and by the Ottoman government on territories at that time under the Turkish sovereignty which had since passed under the sovereignty of either Bulgaria or Greece. The Commission decided at an early date, in interpreting article 12 of the Convention, that its words "in the country which they [the former emigrants] have left" applied not only to property left in the territories originally Greek and Bulgarian but also to that left in territory then under Turkish sovereignty and now under Greek or Bulgarian sovereignty.[13]

The Commission also had to determine the meaning of the words: "the property left by them," namely, the former emigrants, "in the country which they have left." The Bulgarian view was that these words applied to all properties belonging to former emigrants by virtue of the ordinary laws, notwithstanding the modifications introduced into the situation by reason of exceptional laws or administrative measures promulgated or taken against them by the Greek, Bulgarian, or Turkish governments with a political purpose and occasioned by the abandonment of such properties following

11 Rules, article 15, paragraph 2.
12 Procès-Verbaux, viii, 155th meet., October 2, 1923, p. 1012.
13 Procès-Verbaux, ii, 48th meet., July 11, 1921, p. 243.

the emigration of their owners. The Greek view excluded property confiscated, seized, etc., under Turkish sovereignty, by virtue of legislation and administrative measures of the Turkish government.[14] The Greek member thought that the Commission was incompetent to deal with the liquidation of property disposed of by the Turkish government. Legally, his view would seem correct. But the Commission here again, as in the case of the determination of persons entitled to claim under article 12, was not greatly bothered by legal questions. It preferred to pay attention to "the humanitarian aims which the Convention was pursuing." Here were a number of people who had left their properties behind in territories under Turkish sovereignty. These properties were confiscated, seized, or otherwise dealt with by the Turkish government. Then the Bulgarian and the Greek governments succeeded the Turkish government in the same territories. Should these dispossessions be ignored by the Mixed Commission?[15] It could be answered that the duty of the Commission, however pious and humanitarian might be its intentions, was to execute the Convention, and not to write a new one. What was important was the intention of the contracting countries at the time the Convention was made. Now, by no construction of its terms can article 12 be made to mean that the two governments were to cancel the legislative or administrative measures taken by another government on territory over which that government exercised full legal authority before its annexation to the countries concerned. At the time this territory was occupied by Greece and Bulgaria, certain rights had already been disposed of by the Turkish government. These were, accordingly, not disposed of by legislative or administrative measures of Greece and Bulgaria of the sort which were now to be repealed. Of course, properties left by former emigrants and not disposed of by the Turkish government could be claimed by their owners. However, the two neutral members were of

[14] Procès-Verbaux, ii, 36th meet., March 31, 1921, p. 154; 38th meet., April 6, 1921, p. 163; 44th meet., April 28, 1921, p. 210.

[15] The memorandum of the neutral member, de Roover, which formed the basis of the decision of the Commission, attempts also to justify this view by an interpretation of the letter of the Convention; but his arguments are specious and artificial.

the view that the Bulgarian position was more reasonable, and the Mixed Commission adopted it in its decision.[16] In one respect the solution seemed hardly equitable. Properties left by Bulgarians in territories formerly under Turkish and now under Greek sovereignty had been allotted by the Turkish government to Turks who had left the Bulgarian territory after the Balkan Wars. Thus Greece was now bound to restore these properties to Bulgarian former emigrants without receiving in exchange the properties left in Bulgaria by the Turks.

§ 78. Repeal of measures of dispossession. A law repealing all laws and measures of dispossession applied to property left behind by former emigrants in territory now under the Bulgarian sovereignty was passed in Bulgaria on July 27, 1921.[17] A Greek draft law to the same effect was considered by the Commission in a number of its meetings.[18] Following the promulgation of this law by the Greek government, and the promulgation and adoption of laws and decrees in the two countries securing reciprocity, the Commission was satisfied that the Convention was to receive complete reciprocal recognition in the countries concerned.[19] The Rules, accordingly, provided as follows (articles 29 and 30) with respect to properties of former emigrants.

All exceptional measures, taken on the basis of laws, regulations, circulars, or otherwise, and affecting property of persons belonging to the Greek or Bulgarian minority, who had left their country of origin and were now established in the country to which they were naturally akin, were repealed or cancelled. These persons had the right, even if they had not filed a declaration of definitive emigration,[20] to take possession of their property, whether or not such property had been confiscated, sequestrated, abandoned, or the like, and to

[16] Procès-Verbaux, ii, 48th meet., p. 245.
[17] See text of this law in Procès-Verbaux, iii, pp. 367-374.
[18] Procès-Verbaux, iv, 70th, 71st, and 72d meet., December 27 to 29, 1921, pp. 455 ff.
[19] Procès-Verbaux, vi, 115th meet., November 11, 1922, p. 785.
[20] This declaration was only required when such persons desired their property to be liquidated by the Commission. See decision of Oct. 10, 1921 (Procès-Verbaux, iv, p. 432).

dispose of it freely, by using it to their own profit, by transferring it to others, or otherwise, subject to certain restrictions to be considered below. It is to be noted that the Rules thus extended the principle of repeal of extraordinary measures against the property of persons who had left property in their country of origin, and of the reinstatement of such persons in their properties, to persons who filed no declaration of definitive emigration. It is hard to find any basis in the Convention or in the appointment of the Commission for its intervention in favor of persons who were not emigrants. The Commission in this without doubt acted beyond its competence. Such persons, if they had rights, could claim them under the Treaty concerning the Protection of Minorities, with which the Commission had nothing to do. The reason alleged by the Commission, that the failure to reinstate such persons in their properties would bring upon them an indirect pressure to declare their intention to emigrate, in order to have the properties liquidated by the Mixed Commission, would seem weak.[21]

§ 79. Income of, and damage to, property of former emigrants. In case such property had been confiscated or placed under sequestration, the proprietors had a right to the income received by the state or by the sequestrator from the date of confiscation or act of sequestration to the date of restoration of the property to the legally entitled persons. This income was to be paid through the medium of the Mixed Commission.[22]

For any damage to such property done after October 4, 1920, by the act or negligence of the authorities charged with its administration and keeping, an indemnity was due to proprietors. They needed to prove that such damage was done after the above date, and that there had really been, on the part of the competent authority, a negligence which caused

[21] See also Wurfbain, *L'échange Grèco-Bulgare des minorités ethniques* (Lausanne, 1930), pp. 75, 140.

[22] An application for the payment of the income, containing a description of the property for which the state had received revenues, the amount of such revenues, if known, the designation of the administration which might have received them, and any other useful details, was to be presented to the Mixed Commission or Sub-Commission by the interested party (Rules, article 69).

such results as destruction of buildings, vines, plantations, etc.; non-payment of premiums on insurance policies, when the revenue of the property sufficed for their payment; and the like.[23] In cases in which the property in question was used by refugees and the latter paid no rent, no indemnity was due the proprietor. Property taken after October 4, 1920, by eminent domain for reasons of public and social utility might be reappraised by the Mixed Commission on the basis of its previous state and its value at the time of the new appraisal. In this case the price already paid was to be subtracted from the price resulting from the liquidation by the Mixed Commission.

§ 80. Restrictions on property rights of former emigrants. This cancellation of exceptional measures and the right of free disposition of property of former emigrants was subject to the following restrictions:

(1) Property which had been used for the settlement of refugees was not restored to its proprietor; the latter had only the right to the value of such property as determined after liquidation by the Mixed Commission.

(2) Property which had been rented without a clause for cancellation and for which the term did not expire before July 1, 1923, called for special measures by the Commission and the Sub-Commissions, the state being held liable for indemnifying the owner in the future.

(3) In the case of property in dispute between a former emigrant and a third person,[24] the controversy was heard by the competent local Sub-Commission. If the third person claimed a right *in rem* acquired on such property after its seizure by the state, and the Sub-Commission or the tribunals of the state recognized such right, the emigrant owner had a right only to the value of the property as determined by the Mixed Commission. If such right was acquired prior

[23] An application for indemnity, with all necessary specifications and details, was to be presented to the Mixed Commission or Sub-Commission by the interested party (Rules, article 70).

[24] As the Commission understood the term 'third person,' it meant a person, not connected with the dealings in the properties of former emigrants, who had acquired rights by virtue of the ordinary law. Procès-Verbaux, iv, 70th meet., p. 463.

to the seizure of the property by the state, and the Sub-Commission found that such right was a right *in rem* according to the ordinary law, the parties were referred to the tribunals. If the right claimed was not found by the Sub-Commission to be a right *in rem,* the authorities were asked to restore the property to the emigrant.

The following were not considered as creating rights *in rem,* according to the ordinary law: (a) titles created and issued by the Ottoman Commission by virtue of the Law on Abandoned Property (*Emval-l-Metrouké*); [25] (*b*) donations or purchases of a fictitious character or at such a price that the act constituted in substance a disguised donation; (*c*) prescription, except in cases where the Mixed Commission found that the emigrant proprietor had left his country for personal reasons, independently of any compulsory or mass movement of emigration.

(4) If a third person, who had in his possession without legal title the property of a former emigrant during the absence of the latter, had made reasonable improvements, consisting of buildings, plantations, etc., the Mixed Commission, when called upon to liquidate such property, on the application of the former emigrant determined the share of each party in the value of the property. In case the former emigrant did not apply to the Commission for the liquidation of the property, the controversy between him and the third person was decided by the tribunals.

§ 81. Protection by the Treaty concerning the Protection of Minorities. A decision of the Commission made it clear that the fact that a former emigrant availed himself of the provisions of the new law in Greece, abrogating the exceptional measures of dispossession, and took possession of his property, was not to be deemed as implying that the person in question had decided definitively to avail himself of the Convention and had renounced the rights afforded by the Treaty concerning the Protection of Minorities.[26]

The above decision was declared applicable in Bulgaria as

[25] The possession of such a title did not prevent a person from proving his rights in another way, Procès-Verbaux, iv, 70th meet., p. 464.

[26] Procès-Verbaux, iv, 72d meet., December 29, 1921, p. 473.

well as in Greece. The two governments were held bound to preserve and maintain the properties of former emigrants which were already confiscated, placed under sequestration, or deemed abandoned, until the moment of their restoration to the legally entitled persons.[27]

§ 82. **Taking possession of properties.** The procedure for former emigrants in taking possession of properties left by them was the following.[28] The interested person had to obtain from the mayor of the township of his domicile a certificate of membership in a minority and file it, together with an application for taking possession of his property (*demande de reprise de biens immobiliers*), with the Sub-Commission of his domicile or the Mixed Commission. The Sub-Commission, after examination, delivered to such person a certificate (*certificat de droit de reprise de biens*) stating that the person in question fulfilled the conditions required by article 7 (b) of the Rules; namely, that he was a former emigrant, within the meaning of the Convention. Then the interested person applied, directly or through an agent, to the administrative authorities of the place where his property was situated, who were bound to put him in possession of the property. In case a controversy was raised between the former emigrant and the local administrative authorities, or between the former and third persons, in respect to his rights in the property claimed, he might appeal to the Sub-Commission of the place where the property was situated. The latter would then examine his rights according to the rules of articles 29 and 30 of the Rules above considered.

§ 83. **Property occupied by refugees.** The exception concerning property occupied by refugees to the rule of restoration of properties of former emigrants made necessary further regulations as regards, in particular, the period of settlement, the persons to be classed as refugees, and the uses which such property served.[29] The exception applied only to property in which refugees were already finally settled before the presentation of the certificate, issued by a Sub-Commission, of the

[27] Procès-Verbaux, vii, 131st meet., March 3, 1923, p. 841.
[28] See Rules, article 66.
[29] Procès-Verbaux, ix, 182d meet., April 13, 1924, p. 1119.

right to enter into possession. The power of the government to requisition a property for the settlement of refugees was suspended from the date of the presentation of the above certificate until the expiration of the period for direct sale of such property by the emigrant in question. However, in regions where the mass migration of the local population had practically suspended the market for lands and houses, and where a new economic life had not reëstablished such market, the government might refuse to restore property that it desired to reserve for the settlement of refugees.

The Commission defined the word 'refugees' as meaning the persons who had left their country of origin in order to establish themselves in the country to which they were nationally akin on the occasion of a war, a revolution, or a political movement, and who were in a state calling for assistance. The term was also negatively defined, as not including persons who had emigrated in an isolated way, or for personal convenience, or persons who were financially independent. It will be seen that these definitions did not cover all the cases of refugees; they served only for the purposes of the application of the Convention. The right of former emigrants to enter into possession of their properties and dispose of them freely was restricted only in regard to the swarms of destitute refugees who stood in need of immediate settlement and assistance.

Not only were the possessory rights of refugees in the property of former emigrants limited to certain classes of refugees and to certain periods of time; but they applied only to the following classes of property. (1) Productive land allotted to refugees for cultivation and effectively cultivated by them. This excluded land which was not given for cultivation or which was not actually cultivated by the refugees. (2) Meadows allotted to refugees for the needs of their own live-stock and actually used for their pasturage. This excluded meadows allotted or used for other purposes. Thus, for example, if these meadows were used for the pasture of cattle belonging to other persons than the refugees to whom they were allotted, the former emigrants had a right to enter into possession. (3) Any house situated near the lands allotted to refugees and of which half at least was occupied by them. (4) Domestic workshops, stalls, etc., in villages or towns granted to refugees, who employed them for their own subsistence. (5) Any apartment house or private house in a city which was not put to any particular use and of which half at least was occupied by refugees. (6) Building lands on which masonry or wooden buildings exceeding in value the land had been built for refugees. In all cases in which a person had obtained land, lodging, shop, etc., as a refugee and did not use the same himself but rented it to another, he forfeited his special privileges as a refugee; and the property was restored to the proprietor, unless the tenant was a refugee to whom the property in question was indispensable and to whom the government gave definitive possession.

In some cases the settlement of refugees in the properties of former emigrants was considered to have fulfilled its purpose, and such properties were returned to the emigrant proprietors. These cases were (1) when the competent local authority regarded the property as temporarily occupied and as restorable; (2) when the property was of a special character, such as workshops, factories, mills, etc.; (3) when less than one-half of the property was occupied by refugees; and (4) when the tents or wooden buildings constructed for refugees were of a value inferior to the value of the land owned by former emigrants.

§ 84. Taxes on property of former emigrants. In connection with these decisions in favor of former emigrants, the Commission took up also the question of taxes assessed on property left by them. It took the view that these people had been deprived of the revenues of their properties for a long time and that their properties had depreciated in the meantime, and proposed to the two governments the following measures. For the period intervening between the time when the emigrants left their properties and the time they entered again into possession, they should not be asked to pay any taxes in excess of the revenues paid or to be paid to them. Such taxes were to be deducted from the amount of revenues payable by the administration or sequestrator in possession of the property, or should be paid by the third person who had used the property. Descent taxes on successions should be assimilated to other taxes on the property and be due and payable as above, in case the succession passed in the direct line or in the collateral line within the third degree. In all other cases succession taxes should be due in their entirety. Likewise taxes due for the time preceding the date on which the emigrants left their country of origin or after their retaking possession of the property were to be payable in the ordinary way.[30] These measures were adopted by the two governments in accordance with the proposal of the Mixed Commission.[31]

In regard to the payment of the tax on capital, the Commission interpreted the above decision to mean that, for property liquidated by the Mixed Commission, the single tax on capital was not payable by the former emigrants if they had left their property prior to the promulgation of the law imposing the tax. But emigrants in possession of property under liquidation by the Mixed Commission, or former emigrants who had left the property after the enactment of the law, were bound to pay the tax.[32]

[30] Procès-Verbaux, viii, 163d meet., December 29, 1923; ix, 183d meet., April 16, 1924.
[31] Procès-Verbaux, ix, 179th meet., April 2, 1924, p. 1100.
[32] Procès-Verbaux, xxii, 366th meet., September 22, 1927.

CHAPTER VI

THE ESTABLISHMENT OF PROPERTY RIGHTS

§ 85. Distinct operations involved in liquidation. The primary object of the Convention was to insure the free exercise of the right of reciprocal emigration of the Greek and Bulgarian minorities from Bulgaria and Greece. To this end, first, all the facilities for emigration were afforded, as described in Chapter IV. Then, the former emigrants were placed in possession of their property, and their right, as well as that of emigrants, to dispose freely of their property by direct sale was secured and encouraged. It was only in the last place that the Mixed Commission and the Sub-Commissions undertook to liquidate the real property of former and new emigrants. This they might do in two cases: on an application for liquidation, filed within the specified period by an emigrant; and *ex officio,* on the lapse of the period within which direct sales could be made.[1]

[1] Rules, articles 16, 17, 28. 37, 38.

The liquidation of real property involved several distinct operations: the establishment of the rights of property; the land surveying; the appraisal of rural and urban property, buildings, forests, etc.; the compiling of the files; the examination by the Reporting Committee and the Mixed Commission; and the payment. In this chapter the first of these operations is to be considered.

§ 86. Application for liquidation. Any candidate for emigration who desired to have his real property liquidated by the Mixed Commission was to manifest his intention by filing an application for liquidation. Blank forms of such application could be obtained through any agency of the Mixed Commission. The application might be filed in Greek, Bulgarian, or French. It might be deposited at the same time with the declaration of emigration or at a subsequent time. More than one might be deposited by the same emigrant and at different dates in case they concerned different properties. The application should contain a description of the applicant and of the property. The nature of the property, the place where it was situated, a detailed specification of its boundaries, the area (if land) or number of floors (if a building), the titles or proofs of the applicant, and the estimated price were to be indicated.[2]

§ 87. Posting the application. On the receipt of an application for liquidation the Sub-Commission caused a public announcement to be posted at the town hall of the village where the property was situated. This announcement stated that a named person had applied for the liquidation of such a property, and that any person who objected to such liquidation on the ground that he had legal rights on the property in question would be given opportunity to prove his rights before the Sub-Commission prior to the expiration of thirty days from the date of posting the announcement. A third person could plead his rights orally on the day of the appraisal of the property, even though he had not filed his objections in writing within the specified period, in case the Sub-Com-

[2] Rules, article 37.

mission deemed that there were sufficient reasons for justifying such exception.[3]

§ 88. Summoning the interested parties. When a certain number of declarations of emigration and applications for liquidation had been received, the Sub-Commissions worked out a general scheme for the establishment of property rights. This scheme took account of the necessity for the presence of the interested parties in the place where the properties were situated, of the geographical situation of the various localities, and of the means of communication. The Sub-Commissions informed the mayors of the various villages, thirty days in advance, if possible, of the date on which they would visit the villages, in order that the interested parties might be notified. In exceptional cases, arising chiefly from the hurried departure of emigrants, the Sub-Commission might go to the site of the properties and establish the property rights provisionally, without waiting for the expiration of the above thirty-day period. In such case the act of establishment of the rights was conditional upon the failure of third parties to file any objections within that period.[4] The candidates for emigration were also summoned by registered mail by the Sub-Commissions. They could appear personally or by attorney. The relatives or friends of emigrants, the administrators of their properties, as well as members of the bar of each country, could appear as attorneys. Professional representatives of emigrants, not members of the bar, were excluded. The emigrants could communicate, orally or in writing, with the Commission or the Sub-Commissions in any of the three languages; Greek, Bulgarian, or French. So could also their attorneys, with the exception of members of the bar, who were bound to use the French language only.[5]

§ 89. Sittings of Sub-Commissions. After the working out of the itinerary of a Sub-Commission and the proper notification of its visit to a village, as described above, the Sub-

[3] Rules, article 39.
[4] Decision of the Commission, September 2, 1924 (Procès-Verbaux, ix, 195th meet., p. 1194).
[5] Rules, articles 41-46.

Commission went to the village to proceed with the establishment of rights. In the presence of the mayor of the village or his deputy, or of a representative designated by the Communal Council [6] to sit, the Sub-Commission examined the applications for liquidation of the emigrants of the village.[7] Each emigrant had to prove to the Sub-Commission, in public session, his property rights on the real estate for the liquidation of which he had filed an application.

§ 90. **Proof of property rights.** Property rights could be proved by any of the following means of evidence:

(1) By a regular title or deed, conforming to the requirements of the law of the place where the property was situated.

(2) For the territories newly acquired (since 1912) by a title or authentic copy of a title conforming to the requirements of the Ottoman law, accompanied by a translation in Greek or in Bulgarian authenticated by the respective Ministry of Foreign Affairs, or translated into French by a special employee of the Mixed Commission.

(3) By *hudjets* and judgments of tribunals.

(4) By receipts for payment of taxes delivered by the Ottoman authorities, for the territories newly acquired, and supported by the testimony of two persons of the commune where the property was situated.

(5) By the testimony of two inhabitants of the commune where the property was situated, who declared, under oath, before the Justice of the Peace of their domicile, that the property belonged to the prospective emigrant. The report written by the Justice of the Peace on this occasion was produced before the Sub-Commission of the place where the property was situated.

(6) By the testimony of three inhabitants of the com-

[6] The representative of the village could not be chosen among the prospective emigrants. In case the whole village was emigrating, the representative was elected among the inhabitants of another village of the same commune or district, and in case the majority of the commune was emigrating, the representative was elected by the district council among the notables of the neighboring communes (Rules, article 50).

[7] Also of candidates for emigration of small neighboring villages which the Sub-Commission did not visit.

mune, in the presence of the mayor or his deputy or the representative of the village.

(7) By ancient documents having an ascertained date and originating from national authorities or administrations.

(8) By the testimony, under oath, of old inhabitants of the commune in case the property was situated in places which had been abandoned by the old population after 1900 in connection with political events.[8]

§ 91. Difficulties of proof. In order to appreciate the wisdom and effect of these provisions on evidence, one should keep in mind the system of land law prevailing in these countries. It should first be recalled that the emigration of the Bulgarian minority from Greece and consequently the establishment of property rights in real estate of this minority concerned almost exclusively the territories until 1912 under the Turkish sovereignty which now formed part of Greece, in particular, Macedonia and Western Thrace. In Bulgaria the problem was different. The emigration of the Greek minority extended all over the country, although the greatest part came from the newly acquired territories and from the coastal region on the Black Sea. There was no registry of deeds or titles on real property in Macedonia and Western Thrace. There was a registry of lands in Bulgaria, but for fiscal purposes alone, based on declarations of interested parties. A systematic official control of the entries in such registry did not exist, and the Commission decided accordingly that extracts from it could not constitute an authentic title.[9]

Under the Turkish land law, most of the land belonged nominally to the state, but for all practical purposes its possession, use, and disposal belonged to private persons. These persons were supposed to possess the land by virtue of a *tapou* or official title, issued by the Ottoman Title Office (*Defter Hané*) at Constantinople. The authenticity of these titles presented by interested parties was often subject to serious doubt, and the Commission obtained from the Turkish gov-

[8] Rules, articles 47, 48, 49.

[9] Decision of July 31, 1925. Procès-Verbaux, xii, 236th meet., p. 1484.

ernment permission to get in touch with the *Defter Hané* and inform itself as to the authenticity of such titles.[10]

The cases of verification of Turkish titles became so important that the neutral member, M. de Reynier, accompanied by representatives of the two countries, had to go to Constantinople in order to obtain information from the *Defter Hané*.[11] The *Defter Hané* displayed no great haste in answering the questions put by the Commission. M. de Reynier suggested that the Commission send one of its employees to Constantinople to obtain information on titles submitted or objected to as false. This would guarantee a greater truthfulness. The Commission in several instances had conducted direct investigations. The Bulgarian member of the Commission preferred that the party having the burden of proof should produce the information establishing the validity of the documentary evidence. This view was not adopted by the Commission,[12] which sent to Constantinople its agent, M. Girod, for the verification of titles.[13] It appears that M. Girod by direct investigation in the *Defter Hané* found that many *tapous* presented by emigrants were false.[14]

But such titles were not always possessed by the interested parties. Their ownership might be shown by documentary evidence of other sorts, such as judgments of Turkish tribunals recognizing possessory rights, or by tax receipts showing that a person was possessor of a certain property. But all such documents might have been destroyed or lost in the dire years of the war and emigration.[15] The archives of Turkish tribunals, where evidence of ownership could sometimes be found, were often destroyed or inaccessible. And the receipts of payment of taxes on property by emigrants had often been lost.

[10] Procès-Verbaux, vii. 165th meet., January 9, 1924; xxviii, 423d meet., p. 5.

[11] Procès-Verbaux, xxxiii, 474th meet., February 21, 1929, p. 2; 476th meet., March 28, 1929, p. 3.

[12] Procès-Verbaux, xxxiii, 478th meet., April 3, 1929, p. 2; xxxiv, 486th meet., May 24, 1929, p. 6.

[13] Procès-Verbaux, xxxiv, 494th meet., July 25, 1929, p. 7.

[14] Procès-Verbaux, xxxvi, 511th meet., October 12, 1929, pp. 3 ff.

[15] The Commission accepted as evidence even the slenderest documents. An example is the case of the property rights of the inhabitants of certain villages in the region of Florina. Procès-Verbaux, xxx, 443d meet., pp. 2 ff.; xxxi, 452d meet., pp. 6 ff.

Thus the testimony of witnesses was the only possible evidence in many cases. Indeed, this was the evidence habitually resorted to before the Sub-Commissions.[16] In order to secure its truthfulness, testimony of witnesses could only be taken before the mayor or his deputy, or the representative of the commune. The Sub-Commissions, as a rule, did not insist on conclusive evidence of ownership. They were inclined to give the applicant the benefit of the doubt.[17] But when third parties presented evidence of ownership in the property under liquidation by indisputable official titles, testimonial evidence on the part of the applicants was not sufficient for the establishment of their rights.[18]

For the city and suburbs of Saloniki there was a Turkish registry of properties preserved in the Government Translation Bureau at Saloniki. It was admitted that every owner of property in Saloniki ought to be necessarily registered in that registry. However, many properties of Bulgarian emigrants were recognized on the mere testimony of witnesses. The Greek member of the Commission asked the reversal of all such decisions. But as no objection was raised within the period provided by the decisions of the Commission, his motion was overruled.[19]

§ 92. Hearings and decision. The Sub-Commission heard the emigrant and his witnesses and took cognizance of the written documents. It also heard the third parties claiming property rights in the real estate in question. Questions of property rights and succession could be passed upon by the Sub-Commission in accordance with the existing laws. The fact that a case was pending before the courts in regard to a property did not prevent the Sub-Commission from dealing with the case.[20]

[16] Even ownership of large areas, such as pasture land of 30,000 *décares,* was proved by mere testimony of witnesses. See Procès-Verbaux, xxvii, 420th meet., May 29, 1928, p. 14.

[17] See on this Procès-Verbaux, xxiii, 386th meet., pp. 9-10.

[18] Procès-Verbaux, xxv, 400th meet., pp. 17 ff.; 428th meet., p. 6. But this rule was not always followed by the Mixed Commission. Cf. xxvi, 412th meet., pp. 6 ff.

[19] Procès-Verbaux, xxxii, 467th meet., December 18, 1928, p. 11.

[20] When the Sub-Commission thought that it could not deal with a certain case, it might refer the question to the Mixed Commission; the latter,

After the hearing the Sub-Commission withdrew and heard in private the opinion of the mayor or representative of the commune on the allegations of fact as well as on the reliability of the witnesses and on the claims of the emigrant. The mayor or representative of the commune then withdrew, and the Sub-Commission, after discussion, decided the case by a majority vote. It drew up a report certifying the establishment of the rights of each emigrant.[21] A copy of the report [22] was communicated to the emigrant, containing a summary of the decision in a language known to the candidate. The latter might present his objections within thirty days from such communication. The interested third parties might also file their objections within the same period. Each of the two members of the Sub-Commission might deposit a note containing his views.[23]

§ 93. Procedure for properties of former emigrants. What is said above for new emigrants applied also to former emigrants.[24] In view, however, of their absence from the place where their properties were situated, greater facilities were given to them for their individual or collective representation by attorneys. In the boundary region of the two countries or in regions where war operations had taken place the entire population of a great number of villages [25] had emigrated many years before the coming into effect of the Convention. Those villages were either entirely deserted or occupied by refugees when the work of liquidation began. The old boundaries of properties had often disappeared. It was extremely difficult to establish the property rights of such former emigrants

if it decided that the case should go before the courts, informed the Sub-Commission, which notified the interested party. See Procès-Verbaux, xi, 199th meet., September 15, 1924, p. 1239.

[21] In case of distribution of a succession, the Sub-Commission determined the part coming to each of the heirs, whether these were emigrants or not, present or absent. In case of minors, the rights were established in their names. See Procès-Verbaux, xii, 231st meet., June 30, 1925, p. 1441; 233d meet., July 22, 1925, p. 1461.

[22] The act of establishment of rights was drawn up in the language of the country where the property was situated. See decision of the Commission, Procès-Verbaux, ix, 195th meet., September 2, 1924, p. 1195.

[23] Rules, articles 50-58.

[24] Rules, articles 67, 68.

[25] For instance, in the region of Kilkis and the valley of the Struma in Macedonia, the entire population of 70 to 80 villages had emigrated.

with any degree of accuracy.[26] Not all the former inhabitants and owners of real estate of such villages applied for the liquidation of their property, and the delegations of applicants could not be trusted in their testimonies as to the existence and extent of property rights of applicants. The competent Sub-Commission, therefore, made efforts to constitute delegations which should represent the interests of the old inhabitants of the village who did not apply for the liquidation of their properties as well as of those who applied. These delegations, which were summoned in order to aid the Sub-Commissions in the establishment of rights, received a remuneration from the Mixed Commission, and were granted gratuitous passage on the state railroads used in their journey.[27] At the same time, the interested emigrant proprietors were summoned and their journey was facilitated in order that they might assist at the establishment of their rights.[28]

§ 94. Consequences of early departure of emigrants. By the end of 1925, most of the candidates for emigration had left the country of origin, and the provisions of the Rules for their summoning, for communication of decisions of the Sub-Commission, and for objections by third parties could no longer be applied. The Commission caused measures to be taken to preserve the existing boundaries of properties belonging to such emigrants,[29] and on December 23, 1925, a new procedure was adopted.[30] Whenever the emigrants had departed and their actual address was unknown to the Sub-Commissions, they were summoned to the hearing for the

[26] For instance, the delegations of interested former emigrants in the region of Melnik in Bulgaria were not able to testify as to the boundaries of their properties, and the Sub-Commission had to suspend its work in that region. The same difficulties were experienced in Kilkich in Greece. See Procès-Verbaux, xvi, 305th meet., December 8, 1926, p. 2034.

[27] The remuneration was paid for each day these delegations were at the disposal of the Sub-Commissions and for the days of travel. Procès-Verbaux, xiii, 253d Meet., February 17, 1926.

[28] Passes were granted to such former emigrants; and the authorities were informed, that they might take measures for the prevention of any disorders or friction. Procès-Verbaux, xiv, 266th meet., June 10, 1926.

[29] Procès-Verbaux, xi, 202d meet., October 20, 1924, p. 1267.

[30] Procès-Verbaux, xiii, 251st meet., December 23, 1925, p. 1592.

From October 20, 1925, all differences concerning the work of liquidation between properties of new and former emigrants were abolished. Procès-Verbaux, xii, 244th meet., p. 1544.

establishment of their rights through the medium of the appropriate ministry of the country of immigration. At the expiration of sixty days from the receipt of such letter by the appropriate ministry, the Sub-Commissions proceeded to the establishment of rights, even in the absence of the interested parties or of their attorneys. Moreover, the interested parties were no longer summoned individually, but collectively for each village. Through press notices issued by the central Sub-Commissions the emigrants of each village were urged to organize their delegations immediately, and functionaries of the Sub-Commissions were sent to the various villages to explain orally to the interested parties the necessity for appointing their delegations.[31] The decision of the Sub-Commission concerning the determination of rights and the appraisal of the property was communicated to the applicant as above, and the period within which he might file his objections was sixty days from the receipt of the communication by the appropriate ministry. The period for objections by third parties was also extended to thirty or sixty days after the communication of the decision to the interested party, depending on the way the communication was made, whether directly or through the agency of the appropriate ministry. From August 16, 1926,[32] the communication of the decision of the Sub-Commission to the interested party was abolished. The representatives of the two countries in the Centres (Sofia, Saloniki, Comotini) were empowered to make such communication in the form and in the way they desired. Thus the Sub-Commissions had no longer to wait for the expiration of the above period of sixty days before they proceeded to the completion of the file and its transmission to the respective Center.

§ 95. Further simplification of procedure. In the spring of 1927, with a view to speeding up the work of liquidation, further simplifications were adopted.[33] The procedure for villages where the total value of properties under liquidation was small (not exceeding 500,000 drachmas or 900,000 leva,

[31] Procès-Verbaux, xiv, 255th meet., February 25, 1926, p. 1635.
[32] Procès-Verbaux, xv, 280th meet., August 16, 1926, p. 1797.
[33] Procès-Verbaux, xvii, 331st meet., March 30, 1927; and xviii, 332d meet., March 31, 1927.

in the opinion of the President of the Sub-Commission) did not involve local investigation. Each Sub-Commission determined the property rights in such villages in its jurisdiction. The delegations were convened by the Centre. The procedure took place at the Centre or at a secondary Centre. In case the interested parties did not appear, the liquidation was made in their absence. In such case the Sub-Commission tried to establish the rights by all means at its disposal, testimony of inhabitants, other liquidated property, etc. If it did not succeed in establishing the rights, this was noted down in the *procès-verbal* and the name of the applicant was placed on a list of persons who had lost their rights to ask the intervention of the Mixed Commission.[34]

The delegations for larger villages were convoked by the state of immigration. For small villages the minimum number of delegates was fixed at three; for middle-sized or large villages the delegates were proportionate to the number of files, from five to ten per cent of such number. Incompetent or useless delegates were sent back to their countries.

§ 96. Proved rights always liquidated. In case an emigrant should present valid evidence of his property right on real estate which already was recognized as that of another emigrant, the Sub-Commission informed the Mixed Commission. The Commission ordered the reëxamination of property rights in case no payment was yet made. Otherwise, on the establishment of the rights of the new applicant, a new payment might be made and the competent government was informed that it might take the necessary measures for recovering the sums which had been unduly paid.[35]

Family properties presented such difficulties. "They are theoretically partitioned between more than one generation of heirs, though no actual division of the properties has been made. All the shares have to be proved, very often by oral evidence. They not infrequently run into hundreds in one property, Bulgarian emigrants in every village have disputes in which one member of the family is accused of defrauding

[34] Procès-Verbaux, xviii, 336th meet., April 15, 1927, p. 5.
[35] Procès-Verbaux, xvi, 294th meet., October 21, 1926, p. 1898.

the others. The Commission has tried, as far as possible, to refer these numerous disputes to the Bulgarian delegation." [36]

Buildings belonging to an emigrant and located on land which did not belong to him were liquidated by the Mixed Commission, and, therefore, the property rights could be established on such buildings.[37]

§ 97. Quasi-real rights liquidated. The Mixed Commission had authority under the Convention only to liquidate real property of emigrants. Emigrants applying for liquidation, therefore, should prove *ownership* of real property. The Commission, however, interpreted the Convention in a large spirit in this respect also, being influenced by the provision of the Convention (article 2, paragraph 2) that the emigration "shall not affect the pecuniary rights of the emigrants, as these may exist at the moment of emigration." Consequently, whenever a quasi-real right was established by the applicant, the Commission proceeded to its liquidation. This was the case with buildings erected by emigrants on land owned by railroad companies and leased by such companies for an indefinite term. It was proved that such buildings formed the subject of sale.[38]

§ 98. Erazi mirié and metrouké in former Turkish territory. Although all fields and pastures and, in general, most of the land in the newly acquired territories of Bulgaria and Greece were, according to the Turkish law, public lands, *erazi mirié,* the people having only possession and enjoyment thereof, *tessarouf,* the Commission treated rights in such lands as property rights. The land situation in Turkish territories is described fully in a subsequent chapter, in connection with property rights in forests. As will be seen, there existed also a category of *metrouké* lands which could not be owned by any one, being reserved for the public use (such as public highways) or for the use of the inhabitants of a village (such as pasture lands). They corresponded to the *domaine public* in France, in distinction to the *domaine privé* of the state. In

[36] See Memorandum on the Mission and Work of the Mixed Commission on Greco-Bulgarian Emigration, May, 1929, p. 23.
[37] Procès-Verbaux, xiv, 262d meet., May 29, 1926, p. 1696.
[38] Procès-Verbaux, xxiv, 398th meet., January 30, 1928, p. 11.

certain cases official titles, *tapou,* were produced, with the view of establishing property rights in such land. The objection of the Greek member of the Commission to the recognition of such property rights was supported by the Commission.[39]

§ 99. **Rights of fisheries.** The case of fisheries on the Black Sea coast caused a great deal of trouble to the Mixed Commission. These fisheries were called *talian* in the Turkish language, from the name of a fishing instrument consisting of a complicated net attached to the shore and extending for 400 metres into the sea. This served for the capture of migratory fish, especially mackerel. Greek emigrants from the Black Sea coast claimed ownership of (*a*) a certain zone of the sea along the coast, and (*b*) of the buildings and lands on the shore where they practised their calling.[40]

It was not disputed that under Turkish law an ownership, or at least a right *in rem,* on the seashore and in a zone of the adjacent sea was recognized. The claimants could produce official titles or deeds issued by the Turkish government and could prove that they had the right to dispose freely of their property rights in the *talians* by sale, mortgage, etc.

The Bulgarian member of the Commission maintained, however, that any such rights of the Greek fishermen ceased to exist from the time the Black Sea coast ceased to be Turkish territory and became part of the Bulgarian state. Further, he maintained that the Bulgarian Property Law of 1904 not only declared the seashore property of the state, but also gave an exhaustive enumeration of rights *in rem* and real servitudes, which did not include rights of fisheries. No longer could there exist a right in the adjacent sea, which is generally considered as *res extra commercium* and which was for this reason left out by the Property Law of 1904. Moreover, the

[39] Procès-Verbaux, xxi, 358th meet., August 11, 1927, pp. 14-16.

Later, doubts arose as to whether certain lands under liquidation were really *metrouké* lands, and a revision of the cases was ordered by the Commission. See Procès-Verbaux, xxxi, 452d meet., November 2, 1928, pp. 6, 11, and annex 1.

[40] See opposing arguments of Greek and Bulgarian members in Procès-Verbaux, xxxiv, 487th meet., May 30, 1929, pp. 6 ff.

Bulgarian member claimed that the law of December 13, 1921, declared the *talians* to be in the ownership of the State from the beginning of their existence. The Bulgarian member, therefore, concluded that the Greek emigrants had no property right in the fisheries to be liquidated under the Commission. They had only a personal right, similar to that of hunting, with which the Commission was not concerned.

The weakness and contradictions of this argument were brought out very forcibly by the Greek member, who proved that since 1878 the owners of *talians* had been invited by the Bulgarian government to produce and register their titles, and that until 1919 they continued to be in the undisturbed possession and ownership of the *talians*. In 1919, however, they were expelled by the Bulgarian government without indemnity, contrary to articles 67 and 68 of the Bulgarian Constitution. The owners of the *talians,* before their expulsion, were taxed for their rights in the adjacent sea as for real property. The *talians* were registered in the registry of deeds like all real property. Decisions of Bulgarian courts referred to the rights in the *talians* as property rights. The fact that the Bulgarian government recognized property rights in the *talians* was shown from the fact that the law of 1921 declared them property of the state, which disposed of the theory that they were *res extra commercium.*

The Commission for a long time left undecided the question of the nature of the rights in the *talians*. However, it instructed the Sub-Commissions to gather all particulars necessary for the establishment of rights of emigrants in the *talians*.[41] Later it took measures for their appraisal and for the formation of files for the *talians*. The constitution of a special legal committee was contemplated for the solution of the question of the nature of the rights in fisheries. In the first part of 1929 the question was discussed at the meetings of the Reporting Committee, and the neutral members obtained unofficial juristic advice. Lastly, at its meeting of May 30, 1929, the Commission admitted, over the protests of the

[41] Procès-Verbaux, xii, 236th meet., July 31, 1925, p. 1482.

Bulgarian member, that the rights in the *talians* were property rights, and decided that the *talians* were to be liquidated by the Mixed Commission.[42]

§ 100. Mining rights. The question of property rights in mines was not approached by the Commission until July, 1930. There were two kinds of rights to be considered: rights in mining concessions and rights in mining search permits. The two governments admitted the existence of a right *in rem* in the first case. In the second case the Bulgarian delegation contended that a similar right existed, whereas the Greek delegation held that the right was not even a right *in personam,* but rather a legal license, and as such could not form the subject of liquidation by the Mixed Commission.

There were only a dozen files for claims of this kind, and the neutral members served notice that they would deal with these according to equity rather than by application of strict legal principles. The decisive question was whether at the time of the emigration a person possessed a validly acquired right of license to search for mines. In such a case this right had a certain pecuniary value and the question was only one of appraisal. Instructions to this effect were given to the Sub-Commissions by a decision of the Commission.[43]

§ 101. Real property by destination. The Commission also decided that things constituting real property by destination could be liquidated by the Commission.[44] Such property was held to be the equipment serving for the preparation of wine, wine-presses, tubs, and tuns, in structures built specially for this use. Tuns were understood to be receptacles for wine which could be taken out-of-doors without being taken to pieces. Casks and barrels were not held to be real property by destination. Receptacles for wine belonging to merchants or non-producers or those meant for domestic use were considered movable property. Similarly the equipment of industrial distilleries (boilers, stills, etc.) which could be removed only with difficulty was deemed to be real property

[42] Procès-Verbaux, xxxiv, 487th meet., p. 26.
[43] Procès-Verbaux, xl, 561st meet., July 26, 1930.
[44] Procès-Verbaux, xi, 206th meet., November 1, 1924, pp. 1289, 1290.

by destination, but not boilers, stills, etc., meant for domestic use.

§ 102. Abandoned property. Many villages in territories formerly under Turkish sovereignty had been abandoned during the wars of 1912-13. Their inhabitants left sometimes without intention of returning, and, if they came back into the same region, settled in other villages. It was repeatedly contended by the Greek member of the Mixed Commission that, according to article 68 of the Turkish land law, these people had lost their rights in their lands, and that the Commission should not liquidate any such property. This view was not accepted by the Commission, which assumed that the persons in the above cases failed to return to their villages because of the difficulties and dangers of the times, and that no voluntary abandonment had really taken place.[45] In the case of the village of Sitchanli in Thrace this hypothesis did not seem justified. This village was destroyed in the Turko-Bulgarian war of 1912. The Bulgarian inhabitants left the village and on their return at the termination of the war did not attempt to rebuild it although it was included from 1912 to 1920 in the Bulgarian state, and preferred to settle in neighboring villages. It would seem that in this case there was a real abandonment. The Bulgarian member himself did not deny this, but argued that under the Bulgarian law, which was in force in Sitchanli until 1920, the abandoned properties were not lost to the emigrants so long as they were not taken into possession by third persons.[46] Legally, this seemed to be true, but since the abandonment of the village was not a result of emigration, but of destruction during the war, the liquidation of the properties of this village did not seem justified.

§ 103. Liquidation ex officio. The Rules provided that in case an emigrant should not sell directly his property before a specified date, such property should be liquidated *ex officio* by the Mixed Commission.[47] The Commission decided that all

[45] Procès-Verbaux, xxvii, 417th meet.; xxix, 429th meet.; xxx, 440th meet., p. 9.

[46] Procès-Verbaux, xxvii, 417th meet., May 19, 1929, pp. 18 ff.

[47] Articles 16, 38. See on the extension of this period *supra*, p. 125.

properties belonging to emigrants, that is, persons who had deposited declarations of emigration, could be liquidated *ex officio,* if they had not been sold by the proprietors at the time of the visit of the Sub-Commission to the village for the purpose of the establishment of rights. The same rule prevailed for properties the liquidation of which had not been applied for until that moment.[48]

The guiding idea of the Commission was that it was its duty to liquidate all the property of emigrants, whether they had deposited applications for liquidation or not, so long as they had not sold such property directly. It was under the influence of this view that it adopted, later,[49] the procedure of liquidation in the absence of delegations; allowed the examination of supplementary applications for liquidation deposited after the expiration of the specified period;[50] and authorized the acceptance of declarations of emigration deposited after the time-limit in case of claims on shares of property under liquidation.[51]

It was the view of the Commission that if the competent Sub-Commission had already visited a certain village, it could reject any applications for liquidation *ex officio* which were made by the representatives of the two countries or by delegations. It was the assumption that every village would be visited once only by the Sub-Commissions and other agencies of the Commission. In fact most of the villages were visited several times, and the liquidations *ex officio* could therefore be made at any of such visits. This caused great delays in the work of the Commission. In the spring of 1928 a discretionary power was given to the Presidents of the agencies of the Commission to reject applications for liquidation *ex officio,* whenever delay would be caused by their acceptance.[52]

The Sub-Commissions were asked to exercise their judg-

[48] Provided, however, that the emigrants were duly summoned. See Procès-Verbaux, xv, 286th meet., September 3, 1926, p. 1837.

[49] Procès-Verbaux, xviii, 336th meet., April 15, 1927.

[50] Procès-Verbaux, xix, 341st meet., May 25, 1927, p. 8.

[51] Procès-Verbaux, xvii, 322d meet., February 12, 1927, p. 2156; xix, 348th meet., June 17, 1927, p. 6.

[52] Procès-Verbaux, xxvii, 415th meet., May 7, 1928, p. 15.

ment in such cases and to proceed to the liquidation *ex officio* only of those properties the rights in which could be proved, notwithstanding the absence of applications for liquidation, by the means of evidence enumerated in the Rules. The properties in which ownership could not be proved were to be placed on a list to be communicated to the two states. The Sub-Commissions usually did not recognize and appraise such properties unless the property rights were proved beyond a doubt.

When the work of liquidation neared its end, it was found that the compiling of new files of liquidations *ex officio* and supplementary liquidations was being undertaken at the Centre of Saloniki for Bulgarian emigrants. This was brought to the attention of the Commission by the Greek member with a request that an end be put to the formation of such new files. The Commission discussed the matter at its meeting of July 2, 1929.

The Bulgarian and Greek members were in disagreement on the following points:

(1) With respect to properties for which no application for liquidation had been made by emigrants and which could be liquidated *ex officio,* the Greek member maintained that the conditions stated above should remain in effect.

(2) With respect to properties surveyed by land-surveyors but not contained in the applications for liquidation nor declared at the meeting of the Sub-Commission when the property rights were established, the Bulgarian member urged that these properties be liquidated, while the Greek member insisted that it was not possible to grant to a person more than he had applied for.

(3) With respect to the time-limit of liquidations *ex officio,* the Greek member, opposing in this the Bulgarian member, maintained that liquidation *ex officio* should no longer be allowed for properties situated in places where no work remained to be done.

(4) With respect to supplementary liquidations, a confusion had often arisen between these and liquidations *ex officio.* Supplementary liquidations were those proceeding on

supplementary applications of emigrants requesting liquidation of properties omitted in their original applications. The period for the filing of applications expired December 15, 1926, but the Commission, on certain conditions, accepted supplementary applications till January 30, 1928. Such applications were received by the Sub-Commissions, who dealt with them as follows. In case they concerned properties in localities where the property rights had been already established, they were not taken into consideration; in case they concerned properties in localities where the work of establishment of property rights had not been terminated, they could be taken into consideration by the Sub-Commissions as sources of information for the liquidation *ex officio*. From January 31, 1928, such applications were no longer received at all. Consequently, the Greek member maintained, in opposition to the Bulgarian member, that, since from January 31, 1928, the Commission prohibited the emigrants from supplying the Sub-Commissions with information on omitted properties for the purpose of liquidation *ex officio,* this involved a similar prohibition of demands for liquidation *ex officio* after the above date on the part of the Bulgarian members of Sub-Commissions.

At the bottom of this dispute was the fact that there were about 6000 Bulgarian former emigrants from Macedonia and Thrace who, for one reason or other, had not filed at the proper time a declaration for emigration and an application for the liquidation of their properties. The Bulgarian government, through its representatives and the machinery of liquidations *ex officio* and supplementary liquidations, was endeavoring to have the properties of these persons liquidated by the Mixed Commission. The Greek government, on the contrary, sought to defeat this purpose by shutting the door to such liquidations. It should be recalled that the persons in question and the Bulgarian government had more than five years, from November, 1922, to January, 1928, to apply for liquidation, and that to admit these new applications would cause great delay in the work of the Commission. Besides, the persons in question preserved all their rights in their properties under the Greek law and the Treaty concerning the Protection of Minorities.

The Commission, at its meeting of July 2, 1929, accepted the Greek position and stood by its previous decisions, thus putting an end to the formation of new files of liquidation.[53]

[53] Procès-Verbaux, xxxiv, 492d meet., pp. 22 ff.

CHAPTER VII

PROPERTY OF COMMUNITIES

§ 104. Questions raised by the provisions on communities. As is seen in another place, the Convention provided in article 7 that real property, rural or urban, of communities as well as that of individuals should be liquidated by the Mixed Commission. Article 7 referred to article 6 for a definition of the communities whose property was to be liquidated. These comprised the communities which had to be dissolved by reason of the emigration of their members, and included churches, convents, schools, hospitals, or foundations of any kind whatever. The question of defining these communities, and the conditions under which their property was to be liquidated by the Commission, provoked lengthy and often confused discussions in the Mixed Commission, which were terminated by a recourse to the Permanent Court of International Justice for an advisory opinion.

It was generally admitted that there were two main questions of interpretation with regard to the provisions of the Convention on communities: (1) What were the communities referred to in the above articles of the Convention; what was their nature? (2) When were these conventions to be considered dissolved, in which case their movable property could be taken away by their members and the real property was to be dealt with by the Commission?

§ 105. Positions of the national members of the Commission. The position taken on these questions by the members of the Commission appointed by the two governments has not been consistent. Originally the Bulgarian member agreed [1] with the Greek member that the communities referred to in the Convention were the national-religious communities which were created and existed under the Turkish rule, although not recognized by the Turkish law as juristic persons capable of rights or obligations. Soon afterwards, however, the same member sought to apply to such communities the general rules applicable to juristic persons or even to the administrative divisions of a state.[2] In his view, a community should be deemed dissolved when all its members emigrated, or, at least, such a large number that the remaining members could not continue the existence of the community. He argued from the analogy of juristic persons, corporations or associations which continue to exist notwithstanding the reduction of their membership, so long as the remaining members suffice to secure their existence, in conformity with their organization, their charter, or the law. He drew also the analogy of the administrative subdivision or commune, whose inhabitants have no right on its property, as that is destined to the use and benefit of the commune as a juristic person. The Bulgarian member thought, therefore, that a fixed rule should be adopted, and that whenever five members at least of the community had not emigrated it should be concluded that the community was not dissolved and could not claim under the Convention.[3] He also proposed that the inhabitants of an administrative area, as city, village, parish, quarter, etc., who in the year preceding the emigration were considered as forming part of the minority of that administrative area and who continued so to form part, should be regarded as members of a religious or national

[1] Procès-Verbaux, vii, 142d meet., April 25, 1923, p. 919.

[2] See Procès-Verbaux, viii, 148th meet., August 27, 1923, p. 970.

[3] The Bulgarian position was later modified. When the number of the remaining members of the community exceeded one-fourth of the previous total membership, a proportional part of the community property should be left to them. Procès-Verbaux, xv, 286th meet., September 3, 1926, p. 1840.

community. The Bulgarian member cited in support of his argument extracts from the *Jurisprudence générale* of Dalloz on the law of the communautés de droit which was supposed to apply to communities referred to in the Convention.

In this error the Bulgarian member was followed by the Greek member,[4] who, while rightly calling attention to the fact that the Convention included explicitly among the communities churches, schools, hospitals, etc., attempted to apply in the matter the provisions of the French Civil Code and the French administrative law. He proposed to follow their distinction between communal public property (*biens communaux de droit public*), such as streets, squares, forests, or pasture lands, over which a commune has only a *jus utendi et fruendi* and which on the dissolution of the community would remain in the ownership of the state, and communal private property (*biens communaux de domaine privé*), such as churches, schools, etc. These belonged in ownership to the community as in the case of an individual. The Greek member found no theory or principle in the general law of any country justifying the position of the Bulgarian member that the property of the community could not be liquidated so long as five members had not emigrated, thus leaving, for instance, the real estate of a community of 10,000 people to five individuals.

§ 106. Communities as actual conditions. The attempts of the Bulgarian and Greek members of the Commission to apply the French civil or administrative law to the communities in the old Turkish territories were very unfortunate. These communities were actual conditions rather than juristic persons. They had never been recognized as juristic persons by the Turkish law or the Turkish administration. Their existence is explained by the privileges enjoyed by the Greek Patriarchate and later by the Bulgarian Exarchate and the Bishops. Under these privileges, the Christians were allowed to have churches, convents, schools, libraries, etc. Grouped together in a given locality by common race, religion, or language for the purpose of preserving these and their traditions, bringing up their children in the same spirit, rendering mutual

[4] Procès-Verbaux, viii, 150th meet., August 31, 1923, p. 982.

assistance, they formed either communities in general, or independent foundations, or institutions such as churches, schools, and hospitals. The direction, supervision, and financial management of the properties needed for the fulfilment of the aims of these communities was not governed by any rules of Turkish law, but by those established by the Patriarchate or Exarchate and the Councils of Bishops and delegates of the people.

The Greek member of the Commission, Mr. Gheorgopoulos, abandoned in November, 1927,[5] the wrong position of his predecessor, and presented this true conception of the communities. He pointed out that the Convention referred to two kinds of communities: first, the organized national or religious aggregations of persons, which possessed and administered certain properties for the purpose of satisfying certain needs, demands, and interests of their members, and, secondly, the independent autonomous foundations and institutions, such as convents, hospitals, and schools. In the first case a community possessed property of all sorts and with its proceeds it maintained schools, churches, libraries, cemeteries, etc. In the second case the autonomous foundations or institutions possessed property of their own and were maintained with their own resources or from the proceeds of their own property.

With regard to the question when such communities were to be dissolved under the Convention, Mr. Gheorgopoulos maintained that it was not possible to fix an arbitrary rule that when a specified number of members of a community had not emigrated the communities should not be deemed as having to be dissolved. It was an actual condition in each case and it was to be dealt with as such. The creation and maintenance of the community was determined by a certain purpose. Its dissolution ought to be admitted in case such purpose could no longer be fulfilled. Further, the Greek member held that the general principle of article 2 of the Convention, that the "exercise of the right of emigration should not affect the pecuniary rights of the emigrants, as these may exist at the moment of emigration," concerned communities as well as

[5] Procès-Verbaux, xxiii, 381st and 382d meet., annexes.

individuals. But for the provisions of the Convention, it might be argued that the property of the communities, on their dissolution, would go to the state where such property was located. Under the Convention, the property of the communities was to be liquidated in their favor. From this it was concluded, that a community should be dissolved when a sufficient number of its members had emigrated to need a community property in their new settlement.

§ 107. Greek communities dissolved in Bulgaria since 1891. A further question arose in connection with communities dissolved prior to the coming into effect of the Convention respecting Reciprocal Emigration, whose members had emigrated between the year 1900 and the coming into effect of the Convention. The Commission had unanimously decided, as is seen,[6] that the word 'persons' in article 12, which concerned former emigrants, applied also to communities. In the old territory of Bulgaria, before the Balkan war of 1912, the Greek Orthodox communities had been dissolved *de jure* and later *de facto,* in consequence of the so-called Jifkoff Act on Public Education promulgated December 14, 1891. According to this Act, no communities were longer recognized, except the religious Musulman, Israelite, Armenian, etc., communities. The law was applied not immediately, but gradually in the course of the next few years. The Supreme Court of Bulgaria confirmed the abolition of the Greek communities in a case in 1895. In this case the Court affirmed a decision of the tribunal of Varna dismissing a suit of the Greek community of Varna against a Bulgarian tenant of one of its properties on the plea of the latter that there existed no Greek community. The Greek communities in fact went out of existence in the following years; and in 1906, on the occasion of the violent anti-Greek movement in Bulgaria, all property of Greek institutions, churches, schools, hospitals, convents, etc., was confiscated.

In view of the fact that the *de facto* dissolution of the Greek communities in Bulgaria came about mainly after 1906, the Greek member of the Commission maintained that the

[6] See *supra,* p. 88.

property of such communities was also to be liquidated by the Commission under the provisions of article 12 of the Convention and under the decisions of the Commission concerning former emigrants from 1900 to the coming into effect of the Convention.[7] The Bulgarian member of the Commission argued that the latter could not liquidate property of communities which had ceased to exist *de jure* in 1900, since it could not deal with the liquidation of properties of individuals who had emigrated prior to that year. To this the Greek member replied that article 29 of the Rules for reciprocal emigration and liquidation, which provided that all exceptional measures taken against the property of former emigrants were deemed abrogated and cancelled, had a retroactive effect; that the Jifkoff Act should be deemed as one of the exceptional laws passed against property of Greek communities, existing in whatever period, when the members of such communities had emigrated after 1900; and that the Convention considered all communities as existing at the time when their members emigrated.[8]

All this was highly ingenious; but it lost sight of the important provision of the Convention, article 6, paragraph 2, that its provisions applied only to those communities which were dissolved *by reason of the emigration of their members*. Therefore the Convention had nothing to do with communities which were dissolved for any other reason than that of emigration of their members.

§ 108. In whose favor was community property to be liquidated? The questions of dissolution and liquidation raised a further question, that of the payment of the proceeds of liquidation. Both the Greek and Bulgarian members seemed to agree [9] that since both in Bulgaria and Greece the communities are now under the supervision of the government which recognized their existence, the proceeds of liquidation of their properties in the country of origin should be turned

[7] See *supra*, § 37.

[8] Procès-Verbaux, xxiii, 381st meet., November 10, 1927, annex; 382d meet., November 16, 1927, annex; 385th meet., November 24, 1927, pp. 5-7.

[9] Procès-Verbaux, xxiii, 381st meet., annex, and 382d meet., Annex, November, 1927. See also xv, 286th meet., September 6, 1926, p. 1839.

juristic persons were included in the term *communautés* of the Convention:

(1) Associations or corporations proper, such as clubs, societies, etc., founded with the exclusive or main purpose of serving a common interest of their members and not with a lucrative purpose.

(2) Associations in the form of communities, religious or cultural, which, though difficult to define, have always played a considerable rôle in the Balkan provinces of the Ottoman Empire. These groups were united by the religious or cultural kinship alone, without formal incorporation, and without a charter defining the relations of the members between themselves and towards the community. This type comprised school and church communities and sometimes convents and their dependencies (metochies); it possessed a property independent of the contributions of the members. The members or the beneficiaries of these communities had a right in the moral capital of the institutions, but it could not be claimed that they had a right to a specific part of the property in case of the liquidation of the community.

(3) Foundations, that is, corporations to administer a certain property, constituted by an individual or a group of individuals for a definite purpose. These did not cease except at the extinguishment of the capital to which they owed their existence, or at the accomplishment of the purpose for which they were created, or at the disappearance of the object that they served.

These three categories of juristic persons were to be admitted to the same benefits as individuals under the Convention. The Commission was bound to liquidate properties of communities whenever an application was filed. The question in whose favor the liquidation was to be made depends on whether the community belonged to the first or to the other two groups. If the case was of an association or corporation proper, its property was to be divided in whole or in part among the emigrating members. If the case was of foundations, or of associations in the form of communities as defined under (2) above, the members could not receive individually any part of the property, but they should continue to enjoy the benefit of the community property. Consequently, the community property was to be liquidated in favor of the state in which the emigrant members were settled; that state would then be bound to devote the product of the liquidation to the creation in its territory of institutions, the aim of which should be as nearly as possible identical with the aim of the original community.

This second interpretation seemed, indeed, to grasp the real situation, the first being too legalistic and specious, and ignoring the nature and conditions of the communities in question. It should be noted that the first interpretation agreed fundamentally with the Bulgarian position, while the second interpretation confirmed in a great measure the Greek position as it was stated by Mr. S. Gheorgopoulos. The only difference was in the fact that associations or corporations for non-lucrative purposes were included by the memorandum of the neutrals as communities in the provisions of the Convention. Their inclusion would not seem justified, unless they could be brought under the terms "foundations of any kind whatever" of article 6, paragraph 2.

As was to be expected, the Greek and Bulgarian members, being invited to express their views on the above interpretations, favored each the interpretation consonant to his own position. Therefore, no solution acceptable to both parties was found.

§ 110. The recourse to the Permanent Court of International Justice. Under these circumstances, on September 17, 1928,[13] when the Mixed Commission was at Geneva, the President communicated to the members of the Commission the text of a letter that he proposed to send to the Ministers of Foreign Affairs of the two countries, in which he suggested that it would be useful to obtain an advisory opinion of the Permanent Court of International Justice on the question of communities. The members had no objection to the sending of such a letter, but no response to the suggestion was obtained for a considerable time. A year later, in September 1929, when

[13] Procès-Verbaux, xxx, 438th meet., p. 2; 439th meet., pp. 1-2.

the Commission was again meeting at Geneva, the neutral members definitely raised the question of recourse to the Permanent Court. The Greek member declared that the Greek government accepted such recourse. The Bulgarian government was reluctant to do so. However, the President of the Commission prepared, in collaboration with a member of the Legal Section of the Secretariat of the League, a draft questionnaire to be submitted to the Court.[14] At last, in December, 1929,[15] the Bulgarian government signified its consent to a recourse to the Permanent Court for an advisory opinion. As no agreement could be obtained on the questionnaire to be submitted to the Court, the two neutral members prepared their own questionnaire and the Greek and Bulgarian members of the Commission prepared each a separate set of questions.

By a letter dated December 19, 1929, the President of the Commission requested the Secretary-General of the League, in the name of the Greek and Bulgarian governments, to submit to the Council a request that an advisory opinion be obtained from the Permanent Court of International Justice, for the use of the Mixed Commission, with regard to the interpretation of those clauses of the Convention concerning Reciprocal Emigration which related to communities. A resolution to this effect was adopted by the Council of the League on January 16, 1930.[16] By order of January 24, 1930, the President of the Court fixed February 28, 1930, as the date by which written statements, if any, were to be filed with the Registry of the Court. This time was later extended to March 17, 1930. By that time written statements were deposited by the two governments. The Court held public sittings from June 19 to July 1, 1930. The President of the Mixed Commission and the agents of the two governments also addressed replies to certain questions formulated by the Court by order dated June 30, 1930. The two governments availed themselves of the right of choosing each a judge of their nation-

[14] Procès-Verbaux, xxxv, 504th meet., p. 1; 505th meet., p. 2; 506th meet., p. 1; 508th meet., annex No. 7.

[15] Procès-Verbaux, xxxvii, 519th meet., December 3, 1929.

[16] League of Nations, *Official Journal,* February, 1930, p. 109. See the questions to the Court, listed *ibid.,* pp. 187-188.

ality to sit on the case. The Court handed down its decision on July 31, 1930. It is worthy of especial mention that the opinion of the Court was unanimous, even the Bulgarian and Greek judges having agreed with the rest of the Court.

§ 111. The Advisory Opinion of the Court. The opinion of the Court [17] entered first into the consideration of the general purpose of the Convention concerning Reciprocal Emigration. It found that it was desired "by as wide a measure of emigration as possible to eliminate or reduce in the Balkans the centres of irredentist agitation . . . and to render more effective than in the past the process of pacification." Since, then, the Convention was meant to encourage as wide a measure of emigration as possible, and to overcome the hesitation of the minorities to take advantage of its provisions, it provided for the remedy of any material losses which emigration might entail upon both new and former emigrants.

Although it was individuals only who were entitled to take advantage of the terms of the Convention, "nevertheless the material benefits which from time immemorial in the East individuals of the same race, religion, language, and traditions have derived from uniting into communities are well known." The Convention therefore aimed at securing for the individuals the property of the communities dissolved by reason of their emigration.

After these preliminary observations, the opinion of the Court goes into the questions raised by the Mixed Commission. Considering the first and main question, What is the criterion to be applied to determine what is a community within the meaning of the Convention, the Court finds that "the 'community' is the general traditional conception thereof in the East of an exclusively minority character, of a group of persons living in a given country or locality, having a race, religion, or language and traditions of their own, and united by this identity in a sentiment of solidarity with the view to preserving their traditions, maintaining their form of worship, insuring the upbringing of their children . . . and rendering

[17] Permanent Court of International Justice, *Publications,* Series B, No. 17, Advisory Opinion regarding The Greco-Bulgarian Communities.

mutual assistance to each other." The question whether a particular community did or did not conform to the above conception was a question of fact for the Mixed Commission. This incidentally confirmed the Greek argument as propounded by Mr. Gheorgopoulos in the Mixed Commission and as presented before the Court. The Court clearly stated the position of communities in the following terms: [18]

> In order to fulfil the purpose for which they existed, and in order to meet the common needs of their members, it was necessary that the communities should have a patrimony, no matter what legal form their possession of it might take, or what the local law might be as regards the granting or withholding of juridical personality so as to enable them to be capable in law of owning property.
>
> The existence of communities is a question of fact; it is not a question of law. In actual fact the communities ordinarily possessed property. The Convention itself recognizes this by referring expressly to the property, movable or immovable "belonging to communities." It is this situation of fact which the Convention has in mind.

The Court also considered that churches, convents, schools, hospitals, etc., having a separate existence, were to be treated like communities.

With regard to the second question of the Mixed Commission, What conditions must be satisfied to cause the Commission to dissolve a community, the Court held that this also was a question of fact. The Commission was to be satisfied that a community was to be dissolved when the fact had taken place. The conditions to be fulfilled for this were: that the dissolution was the consequence of the emigration of persons who were members of the community; and that as a result of this emigration, of its extent and its conditions, the community was unable to perform its task and fulfil its purpose. In this again the Court accepted the Greek view in the matter.[19] Besides the above two questions submitted by the Mixed Commission, similar questions, differently framed, were sub-

[18] Permanent Court of International Justice, *Publications,* Series B, No. 17, Advisory Opinion regarding The Greco-Bulgarian Communities, p. 22.

[19] Procès-Verbaux, xv, 286th meet., September 3, 1926, p. 1841; xvi, 304th meet., December 3, 1926, pp. 2017-18.

mitted to the Court by each of the two governments. The Court refrained from making remarks or replying separately on the two relevant questions of the Greek government,[20] as it had covered them by its remarks and replies to the above questions, and in fact had accepted, in general, the views of this government. The three questions submitted by the Bulgarian government referred to the above points, what was a community in the meaning of the Convention and when should it be regarded as dissolved. The remarks and replies of the Court to the questions of the Bulgarian government reject the views of the latter. In particular, the Court denied the contention that a community was a legal fiction, existing only in virtue of the laws of a country, and that the dissolution of a community had to be ordered by any one, since as regards the application of the Convention there was no need to ascertain what particular law was applicable. The Court also stated that the communes were not included in the term 'communities.' This already had formed the subject of a decision of the Mixed Commission to the same effect.[21]

The third question of the Commission was, What was to be understood by dissolution, what relations were to be dissolved, and what was the period by reference to which the existence of the relations to be dissolved was to be established? The answer of the Court was that dissolution was the cessation of the existence of the community, and that the period by reference to which the existence of the relations in the community was to be established was the moment immediately preceding the dissolution of the community. If, however, the dissolution of the community took place as the result of several consecutive emigrations, the Commission was to ascertain how far the earlier emigrations had contributed to the dissolution and should be taken into consideration for the purpose of the distribution of the property of the communities.

With respect to the payments of the value of community property liquidated by the Mixed Commission and to movable property of communities, the Court held that, in view of the

[20] Questions 1 and 3 of the Greek Government.
[21] See *supra*, p. 89.

purpose of the Convention to encourage individuals to emigrate by affording them the possibility of benefiting individually from the property of the community, the dividing up of the property of the communities was a favor reserved to such persons. The parties to receive such property were therefore those who established their title and claimed liquidation on the ground of dissolution. If the Commission should not be able to trace the original claimants, it should inform the government concerned of the fact, and the government was to take the necessary steps to insure payment to the persons entitled as above. In this the Court did not follow the view of the two governments, who wished to have the proceeds of the liquidation of immovable property of emigrants turned over to the respective governments. The Court's interpretation was, of course, not based on any provision of the Convention; but it is difficult to disagree with it, although it might be difficult to see why the emigrants should divide the proceeds of the liquidation of a large landed community property acquired in the course of many generations. Nor is it probable that the provision for the liquidation of community property was inserted in the Convention with the intent of having the proceeds of liquidation divided up among the emigrants. However, the liberal interpretation of the Court is certainly in conformity with the spirit of the Convention. It was based not only on the general consideration that emigration ought not to entail material losses to emigrants, but also on the information given by the neutral members that many losses were actually suffered by the emigrants, on account, especially, of the depreciation of the bonds given them in payment by the governments.

On a question of the Greek government concerning property of communities dissolved prior to the Convention concerning Reciprocal Emigration of 1919, the Court held that "just as persons emigrating subsequently to the Convention participate in the property of the community the dissolution of which is brought about by their emigration, so former emigrants ought to have the possibility of participating in the proceeds of the liquidation of property belonging to a community of which they were members and the dissolution of which resulted from their departure." However, the Court pointed out that if a community had been dissolved before the entry into force of the Convention for any other reason than the emigration of its members, it did not fall under the provisions of the Convention.

§ 112. Preliminary decisions of the Commission. During the preliminary stages of the work of the Commission and in the first years of its existence, a number of decisions were taken which did not affect the final determination of the various questions of interpretation raised by the provisions of the Convention on communities. The decision on the interpretation of the word 'persons' of article 12,[22] that excluding administrative communes from the conception of a community,[23] and that on movable property of communities which might be taken away by emigrants,[24] are considered in another part of this study. Other decisions, referring in particular to the liquidation of properties of communities, are considered in the remaining pages of this chapter.

An important practical question raised by the properties of communities was the following. In view of the fact that the communities were not recognized by the Turkish law, and therefore could not have rights and obligations under it, the property which was in fact community property was held in the name and title of a member of the community, a person of known honesty, called in Turkish *mutiveli*. The situation was similar to that of a trust in the Anglo-American law. A person, as trustee, held the title for the benefit of the community. But the trust relation was not recognized by the Turkish law, and the person holding the title was not amenable to the court by any judicial or administrative proceeding tending to enforce the trust. The control over the trustee was not a legal control, but one secured by religion and social custom or ethics.

A first question, therefore, which was presented before the Commission was that of a property for which a new or former emigrant presented a written title, but which was in fact

[22] See *supra,* p. 88.
[23] See *supra,* p. 89.
[24] See *supra,* p. 119.

owned by a community. On the proposition of both the Greek and Bulgarian members, the Commission decided that in such cases the Sub-Commissions should proceed to liquidate such property, viz., establish the rights, survey the land, appraise it, etc., as if the person in question were the real owner. However, on the request of the interested community, or a religious or national administration acting on behalf of such community, or on its own initiative, the government of the country to which the community was nationally akin, and to which its members had immigrated, might through the medium of its representative on the Mixed Commission, seize the proceeds of the liquidation. The apparent owner might have recourse against such seizure before the tribunals of the country with which he was nationally akin. In case such proceeds had already been paid over to the incumbent, the government might take action before the courts. The Sub-Commissions were directed to note, in their decisions, all objections made before them to the effect that the incumbent was only a trustee for the community.

The next question was how to deal with the property of communities when no emigrant applied for its liquidation as property in his name and under his title. This question was connected with the problem of the dissolution of a community in case not all its members had emigrated. The Greek member of the Commission had proposed that each community should be allowed to consider itself as dissolved or not, to make agreements with the remaining members, and to dispose of its property as it saw fit. The Commission would then be bound to liquidate all community property when an application for liquidation was made by the council of a community.[25] The Commission finally decided[26] that the liquidation of real property might be applied for either by the council of the emigrating community or by the member of the Commission representing the country to which the community was nationally akin. When applications for liquidation of community properties were filed, the Sub-Commissions and other agents

[25] Procès-Verbaux, viii, 150th meet., August 31, 1923, pp. 982, 986.
[26] Procès-Verbaux, ix, 187th meet., May 27, 1924, p. 1135.

of the Mixed Commission were directed to proceed to the liquidation of such property in accordance with the procedure prevailing in respect to other property.[27]

Even without such application, however, the Sub-Commissions were authorized, whenever they thought it advisable, to proceed to the appraisal of properties belonging to a community; this was an attempt to simplify the work of appraisal. To this end the land surveyors were directed by the Commission,[28] on their visit to a locality for the purpose of surveying property of private persons, to survey, as a general rule, the community properties situated in such locality. Similar directions were given to expert architects [29] in case of buildings of small importance belonging to communities. No expert examination of important community buildings (of a value above 500,000 drachmas or 1,000,000 leva) was made, however, except by special order of a Sub-Commission.

The difficulties met with in the appointment of proper delegations for the establishment of property rights were even more serious when the property rights of communities were to be proved. Emigrant members of a community were not necessarily settled in the same locality in their new country, and it was difficult to find the persons most qualified to testify.[30]

By the end of 1928 most of the lands and buildings belonging to communities had been surveyed and the property rights were determined or in process of determination. It was in connection with large community properties that much preliminary work remained to be done. There are 57 cases of communities in Thrace, 263 in Macedonia, and 76 in Bulgaria.

§ 113. Difficulties presented by the metochy of Rogen or Rosino. The application for liquidation of the metochy or convent farm of Rogen, in Bulgaria, by the convent of Iveron in Mount Athos raised also certain difficult juristic questions, apart from those concerning communities in general. In another place the question of the admission of the metochy of

[27] Procès-Verbaux, xv, 290th meet., September 15, 1926, p. 1864.
[28] Procès-Verbaux, xii, 235th meet., July 28, 1925, p. 1480.
[29] Ibid.
[30] See, for instance, the case of the community of Tatar-Pazardjik. Procès-Verbaux, xxxii, 468th meet., December 22, 1928, p. 17.

Rogen to the benefits of the Convention is considered.[31] The further question was whether the convent of Iveron of Mount Athos could claim any property rights in the metochy of Rogen.[32] An exposition of the opposing arguments in this respect by the Greek and Bulgarian members is indeed an exposition of the status of the convents of Mount Athos.

The Bulgarian position was that the convent of Iveron could not claim liquidation of its property by the Mixed Commission, even under the provisions for constructive emigration of article 7, remark 1, of the Rules, since this convent as well as the other convents of Mount Athos, with all their dependencies, were *stavropegiac,* their properties belonging to the Oecumenical Patriarchate of Constantinople.

The word *stavropegiac* (*σταυροπηγιακαί*) is composed of the words *stavros* (*σταυρός*) meaning 'cross,' and *pegnymi* (*πήγνυμι*) meaning 'set fast.' It refers to the fact that the cross, which, according to the rules of the Orthodox Church, should be set at the place where a new convent was erected, was sent directly by the Patriarch, who was thus considered the founder of the convent.[33] Such convents were under the direct ecclesiastical jurisdiction of the Oecumenical Patriarchate, whereas all other convents were subject to the jurisdiction of the local bishops. The convents of Mount Athos date from the middle of the ninth century.

According to the Greek argument, the convents of Mount Athos from their original establishment and during the existence of the Byzantine Empire enjoyed a complete independence and autonomy, and formed a sort of independent republic. Their exclusive ownership and possession of their estates was always recognized. This situation continued during the Turkish Empire. The only connection between these convents and the Oecumenical Patriarchate was ecclesiastical or spiritual. Many firmans or decrees of the Turkish Emperors

[31] See *supra,* § 40.

[32] The facts and disputes in the case of this metochy may be seen in Procès-Verbaux, xxii, 369th meet., p. 6 and annex 1; 370th meet., p. 1 and annexes; and xxiii, 374th meet., p. 14; 379th meet., pp. 6 ff.; 380th meet., pp. 1 ff.

[33] For the procedure see John Hackett, *History of the Orthodox Church of Cyprus* (London, 1901), pp. 368-369.

recognized the privileges of these convents. Moreover, the Treaty of Berlin of 1878 (article 62, paragraph 8) added an international security by providing that "the monks of Mount Athos, whatever their country of origin, shall be maintained in their previous possessions and advantages, and shall enjoy, without any exception, an entire equality of rights and privileges." [34]

All this was not disputed by the Bulgarian member of the Mixed Commission. It was also not disputed that the new constitutional charter of Mount Athos, prepared by a special commission, adopted by the Double Extraordinary Assembly of the twenty convents of Mount Athos in 1924, and approved by the decree of June 1, 1926, of the Greek government, affirmed the exclusive property rights of the convents and the purely spiritual jurisdiction of the Oecumenical Patriarchate.[35] What was disputed was the status of the convents

[34] The Treaty concerning the Protection of Minorities in Greece of August 10, 1920, article 13, contains a similar engagement on the part of Greece applying to the non-Greek monastic communities of Mount Athos. League of Nations, *Treaty Series,* xxviii, p. 256.

[35] See text of the charter in the "Journal of the Government" of Greece, 1926, part i. Extracts from the charter are also given, in French translation, in Procès-Verbaux, xxii, 369th meet., annex 1, pp. 5 ff. The following articles are material:

ARTICLE 1. The Hagionymé Mount Athos is composed of twenty holy, sovereign, royal, patriarchal, and stavropegiac convents, classified, conformably to the perpetual order, as follows:

(1) The Convent of Great Lavra
(2) " Vatopedi
(3) " Iveron
(4) " Chilandari
(5) " Dionysiou
(6) " Koutloumousiou
(7) " Pantokratoros
(8) " Xeropotamou
(9) " Zographou
(10) " Docheiariou
(11) " Karakallou
(12) " Philotheou
(13) " Simonos Petra
(14) " Saint Paul
(15) " Stavroniketa
(16) " Xenophontos
(17) " Gregoriou
(18) " Esphigmenou
(19) " Russiko
(20) " Kastamonitou

ARTICLE 2. Outside the above Convents, it is absolutely forbidden to any one to own property in the Mount Athos.

ARTICLE 5. All the Convents of Mount Athos, in so far as they are patri-

before the promulgation of this charter, at the time the Convention respecting Reciprocal Emigration was entered into and the declaration of emigration for the metochy of Rogen was filed in 1923.

It was argued by the Bulgarian member of the Mixed Commission that the Decree on the Administration of the Convents promulgated by the Turkish administration in 1875 (Zihildjé 20, 1294) had changed the status of Mount Athos. The effect of this decree, in the Bulgarian view, was to render the convents of Mount Athos subject to the Oecumenical Patriarchate of Constantinople and to make all their property inalienable, like all church property.[36] The Greek member did not deny the promulgation of the above decree, but he contended that it was never adopted or approved by the convents or their general Council and was never binding upon them;[37] that the prohibition upon alienation of real estate always applied only on property situated on Mount Athos; and that the first authoritative codification of all the *chrysobula, sindhillims, firmans,* and customs governing Mount Athos is in the General Regulations of 1912. These Regulations were

archal and stavropegiac, are subject to the spiritual jurisdiction of the Great Eastern Orthodox Church, no other commemoration being permitted except that of the Oecumenical Patriarch.

It is forbidden to any heretic or schismatic to establish himself in Mount Athos.

Article 13. The administration of all the properties of the holy Convents is placed in the care of the brotherhood of each Convent leading a monastic life.

[36] The text of this decree is found in an abbreviated French translation in George Young, *Corps de droit Ottoman,* ii, pp. 47-56, and in full in a Greek translation in Nicolaides, Ὀθωμανικοὶ Κώδικες (Ottoman Codes) (Constantinople, 1889-91), iii, pp. 2803 ff. The most important articles are:

Article 1. The peninsula of Mount Athos comprises . . . twenty Convents, called *stavropigiaka,* which are subject to the spiritual administration of the Oecumenical Patriarchate of Constantinople . . .

Article 3. The said convents with their dependencies are subject to the Oecumenical Patriarchate and constitute inalienable church property. The monks living therein in their civil administration are subject to His Majesty the Emperor and in their spiritual administration to the Oecumenical Patriarch, their head, on whom they depend.

Article 50. In Mount Athos no one has an individual right of ownership and dominion in real estate . . .

Article 52. No one may ever on any pretext sell, grant, or alienate the property of a convent of Mount Athos or its dependencies, whether in the imperial territories or in a foreign country. . . .

[37] Articles 147, 148, and 150 of the decree seem to make its application subject to ratification or approval.

prepared in Constantinople, revised and approved in 1910 by the Holy Community of Mount Athos, voted in 1912 by the Holy Synod of the Oecumenical Patriarchate, and in force since that time. According to the Bulgarian view, these Regulations have no legal validity and have never been in force, since they have not been submitted to the Turkish Government for approval.

The further contention of the Bulgarian representative was that the real estate of the convent of Iveron being inalienable according to the general rule of the inalienability of property of convents, regardless of the provisions of the Regulations of 1875, the convent in question could not claim the liquidation of its property by the Mixed Commission, which was not different from sale of property. This argument could hardly be taken seriously, since the Convention concerning Reciprocal Emigration expressly provided that real property of communities was to be liquidated by the Mixed Commission, and explicitly included the convents under the term 'communities' (articles 6 and 7). Indeed, the whole dispute over the Rules of 1875 seemed pointless, since their only material provision against alienation of real estate of convents is nullified by the Convention.

§ 114. Effects of the Advisory Opinion of the Permanent Court. It would seem that the case of the metochy of Rogen will be easy to decide after the advisory opinion of the Permanent Court. This opinion recognized that a convent might belong to a community or might be an independent institution, in which case it was assimilated to a community under the Convention. In either case, the emigrants who were beneficiaries of such an institution had the same rights in respect of the property thereof as in respect of property belonging to a community.

The Commission will have to take a number of decisions to carry into effect the advisory opinion of the Court. In general, Greece will obtain a great financial advantage as a consequence of the opinion, in view of the fact that the Greek communities in the territories acquired by Bulgaria after 1912 possessed large landed properties, whereas the properties owned by the Bulgarian communities in the Greek territories were small and unimportant. This was at the bottom the reason why the two states stood for different interpretations of the provisions of the Convention.[38]

[38] Procès-Verbaux, xxiii, 377th meet., p. 18.

CHAPTER VIII

PROPERTY RIGHTS IN FORESTS

§ 115. Turkish Land Law. The complicated character of the Turkish land law raised especial difficulties in the establishment of the property rights in forests of emigrants and communities. A proper consideration of these difficulties and of the decisions adopted by the Mixed Commission requires a preliminary survey of the Turkish land law and of the changes brought about by the succeeding Bulgarian and Greek laws.

The Turkish land law of 1858 (Ramazan 7, 1274), in article 1, distinguishes five categories of lands: [1] (1) lands *memlouké,* which belong in complete ownership, *mulk,* to persons; (2) lands *miri,* or public, belonging in ownership to the state; (3) lands *mevkoufé,* or dedicated, which are inalienable; (4) lands *metrouké,* or abandoned; and (5) *mevat* or 'dead' lands. Articles 2 to 5 define each category of lands.

Lands belonging in complete ownership to persons are of four kinds: (*a*) the building lands situated in villages and towns and lands comprised in their inclosures, which do not exceed one-half *stremma* [2] and are considered as dependencies of houses; (*b*) lands withdrawn from the public lands and

[1] The text of the Turkish law is found in a Greek translation in Nikolaides, Ὀθωμανικοί Κώδικες (Ottoman Codes) (Constantinople, 1889-91), ii, pp. 1005 ff. A French translation is found in Young, *Corps de droit ottoman,* vi, pp. 45-83.

[2] A *stremma* is equivalent to 0.2471 acres.

granted in complete ownership to an individual; (*c*) lands subject to the tithe (*ushriyé*); these represent lands granted, after the conquest of the Byzantine Empire and the other Balkan territories, to the victors in complete ownership; and (*d*) the taxable lands (*haradjié*); these represent lands left in the ownership of the vanquished Non-Mussulman inhabitants.

Public lands, *miri,* are the fields, pasture lands, forests, and the like, which belong in ownership to the state. Possession of these lands was formerly granted to private persons by the owners of military fiefs, but for the last century possession has been granted by the government by a possessory title, *tapou.* The bulk of the landed property in Turkish territories belonged to the state, and the persons in possession of such land had only a possessory title.

The dedicated or mortmain lands were of two kinds: (1) Lands, previously privately owned, which had been dedicated to charitable uses in accordance with the religious law. The ownership and possession of such lands belonged to the *vakouf* or charitable institution. (2) Lands withdrawn from the public lands. In these lands it was the public taxes, such as the tithe, etc., that had been given to the *vakouf.* These lands were not in the full sense *vakouf* lands, since they remained in the ownership of the state. Most of the *vakouf* lands in Turkey belonged to this class.

'Abandoned' lands were those left to the public use, such as public streets, and those left to the use of all the inhabitants of one or several villages or towns, such as pasture lands. 'Dead' lands were those that were in the possession of no one; were not left to the use of the inhabitants; and were situated at a certain distance from inhabited places.

From the subsequent provisions of the land law concerning public lands, *miri,* including *vakouf* lands belonging in ownership to the state, it is clear that the state retains and exercises the ownership (*recambé*) on such lands, and the persons having a possessory title (*tapou*) exercise therein the right of possession and the right of collecting the products (*tessarouf*), rights deemed to be derived from a relation of landlord and tenant (*idjaré*). The land is granted to a person to cultivate or use it, and he has definite obligations or duties towards the state; hence the grant has the designation *ihalé vé tefviz,* which means transferring in trust or in confidence. The tenant is bound to cultivate the land, or to pay an annual fee in case the land is not for cultivation (articles 68 and 84). Moreover he can only make use of the land in accordance with its nature. Thus, pasture lands can be cultivated only on express authorization of the state, given through a *tapou* (article 10). Likewise, land held under this tenure cannot be used for making bricks (article 12), or for planting vines or fruit trees (article 25), without special authorization.

§ 116. Its provisions on forests. With regard to forests and trees, there are special provisions in the land law which may now be considered (articles 25 to 30). In general, the law distinguishes trees of two kinds: those that are planted by the possessor of the land and those that grow naturally on the land. Fruit trees and vines planted in a land by the possessor on the authorization of the state [3] do not follow the condition of the land but belong to its possessor. Similar is the case when the latter grafts or improves trees which grew naturally on the land in his possession. On the contrary, trees growing naturally on *miri* lands, including fruit trees, follow the condition of the land and therefore belong to the state. A tithe is paid to the latter on the products of fruit trees. Such trees cannot be felled or uprooted by any one.

Forests are also of two kinds: first, those that are planted on the authorization of the government, by the possessor of the land; they belong to the said possessor, who has the right to cut them down or uproot them. Secondly, those growing naturally on the land in possession by *tapou.* The possessor of such forests may only cut down trees. Exception is made for forests on common mountains (*djipali moupaha*) and forests left to the use of the inhabitants of villages. The benefit and use of these forests belong to the whole village. They cannot be withdrawn from such use and placed in the possession of private persons by means of a *tapou* (articles 91 and 104).

[3] The case is the same with trees planted without authority, but not uprooted, as by right, by the state within three years.

§ 117. Turkish Law on Forests of 1870. The situation in regard to forests was clarified by the Law on Forests of 1870 (Cheval 11, 1286).[4] The law recognizes four categories of forests: (*a*) forests belonging directly to the state; (*b*) forests attached to the administration of charitable institutions (*vakouf*); (*c*) forests for the use of towns and villages, or communal forests; and (*d*) woods and forests belonging to private individuals (*courou*). Leaving aside the question of permission to cut down trees from public forests, the ownership of such forests is in the state. It is clear, therefore, that forests of this kind in the newly acquired territories of Bulgaria and Greece were outside the scope of the Convention concerning Reciprocal Emigration.

The third category of forests corresponds to the so-called 'abandoned' lands which are left to the common use of the inhabitants of villages and towns. It is not clear to whom the ownership of such forests belongs. The state is not allowed to transfer the possession to individuals, and the inhabitants of the village or town to whose use the forest has immemorially pertained may only cut wood or otherwise get the benefits of the forest. Whenever, however, lumber or wood is cut from such forests for trading purposes by an inhabitant of the village, a tithe is due to the state. This points to the retention of the same mere ownership in such forests by the state as in all public (*miri*) lands.

Forests of the second category, dedicated to *vakoufs*, follow the condition of the lands. As we have said, only a few of the *vakouf* lands belonged in ownership to charitable institutions, most of them remaining public lands, although the use and possession were transferred.

This law does not deal with forests belonging to private persons, which are governed by the provisions of the land law referred to above. As we have seen, these forests may be of two kinds, those planted by a private person, which belong in ownership to such person (articles 25 and 26), and those growing naturally on a land in the possession of a private person

[4] See this law in a Greek translation in Nikolaides, Ὀθωμανικοὶ Κώδικες, iv, p. 3406; and in French, in George Young, *Corps de droit Ottoman* (Oxford, 1905-06), vi, pp. 3-11.

(article 30), or transferred by the state to the possession of such a person (article 3), on which the state retains a naked ownership, as on all public (*miri*) lands.

§ 118. **Forests or trees in pasture lands.** A further complication arises in regard to forests or trees on pasture lands. Of pastures there are three categories: (1) Pasture lands included in the general category of the so-called 'dead' lands (*mavat*) or to the category of *res nullius* (*moubah*), dealt with in articles 1234 ff. of the Ottoman Civil Code. Every person may have his cattle graze therein.

(2) Communal pasture lands, used for the needs of villages and towns and distinguished into *yailak* or summer pasture and *kychlak* or winter pastures (article 97 of the land law). There exists also a kind of half-communal pastures, *otlak,* which may be used by the inhabitants of a village but were originally 'dead' lands (article 105). These cannot be sold or bought and their possession cannot be transferred by *tapou.*

Lastly, (3) private pastures (*mera* or *tchaïr*) which are in the possession of a private person and are in the mere ownership of the state like all public (*miri*) lands (articles 24, 98 and 99). These may be transferred and possession may be acquired by means of a *tapou.* They may also be *yailak* or *kychlak.* These pastures may include trees or forests planted by the possessor or growing naturally on the land. In this respect the provisions referred to above, on trees or forests growing on other lands in the possession of a person, prevail.

The law on this point is quite inexplicable. As we have already seen, the right of private persons on (*miri*) lands is a *sui generis* right. In name and appearance it is equivalent to a tenant's right of possession. The relation corresponds to a feudal relation, with the difference, however, that the landlord here is the state itself. The possessor exercises all the derivative rights or powers of ownership with the exception of the *jus abutendi.* He has more rights than under the emphyteusis or superficies of the Roman law. It is strange, therefore, that while all plants, fruits, and products of the land belong in ownership to the possessor of the *tapou,* the forests and trees growing naturally on the land form an exception and belong in ownership to the state.

§ 119. The iradé of 1870 concerning forests. The unjustness of these provisions was corrected by an *iradé* of January 18, 1870 (Cheval 16, 1286), issued a few days after the publication of the Law on Forests. The text of this *iradé* has never been found. Yet the substance of its provisions has often been referred to in the collections of Ottoman laws, and the decisions of the Turkish courts since 1870 speak of the *iradé* and consider it a law. Moreover, a general decree of 1879 (18 Rebbi oul-evel, 1293) refers expressly to the *iradé* and confirms it.[5] The *iradé* abrogated all the provisions of the land law which reserved the ownership of the state in trees or forests growing naturally on *miri* lands.[6]

The Greek and Bulgarian members of the Mixed Commission were in general agreement on this state of the Turkish law, with the exception of the case of trees and forests growing naturally on private pastures. The Bulgarian member thought that the latter under the land law are *res nullius* and not in the ownership of the state, and that, consequently, the *iradé* of 1870 did not affect their condition, since it dealt only with forests on which the state retained the ownership under the land law. The Greek member maintained that trees and forests in private pastures were in no way *res nullius*. The Bulgarian view seems wrong, in view of the provisions of the land law above referred to, and, especially, in view of the Law on Forests, which abolished the *moubah* forests included, according to the land law, in the category of 'dead' lands or *res nullius*. The *iradé* speaks of trees or forests growing naturally on *miri* lands. And article 24 of the land law says expressly that *yailak* and *kychlak* pastures which are not left to the use of villages but are possessed by virtue of a *tapou* by private persons, "do not differ from fields," which are *miri* lands. Thus, *miri* lands include private pastures as well as

[5] See text of this Decree in Procès-Verbaux, xxxvii, 514th meet., November 1, 1929, annex 1, p. 19.

[6] See, on this *iradé,* the Bulgarian and Greek statements on forests, Procès-Verbaux, ix, 176th meet., March 13, 1924, annexes 1 and 2.

fields. Moreover, the ministerial instructions of 1876 and a circular of September 8, 1911, of the Ministry of Agriculture explicitly provided that the *iradé* of 1870 applied to possessors of private pastures.

This last fact was admitted by the Bulgarian member of the Mixed Commission. It was objected, however, that the instructions and circular could not modify the law, and that they were due to political reasons, with a view of favoring rich Turks who were in possession of *yailaks* and *kychlaks* at the expense of the states which were about to acquire new territories in Bosnia and Herzegovina and in Bulgaria. Besides, the above instructions and circular required the fulfilment of certain conditions, such as payment of a fee, by those persons who desired to avail themselves of the *iradé* of 1870, and there was no evidence that possessors of *yailaks* and *kychlaks* in Bulgaria had fulfilled such conditions. It was replied, first that these ministerial instructions did not purport to change the law, and, secondly, that the fulfilment of the conditions of the instructions was a question of proof of ownership on a particular property, and had nothing to do with the question of principle whether forests in *kychlaks* and *yailaks* were private property.

§ 120. Law of Greece and Bulgaria. Such was, in general, the Turkish law on lands and forests until the time when the Turkish territories were acquired by Bulgaria and Greece. After the annexation of Macedonia and Thrace by Greece, the Turkish land law continued to be applicable in these provinces. So no difficulty arises in respect to Bulgarian property rights in forests in Thrace and Macedonia.

The Turkish land law and the law on forests remained applicable in Bulgaria from the time of its independence to 1904. But the so-called *miri* lands were considered to be in the ownership of their possessors whenever a *bona fide* possession during ten consecutive years could be shown. In 1904 two laws were promulgated in Bulgaria, a land law and a special law on forests of February 25, 1904 (Ukaze No. 29).

The latter law in its first article, paragraph 5, provided that the *yailaks* or summer pastures should become the property of the state. They were taken by eminent domain, their proprietors being indemnified for the pastures. It would seem, then, that this law recognized the right of the possessors in the pasture, as such, but not in the forest growing therein. Was this an arbitrary measure taken by the Bulgarian state, or was it a legislative interpretation of the Turkish law prevailing previously? The latter was asserted by the Bulgarian member of the Commission. In his view, no further question of interpretation of the *iradé* of 1870 and of the instructions issued for its execution could arise. The law of forests of 1904 was applied in the new territories acquired by Bulgaria in 1912-13.

§ 121. **The position of the Greek and Bulgarian members of the Commission.** Thus, in the Bulgarian view, the following trees and forests were private properties and could be liquidated by the Mixed Commission:

1. Forests on *miri* lands possessed on the basis of *tapou* referring explicitly to forests (*orman, courou, tchaililik*).

2. Trees of any kind planted with or without authorization of the government on *miri* lands.

3. Forests for which there existed a *tapou* referring to a field, whether they were planted or grew naturally on the field.

4. Trees or forests which had grown naturally on meadows, but not forests which had grown on pastures, called *yailak* or *kychlak*.

On pastures only rights of pasturage could be claimed.

In the Greek view, to the above four categories of trees and forests a fifth one should be added: namely, all lands having the character of *miri* including, therefore, private *yailaks* and *kychlaks* and all forests which were planted or had grown naturally on private pastures, for which the possessors possessed titles (*tapou*) or copies of titles, Turkish or Bulgarian, referring to '*mera* and *gora*,' '*yailak* and forest,' '*kychlak* and forest,' and the like.[7]

[7] See the exposition of the conflicting views in Procès-Verbaux, ix, 176th meet., March 13, 1924, pp. 1101 ff. and annexes 1 and 2. See also viii, 147th meet., August 10, 1923, pp. 959 ff.

A law on forests passed by the agrarian government in Bulgaria on May 3, 1922, purported to expropriate all private forests on *miri* lands. But this law was passed after the coming into force of the Convention respecting Reciprocal Emigration and was not taken in consideration even by the Bulgarian member of the Commission.

§ 122. Decisions of the Mixed Commission. The Mixed Commission, taking into consideration the above statements of the views of the two countries concerned, adopted a decision on April 2, 1924.[8] The Sub-Commissions were authorized to proceed to the liquidation of forests on the following bases. They were to refer to the Commission all cases in which there was a presumption that they concerned trees or forests which had grown naturally on *yailaks* or *kychlaks*. In cases of titles concerning a *yaïlak* and forest, when the Sub-Commissions found that the *yaïlak* was distinct from the forest, only the former would be referred to the Commission. In cases of Bulgarian titles referring to '*gora* and *mera*,' '*gora* and *pasbichté*' or '*gora* and *pacha*,' the Sub-Commissions should find out if these terms are a translation of the Turkish terms '*yaïlak*' or '*kychlak*' by resorting to the original Turkish title. In all other cases the Sub-Commissions were to establish the property rights.

The decision also provided that property rights in forests could be established by the means of evidence enumerated in article 48 of the Rules. By exception, however, the testimony of witnesses, as a general rule, was to be admittel only in the case of forests of small area and when, in connection with other evidence, such testimony was necessary to establish the real facts. The Sub-Commissions were to recognize as private properties, among others, the following:

(1) Forests on *miri* lands possessed by virtue of a *tapou* referring to forest (*orman, courou, tchalil*), field, or garden.

(2) Trees of any kind, grown with or without authorization on *miri* land.

This decision of the Mixed Commission confirmed the points agreed on by the Bulgarian and Greek members and reserved only the controversial questions.

With a view of speeding up the work of liquidation, it was decided in the fall of 1926 [9] that the Sub-Commissions, on their visits to the various villages, should proceed to the liquidation of forests on the basis of the existing procedure.

[8] Procès-Verbaux, ix, 179th meet., p. 1103.
[9] Procès-Verbaux, xv, 290th meet., September 15, 1926, p. 1864.

Forests on *yailaks* and *kychlaks* were not to be excepted. Property rights therein could be established by the Sub-Commissions, although special mention should be made of them in the *procès-verbal,* reserving the decision of principle to the Mixed Commission. Only on forests of large area the surveying and appraisal were to be left for a subsequent period. In the spring of 1928 the Commission ordered the survey and measurement of large *kychlaks* on which the rights of property had already been established.[10]

§ 123. **Proof of property in forests.** The provisions concerning the evidence admissible for the purpose of establishing property rights in forests were somewhat indefinite. A distinction was made between small and large forests. In respect to the latter, testimony of witnesses, the more fragile means of evidence, was excluded, but only as a general rule. This implied that such evidence could be admitted by the Sub-Commissions as an exception, even in the case of large forests, and whenever it was deemed satisfactory and convincing. In the case of small forests, the testimony of witnesses was always admissible when it was supported by other evidence, such as the production of certificates of payment of taxes.

It appears that the rule in the case of large forests, especially in Thrace, became an exception, and that the line of demarcation between small and large forests was very uncertain and drawn at different points by the various Sub-Commissions. With a view to remedying this situation, the Commission decided later[11] that small forests should be deemed those the area of which did not exceed 100 decares[12] for each proprietor or co-proprietor. The Commission took the view that all cases of establishment of property rights in forests of a larger area would be reviewed by it.

The admission of the testimony of witnesses for establishing property rights in forests ought to have been all the more strictly limited, in view of the fact that, according to the Turkish law, no ownership could be acquired in a forest with-

[10] Procès-Verbaux, xxvii, 419th meet., May 26, 1928, pp. 9 ff.

[11] Procès-Verbaux, xxii, 366th meet., September 22, 1927, pp. 12, 16.

[12] A *décare* is equivalent to 1000 square metres or 1196 square yards, or about one-fourth of an acre.

out the issuing of a title (*tapou*) by the *Defter Hané*, the Registry at Constantinople. No title by prescription could be acquired to forests under the Turkish law.[13] It would seem, therefore, that, with the exception of small forests, where testimony of witnesses corroborated by other documentary evidence might be admitted, official titles of ownership (*tapou*) should always have been required of emigrants.

The danger and abuse of testimonial evidence appeared clearly in the case of the forests of Gabrovo in Thrace, claimed by ten Bulgarian emigrants. These forests, containing thousands of acres, were found by the Sub-Commission to be in the ownership of those emigrants on the sole basis of the testimony of witnesses, including the interested parties themselves. The Greek representative on the Sub-Commission, not expecting that the Sub-Commission would take such a decision, was unable to obtain the contradictory testimony of other witnesses until after the decision was taken. A brother of an emigrant came himself to testify that he never knew his brother to possess any forests. The Mixed Commission, in reviewing the case,[14] saw immediately, notwithstanding the contrary opinion of the Bulgarian member, that it was impossible to recognize property rights in forests of so large an area on the basis of mere testimonial evidence, which was not even uncontradicted. It decided to invite the emigrants to produce documentary evidence in corroboration of the testimony,[15] and to request the *Defter Hané* of Constantinople to transmit to the Mixed Commission any copies of *tapou* issued to the ancestors of the emigrants.

A confirmation of the *tapou* by the *Defter Hané* was also asked in the case of the forest of Begovitza in Bulgaria, although, besides the title, other documentary evidence was produced by the emigrant. The authenticity of the title was disputed by the Bulgarian member of the Sub-Commission.

[13] See Circular of the Ministry of Justice of Safer 28, 1304, in Nicolaides, Ὀθωμανικοὶ Κώδικες, ii, p. 1062.

[14] Procès-Verbaux, xxii, 372d meet., October 8, 1927, p. 4.

[15] The emigrants presented later a Turkish document, which lacked essential parts, such as signatures or titles of the authority which had issued it. The Commission decided that an authentication of the document was necessary. Procès-Verbaux, xxviii, 423d meet., June 25, 1928, pp. 4 ff.

A decision of the Sub-Commission to submit the authenticity of the title to an expert was annulled by the Mixed Commission.[16]

In the region of Florina in Macedonia the local Sub-Commission seems to have required evidence of official titles (*tapou*) for the establishment of property rights in forests, taking the view that testimonial evidence was not admissible in cases of public or *miri* lands. This was not wholly in conformity with the Rules (article 48) and the decisions of the Commission. The Commission referred the cases to the Director of the Centre of Saloniki, with instructions for the reexamination of the rights according to a summary procedure, notwithstanding the protests of the Greek member.[17]

In the case of forests of small size, that is, less than 100 decares, or twenty-five acres, the testimony of witnesses was admitted, even when the corroborating documentary evidence was very slight. Thus, in the case of the forests of Golem-Dervent, in Thrace, a single receipt for payment of the tax *onlak-vergassi* (general tax on property), presented by one among a great many inhabitants of that village claiming ownership, was deemed sufficient corroborating evidence. Indeed, the essential evidence in the case was deemed to be the testimony of witnesses.[18]

§ 124. The question of forests in kychlaks and yailaks. After repeated postponements, the question of *yailaks* and *kychlaks* came up for final decision before the Mixed Commission in November, 1929. The Greek and Bulgarian members entered on November 7 their respective statements on this matter.[19] The Greek statement, proceeding from the un-

[16] Procès-Verbaux, xxiii, 373d meet., October 13, 1927, pp. 1 ff.
[17] Procès-Verbaux, xxx, 443d meet., October 6, 1928, pp. 3, 8.
[18] Procès-Verbaux, xxx, 445th meet., October 15, 1928, pp. 4 ff.
This village consisted of a group of hamlets located in the midst of a *miri* forest, which was rather an area covered with bushes. The claims of the Bulgarian emigrants were supported also by the testimony of Turkish inhabitants of neighboring villages, and were contradicted by testimony of Greek peasants. The Greek member of the Sub-Commission presented also a tax receipt for cutting wood in the communal forest, which would seem to be located in the same place where the private forests were said to be. The neutral members of the Commission were influenced by the small value of the disputed properties.
[19] Procès-Verbaux, xxxvii, 514th meet., p. 2 and annexes 1 and 2.

disputed fact that the Turkish land law in article 3 classified explicitly *yailaks* and *kychlaks* under the general category of *miri* lands, undertook to answer the question to whom the trees grown on *yailaks* and *kychlaks* belonged. Article 28 of the land law provided expressly that:

"All trees . . . growing naturally on *miri* land follow the condition of the land. The product of the trees belongs to the possessor of the land. . . . However, the trees cannot be cut or taken off by the possessor or any one else. For every such tree cut or taken off the value of the tree is to be paid to the state."

This restriction upon the rights of the possessor of the land was abolished by the *iradé* in 1870. Thus the unrestricted right in the trees was recognized in the possessor of *yailaks* and *kychlaks,* in whom, after the issue of the *iradé,* the *jus utendi, jus fruendi,* and *jus abutendi* were united. Documentary proof appended to the Greek statement tended to show that the law was so understood and applied by both the Turkish Empire and its successor, the Greek state. Annexed to the statement were also a mass of documents in support of the Greek interpretation, including a report of a Commission constituted by the Ministry of Agriculture and Public Domain of Bulgaria; extracts from writings of Turkish and Bulgarian legal writers; opinions of two professors of law of the University of Constantinople; decisions of courts, etc.; all agreeing that forests on *yailaks* and *kychlaks* were in the unqualified ownership of the possessor of the land.

The Bulgarian statement, proceeding from the facts that *miri* lands were in the mere ownership of the state, and that *yailaks* and *kychlaks* were *miri* lands concluded that the only rights of possessors of *yailaks* and *kychlaks* were to pasture and water cattle therein and to get the product of the trees. The *iradé* of 1870, in the Bulgarian view, did not grant to possessors of *yailaks* and *kychlaks* any further rights, except that of collecting the indemnity due from third persons felling trees, and that the other restrictions upon the right of the possessors of *yailaks* and *kychlaks* in the trees remained after the *iradé* of 1870. Hardly any authorities were cited in support of the Bulgarian interpretation, which seemed highly artificial.

On December 9, 1929,[20] the Bulgarian and Greek members stated once more their positions in the matter, and the neutral members announced that they had now formed their opinion in the matter in the light of the various documents submitted by the two national members. The Commission, then, decided, by the votes of the neutral and Greek members and over the protests of the Bulgarian member, (*a*) that all *miri* lands, including the *yailaks* and *kychlaks,* were considered private property for the purpose of their liquidation by the Mixed Commission, notwithstanding any laws in the two countries to the contrary; and (*b*) that the trees of all kinds (forests) grown naturally on *miri* lands, and in particular in *yailaks* and *kychlaks,* were also to be considered private property, as above.

[20] Procès-Verbaux, xxxviii, 521st meet., pp. 1-12.

CHAPTER IX

THE LAND SURVEYING

§ 125. Establishment of the surveying service. The Rules worked out by the Mixed Commission provided that, after presenting the evidence of his ownership in a parcel of real estate, the emigrant should also introduce evidence in regard to the price of the property. The Sub-Commission would thereupon proceed to the appraisal of the property on the basis of the data possessed by it or supplied by the emigrant. In practice, things did not prove so easy. The Sub-Commissions had to be limited to a purely judicial task, and the factors for the appraisal had to be found and supplied, through complicated and painstaking work, by various groups of experts.

The first factor necessary for the appraisal of a rural property was the precise area and extent of such property, for instance, the number of acres of land owned by an emigrant, the number of trees or vines, and the like. As we have already said, in the territories newly acquired from Turkey by Greece and Bulgaria, there was no government survey of lands or cadastre, and no way existed for knowing beforehand the exact limits of each property. In the old provinces of Bulgaria the government survey of lands, established for fiscal purposes, afforded a convenient, though not always to be trusted, way of getting at the area of rural properties. The declarations of applicants could hardly be trusted, being very often inexact.

It was necessary, therefore, to attach a surveying service to each Sub-Commission. This service was created early in 1925, under a topographer of neutral nationality. The surveyors were all of neutral nationality, usually Russians, and worked in pairs. The number of pairs sent to each locality varied according to the importance of the work.

§ 126. Original duties of surveyors. Even before the creation of this service, the Commission had caused measures to be taken to preserve the existing boundaries of rural properties of emigrants who had left their country of origin.[1] The first land surveyors were sent to Thrace. Their work was to visit each village, in the order indicated by the central Sub-Commissions, and draw up a preliminary sketch of properties. Each parcel of land and property was to be numbered, the names of owners, ascertained from the notables of the village, were to be noted, and certain descriptive or identifying factors were to be entered.[2] A land survey of each village was drawn up and extracts from the survey were made for each individual file. When the Sub-Commissions had established the property rights of applicants, they were supplied with these extracts from the survey, which were necessary for the appraisal.

In the old territory of Bulgaria no land surveying took place. The Sub-Commissions based their decisions on the areas given in the government fiscal survey of lands of 1911. In the new territory of Bulgaria, acquired after 1912, land surveying has been necessary. Data for the constitution of a registry of lands for this territory were collected in 1922 but were still incomplete.[3]

The work of surveying followed the establishment of the property rights on properties declared by emigrants in their applications for liquidation. The applicants themselves or the delegations representing the emigrating population were supposed to give to the surveyors the necessary indications for the surveying of individual properties.

§ 127. Difficulties of work of surveying. In the previous three chapters the difficulties met in the proof of ownership have been indicated. The work of surveying met with still

[1] Procès-Verbaux, xi, 202d meet., October 20, 1924, p. 1267.
[2] Procès-Verbaux, xi, 222d meet., February 3, 1925, p. 1373.
[3] Procès-Verbaux, xvi, 294th meet., October 21, 1926, p. 1897.

greater difficulties. It should be recalled that many applicants had left their place of origin before the war and as far back as 1900. Some of the villages of such emigrants were destroyed during the war or were entirely deserted. The boundaries of individual properties in such villages had often disappeared. Kilkish, Achtopol, Anchialo, Sitchanli, etc., are some of these villages and towns. On the other hand, property in Southeastern Europe is parcelled out to an extreme degree. One does not own a single large parcel of land, but several small patches of land of various categories, separated from each other by property belonging to others. After an absence of many years, one could not identify such little bits of land, except with the help of all the inhabitants of the villages concerned. Lastly, applicants resident in cities or towns and owning rural properties were not able to point out the exact boundaries of such properties.

Under these conditions, the opinion of the Greek member of the Mixed Commission, that a specific survey of each parcel should be made and that no parcel not so surveyed should be recognized, although theoretically sound, was impossible of application under the existing conditions. It would require the indication of boundaries on the spot by the applicant himself, and at least the evidence of witnesses for each specific parcel. As a matter of fact, most of the establishment of property rights and the surveying of land was made on the basis of the testimony of delegations. This procedure was inherently inadequate. An illustration of the grave errors and abuses to which it gave rise is afforded by the results in the village of Sitchanli in Thrace.[4]

This village was predominantly Bulgarian. There were 450 persons who had applied for the liquidation of their properties. These persons had already emigrated from Thrace, and for the establishment of their rights a numerous delegation appeared on the day the Sub-Commission visited the village. Most of the property rights claimed by the applicants were established on the basis of the testimony of these delegates. Then the land surveying was to be made. As the Bulgarian

[4] Procès-Verbaux, xxvii, 416th meet., May 9, 1928, p. 6.

lands formed blocks, the surveying was made jointly for each block or 'island' of the soil. A map of the village was drawn up, and the surveyors partitioned the properties in each block, in consultation with the same delegation which had testified to the existence of the rights, and taking into consideration the declared areas.

For certain blocks this partition of properties on the map did not cause any difficulties. For other blocks of lands, however, the delegates modified the statements made before the Sub-Commission at the establishment of the rights; they pretended to know nothing of many applicants; and they declared that such applicants possessed no properties in those blocks of lands. Consequently, the surveyors divided the lands of these blocks among a number of applicants much smaller than was called for by the establishment of rights. It followed that applicants whose declarations called for an average of 10 decares received on the survey 60 decares. The surveyors also drew up a list of 'unknown' properties, that is, of properties to which the rights had been established but for which no land could be found. This list was submitted to the Sub-Commission, which revised its first decisions and rejected the rghts of applicants for whom no land was found.

What had happened? Simply that the delegates found an opportunity to give to themselves and to their relatives land which belonged to absent applicants. At the time they testified to the existence of the rights, they were unaware of the mode of distributing the land and told the truth. In the case of this village the abuse was so apparent that a revision was undertaken, but it is a fair inference that in a great many cases grave injustices and arbitrary solutions took place.

§ 128. Surveying of each parcel of land abandoned. In view of the above-enumerated difficulties, the original plan of surveying each parcel of land declared by an emigrant had to be given up in several cases. A contributing consideration was that of saving the enormous amount of time which would have been required for individual surveys.

Thus, in villages of a mixed population, the Bulgarian groups of lands were separated from other lands, and in general no parcel surveying was made of such groups of lands. In the case of homogeneous Bulgarian villages, whose entire population had filed declarations of emigration and applications for liquidation, the surveyors contented themselves with determining the boundaries of the village and the boundaries between private and communal properties.[5]

As the work of land surveying did not progress fast enough, although many teams of surveyors were engaged in the work, the system of detailed surveying of each parcel of land was discarded, in the spring of 1927,[6] in the case of certain remote villages, situated among the mountains, where the value of lands was relatively very low, and where the boundaries had completely vanished, their old inhabitants having emigrated many years before.

The system of detailed land surveying was also forsaken in cases when, by reason of the absence of proprietors or of their delegations, the surveyors were unable to determine the boundaries of the properties.[7] The Sub-Commissions accepted in such cases an approximate area calculated in conformity with the data possessed by them.

Later, the Directors of the three Centres (Sofia, Saloniki, Comotini) were authorized to allow the abandonment of the general rule of land surveying of each parcel by the Chief of the Service of Land Surveying and the adoption of simplified methods, whenever they should appear necessary, either by reason of the local conditions, or to make it possible to terminate the work of land surveying by September, 1927.[8] The most typical cases in which simplified methods were applied were the following: [9]

(1) Cases where the Sub-Commission by the existence of titles or contradictory testimonies was able to form a fair opinion as to the validity of the claims of the applicant in respect to quality as well as to quantity. The approximate area of such lands was not subject to doubt.[10]

[5] Procès-Verbaux, xii, 232d meet., July 2, 1925, p. 1446.
[6] Procès-Verbaux, xviii, 336th meet., April 15, 1927, p. 7.
[7] *Ibid.*, p. 5.
[8] Procès-Verbaux, xviii, 339th meet., May 15, 1927, p. 6.
[9] *Ibid.*, annex 1.
[10] See, for instance, the case of the right of Koutzoglou to one-twelfth

(2) Cases of parcels of land whose boundaries were lost, or which could not be measured by reason of the absence or the departure of the delegations.

(3) Cases of villages where about 50% of the parcels were already measured individually. In these cases, an ocular inspection or rough estimates might afford sufficiently precise results.

In all such cases, the Chief of the Service of Land Surveying supplied to the Sub-Commission a sketch giving the relative situation of the parcel. In villages where no land surveying had been done in the past, one-third of the parcels were measured. Simplified methods of surveying were also applied to large estates.[11]

§ 129. **Unsurveyed lands.** What was to be done with properties ownership of which was proved, but which could not be measured, or whose boundaries were unknown? As stated above, the inability of surveyors to locate or measure such lands did not always mean that the properties did not exist.

Whenever the ownership of *some* land was proved, the Commission, in a generous spirit, often recognized and appraised such properties, although they were of unknown boundaries and not measured.[12] The area in such a case was calculated on the basis of the average area of properties recognized previously and surveyed in the same village. An outstanding case in which the Commission had much difficulty to determine the proportion of lands covered by the expression of the land surveyors, "the delegates do not know the boundaries," was that of Greek lands in Melnik, Bulgaria.[13]

In other cases the Sub-Commissions recognized a category of lands termed *biens à ajouter,* representing parcels not declared by the emigrants, presumably by omission, and of which indications were furnished to land surveyors by delegates of emigrants, with the assistance of local witnesses.[14]

of a property (*tchiflik*) the area of which was given in a title. Procès-Verbaux, xxvii, 420th meet., p. 19; xxviii, 421st meet., p. 16.

[11] Procès-Verbaux, xxviii, 426th meet., p. 4.

[12] Procès-Verbaux, xvii, 321st meet., p. 2145; xxiii, 375th meet., October 21, 1927, p. 5.

[13] Procès-Verbaux, xxviii, 425th meet., pp. 13 ff.

[14] Procès-Verbaux, xxvi, 410th meet., pp. 9 ff., 15 ff.; 413th meet., pp. 2 ff.; 422d meet., p. 27.

In cases where lands were declared and were reported by the surveyors as 'unknown,' it was found that such lands included lands declared by other persons and measured; lands really non-existent; lands which had vanished by reason of floods and inundations; and lands which were not measured because the surveyors omitted them or could not locate them easily, but which probably existed. Lands of the class last named were recognized to the extent of three-fourths of the declared area.

§ 130. The surveying of forests. The surveying and measuring of the area of forests was a difficult and expensive problem. In the case of a large forest, that of Ravadin-Alepou near Sozopol in Bulgaria, it was decided that the expenses were to be distributed equally between the interested parties and the Commission.[15] Later it was resolved that such expenses were to be borne by the Commission alone, which seems more just.[16]

Expert foresters were appointed for the purpose of surveying forests under liquidation. The total area of forests only was measured; but the foresters eventually determined the approximate areas of the various kinds of trees, counted the trees, and measured their sizes.[17]

[15] Procès-Verbaux, xii, 229th meet., May 15, 1925, p. 1420.

[16] Procès-Verbaux, xiv, 264th meet., June 15, 1926, p. 1706. The Commission decided to extend this decision to the case of the forest of Ravadin-Alepou. Ibid., xvi, 300th meet., November 11, 1926.

[17] Procès-Verbaux, xv, 274th meet., July 28, 1926, p. 1763; 279th meet., August 11, 1926, p. 1789.

CHAPTER X

THE WORK OF APPRAISAL

§ 131. Real value of property as basis of appraisal. After the work of establishment of property rights of emigrants and the land surveying, the third stage in the liquidation of real property by the Mixed Commission was the appraisal of such property. This has been the most arduous and difficult task. The Commission in one of its earliest meetings [1] decided that the basis of appraisal of emigrants' properties "shall be their real value at the time of liquidation." This rule was also inserted in the Rules (article 18), with the qualification that the real value "in the state in which the properties shall be found" at the time of liquidation will be taken into consideration.

The finding of such 'real value' was a very difficult problem. In cases of sporadic or partial emigration from certain villages or towns, when the properties of emigrants were located in the midst of similar properties belonging to non-emigrants, it was comparatively easy to find a basis for the real value of properties under liquidation. Different was the case of localities where the whole or the greater part of the inhabitants had emigrated. A great number of villages and towns near the boundary line, especially in the regions of Melnik in Bulgaria and Kilkitsh in Macedonia were almost entirely deserted by their inhabitants several years before the

[1] Procès-Verbaux, i, 16th meet., January 11, 1921, p. 69.

Convention respecting Reciprocal Emigration came into effect. Their inhabitants were Greeks or Bulgarians who had emigrated to the country to which they were racially akin, or Turks compelled to leave Macedonia in accordance with the Greco-Turkish Convention of 1923 for the exchange of populations. Many of these villages were still unoccupied at the time the work of liquidation began, either because the locality was ravaged by malaria or because the houses had been destroyed and the lands rendered unfit for cultivation. In some villages only burnt walls of houses remained. In others the lands were now full of stones or overgrown by bushes, or their soil had been carried away by floods. What was the 'real value' of properties in such unreconstituted villages at the time of liquidation? In other cases the Greek refugees from Asia Minor or the Bulgarian refugees from Macedonia and Thrace were established in deserted villages as new occupants. The old houses were rebuilt, new structures were erected on the ruins of old buildings, the deserted and uncultivated lands were made to return an increase through the labors and expenditure of the new occupants. What was the real value to the old emigrants of such properties?

To these causes new difficulties were added by the wilful and seemingly purposeless destruction of emigrants' properties by the immigrants. Thus the Mixed Commission, on the ground of a declaration of the Greek member, instructed the Sub-Commissions to visit the vines left by Greek emigrants in the region of Burgas in Bulgaria and to consider their state with a view to their subsequent appraisal, as these vines were being destroyed by the Bulgarian immigrants.[2]

§ 132. Inadequacy of provisions of the Rules. In view of the above conditions, the provisions of the Rules concerning the appraisal of emigrants' properties were very inadequate. The Sub-Commissions were to work out a plan for their visits in the various localities to establish rights and appraise properties. They were to hear the evidence of the emigrants or their representatives and witnesses as to whether the price claimed by them was based on prices obtained in recent years

[2] Procès-Verbaux, xii, 239th meet., August 11th, 1925, p. 1499.

for similar properties. They were to proceed to the appraisal of the properties on the basis of data possessed by them, or supplied by the emigrant and by the communal representative, or by an agent charged with collecting information.[3]

At an early date the inadequacy of these provisions became manifest. The Commission decided that the Sub-Commissions should devote an important part of their time to the work of appraisal to be made in regions of different characters. They should take note of the items which might aid in the appraisal and make a comparative study.[4] A little later more elaborate and discriminating rules for appraisal were adopted by the Mixed Commission.[5] For purposes of appraisal, the Sub-Commissions were to divide the properties under liquidation into three categories:

(1) Properties whose prices were not influenced by the former, present, or probable emigration of the Greek, Bulgarian, or Turkish minority.

(2) Properties situated in localities where partial emigrations or the prospect of a future emigration had lowered the market value of real estate.

(3) Properties situated in localities where an important emigration in the past had disorganized or suspended the market for real estate.

For the appraisal of properties of the first category, the Sub-Commissions were to seek the current market price by comparing the properties under liquidation with similar properties recently sold, or by resorting to expert advice, or by using any other source of information at their disposal. For the appraisal of properties of the second category, the Sub-Commissions were to determine the real value by comparing such properties, directly or indirectly, with similar properties situated in similar regions, preferably in the neighborhood, where emigration had not influenced the market prices. The indirect comparison might be used by finding the possible income of the property under liquidation, taking into account the productivity of the soil and the general conditions of the

[3] Rules, articles 41, 49, and 51.
[4] Procès-Verbaux, viii, 149th meet., August 30, 1923, p. 980.
[5] Procès-Verbaux, viii, 167th meet., January 16, 1924, p. 1057.

market, and the ratio of capitalized value to income of properties in neighboring regions. Then by comparing the real value of the properties under liquidation, found by the above methods, with their actual lower price on the market, a local coefficient was to be determined, which might be applied to the local price of all other properties of the same locality.

For the appraisal of properties in localities where an important emigration in the past had disorganized or suspended the market for real property, the methods of appraisal appropriate to properties of the second category were to be applied. In order, however, to secure uniformity of application, the appraisals were to have a provisional character until the Mixed Commission could study them and compare them with each other.

An interesting case of this sort, illustrative of many similar cases, is that of the town of Achtopol. This town was until 1906 a prosperous maritime Greek community on the coast of the Black Sea. At that time its population was driven out in consequence of the anti-Greek movement in Bulgaria. Following this compulsory emigration, the town was deserted and ruined. The native Bulgarians and the Bulgarian refugees were alike disinclined to the life of fishermen. The Mixed Commission thought, rightly, that but for the emigration Achtopol would have retained its former importance, and that although the Bulgarian refugees newly established therein, who came from the Macedonian mountains, had no inclination to the fishing industry, the new generation, born on the sea-coast, would learn to avail itself of the lucrative maritime opportunities of the place. Consequently, the abandonment of Achtopol was not deemed to be a factor in the depreciation of the properties left by the emigrants.[6]

The appraisal was to be made in the money currently used for the purchase of lands and immovables in the region where the property in question was situated. But, as will be seen, immediately after the decision of final liquidation of the Mixed Commission the appraisal price of each property was to be converted into an obligation in dollars, according to the

[6] Procès-Verbaux, xxvii, 417th meet., May 19, 1928, pp. 6 ff.

Plan of Payment. This was, indeed, necessary, in view of the unstable monetary situation in Greece and Bulgaria between 1921 and 1927.

§ 133. Appraisal by experts. When the first liquidation cases came before the Mixed Commission early in 1925, it was seen that the correlation between the prices arrived at by Sub-Commissions in different regions was unsatisfactory. Two remedies were proposed: the revision of the prices by the Mixed Commission in consultation with the Presidents of the Sub-Commissions; and fresh appraisals by a staff of experts.

The Bulgarian member of the Commission was of the opinion that appraisals could not and should not be made by the Sub-Commissions, but by experts. In this view the Greek member concurred, against the opinion of the President of the Commission that this procedure would occasion great delay in the work. The members representing the two countries insisted on applying strictly the letter of the Convention for detailed individual liquidations. Appraisal by special experts instead of summary valuations by Sub-Commissions doubtless would and did cause slowness in the work of liquidation, but at least it promised a like treatment for the two countries.

A first staff of agronomists (*équipe d'évaluation*) was created on January 17, 1925. It was to form an independent agency and was to submit its expert findings to the Sub-Commissions as well as to the Mixed Commission. The appraisals made by it were only findings, which the Sub-Commissions were not compelled to accept.[7] This mode of appraisal did not give entire satisfaction. It was thought that the best way of correlating the appraisals in the two countries and in the different regions of each country would be to determine the bases for finding the actual value of different kinds of property.

Real property was then distinguished into agricultural lands and buildings or building lands. It was decided that for land appraisals the productivity of the soil was to be assessed and capitalized at a certain rate and at the current market

[7] Procès-Verbaux, xi, 255th meet., February 19, 1925, p. 1390.

price for the product. For buildings, such factors as the cost of construction at current prices of materials, labor, and transportation expenses were to be assessed and a coefficient for age and wear and tear should be deducted. For the appraisal of building lands a scale based on population and situation was to be fixed.

On these bases, the establishment of a tariff of prices of lands was decided upon on July 22, 1925. This is considered in the next chapter. The application of this tariff, which was finally adopted February 26, 1926, to properties under liquidation was made by the staffs of agronomists. Their decisions were no longer merely expert findings for the Sub-Commissions and could be modified only by the Mixed Commission.[8] However, the Sub-Commissions were authorized, whenever they should unanimously consider themselves in a position to do so, to proceed by themselves to the application of the tariff.[9]

Buildings and building lands did not lend themselves to the mechanical application of a tariff of prices. Appraisal was based to a certain degree on individual factors and on local conditions. Expert architects were used for assessing values, but they worked on different lines in Macedonia, Thrace, and Bulgaria. An analytical method was employed in Macedonia.[10] A general tariff of basic prices of materials, labor, and transportation expenses was adopted. This, however, served only as a guide to architects to insure a degree of uniformity in the appraisal. They also established a special tariff of local prices for each village. Their appraisals were only expert finding for the Sub-Commissions, which alone could take decisions, subject to appeal and modification by the Mixed Commission.

In Thrace the general tariff of prices for buildings served also as a guide to the expert architects. The architects, a Greek and a Bulgarian, worked together. In agreement they could decide upon the appraisal, but their decision was subject to appeal.

[8] Procès-Verbaux, xv, 272d meet., July 23, 1926, p. 1755.
[9] Procès-Verbaux, xiv, 262d meet., May 29, p. 1689.
[10] Procès-Verbaux, xii, 242d meet., October 9, 1925, p. 1533.

In Bulgaria the appraisal of buildings and building lands was made by a single architect, according to methods adopted by himself. An effort was made subsequently, as will be seen, to establish a uniformity of appraisal between Bulgaria and Greece,[11] although from the difference of procedure unity of method was not possible.[12]

Special methods were used for the appraisal of mills, salt works, etc., which are dealt with below.[13] Forests were appraised by a single neutral expert forester, M. Jaccard, until April 30, 1927. An appeal against his appraisals could be taken by the members of the Reporting Committee within fifteen days from notification by the President of that Committee. At the insistence of the Greek and Bulgarian members, a staff of foresters was created on the above date, and the taking of decisions and appeals therefrom thenceforth followed the rules governing the staffs of agronomists.[14]

The staffs visited each village and appraised on the spot the properties under liquidation. This rule was discarded in the case of villages of which the approximate entire value, in the opinion of the President of the competent Sub-Commission, did not exceed 500,000 drachmas or 900,000 leva. The appraisal in such cases was made in the light of the value of neighboring villages, and according to the method considered most adequate by the President of the staff.[15]

§ 134. **Appeals against decisions of appraisal.** The decision of appraisal taken by the Sub-Commission or the staff of agronomists was communicated to the interested parties or their representatives, at the place where it was taken, if the latter were present, or by registered mail if they were absent. Within a period of thirty days from the receipt of such communication the interested parties or third persons might file their 'objections,' which were transmitted to the Commission.[16]

[11] Procès-Verbaux, xii, 240th meet., October 3, 1925, p. 1505.
[12] On all this see *infra,* Chapter XII.
[13] See *infra,* pp. 244 ff.
[14] Procès-Verbaux, xviii, 333d meet., April 4, 1927, p. 2308.
[15] Procès-Verbaux, xvii, 331st meet., March 30, 1927, p. 2286; see also xxiii, 373d meet., October 13, 1927, pp. 15, 17.
[16] See Rules, articles 57, 58, as amended by the decision of the Commission on June 30, 1925. Procès-Verbaux, xii, 231st meet., p. 1442.

The new procedure adopted December 23, 1925, by reason of the fact that all emigrants had left the country of emigration and that the constitution of delegations presented great difficulties, was applied to the establishment of property rights as well as to the appraisal.[17]

Objections also could be filed by the members of the Sub-Commissions representing the two countries within a period which was successively reduced from thirty to fifteen and eight days.[18] At the expiration of this period, the files were transmitted to the Director of the Centre. To him also were transmitted the objections of the interested parties. On their receipt, the Director of the Centre held the objections at the disposal of the representatives at the Centre of the two countries. The latter were authorized by the Commission, in the case of files of a value of less than 75,000 drachmas or 125,000 leva, to see whether the objection could not form the subject of an amicable agreement, or whether it was necessary to take an appeal. In the latter case, the appeal was presented to the Director within a month from the notification to the representatives of the receipt of the objections. If the appeal was of a technical nature, or against the appraisals, it was examined by the competent neutral expert of the Mixed Commission, who visited each Centre once a month. If it concerned a question of principle, it was sent by the Director to the Mixed Commission. In the latter case, if it were deemed necessary, all further procedure relative to appraisals was suspended by the Director until the Commission should decide on the appeal.[19]

The neutral experts of the Mixed Commission inquired whether the tariff of lands and the local tariff of buildings were rightly applied, and in case they thought proper that

[17] Procès-Verbaux, viii, 251st meet., December 23, 1925. For this procedure see § 94, *supra*.

[18] Procès-Verbaux, xii, 231st meet., June 30, 1925, p. 1442; xviii, 333d meet., April 4, 1927, p. 2307; xxiii, 375th meet., October 21, 1927, p. 5.

[19] Procès-Verbaux, xv, 278th meet., August 10, 1926, pp. 1783 ff.

An appeal against a decision of a staff of agronomists could only be taken on a fact which was brought to the attention of the President of the staff in writing in the place where the appraisal was made.

An appeal against a decision of a Sub-Commission for the appraisal of buildings could only be taken against the local tariff of a village. Errors or omissions in individual files could not form the subject of an appeal.

the prices should be modified, they proposed the corrections to be made. They passed on the appeals in regard to the general classification of the village, the classification of its lands, the coefficients of increase or reduction, etc. Sometimes they gave no reasons for their proposals; sometimes they referred to the reasons stated by the neutral presidents of the agencies of appraisal; in certain cases they gave a short statement of their grounds.[20] The prices proposed by the experts were applied at the Centres without waiting for the decisions of the Mixed Commission. The Reporting Committee of the Mixed Commission, on receiving the files from the Centres, made its report to the Mixed Commission, which decided ultimately on the appeal.[21]

§ 135. Decisions by the Mixed Commission on appeals. The Mixed Commission, as a rule, did not pass on questions of appraisal of individual properties. The individual files of each village, when compiled and verified by the service of auditors, were submitted together to the Commission and its reporting Committee. The points debated at the Commission concerned the application of the tariff of lands in general, including classification, increases for special cultures, reductions for remoteness and malaria, etc., and the correctness of the local tariff of buildings.

The work of the Mixed Commission was too difficult in this respect. There were altogether too many appeals made by the members of the agencies of appraisal. An extract from a report of the neutral expert of the Mixed Commission, Mr. Fluck, is worth quoting:

> It is very surprising to note that the agronomists take so many appeals. . . . These are appeals taken from both sides against the zones. . . . The Greek agronomist classifies them as third-class lands, the Bulgarian as first-class, and the President of the staff as second-class. In most of the cases the agronomists have in their mind only one quality of zones and forget that this is influenced by a great number of factors, such as the quality of the lands, the

[20] See, for instance, reports of the neutral experts in Procès-Verbaux, xix, 346th meet., June 9, 1927, annexes ii, iii, v, and vi.

[21] Procès-Verbaux, 273d meet., July 24, 1926, p. 1758; xviii, 333d meet., April 4, 1927, p. 2307.

distance from the village, the conditions as to moisture, the elevation, the exposure to the sun, the ease of access, the fitness of the soil for special cultures, etc. By appealing against the appraisal of all the zones that the President classifies otherwise than he, the dissenting agronomist practically nullifies the work of the staff and delays the work needlessly. It is possible that the President may err once or several times, but he cannot err in all the cases that he decides against the view of the agronomist.[22]

Furthermore, the Greek and Bulgarian members took up all these appeals at the meeting of the Reporting Committee and of the Commission. They read very long notes, sometimes appallingly long, in support of their respective positions. It is not to be wondered at that the neutral members of the Commission accepted the recommendations of the neutral experts, who, having visited the villages, were in a position to pass an intelligent judgment on the conflicting views of the Greek and Bulgarian members.

§ 136. Scope of arbitrariness of decisions. The decisions of the Commission were not always free from arbitrariness. The tariff of prices had left sufficient discretion in its application. An illustration is offered by the case of the village of Calapodi in Greek Macedonia. This village at the time of the Balkan Wars had a population of 2500 inhabitants and numbered more than 500 houses. It was built on a mountain, part of its lands being on the mountain slopes and part on the outlet to the large valley of Drama, which is famous for the cultivation of a superior quality of tobacco, *Basma*. During the World War this village was almost completely destroyed and was abandoned. A small number of Greek refugees from the Black Sea were settled there and were cultivating tobacco on the lands of the valley. The Greek refugees, in general, could not be persuaded to settle in this mountainous region, the lands being of very poor quality. Under these conditions the neutral President of the staff of agronomists decided that the village should be classified as a 'bad village' and that the small proportion of land planted with tobacco could not justify its being classified as an 'average village.' The neutral member

[22] Procès-Verbaux, xxv, 399th meet., February 11, 1928, p. 5.

of the Commission, Colonel Corfe, thought that Calapodi had not lost the economic possibilities which had formerly given it importance. And, since the tobacco lands of a neighboring village were classified as outside the tariff (*hors barème*) because of their great value for the cultivation of tobacco, the President proposed to increase the prices of all the land properties of Calapodi by 20%, which would, in effect, amount to classifying it as an 'average village.' The Commission decided to that effect over the protests of the Greek member.[23] This decision was taken against the view of the neutral President of the staff and of the neutral expert of the Commission. It was certainly not a liquidation of the "real value at the time of liquidation." It was based on the value of neighboring villages and on future prospects.

§ 137. **Reappraisal of expropriated properties.** Special decisions were taken by the Mixed Commission in respect to properties expropriated, after October 4, 1918, by the Greek or Bulgarian state for public works or for reasons of public or social utility. The Rules already provided (article 18) that such properties would be appraised on the basis of their condition at the time the expropriation was made, and not at the date of liquidation as in the case of other properties. This implied that the Commission would reappraise such properties for the purposes of liquidation under the Convention. In the case of properties of persons who had already emigrated before the coming into effect of the Convention, it was expressly provided by the Rules that, on the application of the interested parties, such properties could be appraised by the Mixed Commission on the basis of their previous condition and their value at the time of the new appraisal. In such case, the price already paid was deducted from the price resulting from the liquidation by the Mixed Commission.

These provisions were not considered entirely adequate for the protection of emigrants, whose properties, especially after the influx into Greece of refugees driven from Asia Minor, had often been expropriated for the settlement of refugees. The emigrants feared that the expropriation was to

[23] Procès-Verbaux, xxviii, 425th meet., June 30, 1928, pp. 9 ff.

put an end to their rights, and were unwilling to emigrate before their property was liquidated by the Mixed Commission. The Commission accordingly adopted the following decision.[24]

In case the prospective emigrant deposited a declaration of emigration before the expropriation of his property, such declaration could not prevent the government from taking possession of such property before payment to him, but the rights of the government by virtue of the general laws were subject to the following restrictions: The expropriated property could not be appraised and paid for unless the owner consented thereto or revoked his declaration of emigration; the Mixed Commission proceeded to the liquidation of and payment for such property according to its own methods. The same was true in case the prospective emigrant, before the decision of expropriation of his property became final, deposited his declaration of emigration and an application for liquidation of his property, or a revocable declaration of emigration, by which he reserved his rights under the Convention and which he might revoke within two months from the date of deposit.

This decision became effective May 5, 1923, but it was applied retroactively to all expropriations made from December 18, 1920, to that date, in case the emigrant filed a declaration of emigration before October 15, 1923, and had made objections before the expropriating authority or taken steps before the Mixed Commission with the view to reserving for himself the benefits of the Convention.

A later decision of the Commission extended the benefits of the Convention to certain properties expropriated before October 4, 1920. Urban properties of emigrants expropriated before the above date, and for which the interested parties were not yet paid at the moment a decision of the competent Sub-Commission was taken, were appraised by the Mixed Commission.[25] This decision was not contrary to the provi-

[24] Procès-Verbaux, vii, 140th meet., April 18, 1923, p. 907.
[25] Procès-Verbaux, xvi, 304th meet., December 3, 1926, p. 2015.

sions of article 18, paragraph 3, of the Rules, which brought under the scope of the Convention only expropriations made after October 4, 1920. For the Commission considered that since no payment was made to the owner of the property the expropriation, according to the public law of most countries, was not definitive.[26]

§ 138. **General estimate of the work of appraisal.** The method of summary appraisal by the Sub-Commissions, as originally contemplated, would probably have been a speedier process than that actually adopted. It would, however, have placed a heavy burden on the shoulders of the Mixed Commission, which would have had to revise the liquidation prices in an attempt to correlate appraisals in the two countries. The individualized appraisal by experts on the bases of definite tariffs at least satisfied the demand of the emigrants, who attached great importance to matters of detail concerning their properties. It also satisfied the two governments that there was reciprocity in the appraisals and that they were both treated in the same way. This is on the assumption that the tariffs were just and corresponded to the real values of the properties in the two countries.

Although there was much outcry in the Commission by the two national members against the tariff of prices for lands, each claiming that his own country was paying too much, the truth is that, generally speaking, the liquidation prices given were just and fair.

What would seem to be well founded protests relate to the appraisal of buildings. The general tariff for buildings in Macedonia was applied for some time too rigidly by the architects. Prices were thus allowed which were found later to be in excess of the real market prices.[27] Mr. Charles B. Eddy, Chair-

[26] As a matter of fact, the Supreme Court of Bulgaria had decided that the expropriation was definitive, although no payment had been made. But it was proved that the owners continued to have the use of the property, and evidence was tendered of the fact that taxes were still paid by the owners.

[27] See statement of Mr. Saunders, delegate of the Mixed Commission at Saloniki, and Mr. Houssa, Director of the Centre of Saloniki, in their report to the Commission. Procès-Verbaux, xxiv, 394th meet., January 20, 1928, pp. 15, 24.

man of the Greek Refugee Settlement Commission, echoes these protests in his report on his tour in Macedonia in March, 1927.[28]

In his report Mr. Eddy wrote:

> Our refugees live in houses abandoned by the Bulgarians. These houses are in bad condition and need repairs, but they have been appraised by the Mixed Commission at prices so high that the refugees hesitate to make repairs, fearing to have to pay big prices. We have examined three of these houses. One appraised by the Mixed Commission at 120,000 drachmas is inhabited by the President of the village. He declared that he could build a better one if we would give him 15,000 drachmas. Two other houses appraised at 85,000 and 105,000 drachmas respectively have also been given too high prices. Taking into consideration the cost of a new house built by the Refugee Settlement Commission, I do not see how one may expect that the refugees should pay for these houses *even the one-third of the prices* given by the Mixed Greco-Bulgarian Commission. Personally I believe these houses are not good to live in, that they have no value at all, and that they should be destroyed and replaced by new buildings. Likewise the land was over-appraised, our figure being ten shillings per *stremma* against five pounds by the Mixed Commission. The acts of this Commission call for investigation. . . .

This was the judgment of the Chairman of the Greek Refugee Settlement Commission on the appraisals made by the Mixed Commission. He knew well the cost of these houses, since tens of thousands had been built under the auspices of the Refugee Commission. When these statements were brought to the attention of the Mixed Commission, Colonel Corfe, its President at the time, registered his protest.[29] He called attention to a statement in the Sixth Quarterly Report of the Refugee Settlement Commission (May 25, 1925) on the various points of view of appraisal. It was stated in the report in question that "the valuation of lands depends on

[28] Rapport de M. Charles B. Eddy, Président, etc., sur son Voyage en Macédoine (Mars 1927), dated April 9, 1927, and addressed to the Financial Committee of the League. This report is no longer confidential, but it has not been printed for publication.

[29] Procès-Verbaux, xxi, 358th meet., August 11, 1927, p. 7.

the point of view on which one is placed. In Greece, all the large and average properties are expropriated in behalf of cultivators at prices fixed by the Greek commissions of valuations and below the prices at which these lands would be sold freely on the market. For instance, the average price paid in Thessaly by these commissions is 150 drachmas, whereas on the market it would be 2000 drachmas per *stremma.* The price at which the Refugee Settlement Commission is selling the land to the refugees approaches the former price and not the latter."

Colonel Corfe thought that the Mixed Commission liquidated the properties of emigrants at prices approaching the free market prices. This might probably explain the divergence between the prices given for lands by the Refugee Settlement Commission and the Mixed Commission, but it certainly did not explain the high prices given in the case of buildings. Colonel Corfe, indeed, could not answer the statement that old and ruined houses were appraised at three times the sum it cost to build new houses. The real truth is that the Mixed Commission and its agencies for a considerable time applied rigidly the general tariff worked out by the architects in Macedonia. Also this Commission was moved in general by the belief that emigrants should be indemnified for their properties as liberally as possible, so that they might reëstablish themselves easily in their new country. In view, however, of the installation of Greek refugees in these Bulgarian houses, the Refugee Settlement Commission was meeting with a difficult problem in such cases as those described by Mr. Eddy.

CHAPTER XI

APPRAISAL OF LANDS

§ 139. The working out of the tariff of prices for lands. On July 22, 1925, the Mixed Commission appointed Mr. Saunders, its delegate at Saloniki, and M. Namèche, President of the second Sub-Commission in Bulgaria, to establish a tariff of prices for the lands situated in the regions of emigration in Greece and Bulgaria, for the purpose of facilitating and simplifying the work of appraisal of lands.[1] Messrs. Saunders and Namèche presented to the Commission on August 22, 1925, a draft worked out by them at Saloniki within the month following their appointment. A little later, September 11, 1925, following their visits to Thrace and Bulgaria, they sent to the Commission certain supplementary notes on this draft. During the months of September, October, and November the Commission studied this draft, and finally adopted it in general, subject to such modifications as the authors might consider useful after listening to remarks to be made by the Greek and Bulgarian members or their respective experts.

At the same time a committee *ad hoc* was appointed, con-

[1] Procès-Verbaux, xii, 233d meet., July 22, 1925, p. 1452.

sisting of the authors of the draft and Mr. Saulus, President of the First Sub-Commission in Bulgaria, and also of two agronomists, a Greek and a Bulgarian, who, however, had no vote in the decisions of the committee.[2] This committee was to proceed to a study of the prices of lands in Greece and Bulgaria and to examine thoroughly the part of the tariff referring to such prices. This examination of prices was to be made by comparing the prices of the proposed tariff with all other factors supplied by the work of appraisal of the Sub-Commissions or the staffs of agronomists. The committee was to present a detailed report, explaining the method of work, the various factors taken into account, such as natural and economic conditions, etc., the calculations made, and also the opinion of the minority in case of decisions taken by majority vote.

The committee met from December 23, 1925, to February 15, 1926, and heard the remarks and objections of the two experts representing the two governments.[3] The authors of the draft came to the conclusion that all these objections and remarks had been taken into consideration by them in the working out of the tariff, and that no new factor had been discovered which might lead to a modification of the project, apart from certain changes of secondary importance. In consequence, the Mixed Commission finally adopted the tariff on February 26, 1926.[4]

The tariff entered into effect on this same day. It was to be applied in its entirety, unless a decision of the Commission suspending or modifying its application should intervene. Such a decision could be taken after consideration of proposals of the Greek and Bulgarian members or of the agencies charged with the application of the tariff.[5]

[2] Procès-Verbaux, xiii, 249th meet., December 18, 1925, p. 1582.

[3] The work of the Committee appears in a volume entitled Commission Mixte Gréco-Bulgare, Comité Barème, Procès-Verbaux des Séances. This was not published. The present writer was granted access to this volume.

[4] Procès-Verbaux, xiv, 256th meet., p. 1654.

[5] The authors of the tariff submitted later an interpretative memorandum on certain parts of the tariff. A part thereof was adopted by the Commission, October 30, 1926, while the rest was merely communicated to the agencies of appraisal, which were left free to exercise their discretion. See Procès-Verbaux, xvi, 297th meet., p. 1917 and annex.

§ 140. Criticism of the tariff. Certainly it would have been better had this tariff been worked out by two neutral persons, with the coöperation of experts representing each of the interested countries, whose suggestions and remarks could have been taken into consideration. The original authors, having arrived with great pains at a solution, were not disposed to begin all over again, when, after the completion of the project, they were confronted with the viewpoints and objections of the experts of the two governments concerned. They preferred to reject, systematically and summarily, all such objections, finding them always without foundation.

A more scientific and sound method of arriving at a just tariff would have been to determine independently the actual and real prices of lands both for Bulgaria and for Greece. However, the authors thought that Bulgaria was a producing and Greece a consuming country; that the monetary situation and rate of interest were different in the two countries; that the winter lasts longer in Bulgaria than in Greece; that there was a free market of land in Bulgaria, while in Greece sales of land were rare; and that the demand for land in Bulgaria was greater than in Greece. The authors, then, gave up absolutely the attempt to determine the actual value of land in Greece.

A basis of the value of land in Bulgaria was sought and found in the classification of land in the government land registries established for fiscal purposes. Although the entries in such registries were not altogether sure guides, they gave, in general, just results. They were based on the productivity of the land and on the price of products. The prices given to the various categories of land were higher than the prices established by the staffs of agronomists and the Sub-Commissions.

In Greece, however, no independent basis for the value of lands was sought. The authors simply transferred the prices found in Bulgaria to lands in Greece, after affixing to such prices a coefficient of increase on the assumption that the land in Greece possessed greater productivity and the products sold higher. Doubtless, in some parts of Greece, such as Eastern Macedonia, the land is more productive, but the situation is altogether different in the greater part of Macedonia and Thrace. The result was that the value of land in Greece was in many cases overestimated.

§ 141. General part of the tariff. The tariff first grouped together the various localities of emigration into centres: great, average, small, and very small centres. In Greece, the localities were grouped as follows: [6]

Great Centres: Saloniki, Kavala.

Average Centres: Drama, Xanthi, Comotini, Alexandroupolis, Seres, Naoussa, Florina, Dedimotika, Edessa, Verria, Soufli.

Small Centres: Langada, Kilkitch, Yenidje Vardar, Gumendje, Kozani, Kastoria, Kailaria, Sorovitch, Demir-Hissar, Negrita, Pravi.

Very small Centres: Zirnovo, Statista.

In Bulgaria the grouping was as follows:

Great Centres: Sofia, Philippopolis.

Average Centres: Varna, Burgas, Yambol, Karvobate, Stara-Zagora, Tatar Pazartjik, Donpritza, Djoumaya.

Small Centres: Railway stations of average importance and small ports, Bila, Messemvria, Anchialo, Sozopoli, Aktopole, Kizil-Agatch, Petritch.

Very small centres: Kavakli, Malko Tirnovo.

This classification of localities attempted to take into account the influence on the prices of lands of population and of the presence or neighborhood of a railway or a port. The very small centres were the localities at a great distance from railways and ports, whose means of communication were poor roads impassable in the winter. The great centres were populous cities on the main lines of communication. Between these two groupings were placed the other two.

A second classification recognized five categories of villages, according to the quality of the lands of each village:

(*a*) *Very good villages,* where lands were very fertile and low and the subsoil contained abundant water;

(*b*) *Good villages,* whose lands were fertile and deep;

(*c*) *Average villages,* whose lands were fertile and deep but high;

[6] The staffs of agronomists were authorized to add any further small or very small centres that the authors of the tariff might have omitted.

(*d*) *Bad villages,* composed of thin, pebbly, or sandy soils, of high elevation, and low fertility;

(*e*) *Very bad villages,* composed of lands of low fertility upon the mountains, mostly uncultivated and pasture lands.

A last classification distinguished the lands of each village into three categories, first, second, and third, according to the quality of the land. This classification had been already applied by the Sub-Commissions and the staff of agronomists before the establishment of the tariff, the lands of each village being classified according to their quality into zones (*lieux-dits*).

§ 142. Figures of the tariff. The tariff, then, was as follows for each *stremma* or decare (1000 square metres or 0.247 acres) for Greece and Bulgaria:

TARIFF OF LANDS

Category of villages	Greece (in drachmas)			Bulgaria (in leva)		
	1st class of lands	2d class of lands	3d class of lands	1st class of lands	2d class of lands	3d class of lands
			Great Centres.			
a.	2685	2085	970	4130	3310	1615
b.	1565	1170	805	2410	1855	1340
c	1240	970	615	1910	1540	1025
d.	1020	760	475	1565	1205	790
e.	600	470	330	925	750	550
			Average Centres.			
a.	2500	1880	865	3840	2980	1445
b.	1440	1050	725	2180	1675	1205
c.	1150	880	555	1770	1395	925
d.	920	630	425	1420	1005	710
e.	535	425	285	820	675	475
			Small Centres.			
a.	2305	1670	765	3545	2650	1275
b.	1270	985	550	1950	1560	915
c.	1060	790	490	1630	1250	820
d.	830	620	340	1275	980	570
e.	475	380	210	730	600	350
			Very Small Centres.			
a.	2045	1430	605	3145	2270	1005
b.	975	710	405	1500	1125	675
c.	845	520	350	1300	825	580
d.	620	432	210	955	685	355
e.	360	270	140	550	425	230

§ 143. **Bases of the tariff.** As we have stated above, the authors of the tariff did not attempt to find the actual price of land in Greece. They found the prices for Bulgaria and applied them with a differential coefficient to Greece. The process for establishing the above tariff was as follows:

The prices for Bulgaria were based on the productivity of lands of the great centres belonging to the five categories of villages and three classes of lands above described. As is seen from the table appearing in the footnote,[7] the produce in kilogrammes of a *stremma* of first-class land in a 'very good village' was multiplied by a unitary price and the product was reduced by one-fourth on account of fallow land; forty per cent of this sum was considered to be the net income of the land; this was further multiplied by ten, it being admitted

[7] TABLE OF PRODUCTIVITY

1st category of land

Category of village	Produce in kilogrammes		Price in leva		Fallow	Net income	Value of product × by 10	Tariff
	Grain	Straw	Grain	Straw				
Very good	200	250	6	0.70	1/4	40%	4135	4130
Good	130	160	6	"	1/4	35%	2340	2410
Average	120	150	5.3	"	1/4	32.5%	1810	1910
Bad	110	140	5.3	"	1/4	30%	1530	1565
Very bad	90	120	5.3	"	2/5	27.5%	925	925
2d category of land								
Very good	160	180	6	0.70	1/4	40%	3256	3310
Good	110	140	6	"	1/4	32.5%	1840	1855
Average	105	135	5.3	"	1/4	30%	1464	1540
Bad	100	130	5.3	"	1/3	27.5%	1140	1205
Very bad	80	110	5.3	"	2/5	25%	750	750
3d category of land								
Very good	120	150	6	0.70	1/3	30%	1650	1615
Good	100	130	6	"	1/3	27.5%	1270	1340
Average	90	120	5.3	"	1/3	27.5%	1025	1025
Bad	80	110	5.3	"	2/5	25%	750	750
Very bad	70	90	5.3	"	1/2	25%	543	550

The unitary price of 6 leva represents the average compound price obtained by taking 2/3 wheat, 1/6 corn, and 1/6 barley.

The price of 5.3 leva represents the average compound price obtained by taking 1/3 barley, 1/3 wheat, and 1/3 corn.

The unitary price of 1 leva adopted for straw is reduced by 3/10, by reason of the corn, whose stalk is of trifling value.

that the rate of capitalization in Bulgaria (and in Greece) was 10%. In this way the basic fifteen prices corresponding to the lands situated in the great centres were established. The prices of the lands of average, small, and very small centres were established by the application of coefficients to the above prices. Such coefficients were adopted by the authors of the tariff after investigation of the general conditions.

When the prices for Bulgaria were thus established, they were transformed by a differential coefficient so as to form the prices for Greece. The authors of the tariff thought that there was a constant relation between the various lands of Bulgaria and the lands of Greece, turning around certain coefficients. They thought that the lands in Macedonia and Thrace, on the whole, had comparatively a greater value than in Bulgaria, for the following reasons:

1. Taking into account the fallow land in these two countries, the production was greater in Macedonia and Thrace than in Bulgaria.
2. It was not clear that the cost of production was larger in the one country than in the other.
3. The prices of the products of the soil were incontestably higher in Macedonia and Thrace than in Bulgaria.
4. The cost of living was higher in Greece.

Since, then, the value of land in Greece was greater, the tariff prices were established by applying a differential coefficient to the prices of lands in Bulgaria. Thus, instead of converting the prices in leva to prices in drachmas at the rate of exchange at the time, which was 1000 leva for 435 drachmas, 1000 leva were considered equal to 650 drachmas in the case of lands of the first class, 630 for lands of the second class, and 600 for lands of the third class. In other words, a price of 1000 leva was converted, on the average, into one of 625 drachmas, which amounted to an application to lands in Greece of a differential coefficient of a little over 43% as compared with the prices of similar classifications in Bulgaria.

These prices were established in February, 1926, and the authors had in mind that the value of the money in either country might subsequently fall, which would have the effect of causing a discrepancy between the value indicated in the prices of the tariff and the one the authors had in mind. The authors accordingly determined the relation between the leva and the drachma and between each of them and the dollar at the time the tariff was established.[8]

§ 144. Reduction of basic prices for remoteness, malaria, and pasture lands. The various prices of the tariff were subject to reduction or increase by reason of various factors. Two important factors for reduction were remoteness and malaria. Reduction was also made for pasture lands and marshes.

Remoteness from the various centres enumerated above, which were centres of consumption or of shipment of products, increased cost of transportation and, consequently, reduced net income. The prices of lands remote from the centres should be diminished to a corresponding degree. The authors admitted a coefficient of reduction corresponding to an increase in the cost of production of 6.50 leva for each *stremma* for a distance of ten kilometres from a centre.

Thus, when the land was at a distance of ten kilometres from the centres, the prices of the tariff were reduced by 5%. Beyond the ten kilometres, the reduction was 2½% per space of five kilometres computed from centre to centre.[9] For vines and mulberry trees the distance from centres had no effect on the prices of lands.

In the region where malaria prevailed with particular intensity, the prices of the tariff were to suffer a reduction of a maximum of 20%. This part of the tariff was amended subsequently by the Mixed Commission, the maximum coefficient of reduction being fixed at only 10%. Such regions existed only in Greek regions of emigration. The application of the

[8] The rates were as follows: two leva and thirty stotinki equal to a drachma; one dollar at Sofia equal to 139 leva; one dollar at Saloniki equal to 62.8 drachmas.

[9] 12½ kilometres were counted as 15 kilometres; 12.3 as 10 kilometres.
In the case of two or more centres between which a choice might be made, preference was given to the centre which was a consuming or exporting market. In case of doubt, the choice was for the centre the most advantageous for the emigrant.
The distance was measured in a straight line on the map published by Artaria & Co. by the application of a coefficient of correction of 1.20. See Procès-Verbaux, xvi, 310th meet., December 10, 1926, p. 2067.

reduction was to be determined, in the first instance, by the staffs of agronomists on their visits in the places. The Commission, however, decided that the reduction was to be applied to cities and villages in Greece where the occurrence of malaria was fixed at 50% or more in the statistics for the year 1924 of the Department of Health of the Greek Ministry of Communications.[10]

Pasture lands were classified as lands of the second or third class and were appraised at the price of the tariff corresponding to such class, but a reduction of 25% was applied to such price. Marshes were classified as third-class lands and the price of the tariff corresponding to that class was reduced by 50%.

§ 145. Increase of basic prices for tobacco lands. Increases of the tariff prices were adopted for tobacco lands, vegetable gardens, irrigated lands and meadows, and rice grounds.

The authors of the tariff and the Greek and Bulgarian experts agreed that an increase of the tariff prices was justified for lands situated in localities where the cultivation of tobacco occupied an important place. The authors of the tariff thought that tobacco was cultivated very generally only in lands of the first and second class and that therefore only the prices corresponding to such classes should be increased. They also thought that the increase should take into account the proportion of land which was cultivated for tobacco in a certain locality. A small proportion of such lands would seem to show that the land of the locality in question was not generally fit for cultivation of tobacco.

Consequently, the following coefficients of increase were proposed by the authors of the tariff. If the area cultivated with tobacco in a certain locality was less than 2½% of the total area, the tariff prices were not to be modified. If such area was more than 2½%, the tariff prices of first- and second-class lands were to be increased by 15%. If the tobacco area was more than 5%, the increase was fixed at 30%, and if more than 10%, the increase was 50%.

In the localities where the tobacco was of special quality,

[10] Procès-Verbaux, xv, 283d meet., August 26, 1926, p. 1821.

as Xanthi, Drama, and Zihna, or where there existed special economic or agricultural conditions, as at Florina, Stanimaka, etc., the tariff was not to be applied. The determination of the existence of such conditions was to be left to the judgment of the staff of agronomists. These regions were called 'outside the tariff' (*hors barème*).

The proportion of area cultivated in tobacco was an important criterion for the application of the above figures. The Commission adopted the suggestion of the authors of the tariff [11] that this proportion was to be established by taking into account the average of the statistical data for 1923, 1924, and 1925 for Bulgaria and Greece, and the statistics of colonization for the same years in Greece. The area effectively cultivated in those years, that is, the lands that gave crops, were only to be considered.

§ 146. Increases for other factors. Vegetable gardens have a higher productivity than ordinary lands when they are irrigated. Accordingly, the tariff provided that they were considered first-class lands of the locality where they were situated, and the general tariff prices were increased from 100 to 200%, regardless of the mode of irrigation used.

Irrigated lands produce more than ordinary lands and their prices are therefore higher. The tariff provided that such lands, whether of the first, second, or third class, were to be appraised at an increase of 50% on the ordinary tariff prices. Land was to be appraised as 'irrigated land' when it was really irrigated and not when it was only irrigable.

Meadows are to be distinguished from mere pasture lands. The former are lands where the grass is regularly mown once or twice a year. They may or may not be irrigated, and may belong to the first, second, or third class of lands. The tariff prices were increased by 50% unless the meadow was irrigated, when the coefficient of increase was 70%. Lands growing lucerne were also considered of a higher productivity. The ordinary tariff prices were increased by 25% in respect to them.

[11] Procès-Verbaux, xvi, 297th meet., October 30, 1926, p. 1917; xviii, 335th meet., April 13, 1927, pp. 1, 9. The staffs of agronomists were to admit the official statistical data; the information given by the Bureaus of Colonization was only a factor for the formation of their judgment.

Rice grounds are cultivated only every other year, but their productivity is much higher than that of ordinary lands, especially when they are irrigated. The tariff provided that they should be appraised according to the class of the land, but the ordinary tariff prices were to be increased by 100%. The staffs of agronomists were to take into consideration, however, whether a constant irrigation was at the disposal of the cultivator.

The increases of prices of land, above indicated, were subject to reductions for the causes enumerated previously, viz., distance from centres, malaria, etc.[12]

§ 147. **Tariff for vines.** Special tariffs were adopted for vines, mulberry trees, and fruit trees. Vines were distinguished into three categories: (1) Those attacked by the phylloxera were appraised as ordinary lands. If they included fruit trees, they were considered as lands of the next superior class. (2) Those which were healthy but were situated in a region which was attacked by the phylloxera were appraised as normal vines, but a reduction of 25% was applied to the prices of the latter. (c) Normal vines were classified as old or Hungarian and American vines, the former being further distinguished as vines bearing fruit and vines without fruit. To the old or Hungarian vines were assimilated vines attacked by phylloxera situated in the sand of the sea coast, as the insect has not much effect on them. The following tariff was applied to the vine stocks of vineyards, including the soil:

Old or Hungarian Vines

Vines without fruit

1 decare: 500 vine-stocks. Bulgaria		1 *stremma:* 900 vine-stocks. Greece	
1st class	10 leva	1st class	5 drachmas
2d "	8 "	2d "	4 "
3d "	6 "	3d "	2 "

Vines bearing fruit

1st class	15 leva	1st class	8 drachmas
2d "	12 "	2d "	5 "
3d "	8 "	3d "	3 "

[12] See decision of the Commission, Procès-Verbaux, xvi, 310th meet., December 15, 1926, p. 2066.

American Vines

1 decare: 500 vine-stocks

	Bulgaria		
	1st class	*2d class*	*3d class*
1 year	14 leva	12 leva	8 leva
2 years	16 "	14 "	10 "
3–4 "	23 "	16 "	12 "
5–8 "	25 "	20 "	16 "
9 and more "	20 "	18 "	14 "

In case an emigrant presented a certificate of the authorities from which it appeared that he owned a number of vine-stocks for each *stremma* higher than the average number indicated in the tariff (500 in Bulgaria or 900 in Greece) and his property rights were recognized, his land and his vine-stocks were appraised separately as follows: [13] The land was estimated at the average rate of 1320 leva in Bulgaria and 835 drachmas in Greece, per *stremma* or decare, in view of the fact that vines are usually planted in mediocre soil. The vine-stocks were appraised according to the number indicated in the certificate and the figures of the tariff.[14]

§ 148. Tariff for mulberry and fruit trees. Mulberry groves constitute an important source of income in some parts of Bulgaria and Macedonia in connection with the feeding of silkworms. A special tariff was provided for them. It was presumed that a *stremma* or decare contained 100 mulberry trees, unless there was an official statement to the contrary. The tariff for each tree, including the soil, was as follows, according to the class of lands:

Bulgaria		*Macedonia*	
1st class	190 leva	1st class	150 drachmas
2d "	150 "	2d "	115 "
3d "	115 "	3d "	75 "

Mulberry groves containing less than 100 trees per *stremma* were considered as containing 100, in case the staff of agronomists deemed it proper. The authors of the tariff thought that the value of a mulberry grove did not always depend on

[13] Procès-Verbaux, xvi, 309th meet., December 14, 1926, p. 2063.

[14] In the region of Stanimaka, which was considered *hors barème* and where valuations of vines were made before the establishment of the tariff, it was decided that a maximum of only 550 old or Hungarian or 500 American vine-stocks for each decare was to be taken in consideration. Procès-Verbaux, xvii, 322d meet., February 12, 1927, pp. 2162-63.

the number of trees on a *stremma*. Trees planted thinly show a greater development and, consequently, give a higher revenue.

Orchards were similarly appraised according to a special tariff. Each tree was appraised as follows, according to the quality of the land on which it grew:

Bulgaria		*Greece*	
1st class	225 leva	1st class	180 drachmas
2d "	190 "	2d "	145 "
3d "	150 "	3d "	100 "

Groups of less than ten fruit or mulberry trees were considered as isolated trees and were not appraised. Similarly no appraisal was to be made of young trees which had not yet borne fruit. The Commission, however, decided, in September, 1926,[15] that in all future appraisals the rule that isolated trees should not be appraised should be discarded in cases of fruit or forest trees presenting a particular character, which by reason of the fruits, or of the wood, constituted an important source of revenue for the emigrant. In such cases the staffs of agronomists and expert architects were directed to take into account the value of these trees, even when they were less than ten for each *stremma*. The value could be estimated by taking into consideration such elements of valuation as productivity, size, or age.

At a late period,[16] the Mixed Commission, on the proposal of its neutral expert agronomist, adopted a tariff for the appraisal of isolated trees, with a view to solving the difficulties presented in the work of the agencies of appraisal and simplifying their work. The Greek member protested against the adoption of a tariff which would result in the appraisal of all isolated trees in Greece, whereas thousands of trees of Greek emigrants in Bulgaria had not been appraised in the past. In the view taken by the Commission, the prices proposed in the tariff were to constitute only a guide for the agencies of appraisal.

§ 149. Procedure of appraisal of lands. The procedure of appraisal of lands, as it developed after the first experiments,

[15] Procès-Verbaux, xv, 287th meet., p. 1846.
[16] Procès-Verbaux, xx, 353d meet., July 9, 1927, pp. 5 ff.

was as follows. The staff went to a village for the purpose of appraising the lands of emigrants. It first ascertained the distance of the village from a certain centre, great, average, or small. Then it considered the general aspect of the village, whether it should be classified as very good, good, and so forth. Next, it had to determine what lands of the village should be deemed to be of first, second, or third class. To this end, the staff went over the lands of the village and classified them in name-places (*lieux-dits*) or zones. These were denominations that the peasants gave always to various parts of the landed property of the village. These same denominations were indicated in the plans of the land surveyors and in the applications for liquidation. The staff then decided that the lands of the zone A, for instance, were first-class lands, the lands of zone B, second-class lands, and so forth.

Thus the staff was able to draw up a report in which it was indicated that, in view of the fact that the village in question is at such a distance from such a centre, and that the general aspect of the village places it in a certain category of villages (very good, good, etc.), the lands of such village are to be appraised at the prices indicated by the tariff for the centre and category in question. The report also indicated the classification of the various zones of the village according to the quality of their lands, and determined the increase for tobacco or the decrease for malaria, etc.

The decisions of the staff were taken by the vote of the neutral President, the Greek and Bulgarian members having only the right of giving their opinions. The latter could take appeal against decisions on each of the above points. But no appeal could be considered, unless it concerned a fact which was brought to the attention of the President of the staff in writing, on the spot where the decision was taken.[17] The appeals were examined by the neutral expert agronomist of the Commission, who reported to it.[18]

The grouping in centres, the classifications, and the scales of coefficients in the tariff for lands were considered by the

[17] Procès-Verbaux, xvi, 297th meet., November 30, 1926, p. 1914.
[18] See also *supra*, § 134.

Mixed Commission to be rigid. The staffs of agronomists were authorized to discard this rule in exceptional cases when they considered it absolutely necessary.[19] Indeed, the authors of the tariff suggested that in certain cases of very special economic conditions the tariff should not be applied and that the agronomists should make independent appraisals. Xanthi in Thrace, Rosna in Macedonia, and Stanimaka in Bulgaria were considered to be such cases. These localities were considered as *hors barème,* outside the tariff.[20]

The classification of lands in three categories, according to the quality of the soil, was made easier in Bulgaria by the existence of the government registry of lands. The Commission decided that the staff of agronomists should follow the classification of the registry in the old territories of Bulgaria and should verify by trial the exactness of such classification. In the new territories of Bulgaria the staff was to consider whether the incomplete data of the registries of 1922 were admissible or not.[21]

The staffs of agronomists were authorized by the Commission [22] to classify in the category of lands corresponding to the quality of their soil the uncultivated lands which might become again productive lands, especially in villages of the old emigration. This decision was not in conformity with the principle of the Rules that the basis of appraisal was the real value of the land at the time of liquidation.[23] The staffs, on the other hand, were authorized to appraise as agricultural lands parcels of lands which had become building lands because of the installation of refugees.[24]

[19] Procès-Verbaux, xv, 290th meet., September 15, 1926, p. 1862.

[20] The basic prices of lands and of the special cultivation in the region of Stanimaka were determined by decisions of the First Sub-Commission in Bulgaria, and an expert examination by the staff of agronomists was made in the spring of 1926. The Mixed Commission adopted the report of the staff of agronomists which proposed prices higher than those of the general tariff. See Procès-Verbaux, xiv, 270th meet., July 19, 1926, pp. 1739-41.

[21] Procès-Verbaux, xvi, 294th meet., October 21, 1926, p. 1897.

[22] Procès-Verbaux, xvi, 301st meet., November 12, 1926, p. 1957.

[23] Such uncultivated lands situated in the zone classified by the staff as irrigated lands benefited by the increase applied to the latter. See decision of the Comission. Procès-Verbaux, xvi, 310th meet., December 15, 1926, p. 2068.

[24] Procès-Verbaux, xvi, 301st meet., November 12, 1926, p. 1958. In case, however, the change was due to the normal growth of population, such parcels were appraised as building lands.

The question of the general character of the village, namely, whether it should be classified as very good, good, average, bad, or very bad, was the most difficult question, and the basis of most of the discussions at the Mixed Commission. The latter almost invariably followed the opinion of its neutral expert on this question, as it also followed, very generally, his recommendations on increases or reductions by a coefficient of the prices given by the agencies of appraisal.

§ 150. **Appraisal of forests.** The tariff of lands adopted by the Commission in February, 1926, did not deal with the price of forests. Subsequently, in August, 1926, the Mixed Commission obtained the services of an expert forester, M. Jaccard, for the appraisal of forests. This expert was left entirely free in the choice of his methods of appraisal. Until April 30, 1927, the appraisals made by this expert were examined only by the Mixed Commission, which generally approved them. At the above date a staff of experts, as in the case of the expert agronomists, was created, presided over by the neutral expert, M. Jaccard. The procedure of the work of this staff was similar to that of the staff of agronomists of lands.[25] The yearly revenue of a forest served as the principal basis of appraisal. A capitalization rate of twenty was generally adopted.

At the end of 1928, the Commission contemplated dispensing with the services of the expert forester, M. Jaccard. This caused loud protests on the part of the Greek member. M. Jaccard had made the appraisals of all the forests of Bulgarian emigrants from Greece, but had not yet appraised many Greek forests in Bulgaria. It was the intention of the neutral members of the Commission to use the only remaining staff of agronomists for the appraisal of the forests in Bulgaria in the spring of 1929, as no work could be done in the winter. The Greek member thought this would not protect the Greek interests, and that reciprocity in the appraisals would not be secured,[26] and threatened to call to the attention of the League of Nations what he called lack of the spirit of jus-

[25] Procès-Verbaux, xviii, 333d meet., April 4, 1927, p. 2308.
[26] Procès-Verbaux, xxxii, 465th meet., December 1, 1928, p. 13.

tice and reciprocity. The Commission, eventually, decided to interrupt the work of the team of foresters during the winter and engaged the services of M. Jaccard again in the spring.[27]

§ 151. Appraisal of fisheries. The fisheries (*talians*) were appraised in a special manner. Their value, indeed, depended on the revenue alone. The interested parties were invited to appoint a representative, an expert or otherwise, within a definite period. If they failed to do so, the interested member of the Mixed Commission was bound to appoint a representative. Another representative was appointed by the member of the Commission representing the country in which the fisheries were situated. These two representatives presented their arguments before the expert agronomist of the Mixed Commission, Mr. Fluck, who decided on the value in the first instance. An appeal from his decision might be taken to the Commission.[28]

The experts representing the two countries, after long discussions, reached an agreement as to the prices of the *talians* in Bulgaria. Mr. Fluck approved this agreement and adopted their appraisals. The Mixed Commission later ratified this agreement.[29]

The rights of Bulgarian emigrants to fish in certain small lakes and ponds in Macedonia were appraised by Mr. Fluck, who heard the views of the Bulgarian and Greek experts. Mr. Fluck's appraisals, although admitted by the neutral members of the Commission to be generous, were ratified by the Mixed Commission over the protests of the Greek member.[30]

§ 152. Appraisal of unsurveyed or unclassified lands. We have seen, in another connection,[31] that the Mixed Commission authorized the liquidation of properties of emigrants whenever their rights were proved before the Sub-Commissions, even if the land surveyors had not been able to locate or measure such properties. Following this decision, the Commission had to adopt a number of arbitrary criteria for giving

[27] Procès-Verbaux, xxxii, 466th meet., December 11, 1928, p. 4.
[28] Procès-Verbaux, xxv, 401st meet., February 20, 1928, p. 8.
[29] Procès-Verbaux, xxxiv, 487th meet., May 30, 1929, p. 27.
[30] See previous note.
[31] See *supra*, § 129.

to such properties a certain area and value. Thus, such lands were supposed to have the average area of all lands recognized and surveyed previously in the same village; if they could not be placed in a certain zone of the village, the lands were considered of the second category in regard to their quality; lands of special cultures were deemed to belong to the single category of the village or otherwise to the second class.

Similar measures were taken for the appraisal of lands which by omission were not classified or appraised by the agencies of appraisement on their visits to the villages. Zones of a village, not classified by the staff, were deemed to be second-class lands.[32]

[32] Procès-Verbaux, xxiii, 375th meet., October 21, 1927, p. 9; xxv, 400th meet., February 14, 1928, p. 9.

CHAPTER XII

APPRAISAL OF BUILDINGS

§ 153. The working out of the general tariff for Greece. The appraisal of buildings was a much more difficult task than that of agricultural lands. It required professional ability and a knowledge of local prices of labor and materials. The Sub-Commissions were not qualified for this task. They sought the services of expert architects. In Bulgaria a single expert was used for the expert appraisal of buildings, Mr. Stavroff, who seemed to inspire confidence in both the Greek and Bulgarian members of the Commission. In Greece no single architect was available who could give the whole of his time to appraisal of buildings of Bulgarian emigrants. Instead, eight architects, chosen among well known foreign architects established in Saloniki, were intrusted each with the task of appraising the buildings of a certain region.

It was soon discovered, however, that neither in form nor substance were the appraisals in Greece alike, and that important divergences of prices existed between the expert findings of the architects in Greece.[1] The differences of appraisal

[1] The report of M. Godineau to the Mixed Commission under date of May 27, 1925, was placed at the disposal of the writer at the offices of the Mixed Commission.

reached sometimes the proportion of 10 to 1. Under these conditions, the expert architects were convened and asked to establish the bases of a unity of method and uniformity of valuation. Mr. Modiano, one of the architects, chosen as Rapporteur, submitted to the Mixed Commission through M. Godineau, President of the Central Sub-Commission in Saloniki, a report on a uniform analytical method of expert examination of buildings in Macedonia, and basic tariffs and formulas reducing to a minimum the differences of appreciation and the divergences of prices between the various expert appraisals.[2]

This method was ratified by the Mixed Commission on October 9, 1925,[3] and the tariffs of prices were approved, so far as Macedonia was concerned. The expert architects of Thrace were also directed to adopt the same method and tariffs for their appraisal.[4]

§ 154. Tariff for buildings and appurtenances. The tariffs established basic price-units for buildings and appurtenances. The price-units were based on three factors: the price of the labor, materials, and transportation which entered into the structure of buildings and their appurtenances. The basic price-units were calculated according to the actual normal average value of the work and were subject to change in accordance with the distance from places of supply, the mode of transportation, and the cost of labor and of materials.

On the basis of the prices of these factors, the basic price-units for various parts of buildings and fixtures were determined in a general tariff. Thus, prices were fixed for foundations, walls, roofs, partitions, floors, ceilings of various kinds, also for ovens, chimneys, wine-presses, flour-bins, wine-casks, etc. Staircases, doors, windows, wells, fruit trees, and climbing vines were left to the appraisal of the expert architects.

The result of the appraisal of a building was subject to reduction for depreciation of the construction and of the acces-

[2] Letter of Mr. Modiano under date of May 27, 1925, in III *Sous-Commission d'Emigration Gréco-Bulgare en Grèce,* Procès-Verbal of the 17th meeting, Saloniki, May 27, 1925, and tariffs dated June 12, 1925.

[3] Procès-Verbaux, xii, 242d meet., p. 1533.

[4] On the appraisal of buildings in Thrace, see *infra,* § 160.

sory fixtures. The coefficient of depreciation was established by taking into account the degree of solidity, the nature of the materials used, and wear and tear. Special mention of these factors was made in the report drawn up by each architect.

The prices of the basic factors were fixed as follows:

Basic factors	Prices
1. *Labor*	Drachmas
Laborer, daily wage	40
Mason, daily wage	70
Carpenter, daily wage	80
Cabinetmaker, daily wage	90
2. *Transportation*	
By mule, per ton-kilometre	50
By cart, per ton-kilometre	6
3. *Materials*	
Field stone, per cubic metre	15
Quarried stone, per cubic metre	30
Sand or gravel, per cubic metre	12
Raw bricks, per cubic metre	60
Bricks, per cubic metre	220
Quicklime (local), per *oka* *	1.25
Rough lumber, per cubic metre	400
Planed lumber, per cubic metre	500
Sawed lumber, per cubic metre	1200
Tiles (local), per square metre	50
Tiles, per square metre	40
Laths for plaster walls per cubic metre of masonry	20

* Equivalent to a little less than three pounds.

§ 155. Tariff for building lands. The tariff for building lands, that is, lands on which buildings were standing and lands belonging to or in the neighborhood of buildings, to the exclusion of cultivated lands, took into account two factors: the population of the village or town in which the land was situated, and the situation in the village or town. With respect to the latter, three categories were established: lands in the centre of the village or town and on the principal streets; lands intermediate between the centre and the outskirts; and lands far from the centre, without streets, or on blind alleys, and lands in the outskirts of the village or town. A fourth category was made only for villages between 4000 and 6000 inhabitants. On these bases the tariff was fixed as follows:

Number of inhabitants	Price per square metre for each category 1st category Drachmas	2d category Drachmas	3d category Drachmas	4th category Drachmas
500	6	4		
1000	8	5		
2000	12	6		
3000	22	11	4.50	
4000	32	16	8	3
5000	42	21	11	4
6000	52	26	13	5
7000	62	31	15.50	
8000	72	36	18	
9000	82	41	20.50	
10000	92	46	23	
11000	102	51	25.50	
12000	112	56	28	
13000	122	61	30.50	

§ 156. Appraisal of buildings in Bulgaria. While these tariffs were established in Greece, the expert architect, Mr. Stavroff, in Bulgaria applied a simplified method for the total appraisal of buildings without a distinct and detailed appraisal of the various constituent parts of a building and its accessories. This method was derived from a previous study of the various types of houses, dependencies, annexes, commercial and industrial buildings, etc. Mr. Stavroff divided the various buildings into well defined categories according to the unit value for each square metre or cubic metre. This classification permited him to obtain more or less precise prices.

As doubts arose as to whether there was reciprocity between the appraisals in Greece and Bulgaria, the Mixed Commission invited Mr. Stavroff to supply, taking account of the expert examinations already made by him, the following documents: a general average tariff of basic prices for all Bulgaria; a special tariff of local prices for each village; a general concise report on the situation of each village and the reasons justifying the non-application of the general tariff; a justification of the prices of building lands; the coefficient of age of buildings; and a sketch of each building, indicating the neighboring properties. These factors were to serve for comparing the appraisals made respectively in Bulgaria and Greece and for bringing about equivalence between the prices given in the two countries.[5] A report with a tariff for Bulgaria was submitted by Mr. Stavroff on December 5, 1925.[6] This tariff concerned only buildings, not building lands. Like the tariff of the expert achitects in Macedonia it gave first the basic prices of the factors of labor, transportation, and materials, and then the price-units for the various pieces of construction, parts of buildings, and accessories. The Commission did not proceed to the approval of this tariff, and did not even consider it until November, 1926, when the question of the obligatory character of the general tariff of buildings for Greece arose.[7] In fact, Mr. Stavroff continued to apply his own method, the reports submitted by him for each appraisal being too short to permit any control of his work.

§ 157. Application of the methods of appraisal in the two countries. It would seem that this difference in methods of appraisal was bound to result in differences in the prices given in Greece and Bulgaria. Classifying a building, according to its nature or its mode of construction, in a certain category, and giving to it a rough price, was totally different from calculating the quantity of materials, stone, wood, etc., used in the construction of a building, estimating the cost of such materials and of constructing the building, as if it were actually to be built, and then diminishing this amount by a coefficient for age and wear and tear. This analytical method has apparently resulted in higher appraisals of buildings in Greece. The expert architects who worked out the tariff of buildings were perhaps influenced by the conditions in Saloniki, a city in which building operations were very active after the war, following the great fire of 1917 and the influx of thousands of Greek refugees from Asia Minor.

During the first year after the date of the adoption of the tariff of buildings, the expert architects in Macedonia who appraised the buildings for the Sub-Commissions applied the tariff rigidly. This resulted in giving exorbitant prices for

[5] See note 3. See also Procès-Verbaux, xiv, 264th meet., June 5, 1926, p. 1706.

[6] Transmitted by letter No. 1/ 322/D I/ I/ dated Dec. 5, 1925, of Mr. Saulus, President of the First Sub-Commission in Bulgaria.

[7] Procès-Verbaux, xvi, 301st meet., November 12, 1926, pp. 1958 ff.

small and cheap houses and for ruins. The protests of the Greek members of the Sub-Commissions were unceasing. At last, a number of investigations on the prices given by the architects for certain villages and confirmed by the Sub-Commissions were ordered by the Mixed Commission. An investigation of the small city of Yénidjé-Vardar, conducted in the summer of 1926 by Mr. Haussa, President of the Third Sub-Commission and later Director of the Centre of Saloniki, proved the arbitrariness of the appraisals made and their conflict with the actual market prices of the buildings in question. The prices of the tariff were found to be too high for the city of Yénitzé, a city of 10,000 inhabitants in the neighborhood of Saloniki, which proved *a fortiori* that the same prices for small towns and villages in the interior of Macedonia, where labor was cheaper and the materials were at hand in the neighborhood of the village, had no basis at all. This investigation proved, in the words of the expert architect, Mr. Arrigoni, who made the original appraisals, "that by reason of the system of construction the result of the calculation was above the intrinsic commercial value." Mr. Haussa decided that the prices given by the tariff were maximum prices, and that it was necessary to reduce by 15% the prices given by the expert architect for the buildings of Yénidjé-Vardar.[8]

After the summer of 1926 the Sub-Commissions did not hesitate to reduce the prices proposed by the expert architects. The Commission, on the proposal of its neutral expert, reduced on many occasions the prices on buildings as fixed by the Sub-Commissions. These reductions have extended from 10% to 25%.

In order to secure reciprocity in the appraisals of urban buildings in the two countries, it was decided by the Commission to have Mr. Stavroff go to Saloniki and communicate his methods to the architects designated by the Commission for the expert appraisal of urban buildings and building lands of Bulgarian emigrants in Macedonia and Thrace. Mr. Modiano was to be charged with the expert appraisal of prop-

[8] Procès-Verbaux, xxiv, 344th meet., January 20, 1928, annex 1.

erties in Saloniki.[9] The Commission asked a report from Mr. Stavroff and Mr. Modiano on the methods applied by them for the expert appraisal of urban properties in Bulgaria and Saloniki respectively.[10]

These experts expressed the view in their report of October 12, 1926, that in the particular case of Saloniki, the non-analytical method adopted by Mr. Stavroff could not be easily applied, as the properties were not numerous and their construction varied greatly. It was preferable, in their opinion, to follow in Saloniki the analytical method applied in Macedonia. The important thing was that the two experts should estimate in the same manner the age and depreciation for wear and tear of buildings. For this purpose they visited and examined together a number of buildings in Saloniki and found their points of view alike.

Concerning the building lands, the two experts were in agreement that their appraisal should be based primarily on the value of the neighboring lands as verified by sales. When this basis was lacking, the net annual income of a property capitalized at 10%, minus the value of the building, should form the basis of appraisal.

The Commission concluded from this report that there existed reciprocity between the two countries as regarded the appraisal of urban buildings and building lands.[11]

§ 158. Local tariffs. In view of the results that the general tariffs produced in Greece with respect to buildings and building lands in villages and towns, the Mixed Commission, after long discussions, took a decision on November 12, 1926,[12] to the effect that the general tariffs for the expert appraisal of buildings and building lands in Greece, worked out by the experts in Macedonia, and those for Bulgaria, prepared by Mr. Stavroff, were only to be used as guides by the expert architects.

For each village the experts were directed to establish a local tariff, and to correct the prices on the basis of informa-

[9] Procès-Verbaux, xv, 279th meet., August 14, 1926, p. 1794.
[10] Procès-Verbaux, xv, 285th meet., August 30, 1926, p. 1829.
[11] Procès-Verbaux, xvi, 298th meet., November 2, 1926, pp. 1920 ff.
[12] Procès-Verbaux, xvi, 301st meet., November 12, 1926, pp. 1958 ff.

tion gathered on the place. They might also show that the prices of the general tariff should be applied in a certain village. In the latter case, the general tariff should constitute the local tariff for the village in question.

§ 159. **Procedure of appraisal.** Each building was examined and appraised by itself, and a plan and rough sketch were drawn up. The expert appraisal was made by the architect and communicated to the members of the Sub-Commissions with a view to its discussion and adoption. The national members of the Sub-Commissions sent to the place their technical advisers, who made expert counter-examinations and addressed reports to the members to whom they were responsible. The Sub-Commission subsequently held a meeting, when the members presented their objections and asked a general reduction or increase on all the expert appraisals of a village. The members had a right of appeal to the Mixed Commission against the decisions of the Sub-Commission. Such appeal could, however, only refer to the local tariff. Any error or omission in an individual file could only be brought to the attention of the President of the Sub-Commission, who passed on it definitively.[13]

The Commission sent to the place its neutral expert, to report to it on the appeals. This expert from October, 1926,[14] was M. Savoie. The Sub-Commissions did not approve all the expert appraisals of the architects individually, but only the local tariff. The adoption of the latter by the Sub-Commission carried with it *ipso facto* the adoption of the corresponding individual expert valuations. The objections for omissions, material errors, or the coefficient of age and wear and tear which might be raised in regard to individual expert appraisal, and which could not be examined by the Sub-Commissions, might be presented before the Mixed Commission by the interested members until the day of the examination of the files by the Commission.[15]

The work of examination of all the appeals against deci-

[13] This restriction of appeals was decided upon by the Commission on November 12, 1926. See previous note.

[14] Procès-Verbaux, xvi, 295th meet., October 23, 1926, p. 1905.

[15] Procès-Verbaux, xx, 352d meet., June 30, 1927, p. 8.

sions of the Sub-Commissions concerning the local tariff for buildings and building lands has been a difficult task. M. Savoie, the neutral expert architect of the Mixed Commission, was not able to attend to all this work. Accordingly the Commission appointed on May 7, 1928,[16] as its second expert, Mr. Stavroff, who was sent to Saloniki and placed at the disposal of the Director of that Centre with authority to examine all appeals not yet examined on the appraisals of buildings in Greece. M. Savoie was retained in Sofia for the appeals against decisions of appraisal of buildings in Bulgaria.

§ 160. Procedure of appraisal in Thrace. In Thrace the procedure of appraisal of buildings and building lands was different. Such appraisal was not made by the Sub-Commissions, acting on the advice of expert architects, but by a staff of two architects, a Greek and a Bulgarian. It was thought that by the collaboration of the representatives of the two countries the expert work might be simplified and speeded up.[17] In case, however, the two experts did not agree, decisions of appraisal were taken by the Sub-Commissions of Thrace. These architects submitted to the Commission a report on their method of expert appraisal, including the establishment of a local tariff for each village. This method, which was approved by the Commission,[18] was as follows. On arriving in a village for the appraisal of buildings, the experts analyzed, on the basis of the general tariff, a number of typical buildings of the village. This computation gave the average price per cubic metre of a building. For the remaining buildings it was sufficient to find the cubic metres and apply the average price found by the typical buildings. The annexes and accessories were appraised separately for each immovable property and their value was added to the value of the principal building. Thus, the expert findings dealt distinctly with: (1) the value of the land; (2) the value of the principal building; (3) the value of the accessories; and (4) the value

[16] Procès-Verbaux, xxvii, 415th meet., pp. 6-7, The Greek member agreed to this appointment. See also Procès-Verbaux, xxviii, 428th meet., July 12, 1928, p. 4.

[17] Procès-Verbaux, xv, 292d meet., September 18, 1926, p. 1881.

[18] Procès-Verbaux, xvii, 316th meet., January 14, 1927, pp. 2102, 2103.

of annexes. Lastly, the reports of the expert examination of each village were accompanied with a descriptive note upon the village and a list indicating the price-units of all the materials entering into the construction of the buildings of the village. This was the local tariff, and rendered possible the control of the work of the experts at every step.

The system of expert appraisal in Thrace by the two experts representing the two countries did not prove entirely satisfactory. The Greek member of the Commission asked the substitution of Mr. Mavromatis for the original Greek representative, Mr. Bogatsoglou; then he became dissatisfied with Mr. Mavromatis, and asked that he be replaced by a third architect. The Commission refused to accept the resignation of Mr. Mavromatis, since this would necessitate the remaking of 2000 appraisals actually in progress.[19]

§ 161. **Value at the time of liquidation.** The appraisal of buildings was, in general, the most difficult task in the process of liquidation. A great deal of arbitrary judgment prevailed in finding the "real value at the time of liquidation." The term "time of liquidation" was interpreted to mean the time when the expert architects visited the villages where such buildings were situated. The real value of ruined or destroyed buildings was found by taking into account all kinds of factors, such as the possibility of rebuilding a certain village, the use of the ruins by the inhabitants of such village, etc.[20] Thus, in the case of Achtopol, a fishing town, deserted by the Greek emigrants in 1906 and ruined since, no depreciation of the ruins was admitted by the Commission by reason of abandonment and the disinclination of Bulgarians for the fishing industry. It was thought that the new generation born on the seacoast would adapt itself to the lucrative maritime conditions of the place.[21]

To buildings which were not examined and appraised by the architects on their visit to a village, the average value of

[19] Procès-Verbaux, xx, 353d meet., July 9, 1927, p. 14.
[20] Reports of the neutral expert architect under dates of November 29, 1927 (M.29), and December 5, 1927 (M.30), concerning the ruins of Zarovo and Moutoulovo.
[21] Procès-Verbaux, xxvii, 417th meet., May 19, 1928, pp. 6 ff.

similar buildings examined by the architects in the village was assigned.[22]

§ 162. Honoraria of architects. The expert architects received honoraria for their expert examinations of buildings and building lands. A specific sum for each building examined and appraised by them was paid by the Commission, this sum being proportional to the importance of the building. Thus, for a two-story house with annexes and accessories forming part thereof, the honorarium was 300 drachmas in Macedonia; for a one-story house with annexes and accessories, the honorarium was 250 drachmas; for annexes located outside the residential sections and lands of such annexes, 75 drachmas; and for lands without buildings, 50 drachmas.[23]

§ 163. Appraisal of salt works. Certain classes of industrial buildings could not be dealt with by the above ordinary methods of appraisal. The salt works on the coast of the Black Sea, especially in the region of Anchialo, were properties of this kind. Their value depended on their product, the general expenses, the cost of the product, etc. A functionary of the Secretariat of the Commission, Mr. Tarnovsky, was charged with making a study of the above factors of the value of salt works. He was directed to examine, among other things, the accounts of the German firm of Mannesmann at Anchialo.[24] All appraisals of salt works made in the meantime by the expert architect Mr. Stavroff were held in suspense,[25] with the exception of some salt works of small importance[26] which had none of the industrial elements with which the Mixed Commission was concerned.

Mr. Stavroff's appraisals and Mr. Tarnovsky's thorough study of the general conditions of exploitation of the salt works at Anchialo, together with a report by M. Savoie, the

[22] Procès-Verbaux, xxiii, 375th meet., October 21, 1927, p. 9; xxv, 400th meet., February 14, 1928, p. 9.

[23] Procès-Verbaux, xii, 242d meet., October 9, 1925, p. 1533. Equivalent honoraria were paid to Mr. Stavroff for his expert work in Bulgaria; the two experts in Thrace divided between themselves honoraria equal to those paid to expert architects in Macedonia. The honoraria were raised and modified in November, 1926. Procès-Verbaux, xvi, 298th meet., p. 1925.

[24] Procès-Verbaux, xxiii, 381st meet., November 10, 1927, p. 2.

[25] Procès-Verbaux, xxvii, 420th meet., May 29, 1928, p. 2.

[26] Procès-Verbaux, xxviii, 425th meet., June 30, 1928, p. 3.

expert architect of the Mixed Commission, formed the subject of discussion by the members of the Mixed Commission.[27] These experts did not agree either on the annual production of salt, on the selling price of salt, or on the expenses of production and the maintenance of the salt works. The Commission distinguished the salt works called Golem-Gheren, which had the character of large industries, from the smaller salt works.

Concerning the former, the Greek member maintained that the annual average production of the seven years 1921-27 was 18,700 sacks of salt; that the average price was 96 leva for 100 kilogrammes; that the general annual expenses amounted to about 600,000 leva; and that the annual net revenue was 1,178,000 leva. He thus estimated the real value of the salt works of Golem-Gheren, with a capitalization rate of twenty, as in the case of forests, as 23,562,000 leva. On the contrary, the Bulgarian member of the Commission contended that the annual production was 13,000 sacks of salt, the price 81 leva per 100 kilogrammes, and the net revenue 403,000 leva. By capitalizing this revenue at the rate of ten, as with ordinary buildings, he estimated the real value of the same salt works as 4,030,000 leva. The neutral members of the Commission adopted the view that the capitalization rate should be ten, and that on the basis of the accounts of the owners of Golem-Gheren the annual average production was 14,570 sacks of salt. They proposed the price of 7,713,000 leva for the liquidation of the salt works in question. This proposal was accepted as the decision of the Commission by the majority vote of the neutral member and the President and against the protests of the Greek and Bulgarian members.

The small salt works formed the subject of expert appraisal on the part of the architect Mr. Stavroff. Appeals against his findings and the decisions of the Sub-Commissions were taken by both the Greek and Bulgarian representatives. The expert architect of the Mixed Commission, M. Savoie, went to the place and made a study of the various factors on which the appraisal was based, and proposed an increase of

[27] Procès-Verbaux, xxxi, 451st meet., October 31, 1928, pp. 1-12.

12% on the prices fixed by Mr. Stavroff. The average annual production of each salt work was estimated to be 20 sacks of salt, the expenses of production 45 leva for each sack, and the price of the salt 90 leva per 100 kilogrammes. It was proposed to adopt a capitalization rate of twenty. The Commission thought that the increase proposed by M. Savoie was too generous, and adopted instead an increase of 8% on the appraisals made by Mr. Stavroff.[28]

The salt works of Malak-Gheren were reckoned intermediate between the large and small salt works. They comprised 150 wells, 16 reservoirs, 2 deposits, and an oil motor. Mr. Stavroff had proposed the price of 1,755,480 leva. M. Savoie proposed an increase of 12% of this amount.[29] The Commission adopted this increase and liquidated the property for 1,966,137 leva.

§ 164. **Appraisal of mills.** Special difficulties also arose in connection with the appraisal of mills. There were in Greece as well as in Bulgaria two categories of mills; the modern mills with modern machinery and the rustic mills with one, two, or more mill stones on wooden axes. They presented difficult questions, such as value of construction, advantages in the position of the mill, the importance of its commercial outlets, the existence and value of water rights, etc. Fundamentally the mills were all industrial undertakings, and their revenue capitalized would always give their real value.

But this revenue was not easy to find. Owners of small mills kept no books of accounts, and their testimony could not be sufficient proof. Besides, many mills had been abandoned, and their value at the time of the liquidation had to be determined on another basis than that of revenue.

Necessarily, then, the appraisal should take into account, besides the value of buildings, machinery, and accessories, certain other factors. The land, for instance, on which a mill was erected had a special value as being in a place where water was available.

The appraisal of mills, as of other buildings, was made by

[28] Procès-Verbaux, xxxi, 456th meet., November 14, 1928, p. 18.

[29] The Greek member maintained that the real value amounted to 5,020,000 leva; the Bulgarian member argued for the price of 877,740 leva.

the Sub-Commission with the aid of the expert architects. The lands on which mills were erected were appraised as building lands of the first category of the village concerned.[30] In the case of ruined mills, the reasons for their abandonment were considered, that is, whether the abandonment was compulsory or came from the fact that the mill could no longer be used because of the change of natural or economic conditions. Whenever the revenue could be ascertained, it was capitalized at the rate of 10%.[31]

For some time water rights were not taken into account in the appraisal of mills in Macedonia, on the assumption that the use of water belonged not to the owner of the mills exclusively but to all riparian owners who irrigated their lands.[32] However, Mr. Stavroff, the expert architect in Bulgaria, included water rights in the appraisals made by him of Greek mills in Bulgaria.[33] Consequently, M. Savoie, the neutral expert architect, was asked to make a report on the method of appraisal of mills and in particular of their water power. This report, suggesting certain general coefficients of increase of prices, was submitted by M. Savoie and Mr. Houssa, Director of the Centre of Saloniki, to the Mixed Commission on February 7, 1928, and approved by it February 24, 1928.[34]

Since it was found that the appraisal of mills was made differently in Bulgaria and Greece, M. Savoie and Mr. Stavroff were asked to go over these appraisals and revise them so as to achieve a reciprocity. This was done, as the two experts informed the Commission by their report of November 17, 1928. This revision seemed to have resulted in low prices for mills in Greece and Bulgaria alike; and the Commission, by the vote of the two neutral members, increased by 10% all the prices proposed by the two experts.[35]

[30] Letter of M. Savoie to the President of the Mixed Commission, No. 7372/10-28, of May 26, 1927, and annexed Note A, dated May 24, 1927.

[31] M. Savoie's Notice No. 2 concerning the appraisal of mills in Macedonia, Thrace, and Bulgaria, dated July 25, 1927.

[32] Letter No. 9131/I-397, dated September 13, 1926, of the Director of the Centre of Saloniki to the President of the Mixed Commission.

[33] Letter No. 390, August 8, 1927, of the Bulgarian member to the President of the Mixed Commission.

[34] Procès-Verbaux, xxv, 401st and 402d meet.

[35] Procès-Verbaux, xxxiv, 485th meet., May 23, 1929, p. 21.

CHAPTER XIII

DEBTS, TAXES, INDEMNITIES, RENTS, AND PENSIONS

§ 165. Filing claims for debts of emigrants. The final liquidation of an emigrant's property involved certain other matters. The emigrant might have money obligations in the country of his origin or he might owe taxes to the treasury of that country. On the other hand, the state might owe him money on account of rent or indemnity for the use of his property. These factors affected the final liquidation.

It has been already seen in another connection [1] that candidates for emigration, unless they were indigent persons, were granted passes by the Sub-Commissions for their emigration only on the presentation of a certificate of the fiscal authorities showing that their taxes were paid. Furthermore, the Sub-Commissions, on the receipt of applications for the liquidation of the properties of emigrants from a village, had a notice to the public posted in the town hall of that village, inviting persons claiming rights in the properties to present their objections to the liquidation within a specified period. Among such rights mortgages were included. In view of the

[1] See Chapter IV.

departure of many emigrants before the liquidation of their properties, the Commission instructed the Sub-Commissions to ask the emigrants to file a certificate of a public administration showing their debts to the Treasury and the National and Agricultural Banks and those registered in the Mortgage Office. In many cases the emigrants complied with this instruction, and on depositing the above certificate added their consent for the payment of the amount of such debts from the amount of the liquidation of their properties.

From January 1, 1926,[2] for the determination of the amount of the debts of emigrants to the Treasury authorities and the National Bank or Agricultural Bank and of debts registered at the Mortgage Office, the Sub-Commissions based their decisions on the certificates issued by the above administrations. These certificates were filed by the emigrants at the time of their departure, or, on their failure to do so, procured by the Sub-Commissions by addressing a letter to the public administrations. This letter informed the latter that the certificate should be sent in within thirty days.[3]

After December 1, 1927,[4] the claims of public administrations were addressed to the Centres, where the files of the emigrants were being compiled. Any claims from this source, reaching the Centre after the expiration of the period of one month from the date on which such administrations were requested to communicate the taxes or debts due by the emigrant, were not taken in consideration.

As objections of interested parties and third persons generally could be received, according to a decision of the Commission of February 12, 1927,[5] until the moment of the examination of the files by the Reporting Committee, bilateral

[2] Procès-Verbaux, xiii, 251st meet., December 23, 1925, p. 1595.

[3] On the explicit request of the interested administration, the Sub-Commission might, by exception and in concrete cases, extend this period to sixty days. The Commission reserved the right to take into consideration claims of a public administration filed after the expiration of the above period but before the liquidation of the property of the emigrant. See, for instance, cases in which late claims were taken into consideration, in Procès-Verbaux, xvi, 303d meet., November 27, 1926, and cases in which the Commission refused to accept such claims, ibid.

[4] Procès-Verbaux, xxiii, 382d meet., November 16, 1927, p. 8.

[5] Procès-Verbaux, xvii, 322d meet., p. 2158.

agreements for payments of debts were received within all this period. In fact, the Commission received directly a great number of bilateral agreements after the completion of the files and while they were before the Reporting Committee.

This situation was changed after July 15, 1928.[6] Claims of third parties or emigrants reaching the Mixed Commission directly were not taken in consideration. Claims reaching the chief of the compiling service were taken into account only if they were received before the final completion of the files.

The amount of the debts, determined as above, was debited to the emigrant and communicated to him with the decision of appraisal.[7] His objections were received until the expiration of the time fixed for the filing of objections in regard to the appraised value and the establishment of the property rights.

§ 166. Suspension of execution by creditors. In the meantime the Commission took measures for preventing the execution of judgments or attachments against properties of emigrants. It adopted a decision to the effect that it would pay private debts of emigrants, recognized by the emigrant or for which a decision for seizure had been obtained and notice thereof given to the Commission, at the time of liquidating their properties.[8] Following this decision, the two contracting countries took steps for suspending all measures of execution by creditors of emigrants.[9]

§ 167. Uncontested or non-contestable and contested debts. The Plan of Payment adopted August 14, 1926,[10] made

[6] Procès-Verbaux, xxviii, 424th meet., June 26, 1928, pp. 4, 9.

[7] Although, in general, no emigrant could leave his country of origin without presenting a certificate of payment of taxes, the Sub-Commissions and later the compiling services always asked from the public administrations a certificate of the position of the emigrant. For the property was usually not transferred to the state until long after the emigration of the emigrants, and therefore continued to be taxable.

[8] Procès-Verbaux, xii, 231st meet., June 30, 1925, p. 1443.

[9] See, however, the important case of the Greek emigrant Theodor Nikoloff of Hashkovo in Bulgaria, in which everything was done to prevent the Commission and its agencies from proceeding to the liquidation of the emigrant's property; finally the whole folder was stolen while it was being transferred by his attorney from the Centre of Sofia to the competent Sub-Commission. Procès-Verbaux, xx, 354th meet., August 26, 1927, annex 5.

[10] Although this Plan was not approved by the two governments, its pro-

a distinction between non-contested (acknowledged private debts) [11] or non-contestable debts (debts to public administrations, debts established by final judgment and followed by seizure with notice to the Commission, and mortgage debts), and debts which were disputed by the emigrant. Debts of the first class were charged against the emigrant by the Sub-Commissions and were deducted from his credit account.[12]

As regards the debts which were contested by the emigrant, the Mixed Commission did not intervene except in two cases: (1) when the competent judicial authority had allowed to the creditor the seizure of the emigrant's property and official notice of this was sent to the Commission before its decision for liquidation; and (2) when a judgment of the court of first instance had been handed down against the emigrant and notice thereof sent to the Commission before its decision for liquidation, but the emigrant had taken an appeal therefrom.

In these two cases the question of the payment of the debt was postponed until a final decision or an agreement of the parties was reached. The Commission reserved temporarily a part of the liquidation amount due the emigrant sufficient to cover the debt, interest, and court costs.[13] These were the only cases of debts contested by the emigrant in which the Commission intervened in favor of creditors. The latter were compelled, therefore, to prosecute their claims, in case they were contested by the emigrant, so as to secure a decision allowing the seizure or a judgment of the court of first instance recognizing their claim. If they succeeded in either measure and notified the Mixed Commission, the amount necessary for the payment of their debts was reserved by it.

visions concerning the debts of emigrants entered into effect, by specific decision of the Commission, on August 14, 1926. See Procès-Verbaux, xv, 279th meet., p. 1789.

[11] Such debts were not the mere promises of the debtor to pay his debt, but explicit agreements of the debtor to settle his debt by means of the liquidation amount of his property. When such explicit agreement did not exist, the debt belonged to the second category of contestable debts. See Procès-Verbaux, xxviii, 421st meet., June 12, 1928, p. 4.

[12] The method of payment of these debts is dealt with in Chapter XV.

[13] In case the final judgment was against the creditor, the retained sum was returned to the emigrant. See Procès-Verbaux, xxviii, 421st meet., June 12, 1928, p. 5.

§ 168. **Abuses with respect to acknowledged debts.** The category of debts acknowledged by the emigrants, which the Commission deducted from the liquidation amount, gave rise to difficulties and abuses. On the one hand, as these acknowledgments were embodied in writings of various forms which were sometimes repudiated by the emigrants, it was necessary to examine the genuineness of these documents. On the other hand, as the Plan of Payment provided that debts were paid entirely in cash, although the cash payment to the emigrant could not exceed 10%, fictitious acknowledgments of debts were presented by third parties in collusion with the emigrants. The Commission considered the desirability of giving up the attempt to pay debts of emigrants merely acknowledged by them and of paying only the debts to the public administrations (state, commune, etc.), the National and Agricultural Banks, and those registered at the Mortgage Offices.[14]

On December 18, 1928,[15] the Commission decided that acknowledged debts of emigrants to third persons in the country to which they were emigrating were not to be considered unless these persons were lawyers and claimed fees for their services. This decision, taken at so late a time, was deemed by the Greek member to concern especially liquidations of Greek emigrants and to favor Bulgarian creditors more than Greek creditors and caused many protests on his part. The Bulgarian government apparently had paid a large sum of money over the 10% for debts of Greek emigrants to creditors in Greece.

§ 169. **Abuses with respect to debts to public administrations.** The debts of emigrants to public administrations were accepted for a long time by the Mixed Commission as noncontestable and were deducted from the liquidation amount of the emigrant. No serious difficulties arose in the first two or three years of the work of liquidation. In the following years the claims of public administrations in Bulgaria against Greek emigrants increased to such an extent that at one time the Greek representative at the Centre of Sofia refused to

[14] Procès-Verbaux, xxvii, 416th meet., May 9, 1928, pp. 2 ff.
[15] Procès-Verbaux, xxxii, 467th meet., p. 30.

sign the files. An explanation was asked by the Mixed Commission; and an investigation by the neutral member of the Commission followed, which disclosed the following facts.[16]

The average debts of Bulgarian emigrants claimed by the Greek administrations from September 15, 1924, to August 27, 1926, amounted to 0.144% of the appraisal of their properties. In the first quarter of 1927 this average was further decreased to 0.04%. On the contrary, the Bulgarian administrations claimed against Greek emigrants debts from taxes amounting for the period from March 31, 1924, to November 20, 1926, to an average of 1.35%, for the period from February 12 to March 2, 1927, to an average of 2.61%, and from October 8, 1927, to December 24, 1927, to an average of 6.04%. Not only had the average of charges so increased, but there were cases where the Bulgarian treasury authorities claimed a charge of 10, 20, 30, 50, and more than 100% of the value of the property. The neutral member concluded that it was difficult to understand this increase in charges, and that the existing situation could not be allowed to continue. The Bulgarian member argued, in particular, that as the date of transfer of the properties to the state in Bulgaria was later than in Greece, since Greek emigrants left Bulgaria at a later period, the taxes charged against them were higher. However, the neutral member stated that the explanations given by the Bulgarian administrations for the heavy charges were inadmissible.

In view of these conditions, the Commission decided that the principle of non-contestability of debts of emigrants to public administrations should be qualified as follows.[17] The amount of the claim exceeding 3% of the liquidation amount of the properties of the emigrant would not be taken into consideration or debited to the emigrant. Moreover, in the case of new emigrants, if the file contained a certificate of payment of taxes which was issued after the transfer of the property to the state, no claim of the public authorities was to be taken into consideration. In the case of former emi-

[16] Procès-Verbaux, xxv, 402d meet., February 24, 1928, pp. 10 ff.
[17] Procès-Verbaux, xxv, 403d meet., February 25, 1928, pp. 10 ff.

grants, if the transfer of their property to the state was made after January 1, 1925, and there existed in the file a certificate of any date showing that the owner paid his taxes, no claim of the administrations was to be taken into account. If the date of transfer was a date prior to January 1, 1925, no taxes were due by former emigrants.[18]

The above decision dealt with claims of public administrations in general. The modes of application of the decision were determined by the President of the Commission, who was charged with this task. Against the protests of the Bulgarian member, the Commission approved [19] the procedure adopted by the President, which restricted the claims of the administrations to 3% of the liquidation amount, whether they represented taxes imposed on the liquidated property or other kinds of taxes, fines imposed by taxation laws, or other debts of the emigrant to the state. Indeed, only the interpretation of the decision in this way could secure the emigrant against excessive claims on the part of the administration.

§ 170. Principles of equity applied by the Commission. In the solution of the question arising in respect to debts of emigrants the Commission followed rules of equity more than strict legal principles. In cases, for instance, of mortgage debts or taxes encumbering a property belonging in part to an emigrant and in part to a non-emigrant, the former was charged with the part of the debt proportional to his part of the estate, although, according to the law of the country where the property was situated, the creditor and the state had the right to claim payment of the entire debt or tax from the one of the co-debtors, namely, the emigrant. If the emigrant had been compelled to pay the entire amount of the debt, he would have had difficulty after his emigration in collecting the part due by the co-owner.[20]

The payment of the debts was governed by the law of the

[18] By a decision of the Commission, December 29, 1923, the two governments were asked, on the basis of reciprocity, to claim no taxes against former emigrants and refugees, for the time intervening between the abandonment of their properties and their reinstallation, in excess of the revenues which they received or were to receive. Procès-Verbaux, viii, 163d meet., p. 1048.

[19] Procès-Verbaux, xxvi, 409th meet., April 4, 1928, pp. 9 ff.

[20] See such case in Procès-Verbaux, xxvi, 407th meet., March 24, 1928, p. 7.

country where the debt was to be paid. Thus, the obligation to pay interests on the debt ceased if there was a moratorium in the country in question. Similarly, a debt in gold was payable by the Commission in currency notes, if the law of the same country was to this effect.[21]

§ 171. Mortgage debts. Mortgage debts were further dealt with as follows: [22] (1) if both the creditor and the debtor emigrated, the mortgage was cancelled by payment of the creditor made through the liquidation accounts of the two parties. The debtor was debited and the creditor credited with the amount of the debt; (2) if the creditor did not emigrate, the debtor's liquidation account was debited with the amount of the debt and the property passed to the state encumbered with the mortgage; (3) if the creditor only emigrated, his relations with the debtor were not modified. He continued to have the right to proceed against the debtor.

§ 172. Debts to attorneys of emigrants. A special category of claims settled by the Commission were those arising from services of lawyers to emigrants. A decision of June 30, 1925,[23] provided that the debts of emigrants to attorneys, members of the bar of the two countries, could be paid by the Commission in case there was a bilateral agreement between attorney and emigrant and such agreement was included in the file. Powers of attorney and revocations of such powers could be filed with the Mixed Commission until the time of examination of the files by the Reporting Committee.[24] A result of the revocation of the power was the annulment of the bilateral agreement concerning the payment of the fee due an attorney. From July 15, 1928, claims of attorneys, as well as powers and revocations, could not be taken into consideration unless received by the compiling service before the final completion of the corresponding file.[25]

[21] Procès-Verbaux, xxvi, 411th meet., April 11, 1928, p. 19; xxvii, 420th meet., May 29, 1928, pp. 17-18; xxx, 440th meet., September 28, 1928, pp. 5-6.
[22] Procès-Verbaux, xii, 235th meet., July 28, 1925, p. 1481.
[23] Procès-Verbaux, xii, 231st meet., p. 1443.
[24] Procès-Verbaux, xxii, 372d meet., October 8, 1927, p. 9.
[25] The Commission reduced by a certain percentage the fees of attorneys, taking into account the depreciation of the bonds received by emigrants. See Procès-Verbaux, xxx, 442d meet., October 3, 1928, p. 14.

§ 173. Indemnities and revenues due emigrants. As we have seen in another connection, the Rules cancelled all exceptional measures taken against properties of persons who had emigrated before the coming into force of the Convention respecting Reciprocal Emigration. They provided that such persons had a right to the revenue received by the state or by the sequestrator from the date of confiscation or act of sequestration to the date of restoration of the property to the legally entitled persons.[26] This revenue was to be paid through the medium of the Mixed Commission. For any damage to such property done after October 4, 1920, by the act or negligence of the authorities charged with its administration and keeping, an indemnity was due to the proprietors.[27]

Further decisions of the Commission taken after the adoption of the Rules specified other cases in which emigrants had a right to receive payment from uses made of their properties. Thus, they were entitled to the payment of rent on properties used by public administrations for all the time such use continued. The amount of such rent, whenever it was not fixed at the time by the administration or the sequestrator, was estimated by the Mixed Commission, in accordance with the prevailing rent at the particular period and in the rate of exchange of the money at that time.[28]

The farmers who were candidates for emigration were advised by the Sub-Commissions not to emigrate before the harvesting of their fields. In case, however, they wished to depart at an earlier time, and the local authorities were disposed to settle refugees competent to do the harvesting, the candidates for emigration could leave without gathering the crops of their fields. In such cases the Sub-Commissions, at the time of appraising the lands, determined separately the value of the soil and the value of the crops at the stage in

[26] The state determined the revenue which was due to the emigrant for the specified period. This was to be paid to the emigrant regardless of whether the state had collected it or not. See decision of the Commission, Procès-Verbaux, xiii, 252d meet., February 3, 1926, p. 1603.

[27] Rules, articles 69, 70. For the conditions and limitations of application of these rules see *supra*, Chapter V, pp. 131 ff.

[28] Procès-Verbaux, viii, 153d meet., September 22, 1923, p. 1002.

which they were at the date of the emigration. The same rule prevailed, by exception, in other cases where serious reasons had caused the sudden emigration of the owners before the harvest.[29]

§ 174. Indemnity for dispossession of emigrants. As has been seen above,[30] the Commission took special measures in favor of candidates for emigration at the time the Greek refugees from Asia Minor poured into Macedonia and Thrace, and the Bulgarian refugees from these last provinces took possession of properties of Greeks in Bulgaria. It intervened in order to distribute the refugees in the best possible way and to place the soil at the disposal of the refugees, in case the emigrants were not desirous of cultivating it before their emigration. It also decided to indemnify the emigrants who, although remaining in their homes, were deprived of their lands and so unable to procure subsistence. The payment of a special indemnity in such cases was decided upon by the Commission on February 3, 1925.[31] This indemnity was rather high, and was intended at the same time to indemnify persons deprived of their lands and to encourage them to leave the country of origin and search for new lands in the country of immigration, since after the settlement of the refugees both populations could not live on the same lands. If such candidates for emigration were willing to leave after April 15, 1925,[32] they were granted a special indemnity equal to 12% of the value of their lands as this value was determined by the Mixed Commission at the liquidation. Such indemnity, however, could not exceed 20,000 leva in Bulgaria and 8000 drachmas in Greece per family of farmers.

The indemnity was paid because the candidates for emigration were dispossessed of their lands and were unable to cultivate them for their subsistence for the year 1925. But the dispossessions continued after the above decision of February 3, 1925, and lands sown by candidates for emigration were granted to refugees in both countries. In such cases,

29 Procès-Verbaux, ix, 188th meet., June 2, 1924, p. 1137.
30 See *supra,* Chapter IV, pp. 108 ff.
31 Procès-Verbaux, xi, 222d meet., p. 1371.
32 And by special approval of the Sub-Commissions after March 1, 1925.

the Commission decided on May 2, 1925,[33] the above indemnity of 12% of the value of the lands was paid without the maximum limit, and to this was added the value of the seed. And as emigrants continued to be dispossessed in the years following 1925, while they still remained in the country of origin awaiting the liquidation of their properties, the Commission, in order to give effect to article 20 of the Rules, which provided that no emigrant should be dispossessed of his property before receiving entire payment, decided[34] that the indemnity of 12% should bear interest from the first day of November of the first year of dispossession. To emigrants who were deprived of their harvest or vintage, without being dispossessed of their properties, an indemnity of 6% on the value of their lands was allowed.

The Sub-Commissions were instructed to collect all necessary information from interested parties, delegations of emigrants, members of Sub-Commissions, local authorities, etc., and to take decisions as to whether the indemnity was due to all the emigrants of a village or to some among them, and as to the total proportion of cultivable lands to which the indemnity should be applied. No appeal from these decisions of the Sub-Commissions could be taken.

§ 175. Applications of emigrants. Save for these *ex-officio* investigations and decisions of the Sub-Commissions, the interested parties were required to file applications for the payment of revenues collected by the state from the property of emigrants and for indemnities. These applications contained a description of the property; they specified the amounts of revenues, if known, or the damage done, and all other necessary factors. The applications were submitted to the Mixed Commission or the competent Sub-Commission. The period within which applications should be filed was step by step extended until December 15, 1926, for Bulgarian emigrants from Greece. The Commission continued to accept applications after the expiration of this period in exceptional cases until August 1, 1928.[35]

[33] Procès-Verbaux, xii, 228th meet., p. 1411.
[34] Procès-Verbaux, xix, 349th meet., June 18, 1927, pp. 4 ff.
[35] Procès-Verbaux, xxvii, 420th meet., May 29, 1928, p. 22 and annex 5.

§ 176. Transfer of possession to the State. The question of taxes due by the emigrant in his country of origin and of indemnities and rents due to the emigrant by reason of the use of his property was connected with the question of the transfer of the emigrant's property to the state in the territory of which it was situated. At the moment of such transfer the liabilities and rights of the emigrant ceased. Article 21 of the Rules, in accordance with the last sentence of Article 10 of the Convention respecting Reciprocal Emigration, provided that after the payment by the Commission of the price of his property to the emigrant, such property was acquired by the state in whose territory it was situated.

Although the ownership of the liquidated property was transferred as provided by the Rules, possession by the state of emigrants' property might be acquired earlier or later. The liabilities and rights of emigrants were determined by the transfer of possession rather than of ownership. A decision of the Commission,[36] at an early period, provided that emigrants could continue to live in, or possess, property liquidated and transferred to the state without any charge until the day when the competent authority should present itself to take possession. This decision received hardly any application, the emigrants having, as a rule, left their homes long before the liquidation of their properties and the payment. Later [37] the Commission laid down the principle that the date of transfer of possession of liquidated properties was the first day of the second month that followed the meeting of the Commission at which the decision of liquidation of the property in question was taken. A general exception, however, was made of the cases in which the competent Sub-Commission had proposed a definite date for the transfer of possession. The Commission ratified such proposals of the Sub-Commissions, and the date proposed by them remained in effect.

The exception concerned very numerous cases of emigrants who left definitively their country of origin without waiting for the liquidation of their properties. In such cases

[36] Procès-Verbaux, ix, 187th meet., May 27, 1924, p. 1135.
[37] Procès-Verbaux, xv, 290th meet., September 15, 1926, p. 1862.

the Sub-Commissions informed the competent administrative authorities and invited them to take possession of the properties.[38] Possession could thus be taken by the state before payment of the liquidation price of the property. In case possession was taken by the state, the Sub-Commissions were instructed to fix the date of the transfer of possession.[39] Notice of the fixing of this date was sent to the competent authorities as well as to the interested parties.

§ 177. Consequences of transfer of possession. By the transfer of possession of the property to the state, all the benefits of the property were transferred, although the state did not acquire ownership until payment of the liquidation price. Consequently, the Commission determined as follows the consequences of the transfer of possession: [40]

(1) The risks were no longer borne by the emigrant. Any deterioration of the property or total or partial destruction concerned only the state.

(2) The emigrant was no longer liable for taxes on the property.

(3) The leases previously made by the emigrant had no longer any effects as regarded him. He was free for the future from all obligations to the tenant. The future rents were payable to the state.

(4) The interest on the liquidation price ran from this date.[41]

In the case of properties of emigrants expropriated by the state, which were reappraised by the Mixed Commission,[42] the date of transfer of possession was deemed to be the day on which the emigrant lost the enjoyment of his property, namely, the day on which possession was taken by the authori-

[38] Procès-Verbaux, ix, 195th meet., September 2, 1924, p. 1194; xi, 203d meet., October 22, 1924, p. 1271.

[39] Procès-Verbaux, xi, 211th meet., November 14, 1924, p. 1308. In case an emigrant possessed several pieces of property which were transferred to the possession of the State at various periods, the Sub-Commissions could fix a single date of transfer for all. See xii, 231st meet., June 30, 1925, p. 1443.

[40] Procès-Verbaux, xii, 242d meet., October 9, 1925, p. 1637; and xv, 290th meet., September 15, 1926, p. 1862.

[41] In case the date of transfer of possession was fixed by the Sub-Commissions, the interest began from the first day of the second month following such date.

[42] Procès-Verbaux, vii, 140th meet., April 18, 1923, pp. 907-910.

ties of the state.[43] Consequently, all rents or revenues of such properties paid by the state to the emigrant for the time following such date were refunded to the state by the Commission at the moment of liquidation.

§ 178. Pensions of emigrants. An indemnity was also to be granted to emigrants for the paid-up value of their pensions. The Commission thought that pensions were "pecuniary rights" of emigrants, and should not be affected by "the exercise of the right of emigration" as provided for in article 2 of the Convention. An early decision of the Commission [44] made the following provisions:

1. The officers and employees of the state and invalids enjoying a pension allowance and emigrating under the Convention were to lose their right to the allowance from the date of the declaration of emigration and to have a right to indemnity by the state for the paid-up value of the pension due them.

2. The monthly payments of pension made to the emigrant after the filing of the declaration of emigration were to be deducted from the above indemnity.

3. For the determination of the rate of indemnity, the following scale and method were recommended. Retired officers and employees of state who had already received a pension for ten full years were to receive as indemnity a sum equal to the total of payments made by them or of stoppages of wages for the pension fund. In case they had received a pension for less than ten years, their indemnity would be calculated by capitalizing at compound interest at 7% the total of payments made by them or of stoppages of wages for the pension fund. For invalids the amount of indemnity was to be ten times the amount of the annual pension.

This indemnity for pensions was to be paid in the same way as the other payments under the Plan of Payment. The decision was transmitted by the national members of the Commission to the two governments for their observations. It was understood that in case no objection should be formulated, the decision was to stand as accepted.

[43] Procès-Verbaux, xvii, 314th meet., December 24, 1926.
[44] Procès-Verbaux, viii, 148th meet., August 27, 1923, p. 968.

The two governments formulated no objections and this decision went into effect. It proved defective and inadequate.

First, with regard to the persons admitted to its benefits: (*a*) it dealt only with employees of the state and not with those of other public administrations, such as communes; (*b*) it concerned specifically only persons emigrating after the coming into effect of the Convention and not persons who had emigrated before that time; and (*c*) it was restricted to persons who at the time of the declaration of emigration enjoyed the right to a pension allowance, and left out persons who had already made payments or allowed stoppages out of salaries for the benefit of the pension fund.

Secondly, with regard to the loss of the right to a pension allowance in exchange for a right to indemnity. (*a*) The decision provided that the right to the pension was lost from the date of filing the declaration of emigration. Many emigrants did not leave the country until long after the filing of their declaration of emigration. During that time they did not receive the pension allowance, neither were they paid the indemnity. (*b*) It was provided that the monthly payments of pension allowance made to the emigrant after the filing of the declaration of emigration were to be deducted from the amount of indemnity. It happened that sometimes these deductions not only swallowed up the amount of the indemnity but made the beneficiary a debtor to the state. (*c*) As the indemnity was payable in the same way as other property of emigrants under the Plan of Payment, beneficiaries were to receive 10% in cash and 90% in bonds. In view of the depreciation of the bonds by 25 to 50% of their normal price, the beneficiary was unable to obtain in an insurance company in his new country an annuity equal to his pension.

Thirdly, the decision provided that the indemnity for invalids was to be ten times the amount of the annual pension. The term 'annual pension' was interpreted in one of the states to mean the initial pension allowance without the increases granted later on account, for instance, of the depreciation of the currency.[45]

[45] Procès-Verbaux, xxxii, 465th meet., December 1, 1928, annex 1.

The neutral members of the Commission agreed with the Greek member that the above decision ought to be revised.[46] A draft arrangement prepared by the Financial Committee of the League at the request of the neutral members of the Mixed Commission and submitted by these members to the Commission on December 1, 1928,[47] proposed the sound principle that emigrants "entitled at the time they left their country of origin to a pension allowance, had the right to continue receiving such pension in their new country." It also defined 'pensions' as including old age and invalid pensions granted by the state or other public administration, pensions of widows and orphans, as well as permanent, temporary, or exceptional allowances which by virtue of the laws were granted to persons to supplement their ordinary pensions.

The question of pensions was of concern to Greek emigrants from Bulgaria much more than to Bulgarian emigrants from Greece. There were only 54 claimants among the latter, mostly dependents of soldiers. Greek claimants from Bulgaria were 321. After repeated postponements, this question came up at last for final decision in July, 1930.[48] The following decision was then adopted, abrogating the decision of August 27, 1923:

> The emigrants entitled at the time of emigration to a pension allowance will receive a paid-up pension indemnity in their new country. This will be appraised by the Mixed Commission. There are included among the pensioners those emigrants who, being in a position to obtain a pension, were refused it for the sole reason that they were emigrants. Each state is to credit the other with an amount equivalent to the total value of paid-up pension indemnities fixed by the Mixed Commission.

The Mixed Commission then fixed the total amount of paid-up indemnities at the charge of the Bulgarian government at 8,874,375 drachmas and that at the charge of the Greek government at 1,619,375 drachmas.

[46] Procès-Verbaux, xxxii, 465th meet., December 1, 1928, p. 13; 466th meet., December 11, 1928, p. 9.
[47] *Ibid.*, annex No. 1.
[48] Procès-Verbaux, xl, 559th meet., July 22, 1930.

CHAPTER XIV

THE LIQUIDATION

§ 179. Final stages of the liquidation. After the property rights of emigrants had been established by the Sub-Commissions, the landed property measured by the surveyors, and the decisions as to the appraised value taken by the proper agencies, all the data necessary for the final liquidation were collected. Yet before the final decision of the Mixed Commission to issue the order for liquidation, there was still work to be done by various agencies. The files of each emigrant and of each village were to be compiled, audited, and submitted to the Reporting Committee and the Mixed Commission. After the vote of the Mixed Commission there was the final work to be done by the Liquidation Service. All these matters will be considered in this chapter.

I. Compiling Services

§ 180. Work of the compiling services. Article 59 of the Rules provided that after the communication of the decision of the Sub-Commission to the emigrant, the Secretary of the Sub-Commission was to set up a file relative to the appraisal of the properties which this decision concerned. The file was to contain: (1) the application for liquidation and the declaration of emigration; (2) the report relative to the appraisal by the Sub-Commission; (3) the notes of the members of the Sub-Commission; (4) the objections of the emigrants, or a note from the Secretary that there were no such objections; (5) the objections of third parties; (6) the titles or other documents establishing the property rights of the emigrant; (7) a certificate of the notary public or other authority showing that the property was free from mortgage or attachment; (8) a certificate of the National Bank and the Agricultural Bank of the country where the property was located that the emigrant owed them no debt; and (9) a certificate of the tax collector showing that the taxes were paid.

Following the many changes of the method of appraisal and liquidation adopted later, and, especially, the separation of the work into several operations, the number of documents comprised in a file increased. It was the duty of the Secretary or an under-secretary of each Sub-Commission to make up the file of each emigrant and to gather all the information relative to the objections, debts, etc.

Three compiling services were created at the three centres: Saloniki, Comotini, and Sofia. The materials furnished by the different agencies were collected by these services under the supervision of the Presidents of the Central Sub-Commissions and the Greek and Bulgarian representatives at the Centres. In order to speed up the work, after the fall of 1926,[1] the files were compiled by the application of a 'liquidation sheet.' On this were noted the name of the claimant in whose favor the property was liquidated; the details of the property recognized; its area as surveyed by the land surveyors; the category

[1] Procès-Verbaux, xvi, 294th meet., October 21, 1926, p. 1895.

in which the property was classified by the staff of agronomists; the unit prices fixed by the architects and their application to the buildings of the emigrant in question; and the prices given by agronomists and foresters to the properties in question. When the value of each rural property had been thus calculated on the sheet the amount of the appraisal of all the real property of the emigrant was found by addition.[2] Lastly, the indemnity due the emigrant, if any, was added, and the debts of the emigrant, and the taxes due by him, were deduced from the amount. The balance constituted the sum payable to the emigrant. The 'liquidation sheet' was made in four copies, one for the Mixed Commission, one for the archives of the Sub-Commission, one for Bulgaria, and one for Greece.[3] It was drawn up in French and signed by the Secretary or under-secretary of the Sub-Commission and the Greek representative in the Centre in Bulgaria or the Bulgarian representative in the Centres in Greece.

When completed, the files were checked, as will be seen later in this chapter, and were then sent to the Commission. They included a general file for each locality, comprising the minutes of the Sub-Commission, reports of the staffs of agronomists, appeals, experts' opinions, etc., and the individual files of each property owner.

The claims of about 138,000 emigrants from Bulgaria and Greece occasioned the setting up of about 48,000 files.

§ 181. Difficulties presented. From the nature of things, that is, from the separation of the work of liquidation among various agencies: surveyors, architects, staffs of agronomists, Sub-Commissions, Direction of Centres, etc., the compilation of the files became an arduous task and often fell behind. In the Centres of Sofia and Saloniki chiefs of the service of compiling files had been appointed. The work was complicated. Many omissions were found and questions of application or interpretation of decisions of the Commission with respect to each of the documents contained in a file needed solution. For

[2] Only in exceptional cases was the compiling of separate files for various properties of an emigrant permitted. Procès-Verbaux, xvii, 314th meet., December 23, 1926, p. 2095.

[3] Procès-Verbaux, xvii, 331st mt., March 30, 1927, p. 2283.

instance, the debts of an emigrant might not be listed; or the prices of buildings were to be modified in accordance with a decision of the Sub-Commission or of the neutral expert; or certain properties of the emigrant were noted as "unknown" or "boundaries lost" or "sold" and the fate of these properties was to be determined; or certain zones of a village were not classified and certain buildings were not appraised by the architects; or the trees which should be appraised were omitted, etc.[4] The Commission decided [5] that the chiefs of the compiling service at each Centre were to have power to decide all questions necessary for the completion of the files. In case they should find that a decision of the Sub-Commission or the staff of agronomists was missing, they were to convene the Greek and Bulgarian representatives in a Committee qualified to take proper steps.[6]

§ 182. Neutrals blamed for slowness of work. The Greek and Bulgarian members of the Commission agreed on a plan for the compiling of the files which was calculated, in their view, to accelerate the work. The compiling of the files of Bulgarian emigrants in the Centres of Saloniki and Comotini was to be left to the responsibility of the Bulgarian delegation and that of the files in the Centre of Sofia to the responsibility of the Greek delegation. An observer of the other delegation would be in each Centre to watch the operation of the service. A neutral arbiter would also be appointed in each Centre, to solve alone all questions referred to him by the chief of the service or the observer. When fully made up, the files would be submitted to the auditing service and thence go to the Mixed Commission.

Unfortunately, their view was not shared by the neutral members of the Commission, who detected in this proposal a certain reproach to the Commission and to its neutral agents charged hitherto with the completion of the files. There is no doubt that the Greek and Bulgarian members were dissatisfied with the slowness of the compiling service. Whether the neu-

[4] Procès-Verbaux, xxv, 400th meet., February 14, 1928, annex No. 3.
[5] Procès-Verbaux, xxiv, 395th meet., January 21, 1928, p. 4.
[6] The sort of decisions taken by the chief of the compiling service is seen in Procès-Verbaux, xxx, 440th meet., annex 1.

tral members of the Commission were justified in defeating the desire of the representatives of the two countries to have the work completed as soon as possible and to allow no further delays, is very questionable. The President of the Commission resorted again in this instance to the curious argument that the neutral members of the Commission were responsible to the Council of the League of Nations which had appointed them, and could not leave the responsibility of the work to the two delegations.[7]

The neutral chiefs of the service, who were retained, supervised the work of the various staffs occupied with compiling files in each Centre. Each of the Sub-Commissions had its own staff. Thus in the winter of 1928 there were six staffs in the Centre of Saloniki, one staff at Comotini, and four staffs at Sofia.[8]

In order to secure a greater efficiency in the work of compiling, which always lagged, it was suggested by Colonel de Reynier that premiums be granted to the staffs. This suggestion was eventually adopted by the Commission.[9]

II. Verification Services

§ 183. Work of verification. In June, 1925, a Section of Verification of the Files was created at the Secretariat of the Mixed Commission, for the purpose of verifying the various documents of the files before the submission of the files to the Reporting Committee. Soon afterwards experience showed the necessity of decentralizing this service. The chief of the service, Mr. de Tarnovsky, was successively sent to Saloniki, Comotini, and Sofia, and this system of verification at the Centres proved most practical.[10]

Subsequently, at the proposal of the Greek and Bulgarian members of the Commission, Mr. Tarnovsky was nominated

[7] Procès-Verbaux, xxiv, 396th meet., January 25, 1928, pp. 1 ff.; 397th meet., January 27, 1928, pp. 2 ff.

[8] Procès-Verbaux, xxv, 400th meet., February 14, 1928, p. 4.

[9] Procès-Verbaux, xxvi, 409th meet., April 4, 1928, pp. 2 ff. and annex; xxvii, 415th meet., May 7, 1928, p. 8.

The premiums were paid on the number of files completed and transmitted to the Commission in perfect state.

[10] Procès-Verbaux, xiv, 255th meet., February 25, 1926, p. 1640; xv, 273d meet., July 24, 1926, p. 1760.

inspector of the service of verification. He had the technical direction of the three staffs of checkers, consisting each of a Greek and a Bulgarian functionary and established at each of the three Centres.[11] The Director of each Centre delivered to these functionaries the files for verification.[12]

The verification followed the completion of the files. The completed files were transmitted to the verification service. The business of that service was to verify the application of the decisions. The Bulgarian and Greek checkers were deemed to be 'neutral' employees, that is, their duty was to make a statement of all errors or omissions found by them. In case of temporary absence of one of them, the verification was pursued by the other so long as no substitute was designated by the interested Representative at the Centre. The staff conferred directly with the President or Secretary of the competent Sub-Commission for the correction of the errors or omissions. In case of disagreement on a proposed correction, the disputed points were examined by the Inspector; in case of conflict between the latter and the President of the Sub-Commission, the Director of the Centre intervened. The Inspector alone might refer the case to the Mixed Commission.[13]

The Inspector was mainly responsible for conformity between the description of the properties and the corresponding decisions of the appraisal: the exactness of the distribution of properties owned by several persons, the accuracy of the area assigned to each property, etc. An important subject of verification was the correspondence between the local tariff adopted by the architects and the individual appraisals of each building in a village, in view especially of the fact that the decisions of the Sub-Commissions referred only to the local tariff. The

[11] The technical direction of the service of verification belonged to the Directors of the Centres from April 2, 1927. Procès-Verbaux, xviii, 382d meet., p. 2300.

[12] Procès-Verbaux, xv, 274th meet., July 28, 1926, p. 1762. A second staff for the Centre of Sofia was created, March 31, 1928 (Procès-Verbaux, xxvi, 408th meet., pp. 23-24), in order to speed up the work at this Centre, which progressed very slowly. Against the combined vote of the Greek and Bulgarian members, the Commission decided later that, at the direction of the neutral members, the Inspector could proceed, by himself, to the verification of the files in lieu of the Bulgarian and Greek checkers. See Procès-Verbaux, xvi, 302d meet., November 20, 1926, pp. 1970, 1973.

[13] Procès-Verbaux, xv, 282d meet., August 20, 1926, p. 1807.

architects were directed by the Commission to give sufficient indications in the individual appraisals to permit their comparison with the local tariff by the service of verification.[14]

The files, verified as above, were transmitted, by order of the Inspector, under seal to the Director of the Centre, who saw to their secure transmission to the Mixed Commission.

The processes of completion and verification of files remedied the defects, omissions, or errors observed in the work of the agencies of establishment of rights and appraisal of properties, and rendered rare the cases where the Mixed Commission had to send back the files to the Centres or Sub-Commissions.[15]

III. The Reporting Committee

§ 184. Functions of the Reporting Committee. The files of a whole village, duly compiled and verified, were transmitted to the Mixed Commission. On their receipt, they were registered with the Secretariat, in accordance with article 60 of the Rules and were taken up by the Commission in the order of registration. In exceptional cases, certain files were discussed out of the regular order.

The roll of liquidations was posted at the Secretariat of the Mixed Commission and the Sub-Commissions. All the procedure before the Mixed Commission was in writing. The interested parties could not ask to be heard orally.

From the end of the summer of 1926 [16] a Reporting Committee was created at the Mixed Commission with the view of lightening the work of the latter. This Committee was composed of the neutral member of the Commission, or a substitute designated by him, and representatives of the members of the Commission appointed by the two countries. The Secretariat submitted the files to this Committee. The discussion in it did not deal with the individual files, but with the village

[14] Procès-Verbaux, xx, 352d meet., June 30, 1927, pp. 8-9.

[15] See such cases, prior to the creation of the services of completion and verification of files, in Procès-Verbaux, xii, 237th meet., August 4, 1925, p. 1490; 238th meet., p. 1493; 244th meet., November 3, 1925, p. 1571; 246th meet., p. 1572; xiii, 252d meet., February 3, 1926, pp. 1599 ff.; xiv, 254th meet., February 18, 1926, pp. 1630, 1631.

[16] Procès-Verbaux, xv, 278th meet., August 10, 1926, pp. 1785-86.

in general. Sometimes a coefficient of increase or reduction of the prices of each file was agreed upon. In case the Committee was unanimous, whether an appeal had been previously taken or not, the liquidation order (*bon à liquider*) was issued by the Committee. Note of this was taken by the Mixed Commission later. But such cases were very rare.

IV. The Mixed Commission

§ 185. Decisions of liquidation. In general, the neutral Chairman of the Reporting Committee reported the files of each village to the Commission. The latter discussed once more all the questions raised before the agencies of the Commission and the Reporting Committee; the establishment of rights, the surveying of lands, the appraisals of lands and of buildings, etc. The discussion was of a rather academic and idle character. Rarely was any change made. On technical questions of appraisal the Commission adopted the reports of its neutral experts. On all other questions the President accepted the views of the neutral member who was Chairman of the Reporting Committee, and the two constituted a majority in the Commission. However, the Greek and Bulgarian members read notes of many pages and argued on their views.

The neutral members were never able to obtain a unanimous vote on the final liquidation of any village. Both the interested members would vote against the proposals of the neutral members, and often both would protest against the decisions taken by the majority vote of the two neutrals. The Commission was not a judicial body of four disinterested members. The members representing the two governments were two lawyers whose arguments were always contradictory and irreconcilable. The two neutrals usually had to make a compromise between the two opposing parties, both of whom naturally protested.

The decision of the Mixed Commission stated that a liquidation order (*bon à liquider*) was to be issued for the files whose lists were annexed to the minutes of the meeting. Whenever a coefficient of increase or reduction of the prices of each file was adopted, the liquidation order was issued after the coefficient in question had been applied on the prices. Extracts from the decisions were communicated to the government on the territory of which the properties under liquidation were situated, and to the interested parties.

V. Liquidation Service

§ 186. Organization of the service. Following the decision of the Mixed Commission the files were transmitted to the liquidation service.

This service formed, at first, a part of the Secretariat of the Commission, and its working left much to be desired. The Director of the Financial Section of the Secretariat of the League of Nations, Sir Arthur Salter, and the Société Anonyme Fiduciaire Suisse advised a reorganization of this service. By a decision of November 11, 1926, the Commission asked the above-named institution to put at its disposal a high functionary, who was to study the whole of the auditing operations of the Commission.[17] The Vice-Director of the Société, M. Würmli, came to Sofia in the first days of December, and, after a study of the organization and work of the Commission and the Sub-Commissions, presented a report to the Commission on the general lines of a simplified system of the liquidation service. It was agreed that a functionary having control of the service of liquidation and accounting of the Secretariat should be appointed, and that a candidate should be proposed by the Swiss Company to serve under its responsibility.[18] The Société Anonyme Fiduciaire Suisse agreed to undertake the direction of the service of liquidation and the supervision of the internal accounts of the Commission, and to hold itself responsible for any error due to a professional omission and for all material consequences of such error. M. Brönimann, a reviser of the Swiss Company, was appointed to the charge of the direction and supervision, and took up his duties on February 1, 1927.[19]

[17] Procès-Verbaux, xvi, 300th meet.. pp. 1934, 1936.

[18] Procès-Verbaux, xvi, 307th meet., December 10, 1926, p. 2047; 312th meet., December 17, 1926, p. 2076; 313th meet., December 18, 1926, p. 2085; 314th meet., December 23, 1926, p. 2094.

[19] Procès-Verbaux, xvii, 317th meet., January 22, 1927, p. 2118; 319th meet., February 3, 1927, p. 2134.

§ 187. **Work of the service.** The service of liquidation was charged, in particular, with (*a*) the deduction of the debts of emigrants to the state or to third parties; and (*b*) the preparation of the memoranda of liquidation (*bordereau de liquidation*) which were sent to the two governments and served to specify the liquidated properties and to indicate the sums which were to be paid in cash and in bonds. These memoranda served also as liquidation accounts. In connection with decisions of liquidation concerning community properties, the question arose, in view of the failure of the Commission to reach a decision on the questions of principle regarding communities, in whose name the instruments of payment should be issued. The Commission adopted here, as in other matters concerning community properties,[20] a provisional decision. The orders of payment were issued by the liquidation service in the name of the particular communities or institutions of such communities, and were placed in the hands of the government of the state to which the members of such communities had emigrated to be kept by it pending a final decision in the matter.[21] Following the advisory opinion of the Permanent Court of International Justice, the Commission was to decide on the persons entitled to receive, as members of communities dissolved by reason of the emigration, the proceeds of the liquidation of community properties.

The service of liquidation was also charged with two important tasks. It calculated the interest due an emigrant on his credit account resulting from the liquidation of his property, and the indemnities, revenues, or rents to which he was entitled. It also converted the credit account to dollars for the purpose of payment to the emigrant.

§ 188. **Calculation of interest.** As regards the calculation of interest the Plan of Payment, adopted in August, 1926,[22]

[20] See *supra,* p. 173.

[21] Procès-Verbaux, xxi, 357th meet., August 4, 1927, pp. 5-6; xxii, 367th meet., September 23, 1927, pp. 8-9. Instruments of payment were, for instance, issued in the name of the "Church of the village of Karydia," "School of the village of Tchobankeoy," "Building lands and forests of the village of Dervent," etc. etc.

[22] Although the plan of 1926 was not approved by the two governments, its provisions on calculation of interests and on conversion of the liquidation

distinguished between credits on which interest was due, according to decisions of the Mixed Commission, from a date prior to the date of the decision of liquidation, and credits on which interest was due after such date. In the first case, the interest was calculated at 6% on the total credit in dollars from the date of loss of possession of the property by the emigrant until the beginning of the current half-year. The amount of the interest was added to the credit. In the second case, after the credit of the emigrant was divided into the 10% cash payment and the 90% payable in 'provisional bonds,' the interest of these bonds was calculated for the months between the beginning of the half-year during which the decision of liquidation was taken and the date at which the possession was lost to the emigrant. The amount obtained in this way was subtracted from the part of the credit payable in cash.[23]

The emigrant was considered to have lost the enjoyment of his property prior to the decision of liquidation, and was therefore entitled to receive interest on the liquidation price of his property when such property was occupied by the refugees or placed in possession of the state. The date of loss of possession was the date of departure from the country of origin in the latter case, and the date of occupation by the refugees in the former case, if this preceded the departure of the emigrant. A former emigrant, owner of a property of which he had lost possession, was considered to have lost the enjoyment on January 1, 1925.[24]

An emigrant who left his country of origin after the liquidation of his property, or who, having left before such liquidation, did not permit the taking possession of his property by the state or refugees,[25] or who remained in or retook possession of the property until the liquidation, was considered to have lost the enjoyment of his property on the first day of the second month following the decision of liquidation.

amount had formed the subject of previous decisions of the Commission and were applied by it.

[23] Plan de Payments, decision 2; see also Procès-Verbaux, xiv, 258th meet., March 11, 1926, p. 1667.

[24] See on this a decision of the Commission in Procès-Verbaux, xi, 206th meet., November 1, 1924, pp. 1282-85.

[25] For instance, by renting his property to a non-emigrant.

From that date the interest was due on the 'provisional bonds' received in payment for his property. In case, however, such an emigrant had a legitimate reason for continuing to remain in possession of his property—for instance, the purpose of harvesting or vintage—he could ask that a date be set subsequent to the first day of the second month following the decision of liquidation. The Commission, if it deemed such a request justifiable, fixed that date as the date of loss of enjoyment of the property by the emigrant. And in such case, the interest on the bonds for the months during which the owner emigrant remained in possession of the property was subtracted, as mentioned above, from the part of the liquidation amount payable in cash to the emigrant.

All payments made to an emigrant on account of revenues, rents, indemnities, and so forth, being included in the amount payable in provisional bonds, were considered as bearing interest from the first day of the second month following the decision of payment, and therefore no calculation of interest was made by the service of liquidation on their account.

§ 189. **Conversion of liquidation amount.** The second task of the service of liquidation was the conversion of the liquidation amount from the currency of the country of origin to dollars and from dollars to the currency of the country of immigration. The rate of conversion, which is the important element in this respect, was determined by a series of decisions of the Mixed Commission which need to be analyzed.

As we have said in another connection, the authors of the tariff of prices for lands, in fixing the prices for Bulgaria and Greece in leva and drachmas respectively, had, of course, in their minds the actual value of these moneys at the time of the establishment of the tariff. They took care to indicate that at that time the rate of exchange was 139 leva for one dollar and 62.8 drachmas for one dollar. It is clear that if the value of the drachma and leva should fall in subsequent times, the prices fixed by the tariff in these moneys did not represent the value and the purchasing power estimated by the authors of the tariff, and that an increase of the prices corresponding to the depreciation of the money should be made. The relation also between the drachma and the leva, which the authors of the tariff took into consideration, was liable to change. It was thought then that these difficulties would be overcome if the liquidation price of emigrants' properties should be converted into dollars.

§ 190. Rate of conversion. The rate of conversion was determined by decisions of the Commission,[26] the substance of which was annexed to the Plan of Payment adopted August 14, 1926. In case the appraisal was made in gold, the conversion in dollars was made at par. In case the appraisal was made in paper money, the conversion in dollars followed these rules:

1. In case the Commission affirmed the decision of appraisal of the first instance (Sub-Commission, staff of agronomists, staff of foresters, etc.), or if it modified it, basing its modification on the established facts and reports of experts on which the decision of first instance was founded, the rate of conversion was the following:

   (*a*) If the decision concerned lands, the average of the average rates of the six months preceding the drawing up of the tariff.

   (*b*) If the decision concerned buildings and building lands, the average of the average rates of the six months preceding the report of the expert.

   (*c*) If the decision of appraisal referred both to lands and to buildings (or building lands), the Commission adopted a distinct rate of conversion for each category of property.

2. In case the Commission modified the price adopted by the decision of the first instance, basing its action on new data, it adopted as the rate of exchange the average of the monthly average rates of the six months preceding the date of the report of the expert attached to the Mixed Commission.

3. In the case of credits arising from the restitution of revenues or rentals, the rate of conversion was the average of

[26] Procès-Verbaux, viii, 167th meet., pp. 1057-60; xiv, 267th meet., June 12, 1926, p. 1722; and xv, 271st meet., July 21, 1926, p. 1748.

the monthly average rates of the six months preceding the decision of payment of the Mixed Commission.

As will be seen, the credit balance of the liquidation account of emigrants was divided into two parts, one of 10% payable to the emigrant in cash, and another of 90% payable in bonds. The cash payment was made in dollars, as it resulted from the aforesaid conversion. The 90% was to be paid in bonds issued in the national money of the country of immigration. This 90% of the dollar credit balance was converted into that money (drachmas or leva) by taking as the rate of conversion the average of the monthly average rates of the six months preceding the decision of liquidation.

These rules were adopted by unanimous decisions of the Commission, and seem to be sound in attempting to give to the liquidation price a value free from the fluctuations of the national currencies. By taking the monthly average rates of six months and calculating the average of these rates, the conversion from the national money to the dollar followed as closely as possible the true value of the money. The six months on whose monthly average rates of exchange the rate of conversion was based, were differently defined in the case of lands and in the case of buildings (or building lands).

In the first case, the six months preceding the establishment of the tariff of prices were taken into consideration for calculating the rate of conversion. This was fair, since the tariff of prices for lands was established by its authors, as mentioned above, by taking into account the prices of lands during the six months preceding its establishment and a fixed relation between the leva and the drachma. Besides, the tariff was rigidly applied by the staff of agronomists, who also determined the classification of the lands and the coefficients of increase and reduction on the basic prices. The rate of conversion of the price of lands was, accordingly, fixed by the Commission at 60.08 drachmas for a dollar, which was the average, calculated as above, of the six months preceding the month of August, 1925, when the tariff was drawn up.

In the case of buildings and building lands, to quote the

President of the Commission, "the tariffs of prices were established by the expert architects in Bulgaria and Greece. But these tariffs are not of the same character as the tariff of lands. They do not give fixed and invariable prices like those fixed for the various categories of lands. Their formulas allow variable factors, for which the expert has always the power to propose modifications of the prices and justify them by considerations of place and time. The date of the establishment of these tariffs does not play, therefore, the same role as that of the tariff of lands." [27] Since, therefore, the value of buildings and building lands was determined by the architects, according to the data gathered by them in each place at the moment of their visit in each locality, it was rightly decided that the six months preceding the date of the report of the architect should constitute the basis for calculating the rate of conversion. It should be recalled that while the tariffs of prices for buildings were established by the architects in 1925, the actual expert appraisals of each village by the expert architects were made in 1926, 1927, and 1928, and the rates of exchange in these various periods were not at all alike.

§ 191. Modification of the rate for buildings. But this rule for the conversion of the prices of buildings and building lands was modified by a decision of the Commission taken July 9, 1927,[28] under conditions which occasioned great protests from one of the national members of the Commission.

In the first days of July, 1927, the Secretariat circulated a draft plan concerning the rate of conversion of buildings. This draft was presented under the form of a proposal "aiming at simplifying the work of the service of liquidation." As explained by the President of the Commission, Colonel Corfe, at the meeting of July 9, in view of the different times at which the buildings or building lands of an emigrant were appraised by expert architects, it might happen that the service of liquidation had to apply two, three, or four rates of conversion for the same file. Now, it should be pointed out immediately that such cases were rare. The expert architects

[27] Procès-Verbaux, xiv, 267th meet., June 12, 1926, p. 1721.
[28] Procès-Verbaux, xx, 353d meet., pp. 4-5.

when visiting a locality made a report of appraisal on all the buildings of such locality. It is only in case of owners possessing buildings in various localities, or of repeated visits of architects in a certain important locality, that appraisals of buildings of the same file were made at different periods. On the assumption, however, that the existing situation was complicated, the President of the Commission proposed that the service of liquidation should adopt a single conventional rate of conversion of the appraisal price of all properties of emigrants.

Mr. Stavroff, the expert architect, who made the appraisals of buildings in Bulgaria, on being consulted on the proposed innovation, declared that the adoption of a conventional single rate of conversion *would not present any inconvenience,* so far as Bulgaria was concerned. The same view was expressed by M. Savoie, the neutral expert architect attached to the Commission for the appraisal of buildings in Greece.[29] It should be noted that these experts merely declared that no inconvenience would result, and that they were thinking, in general, of a conventional single rate of conversion and not of a particular rate. Besides, Mr. Stavroff's appraisals were made and completed for almost the whole of the localities of emigration in Bulgaria before the end of the year 1925, so that the question of appraisals at different epochs, and, consequently, of the influence on such appraisals of the fluctuations of the value of the leva did not arise.

Under such conditions, the President of the Commission, Colonel Corfe, the same who at the 267th meeting of June 12, 1926, had differentiated, in the terms quoted above,[30] the case of lands and of buildings for the purpose of conversion of the prices of appraisal into dollars, proposed the following decision: "The rate of conversion of credits relative to buildings and building lands shall be that which is fixed by the decision of the 267th meeting for the conversion of credits relative to lands." This decision was adopted unanimously. The Greek member was absent from Sofia at that time and a secretary

[29] Letter of the President No. 9521, of June 27, 1927, and reply of M. Savoie under date of June 29, 1927.

[30] See *supra*, pp. 277-278.

sat in his place.[31] The latter did not realize the effect of the decision, being, the Greeks contended, misled by the anticipation of simplification of the work of liquidation on which the modification was based.

§ 192. **Consequences of the change.** This change of the rules of conversion of prices of buildings may, indeed, have meant a simplification. But it meant something else besides. The rate of conversion fixed by the decision of the 267th meeting (June 12, 1926) for the prices of lands was 60.08 drachmas for one dollar. In 1926 the value of the dollar in Greece fluctuated between 70.10 and 83.74 drachmas, and in the first seven months of 1927 between 83.48 and 75.60.

Thus, suppose the case of a village in Greece whose buildings and building lands were appraised by the architects in July, 1926, at 1,000,000 drachmas. According to the prior rule as to the conversion of this amount in dollars, the average of the monthly average rates of the six months preceding July, 1926, that is, 75.30 drachmas to a dollar, would be the rate of conversion. The 1,000,000 drachmas would be converted into $13,280. With the new rule of 'simplification,' the rate of conversion being 60.08 drachmas for a dollar, the 1,000,000 drachmas would be converted into $16,644. That is, the Greek treasury, for the sake of simplification, was made to pay an extra $3,364, or a difference of 25%. If the village was appraised in March, 1927, the 1,000,000 drachmas price would be converted into $12,470 according to the old or $16,644 according to the new method, an excess of $4,174, or 33.5%.[32]

Now, of course, Mr. Stavroff and M. Savoie may have declared that the adoption of a single conventional rate of

[31] M. de Reynier was also absent at this time, M. Lagrange, the Secretary-General of the Commission, being his substitute.

[32] Procès-Verbaux, xxi, 362d meet., August 25, 1927, annex no. i. A still more flagrant case of the strange results of this decision is the following: Take, for example, a building for which a price of 100,000 drachmas was given by the architect of the Sub-Commission. On appeal, the neutral expert architect of the Commission visits the village, finds the price of 100,000 drachmas excessive, and proposes a reduction of 10%. The Commission approves this reduction and the building is liquidated for 90,000 drachmas. Under the new decision for conversion, the 90,000 drachmas would be converted to dollars at the low rate of 60.08 drachmas for a dollar of 1925 and not at the rate of about 75 of 1927. The sum of dollars thus obtained would be worth 115,000 drachmas, that is, 15,000 drachmas more than the price that the neutral expert had considered excessive.

conversion would not cause any 'inconvenience,' but surely they did not mean that the results of both methods would be alike. Clearly, this was not a simplification alone. It was an increase of the appraisal of buildings by a coefficient which might reach as high as 33.5%.[33] It should be added that the chief of the service of liquidation, the person whose opinion should properly have been asked as to the effects of the proposed change, knew nothing of the proposal.[34]

The change contravened also the fundamental principle of the Convention, the Rules, and practically all relative decisions, that the basis of liquidation should be "the real value of properties at the time of liquidation." This phrase was understood by the Commission to mean the time of the visit of the agencies of appraisal in the village. When such visit and appraisal were made in 1926 or 1927, the adoption of a rate of conversion referring to the first half of 1925 was without any foundation. The protests of the Greek member would therefore seem entirely justified, and the consent of the Greek representative at the meeting at which this decision was taken could certainly not be held to have estopped the Greek member from protesting against a decision which was explicitly adopted for the sole purpose of simplification of the work of the service of liquidation.

Such crude arbitrariness, to call it nothing worse, was at the root of the loss of confidence in the fairness or wisdom of the proposals and attitude of the neutral members of the Commission, and was responsible in great measure for the partisan spirit and lack of good will shown by the Greek and Bulgarian members.

§ 193. Revision of the decision as to rate of conversion. According to a rule adopted at an early period [35] by the Com-

[33] The Greek member maintained that this increase might reach as high as 39%. Procès-Verbaux, xxii, 365th meet., September 1, 1927, pp. 4, 8.

[34] Procès-Verbaux, xxi, 362d meet., August 25, 1927, annex i, Letter to the President, August 23, 1927; also Procès-Verbaux, xxii, 365th meet., September 1, 1927, p. 20. At this last meeting, Colonel Corfe stated that the Chief of the Service of liquidation, M. Brönimann, was consulted on the change. This was denied by the Greek member, who declared that M. Brönimann had assured him of the opposite, and proposed that M. Brönimann be invited before the Commission to state the truth. This proposition was not supported by the neutral members.

[35] Procès-Verbaux, i, 11th meet., January 4, 1921, p. 49.

mission, a decision taken by it could not be modified subsequently, nor could the discussion thereon be reopened. In exceptional cases, however, a member of the Commission could send a memorandum to the President and the other members, setting forth a proposal for reconsideration and the reasons for it; at the first meeting of the Commission after three days from the delivery of the memorandum the President was to put to vote the question of reconsideration, and if three-quarters of the votes were in favor of the proposition, the discussion might be reopened.

The proposition of the Greek member to reopen the discussion on the above decision of July 9, 1927, obtained a unanimous favorable vote on September 1, 1927,[36] although it was placed on the agenda of the meeting of August 25. The Commission refused to take a vote on August 25 because of the refusal of the Greek member to sign certain liquidation accounts resulting from the application of the decision under question. It was his contention that the decision was so fundamentally wrong and defective that the Commission could not properly apply it, and that the discussion should be reopened immediately.[37] As the Greek member persisted in refusing to sign the liquidation accounts, the Commission decided unanimously that the discussion on the decision of July 9 should be reopened.

On the reopening of the discussion on September 1, 1927,[38] the Greek member took his position squarely on the established fact that the decision of July 9 was taken for the sole purpose of simplifying the work of the service of liquidation, and that its actual effect was an increase of the price of liquidation of buildings as high as 39%. Since the consequences of the decision were totally different from the anticipations upon which its adoption was based, the decision should be annulled.

[36] Procès-Verbaux, xxii, 365th meet., September 1, 1927, p. 1.
The Greek member, Mr. Gheorgopoulos, on his return to Sofia, realizing the effects of the decision of 'simplification' expressed orally to the President, on August 15, 1927, the reasons for which he asked the revision of the decision. On August 7 and 15, notes were addressed to the President by the Greek member.
[37] Procès-Verbaux, xxi, 362d meet., August 25, 1927, pp. 1 ff.
[38] Procès-Verbaux, xxii, 365th meet., pp. 7 ff.

Colonel Corfe and the Bulgarian member of the Commission looked at the question in a very different manner. They thought that the decision should be revised or annulled only if it proved to be inequitable and unjust. They argued, on the basis of the liquidation of twenty-three villages in Macedonia, that the architects did not give different prices in drachmas in 1926 or 1927 from 1925, and that, consequently, they were not influenced in their appraisals by the fluctuations of the exchange; that, on the contrary, Bulgarian emigrants from Greece, being paid in 1926 or 1927 prices in drachmas established in 1925, were in fact losing in the settlement, since the drachma had depreciated in those years; and that, consequently, the decision of July 9, 1927, tended to do justice to these emigrants by paying them an equivalent in dollars which was not affected by the loss of the value of the drachma.

The Greek member, drawn into this discussion, argued that the prices of the general tariff of buildings established in 1925 were so enormously high that it was only natural that, after the decision of the Commission to the effect that these were merely maximum prices, the architects should not exceed them. He cited on this point the opinion of M. Brönimann, Chief of the Service of Liquidation, namely, that the fact that the architects had not modified their prices, notwithstanding the depreciation of the drachma, was explained by the exaggerated prices of the tariff of buildings. Moreover, the question of injury to Bulgarian emigrants by the depreciation of the drachma had never been raised before, either by the Bulgarian or by the neutral members. The neutral members, now basing the decision of July 9 on grounds discovered or disclosed after its adoption, refused to consent to its revision. However, the President, M. de Reynier, made the reservation that he would continue the investigation of the question through the intermediary of the Delegate of the Mixed Commission at Saloniki, Mr. Saunders, and the Director of the Centre of Saloniki, Mr. Houssa.

This investigation was carried on by these neutral agents of the Commission through the following four months. In the latter part of December they submitted a very full report, which formed the subject of discussion by the Commission at its meeting of January 20, 1928.[39] The report justified to a very large degree the contention of the Greek member. It was concluded that the prices of the general tariff of buildings for Macedonia and Thrace exceeded the real prices of the market during the years 1925 and 1926 by 15%, and that, therefore, the rate adopted by the decision taken on July 9, 1927, should receive an equivalent reduction. In other words, the rate of conversion of 60.08 drachmas for a dollar should be changed to a rate of 67 drachmas for a dollar. On the other hand, the valuations made after November, 1926, when the Commission decided that the prices of the tariff were maximum prices, ceased to be excessive, since the drachma was depreciated; the appraisal prices, therefore, of this period should be converted into dollars according to the old rule, which took into consideration the rate of exchange during the six months preceding the report of the architect. It was proposed that this rate should be fixed at 75.65 drachmas per one dollar.

In view of these considerations and of the proportion of files appraised in the above two periods, the authors of the report proposed a single conventional rate of conversion of appraisal prices of buildings of 70.13 drachmas for one dollar. The Greek member, arguing from the facts cited in the report, concluded that the rate should be 73.50. On the contrary, the Bulgarian member was opposed to any change of the decision of July 9, 1927. A decision taken by the majority of the two neutral members over the protests of the two interested members fixed for the future liquidations the rates of conversion as follows:

For lands, 60 drachmas for one dollar.

For buildings and building lands, 70 drachmas for one dollar.

§ 194. Rate of conversion for forests. Following this decision, the question arose of the rate of conversion of appraised values of forests. The appraisal of forests was made for a time by the expert forester, M. Jaccard, alone, and later by a staff

[39] Procès-Verbaux, xxiv, 394th meet., January 20, 1928, pp. 2-36.

of foresters under the chairmanship of M. Jaccard. No tariff or definite methods of appraisal of forests were adopted by the Commission. The staff chose the methods deemed best by it. When the files of appraisal of small forests came to the Mixed Commission, the service of liquidation raised the question of the conversion of the appraisal figures. The Secretariat gave the opinion that forests were to be included in the category of lands, and that, therefore, the rate of 60 drachmas for a dollar should be applied. However, M. Jaccard sent a note to the Commission, stating that all the appraisals of forests were made in the two countries at the price of the date of appraisal and the nearest market, and that, as there was no tariff, no account was taken of the relation existing between the drachma and the leva.

At the request of the Greek member, the Commission took up the question of establishing a rate of conversion for appraisals of forests. It was admitted that the appraisals were now made in money which was stabilized in both countries, and that the Greek drachma for more than a year had been stable at the rate of 77 drachmas for one dollar. In view of this fact, and of Mr. Jaccard's statement that the appraisals were made with regard to the actual market prices, one must agree with the Greek contention that the rate of conversion for forests should be fixed at 77. The neutral members thought that the rate should be 70 drachmas for a dollar on the grounds, which are difficult to support, that forests were technically included in the category of lands, for which the rate of conversion was fixed at 60, and that the adoption of three various rates of conversion for lands, buildings, and forests, should be avoided. The consideration that forests may logically be put within the category of lands is without force, in view of the facts that lands were appraised according to a tariff adopted in 1925, while forests were appraised in the stable money prices of 1928. The complications to which three different rates of conversion for three different categories of properties would give rise were infinitesimal, in view of the small number of forest appraisals. The adoption, therefore, by the Commission of the rate of 70 drachmas for a dollar for forest appraisals seems altogether arbitrary and unjustifiable.[40]

§ 195. Statistics. The claims of 138,000 emigrants from Bulgaria and Greece gave rise to the formation of some 48,000 files. Of these 38,737 were examined by the Mixed Commission to April 30, 1929. They resulted, after cancellations and regrouping, in 34,298 liquidations, or 10,409 files of Greeks from Bulgaria and 23,889 files of Bulgarians from Greece. For each year the number of liquidations was as follows:

Years	*Greeks from Bulgaria*	*Bulgarians from Greece*
To 1925	4	3
1926	1050	1435
1927	3955	8341
1928	4684	12087
1929 (to March 31)	481	1381
	10,174	23,247

On April 30, 1929, the liquidations remaining to be done amounted to 4938 files of Greeks from Bulgaria and 5602 files of Bulgarians from Greece. The monthly output of the Mixed Commission is shown in the graph on the next page.[41]

In August, 1928, a request was addressed to the Commission by the Bulgarian member, referring to about 6000 new declarations of emigration involving 30,000 Bulgarians who had emigrated from Greece and who had declined to file declarations and avail themselves of the benefit of the Convention within the time-limit fixed by the Commission. It was outside of the competence of the Mixed Commission to decide whether the Commission should accept these declarations and liquidate the properties involved, and it was left to be determined by agreement between the two governments. The possibilities of such an agreement are considered elsewhere.[41a]

§ 196. Plans for total liquidation of remaining work. At the end of 1929 the work of establishment of property rights, of survey, and of appraisal of lands and buildings was nearly

[40] Procès-Verbaux, xxxi, 457th meet., November 15, 1928, pp. 1-8.

[41] This graph and the data cited above are borrowed from the Memorandum on the Mission and Work of the Mixed Commission on the Greco-Bulgarian Emigration, May, 1929, prepared by the neutral members of the Commission.

[41a] See *infra*, p. 723.

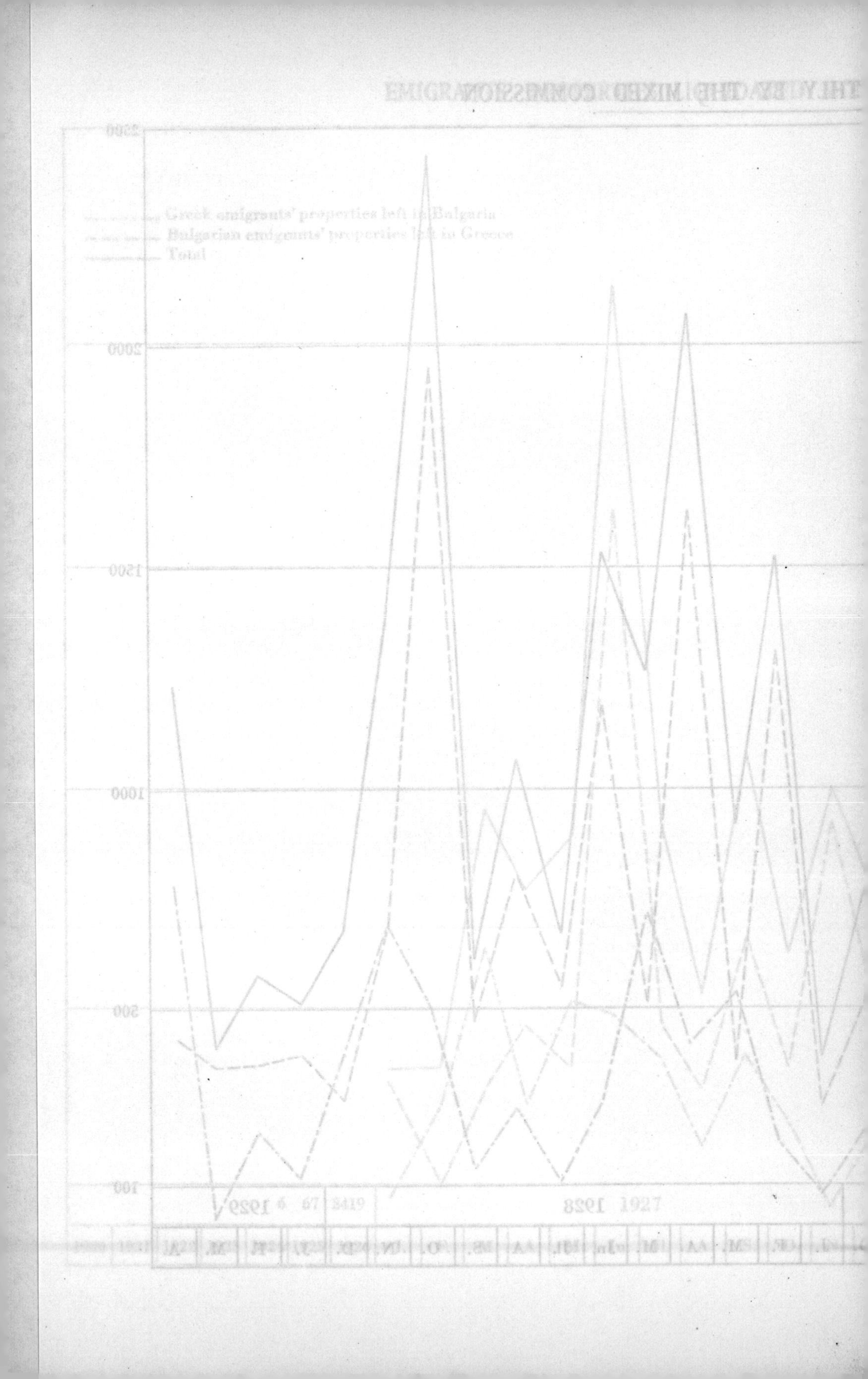
Greek emigrants' properties left in Bulgaria
Bulgarian emigrants' properties left in Greece
Total

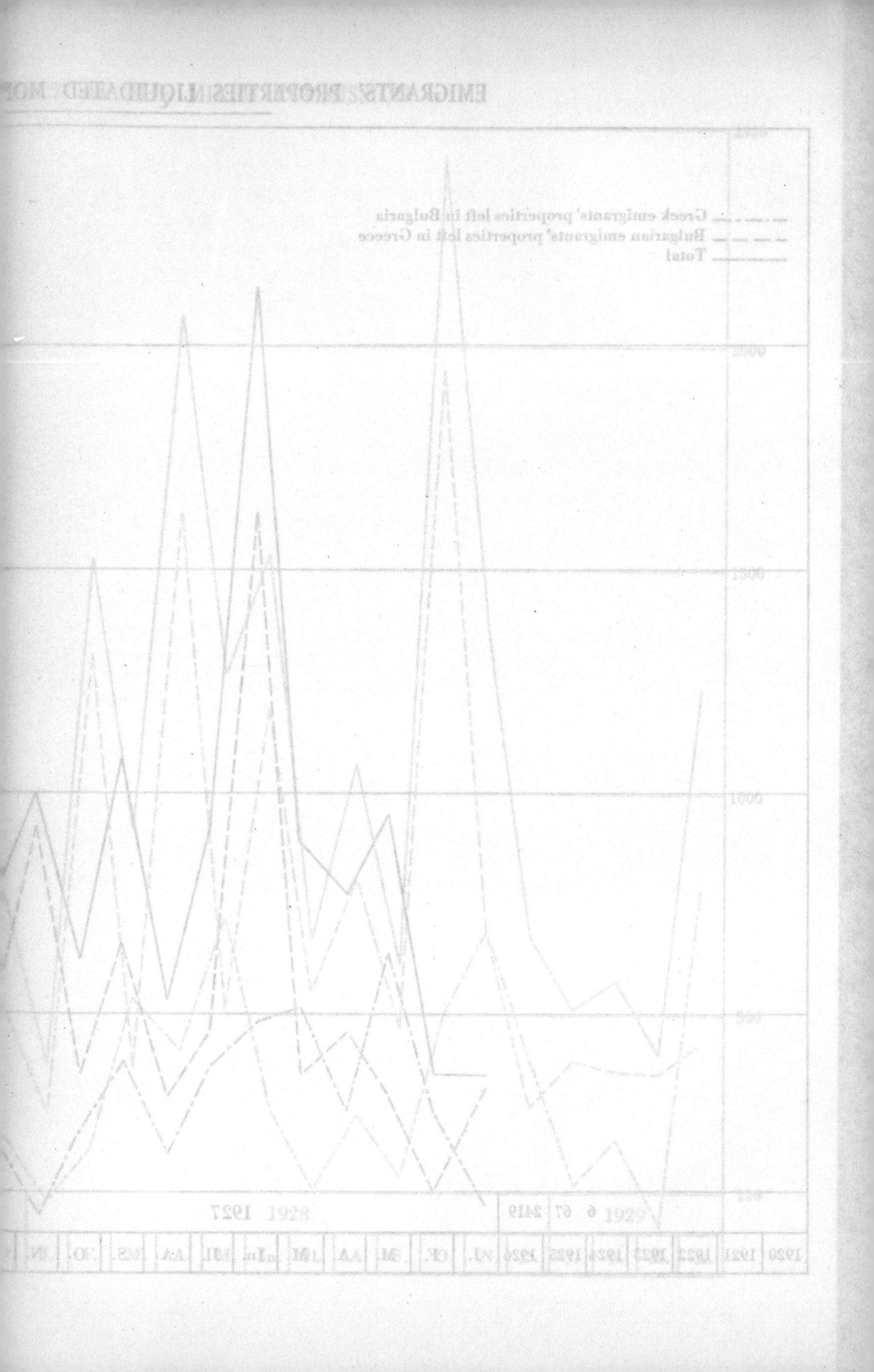

completed. Only the work of compiling the files remained in arrears. It was then decided to concentrate all the services of the Commission in Bulgaria and Greece at Athens on May 1, 1930,[42] with the view of effecting a fusion between the various services previously existing in Bulgaria and Sofia, and between them and the Secretariat of the Mixed Commission. This concentration took place on the date set, and the whole work previously done by the various agencies of the Commission was divided up between four services: (1) a Direction of the agencies of the Commission, something like the old Direction of the Centres; (2) a Service of File-Compiling for both countries; (3) a Sub-Commission for both countries; and (4) a delegation of the Mixed Commission at Sofia.[43]

As the original plan of the Commission that at the end of 1929 its work should be entirely finished did not materialize, the two neutral members in the last months of 1929 considered plans for a final liquidation of the remaining work. Each of the two neutral members deposited a plan on November 29, 1929.[44]

Colonel Corfe's plan took into consideration the fact that by the end of 1929 a total of

31,114 Bulgarian properties out of 32,693, and
15,180 Greek " " " 15,861,

would be liquidated, and that, consequently, 95% of the liquidations to be made would be completed. Besides this matter, the following questions needed solution:

1. That of the properties of communities.
2. The interpretation of the Caphandaris-Moloff Agreement, which, however, belonged to the Council of the League.
3. The question of pensions.
4. That of the revision of appraisals of certain properties.
5. That of supplementary applications for liquidation.

[42] Procès-Verbaux, xxxviii, 528th meet., December 21, 1929, p. 1; 531st meet., January 29, 1930, p. 14.
[43] Procès-Verbaux, xxxix, 540th meet., April 2, 1930, p. 18.
[44] Ibid., 518th meet., p. 6 and annexes.

Colonel Corfe queried whether all these questions could not be solved by a general solution.

He interpreted the points of view of the two governments as follows: The Bulgarians alleged that the value of Bulgarian properties left in Greece by Bulgarian emigrants was much greater than the value of properties left in Bulgaria by Greek emigrants, and that consequently the Bulgarian government should receive an important balance from the Greek. The Bulgarians feared that this balance would gradually be reduced as the work of liquidation went on. The Greeks, on the other hand, sought to reduce this balance by the revision of various appraisals, holding the view that the Bulgarian emigrants had been favored by the appraisals of the Commission. The Greeks wished to have all the properties of the communities liquidated, believing that the properties of Greek communities in Bulgaria were of a greater value than the properties of Bulgarian communities in Greece. The Bulgarians saw a political advantage in leaving the properties of their communities in Greece unliquidated, whereas the point of view of the Greeks was totally different.

The proposal of Colonel Corfe was to decide by arbitration the final amount of the balance due by the Greek government to the Bulgarian, after all liquidations should be discontinued at the end of February, 1930. The question of the properties of the communities was not to be examined by the Commission at all, and such properties were to pass definitively to the government of the country where they were situated. Similarly the questions of pensions, revisions, and supplementary liquidations were not to be touched upon by the Commission. Each country was to be free to determine such questions with its own nationals by the creation of a special service for this purpose.

M. de Reynier, in the counter-plan which he submitted, remarked that Colonel Corfe's plan went far beyond the province of the Mixed Commission, and predicated the amendment of the Convention and of the Caphandaris-Molloff Agreement, and also an agreement for submission to arbitration. So large a plan, he thought, was too difficult to carry out within a short time, and, therefore, it could not be hoped that the Mixed Commission could be dissolved within a limited space of time. He proposed, instead, that on December 31, 1929, the Commission should close provisionally the accounts between the two countries on the basis of the liquidations already made, in accordance with article 5 of the Caphandaris-Molloff Agreement.[45] As soon as this was done, the debtor state was to deliver the proper amount in checks to the neutral bank, as provided for by the said article 5. In the meantime the Commission would continue the liquidations. As soon as the provisions of article 5 were complied with, the Commission would decide on the amount of the appraisal for the liquidations still pending at the time, which would probably not exceed 1000 files. In the meantime, also, the question of the communities would either be referred to the Permanent Court of International Justice or decided upon by the Mixed Commission. The latter would also give a final solution to the question of revisions of liquidation decisions. Under such conditions, the Commission would then be able to determine the final balance of the account between the two governments, and would be in a position to dissolve.

Nothing came of these plans. At the time these lines are written (July, 1931) the Commission is still at work. No provisional balance of the accounts has yet been established. In the meantime the question of communities has been submitted to the Permanent Court of International Justice, which has rendered thereon its advisory opinion No. 17. The question of revisions of liquidation decisions on the ground of material errors causing losses to the treasuries of the two countries is probably to be solved soon.

In June, 1930,[46] the neutral members forced through a decision requiring the two governments to present lists of those liquidations made from the beginning to April 1, 1930, for which either government desired a revision. About 33,000 files had been liquidated to that date, and the two national members in the Commission protested that it was impossible

[45] See on this *infra*, p. 311.
[46] Procès-Verbaux, xl, 551st meet., June 12, 1930, pp. 6-10.

for them to present these lists by August 15, 1930, as the decision required. It is probable that the Mixed Commission will award a lump sum of money to one or the other government on account of liquidation decisions which should be revised.

CHAPTER XV

PAYMENTS UNDER THE CONVENTION

§ 197. Working out of the Plan of Payment. In the preceding chapter matters were carried to the stage where the liquidation service calculated the amount payable to the emigrant and converted the liquidation amount into dollars at the fixed rate of conversion. It is now necessary to describe the further action of this service, leading to the payment to emigrants and the regulation of the accounts between the two countries. Before this it is necessary to trace the history of the question of payments.

More than a year after the constitution of the Commission, it was decided to appoint one of the neutral members Rapporteur to conduct negotiations between the two governments and to prepare a Plan of Payment.[1] M. de Roover, as Rapporteur, carried on preliminary negotiations with the two

[1] Procès-Verbaux, iv, 75th meet., January 11, 1922, p. 516.

governments as to the principles on which the Plan was to be based. A draft was prepared by him on June 13, 1922.

There were two main financial problems at the threshold of the question of payments: the placing by each government at the disposal of the Commission of funds sufficient for the payment for emigrants' properties as soon as they were liquidated; and the exportation of such funds from the state of origin of the emigrants to the state of settlement. It was presumed that either the one or the other government would finally have to pay between one and two million dollars more than the other on account of liquidation of emigrants' properties. The Commission wished to make the burden of the two governments as little onerous as possible and at the same time protect the interests of the emigrants. With this double end in view the following principles were agreed upon:

(1) The two governments were not to be compelled to pay immediately the full value of the liquidated properties in cash. Only 10% was to be paid in cash and 90% in public bonds. But such bonds were to be guaranteed, so that their full nominal value should be preserved, and they were to be redeemed within a relatively short time.

(2) The two governments were to be responsible each for the bonds to be issued to emigrants from the country of the other. In this way, the emigrant would have nothing to do any longer with the government of the country which he left, and payments on the bonds were to be made by the government of his new country. This substitution made necessary guarantees of payment of the balance resulting from the adjustment of accounts between the two governments.

(3) A stable money was to be chosen for the credits between the states which the execution of the Convention would require. The American dollar was to serve for the conversion of such credits.

M. de Roover gained the adhesion of the Greek government to his draft Plan of Payment on July 15, 1922.[2] The Bulgarian government gave its approval on October 6, 1922,

[2] All this may be seen in Procès-Verbaux, v, 92d meet., February 23, 1922, annex; 95th meet., March 3, 1922, p. 95; vi, 107th to 111th meet., June 22 to July 15, 1922, pp. 750 ff., 759, 763 ff., 766.

subject, however, to three reservations: (1) that the mode of payment of the obligations of the one government to the other was definitively to be as provided in the draft; (2) that any debt between the two National Banks on account of cash payments was to be paid in bills payable in three months; and (3) that the sums due by one to the other government according to the Plan could not form the subject of any compensation or sequestration, either between the two states or between Bulgaria and any other state.

It was necessary also to secure the agreement of the Inter-Allied Commission in Bulgaria for the financial engagements that Bulgaria was to undertake under the Plan of Payment. The terms of the Treaty of Neuilly (article 132) raised certain difficulties and the Conference of Ambassadors had to intervene.

In the meantime a change of ministry took place in Greece, and the Minister of Foreign Affairs, Mr. Politis, wished to study the Plan in greater detail.[3] He requested certain modifications, and an agreement was obtained on new proposals of the Rapporteur, M. de Roover. Thus, the period for amortization of the bonds was increased from six to twelve years. The period for the payment of the bills representing the debts between the National Banks of the two countries was fixed at six months. A proposal of the Greek government to substitute for the guarantees of the bonds provided for in the Plan the guarantee of the National Bank of Greece or a deposit of gold bonds was referred to the Bulgarian government for its agreement.[4] At that time the Commission estimated that each of the two countries would have to pay finally to emigrants a sum between $1,500,000 and $3,000,000.

Subject to future agreement on such substitution of guarantees, the Plan of Payment was adopted unanimously by the Commission at its meeting of December 8, 1922.[5] The Plan was then approved by the two governments and promulgated in the official journals of the two countries. A number of its

[3] Procès-Verbaux, vi, 113th meet., November 7, 1922, pp. 773 ff. and annexes.
[4] Procès-Verbaux, vi, 126th meet., December 4, 1922, pp. 819 ff.
[5] Procès-Verbaux, vi, 127th meet., pp. 821, 827.

provisions were modified by subsequent decisions of the Commission.[6]

In this form it consisted of nineteen articles and governed the matter of payments until September, 1927, when the intervention of the Financial Committee of the League of Nations was sought, as the Plan was not wholly executed and in certain respects was not in accord with developments.

§ 198. General scheme of payments under the Plan. Article 2 of the Plan provided that the payments to emigrants dealt with by the Plan were on account of (1) principal claims, being the value of the properties liquidated by the Mixed Commission; and (2) secondary claims, comprising revenues, rents, and sale prices received by the Treasury and certain indemnities. These claims, expressed in the legal money of the country where the properties were situated, were converted into credits in dollars at the rate of conversion fixed by the Commission, and were due and payable to the persons entitled thereto as follows (articles 4 to 11 and 13 to 17):

Payments were made in cash and in public bonds. As a rule 10% of the amount due the emigrant was paid in cash. The Mixed Commission issued for such payment a check in dollars on the National Bank of the country in which the property was situated. This check was cashed in the currency of the country where it was paid at the rate of exchange of the day of its presentation. The Banks received the funds necessary for these cash payments from each government.

For the payments in public bonds, each of the two governments was substituted for the other. By this substitution the claim of each emigrant against the state whose territory he quitted was converted into a claim against the state whose subject he became. Simultaneously, each government became creditor of the other government for the total amount of the transferred debt.

The credit and debit accounts thus created between the two governments balanced each other partially; and the whole

[6] Procès-Verbaux, viii, 154th meet., September 28, 1923, p. 1009; 156th meet., October 26, 1923, p. 1017; ix, 171st meet., February 6, 1924, p. 1077; xiv, 258th meet., March 11, 1926, pp. 1667 ff.

deferred debt of the two governments to all the creditor emigrants was composed, in the last analysis of (1) the debt of each government to its new nationals, and (2) the debt of one of the governments to the other, and an identical debt of the latter to its new nationals, the amount of which was equal to the difference of the claims of the two groups of emigrants.

The deferred payments of 90% were made at the moment of liquidation of their properties to emigrants in the form of 'provisional bonds,' which were to be exchanged later for 'final bonds.' The provisional bonds issued by the state of settlement of the emigrants were distributed through the intervention of the Mixed Commission, which kept account of the bonds issued by each government. The provisional bonds bore interest at 6% from the date of the transfer of possession to the State in the properties liquidated by the Commission. The interest was payable semi-annually.

At the termination of the liquidation of all immovable property of emigrants, and after the issue of all the provisional bonds necessary for their payment, the Mixed Commission was to declare the accounts closed, and to invite the two governments to liquidate or fund their respective debts within three months. The two governments were either to pay in cash the value of the provisional bonds, or place under the control of an international financial organization fixed and sufficient revenues for the service of the debt represented by the provisional bonds. As soon as these revenues were determined the Commission was to replace the provisional with final bonds, or to transform the former to final bonds by appropriate inscriptions.

The final bonds were to yield interest at the rate of 6% per year and be redeemable within a short period, not exceeding 12 years, and beginning from July 1, 1926. The service of these bonds was to be insured by an annual revenue guaranteed as is said above.

The form of the provisional and final bonds, the privileges to be enjoyed by them in the country issuing them, and the duration of amortization of the final bonds, were to be determined by agreement between each of the governments and the Mixed Commission.

The bonds were to be accepted in place of money in certain categories of payments by the emigrant to the issuing government. In particular, they could be given in payment for properties which the possessors of the bonds wished to acquire from the state on whose territory they were settled; also, as a guaranty for all contracts entered into with such state.

§ 199. Accounts between the National Banks. At the time the Plan was drawn, it was believed that the emigration and liquidation would cause the export of funds from the one country to the other. Such export might be prohibited by the law. The Plan therefore authorized the export of cash payments under the Convention and of money coming from direct sale of properties or from personal economics. This export was to be made as follows. The National Banks of the two countries were to open mutually a credit in dollars, which was to be used for the benefit of emigrants. Bulgarian emigrants from Greece could deposit their money in drachmas at the National Bank of Greece and obtain a check in dollars on the National Bank of Bulgaria. The exchange was made at the average rate between the rate of purchase and the rate of sale of the day. The check was payable at the National Bank of Bulgaria at the average rate between the rate of purchase and the rate of sale of the day of presentation. Similar advantages were enjoyed by the Greek emigrants from Bulgaria.

At the beginning of each month the two Banks drew up a statement of mutual debits and credits, in dollars, resulting from the operations of the preceding month. The Bank having a credit balance received a 'provisional acknowledgment' (*reconnaissance provisoire*) for the amount of the balance. These acknowledgments were issued in dollars and bore interest at 6% yearly. They were to be liquidated and consolidated in the same way as the 'provisional notes' issued by the two governments for their mutual accounts.

§ 200. Accounts between the two governments. At the beginning of each month the Commission determined the amount of provisional bonds issued, at its request, during the preceding month by each of the two governments. Each government being creditor of the other to the extent of this amount, the Commission balanced the debit and credit accounts thus created between the two governments. For the amount of this balance the debtor state issued to the creditor state, through the intermediary of the Commission, a provisional note (*bon provisoire*) in dollars bearing 6% interest.

At the closing of the accounts, on the termination of the work of liquidation, the Commission was to determine the totals of the credits and debits between the two governments from the provisional notes and the capitalized interest thereon. The set-off between these debits and credits would give the final debt of the one of the governments to the other on liquidation accounts.

At the same time the Commission was to find, in agreement with the two National Banks, the totals of the credits and debits occasioned by the provisional acknowledgments issued by these Banks and the capitalized interests thereon.

The possible debt of the one state to the other in the liquidation accounts and the possible credit of its National Bank in the accounts between the Banks could be set off the one against the other. The resulting balance would constitute the final debt of the one government to the other or of the one Bank to the other. There was to be a direct agreement between each state and its National Bank with regard to the balance. The final debt between the governments or between the Banks was to be paid or funded, as seen below. The debtor country could not set off against this debt any other account pending between the two countries.

§ 201. Final liquidation of accounts. If the setting off referred to above should result in a final debt of the one Bank to the other, it was to be paid by the debtor Bank to the creditor Bank within three months from the closing of the accounts in checks in dollars bearing interest at 6% yearly, payable not later than three months from date.

If the one of the two governments should finally be found debtor to the other, it could pay this debt in a small number of annual payments according to a method to be agreed upon by the parties with the interposition of the Mixed Commission. In the absence of such agreement, the debtor government was bound within three months from the closing of the accounts to remit the amount of its debt to the creditor government in bonds to the bearer, in dollars, bearing 6% interest, and redeemable in six years beginning with the first of July, 1926. These bonds were to be payable, principal and interest, by check on New York. The interest, payable semi-annually, and the service of the bonds were to be guaranteed by sufficient revenues placed under the control of an international financial organization. In case the debtor government should obtain an external loan for the consolidation of its floating debt before the complete amortization of these bonds, it should be bound to redeem by anticipation the above bonds from the produce of such loan.

§ 202. **Guarantee funds.** Besides the fixed and sufficient revenues that each government was required to place under the control of an international financial organism as a guarantee of the obligations resulting from the Plan of Payment, it was further provided by the final article of the Plan that the liquidated properties of emigrants were to constitute in each of the two countries a special guarantee fund, from the time of the payment to emigrants in provisional bonds to the time of the consolidation of the bonds.

This fund was to be under a special administration acting under the control of the Mixed Commission. Each of the governments was to have the possession and enjoyment of the properties constituting each fund, but it could not transfer the ownership of any of these properties except by paying to the administration of the fund the price of the property as determined by the Mixed Commission at the liquidation, or any other price agreed upon by the Commission.

In case one of the governments should not entirely comply with its obligations concerning the consolidation of its debt, the Mixed Commission was to have the right to sell the properties belonging to the fund or to transfer their administration to an institution existing or to be created. On the contrary, from the moment the debt of a government should be consolidated, as provided by the Plan, the control of the Commission over the fund was to cease and the government could dispose freely of the properties constituting such fund.

The governments were given the power to acquire the full ownership of all or part of the properties liquidated by the Commission by offering to the latter to substitute for the guarantee of these properties other equivalent guarantees. The Mixed Commission was competent to decide whether the guarantees offered were sufficient, and to reject them if it should consider them insufficient.

§ 203. **Working of the Plan.** The Plan of Payment proved to be too complicated and not in accord with the facts as they developed.[7] The liquidation did not progress so fast as had been anticipated. To June 30, 1925, seven payments only had been made by the Mixed Commission: three liquidations in Bulgaria, one liquidation in Greece, and three restitutions in Greece. Moreover the emigrants left their country of origin before the liquidation of their properties. Thus the provisions of the Plan concerning cash payments, the exchange account between the two National Banks, and the issuing of provisional bonds did not conform with actual conditions.

The Commission decided to prepare a new Plan. It adopted such a Plan on August 10, 1926; [8] but this was never approved by the two governments and need not be studied here.

With regard to the payments themselves, the following procedure was developed. From the 'liquidation sheet' [9] contained in each file, the liquidation service of the Commission extracted the necessary data and carried them to the 'calculation sheet' on which the amount of the claim of the emigrant was reckoned. The capital of the claim plus the special indemnity due him for dispossession was converted into dollars. To this was added the interest due the emigrant in case possession of his property had been transferred to the state prior to

[7] This accords with what is said in another place (*supra,* § 13) with respect to the theoretical character of the plans of M. de Roover.
[8] Procès-Verbaux, xv, 279th meet., p. 1788.
[9] See *supra,* § 180.

the liquidation.[10] The total constituted the emigrant's total claim.

From this total claim were deducted all debts of the claimant to the state where the property was situated.[11] The remainder was divided into two parts: 10% and 90%. From the 10% were deducted the debts to creditors which were to be paid by the state of origin and certified debts to local administrations, to the National and Agricultural Banks, to lawyers, etc. In case these deductions should exceed the 10%, an additional amount was taken from the 90% part of the claim, which was thus reduced by the same amount.

For the cash payment a check was issued by the Mixed Commission on the National Bank of the country where the property was situated. As the emigrants had left their country of origin, these checks were payable at either the National Bank of Greece or the National Bank of Bulgaria. The Banks notified the Mixed Commission each month of the checks that had been paid during the preceding month.

The 'calculation sheets' prepared by the liquidation service were brought together in 'liquidation lists' which contained the most important data from the sheets. Statistical sheets could be made from these lists, giving at any moment the situation as to payments. The lists were summed up semi-annually and communicated to each government. On the basis of these lists the checks on the National Banks were issued and the emigrants were notified by letter of such issue.

Two copies of the 'liquidation list,' together with the checks and the letters of notice to the emigrants and a copy of each liquidation sheet, were sent to the two governments,[12] which were entrusted with delivery to each emigrant of his check and letter of notice. At the same time the two governments were asked to remit to the emigrants in question the amount of leva or drachmas in bonds. Copies of the lists of

[10] See *supra,* § 188.

[11] See on these debts *supra,* § 248. These debts were deducted from the total claim before its division into cash payment and deferred payment, so that payment of these debts did not reduce the cash payment of 10%.

[12] To the Bulgarian Public Debt, in the case of Bulgarians from Greece, and to the General Office for Refugee Settlement in Greece, in the case of Greeks from Bulgaria.

checks issued were sent at the same time to the two National Banks and to the Bulgarian Public Debt and the Greek Ministry of Finance.

Greece and Bulgaria remitted to the emigrants bonds of two internal loans of 1923 which they contracted for this purpose. They also remitted to them the checks sent by the Mixed Commission. They received from the emigrants receipts in triplicate for the checks and for the bonds. Two copies of each receipt were sent to the Mixed Commission. A receipt service at the Mixed Commission checked these receipts on the liquidation lists, on which also the payment of the checks was noted. This permitted the Commission to have a rapid and clear picture of the situation of payments at any moment.[13]

This, then, was the mechanism of payments. It remains to be considered how far the two states were diligent in making the cash payments and the remitment of bonds, how far these bonds were guaranteed and preserved their nominal value, and how the accounts between the two governments were balanced.

§ 204. Delays in cash payments. For making the cash payments to emigrants from Greece, an account called "Advances to the Mixed Commission of Greco-Bulgarian Emigration" had been opened at the National Bank of Greece on December 30, 1922. The Mixed Commission drew on this account by a check in the name of the emigrant. In Bulgaria, an account was opened at the National Bank of Bulgaria in the name of the Section of Control of the Bulgarian budget. The Commission asked the Bulgarian Public Debt to issue a check in the name of the emigrant.

In Bulgaria cash payments were often greatly delayed. The Bulgarian Public Debt, which was asked by the Commission to issue the checks on the National Bank in the name of the emigrants,[14] delayed the delivery of the checks to

[13] On the mechanism of payments the writer has availed himself freely of the information contained in the Memorandum on the Mission and Work of the Mixed Commission on Greco-Bulgarian Emigration, May, 1929, pp. 25 ff., prepared by the two neutral members of the Commission.

[14] This procedure was consented to by the Mixed Commission at the request of the Bulgarian Government, but under the reservation that no

Greek emigrants from Bulgaria. For example, of a total of 27,000 dollars for which the Commission asked the issuance of checks from April 29, 1926, to December 10, 1926, checks for a little over 300 dollars only were issued. It was alleged that formalities with respect to auditing caused this delay. The Commission decided, December 10, 1926,[15] that the cash payments to Greek emigrants would be made from January 1, 1927, in the same way as the similar payments to Bulgarian emigrants from Greece, that is, by checks issued by the Commission itself on the National Bank of Bulgaria. These checks were to be payable at sight by the Bank and its branch offices, without any formality except the verification of the signatures of the Commission on the check. Furthermore, the Commission decided that on all checks asked of the Bulgarian Public Debt before January 1, 1927, the issuance of which was delayed for more than fifteen days after the letter of the Commission, interest of 6% was to be paid. Within ten days from this decision the Bulgarian Public Debt issued most of the delayed checks, which would tend to prove that the alleged auditing difficulties were not very serious.[16]

§ 205. Changes in the provisional bonds. The provisional bonds were to be exchanged for the final bonds as soon as the liquidation of all the properties and the cash payments were terminated. The Plan of Payment of 1922 provided that these bonds were to be redeemed in twelve years beginning January 1, 1925. This date was fixed in view of the assumption that the budgets of the previous years 1923-25 were to bear the whole of the cash payments for the 10% of the value of liquidated properties. By reason of the delays in the work of liquidation no payments were made out of the budget of

delays would be caused thereby. As delays were often noticed, the Mixed Commission wrote repeatedly to the Foreign Minister of Bulgaria calling his attention to the fact. Procès-Verbaux, xvi, 307th meet., p. 2041.

[15] Procès-Verbaux, xvi, 307th meet., p. 2042.

[16] Procès-Verbaux, xvii, 314th meet., December 24, 1926, p. 2095. As a result of this quick action, the Commission decided that no interest would be charged. As a number of checks asked before January 1, 1927, were still delayed, the Commission decided that after May 31, 1927, it would issue checks, thus applying retroactively the above decision of December 10, 1926. Procès-Verbaux, xix, 341st meet., May 25, 1927, p. 17.

1922-23, whereas the budgets of 1924-25, 1925-26, and 1926-27 carried the burden of cash payments. Accordingly decisions of the Commission fixed, first, July 1, 1926, and later January 1, 1928, as the beginning of the twelve-year period for the redemption of the final bonds.[17] These bonds carried interest at the rate of 6% a year. Either government had the right to begin the redemption of the bonds earlier than January 1, 1928. As to the provisional bonds were attached coupons for semi-annual interest only to January 1, 1924, eight additional coupons, payable July 1, 1924, January 1, 1925, July 1, 1925, January 1, 1926, July 1, 1926, January 1, 1927, July 1, 1927, and January 1, 1928, were delivered to bearers of provisional bonds or were attached to such bonds retained by the Mixed Commission.

The emigrants were paid in Bulgaria by bonds of the Bulgarian loan of 6% of 1923 and in Greece by bonds of the Greek loan of 6% of 1923. These bonds were payable to the bearer and consequently negotiable. They were exempt from all taxes or fees whatsoever. However their market value dwindled to 50% of the nominal value.

To July 31, 1927, the Commission had asked the remittance of bonds to the amount of 200,000,000 drachmas from the Greek government and of 580,000,000 leva from the Bulgarian government. The delivery of the bonds to emigrants was made with great delays by the two governments, owing, in part, to administrative formalities and to the difficulty in getting into contact with the interested parties.

The Commission had called upon the two governments to extend the privileges of the bonds so as to prevent their depreciation. The Greek bonds were accepted in payment of debts to the Refugee Settlement Commission and to the state. The Bulgarian bonds could not be used in payment of all debts to the Direction for the Settlement of Refugees, but only of debts for the acquisition of lands.[18]

[17] Procès-Verbaux, viii, 156th meet., October 26, 1923, p. 1017; xiv, 258th meet., March 11, 1926, p. 1669.

[18] See Report of the President of the Mixed Commission in League of Nations, *Official Journal,* October, 1927, pp. 1221 ff., and Procès-Verbaux, xxii, 366th meet., September 22, 1927, annex 3.

§ 206. Changes in the accounts between the two governments. The Plan of Payment of 1922 provided, in article 11, that at the beginning of each month the Commission was to draw up the account of provisional bonds paid during the past month by each of the two governments and the balance of their debit and credit accounts. For the amount of this balance the debtor state was to deliver to the creditor state through the intermediary of the Commission a provisional note. No such balance was drawn up until the end of the first half of 1925 by reason of the very few payments made to that time. An account of the payments in provisional bonds to this date was communicated to the two governments, and the Bulgarian government was asked to issue two provisional notes for its debit balance.[19]

On March 11, 1926, it was decided that the provisional notes should be issued semi-annually, instead of monthly, and that these notes should bear interest from the first day of the half-year during which the provisional bonds were issued whose balance the notes represented.[20] Since the creditor state was paying interest on the provisional bonds to the emigrants, it should recoup itself from the state on whose account the bonds were issued. The date of issue of each provisional bond was considered to be the date of the decision of liquidation of the Mixed Commission. The interest yielded by the provisional notes was capitalized.

§ 207. Disappearance of the guarantee funds. The provisional bonds remitted to emigrants were to enjoy, according to the Plan of Payment, a special guarantee of the nature of a mortgage on a fund constituted by the properties liquidated by the Commission in either country. These properties could not be sold by the two states without the consent of the Commission unless the interested government paid the value of the properties to the above fund.

The settlement of refugees in the two countries gave rise to problems which required immediate solution. In particular,

[19] Procès-Verbaux, xiv, 258th meet., March 11, 1926, p. 1668. The account is annexed to a report by the neutral member, M. de Roover, appended in Procès-Verbaux, xiii, 249th meet., December 15, 1925, annex no. 2.

[20] Procès-Verbaux, xiv, 258th meet., p. 1667.

it was indispensable to settle the refugees in the properties left by the emigrants and to give guarantees for the loans obtained for the settlement of refugees. Greece promulgated a legislative decree under date of July 26, 1924,[21] authorizing the inscription in favor of the Mixed Commission of a mortgage on all the properties liquidated by it in Greece, with a view of guaranteeing the debit balance which might eventually result from the liquidation of these properties. The Greek Minister of Foreign Affairs brought this legislative measure to the knowledge of the Mixed Commission, and proposed that this guarantee be substituted for the ownership or possession of these properties by the Mixed Commission, in view of the fact that the government wished to dispose of these properties in favor of the refugees. The Greek offer was conditional on the application of a similar measure in Bulgaria. The Commission decided [22] that the proposed mortgage was a satisfactory guarantee, and called upon the Bulgarian government to take a similar measure. As the latter government did not reply to that offer, the Greek proposal remained without effect.

Subsequently, the properties liquidated or under liquidation by the Mixed Commission were given by the Greek government, without prior agreement with the Mixed Commission, to the Greek Refugee Settlement Commission, in partial guarantee of certain advances made under the auspices of the League of Nations for the settlement of the refugees.[23] In Bulgaria, the properties of the same category were placed, without any previous agreement with the Mixed Commission, at the disposal of the Direction for the Settlement of Refugees.[24]

The Bulgarian government claimed absolute ownership of these lands, notwithstanding the contrary provisions of the Plan of Payment. Indeed, according to the Protocol for the Establishment of Bulgarian Refugees (art. VIII) the lands

[21] Published in the Official Journal of July 30, 1924, No. 174.
[22] Procès-Verbaux, xii, 233d meet., July 22, 1925, p. 1456.
[23] See *infra,* § 411.
[24] Procès-Verbaux, xix, 341st meet., May 25, 1927, pp. 18, 20. There were 280,000 decares of lands of Greek emigrants from Bulgaria.

placed at the disposal of the Director of Establishment should be lands belonging in absolute ownership to the Bulgarian government.

The Commission refused to relinquish its lien on the liquidated properties unless other satisfactory guarantees should be substituted. However, the guarantees mentioned in the bonds granted to the emigrants were in fact non-existent. Since the economic and financial situation in the two countries was not very favorable, the market of the bonds given to emigrants was affected correspondingly.[25]

§ 208. Proposed substitute guarantees. The neutral members of the Mixed Commission considered the substitution of other guarantees for those that had ceased to exist. At the suggestion of the Greek government, they decided that the guarantee of each state jointly with the Bank which would be charged with the payment of the interests and the redemption of the bonds would be desirable. Such Banks would be the National Bank of Greece and the Agricultural Bank of Bulgaria. After the dissolution of the Mixed Commission the control of the administration of the funds would be exercised by an international financial agency. The neutral members asked also that the privileges of the bonds be enlarged, so that their value might be kept as high as possible.[26]

In March, 1926, the Ministry of Finance of Greece informed the Commission of its intention to redeem a first portion of the 6% loan of 1923, in conformity with an agreement entered into with the National Bank of Greece, and ratified by the legislative decree of November 14, 1924. In April, 1926, the same Ministry asked the Commission concerning the form which should be given to the definitive bonds, in accordance with article 15 of the Plan of Payment of 1922. The Mixed Commission advised the Ministry of its point of view, and stated that the service of these bonds should be placed under the control of an international financial agency. The Greek Ministry of Finance replied that it

[25] Procès-Verbaux, xix, 323d meet., February 21, 1927, p. 2165; 324th meet., February 24, 1927, p. 2168 and annexes 2, 3, 4; 325th meet., March 2, 1927, p. 2184.

[26] Procès-Verbaux, xix, 341st meet., May 25, 1927, pp. 18-22.

could not place an internal loan under the control of an international financial agency, but that it would secure the service of the bonds through the National Bank.

A year later, in May, 1927, the Greek member of the Commission, in the name of his government, reaffirmed the readiness of the Greek government to redeem a portion of the bonds equal to about 50,000,000 drachmas, and offered to use for the service of the bonds certain special revenues which were to be deposited at the National Bank definitely and irrevocably. The neutral members expressed their pleasure at the proposals of the Greek government, and asked the Bulgarian member to present the corresponding proposals of his government.[27]

On June 30, 1927,[28] the neutral members of the Commission stated that, after receiving competent advice, they considered the proposed new guarantees by the Greek government satisfactory and asked certain additional information. They reiterated their request for concrete proposals of the Bulgarian government, and this request was again repeated in August, 1927, in view of the fact that the President was to present a report on these questions to the Council of the League of Nations at its request.[29]

§ 209. Intervention of the Financial Committee of the League. The Council of the League of Nations, being advised that the question of payment to emigrants and of guarantees of the bonds presented difficulties, adopted a resolution, September 3, 1927,[30] referring this question to the Financial Committee, which was directed to give its opinion on all the technical aspects of the problem in regard to which the President of the Commission should wish to consult it. On the invitation of the Secretary-General, the President of the Commission went to Geneva and informed the Financial Committee of the various questions on which the Commission desired its opinion. Sir Otto Niemeyer was appointed

[27] Procès-Verbaux, xix, 342d meet., May 26, 1927, p. 1.
[28] Procès-Verbaux, xx, 352d meet., pp. 1 ff.
[29] Procès-Verbaux, xxi, 359th meet., August 12, 1927, p. 10.
[30] Document C. 450. 1927. VII; League of Nations, *Official Journal,* October, 1927, pp. 1112-13.

Rapporteur for the questions which concerned the Mixed Commission.[31]

The President of the Commission referred the Financial Committee to the Report which the Mixed Commission addressed to the Council under date of August 20, 1927, in which the technical financial questions waiting solution were enumerated. These were: (1) guarantees; (2) redemption of the bonds; (3) privileges and utilization of the bonds; and (4) payments in cash and fixed term payments.[32]

According to the information given by the President to the Committee, the Mixed Commission on August 1, 1927, had issued directly, or applied for the issue of, cash warrants for a total of $726,078 ($457,433 for Bulgarian and $268,645 for Greek emigrants). Of this amount a minimum of $261,000 had been paid by the two governments to April 1, 1927. It was expected that the two governments would be requested to pay a further $850,000 in cash to the end of 1927 and $1,785,000 to the end of 1928, for the entire liquidation of about 40,000 files of the emigrants of the two countries. The monthly payment for the two countries would amount to about $261,000 from August 1, 1927, to January 1, 1928, and about $170,000 thereafter.

§ 210. Agreement of September 12, 1927, on cash payments. Through the intervention of the Financial Committee a first result was obtained with respect to cash payments. On September 12, 1927, a memorandum was signed at Geneva by the representatives of the two countries regulating the procedure to be followed for insuring the regularity of cash payments. The Bulgarian Minister of Finance, Mr. Moloff, made the reservation that the necessary credits should be granted by the Sobranié or National Assembly.

According to this agreement, the Commission was to notify each government, one month in advance, of the probable amount of the orders for cash payment to be issued by the Commission during the following month. Copies of this notification were to be sent to the National Banks of the two

[31] Procès-Verbaux, xxii, 366th meet., September 22, 1927, annexes.

[32] Procès-Verbaux, xxi, 362d meet., August 25, 1927, annex 3. See also League of Nations, *Official Journal,* October, 1927, pp. 1221-24.

countries. The two governments were to put at the disposal of the two Banks the required funds and the latter were required to notify the Commission of the receipt of the funds.

§ 211. **Caphandaris-Molloff Agreement.** At the session of the Financial Committee of December, 1927, the President of the Mixed Commission was invited to Geneva to state his opinion concerning a note, prepared by the President of the Committee, Mr. Otto Niemeyer, which outlined in general terms a financial agreement between the two parties and the Mixed Commission. The President of the Commission was not entirely satisfied with the solutions proposed, as they did not afford a complete security to emigrants. The period of thirty years contemplated by Mr. Niemeyer for the amortization of the final bonds seemed too long. No guarantees were provided, except the engagement of the two states to provide the necessary credits in their budgets. And no privileges were attached to the bonds, not even that of acceptance in payment for lands belonging to the government. A few days later the Ministers of Finance of the two countries, in coöperation with the President of the Commission, succeeded in arriving at an agreement on all the questions under consideration, which was approved later by the Council of the League. This is the Financial Agreement of December 9, 1927,[33] known as the Caphandaris-Molloff Agreement from the names of the Ministers of Finance of the two countries concerned.

The Caphandaris-Molloff Agreement replaced article 9, paragraphs 2, 3, and 4, and articles 11-19 of the Plan of Payment of December 8, 1922. These articles dealt with the final bonds, the accounts between the two governments and the National Banks, and the guarantees.

The effect of the provisions of this Agreement was as follows:

As soon as the agreement was approved by the two governments, the issuing of provisional bonds would cease and the existing provisional bonds would be exchanged for final

[33] The discussions at Geneva and the Accord are found in Procès-Verbaux, xxiv, 388th meet., December 19, 1927, annexes 1, 2, 3, 4, and 5. See also League of Nations, Document C. 643. M. 211. 1927, p. 6; and League of Nations, *Official Journal,* February, 1928, pp. 182, 243, 244.

ones. In case any provisional bonds were to be issued after January 1, 1928, they were to follow the forms annexed to the agreement. The text of the final bonds, identical for the two countries, was to be determined by direct agreement between the two governments and the Mixed Commission. These bonds were to be issued in leva or drachmas respectively, to bear interest at 6% a year, payable semi-annually January 1 and July 1, and to be amortized by means of a redemption fund available from July 1, 1928.

The period of amortization was to be thirty years. The two states engaged to redeem each half-year, beginning on July 1, 1928, one-sixtieth of the total nominal value of the bonds issued. A bond would be deemed issued, for the purposes of this provision, one month after the date at which the Mixed Commission had notified the two governments of the name of the interested party and of the amount due him. This solved the difficulty of delays in issuing the bonds. In case the necessary bonds for redemption could not be obtained on the market, or in case their market price was above par, they were to be drawn for payment at par. The buying and drawing was to be made by the National Bank of Bulgaria and the Bank of Greece respectively.

No other guarantee was given for the amortization of the bonds than the engagement of the two countries to transfer to the above Banks on January 1 and July 1 of each year the sums necessary for the redemption. The Banks, however, were to notify the Mixed Commission and the Council of the League of Nations, at the end of each half-year, of the amounts paid as interest upon the bonds, the amounts received in respect of the redemption fund, and the sums paid by them for the redemption of bonds. Thus while the susceptibilities of the two governments were protected by the non-insertion in the Agreement of any material guarantees for internal loans, the important guarantee was provided of the supervision by the Council of the League, through the Financial Committee, of the execution of these provisions of the Agreement.

Article 4, paragraph 6, recognized the right of each government to redeem the whole or a part of the bonds (in addition to the one-sixtieth each half-year) at any time, after one month's notice. The two governments undertook to obtain without delay all legislative authorizations necessary for securing the annual inscription in the ordinary budget of the state of the sums required for the service of the bonds.

The bonds and their coupons were to be exempt from any taxes, fees, or charges whatsoever, present or future, in the issuing country. They were to be accepted in such country, at their face value, as pledge for all contracts entered into with the state. The Greek Refugee Settlement Commission and the Directorate for the Settlement of Bulgarian Refugees were to enter into arrangements with the respective governments for the purpose of accepting from the refugees, at par, the bonds issued by the respective governments for the payment of sums due to these organizations.

As soon as all the final bonds had been issued, or, if possible, at an earlier period, the Mixed Commission would fix the total of the balance of the debtor state. It would also compute the amount for interest and amortization corresponding to that total (article 5). The debtor state should then deliver to a neutral bank, designated by the Council of the League as its agent, sixty bonds bearing respectively the dates of December 15 and June 15, and payable in the money of the creditor state. The agent bank was to present these obligations, as they became due, to the debtor state and remit the sums received to the creditor state. This was the guarantee provided by the Agreement for the payment of the debit balance to the creditor state.

Until the Commission should fix the total of the balance of the debtor state, when the above provisions (article 5) were to be applied, a transitory regime was to prevail. On December 31, 1927, and at the end of each subsequent half-year, the Mixed Commission was to fix, in agreement with the Ministry of Finance of each country, the total nominal value of bonds issued. The definition of the term 'issued' above referred to applied in this case also. The Commission would compare the two totals, and the government found debtor would immediately remit to the creditor government a sum representing the semiannual interest corresponding to the amount of bonds equivalent to its debt. In case the redemption of the bonds should begin, the sum to be paid by the debtor government would be increased accordingly.

The functions of the Mixed Commission by virtue of the agreement could be transferred to any other persons or organization which might be designated by the Council of the League. The last article provided that the Agreement was to be ratified and the ratifications deposited at the Secretariat of the League of Nations. The Council also was given power to decide on all differences of interpretation of the Agreement. In general, the Agreement was placed under the authority and supervision of the Council of the League, when ordinarily it would come under that of the two governments or of the Mixed Commission.

§ 212. **Observations on the Caphandaris-Molloff Agreement.** It appears that Bulgaria was more satisfied with the Caphandaris-Molloff Agreement than was Greece, who delayed ratification for a long time. The explanation lies in this reason. Under the Plan of Payment of 1922 (article 11), at the beginning of each month the Commission balanced the accounts between the two governments with respect to the amount of provisional bonds issued by each of them to emigrants. For the amount of this balance a provisional note was delivered by the debtor to the creditor state. Only at the termination of the work of liquidation were these provisional notes to be paid or funded by the State finally found debtor. On the contrary, under the Caphandaris-Molloff Agreement, at the end of each half-year the Mixed Commission was to determine the debit balance on the accounts between the two governments with respect to the issue of provisional bonds, and the debtor state was to remit immediately to the creditor state a sum representing the semiannual interest corresponding to the amount of bonds equivalent to its debt. And in case the redemption of the bonds should begin, the sum to be paid by the debtor state would be increased accordingly.

There was, therefore, an obligation for immediate payment by the debtor state under the new Agreement which did not exist under the previous Plan. And, although the Plan provided for the ultimate payment or consolidation of the total debit balance by the debtor state, and this under more severe conditions than the Agreement of 1927, this obligation seemed remote. The original assumption of the Greek government was that ultimately Bulgaria would be the debtor on the liquidation accounts, as it was presumed that a greater number of Greeks would remove from Bulgaria than Bulgarians from Greece.[34] When this assumption was overcome by the greater number of Bulgarian applications for liquidation of properties, it was still expected that the final termination of the liquidation of the rich Greek community properties and forests in Bulgaria, and the revision of material errors committed during the liquidation, would, if they did not entirely balance the accounts between the two states, at least postpone final settlement until a later period.

Aside from this difference between the Plan of Payment of 1922 and the Caphandaris-Molloff Agreement, which was distinctly to the advantage of Bulgaria, the other provisions concerning final payment were favorable to the debtor state and therefore to Greece, if she should be finally found to owe a debit balance to Bulgaria. The differences in this respect between the Plan and the Agreement are the following:

(1) The Plan provided that the debtor government at the closing of the accounts was to remit to the creditor government bonds payable to bearer in dollars bearing 6% interest, redeemable within six years by drawings at par. This implied great inconvenience and financial dangers for the debtor state. If the debit balance should amount to a considerable sum the service of these short term bonds might be very onerous. Moreover, the bonds were negotiable, and if thrown unseasonably or deliberately on the market they might endanger the credit of the debtor state. On the contrary, under the Agreement of 1927, the debtor state was to deliver to a

[34] See discussions at the Greek Chamber, Βουλή *τῶν* ʽΕλλήνων Β Περίοδος Α *Σύνοδος*, meeting of June 28, 1929, pp. 5, 7.

neutral Bank [35] sixty bonds payable in the money of the creditor state, which were to be presented semiannually during a period of thirty years to the debtor state for payment. These bonds were not negotiable and they were redeemable within a long period. The danger, therefore, to the credit of the debtor state was eliminated and the burden was minimized.

(2) Under the Plan of 1922, the service of the bonds remitted to the creditor state was to be guaranteed by sufficient revenues placed under the control of an international financial institution. The Agreement does away with the obligation of guarantees and international control of revenues, and provides merely for the interposition of the neutral bank for the collection of the sums due on the obligations.

(3) The Plan provided that the properties liquidated by the Mixed Commission were to constitute a guarantee fund for the service of the bonds issued to emigrants in each state as well as for the liquidation of the accounts between the two governments. No such provision is contained in the Agreement.

(4) The most important difference, perhaps, is this: Article 16 of the Plan of 1922 (last paragraph) stipulated that the debt due to the creditor state could not be counterbalanced by the debtor state by any other account pending between the two countries. The Agreement of 1927 omitted this provision. It should be recalled that the Agreement replaces, as is explicitly declared in it, articles 11-19 of the Plan of 1922. The provision of article 16, above referred to, was thus abrogated from the coming into force of the Agreement.

It is possible to argue that the omission of the provision in question in the Agreement of 1927 shows that the intention of the parties was that the counterbalancing of the debt due under the Agreement against other debts between the two states should be allowed. But this interpretation would not seem very strong. The question of counterbalancing should be decided by the application of general rules of equity and good faith, which are applicable in a case where positive international law is not available.

[35] The Council of the League designated in this connection the Banque Nationale Suisse.

Here were two states, having between them mutual debts arising from treaty obligations. At a certain moment both states are bound to make a payment on such debts. Suppose one of the states, for one reason or another, does not make such payment. Why should the other be compelled to execute its obligation? In such a case only an express agreement should be permitted to exclude the counterbalancing of the mutual debts.

Such an express agreement certainly did not exist. It is true, however, as we have seen above, that at the time the draft Convention was submitted to the Bulgarian delegation at the Peace Conference in Paris, the delegation put to the Committee on New States the very question of such a counterbalancing. It was maintained by the delegation that no counterbalancing should be allowed, and that it so understood the provisions of the Convention. The Committee on New States in its reply to the Bulgarian delegation confirmed this understanding. Greece, however, could claim that this reply in no way bound her since she never was advised of or consented to it. And in view of the facts that the clauses originally submitted by Mr. Venizelos dealt with questions of indemnities and reparations as well as with reciprocal emigration, and that the draft Convention was prepared by Mr. Politis, it could not be asserted that the interpretation by the Committee on New States had any important weight.

§ 213. Execution of the agreement of September 12, 1927. The agreement for insuring the regularity of cash payments, adopted September 12, 1927, was duly executed by the two countries. A statement of the President of the Commission, in a note addressed to the Financial Committee under date of March 2, 1928, to the effect that on the Greek side, the payments had not been sufficient to meet the drafts issued to February 20, 1928, "and the total liability on unpaid drafts reaches a high figure," [36] was challenged by the Greek Minister at Berne, Mr. Dendramis.[37] The President had to ask supplementary information from the Secretariat of the Com-

[36] League of Nations, *Official Journal,* April, 1928, p. 477.
[37] Doc. F. 529, May 29, 1928.

mission, and reported that all checks issued by the Commission had been paid by the National Bank of Greece, although on February 20, 1928, there was a debit balance of the Greek government at that Bank. In a subsequent communication, the President of the Commission stated that by April 30. 1928, the funds deposited at the Bank by the Greek government exceeded by $201,000 the sum required for the payment of the checks of emigrants.[38]

The distribution of the checks by the state authorities to the interested persons was in some cases delayed. To August 1, 1928, 75% of the checks were distributed in Bulgaria to the Bulgarian emigrants and 83% to the Greek emigrants in Greece.[39]

§ 214. Execution of the Caphandaris-Molloff Agreement. The execution of the Caphandaris-Molloff Agreement was delayed because of its late ratification by the Greek government. The Bulgarian government ratified the Agreement as early as April 3, 1928. In Greece public opinion was agitated against it, and for some time the government was prevented from submitting it to the National Assembly or pressing for its ratification by difficulties of internal character, notwithstanding the pressure of the neutral members of the Commission and of the Financial Committee of the League.[40]

By reason of this delay, certain provisions of the Agreement, whose execution should have commenced in the beginning of 1928, remained without effect. Thus, articles 1 and 3 provided that all provisional bonds to be issued after January 1, 1928, were to follow the forms annexed to the Agreement, and that the text of the final bonds was to be identical for the two countries and fixed by agreement between the two countries and the Commission.

With regard to the first question, the Greek government

[38] Procès-Verbaux, xxviii, 422d meet., June 23, 1928, pp. 3 ff., and annexes 1, 2.

[39] Procès-Verbaux, xxx, 444th meet., October 10, 1928, pp. 1 ff. and annex 2.

[40] Procès-Verbaux, xxvi, 406th meet., March 17, 1928, p. 1 and annexes 1, 2, 3; xxvii, 418th meet., May 23, 1928, pp. 1 ff.; xxviii, 422d meet., June 23, 1928, pp. 3 ff. and annexes 1, 2; xxx, 444th meet., October 10, 1928, pp. 1 ff. and annex 2. See also League of Nations, *Official Journal,* April, 1928, pp. 449-450, 464, 477-478; July, 1928, p. 1031; October, 1928, pp. 1651, 1738.

issued provisional bonds after February 1, 1928, in the new form, but these were not distributed till the ratification of the Agreement. The Bulgarian government issued no provisional bonds of the new form.

On June 26, 1928, the Mixed Commission adopted, the Greek member abstaining, the text of the final Bulgarian bonds, which was agreed upon by the Financial Committee of the League, the Direction of the Bulgarian Public Debt, and the Secretariat of the Commission.[41] But these bonds were not issued by the Bulgarian government pending the ratification of the Agreement by Greece. The text of the Greek final bonds was adopted by the Commission at its meeting of August 10, 1928.[42]

In the meantime the distribution of the provisional bonds to emigrants by the two governments went on as before. By August 1, 1928, the Bulgarian government had distributed only 264,000,000 leva in bonds out of 1,636,000,000 leva asked by the Commission, or only 16%. On the same date the Greek government had distributed 250,000,000 drachmas in bonds out of a total of 320,000,000 drachmas asked by the Commission, or 78%.[43]

According to article 4 of the Agreement the Commission had found the Greek state debtor to the amount of 18,000,000 leva for the half-year ending December 31, 1927, and had asked it to pay the interest thereon to the Bulgarian government.[44] This payment was not made while the Agreement remained unratified.

In the meantime Mr. Venizelos became Prime Minister in Greece and Mr. Caphandaris, who had signed the Agreement of December 9, 1927, and had vainly tried to bring about its ratification, went out of office. At the session of September, 1928, the Financial Committee had urged the immediate ratification of the Agreement and the Council postponed examination of the question to the December session.[45] The Agree-

[41] Procès-Verbaux, xxviii, 424th meet., pp. 2, 4. See text of the bond, ibid., annex.
[42] Procès-Verbaux, xxix, 433d meet.
[43] Procès-Verbaux, xxx, 444th meet., October 10, 1928, pp. 1 ff. and annex 2.
[44] League of Nations, *Official Journal,* April, 1928, p. 478.
[45] See League of Nations, *Official Journal,* October, 1928, pp. 1651, 1738.

ment was finally adopted by the Greek Parliament on December 9, 1928, and ratified by the Greek government. This was announced to the Financial Committee of the League at its December session.[46]

Soon afterwards, two further difficulties arose. A Greek law adopted January 24, 1929, provided that the 6% loan of 1923 was to be redeemed within fifteen years at par by drawing by lot. The Bulgarian government considered this a violation of article I of the Agreement, which provided for redemption of the bonds within thirty years. However, paragraph 6 of the same article permitted any of the governments to redeem the whole or part of the bonds, in addition to the sixtieth part of the total amount of bonds due each half-year. And there is no doubt that it was to the advantage of the emigrants to have the bonds redeemed as the new Greek law provided.

The purpose of the Greek government, in taking this step, was to present at each semiannual balancing of payments made by each government, as provided in article 4, a larger sum paid by Greece for the redemption of bonds. In this way the balance between the payments by the two governments would be eliminated or minimized, and the obligation under the Agreement of the Greek government to pay to Bulgaria the interest on the balance would be correspondingly affected. The Bulgarian government, indeed, was not financially able to follow the Greek government in the policy of applying to the amortization of bonds more than the required minimum sum.

The Financial Committee of the League undertook to settle this difficulty; and it appears that the Greek government was allowed to print the final bonds with the legend that they were redeemable in fifteen years at par and by drawing by lot.

The other difficulty arose in connection with the moratorium obtained by Bulgaria in connection with the payment of reparations. By virtue of the Treaty of Neuilly, Greece was entitled to a part of the reparations due from Bulgaria. Al-

[46] *Ibid.,* January, 1929, pp. 182-183.

though a moratorium was granted in 1928 by the Reparations Commission, Greece received her part for that year from that Commission from funds at its disposal. In 1929 a new moratorium was to be granted to Bulgaria; and as the Reparations Commission could not make the payments due Greece on account of reparations, the Greek government asserted that it could set off the payment due it by Bulgaria on account of reparations against the payment of interest due by Greece to Bulgaria on its debit balance resulting from the bonds issued, which was required by article 4 of the Agreement. In the meantime the Bulgarian government had notified the Mixed Commission on February 27, 1929, that it would be compelled to suspend the service of the bonds issued to emigrants if the Greek government did not make the payments imposed by the Agreement.[47]

§ 215. Payment of debit balance by Greece. At the session of the Council for March, 1929,[48] Sir Austen Chamberlain asked whether Greece was meeting or would meet without delay the bonds issued by the Mixed Commission in favor of Bulgarian emigrants. The question shows that Sir Austen was not entirely aware of the scheme of payments and of the effect of the Caphandaris-Molloff Agreement. On the one hand, bonds to Bulgarian emigrants were not issued by the Mixed Commission but by the Bulgarian state. On the other hand, Greece was not bound to meet the service of the bonds issued for Bulgarian emigrants from Greece. Payments on these bonds were made by the Bulgarian government, and only in case these payments exceeded those made by the Greek government to Greek emigrants from Bulgaria was Greece bound to pay to Bulgaria the interest on the difference. The obligation, therefore, of Greece was only to ease the Bulgarian budget for the payments to Bulgarian emigrants.

Answering Sir Austen's question, the Greek representative, Mr. Carapanos, said that it was impossible for him to fix any particular date for putting the bonds into circulation, as this was a technical matter. The reply shows that Mr.

[47] Procès-Verbaux, xxxiii, 476th meet., March 28, 1929, p. 2.
[48] League of Nations, *Official Journal,* April, 1929, p. 549.

Carapanos did not understand Sir Austen's question and was simply speaking of the issue of the final bonds, the form of which had to be agreed upon with the Mixed Commission and which were to be printed. Besides, these bonds were to be distributed to Greek emigrants from Bulgaria, and had nothing to do with the bonds for Bulgarian emigrants from Greece, which were to be issued and distributed by the Bulgarian Government.

Here, then, was a perfect case of complete misunderstanding and confusion. However, Sir Austen Chamberlain permitted himself to express the view that the answer was not satisfactory; that "it was of the first importance that arrangements for the payment of the bonds should be made at once"; and that "he would urge . . . upon the Greek Government that this was a matter which admitted of no delay, and that it was really a point of honor to give satisfaction at the earliest possible moment."

Thereupon the representative of Bulgaria, Mr. Bouroff, thanked Sir Austen for the question he had raised and remarked that the Bulgarian government would not be in a position to pay regularly the interest and amortization of the bonds unless it were to receive the balance owing from Greece. Mr. Carapanos pointed out "that the Greek budget would also require certain funds due to it from Bulgaria if it were to be balanced, and he thought that the Financial Committee might examine this question."

These remarks of the representatives of the two countries placed the question in its right place, that is, as a question of the obligations existing on the part of Greece and Bulgaria under two different international agreements to make budgetary payments to each other: on the part of Greece under the Caphandaris-Molloff Agreement; on the part of Bulgaria under the arrangements for reparations.

However, Sir Austen Chamberlain went on to say that he thought "that the discussion had passed outside the limits of the question raised." That was not true; it was a question of budgets, as the representatives of the two countries were agreed. Sir Austen next remarked that "the point that concerned the Council was that an obligation undertaken by the Greek Government at the request of the Council and declared before the Council should be honorably met."

To this, Mr. Carapanos, avoiding discussion, answered that he believed he had replied to this point. His proper answer, of course, should have been that either Sir Austen was not fully informed on the nature of the obligation Greece had undertaken under the Agreement of December 9, 1927, or else his attitude was almost high-handed in attempting to compel the Greek government to increase the resources of the Bulgarian budget, while Bulgaria was allowed by moratorium to postpone payment of reparations and to deprive the Greek budget of equivalent resources.[49]

In the meantime, the Bulgarian government eliminated this question by paying the reparations due to Greece for the first half of 1929. Under such conditions the Greek government had no reason to insist on the question of compensation. At its session of June, 1929,[50] the Council was informed that the Caphandaris-Molloff Agreement was being carried out, the Greek government having made the first payment due under this Agreement. As Mr. Politis explained at the meeting of the Council, the Greek government had had to overcome some very real difficulties, "as public opinion in Greece found it difficult to understand why there should not be a perfect equality of treatment in the execution of the international obligations of the various countries, and why a state should be obliged to pay its debts, while it was not receiving payment from its creditors." Mr. Politis added significantly that the Greek government hoped "that it would be able, upon recovery of the sums which were due to it, to continue to discharge its obligations punctually."

The payment then made by Greece amounted to 140,235,034 leva and covered interest and amortization of capital for the difference in amount of the bonds issued by the two countries until December 31, 1928.

[49] It must be recalled that in the meantime Bulgaria had raised a loan for the settlement of refugees at London and British interests favored the alleviation of the Bulgarian budget.

[50] League of Nations, *Official Journal,* July, 1929, pp. 1015, 1181.

From the time when all the final bonds have been issued, or, in the opinion of the Mixed Commission, a sufficient number of them, the provisions of article 5 of the Caphandaris-Molloff Agreement will be applied. That is, the Mixed Commission will calculate the half-yearly service (interest and amortization) for the total balance due from the debtor state. The debtor state will then remit to the neutral bank designated by the Council of the League bonds payable on December 15 and June 15, one bond for each half-yearly payment. The amount received will be remitted by the agent bank to the creditor state.

§ 216. **Statistical data.** As was noted above, the Commission estimated at the time the Plan of Payment was adopted that each of the two countries would have to pay for liquidation of emigrants' properties a sum between $1,500,000 and $3,000,000. In 1927, when the Plan of Payment was modified by the Caphandaris-Molloff Agreement, the estimates were, exclusive of community properties, pensions, and some other items, a total of $22,000,000 for Greece and $15,000,000 for Bulgaria.

The table below shows the value of liquidations made by the Commission to April 30, 1929, and payments thereon by the two states. At that time there remained unliquidated 4938 files of Greeks from Bulgaria and 5602 files of Bulgarians from Greece, of an estimated liquidation value of $2,770,218 and $4,123,072 respectively.

The most unsatisfactory point in the question of payments was the market price of the bonds delivered to emigrants in payment of the 90% of their liquidation account. The fluctuations of the market price of the Greek and Bulgarian bonds remitted to emigrants is shown in the graph below.[51] Before 1927 the market prices had reached lower levels, but only a small part of the payments under the Convention were made before September, 1927.

In view of the great depreciation of the Bulgarian bonds

[51] This graph and the previous table are borrowed from the Memorandum on the Mission and Work of the Mixed Commission on Greco-Bulgarian Emigration, May, 1929, prepared by the neutral members of the Commission.

	Liquidations to April 30, 1929	Value of liquidations	Checks for cash payments issued by the Commission	Checks remitted to emigrants	Checks paid to emigrants	Bonds of 6% 1923 loan asked to be issued	Bonds remitted to emigrants
Greeks from Bulgaria	10,409 files	$ 5,841,193.70	$ 481,905.43	$ 429,172.14	$ 417,252.12	$ 5,010,813.88 (Drs. 382,818,000)	Drs. 343,145,000
Bulgarians from Greece	23,889 "	17,579,505.97	1,728,344.89	1,419,640.75	1,419,640.75	$15,764,817.31 (Leva 2,186,825,000)	Leva 512,460,500

of the 6% loan of 1923, the President of the Commission, Colonel de Reynier, put the question before the Financial Committee of the League in January, 1930, and asked for technical advice on the measures that should be taken to raise the market price of the bonds.[52] At the time of the signature of the Caphandaris-Molloff Agreement these bonds sold at 62% of the nominal value, their price falling thereafter and gradually reaching 47.8%. At the same time the Greek bonds sold at 75% of the nominal value. The reasons of the depreciation of the Bulgarian bonds seemed to be, first, a larger issue of such bonds for Bulgarian emigrants from Greece, and, secondly, the lack of confidence on the part of the emigrants, who preferred to sell the bonds at any price.

[52] Procès-Verbaux, xxxviii, 532d meet., February 11, 1930, p. 3 and annexes nos. 2-4.

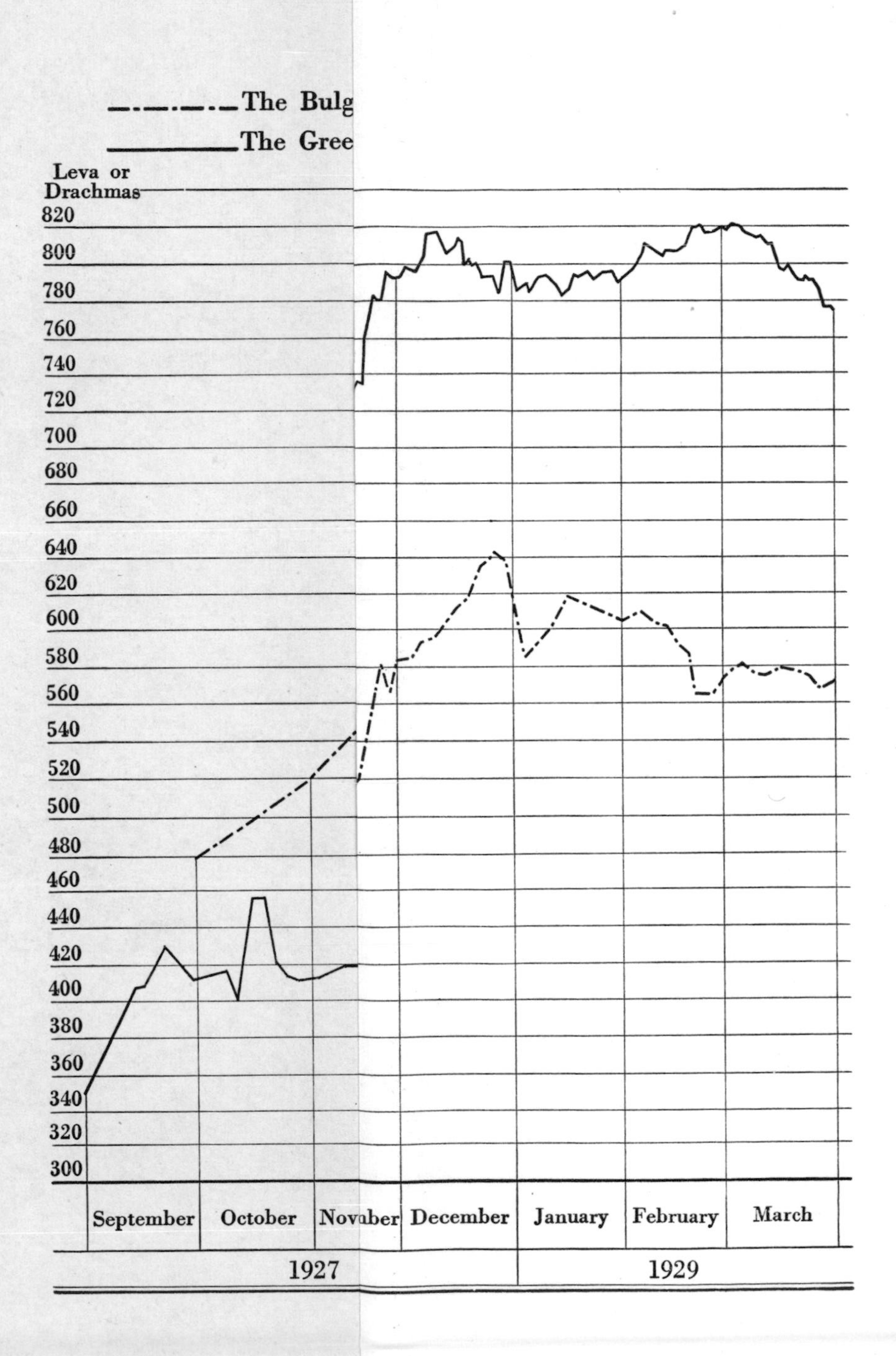

The Bulg
The Gree
Leva or Drachmas
820
800
780
760
740
720
700
680
660
640
620
600
580
560
540
520
500
480
460
440
420
400
380
360
340
320
300
September
October
Novuber
December
January
February
March
1927
1929

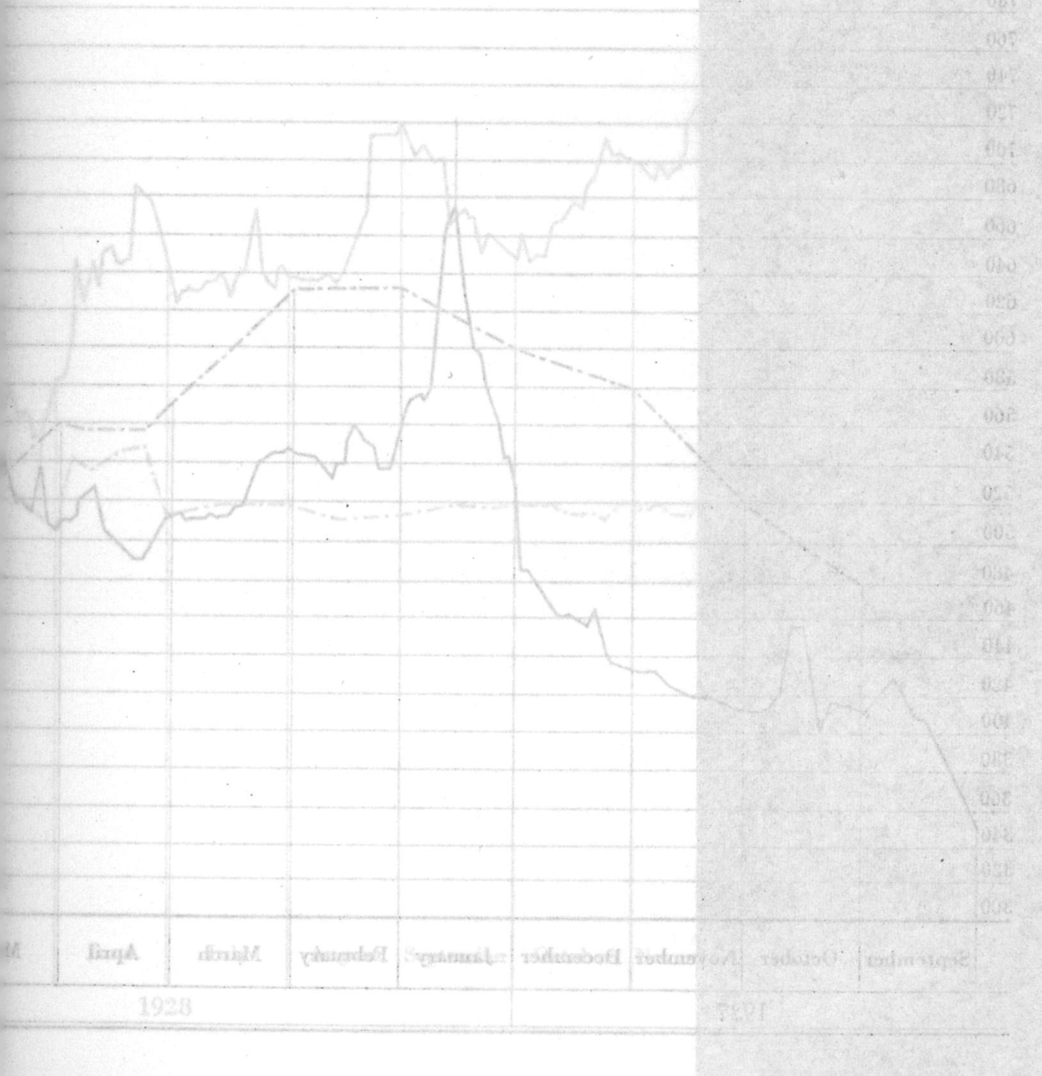

CHAPTER XVI

FINANCES OF THE COMMISSION

§ 217. Decisions for, and administration of, expenditure. At an early date,[1] the Mixed Commission decided that the expenditure for its operation and maintenance was under its own control, and that it might take, by a majority vote, decisions involving expense or pecuniary charges. Such decisions were written out and were called conventionally *arrêtés* or decrees. The original text of every *arrêté* was signed by the President and the members, and was kept by the Secretary in a numbered collection. The President was given power to authorize the current expenditure of the Secretariat. The funds of the Commission were administered by the President and Secretary jointly, who arranged for all payments undertaken in the name of the Commission. The account books were always open to the examination of the members. Once a month, at least, the Greek and Bulgarian members verified all the items and affixed their signatures in token of approval. Four times a year the President drew up a summary of the accounts, which, after approval by the Commission, was sent, for the purpose of information only, to the Greek and Bulgarian governments.[2]

[1] Procès-Verbaux, i, 19th meet., January 14, 1921, p. 90.

[2] The expenses and accounts of the Sub-Commissions were placed under the immediate supervision of the Presidents of the Central Sub-Commissions, who transmitted all the documents to the Mixed Commission. For every expense, a decision was taken by the Sub-Commission, which was submitted to the Mixed Commission for its approval. See Procès-Verbaux, xii, 240th meet., October 3, 1925, p. 1503; xiii, 248th meet., December 15, 1925, p. 1577.

§ 218. Apportionment of the expenditure between the two states. Article 13 of the Convention respecting Reciprocal Emigration provided that "the expenses of the maintenance and working of the Mixed Commission and its agencies shall be borne by the Governments concerned in proportions to be determined by the Commission." The Greek and Bulgarian members developed different points of view relative to the apportionment of such expenses between the two states. From the Bulgarian side it was argued that, in determining the apportionment, account should be taken of the capacity of payment and number of inhabitants of each country, also of the political interest that each country had in the application of the convention, and that on the basis of these three elements the contribution of Bulgaria should be less than that of Greece. The Greek member, on the other hand, asked that the contribution of Greece should be the lesser. The Commission at its meeting of December 2, 1922,[3] decided to take no account of the fact that the convention might be less profitable to the one country than to the other. Greece and Bulgaria were placed in the same class with regard to their contribution to the expenses of the League of Nations. It was thought that a similar system would be equitable in regard to the expenses of the Commission and its agencies. In view, however, of the conditions under which the work of the Commission developed during the first two years, a certain reduction in favor of Bulgaria was allowed by charging to the Greek government one-half of the remuneration of the Bulgarian member during these two years, which had been paid by the Commission.

§ 219. Budgets of the Commission, 1921-29. The budget of the Commission grew steadily from 1921 to 1927, with the multiplication of its work and the increase of its agencies and personnel. In the first year, 1921, its personnel consisted only of a Secretary-General, a First Secretary, and three other employees. In 1922 and 1923 a Sub-Commission was added, and in 1924 a second Sub-Commission was created for the application of the Convention in Western Thrace. The personnel of the Commission rose to 77.

[3] Procès-Verbaux, vi, 125th meet., pp. 814-816.

In 1925 the work of establishment of property rights, of survey of lands, and of appraisal by staffs of agronomists and expert architects began to be carried out. These various agencies, with the increase of the Sub-Commissions to nine for Greece and Bulgaria, raised the personnel to a total of 243. In 1926 and 1927 the Directions of the Centres, the two additional Sub-Commissions, the neutral experts, foresters, and other agencies increased the personnel to 380.

The budget for each of these years then was as follows:

	£ s. d.
1921	10.163.10
1922	12.463. 4.3
1923	13.841.10.3
1924	22.840. 1.7
1925	47.162.16.4
1926	69.195.14.1
1927	110.475. 9.8

In the last year the expenses of the Commission exceeded the budgetary provisions. A committee on economy was created under the chairmanship of M. Brönimann, the chief of the liquidation service, and important económies were made effective in January, 1928. A number of agents of the Commission were dispensed with and the personnel of the Commission was thus reduced to 270. As a result the budget was reduced to £78,263.3*s.*1*d.*

A further reduction of the personnel was effected in 1929. Two Sub-Commissions were left in Bulgaria and one in Greece to finish up the remaining cases of property rights. The Direction of the Centre of Comotini was abolished. All the appraisal experts were released. Only the compiling services remained in full force. The total personnel was 222. The estimated budget for this year was £63,835.

This brings the total expenditure of the Mixed Commission from its constitution to the end of 1929 to £428,240.9*s.*9*d.*

Allowances of one month's salary after dismissal were granted to employees of the Centres by the Director. Allowances were also granted to the teams of the compiling services with the view of obtaining greater efficiency. High functionaries of the Commission were not granted such allowances, the Greek and Bulgarian members having opposed a proposal of the President.[4]

Trips to Geneva by the neutral members were often an unnecessary cause of expenditure. The Greek member usually objected to such trips. His objections, however, were overruled, the neutral members believing that he was actuated by the desire to prevent their contact with the League.[5]

The salaries of representatives of the two governments at the Sub-Commissions or other agencies of the Commission were not included in the expenditure of the Commission. In case payments were made by the Commission to such employees, which properly had to be charged specifically to the one government or the other, reimbursement was asked at the time the regular contribution of each government was due.[6]

By an understanding between the Commission and the Greek government, the former had agreed to administer the sums expended by the Greek government for the remuneration of the personnel of the Greek delegation and of the Greek members and secretaries of the Sub-Commissions. The sums for this purpose were sent by the Greek government to the Commission together with the contribution for the Commission's expenses. From February, 1927, the Commission declined to administer the above sums. It decided to remit them to the Greek delegation for their distribution, and later called upon the Greek government to send separately the funds destined to the Commission and to the Greek delegation.

§ 220. **Receiving funds from the two countries.** From November 1, 1922, the expenditure for the maintenance and functioning of the Commission and its agencies was borne equally by the two countries. Until that time the Commission had asked at five different times, at irregular intervals, for funds from the two governments. From the above date until

[4] Procès-Verbaux, xxxii, 463d meet., November 29, 1928, p. 5.

[5] See, for instance, Procès-Verbaux, xxxii, 465th meet., December 1, 1928, pp. 2-12.

[6] Procès-Verbaux, vi, 125th meet., December 2, 1922, pp. 814-816; xiv, 266th meet., June 10, 1926, p. 1718; xvi, 300th meet., November 11, 1926, p. 1941.

June, 1926, the Commission received funds from the two governments at the end of each half-year. After June, 1926, each of the two governments was asked to send a monthly contribution, at the end and later at the beginning of each month.

The Commission was frequently short of funds, the two governments often delaying remittance of their respective contributions towards its maintenance and functioning. The procès-verbaux of the meetings of the Commission are full of discussions on this matter. The delay was sometimes caused by the fact that the expenditure of the Commission exceeded the monthly sum originally asked of each government and the latter had not secured the necessary appropriations. The excess of expenditure was due to unforeseen disbursements and the increase of the agencies of the Commission. In order to avoid the interruption of the work of the agents of the Commission, the President was empowered by the Commission to obtain loans from banks at Sofia or Athens. These loans were obtained by the signatures of the two neutral members. The deficit was then covered by supplementary contributions asked of the two governments. At one time the advances of the bank rose to a large sum, and the Commission, being unable to obtain further advances, was placed in a very difficult position. The work of its agencies was often interrupted on this account.[7]

In view of the fact that an important part of the funds was expended in the national currency of each country, leva and drachmas, and that the treasury authorities of the two countries met with difficulties in the purchase of foreign money, the Commission decided that in case either of the two countries should desire to pay a part of its contribution in national currency, it might do so to the extent of one-third of the contribution.[8] This measure was taken especially with the hope that the contribution of each government would be

[7] Procès-Verbaux, xvi, 298th meet., November 2, 1926, p. 1918; 300th meet., November 11, 1926, p. 1940; xvii, 319th meet., February 3, 1927, p. 2135; 328th meet., p. 2250; xxvi, 410th meet., April 9, 1928, p. 17; xxxi, 459th meet., November 22, 1928, p. 2.

[8] Procès-Verbaux, xvi, 312th meet., December 17, 1926, p. 2076.

sent to the Commission without delay. This hope was not realized. At times more than two monthly contributions were in arrears. At one time the President of the Commission withheld the sums which were sent by the Greek government for the use of the Greek delegation through the Commission. This arbitrary action did not meet with the approval of the Commission.[9]

As a rule the estimates of the Commission were always short of the expenditure. To this were due the embarrassments of its position more than to the unwillingness of the states to send funds. The national members of the Commission were bitter at times in commenting on this inability of the neutral members in charge of financial affairs to avoid deficits.[10]

§ 221. **Verification of accounts.** As has been said in another connection,[11] the Société Anonyme Fiduciaire Suisse undertook, by agreement with the Commission, the direction of the liquidation service and the supervision of the internal accounts of the Commission. M. Brönimann, the reviser of that Company, was put in charge of the direction and supervision and took up his duties on February 1, 1927. Early in April, 1927,[12] he submitted a report to the Commission on his verification of the accounts from the constitution of the Commission.

In May, 1927, M. Brönimann was asked by the Commission to go and examine summarily the accounts of the Centres at Saloniki and Comotini. He discovered at Comotini great frauds committed by the expert architects in that Centre.[13] It should be recalled that this agency for the valuation of buildings and building lands in Thrace was the only agency of the Mixed Commission made up of representatives of the two countries without the participation of a neutral. The

[9] Procès-Verbaux, xix, 341st meet., May 25, 1927, pp. 1 ff.
[10] See, for instance, Procès-Verbaux, xxix, 434th meet., August 16, 1928, pp. 2 ff.
[11] See *supra*, p. 272.
[12] Procès-Verbaux, xviii, 332d meet., April 4, 1927, p. 2304.
[13] See M. Brönimann's report in Procès-Verbaux, xviii, 340th meet., May 19, 1927, annex 6; and the discussion thereon in the Commission, xix, 341st meet., May 25, 1927, p. 12.

expert architects in Thrace, as well as in the other centres, were not paid a salary, like other agents of the Commission, but honoraria on the basis of the expert appraisals made by them.[14] The architects in Thrace had collected unduly several honoraria for single expert appraisals. On the whole it appears that, especially under the direction of M. Brönimann, the accounts of all services of the Commission were checked and verified, and, except in the case referred to above, no disorder or abuse of any kind took place.

[14] See *supra,* p. 244.

PART II

THE COMPULSORY EXCHANGE OF GREEK AND TURKISH POPULATIONS

CHAPTER XVII

THE CONVENTION FOR THE EXCHANGE OF GREEK AND TURKISH POPULATIONS AND OTHER AGREEMENTS CONCLUDED AT LAUSANNE

§ 222. Origin of the Convention. Like the Convention concerning Reciprocal Emigration between Greece and Bulgaria, the Convention concerning the Exchange of Greek and Turkish Populations of January 30, 1923, is a part of the peace settlement with Turkey in 1923. However, unlike the former, which was worked out by the Committee on New States and for the Protection of the Rights of Minorities and accepted by Greece and Bulgaria, the latter is the fruit of long and laborious negotiations at the Conference of Lausanne.

As a result of the Greek military disaster in Asia Minor in September, 1922, hundreds of thousands of Greeks were driven out from Asia Minor and Eastern Thrace and came to swell the great numbers of Greek refugees who had fled from those provinces during the period 1912 to 1920. In the session of the Assembly and Council of the League in September, 1922, Dr. Fridtjof Nansen was intrusted with the question of relief for the refugees from the Greco-Turkish war.[1] In Constantinople and Athens he carried on certain negotiations for the exchange of Greek and Turkish populations; later he came to Lausanne and put forward a proposal for the adoption of a separate convention for this purpose between Greece and Turkey.

[1] League of Nations, *Official Journal,* November, 1922, pp. 1140-41.

There has been a good deal of dispute as to how the idea of an exchange of populations, and, in particular, its compulsory character, originated, and it is important to trace this development here.

Dr. Nansen on September 27, 1922, after his appointment by the Assembly of the League, telegraphed to Mustapha Kemal Pasha, Head of the Revolutionary Government of Angora, expressing his earnest desire to enter into relations with the authorities of the Angora government with respect to the questions of relief intrusted to him. Arriving in Constantinople in the first week of October, he met several times Hamid Bey, diplomatic representative at Constantinople of the Angora government. On October 12 and 14 Dr. Nansen sent to Hamid Bey a memorandum and a letter, setting forth "the various questions with which I wished to deal, particularly that of an exchange of populations between Greece and Turkey."

In the meantime, on October 13, Mr. Venizelos, diplomatic representative of the Greek government in London and later President of the Hellenic Delegation at the Conference of Lausanne, sent a telegram to Dr. Nansen. In this, Mr. Venizelos stated that the Minister of Interior of the Angora government had declared, a fortnight previously, that the Turks had decided not to allow the further presence of Greeks on Turkish soil, and would propose at the forthcoming conference the compulsory exchange of Greek and Turkish populations. Mr. Venizelos then pointed out that the question of housing the refugees would be even more difficult than that of their alimentation, and added: "I take the liberty of requesting that you will endeavor to arrange that transfer of the populations begin before signature of peace." Mr. Venizelos thought that the problem of housing the refugees in Greece would be facilitated if the 350,000 Turks in Greece could be immediately transferred to houses that the Christians in Asia Minor had already left. It appears, therefore, that Mr. Venizelos was proposing a total exchange, and probably a compulsory one, since he was calculating on the immediate transfer of all Turks from Greece.

On October 15, the High Commissioners of France, Great Britain, Italy, and Japan at Constantinople formally invited Dr. Nansen "to take all possible steps to endeavor to reach an agreement with regard to an exchange of populations between the Greek and Turkish governments as soon as possible, independently of the peace negotiations." Inasmuch as the question of exchange was essentially connected with the problems with which Dr. Nansen was intrusted, he accepted the mission which he was invited to undertake by Mr. Venizelos and the High Commissioners. He also advised the Secretary-General of the League to this effect.

Soon afterwards Dr. Nansen went to Athens, where the Greek government told him "of its desire that he should attempt to establish an agreement on the subject of the exchange of populations." On his return to Constantinople on October 23, Dr. Nansen received a telegraphic communication from Mustapha Kemal Pasha, informing him that "the exchange proposed . . . is acceptable in principle," but that the matter must be considered with the government. On October 30, a telegram from the President of the Council of Ministers at Angora to Refet Pasha, Turkish Governor of Thrace, confirmed likewise the agreement in principle to the exchange of populations, excluding Western Thrace.

Hamid Bey, being instructed to negotiate with Dr. Nansen, informed him on October 31 that "his instructions only permitted him to negotiate on the basis of a total and enforced exchange of populations, from which the population of Constantinople would not be excepted." Dr. Nansen was opposed both to the compulsory exchange and to the inclusion of the Greeks of Constantinople. He was only thinking of a voluntary emigration similar to that between Greece and Bulgaria. He notified the Greek government of Hamid Bey's communication. The reply of that government was "clearly unfavorable" to the exchange of the Greeks of Constantinople. It would seem that the Greek government was not "clearly unfavorable" to compulsory exchange.[2] Dr. Nansen

[2] The quotations in the text and other information are taken from two reports by Dr. Nansen, with annexes, to the Council of the League, under

was unable to carry any further his negotiations in Constantinople. In the meantime the Peace Conference of Lausanne convened.

§ 223. Discussion at the Conference of Lausanne. At the meeting of December 1, 1922,[3] of the Territorial and Military Commission of the Conference, and while that Commission was dealing with the question of prisoners of war, a statement prepared by Dr. Nansen was read by Lord Curzon. It was declared in the statement that the four Great Powers were favorable to the proposal of exchange of populations, believing "that to unmix the populations of the Near East will tend to secure the true pacification of the Near East and because they believe an exchange of populations is the quickest and most efficacious way of dealing with the grave economic results which must result from the great movement of populations which has already occurred." Dr. Nansen understood that the two interested governments were also in favor of the proposal.

Dr. Nansen was not unaware of the grave difficulties "involved in the displacement of populations of many more than 1,000,000 people, in uprooting these people from their homes, transferring them to a strange new country" and of the hardships "upon great numbers of the individual citizens." But he was impressed by the fact that these hundreds of thousands of people had left their productive employment in Turkey and were without any chance of securing other productive employment in Greece, and that the exchange would provide Turkey immediately with the population necessary to continue the use of the cultivated lands which the Greeks had abandoned, while the departure from Greece of her Moslem citizens would make it possible to render self-supporting a great proportion of the refugees. He also pointed out that "it would be easier from the political and psychological point of view to carry through an exchange of populations at a mo-

dates of October 16 and November 15, 1922. League of Nations, Doc.C.729. M.441.1922; *Official Journal,* January, 1923, pp. 126-132.

[3] See Great Britain, *Parliamentary Papers, Turkey No. 1 (1923) Lausanne Conference on Near Eastern Affairs, 1922-1923, Records of Proceedings and Draft Terms of Peace* (Cmd. 1814) (London, 1923), pp. 113-123.

ment such as the present, . . . than it will be when affairs have settled down to a quieter routine."

He proposed that the exchange should be carried out within three months, or by the end of February, 1923; that the Convention respecting Reciprocal Emigration between Greece and Bulgaria should serve as a model; and that a machinery such as the Mixed Greco-Bulgarian Commission should be set up. The political questions to be solved before an agreement could be made were the following: (1) whether the treaty should be based on the principle of compulsory or of voluntary emigration; (2) what should be the area of its application; and (3) what should be the nature of the Mixed Commission or other machinery to be set up.

A discussion followed in the Commission on this statement, during which Mr. Venizelos, President of the Hellenic Delegation, declared that, while what he had in mind was a voluntary exchange of populations, "he was ready to consider an exchange of populations either obligatory or voluntary,"[4] and that he was opposed to the departure of the Greeks from Constantinople. The President of the Turkish Delegation, Ismet Pasha, although in no haste to discuss this problem, consented to its consideration conjointly with the question of immediate release of Turkish civilian prisoners and prisoners of war by Greece. He declared that the Greeks of Constantinople should be included in the exchange. Lord Curzon expressed his preference for a compulsory exchange, as in this way only the results expected would be obtained. On a voluntary basis the exchange would take months, "whereas what was wanted was firstly to get the Turkish population into Eastern Thrace . . . and, secondly, to provide for the accommodation in Greece of the refugees." He also proposed to exempt the Greeks of Constantinople from the exchange in the

[4] Mr. Theotoka, in an address before the Lawyers' Association at Athens, April 26, 1928, entitled "Ta Symvatika dikaiomata ton Hellinon en Turkia kai ton Turkon en Helladi" ("Treaty Rights of Greeks in Turkey and Turks in Greece"), describing the discussions at the Lausanne Conference, states that, after Dr. Nansen's statement, Mr. Venizelos expressed his willingness to negotiate only on the basis of a voluntary exchange of populations. This is not borne out by the Minutes of the Conference, as is shown by the quotation of Mr. Venizelos's statement in the text.

interest of Turkey herself, and to set against these people the Turkish population of Western Thrace.

§ 224. **Compulsory or voluntary exchange?** At last, the Commission decided that the question of exchange should be examined by a Sub-Commission consisting of representatives of each of the three inviting Powers (France, Great Britain, and Italy), of Turkey, and of Greece, under the chairmanship of an Italian delegate. This sub-commission was to hear Dr. Nansen on the question, and collect such evidence as it might think fit. While this Sub-Commission was working, the question of protection for minorities was taken up by the Commission. During this discussion the question of the voluntary or compulsory character of the exchange came up repeatedly. Public opinion among the refugees in Greece was highly aroused. Notwithstanding all their sufferings, they were attached to the land of their birth by many ties, and revolted against the idea of being forbidden to return thither. The Turks in Greece also protested. It could not be denied that they enjoyed complete protection of life and property in Greece, and they abhorred the idea of being compelled to leave their homes. Moreover, to the public opinion of the world the idea of the compulsory exchange of populations was offensive.

As a result of this unfavorable public response, there was a manifest attempt in the Commission to shift responsibility for the origin of the idea of exchange and for the proposal for a compulsory exchange. Ismet Pasha stated that the proposal of exchange had first been made by the Greek government, which seems to be substantiated by Dr. Nansen's reports above referred to. However, he admitted that precedents for the exchange may be seen in the Convention concluded at Adrianople between Turkey and Bulgaria on November 2/15, 1913, as well as in the negotiations entered upon between Greece and Turkey in 1914.[5] On the other hand, Ismet Pasha declared that the compulsory exchange of populations was accepted by Lord Curzon and Mr. Venizelos at the meeting of the Commission of December 1, before he had any chance to

[5] See on these *supra,* § 10.

speak on the subject.[6] In this he was forgetting the fact that Hamid Bey had put the compulsory character of exchange as a condition *sine qua non* to negotiating with Dr. Nansen at Constantinople.

Mr. Venizelos read a declaration before the Commission to the effect that the Greek delegation were willing to give up all idea of a compulsory exchange, subject to the conditions that the Greek population remaining in Asia Minor should not be compelled to leave; that the refugees in Greece should be allowed to return to their homes, and likewise the refugees from Eastern Thrace, as soon as such a return should be compatible with the interests of Turkey, and as soon as the difficulties created by the war should disappear. Mr. Venizelos said that he would even be disposed to accept any date that the Turkish delegation might fix for the return of the refugees to their homes. He wished also to reserve the right of the Greek government to limit the application of the agreement respecting compulsory exchange to those districts of Greece for which it considered the system indispensable.

When Ismet Pasha expressed his surprise at hearing Mr. Venizelos contradict his previous statement, the latter repeated that he had accepted Dr. Nansen's proposals for a compulsory exchange only because he had become fully convinced that any other settlement of the refugee problem would be rejected by the Ottoman delegation. He added: "if there was a misunderstanding on this subject, and if the Ottoman delegation were prepared to consider another solution of the problem based on principles which were more humane, he was prepared to withdraw his consent to the method of compulsory exchange—a method which he had only accepted under stress of necessity." [7]

Lord Curzon declared [8] that he deeply regretted that the solution should be the compulsory exchange of populations, "a thoroughly bad and vicious solution, for which the world would pay a heavy penalty for a hundred years to come." He

[6] *Lausanne Conference,* pp. 203, 218.
[7] *Lausanne Conference,* pp. 223-227.
[8] *Ibid.,* pp. 212, 218.

"detested having anything to do with it. But to say it was a suggestion of the Greek government was ridiculous. It was a solution enforced by the action of the Turkish government in expelling these people from Turkish territory." In reply to this Ismet Pasha remarked that "Lord Curzon had said that he detested the compulsory exchange of populations; but at the meeting of the Commission on the 1st December, Lord Curzon had declared that no solution was possible except the exchange of populations, and that, as voluntary exchange could not give any result, recourse must be had to compulsory exchange."

It must be admitted that Mr. Venizelos was too hasty in indicating his willingness to consider the principle of compulsory exchange of populations. When the question was first brought up before the Commission on December 1, and Dr. Nansen and Lord Curzon reluctantly accepted this principle, Mr. Venizelos voiced his agreement. Later, under the pressure of strong protests from Greece, he went back on his proposal, and raised the question of voluntary exchange in the Sub-Commission.

The idea of an exchange of populations was always welcome to Mr. Venizelos. This is evidenced by his memorandum of January, 1915, to King Constantine, urging the entry of Greece into the war on the side of the allied powers and against Turkey, which is referred to in another place.[9]

§ 225. Drafting of the Convention. The Sub-Commission appointed for drafting an agreement on the exchange of populations met under the presidency of Mr. Montagna, former Italian Minister to Greece, on December 2, 1922.[10] It devoted its first meeting to hearing a full exposition by Dr. Nansen of the results of his investigations and of his suggestions. It then proceeded to the discussion, as requested by Ismet Pasha, first of the questions of the return of civilian hostages and of the exchange of prisoners of war, and then of the question of exchange of populations. An agreement was reached on the first two questions. The question of exchange

[9] See *supra,* p. 29.

[10] *Lausanne Conference,* pp. 328-337. See also Conférence de Lausanne, *Recueil des actes* (Paris, 1923), première série, i, pp. 250-259, 272-278, 577-637.

necessitated "the keenest and most closely disputed negotiations."

While in the Commission itself the necessity of compulsory exchange was reluctantly admitted by all the delegations, and Mr. Venizelos declared his readiness to consider it, in the Sub-Commission the Greek delegation, doubtless under the pressure of public opinion in Greece, proposed that the exchange should be voluntary. The Turkish delegation "definitely opposed this proposal," and the previous decision was maintained.

A serious disagreement arose with respect to the demand of the Turkish delegation that the Moslems established in Western Thrace should be exempted from the exchange, and that all the Greeks established in Turkey, including those in Constantinople, should depart. After long discussions continuing during several meetings, the Turkish delegation agreed, in principle, that the exemption should be extended to the Greeks of Constantinople. The Turks insisted, however, on the removal of the Oecumenical Partiarchate from Constantinople, with all its organizations and constituent bodies. This demand, vigorously opposed by the Greek delegation, and also by the British and American representatives, formed a stumbling-block to the Sub-Commission, which had to leave its work unfinished and refer the question to the Commission.

In the meantime an agreement, in principle, was reached on certain points. The first step was to be the despatch from Anatolia to Greece of the men who were interned at the time of the Greek exodus and separated from their families; the exchange of populations was not to take place until the month of May, 1923; the properties of the exchanged population would be appraised by special commissions with a view to compensation, and if the value of the property left in one country should exceed that in the other, the surplus was to be paid by the state concerned to the commissions.

The Territorial and Military Commission took up again the question of the exchange of populations at its meeting of January 10.[11] The first question brought up was that of the

[11] *Lausanne Conference,* pp. 313-337.

Oecumenical Partiarchate. Lord Curzon and, after him, the heads of the French, Rumanian, Jugoslavian, and Greek delegations voiced their opposition to the Turkish demand for the removal of the Patriarchate from Constantinople, where it had remained as an Oecumenical Patriarchate since the fourth century of our era. All agreed that the Patriarchate should in future lose its political and administrative character and that it should remain a purely religious institution. Mr. Venizelos agreed also, if the Patriarchate might remain at Constantinople, to take steps with a view to the retirement of the Patriarch then in power. However, he insisted upon the reservation to the ecclesiastical authorities alone of all questions concerning marriage. Ismet Pasha yielded to the proposal that the Patriarchate should remain in Constantinople, confining itself within the limit of purely religious matters. As this problem was now solved, the matter of drafting an agreement on the exchange was remanded to the Sub-Commission.[12]

Such an agreement was at last drafted, after arduous and long discussions, and was submitted to the Commission on January 27. At the meeting of the Commission Mr. Venizelos once more paid lip-service to the right of the populations concerned to remain in their country of origin and not to be exchanged compulsorily. The Greek delegation once more made a proposal for the abandonment of the principle of compulsory exchange, but this was done rather to satisfy the Greek public than with a serious view to its consideration by the Commission.[13]

A separate agreement, in the form of a Protocol with regard to Greeks of military age whose families were already in Greece and whom Turkey had agreed to set free to rejoin their families, was to come into force as soon as peace was signed.

§ 226. Provisions of the Convention. The Convention and the Protocol were signed at Lausanne on January 30, 1923.[14]

[12] *Ibid.*, p. 328.

[13] *Lausanne Conference,* pp. 406-413, 419.

[14] *Ibid.*, pp. 425-426, 817-827. The texts are printed also in League of Nations, *Treaty Series,* xxxii, pp. 76-87.

The Convention was to come into force, in accordance with its nineteenth article, immediately after the ratification of the Treaty of Peace by Greece and Turkey. The Treaty of Peace between the British Empire, France, Italy, Japan, Greece, Rumania, the Serb-Croat-Slovene state, and Turkey, signed at Lausanne on July 24, 1923, was ratified by Turkey on August 23, 1923, and by Greece on August 25, 1923.[15]

The Convention concerning the exchange of Greek and Turkish populations consisted of nineteen articles. Its first article laid down the principle of compulsory exchange by providing as follows:

"As from 1st May, 1923, there shall take place a compulsory exchange of Turkish nationals of the Greek Orthodox religion established in Turkish territory, and of Greek nationals of the Moslem religion established in Greek territory.

"These persons shall not return to live in Turkey or Greece respectively without the authorization of the Turkish Government or of the Greek Government respectively."

Article 2 defined the persons who were not to be included in the exchange. These were the Moslems of Western Thrace and the Greeks of Constantinople. Article 3 stipulated that the Moslems and Greeks who had left the Greek and Turkish territories respectively since October 18, 1912, were to be considered as included in the exchange. The first instalment of Greeks sent to Greece were to be all able-bodied men belonging to th Greek population detained in Turkey and whose families had already left Turkish territory. In this respect the Protocol annexed to the Convention provided that, by way of exception to article 1 of the Convention, such able-bodied Greeks were to be released by the Turkish government on the signature of the Treaty of Peace, means for their departure being provided at the same time. It was further stipulated, in article 16, that no pressure should be exercised on the populations to leave before the date fixed for their departure by the Mixed Commission. Also persons exempted from the ex-

[15] The text of the treaty is printed, with an English translation, in League of Nations, *Treaty Series,* xxviii, pp. 12-113.

change were to be free to exercise their right to remain or return to the excepted districts.

No obstacle was to be placed in the way of the departure of a person belonging to the populations which were to be exchanged. Convicts and persons to be tried for crime were to be handed over to the authorities of the country whither they were going. Persons who had already departed were to acquire the nationality of the country of destination on the date of the signature of the Convention. Persons who should leave in the future would lose the nationality they had and acquire the nationality of the country of destination upon their arrival in the territory of the latter country (articles 6 and 7).

The exchange was not to prejudice the rights of property and monetary assets of the exchanged people. They were to be free to take away or arrange for the transport of their movable property. They could also leave such property behind, in which case the local authorities were to draw up an inventory and valuation of such property. Immovable and movable property of the exchanged populations was to be liquidated by a Mixed Commission. This included property of persons who had already departed since October 18, 1912, independently of any measures taken with respect to such property, such as confiscation, forced sale, etc. Expropriated property was to be appraised afresh by the Mixed Commission. Damages to or revenues from such properties of refugees were to be appraised by the Mixed Commission (articles 5, 8, 9, and 10).

Juridical as well as physical persons were included in the provisions of the Convention. Specific provisions were made for communities (articles 3, par. 2, 8, par. 2, 9, and 10, par. 4).

A Mixed Commission to supervise and facilitate the execution of the Convention was to be set up within a month from the coming into force of the Convention. Its constitution, duties, and powers were determined by articles 11, 12, and 13.

The sum due the exchanged population of each country on account of property liquidated by the Mixed Commission was to constitute a government debt from the country where the liquidation took place to the government of the country to which the proprietors emigrated. The exchanged populations were entitled, in principle, to receive in their new country property of a value equal to and of the same nature as that which they had left behind. Provisions were made for the settlement of the accounts between the two governments as a result of the liquidation (article 14).

§ 227. Declaration as to Moslem properties in Greece. Besides the Convention concerning the Exchange of Greek and Turkish Populations, two other acts signed at the close of the Conference of Lausanne should be dealt with here, for they are related to the question of exchange of populations and their execution has been connected with the execution of the above Convention. In the Turkish Counter-Proposals to the Draft Treaty of Peace, submitted at the second period of the Conference of Lausanne, an additional article, 159 *quater*, was proposed in the last part of the treaty, "Clauses diverses." This article provided that "the Moslems residing outside of Greece, as well as those who emigrated from Greece or the island of Crete, and who possess properties therein, shall enjoy, with respect to their properties situated in Greek territory, exclusive of Western Thrace, the benefits of the Convention concerning the Exchange of Populations." [16] This was meant to extend the benefits of the above Convention to Moslems who had left Greece prior to 1912, and imposed on the Greek government the obligation to buy the properties of such persons situated in the old provinces of Greece. Mr. Venizelos voiced his opposition to such a stipulation in the Treaty. But the Turkish delegation threatened to take measures against the Greek subjects residing in Turkey.[17] In view of this danger, the Greek delegation had to yield, and consented to sign a special declaration which put the Turkish demand in a milder form.[18] This is the Declaration as to Moslem properties in Greece, signed at Lausanne on July 24, 1923.[19]

[16] Conférence de Lausanne, *Recueil des Actes,* première série, iv, p. 50.
[17] *Ibid.,* 2e série, i, pp. 75-77.
[18] *Ibid.,* pp. 80, 112, 117.
[19] *Ibid.,* 2e série, ii, pp. 115-116.

This declaration consisted of four paragraphs. The first stipulated that the property rights of Moslems who were not included in the provisions of the Convention concerning the Exchange of Populations, and who had left Greece, including the island of Crete, before October 18, 1912, or who had always resided outside Greece, should not be prejudiced. These persons were to have the right to dispose freely of their properties.

The second paragraph provided that all exceptional measures against the properties of such Moslems were to be cancelled. Any claims with regard to such properties and their revenues, in case these had been collected by the Greek authorities, were to be considered by the Mixed Commission for the exchange of populations, provided such claims were filed with the Commission within six months from the coming into force of the Treaty of Peace.

The above persons might ask the "good offices" of the Mixed Commission for the sale of their properties. This would not involve any obligation of the Greek state to buy such properties.

The last paragraph stipulated that the Declaration was made on condition of reciprocity in favor of Greek proprietors who had left Turkey before October 18, 1912, or who had always resided outside Turkey. The Declaration in substance was a confirmation of the principle of restitution of properties seized during the war which applied to all the Allied Powers and to Turkey under the Treaty of Peace. In addition, however, the Declaration referred to the Mixed Commission instituted by the Convention concerning the Exchange of Populations for the application of its provisions. This is really the only element in the Declaration which constituted a difference in the treatment of properties of Moslems and Greeks in Greece and Turkey respectively from the treatment of properties as between Turkey and the other signatories of the Treaty of Lausanne.

§ 228. The Declaration on Amnesty. Another act signed at Lausanne (July 24, 1923) which should be mentioned here is the Declaration concerning the Amnesty and the annexed

Protocol.[20] The first article of this Declaration provided that no person residing or having resided in Turkey and reciprocally in Greece was to be disturbed or molested, under any pretext, by reason of his military or political conduct, or by reason of any assistance given to any foreign power signatory of the Treaty of Peace, or to its nationals, between August 1, 1914, and November 20, 1922. The annexed Protocol made a reservation to the stipulation of this paragraph. The Turkish government reserved the right to prohibit sojourn in and access to Turkey to one hundred and fifty persons of the category referred to in the Declaration. The names of these persons were to appear in the proclamation for amnesty to be issued by the Turkish government. Such persons were to be allowed nine months to liquidate their properties; at the expiration of this period the Turkish government was to liquidate such properties and remit the sale price to the interested persons.

When the declaration concerning amnesty was being discussed, it was proposed to insert a phrase in the first paragraph making it clear that Turkey and Greece reciprocally were not to prohibit access to their respective territories to former inhabitants thereof who were not subject to exchange.[21] While these two countries were to be free to prohibit the return of persons who were to be exchanged according to the Convention concerning the Exchange of Populations, the Greeks of Constantinople or the Armenians, who were not included in the exchange, were to be free to return to the homes from which they had departed in the past. The delegates of Great Britain, France, and Italy pointed out that permisison to such persons to return to Turkey was a corollary to the amnesty provided for in the Declaration. They stated that the Turkish authorities already prohibited the return of Greeks of Constantinople and of Armenians, while their properties were considered as abandoned and were subject to seizure and confiscation. The Turkish authorities alleged that these persons left Constantinople without regular Turkish

[20] *Ibid.*, pp. 111-114.
[21] *Ibid.*, 2ᵉ serie, i, pp. 97 ff., 109.

passports. This act, however, was not serious enough to entail upon them the severe penalty of perpetual banishment; they ought to be amnestied, like those guilty of all other political or military offences. Moreover, it was recalled that the persons in question had left Constantinople in the panic that prevailed in Constantinople in the months of October and November, 1922, upon the change of regime in Constantinople, and before the Angora government installed itself at Constantinople and was in a position to grant regular passports.

Ismet Pasha made only an evasive reply to the demand that the Turkish government put no obstacle to the return of the above-mentioned persons.[22] Mr. Venizelos thought that, with respect to the Greeks of Constantinople, no question of their right to return to Constantinople could arise, in view of the provisions of the Convention concerning the Exchange of Populations. Indeed, article 2 of the Convention exempted the Greeks of Constantinople from the exchange, and article 16, paragraph 2, provided explicitly that "no obstacle shall be placed in the way of the inhabitants of the districts excepted from the exchange under article 2 exercising freely their right to remain in or return to those districts and to enjoy to the full their liberties and rights of property in Turkey and in Greece." [23]

With respect to the Armenians who wished to return to Constantinople, in spite of the entreaties of all the delegations at Lausanne, the Turkish delegates insisted to the end that they could not take any engagement in the name of the Turkish government, and that "their Government preserved the right to take any measures of security against disorderly elements and trouble-makers." [24]

Concerning the Greeks of Constantinople there was a general agreement expressed that their right to return was guaranteed by the Convention concerning the Exchange of Populations. Mr. Venizelos stated at the meeting of the First Commission (Military and Territorial) of June 4, 1923, that

[22] *Ibid.*, p. 99.
[23] *Ibid.*
[24] *Ibid.*, p. 131.

Riza Nour Bey and himself had discussed the question in the Sub-Commission of experts and were agreed on this point. Riza Nour Bey had also assured Mr. Venizelos that the 150 persons excepted from the benefit of the Declaration concerning the Amnesty, according to the Protocol annexed thereto, were all to be Moslems. In order to confirm this agreement between the Greek and Turkish delegations, Mr. Venizelos read the following declaration:

"The Greek delegation ascertains with satisfaction that the Turkish delegation has declared repeatedly, with respect to the return of the Greeks who have left Constantinople during recent months and, in general, the Greeks who moved from Constantinople temporarily, that they may return to their homes without any obstacle and remain there, enjoying all their property rights and other rights, in conformity with article 16 of the Convention signed between Turkey and Greece concerning the exchange of populations. The Greek delegation takes fresh note of this declaration . . . also of a declaration of the Turkish delegation that no Greek is to be included in the list of 150 persons to be excepted from the amnesty by the Turkish government." [25]

Mr. Venizelos asked the Turkish delegation to confirm this declaration. Ismet Pasha noted that the declaration did not mention the Turks of Western Thrace. When a satisfactory reply was given by Mr. Venizelos, he affirmed that the Convention concerning the Exchange of Populations would be respected by Turkey, but that the Turkish government reserved the right to take the necessary measures for insuring public order by forbidding access to Turkish territories of trouble-makers. Mr. Venizelos having expressed his dissatisfaction with the lack of precision of this answer, Ismet Pasha replied that the Convention was to be respected in principle, and that "if special cases [*des cas d'espèces*] should arise, it would be expedient that the two interested governments come to a preliminary understanding." [26]

The above declaration and the whole discussion in the

[25] *Ibid.*, pp. 131-132.
[26] *Ibid.*, p. 132.

Commission leave no doubt that the Declaration of Amnesty had in no way the effect of limiting the power of the Turkish government to prohibit the return of all kinds of refugees with the exception of the Greeks of Constantinople. It was agreed that the right of these last persons to return was secured by the Convention concerning the Exchange of Populations. At the same time, the Turkish government desired to come to an agreement with the Greek government whenever special cases might arise of persons to whom the Turkish authorities might wish to refuse the right to return to Constantinople.

It should also be pointed out that the Convention concerning the Exchange of Populations had been signed on January 30, 1923, whereas the above discussion took place on June 4, but was to come into force only with the ratification of the Treaty of Peace. This was signed in July and ratified in August, 1923. Thus the above discussion may well be considered as part of the work preparatory to the Convention concerning the Exchange of Populations.

CHAPTER XVIII

THE MIXED COMMISSION AND ITS AGENCIES

§ 229. Constitution of the Commission. The Convention concerning the Exchange of Greek and Turkish Populations provided, in article 11, that within one month from its coming into effect a Mixed Commission was to be set up for the supervision of the exchange and the liquidation of the movable and immovable property referred to therein. The Commission was to consist of four members representing Greece, four representing Turkey, and three chosen by the Council of the League of Nations from among nationals of Powers which did not take part in the war of 1914-1918.[1]

[1] Originally two commissions were proposed at the Conference of Lausanne, one sitting at Constantinople and the other at Athens, each consisting of a neutral President and a Greek and a Turkish member. The Turkish delegation proposed that each of the two countries should be represented by three members on the Commission, while the Greek delegation expressed its preference for a single Commission. A provisional agreement was made that there should be one Commission with a neutral President and three members for each country. Subsequently, when the provisions for the liquidation of and payment for the properties of emigrants were discussed, it became apparent that the work of the Commission would be complicated and varied, and Mr. Montagna proposed that three neutral members instead of one be placed on the Commission. This proposal was adopted, the number of the national members being increased to four for each country. See Conférence de Lausanne, *Recueil des actes,* première série, i, pp. 586, 617, 618.

The Council, being called upon to appoint the neutral members of the Mixed Commission, chose on September 17, 1923, in secret session, after a report by Viscount Ishii, the following: Mr. Erik Einar Ekstrand, a high functionary in the Ministry of Foreign Affairs of Sweden; Don Manuel Manrique de Lara, a Spanish general; and Mr. Karl Marius Widding, a Danish diplomat. In the meantime the two governments had appointed the members representing their countries. The Greek members were Mr. Jean Papas, minister plenipotentiary; Mr. Alexander Pallis, former delegate of the Greek government at Constantinople for the assistance of refugees; Mr. Antonius Calvocoressi, former director of the Mediterranean Bank at Constantinople; and Mr. P. Canaginis, Director of Immigration at the Ministry of Agriculture. The Turkish members were Dr. Tevfic Ruchdi Bey, former Minister of Health; Hamid Bey, of the Ministry of Health, deputy of Erzengan; Ihsan Bey, Inspector of Finance; and Senieddin Bey, from the Ministry of Evkaf (religious foundations).[2]

The Commission was constituted on September 17, 1923, less than a month after the coming into force of the Convention,[3] and met for the first time at Athens on October 8, 1923.

The Convention provided that "the Presidency of the Commission shall be exercised in turn by each of these three neutral members." Viscount Ishii, in his report to the Council, had recommended that the office of President be held by each of these three members for a period of four months, the order of rotation in office to be decided by lot at their first meeting. Such a meeting was held at Geneva on September 24, 1923, in the offices of the Secretariat of the League and in the presence of three members of the Secretariat. Mr. Ekstrand was the first President drawn, but as he was to be retained by his work at the Ministry of Foreign Affairs of Sweden for some time, General de Lara assumed the Presidency. He was to be followed by Mr. Widding at the expiration of four months.

[2] League of Nations, *Official Journal,* November, 1923, pp. 1312-13, 1466-68.

[3] The Convention came into force August 25. See *supra,* p. 345.

Mr. Elkstrand was to hold office after Mr. Widding; he joined the Commission on October 29, 1923.

§ 230. **Changes in membership.** There have been several changes in the membership of the Mixed Commission. Two of the three neutral members originally appointed resigned before the end of the work of the Commission and the third died. Mr. Ekstrand resigned February 3, 1926, having been appointed Minister of Sweden to Argentina, Chile, Paraguay, and Uruguay.[4] Captain Hans Holstad, a Norwegian lawyer and business man, was appointed by the Council on March 20, 1926, in place of Mr. Ekstrand.[5] Mr. Holstad took his seat in the Commission on April 17, 1926. On March 13, 1928, Mr. Widding resigned his post in the Mixed Commission, having been appointed a member of the Memel Harbor Board.[6] The Council of the League appointed Señor Manuel de Rivas Vicuña Sperlier, a Chilean, to fill the place of Mr. Widding.[7] General Manrique de Lara died on February 27, 1929.[8] Mr. Holger Andersen, a Dane, was appointed to succeed General de Lara in December, 1929.

The Greek and Turkish members of the Commission changed too often. These members formed the Greek and the Turkish delegations, one of the four members representing each of the two countries being the president of the respective delegation. The presidents of delegations changed as follows: Mr. Jean Papas was replaced by Mr. G. Exintaris from September 24, 1924, and by Mr. J. Politis from September 8, 1925. He returned to the Commission on February 12, 1926, and was replaced by Mr. K. Diamantopoulos, who was appointed on November 22, 1926, and began his work in the Commission in January, 1927. A Greek delegate of long service on the Commission is Mr. Aristide Phocas, member of the Commission since April, 1925.

As regards the Turkish delegation, its President, Tevfic Ruchdi Bey, became Minister of Foreign Affairs in March,

[4] League of Nations, Doc.C.56.M.32.1926.I, and C.1914.1926.I.
[5] League of Nations, Doc.C.206.1926.I.
[6] League of Nations, Doc.C.177.1928.I.
[7] League of Nations, Doc.C.262.1928.I.
[8] League of Nations, Doc.C. 87.1929.I.

1925. Hamid Bey remained President *ad interim* of the Turkish delegation until June 9, 1925, when Saradjoglou Chukri Bey was nominated to the post. The latter became Minister of Finance in November, 1927, and was replaced by Djemal Husni Bey from March, 1928. The latter left the Mixed Commission in May, 1929, having taken the post of Minister of Public Education.

On July 7, 1927,[9] by agreement between them, and with the view of reducing the expenditure caused by the maintenance of the Mixed Commission, the Greek and Turkish governments decided to reduce their representation on the Commission to two members for each country. Thus the Mixed Commission since that day has had seven members, instead of eleven as previously. Mr. Diamantopoulos and Mr. Phocas were retained as the Greek members and Saradjoglou Chukri Bey and Ihsan Bey as the Turkish members at that time.

§ 231. Substitutes. The Convention made no provision for the temporary absence of one of the members of the Commission. Viscount Ishii's report recommended giving the right to the members appointed by the Council to nominate substitutes, if necessary, for the case of temporary absence, provided no objection was raised on the part of other members of the Commission. The substitutes must possess the qualifications provided in the Convention for the regular members of the Commission. The Secretary-General of the League and the two governments were to be informed by telegram of any nomination of substitutes.

The Commission soon after its constitution discussed the question of appointing substitutes for the neutral members of the Commission. The President of the Greek delegation thought that the private secretaries of the members should replace them in their absence, for reasons of economy. The Turkish delegation did not assent to this accumulation of duties.

Captain Petensen and Mr. B. Spottorno were appointed substitutes for Mr. Ekstrand and General de Lara; Mr. Widding used as his substitute, during his leave of absence in 1924, Count Frederik Moltke, a Dane. Mr. Spottorno resigned

[9] Commission Mixte, Procès-Verbaux, xii, 126th meet.

his post at the Commission at the end of 1924, and Captain Petensen in February, 1925. No new substitutes were appointed. Instead, at certain times the absent neutral member left his vote with one of the other neutral members.

With regard to substitutes for the members of the two national delegations, it was agreed that counsellors of the delegations could serve as such. In case the absence of a member did not exceed one month, the authorization of the President of the delegation was sufficient for his replacement by a counsellor. For a longer absence, authority by the government concerned was to be required.[10]

§ 232. Seat of the Commission. The Commission met first at Athens on October 8, 1923, although it was originally decided to meet at Saloniki as was requested by the Turkish government. It sat at the New Phaleron, in Athens, until June 21, 1924, with the exception of a short visit to Saloniki, where it held four meetings in the latter part of February, 1924. At the above date it moved to Constantinople, where its seat has remained continuously ever since.

When the Commission was sitting in Athens, the work of departure of the exchanged populations was being carried out. It was then requested by the Turkish delegation that the Commission should transfer itself to Saloniki. Instead, it was decided that a Delegation of the Mixed Commission should be sent there, and another to Turkey for the study of the local situation. In accordance, however, with the insistent demands of the Turkish delegation, the Commission went to Saloniki later on and held a few meetings there.

In the fall of 1928, the Turkish delegation insisted that the seat of the Mixed Commission be transferred from Constantinople to Comotini, the city where the Sub-Commission for Western Thrace was sitting. This was a tactical diversion. The Commission at Constantinople was in the midst of the Greeks of that city and their condition there was easily noticed by the neutral members. It was desired by the Turks to have the Mixed Commission in the midst of the Turkish population of Western Thrace, where, the Turks asserted, the Commis-

[10] Procès-Verbaux, i, 15th meet., November 5, 1923.

sion would be in a better position to realize the condition of this population. Comotini is a small and drab city, lacking entirely in accommodations. The neutrals, it is to be presumed, were horrified at the thought of being compelled to live there.

At first, it was urged that a decision for such transfer was premature, and that a delegation of the Mixed Commission should first be sent to Western Thrace to collect all useful information. Such a delegation, under the chairmanship of Mr. Holstad, went to Western Thrace on October 18, 1928.[11] Later, in view of the insistence of the Turkish delegation, the Commission decided to transfer its seat to Greece, and to ask the Greek government to provide it with accommodations in Western Thrace, where the Commission planned to sit on February 1, 1929.[12] In the meantime negotiations of great importance began between the two governments at Angora, and the Greek government did not reply to the request of the Mixed Commission. The neutral members agreed that, in view of the negotiations in course and the uncertainty as to the future of the Mixed Commission and its organization, it was not wise to move to Western Thrace.[13] Notwithstanding the further insistence of the Turkish delegation, the Commission decided that for technical reasons the transfer of the seat could not be made for the time being. Later, on February 6, the Greek government called attention to the lack of accommodations in Western Thrace, and gave the Mixed Commission the choice between Athens and Saloniki as its seat.[14] The question of transfer of the seat was not reopened again.

§ 233. Qualifications of members. Viscount Ishii's report pointed out that for membership in the Mixed Commission "a number of high qualifications were required" and that "men with wide experience and an unimpeachable record must be chosen. Their task will be of great magnitude and heavy responsibility and one which will have to be fulfilled as expeditiously as possible." It does not seem that the three neutral

[11] Procès-Verbaux, 171st meet., October 9, 1928.
[12] Procès-Verbaux, 174th meet., December 22, 1928.
[13] Procès-Verbaux, 175th meet., January 21, 1929.
[14] Procès-Verbaux, 176th meet., February 7, 1929.

members originally appointed by the Council were so well qualified as they should have been.

They were generally without experience in Near Eastern affairs, or in the political history and diplomacy of Greece and Turkey. Two of them, Mr. Ekstrand and Mr. Widding, were able diplomats, but they were neither jurists, with a judicial attitude for the solution of legal questions in a judicial manner, nor 'practical men' in the sense of being able to devise practical solutions of problems. Their work on the Commission lacked initiative, authority, and aggressiveness of purpose. Ever mindful of diplomatic tact, and forgetful of their true mission, they refused to take any decision when the positions of the Greek and Turkish members of the Commission differed. By postponing decisions they allowed disputed questions to drag along until decisions, if made, had no practical effect. As one of these members admitted to the writer at Constantinople in the summer of 1927, the Commission had come to be a kind of 'lightning conductor' in the relations between the two governments. This was an entirely false position for the Commission to be in.

Worse yet, it is not going too far to say that the neutral members lacked courage enough to put an end to the diversions and filibusters in which the national members indulged when they wished to prevent any action or decision by the Commission. Indeed, these members, and in particular the Turkish delegation, often supported interpretations of the Convention wholly untenable; the neutral members knew well enough, as a neutral admitted in a frank talk with the present writer, that these interpretations were maintained not with an honest belief in their reasonableness but as a filibuster. Yet the neutral members did not dare to back the opposing delegation and help defeat the attempts that nullified the work of the Commission.

Specifically, the part played by each neutral member would seem in general to be as follows: Mr. Ekstrand was at first very active, but became later indecisive and discouraged. Mr. Widding was too much of a diplomat. He could be carried along by the view of one of the national delegations and a moment later by that of the other. Mr. Holstad lacked initiative and was not disposed to exert himself. The dissatisfaction of the two governments with the inefficiency of the Commission reached such a point that the Turkish government, in asking the Council of the League in May, 1928, to appoint a successor to Mr. Widding, deemed it necessary to add that "in view of the nature of the duties attached to the office, it would certainly be highly desirable that a person having the necessary economic and legal knowledge, as well as other qualifications, should be selected." [15]

Señor de Rivas Vicuña was the outstanding member of the Commission; and it is to be regretted that he came too late, after the inexperience and inefficiency of his predecessors had all but destroyed the prestige of the Commission. He had a real appreciation of his position and his duties. In less than two months he became thoroughly acquainted with all the pending problems in th Commission and understood the difficulties better than any of the members of the Commission. He had initiative and knew how to make the Mixed Commission follow his lead. He had views and stood by them.

§ 234. Case of General Manrique de Lara. General Manrique de Lara is the only member of the Commission against whom complaints of lack of impartiality appear to exist. The writer, keeping within the strict bounds of official documents, considers it necessary to state the following facts.

(1) When the question of *établis* was first discussed by the Mixed Commission,[16] General de Lara, who had already signed with his two neutral colleagues the Opinion on the interpretation of article 2 of the Convention, receded from this opinion, in view of the refusal of the Turkish delegation to accept the view of the neutral members or even to take part in any vote of the Commission on the matter. General de Lara's allegation that the new law on the census, referred to by the Turkish delegation, threw a new night on the question of the *établis,* was in entire disagreement with the opinion of the neutral members, which he had previously signed, and which

[15] League of Nations, Docs. C.209.1928.I, C.262.1928.I.

[16] Procès-Verbaux, vi, 68th meet., September 4, 1924. On this question see *infra,* p. 403.

stated that "même au cas où une loi de l'un ou de l'autre des pays contractants règlementerait la notion d'établissement, le criterium d'application de la Convention par la Commission Mixte ne devrait pas nécessairement suivre ses dispositions, car . . . la Convention ne tient compte de la législation de l'un ou de l'autre des pays contractants. . . ."

According to this opinion, the law referred to by the Turkish delegation need not be taken into consideration even if it tended to regulate establishment. General de Lara's abandonment of the position that he had taken concurrently with his two neutral colleagues remained inexplicable.

(2) At the session of the Council of the League in October, 1924, when the Greek government called attention to the encroachment of the Turkish authorities upon the powers of the Mixed Commission, General de Lara, then President of the Commission, denied explicitly that there had been any such encroachment.[17] This the Greek delegation considered an act of partiality on the part of General de Lara. When the question was raised of his undertaking a trip to Rome for the session of the Council in December, 1924, at which the question of the minorities in Greece and Turkey was to be considered, the Greek delegation objected thereto, not finding sufficient reason for the trip, in view of the fact that no invitation had been extended to the Commission by the Council or by the Secretariat of the League. General de Lara did not hesitate to discover in the words of the Greek delegation "a manifest effort to avoid the personal participation of the President of the Commission [General de Lara himself] in the projected mission to the session of the Council." He insisted on going to Rome, and put the question to vote, obtaining the unanimous vote of the Commission, the four members of the Greek delegation abstaining from the vote.[18]

(3) At about this time General de Lara's impartiality was openly attacked by the Greek press at Athens and Constantinople. General de Lara provoked a discussion on this subject at the Mixed Commission, asserting that there was some source

[17] See on this *infra*, p. 405.
[18] Procès-Verbaux, vii, 80th meet., December 8, 1924.

of calumny against his person.[19] It is, however, remarkable that only General de Lara was the subject of such attacks, and it is even more remarkable that he did not consider the attacks sufficient cause for his resignation from the Commission.

(4) In June, 1927, General de Lara alone supported, with regard to the *établis* of Constantinople, an opinion entirely opposed to Decision XXVII of the Commission, the text of which was agreed upon by the two governments in the Agreement of Angora of June 21, 1925.[20] This decision provided that all Greeks of Constantinople there present were to be considered as *établis* within the meaning of article 2 of the Convention, provided they were there prior to October 30, 1918; and that the fact that these people came to Constantinople prior to that date could be proved by any means of evidence. General de Lara supported the view that the mere fact that such persons came to Constantinople prior to October 30, 1918, was not sufficient to constitute the proof of establishment, and that it was only a presumption in favor of the establishment.[21]

This opinion was in such opposition to the clear meaning of Decision XXVII that the Greek delegation felt necessary to protest.

(5) The same partiality on the question of the *établis* seems also to have been at the bottom of General de Lara's quarrel with his two neutral colleagues in the fall of 1928. As we shall see in another chapter, while General de Lara was under treatment in a hospital at Salzo Maggiore, his two neutral colleagues, desirous of putting an end to the interminable recriminations between the two delegations and of solving the problems pending before the Commission, took the step of submitting to the two delegations a comprehensive memorandum of their views with definite proposals. General de Lara, learning of the memorandum, left his hospital, at grave danger to his health, and started for Constantinople, with the

[19] General de Lara related, among other things, that at the home of an Athenian lady he had been openly accused of having departed from his neutrality and sustained the case of the Turkish Government. See Procès-Verbaux, vii, 86th meet., February 23, 1925.

[20] See on this *infra,* p. 410.

[21] Procès-Verbaux, xii, 125th meet., June 16, 1927.

hope of preventing his colleagues from putting into their memorandum proposals with which, especially with regard to the *établis,* he totally disagreed. He arrived in Constantinople on September 20, eight days late, the memorandum having been deposited at the meeting of the Mixed Commission of September 12. Then, at the next meeting of the Commission [22] General de Lara declared that Señor Rivas had promised him to wait for his return before touching on the question of *établis.* Señor Rivas, who was then on leave and was informed of this declaration, telegraphed to the President of the Mixed Commission, Mr. Holstad, as follows: "Surprised that advantage is taken in my absence to make erroneous affirmations." He received this reply from General de Lara: "I have spoken only of my request to you with regard to the question of the *établis;* no word from your part indicated to me your disagreement." As de Lara explained to the Commission, he had asked Señor Rivas not to touch the question of the *établis* during his absence and Rivas had given him no answer. Was General de Lara justified in interpreting a failure to reply as an affirmative answer to a categorical request? Señor Rivas, on receiving the above telegram from General de Lara, wired to him the following: "I never promised to postpone the affair of the *établis.* On the contrary, I asked you to send your opinion. In view of your refusal to rectify your error, I wait the text of your declarations in order to do so myself, with the aid of documents, before the Commission and the Council of the League."

This message placed General de Lara in a most uncomfortable position. He could no longer evade the question of retracting his declaration. Instead of doing so he preferred to affirm anew that Rivas had actually and explicitly given him the promise above referred to. Soon afterwards, General de Lara again left Constantinople for Salzo Maggiore. A few months later he died at the sanatorium of Saint Blasien.

§ 235. Functions and character of the Commission. The main duties of the Commission were administrative, legislative, and judicial. The transfer of the populations from one of

[22] Procès-Verbaux, 171st meet., October 9, 1928.

the countries to the other was the main administrative work. The question of the appraisal of immovable properties involved both legislative and judicial duties. The determination of the methods of appraisal and the taking of measures necessitated by the execution of the Convention involved some kind of legislation. The appraisal of individual and communal properties, the determination of the persons exempted from the exchange, etc., were tasks of a judicial character.

As in the case of the Greco-Bulgarian Mixed Commission, the Council of the League, in adopting the report of Viscount Ishii, made it clear that the neutral members appointed by it "will draw their authority from the Convention and always act in strict accordance with the views of the two contracting countries as therein laid down."

It should be noted that, in contrast to the Greco-Bulgarian Commission, where the neutral members constituted a majority over the members representing the two countries, since one of them had the decisive vote of the President, in the case of the Greco-Turkish Mixed Commission the neutral members by themselves constituted a minority. Therefore their dependence on the views of the two countries, when these were in agreement, was absolute.

Soon after the constitution of the Commission, namely, in November, 1923,[23] the two countries appealed over the heads of the Commission directly to the Council of the League, each government complaining that the other was not carrying out its obligations under the Convention. This was putting the responsibility for the execution of the Convention upon the Council, which had expressly denied it when it accepted responsibility for appointing the neutral members to the Commission. This seems to have been called to the attention of the two governments, and, as a result, the Greek and Turkish delegates in the Commission, on instructions from their respective governments, made identical declarations expressing their confidence in the Mixed Commission and their conviction that it would overcome all the difficulties of its task.

The Greek and Turkish members of the Commission were

[23] League of Nations, *Official Journal,* February, 1924, p. 324.

designated respectively as the Greek and Turkish delegation. This was for more than administrative purposes. The President of each delegation expressed the position of the delegation during the discussions. In his absence a member of the delegation was designated as the President *ad interim*. However, when the discussion was closed and a question was put to vote, each of the eleven members of the Commission had a distinct and personal right to vote. It was this fact which caused the Permanent Court of International Justice in its Advisory Opinion No. 16, referred to below,[24] to conclude that, notwithstanding the designations 'Greek delegation' and 'Turkish delegation,' each member of the Commission was independent and voted individually within the Commission. The truth is, as the writer has found from reading all the minutes of the meetings of the Commission in the seven years of its existence until 1930, that there was no such thing as independence of the various members comprising the two national groups in the Commission. The Permanent Court ignored this actual situation in reaching the above conclusion. In only a very few cases concerning questions of administrative detail, five at most in all the above seven years, did the members of a delegation vote differently.

The principle of the delegation of the right to vote in the Mixed Commission was admitted.[25]

The question as to when the Commission was legally meeting was raised on a certain occasion when only two of the neutral members, two of the Turkish members, and one Greek member were present. A substitute Greek and a substitute Turkish member also attended. It was implicitly agreed that a quorum of the eleven regular members of the Commission made a meeting legally constituted. But it was disputed whether substitute members could make up this quorum. In the case in question only five regular members were present and two substitutes. The single Greek member argued that the Commission thus constituted could not properly meet and take decisions, inasmuch as substitutes were ignored by the Con-

[24] See *infra,* § 348.
[25] Procès-Verbaux, ix, 99th meet., January 9, 1926.

vention. This view was not shared by the neutral members and the Turkish delegation, who voted down a proposal to call off the meeting.[26]

§ 236. Secretariat of the Commission. The Commission needed a personnel for the fulfilment of its task. This personnel increased with the development of the work of the Commission. The first to be appointed was the Secretariat.

Mr. Carl Bratli, a Dane, was appointed and acted as Secretary-General for three months, becoming in January, 1924, Chairman of a Sub-Commission.[27] He was replaced by M. Haller, a Swiss, who had in the meantime been chairman of another Sub-Commission. He was replaced, after a short interval during which M. Philippe Briquet acted as Secretary General, by M. F. E. Simond, also a Swiss. Two first secretaries of the Commission were also appointed, a Greek and a Turk, on the proposal of the interested delegations.[28] On the other hand, private secretaries were appointed for the neutral members of the Commission.

§ 237. Sections or Bureaus of the Commission. The Mixed Commission created at first three sections or committees at its seat: one for the determination of the methods of exchange; another for the adoption of the bases for the liquidation of the properties of emigrants; and a third for the study of the measures to be taken in each country for putting the legislation in harmony with the Convention. These sections consisted each of a Greek and a Turkish member and a neutral member as president.[29] Later a financial section and a juristic section were set up.[30] The former was to deal with all questions of finances of the Commission and was later to take up the question of the appraisal of properties. The latter was to study the legal questions presented to the Commission and to advise it thereon.

It should be noted that the establishment of these sections was proposed by the delegations of the two countries, who had

[26] Procès-Verbaux, ix, 102d meet., February 22, 1926.
[27] Procès-Verbaux, ii, 29th meet., January 4, 1924.
[28] Procès-Verbaux, i, 1st meet., October 8, 1923.
[29] Procès-Verbaux, i, 2nd meet., October 8, 1923.
[30] Procès-Verbaux, i, 16th meet., November 7, 1923.

generally the initiative in the early period of the Commission, as also in the later periods. All decisions of principle in the sections had to be ratified by the Commission. Rulings on particular cases through the application of decisions of the Commission became effective as soon as signed by the members of the sections.[31]

In July, 1928,[32] there took place a much needed reorganization of the services of the Mixed Commission. The Committees or Sections were abolished and five permanent Bureaus were created. The first Bureau was to receive complaints of interested parties, give to their claims the necessary attention, and refer them to the competent Bureau. The second Bureau replaced the second Section and supervised the appraisal committees. The third Bureau, replacing the third Section, had charge of the affairs of the Sub-Commissions of Constantinople and Western Thrace. The Fourth and Fifth Bureaus assumed the functions of the fourth and fifth Sections and took up the financial and legal questions respectively. The committee *ad hoc* created under the Agreement on Properties of Athens [33] was maintained.

The Second, Third, and Fifth Bureaus were presided over by a neutral member of the Mixed Commission. The President of the Commission presided over the Fourth Bureau, and the Secretary-General over the first Bureau. A member or a counsellor from each delegation formed part of the Bureaus. These worked every day and took decisions by unanimity. They kept no minutes of their meetings. Questions not decided by the competent Bureau were referred to a Committee of the three Presidents (the President of the Mixed Commission and the Presidents of the two delegations), with a summary statement of the case and the opinions advanced in the Bureaus. This Committee met three times a week and discussed the questions referred to it in the presence of the chairman of the competent Bureau. All questions not decided by this Committee were referred either directly to the plenary assembly of the Mixed

[31] Procès-Verbaux, ii, 29th meet., January 4, 1924.
[32] Procès-Verbaux, 163d meet., July 14, 1928. This was proposed by the Turkish delegation.
[33] See on this *infra,* § 347.

Commission or to a special committee or reporter designated in such case.

§ 238. Plenary meetings and Meetings of the Five. The Commission met at plenary meetings at the invitation of the President. As will be seen in another place, these meetings were very irregular. The most important questions were not usually solved in the plenary sessions of the Commission. They were usually the subject of conversations and compromises in private meetings of the five 'Presidents' of the Commission, that is, the three neutral members and the Presidents of the two delegations.

The plenary meetings had the purpose either of recording an agreement which had already been reached, or of recording a disagreement and allowing each member to put down in the minutes his position on disputed questions. They also served for the reading of notes addressed to the Commission by the two national delegations and the supporting of such notes by oral statements.

The reading of the minutes of the plenary sessions is not a very enjoyable task. Nor does it tell the whole story of the questions before the Mixed Commission, since much was done in informal conferences. However, the minutes are very instructive as showing the impediments in the work of the Commission; the lack of initiative and courage of most of the neutral members of the commission; and the narrowness of spirit and absurd complaints and counter-complaints of the national delegations.

§ 239. Decisions of the Commission. The rule was adopted that the decisions of the Mixed Commission, taken in plenary sessions, were to be considered final. This was so even when the minutes of the meetings were not read and approved. All such decisions were communicated to the two governments.[34]

The Commission could review its own decisions whenever new elements were produced by one of the delegations tending to prove that a decision previously taken was wrong or was based on false premises.

[34] Procès-Verbaux, i, 22d meet., December 7, 1923, p. 171.

The Commission took decisions of principle, administrative decisions, and decisions on particular cases. Only the first were numbered and collected together. The Convention provided in article 12 that decisions were to be taken by majority vote. This stipulation was not carried out, and, in fact, was violated by the Commission. The neutral members of the Commission not only allowed the violation, but indeed occasioned it by the absurd position which they took. With the exception of questions of minor importance, they never undertook to express clearly their own opinion and to add their vote to that of one of the two national delegations so as to reach a decision by majority. They allowed a tacit rule to be established that decisions on any question of importance could be taken only by unanimous vote. Whenever a difference of opinion existed between the two delegations, they conceived their task to be that of attempting to mediate between the two delegations, to reconcile their views, and to reach a compromise which would allow of a unanimous decision. This frustrated the whole purpose of the Convention and rendered the work of the Commission practically nil.

It will be recalled that the situation was different in the Greco-Bulgarian Mixed Commission,[35] where the neutral members stood by their views and either took decisions by their joint vote or added their vote to that of one of the two delegations. The neutral members in the Greco-Turkish Mixed Commission justified their position on the ground that majority decisions, taken against the opinion of one of the delegations, would not be executed by the country of that delegation. This is a slender excuse. The neutral members had other correctives to such a situation; namely, their resignation, or an appeal to the Council of the League.

§ 240. Sub-Commissions. Article 11, paragraph 2, of the Convention provided that the Mixed Commission should have the right to set up, in places where it might seem necessary, Sub-Commissions working under its orders. Each Sub-Commission was to consist of a Turkish member, a Greek member, and a neutral President to be designated by the Mixed Com-

[35] See *supra*, pp. 57, 60.

mission. The Mixed Commission was to decide on the powers to be delegated to the Sub-Commissions.

Five Sub-Commissions were first created [36] to supervise the departure of Moslems from the Greek territories. The Greek and Turkish members of those Sub-Commissions were chosen among the persons residing in Greece and having knowledge of the local conditions. The Greek delegation proposed that the neutral presidents be also chosen from among foreigners established in Greece. This was objected to by the Turkish delegation, and the choice was made from a list prepared by the Secretariat of the League of Nations. Two secretaries, a Greek and a Turk, were attached to each Sub-Commission.

The Commission prepared a set of instructions to direct the Sub-Commissions in the performance of their task. Later it was decided to establish six more Sub-Commissions, three for Greece and three for Turkey.[37]

The eight Sub-Commissions for Greece were distributed as follows: two in the island of Crete (Canea, and Candia or Heracleion); two in Eastern Macedonia (Drama and Kavala); one in Central Macedonia (Saloniki); two in Western Macedonia (Kojani and Kaylar); and one in Western Thrace (Comotini). The three Sub-Commissions for Turkey were located as follows: one in Constantinople; one in Mersina, covering the regions of Smyrna, Aidin, Adana, Koniah, and Kaisariyeh; and the third in Samsun, covering the regions of Trebizond, Erzerum, and Sivas. Each Sub-Commission could be charged with duties in neighboring regions or transferred from one region to the other.[38]

In June, 1924, when Crete and Eastern Macedonia had been almost completely evacuated and the work of evacuation of Asia Minor began, the number of Sub-Commissions was increased to twelve, seven for Greece and five for Turkey.[39] These Sub-Commissions were discontinued gradually as the work of evacuation of the various districts was terminated.

[36] Procès-Verbaux, i, 9th meet., October 24, 1923.
[37] Procès-Verbaux, i, 18th meet., November 21, 1923.
[38] Procès-Verbaux, i, 23d meet., December 11, 1923.
[39] Procès-Verbaux, iv, 56th meet., June 12, 1924.

The Sub-Commissions took decisions in accordance with the instructions of the Mixed Commission. Within the province of these instructions they could take final decisions whenever there was unanimity. Otherwise they referred the case to the Mixed Commission. This was especially so with respect to the exchangeability of persons. The Mixed Commission did not question a decision of a Sub-Commission declaring that a person was exchangeable or non-exchangeable, unless the decision was not unanimous.

§ 241. The periods of the work of the Commission. The work of the Mixed Commission may be divided into five periods. The first begins from October 8, 1923, the date on which the Commission met at Athens for the first time, to April 2, 1925. During this period the work of exchange of the populations of the two countries was completed; the Permanent Court of International Justice handed down its decision on the interpretation of article 2 and of the term *établis* of the Convention; and the Council of the League appointed the three neutral members of the Commission to make an inquiry on behalf of the League of Nations concerning the treatment of the Greek minority in Constantinople and of the Turkish minority in Western Thrace. At the end of this period, the Greek and Turkish governments carried on laborious negotiations, which terminated with the signature of the Agreement of Angora of June 21, 1925.

The second period begins on July 8, 1925, when the Commission met again after an interruption of upwards of three months. All through this period the two governments negotiated with the view, first, of overcoming the refusal of the neutral members to adopt a draft decision, agreed upon by the two governments, which sacrificed the rights of Greeks established in Constantinople who were absent from that city, and later of modifying and supplementing the Agreement of Angora. The Presidents of the two delegations were for most of this period absent from the seat of the Commission. The neutral members themselves were invited to mediate between the two governments at Angora and Athens. Little important work was done all through this period, the rare meetings of the Commission being consumed by individual cases of small importance or urgent nature. Such meetings were often separated by the space of three, four, or six weeks. Indeed, from July 15, 1926, to the end of the year only three meetings were held, on September 6, October 16, and November 17, all of them without importance. This period of the work of the Commission terminated with the end of the year 1926, the Agreement of Athens being signed on December 1, 1926.

The third period begins with the 115th meeting of the Commission on January 15, 1927. Soon afterwards the two governments, through the respective delegations on the Commission, announced the ratification of the Agreement of Athens of December 1, 1926, and the Commission at its 116th meeting, on March 19, 1927, agreed to undertake the execution of this new agreement, which considerably enlarged its sphere of activity and competence. From this date the Commission decided to meet every Thursday, a practice which was not kept up. In the first meetings thereafter many questions of principle were solved, such as the standing from the point of view of exchange of married women and widows, and the determination of the criterion of religion.

The serenity of the work was once more disturbed when the periods fixed by the Agreement of Athens passed without full execution on the two sides. The Turkish government openly began reprisals for the delay in the restoration of Turkish properties by the Greek government. In the meantime a serious dispute arose with regard to the persons who were beneficiaries of the Agreement of Athens, and in October, 1927, the work of Section V of the Commission, which was especially charged with the execution of the Agreement, was interrupted, and the Greek government had to enter into negotiations with the Turkish government, with a view to ending what it considered an unwarranted position taken by the Turkish delegation on the Commission.

From this time on a fourth period in the work of the Commission may be seen. During this period, while the two governments were engaged in negotiations, the Commission worked on as best as it could, postponing decisions on questions of principle, until March, 1928. At the request of the Turkish delegation further discussions were then postponed until the arrival of the new President of the Turkish delegation, Djemal Husni Bey. The meetings were resumed in the latter part of June, 1928.

It was only then that General de Lara declared that it was necessary to work out regulations to determine the general outlines of the work of the Mixed Commission and of the Sections. After almost five years of undisciplined activity, it was coming to be understood that the Mixed Commission needed a set of regulations for its work. The Commission was growing sensitive to criticisms from the Press to the effect that its progress was slow and its action procrastinating.[40]

With the coming of Señor Rivas Vicuña to the Commission, in June, 1928, a fifth period in the work of the Commission begins. Señor Rivas Vicuña, within the shortest possible time after his arrival at Constantinople, grasped the situation and applied himself to the mending of it. He requested the two delegations to prepare a brief statement of the problems pending before the Commission and of their points of view, and proposed that a programme be worked out for the discussion and solution of these problems. These statements were made by the two delegations. Señor Rivas concluded [41] that there was evident correlation between the measures taken in the two countries, the inadequate execution of its obligations by the one government being a result of the incomplete action of the other. He pointed out the absurdity of two countries bound by agreements having recourse to reprisals in time of peace. Shortly thereafter, and after General de Lara went on a leave of absence because of ill health, the two remaining neutrals, Señor Rivas Vicuña and Mr. Holstad, bestirred themselves and presented to the Commission definite proposals intended to clear up the misunderstandings between the two countries.[42] This relatively short period in the work of the Commission presents a greater amount of achievement than the whole five preceding years. All, it may be said without

[40] Procès-Verbaux, 158th and 159th meets., June 21 and 28, 1928.
[41] Procès-Verbaux, 159th and 160th meets., June 28 and July 5, 1928.
[42] Procès-Verbaux, 162d to 167th meets., July 12 to September 4, 1928.

hesitation, was due to the untiring energy and activity of Señor Rivas Vicuña.

On September 12, 1928, the same neutral members, Rivas Vicuña and Holstad, laid before the Commission an important memorandum, stating their views on all the questions pending before the Commission. Following this memorandum, new negotiations began between the two governments, terminating in the abortive agreements of the summer of 1929 and the final agreement of 1930 referred to below.

§ 242. General criticism of the work of the Mixed Commission. The great evil from which all the work of the Commission has suffered is that no preparatory work of any kind was done either by the Mixed Commission itself, by the delegations of the two countries, or by the respective governments. This was of no great consequence in the first part of the work of the Commission, namely, the transfer of the populations. When, however, the main task of the Commission became the restoration and appraisal of the properties of the various categories of persons covered by the Convention concerning Exchange and the subsequent Agreements, involving also problems of seizures and indemnities, the lack of preparatory work and precise data divorced the discussions in the Commission from reality, and often turned them into senseless and preposterous discussions of questions of principle.

Another evil was the total inexperience and mental insufficiency of the neutral members of the Commission as respects questions arising in its work. It is enough to point out that General de Lara, trained in the wars of Morocco, presided over the Legal Section of the Commission, which had to deal with intricate legal problems of international law, conflicts of law, and the municipal law of Turkey and Greece.

The Convention provided explicitly that the Commission was to decide by majority vote. Yet after the Commission had worked fairly well for the first year, from October, 1923, to September, 1924, taking at times decisions by majority vote, the neutral members adopted implicitly the curious position that decisions should henceforth be taken unanimously, since otherwise the government whose view, as expressed by its delegation on the Commission, was not adopted, would not execute the decisions of the Commission.

This was a very serious mistake of the neutral members, and one which had profound consequences in the work of the Commission. Instead of a judicial, legislative, or administrative body, the Commission was turned into a permanent conference, where questions were discussed interminably in an effort to attain a unanimity which was seldom reached.

It is clear that the neutral members ought to have had the courage to throw the weight of their opinion in favor of that of the delegation which they conceived to be right. By their indecision they encouraged dissension. It may be that the decisions of the Commission would not have been executed. But to what did the other course lead? To failure to execute the Convention and the Agreements, to the inactivity of the Commission, and to a total loss of its prestige and authority. A formal decision of the Commission by majority vote, solving a question against the opinion of one of the two governments, would have had one of two effects. Either it would have morally compelled the government in question to abandon its position, or it would have exposed the Mixed Commission to the risk of dissolution. This risk ought to have been taken by the neutral members. They should have declared that they felt a moral responsibility to the Council of the League of Nations, which had appointed them, and to the persons whose interests were intrusted to their care, to express their own views and to help take the decisions that in their conscience they felt to be right.

A perusal of the *procès-verbaux* of the meetings of the Commission discloses a disheartening scene. The two delegations talked at length. On the Turkish side, the Presidents of the delegations changed very often. Every new President took pleasure in arguing about many things at vast waste of time. The *procès-verbaux* registered all their words, which were often ridiculously insignificant. These members several times in correcting the minutes made long additions to what they actually said, thus immortalizing their words! The neutral members let the two delegations talk and recriminate. They only intervened to reconcile and mediate, or to refer questions for study. to sections and committees, where they usually were buried. The minutes do not disclose the use of strong or decisive language in any case by the neutral members. Hardly any initiative appears until the arrival of Señor Rivas Vicuña.

A last handicap to the work of the Commission lay in the long interruptions brought about by the negotiations between the two governments, described below. For many months, three, six, eight, and ten at one time, all activity of the Commission stopped on account of such negotiations. Thus a most expensive machinery was allowed to remain idle and useless. But the negotiations themselves were the result of the situation created by the inefficiency and incapacity of the Commission. The two governments, finding that it was impossible to solve their differences through decisions of the Commission, resorted to direct negotiations.

In conclusion it may be said that the usefulness of the Commission terminated with the completion of the transfer of the exchanged populations from the two countries. Thenceforth the Commission did little, if anything, at least until Señor Rivas Vicuña came to the Commission in June, 1928. Whatever was done by the Commission in the way of minor decisions or of mediation between the two governments could have been accomplished by a single neutral arbitrator. The maintenance of such an expensive [43] institution for so many years had practically no purpose whatever; and it is to be regretted that the two countries, amidst their disputes, did not see the advisability to putting an end to the Commission.

[43] On the expenditures for the maintenance of the Mixed Commission, see *infra*, § 382.

CHAPTER XIX

PERSONS SUBJECT TO EXCHANGE

§ 243. Criteria of exchangeability. The Convention concerning the Exchange of Populations defined in its first article the persons that were subject to compulsory exchange as follows: "Turkish nationals of the Greek Orthodox religion established in Turkish territory and Greek nationals of the Moslem religion established in Greek territory." Article 3 included in the exchange Greeks and Moslems who had already, and since October 18, 1912, left the Greek and Turkish territories. In the following articles the two populations to be exchanged are shortly defined as the "Greeks" and the "Moslems," [1] which stand for the above terms "of the Greek Orthodox religion" and "of the Moslem religion."

It would seem, therefore, that the only criterion of the exchangeability of a person, besides the fact that he was a national of the country which he was compelled to leave, was that of religion. The result would be that the Albanian Mos-

[1] This is also the case in article 2, which defines the persons exempted from the exchange.

lems established in Greece and the Armenians, Syrians, Russians, Rumanians, etc., of the Greek Orthodox religion in Turkey would be compelled to emigrate. This consequence would be avoided if the above criterion of religion were understood in a broader sense. Indeed, it was not meant to be strictly taken as an equivalent to faith or creed, but as a compound of ethnological, political, and religious elements.

As we have seen above,[2] the Convention respecting Reciprocal Emigration of 1919 between Greece and Bulgaria employed three criteria for defining the persons having the right to emigrate: race, religion, and language. Under that Convention also it was noted that the religious criterion was the surest in view of the mingling of races in the Balkans and the adoption by minorities of the language spoken by a strong majority or imposed by ruthless propaganda. In the case of Turkey and Greece the racial and linguistic criteria would be sure to break down in their application. A very large majority of the Moslems in Greece spoke Greek and racially had nothing in common with the Moslems of the interior of Asia Minor. On the other hand, the Greeks of many parts of the interior of Asia Minor spoke Turkish and belonged by no means to a single race.

§ 244. Religion as a criterion in the Convention. Religion was a safe criterion less as a demarcation between the followers of two different faiths than as a sharp dividing line between two ethnic and to a certain extent political entities. The Greek Orthodox religion was an ethnic entity within the Turkish Empire, having as its head the Greek Oecumenical Patriarch of Constantinople and possessing its own organization and administration through the bishops and communities all over the Empire. The Patriarch was from the morrow of the fall of Constantinople recognized by official acts of the Empire as the head of the Greek church as well as of the Greek nation, and he was given not only religious but also administrative and judicial powers within that nation. When Greece became an independent state in 1830, its people maintained a spiritual connection with the Greek Oecumenical

[2] See *supra*, p. 77.

Patriarch and the part of the Greek nation remaining under Turkish rule. Thus the Greek Orthodox religion was in a sense the external link of union between the two parts of the Greek nation, the free and the unredeemed. As such, it was the best criterion for defining the Greek national minority in Turkey.

In the Mixed Commission, when the case of the Arabians of Cilicia of the Greek Orthodox religion arose, the Turkish delegation contended that the term of the Convention "the Greek Orthodox religion" pertained to religion and not to nationality, and that it comprised all those who shared the faith of the Greek Orthodox religion. This would have had the effect that even Russians, Serbs, Rumanians, etc., provided they were Turkish subjects, would be included in the exchange, since the term "Greek Orthodox religion," if used strictly of matters of faith, clearly applied to them. But it could not possibly be admitted that Greece was bargaining by the Convention for the exchange of such persons, who had nothing in common with the Greek nation as such. The Greek delegation asserted that a person to be included in the exchange should be a Greek as well as an Orthodox.[3]

§ 245. The political criterion implied. This interpretation is indeed imposed by the whole spirit of the Convention. It finds also support in the preparatory work of the Conference of Lausanne. Indeed, at the discussion in the Sub-Commission on Minorities of article 1 of the draft convention prepared by Mr. Montagna by combining together the Greek and Turkish drafts, Riza Nour Bey, the Turkish delegate, objected to the proposed expression "ressortissants turcs de religion grecque orthodoxe." He recalled the true reason which caused the Turkish government to propose an exchange of populations. "The Turkish government," he said, "desires to suppress the Greek irredentism in Turkey." For this reason, Riza Nour preferred the expression "les grecs ressortissants turcs" instead of the proposed one, which eventually remained in the text of article 1.[4] His purpose, as the discussion that followed disclosed, was to expel from Turkey the Greeks of the Catholic

[3] Procès-Verbaux, iv, 56th meet., June 12, 1924.
[4] Conférence de Lausanne, *Recueil des Actes, première série,* i, p. 577.

or Protestant religion as well as the Orthodox Greeks. What, therefore, the Turkish delegation had in mind was not the exchange of the followers of a certain religion, but of the persons constituting the Greek irredentism in Turkey, that is, of the ethnical Greek minority. It is clear that Serbs, Rumanians, Russians, or Arabs had no relation whatsoever to Greek irredentism and were not covered by the expression "Greek Orthodox" of article 1.

Riza Nour Bey insisted also on adding the words "et helléniques" after the words "ressortissants turcs" so that this phrase would become "des ressortissants turcs et helléniques de religion grecque orthodoxe." His intention was to expel from Turkey all Greeks of whatever religion and of Hellenic as well as Turkish nationality. By the defeat of these amendments the Sub-Commission intended to limit the exchange to Greeks, Turkish subjects, of the Orthodox religion. At a subsequent meeting of the Sub-Commission at the Conference of Lausanne Mr. Montagna, the Italian delegate, noted that the expression "ressortissants grecs de religion musulmane" might be applied to Albanians in Greece, who evidently should be excluded from the exchange. He proposed that the expression be changed into "ressortissants grecs de religion turque musulmane." [5] The expression "turque musulmane" apparently was considered equivalent to "grecque orthodoxe" as suggesting an ethnical plus a religious criterion. Mr. Montagna's proposal was withdrawn at Mr. Caclamanos's declaration that the Albanians of Epirus were to be excluded, since "s'ils sont les coréligionnaires des Turcs, ils n'en sont nullement les compatriotes." These words, indeed, make the matter quite clear. It was not with coreligionists that the Convention was dealing with but with compatriots of the two contracting countries. It should be also noted that the title of the Convention is "Convention concerning the Exchange of Greek and Turkish Populations."

In view of the compulsory character of the exchange, the question whether or not a person was subject to exchange arose with respect to persons only who asserted that they were not

[5] *Ibid.*, p. 604.

properly included in the exchange. This question was naturally to be decided upon by the Mixed Commission, which, according to article 12, paragraph 3, had "full power . . . to decide all questions to which the Convention might give rise." Indeed, the Commission decided on April 4, 1924, that it was "alone competent to determine whether a person is or is not subject to the exchange." [6]

§ 246. Interpretation by the Commission. The Commission did not undertake to interpret the terms "Turkish nationals of the Greek Orthodox religion" until the last part of May, 1927.[7] All cases presented in the meantime were either held in abeyance or a solution was given by virtue of other provisions of the Convention.[8] For instance, persons established in Constantinople prior to 1918 were exempted from the exchange as such and without regard to their ethnic affiliation. At the 124th meeting of May 26, 28, 30, and 31, 1927, the question of exemption from the exchange of ethnical minorities was debated at great length. The Turkish delegation insisted on placing a wholly literal translation to the terms "Greek Orthodox religion." Such an interpretation, which would have the effect of including in the exchange Serbs, Rumanians, Russians, Arabs, etc., who would have to be sent to Greece, seemed, indeed, so unreasonable that it was opposed not only by the Greek delegation but also by the neutral members. The latter did not think that the term "Greek Orthodox religion" was to be understood as consisting of two terms "Greek" and "Orthodox religion" and as implying any element of race. The fact that no racial element was taken into account in the exchange of Moslems from Greece seemed opposed to any such discrimination in Turkey. Yet it was recognized that all Moslems in Greece of whatever origin (with the exception of Albanians) had a Turkish national consciousness, whereas the same was not true of all followers of the Orthodox religion in Turkey. It was clear to the neutral

[6] Decision XVII of the Commission.

[7] For prior discussions see Procès-Verbaux, iv, 50th meet., June 12, 1924; v, 57th meet., June 18, 1924; vi, 72d meet., September 23, 1924.

[8] Such cases were: a small number of gypsies of the Orthodox religion; Albanians of the Orthodox religion; Bulgarians of the Orthodox religion; and Arabs of the same religion from Cilicia.

members of the Commission that the Arabs of Orthodox religion of Cilicia did not have an Hellenic consciousness.

§ 247. **Orthodox Churches distinguished.** This consideration caused the neutral members to look into the affiliation of persons of the Orthodox religion to the different autocephalous Orthodox churches of the East and into the ties and relations between these churches. The President of the Commission sought for this purpose the guidance of the *Encyclopaedia Britannica,* according to which the Eastern Orthodox Church was a great ecclesiastical federation comprising a number of churches reciprocally independent. These churches were the four ancient Patriarchates of Constantinople, Antioch, Jerusalem, and Alexandria, and the following churches:

	(1)	The Church of Cyprus
	(2)	" " " Mount Sinai
	(3)	" " " Greece
	(4)	" " " Serbia
	(5)	" " " Rumania
	(6)	" " " Montenegro
	(7)	" " " Austria-Hungary
	(8)	" " " Russia
	(9)	" " " Albania since 1922
and possibly	(10)	" Schismatic Church of Bulgaria.

The President of the Commission thought that the term "Greek Orthodox religion" of article 1 of the Convention could not possibly apply to more than the Church of Greece and the Patriarchate of Constantinople.

In accordance with these views, the Mixed Commission adopted two decisions on May 31, 1927.[9] First, that the terms "Greek Orthodox religion" should be interpreted and applied as they have been with regard to Moslems in Greece, without regard to race. Secondly, that the terms "Greek Orthodox religion" of article 1 of the Convention should not be applied to all the Eastern Orthodox religions.

At a later meeting, in December, 1927,[10] the Commission

[9] Procès-Verbaux, xii, 124th meet.

[10] Procès-Verbaux, xiv, 137th meet., September 15, 1927; 142d meet., December 20, 1927; 144th meet., December 27, 1927.

decided, over the protests of the Turkish delegation, that the term "Greek Orthodox religion" could not be applied to: (1) the Patriarchates other than the Oecumenical Patriarchate with its seat at Phanar in Constantinople, namely, the Patriarchates of Antioch, Jerusalem, and Alexandria; (2) the autocephalous churches, such as the Church of Cyprus, the Church of Mount Sinai, the Serbian Church, the Rumanian Church, the Montenegrin Church, the Church of Austria-Hungary, the Russian Church, the Albanian Church, and the Exarchist Church of Bulgaria.[11]

The exclusion in the above decision of the Patriarchates of Antioch, Jerusalem, and Alexandria arose from the case of the Orthodox Arabs, who, indeed, had nothing in common with the Greeks of Greece proper and could not possibly be taken as included in the term of the Convention "Greek Orthodox religion." Many of these people, however, were compelled to leave Turkey and come to Greece in the early stages of the exchange. Seven hundred inhabitants of the region of Mersina, of the Greek Orthodox religion but speaking Arabic, desired to be exempted from the exchange, but the Turkish delegation considered them, in February, 1924, subject to exchange, and asked that the Sub-Commission at Mersina be instructed to send them to Greece. A portion of them still remained in Turkey in 1927, and the Turks fought hard to have the Commission decide that they were subject to exchange. The Commission made the concession, hardly permissible, that the above decision was not applicable to persons who had already left Turkey.[12]

§ 248. Greeks of Protestant and Catholic religion. In view of the explicit provisions of the Convention providing for the exchange of persons of the "Greek Orthodox religion" in Turkey, Greeks of Protestant and Catholic religion were excluded. Indeed, these persons, by not recognizing the Oecumenical Patriarch of Constantinople as the head of their church, were not supposed to form part of that national and semi-political entity of the "Greek unredeemed people" in

[11] Decision No. 35 of the Commission, taken at the meeting of December 27, 1927.

[12] Procès-Verbaux, 146th meet., January 3, 1928.

Turkey, against whom the wrath of the new rulers of Turkey was directed.

Any Greeks claiming to be of the Protestant or Catholic church were provisionally excluded from the exchange, and their cases were examined by the competent Sub-Commission, and, in case of difficulties, by the legal section of the Mixed Commission. Baptismal acts for the Catholics and extracts from church registries for the Protestants served usually as evidence.[13]

Members of the Greek Orthodox religion and of Albanian origin in Turkey should be exempted from the exchange on two grounds, because they were not members of the Greek minority in Turkey according to the meaning of the Convention, and in reciprocity to the exclusion from the exchange of Moslems of Albanian origin in Greece. The Turkish delegation in the four cases that were presented was not willing to take this view, but the Commission decided in favor of the exemption.[14]

§ 249. Albanian Moslems in Greece. The case of the Moslems of Albanian origin arose in the Mixed Commission at an early date.[15] Their claim to exemption from exchange was based, not on the interpretation of the Convention, but on the declaration made by the Greek delegation at the Conference of Lausanne during the discussions in the Sub-Commission. As we have seen above,[16] Mr. Caclamanos, answering a proposal of Mr. Montagna, declared that the Albanians of Epirus were not to be included in the exchange. The declaration by Mr. Caclamanos did not amount to a promise of the Greek government to the Albanian government to exclude Moslems of Albanian origin, but it would seem that it did amount to an undertaking for the benefit of the Albanian minority in Greece.

When the Mixed Commission was constituted and the partial evacuation of Moslems in Macedonia and Epirus began, the question of what was to be done with the Albanians was raised. In the notifications to the Moslem population, no

[13] Procès-Verbaux, v, 64th meet., August 8, 1924.
[14] Procès-Verbaux, v, 65th meet., August 16, 1924.
[15] Procès-Verbaux, i, 21st meet., November 29, 1923.
[16] See *supra*, p. 380.

specific provisions were included concerning the Albanians. The neutral member, Mr. Widding, proposed that the question be left to be determined between the Greek and Albanian governments. Both the Greek and Turkish delegations, however, thought that the Albanian government had no right to intervene in this matter, which was within the exclusive competence of the Commission.

It would seem that the Greek authorities tended to adopt the criterion of place of birth to determine Albanian race. Thus, only persons who were proved to have been born in Albania were declared by the local authorities in Epirus to be exempted from the exchange.[17] This was not considered satisfactory by Albania, as it would result in transferring to Turkey a great part of the Albanians established in Greece. Albania brought the question to the attention of the Council of the League, which, in its session of December, 1923, adopted a resolution expressing the opinion that the Mixed Commission for the Exchange of Greek and Turkish Populations should decide on this matter.[18] This had already been proposed to Albania by the Greek government.[19]

The Mixed Commission at its meeting of March 14, 1924, decided that Greek nationals of the Moslem religion who were of Albanian origin and had settled in Epirus were to be exempted from the exchange. It further decided that, if necessary, it would appoint a special body to obtain on the spot the information necessary to determine which persons should be so exempted. Pending the decision of the Mixed Commission in any special cases submitted to it, the competent Sub-Commissions were to postpone provisionally the departure of all persons who, in their view, were entitled to lay claim to Albanian origin.[20]

A delegation of the Mixed Commission, composed of Mr. Ekstrand as chairman, Hamdi Bey, and P. Metaxas, was sent

[17] See Letter of the Permanent Albanian Secretariat accredited to the League of Nations, dated December 6, 1923. League of Nations, Doc. C. 752. 1923.VII.

[18] League of Nations, *Official Journal,* February, 1924, pp. 364-368.

[19] Letter from the Greek Chargé d'Affaires in Albania to the Prime Minister of Albania, dated October 3, 1923. *Ibid.,* p. 365.

[20] Procès-Verbaux, iii, 43d meet., March 14, 1924.

to Epirus and Macedonia to carry out the above decision. It convened various groups of persons, especially those appointed for the purpose by the Albanian representative at Athens. The delegation was "of the unanimous opinion that all who came before it did so of their own free will and freely expressed their opinion without any pressure from any source whatever." It examined the various data which might be used as criteria of origin, namely, place of origin, language, customs, and dress. From the point of view of relative importance as an index of origin, place of origin was first of all taken into consideration. National consciousness of an individual and the desire expressed by the people to be included in the exchange were also regarded. Language, habits, and customs were considered as of secondary importance.

The delegation reported that the "vast majority of Moslem Greek subjects inhabiting Epirus and Macedonia state without hesitation that they are of Turkish origin and consequently desire to be included in the exchange." On the strength of this report the Mixed Commission issued instructions to the Sub-Commissions to the effect that place of origin was to be the main criterion, and that language and national consciousness were also to be considered.

The Albanian government was not satisfied with these findings and action of the Mixed Commission. It asserted that certain regions in Epirus were populated by people belonging to the Albanian nation and that the only criterion should be the language spoken. People speaking the Albanian and not the Turkish language ought to be exempted from the exchange. It was claimed that the criterion of the expressed wishes of the population could not be trusted, as the wishes were not expressed freely. Consequently, the Albanian government brought up the question again before the Council of the League of Nations at its session of September, 1924.[21]

Mr. Politis pointed out at the meeting that language assuredly could not be made the criterion for Albanian race,

[21] The above facts are taken from a memorandum prepared by the Secretariat of the League of Nations for the use of the Council. League of Nations, Official Journal, October, 1924, pp. 1600-02. See also Procès-Verbaux, iv, 56th meet., June 12, 1924; v, 57th meet., June 18, 1924, and annex 2.

since Greek was the language of the Albanian representative, Monseigneur Fan Noli, while the President of the Greek Republic at the time, Admiral Kondouriotis, spoke Albanian in the intimacy of his home. He agreed, however, that the question of the Albanians in Greece was a question of the treatment of minorities, and as such a subject for the supervision of the League of Nations.[22]

§ 250. Protection of Albanian Moslems as a national minority. The Council, after hearing a report by Señor Quiñones de Léon, decided to treat the matter as a question of minorities and to collect information.[23] In the meantime the Mixed Commission had decided on the exchange of 1500 Moslems of Epirus as not of Albanian origin. The Greek government scrupulously asked the Council to decide what should be done as regards these people. The Council had no objection to their being transported to Turkey on the responsibility of the Mixed Commission.[24] In its session of December, 1924, the Council decided that both the League and the Mixed Commission had duties to fulfil in regard to the Albanians in Greece, the former under the Treaty concerning the Protection of Minorities and the latter under the Convention. The neutral members of the Mixed Commission were, consequently, appointed mandatories of the Council for the protection of the Albanian minority in Greece. It was also thought expedient and desirable that the Chairmen of the Sub-Commissions in Epirus and Macedonia who should be intrusted by the neutral members with the execution of the work should each have at his disposal a person of Albanian origin whom he himself should select.[25]

The Greek and Turkish governments signified their assent to the above procedure, and the three neutral members of the Mixed Commission agreed to act as mandatories of the Council.[26] The latter appointed as their agents the neutral chairmen of the Sub-Commissions in Epirus and Macedonia, and undertook a tour of inspection in regions inhabited by Albanians in

[22] League of Nations, *Official Journal,* October, 1924, pp. 1354-55.
[23] *Ibid.,* pp. 1367-1368.
[24] League of Nations, *Official Journal,* November, 1924, p. 1655.
[25] League of Nations, *Official Journal,* February, 1925, pp. 145, 234.
[26] *Ibid.,* March, 1925, p. 338.

the summer of 1925. They also appointed persons of Albanian origin to assist the neutral chairmen of the Sub-Commissions in their work. These persons were recommended by the Albanian Minister at Athens. In the meantime the Sub-Commissions were supplied with fresh instructions on certain principles for establishing origin. In these, the criterion of national consciousness was relegated to a secondary place, as likely to be the expression of ephemeral changes and conditions, while the criteria of language, dress, customs, and habits were reckoned more reliable, as governed by tradition and as little affected by passing events and tendencies.[27] This was a decided change from the earlier views of the Mixed Commission and the delegation sent to Epirus.

The duties of the mandatories were to give decisions as to the origin of the Moslem population in order to secure the exemption from exchange of persons entitled to such exemption, in accordance with the Greek declaration at the Conference of Lausanne. In case, therefore, a decision as to origin was taken by the Mixed Commission which, if executed, would not conform to that declaration and would hence be contrary to the provisions of the Treaty concerning the Protection of Minorities, such decision could be nullified by a contrary decision of the mandatories. These notified the Greek government of the names of the persons whose exemption from exchange was secured.[28]

The Moslem population of Epirus amounted on June 11, 1925, to 20,160 inhabitants, distributed throughout 63 towns and villages. To that date 2993 persons had been declared exchangeable and had left the Greek territory.[29] When a claim was made by a person that he was of Albanian origin or when one was not recorded as of Turkish origin, the competent Sub-Commission proceeded to examine his origin and excluded him provisionally or permanently from the exchange.

While this orderly process was going on, the Albanian

[27] See supplementary instructions to the Epirus Sub-Commissions and Fifth Report of the Mandatories of the Council in League of Nations, *Official Journal,* September, 1925, pp. 1218-19.

[28] League of Nations, *Official Journal,* November, 1925, pp. 1682-83.

[29] *Ibid.,* September, 1925, p. 1218.

Foreign Minister and the Albanian Minister at Athens were deluging the Secretariat of the League with telegrams and memoranda, accusing the Greek and Turkish governments of conspiracy to transport to Turkey the Moslem Albanians of Epirus.[30] All this had the purpose, apparently, of creating an atmosphere of prejudice and of influencing the work of the mandatories of the Council. Indeed, as the mandatories reported on August 3, 1925, after their tour of Epirus, many Albanians, in view of the measures to which large landed properties were subjected in Greece, regarded emigration to Turkey under the system of exchanges as a means of obtaining land, "and preferred to go to Turkey." Besides, many people mentioned their attachment to Islam as a plea for emigrating to Turkey, which they said was preëminently the home of Mohammedanism. The mandatories and their agents were very careful about the matter, and made exhaustive search and cross-examination before including Albanians in the exchange. This they confirmed once more in answer to the protests and appeals of the Albanian government, while at the same time they denied its various allegations.[31]

At the session of the Council in December, 1925, General Manrique de Lara, President of the Mixed Commission and one of the mandatories of the Council, was invited to Geneva. He denied all the allegations of the Albanian government.[32] He also protested vigorously against the attacks made in the memorandum of the Albanian Minister at Athens upon the members of the Mixed Commission and certain of its officials.[33]

A few months later the work of the exchange was terminated. The Greek government found it desirable to allow the inhabitants of certain villages in Epirus, whom the Albanian government claimed to be Moslems of Albanian origin, to

[30] See League of Nations, Doc. C.695.M.250.1925.I; Doc. C.713.M.262.1925.I; C.741.1925/I/; C.765.1925.I. See also the Greek reply, Doc. C.37.1926.I.

[31] See League of Nations, Doc. C.729.M.263.1925.I, communicating a letter from General de Lara to the Secretary-General, dated November 23, 1925.

[32] See the opinion of the Mixed Commission on the reports of the Albanian government, which it considered to contain untruthful statements and insulting insinuations. Procès-Verbaux, v, 67th meet., August 26, 1924.

[33] League of Nations, *Official Journal,* February, 1926, pp. 153-158.

remain in Greece. Consequently, the Council in June, 1926, advised its mandatories to consider their work at an end and to forward a final report, which they did on July 14.[34]

§ 251. **Determination of nationality and religion.** The persons to be exchanged should have the nationality of the country which they were to leave. Thus, Moslems in Greece, not Greek subjects, and Greeks in Turkey, not Turkish subjects, were not included in the exchange. When a person who *prima facie* was subject to exchange alleged that he was not a Greek or a Turkish national, as the case might be, and documents were produced giving a likelihood of truth to the allegation, the departure of such person was suspended until a final decision could be taken. The Mixed Commission decided in such cases after reference to its Legal Section.[35]

In case a dispute arose between Greece or Turkey and a third state as to the nationality of a person, the Commission suspended its decision until an agreement was arrived at by the two states concerned, when, on the basis of such agreement, it determined whether such person was subject to exchange or not.[36]

The religious affiliation of a person was determined, as a rule, on the basis of entries in civil registries. These were conclusive, unless it was alleged that they were erroneous or incomplete. This allegation was to be proved by convincing evidence, such as official documents or certificates of religion issued by the church of which the claimant alleged to be a follower. The Commission decided on each individual case on the basis of all the evidence.[37]

§ 252. **Change of nationality before emigration.** Moslems of Greece and Greeks of Turkey were subject to exchange in case they were nationals of the country which they were compelled to leave. A material question, therefore, was to decide that a person was a Turkish or Greek national on a certain

[34] *Ibid.*, July, 1926, pp. 867-868, 947-948; September, 1926, pp. 1137-38; October, 1926, p. 1405.

[35] Procès-Verbaux, iii, 44th meet., March 18, 1924.

[36] Decision No. XVII of the Commission, taken at the 47th meet., April 4, 1924.

[37] Decision XXX, taken at the meeting of March 24, 1927.

date at which the principle of exchangeability was effective. There were three possible dates to be considered. The date of the coming into effect of the Convention; that of May 1, 1924, as the day from which the exchange was to take place; or the date on which the notification provided for in article 16, paragraph 1, was to be made to persons who were to leave the territory of Turkey and Greece under the Convention. This question was material for persons who, before one of the above dates, changed their nationality and ceased to be Turkish or Greek nationals.

The Sub-Commissions in Greece solved this question summarily. In Turkey a test case was presented by Lady Tahindji of Mersina, who at the time the Convention entered into effect was a Turkish national of the Greek Orthodox religion, and who subsequently married a Swiss national, thus acquiring the Swiss nationality.[38] It was admitted that the marriage took place after the Sub-Commission began the work of evacuation at Mersina. For this reason the Mixed Commission decided that the person in question was subject to exchange.[39] The Commission left open the question whether a marriage after the coming into effect of the Convention, but before the beginning of the work of evacuation, could influence the question of exchangeability.

Subsequently, the Commission adopted a decision which accepted as criterion the date of the coming into effect of the Convention. Indeed, by the terms of this decision,[40] "married women were to follow the destiny of their husband, from the point of view of exchangeability, if the marriage took place before the coming into effect of the Convention."

§ 253. Change of religion before emigration. There have been cases of Moslems in Greece who embraced Christianity in order to avoid being transferred to Turkey. In the case of some

[38] Procès-Verbaux, x, 111th meet., July 1 and 6, 1926.

[39] Procès-Verbaux, x, 112th meet., September 6, 1926. At the same time the Mixed Commission addressed a letter to the Turkish government, relating the peculiar circumstances of the case, and expressing the wish that the person in question, who was engaged to the Swiss national before the signature of the Convention, be allowed to remain in Turkey.

[40] Decision No. XXIX of March 24, 1927 (Procès-Verbaux, xi, 117th meet.).

Moslems of Crete, the Commission sought to find whether these persons were of age, and if so, at what time their conversion took place.[41] It was agreed that conversions taking place after the signature of the Convention were not to have any effect. For the same reason it was decided that the conversion to Christianity of fifteen Moslems of Serres was not to prevent the compulsory departure of such persons.[42] This decision was hardly logical. The Convention was effective from its coming into force on August 25, 1923, and not from its signature on January 30, 1923. It could not govern events taking place between the latter and the former dates. No provision to the contrary existed in the Convention. Subsequently, the Commission adopted a general decision [43] by the terms of which "the fact that Moslems or Greeks subject to exchange by virtue of the provisions of the Convention changed their religion after January 1, 1922, was not to be taken into consideration."

The Turkish delegation, of course, was not disposed to look with favor upon persons giving up their Moslem faith and embracing Christianity. The Greek delegation also had not much sympathy with such late converts, since their exclusion from the exchange would prevent Greece from taking possession of their immovable property and settling the refugees therein. In this may be found the reasons for the above decision.

§ 254. **Former emigrants.** Even before the coming into effect of the Convention of Lausanne and the constitution of the Commission there had been many currents of emigration between Greece and Turkey, including the great exodus of over a million Greek refugees who, fleeing the Turkish territories, reached Greece in the last months of 1922 and in 1923, after the disaster to the Greek arms in Ionia. Inasmuch as the Convention was meant to clear up the whole situation created by these racial migrations, article 3 provided that "the Greeks and Moslems who have already, since October 18, 1912, left

[41] Procès-Verbaux, v, 57th meet., June 18, 1924.
[42] Procès-Verbaux, 64th meet., August 8, 1924.
[43] Decision XXX, last paragraph, of March 24, 1927 (Procès-Verbaux, xi, 117th meet.).

the territories of which the Greek and Turkish inhabitants are to be respectively exchanged, shall be considered as included in the exchange provided for in article 1."

This provision set the date of October 18, 1912, for the application of the provisions of the Convention concerning the compulsory exchange and the liquidation of the properties of emigrants. All persons (Greeks or Moslems respectively) having left after that date the territories of the two countries were to be deemed subject to exchange and their property was to be liquidated by the Mixed Commission. The aforesaid date is that of the declaration of war between Greece and Turkey in the First Balkan War of 1912. The figures relating to these emigrants and refugees are given in another place.[44]

It is to be noted, however, that not all persons who had emigrated after the above date were to be considered exchangeable, but only those who had left the regions included in the exchange. Consequently, Greeks who had left Constantinople or Moslems who had left Western Thrace after October 18, 1912, were included in the exception of article 2 of the Convention and were not subject to exchange.

Article 3 of the Convention spoke only of "Greeks and Moslems." These terms must be understood with reference to the provision of article 1 to mean Turkish subjects of the Greek Orthodox religion in Turkey and Greek subjects of the Moslem religion in Greece. Consequently, Moslems who had left since October 18, 1912, would seem to be included in article 3 only in so far as they were Greek subjects at the time the Convention of Lausanne went into effect.

§ 255. Angora Protocol No. II of 1925. Most of these Moslems, however, had filed an option in favor of Turkish nationality, in conformity with the Treaty of Athens of 1913.[45]

[44] See *infra*, § 289.

[45] Treaty of Peace between Greece and Turkey, signed at Athens, Nov. 1/14, 1913, and ratified Nov. 16/29, 1913. Article 4 made the following provisions:

"Les individus domiciliés dans les territoires de l'Empire Ottoman passant sous la domination de la Grèce deviendront sujets hellènes.

"Ils auront le droit d'opter pour la nationalité ottomane moyennant une déclaration à l'autorité hellénique compétente dans l'espace de trois ans à partir de la date de ce jour déclaration qui sera suivie d'un enregistrement aux consulats Impériaux ottomans. . . . Toutefois, l'exercice de ce droit d'op-

Their inclusion in the exchange was accomplished by virtue of Protocol No. II, signed, with other arrangements, at Angora on June 21, 1925. This Protocol provided that all Moslems who had left the territory of Greece (with the exception of Western Thrace) after October 18, 1912, were to be included in the exchange, by application of article 3 of the Convention of Lausanne, notwithstanding all the formalities with which they might have complied by virtue of treaties or conventions, and in particular the option in favor of Turkish nationality that they might have exercised in conformity with the Treaty of Athens.

The Protocol was clearly a modification of article 3 of the Convention of Lausanne. It further provided that persons who had left Greece prior to October 18, 1912, and who returned there after this date for a brief sojourn, without the intention of establishing themselves there anew nor of preserving the former Greek nationality, were not to be included in the exchange. The fact that such persons were provided after 1913 with a Greek passport for travel in Greece did not constitute in itself a proof that those persons preserved the Greek nationality, unless this fact was corroborated by other evidence, such as a sojourn in Greece for more than a year; a participation in the political life in Greece as voter, candidate for an elective office, or public functionary; a purchase or sale of immovable property as a Greek subject; taking part in a judicial, quasi-judicial, or administrative proceeding as a Greek subject.

Protocol No. II of June 21, 1925, was communicated to the Mixed Commission on March 19, 1927, the latter undertaking on the same date to carry it into effect. It raised, how-

tion est subordonné au transfert du domicile des intéressés et à leur établissement hors de Grèce.

"Les personnes qui, pendant ce délai, auront émigré dans l'Empire Ottoman ou à l'étranger ou y auront fixé leur domicile, resteront Ottomanes. Elles jouiront de la franchise des droits de sortie pour leurs biens meubles. . . ."

By article 6 of the same treaty these persons were allowed to retain their properties in Greece and to give them in lease or to administer them through agents. No one was to be deprived of his property, "in whole or in part, directly or indirectly, except for public utility and on the payment of a just and previous indemnity." Martens, *Nouveau Recueil Général de Traités,* 3e série, viii, pp. 94-95.

ever, difficulties of interpretation.[46] The Turkish delegation asserted that Moslems, Turkish nationals, who left Greece after October 18, 1912, were not included in the exchange, and that only those who became Greek subjects through the annexation of the new provinces by Greece in 1912 and 1913 and subsequently chose Turkish nationality under the Treaty of Athens were comprised in the exchange under Protocol II of Angora. The Greek delegation opposed this restrictive interpretation, and maintained that the terms "tous les Musulmans" of Protocol II meant that all Moslems, whether Greek or Turkish subjects, who left after October 18, 1912, were included in the exchange. This view was based on the following considerations.

The Moslems who left before the Treaty of Athens of 1913 the territories occupied by Greece in 1912 and 1913 never became Greek subjects. Those who left after that Treaty by filing an option for Turkish nationality became Turkish subjects on transferring their domicile and establishing themselves outside Greece. Both categories were to be included in the general expression "tous les Musulmans" of Protocol II. The Turks who left Greece before the Treaty of Athens were subject to exchange by the fact that by the Treaty of Athens it was prohibited to them to establish themselves in Greece. If it should be possible for these persons to return to Greece, they would be Hellenic subjects and, as such, subject to exchange.

The second paragraph of Protocol II excluded from the exchange the Moslems who left the Greek territories before October 18, 1912, and had returned there after that date for a short sojourn. On the contrary, if such persons returned with the intention of establishing themselves there anew (referring to persons coming from provinces annexed by the Treaty of Athens) or of preserving their old Hellenic nationality (referring to Moslems from Thessaly who had left before 1912) they are included in the exchange. Leaving aside the Thessalian Moslems, according to this second paragraph of Protocol II the mere fact that a Moslem coming from the territories

[46] Procès-Verbaux, 156th meet., March 12, 1928.

annexed by the Treaty of Athens returned there after October 18, 1912, with the intention of establishing himself there anew, and left after that date, rendered him exchangeable. The Moslem in question was presumably a Turkish subject who left originally before 1912, went back after 1912, and left again. If this Turkish national was subject to exchange, it seemed reasonable that a Turkish national who left once and for all after 1912 was to be deemed subject to exchange by virtue of the first paragraph of Protocol II.

§ 256. Juristic persons and communities. The second paragraph of article 3 of the Convention of Lausanne provided that "the expression 'emigrant' in the present convention includes all physical and juridical persons who are required to emigrate or who have emigrated since October 18, 1912." In conformity with this provision, Decision No. XVIII of the Mixed Commission, taken on April 4, 1924, held that "all the decisions of the Mixed Commission concerning physical persons are equally applicable to juridical persons."

The extension of the provisions of the Convention and the decisions of the Mixed Commission to juristic persons was material from the point of view of the liquidation of their properties by the Mixed Commission, and of the right of such persons to take away or arrange for the transport of their movable property.

Especial mention is made in the Convention of communities. It was provided that these included the personnel of mosques, *tekkés, medressés,* churches, convents, schools, hospitals, societies, associations and juridical persons, or other foundations of any nature whatever. These communities have not given rise to the disputes the same term occasioned in the Greco-Bulgarian Mixed Commission,[47] presumably because the question of liquidation of any of their properties never came before the Commission.

§ 257. Married women and minors. The Convention of Lausanne contained no provisions similar to those of article 4 of the Convention of Neuilly, which recognized the right of emigration as pertaining to persons over eighteen years of

[47] See *supra,* pp. 157 ff.

age and prescribed that a declaration by a husband implied that of his wife and a declaration by parents or guardians that of their children or wards under eighteen years of age. The reason for this difference was that under the Convention of Lausanne the exchange was compulsory, and all persons, regardless of age or status, were to be exchanged if they were 'Greeks' in Turkey or 'Moslems' in Greece. However, the Convention excepted certain persons from the exchange when they fulfilled certain conditions of establishment. Also there might be cases of difference of nationality or religion between members of a family. For such cases the Commission established certain rules calculated to secure the integrity of the family or personal independence as the case might be.

Thus, it was decided that married women followed the destiny of their husbands if the marriage took place before the coming into effect of the Convention.[48] Widows were subject to exchange or not, according to their personal status. But when they had minor children (under eighteen years) at the time their case was examined by the Commission, they followed the destiny of these children. This applied only in the regions whose inhabitants were subject to exchange.[49]

The existence of marriage in the above cases might be a disputed question. The entries in civil registries were considered conclusive proof. Allegations that such entries were erroneous or incomplete might be proved by convincing proof. Information in official documents or certificates of religious authorities were accepted as such proof, but were not, in themselves, conclusive.[50]

In certain cases where the hardship of the rules ought to bend to humanitarian considerations, the Commission asked the two governments to allow exceptions. This was done, for instance, in the case of a young Christian girl, whose mother, a Moslem, was exchangeable and asked to take her away.[51]

[48] Procès-Verbaux, vi, 68th meet., September 15, 1924; also Decision XXIX, taken at the meeting of March 24, 1927.

[49] Decision XXXI, taken at the meeting of March 24, 1927.

[50] Decision XXXII, taken at the meeting of July 25, 1927.

[51] Procès-Verbaux, ii, 29th meet., January 4, 1924.

§ 258. Acquisition of new nationality by exchanged persons. Article 7 of the Convention provided that the emigrants were to lose the nationality of the country which they left and acquire the nationality of the country of their destination upon their arrival in the territory of the latter. The moment such persons reached the territory of the country of destination was the moment at which the change of nationality took place.

Prior to the coming into force of the Convention, and as far back as 1912, great numbers of Greeks had left the Turkish territory seeking refuge in Greece, while many Turks had left the Greek territories after the Balkan wars. At what time did these people change their nationality? The above rule could not properly apply to them, as they had not left with the intention of never returning again to their country of origin. The second paragraph of article 7 prescribed with respect to these persons that, in case they had not yet acquired their new nationality, they were to acquire it on the date of the signature of the Convention, namely, on January 30, 1923.

There was still another category of persons to be considered, those subject to exchange who had left Turkey or Greece for a third country prior to or after the coming into force of the Convention. The Commission decided, in view of the above rules, that the fact that the persons in question emigrated to a third country instead of to Turkey or Greece respectively made no difference. If such persons left one of these countries prior to the signature of the Convention of Lausanne, they acquired at the date of January 30, 1923, the nationality of the country to which they were nationally akin; if they left after the signature of the Convention they acquired such nationality at the time they reached the territory of a third country.[52]

[52] Decision No. XXII, taken at the 52d meet., May 9, 1924. This was applied, for instance, to Greeks who had left Turkey after 1912 and were established in the United States. See Procès-Verbaux, xi, 117th meet., March 24, 1927.

CHAPTER XX

PERSONS EXEMPTED FROM THE EXCHANGE

§ 259. Provisions of the Convention. While article 1 of the Convention of Lausanne provided for the compulsory exchange of Moslems in Greece and Greeks in Turkey, an exception to this rule was made with respect to Greeks established at Constantinople and Moslems in Western Thrace. The laborious discussions at the Conference of Lausanne concerning this exception are described above.[1] The exception was contained in article 2 of the Convention, which read as follows:

"The following persons shall not be included in the exchange provided for in article 1:

"(*a*) the Greek inhabitants of Constantinople.

"(*b*) the Moslem inhabitants of Western Thrace.

"All Greeks who were already established before 30th October, 1918, within the areas under the Prefecture of the City of Constantinople, as defined by the law of 1912, shall be considered as Greek inhabitants of Constantinople.

[1] See *supra*, p. 343.

"All Moslems established in the region to the east of the frontier line laid down in 1913 by the Treaty of Bucharest shall be considered as Moslem inhabitants of Western Thrace."

The second and third paragraphs of this article serve to define the two categories of persons included in the first paragraph. What is to be understood by the term "Western Thrace" is explained by the third paragraph. The line of the Treaty of Bucharest is accepted as the western boundary of this region. This is formed mostly by the river Mesta. The Turkish delegation at the Conference of Lausanne asserted that the boundary of Western Thrace should be the river Struma. There was no ground for this demand, except the fact that the Turks desired to leave in Greece a greater number of Moslems. Western Thrace proper did not include more than 130,000 Moslems against the 300,000 Greeks of Constantinople, according to the figures given by the Turkish delegation.[2] Subsequently, in exchange for other concessions on the part of the Greek delegation, the Turkish delegation abandoned this demand. At the same time, the Montagna Sub-Commission included in its minutes a recommendation to the Mixed Commission that the Moslem population of the region between the rivers Mesta and Struma form the last contingent of persons to be exchanged.[3]

The definition of Greek inhabitants of Constantinople is given in the second paragraph of article 2. The area of the prefecture of the city of Constantinople is defined by the Turkish law of 1912. At the Conference of Lausanne, the Turkish delegation was strongly urged by the Allied delegations to accept the extension of this area to the city of Pendik on the Anatolian Railway. This city did not belong to the prefecture of Constantinople but formed part of its suburbs. The Turkish delegation then had refused to accept this proposal as well as that of the Greek delegation that the inhabitants of Pendik, about 15,000, be allowed to transfer themselves within the district of Constantinople.[4]

[2] Conférence de Lausanne, *Recueil des actes,* première série, i, pp. 579, 605. [3] *Ibid.,* pp. 627, 628.

[4] Conférence de Lausanne, *Recueil des actes,* première série, i, pp. 579, 605, 610, 613, 621, 626.

The date of October 30, 1918, as the day *ante quem* the Greeks should have been established in Constantinople in order to be exempted from the exchange was adopted reluctantly at the Conference of Lausanne. The Montagna Sub-Commission had originally adopted a provision that "all Greeks established in Constantinople" should be exempted. This provision and a proposal by Mr. Montagna that the date of 1920 be adopted were resisted by the Turkish delegation.[5]

§ 260. **The *établis* at Constantinople.** The term in article 2 which caused sharp difference of opinion between the two governments, provoked the greatest animosities, and led ultimately to recourse to the Permanent Court of International Justice, is the term *établis* ('established') in the second and third paragraphs. As a matter of fact, the dispute arose only with respect to the second paragraph, concerning Greeks 'established' in Constantinople. The disagreement had continued for some time when, in August, 1924, at the request of the neutral members of the Mixed Commission, the two national delegations presented opposing arguments with respect to the definition of the persons included in the exception of article 2 and the procedure to be followed for their exemption from the exchange. On the basis of these arguments, the neutral members rendered a unanimous opinion recording their conclusions. The memoranda of the two delegations and the opinion of the neutral members were read at the 68th meeting of the Commission on September 4, 1924.[6]

It will be noted from reading article 2 that the persons exempted from the exchange are the 'inhabitants' of the two specified areas. The term 'inhabitants' of the first paragraph is defined by the other two paragraphs. In this definition, for the territorial limits of the area explicit reference was made by the Convention to the Turkish law of 1912, and for the limits of the period of establishment the date of October 30, 1918, was provided. No reference was made to the law of any country with regard to the definition of the term 'established' (*établis*).

[5] *Ibid.*, p. 579.
[6] Procès-Verbaux, vi.

§ 261. **Greek and Turkish arguments.** The argument of the Greek delegation was very simple. The word 'establishment' was not to be confused with the term domicile; it referred to an actual situation and not to a legal condition. Therefore, it was to be interpreted regardless of any Greek or Turkish law prescribing the fulfilment of formalities for the acquisition or transfer of domicile in the city of Constantinople or in Western Thrace. The word establishment did not imply the fulfilment of any legal formality and signified only a continued residence in a certain place where the activity of a person and the conduct of his business were centred. The preparatory work of the Conference of Lausanne reënforced this argument. It was clear that what the Turkish delegation then wished to leave out from the exception of article 2 were the Greeks who came to reside in Constantinople after October 30, 1918.

The Turkish argument identified the word 'establishment' with domicile. Indeed, it was maintained that a person is to be deemed established in a certain place "when he goes to reside there with the intention of remaining there permanently." The conclusion was drawn that Greek inhabitants of Constantinople residing there before 1918, whose families were established in regions of Turkey subject to exchange, did not come to Constantinople with the intention of remaining there permanently, and, therefore, were not to be exempted from the exchange. Further, the Turkish delegation contended that the term *établis* was to be interpreted in connection with the Turkish law on civil status. This law did not consider any person leaving his place of origin to have established a domicile in another place except after the fulfilment of certain formalities. So long as these formalities were not complied with by Greek inhabitants of Constantinople, they were not to be considered as *établis* in Constantinople.

§ 262. **Opinion of the neutrals.** The opinion of the neutral members brought out the confusion of 'establishment' and 'domicile' in the Turkish argument and supported the view that only the word 'establishment' belonged to the terminology of international law. The Turkish law on civil status referred to domicile and was therefore inapplicable. The Convention did not take account of the legislation of the contracting countries except when it explicitly referred to it. The neutral members concluded that all Greeks inhabiting Constantinople and Moslems inhabiting Western Thrace before October 30, 1918, were to be exempted from the exchange, unless it was proved that such persons, before the above date, did not have the intention of remaining there. A number of criteria were cited which were to be used in case of dispute as to the existence of such intention. It was further stated that in the opinion of the neutral members married women and minors were to follow the condition of their husbands and fathers.[7]

This opinion and the conclusions of the neutral members did not please the Turkish delegation, which, through its President, Tevfic Ruchdi Bey, did not mince words in expressing its displeasure. It declared expressly that the view of the neutrals, which was also the Greek view, was manifestly contrary to the Convention, and that "it would not be accepted by the Turkish delegation even though the majority should so decide." It further threatened that "it [the Turkish delegation] would not even take part in the work of the Mixed Commission." Invited by Mr. Papas to state whether the Turkish delegation or the Mixed Commission was competent to interpret the Convention, Tevfic Ruchdi Bey declared that the Turkish delegation considered that article 2 of the Convention needed no interpretation, and that the local Turkish authorities should decide who were to be excluded from the exchange as 'established' in Constantinople.

During this discussion, Tevfic Ruchdi Bey admitted the distinction between domicile and establishment, and gave up the contention that the Turkish law on the civil status of persons was to determine the persons established in Constantinople. But he now contended that another law, that on the census, was to be taken into consideration. This furnished an opportunity to General de Lara to declare that this threw a new light on the matter, and that the conclusions of the neutrals were to be taken only as "a beginning of discus-

[7] League of Nations, *Official Journal,* November, 1924, pp. 1674-76.

sion." This was not the view of the other two neutral members, and as the request of the Turks that the Legal Section of the Commission should study the question of interpretation of article 2 was not accepted, the President of the Turkish delegation resigned his post at the Commission. A few days later, under instructions from his government, Tevfic Ruchdi Bey withdrew his resignation, resumed his seat on the Commission, and reiterated his request that the question at issue be referred to the Legal Section. The Commission, in a conciliatory spirit, on this occasion granted his request.[8]

The Legal Section held long discussions on this subject, but without result, as the Greek and Turkish delegations held to the views already expressed. The Turkish members persisted in granting the status of 'established' persons only to those who had fulfilled the formalities of registration provided for by the law of 1914, while the Greek members continued to assign this status to all persons who by the exercise of their profession, the carrying out of various undertakings, and, in general, in any other definite way, had sufficiently shown their intention of remaining 'established' at Constantinople. The neutral president of the Legal Section, Mr. Ekstrand, although he considered that a clear intention of remaining 'established' at Constantinople should be shown, did not admit that the fulfilment of registration formalities should constitute the only proof of such intention. In other words, he agreed with the Greek interpretation.[9]

The report of the Legal Section was communicated to the members of the Commission on October 1, 1924. The Mixed Commission met to take a final decision on October 3. Tevfic Ruchdi Bey did not appear, and sent word that, for reasons of health, he was again obliged to tender his resignation.

§ 263. Arbitrary conduct of the Turkish authorities. In the meantime the Turkish government undertook to decide the question for itself and forcibly to expel the Greeks whom it considered exchangeable. A letter from the Greek delegation under date of October 12 warned the Commission of the

[8] Procès-Verbaux, vi, 69th meet., September 8, 1924.

[9] See the report of the Legal Section in League of Nations, *Official Journal,* November, 1924, p. 1676-78.

impending arbitrary action. From October 18 to 22 the Constantinople police, without paying any attention to the presence of the Mixed Commission, proceeded to arrest 4452 persons, who were interned in a concentration camp pending embarkation for a Greek port. Of this number 765 persons were clearly nonexchangeable, having been established at Constantinople before October 30, 1918. The rest were exchangeable Greeks to whom the competent Sub-Commission had not yet delivered the necessary passports. The tensity of the situation was relieved by a special agreement between the Presidents of the two delegations, concluded on October 21 under the auspices of the neutral members. The Constantinople Sub-Commission proceeded to the camp to deliver passports to the exchangeable Greeks and to despatch them to Greece, and to set free those who were undoubtedly not liable to exchange.[10]

§ 264. The question before the Council of the League. The whole affair shows clearly that the Turkish government had interfered with the work of the Commission and had encroached upon its powers. For this reason the Greek government brought the question of the Greeks 'established' at Constantinople before the Council of the League at its Brussels session of October, 1924.[11] The Council, after hearing the Turkish and Greek representatives and the President of the Mixed Commission, General de Lara, who, among other things, and in the face of the above facts, denied that any attempt at encroachment upon the powers of the Commission had been made, adopted a report by Viscount Ishii, which suggested that points of great legal difficulty, if the members of the Commission doubted whether they had sufficient juridical knowledge to interpret them, might be referred to the Permanent Court of International Justice.[12] This suggestion was

[10] It is to be noted that the *Procès-Verbaux* of the Commission give no intimation of this conduct of the Turkish delegation and government. The facts are related in documents published in League of Nations, *Official Journal,* November, 1924, pp. 1672-79.

[11] The special agreement of October 21 was not carried out completely. By October 31, or ten days later, 195 persons, not liable to exchange, still remained under arrest, and new persons were being arrested. See Procès-Verbaux, vi, 75th meet., October 26, 1924; and League of Nations, *Official Journal,* November, 1924, p. 1665.

[12] League of Nations, *Official Journal,* November, 1924, pp. 1669-70.

followed by the Mixed Commission, which, after a laborious discussion, decided at its meeting of November 16, 1924, to ask the Council "to request the Permanent Court to give an advisory opinion on the dispute concerning article 2 of the Convention of Lausanne." [13] Meanwhile, and until the time the advisory opinion should be handed down and the Mixed Commission should decide, Tevfic Ruchdi Bey gave the assurance that no prejudicial measure would be taken against the persons whose condition was in dispute.

The Council decided at its meeting of December 13, 1924, to ask the Permanent Court of International Justice to give an advisory opinion on the following question: [14]

"What meaning and scope should be attributed to the word 'established' in Article 2 of the Convention of Lausanne of January 30th, 1923, regarding the Exchange of Greek and Turkish Populations, in regard to which discussions have arisen and arguments have been put forward, which are contained in the documents communicated by the Mixed Commission? And what conditions must the persons who are described in Article 2 of the Convention of Lausanne under the name of 'Greek inhabitants of Constantinople' fulfil in order that they may be considered as 'established' under the terms of the Convention and exempt from compulsory exchange?"

§ 265. Advisory Opinion of the Permanent Court of International Justice. Owing to the urgency of the question an extraordinary session of the Court was convoked on January 12, 1925. Oral arguments were made by Mr. Politis, Minister of Greece at Paris, and Tevfic Ruchdi Bey, President of the Turkish delegation to the Mixed Commission. The unanimous opinion of the Court was handed down on February 21, 1925.[15]

The Court thought that the meaning of the word *établis* was to be determined, not in the abstract, but as the word had been used in article 2 of the Convention. This was held to be a question of international law. The meaning of the French word *établissement* was considered, and its use with reference

[13] Procès-Verbaux, vi, 77th meet.; and League of Nations, Doc. C.694. 1924.I.
[14] League of Nations, *Official Journal,* February, 1925, p. 155.
[15] Permanent Court of International Justice, *Publications,* series B, no. 10.

to a situation of fact rather than in a legal sense was brought out. Hence the Court did not approve the Turkish contention that the Convention required the Greeks to be established according to the Turkish legislation, nor the contention that the Turkish courts should be left to decide the question, in view of the provisions of the Convention referring this function to the Mixed Commission.

Answering the Turkish theory of an implicit reference by article 2 to local legislation, since a contrary solution would involve consequences affecting Turkey's sovereign rights, the Court said:

> The right of entering into international engagements is an attribute of State sovereignty. In the present case, moreover, the obligations of the contracting states are absolutely equal and reciprocal. It is therefore impossible to admit that a convention which creates obligations of this kind, construed according to its natural meaning, infringes the sovereign rights of the High Contracting Parties.

Accordingly, the Court did not feel it to be necessary to consider "whether any particular provisions of the Turkish laws of 1902 and 1914 were or were not contrary to the Convention." It further held that the Mixed Commission was "alone competent to investigate, in each individual case, whether a Greek inhabitant of Constantinople was 'established' in conformity with Article 2 of the Convention and could be exempted from the compulsory exchange."

As regards the second part of the question referred to the Court, concerning the conditions to be fulfilled by Greek inhabitants of Constantinople in order that these might be considered as 'established' and exempt from compulsory exchange, the Court was unwilling to define exactly the degree of stability required of persons 'established' at Constantinople. It thought that this would be satisfied by a person who came to Constantinople to make his fortune, though he intended subsequently to return to his place of origin. The origin of persons concerned was of no consequence.

Hence the Court answered the two questions before it by

saying that the purpose of the word 'established' in article 2 of the Convention of Lausanne was to refer to a situation of fact constituted by residence of a lasting nature, and that to be exempt persons must reside within the boundaries of the prefecture of the city of Constantinople as defined by the law of 1912, having arrived from any other place prior to October 30, 1918, with intention to remain for an extended period.[16]

The advisory opinion was communicated to the Council, which considered it at its session of March 11, 1925, and directed the Secretary-General to communicate it officially to the Mixed Commission, having no doubt that the latter "would attribute to this Opinion the same high value and authority which the Council always gave to the opinions of the Permanent Court of International Justice." [17]

§ 266. Agreement of Angora and the Decision of the Mixed Commission. At this time the Greek and Turkish governments were carrying on negotiations with respect to other matters concerning the exchange. The definition of *établis* formed part of these negotiations, no longer as a legal question but as a political question subject to solution by concession and compromise. One of the arrangements signed at Angora on June 21, 1925, concerned the definition of *établis,* and this, after many vicissitudes described below, took the form of a decision of the Mixed Commission on March 19, 1927.[18]

According to this, which is Decision XXVII of the Commission, the following were to be considered persons established at Constantinople and in Western Thrace in the meaning of article 2 of the Convention:

(1) All the Greeks at Constantinople and the Moslems in Western Thrace who were present at these places at the time of the Decision and were also present there prior to October 30, 1918, and January 30, 1923, respectively. The fact that a person had come to Constantinople and to Western Thrace prior to these dates could be proved by any appropriate evidence before the Mixed Commission.

As an exception to this rule, Greeks or Moslems of the

[16] *Ibid.*
[17] League of Nations, *Official Journal,* April, 1925, pp. 441-442.
[18] The history of these negotiations is described below, Chapter xxvi.

aforesaid regions without profession, property, or means of subsistence could be included in the exchange. These could not exceed one hundred and twenty for each state, and a list of them was to be presented to the Mixed Commission within a period of four months from March 19, 1927.

(2) Also the Greeks of Constantinople and Moslems of Western Thrace absent from these regions at the time of the Decision, who were present there prior to October 30, 1918, and January 30, 1923, respectively, and who, in addition, at the above dates (*a*) were registered in the civil registries of these regions; or (*b*) had a fixed residence in these regions and intended to remain there permanently. This intention was to be gathered from various circumstances, such as the permanent exercise of a profession, a trade, or an industry; the entering into a contract for a work of durable character; the adoption of a profession implying durable residence; and, in general, any other fact proving that the person had the centre of his occupations in the aforesaid regions and intended to remain there permanently. In each case the Commission was to decide.

(3) Wives, minor children of both sexes, and unmarried daughters were to follow the condition of their husband or father and mother.

This decision, in its first paragraph, certainly went further than the advisory opinion of the Permanent Court of International Justice, since it did not take into account the intention of the persons present in Constantinople prior to October 30, 1918, but required simply presence at Constantinople at that date and at the time the decision was taken, on March 19, 1927. But it must be remembered that by this time the police of Constantinople had discovered and caused the departure to Greece of practically all persons who had arrived at Constantinople after October 30, 1918, and that very few, if any, had succeeded in escaping and remaining in that city. In fact, therefore, no real concession was made by the Turks in this case.

§ 267. Proving establishment at Constantinople. Decision XXVII simplified the question of the *établis* of Constantinople. Greeks present at Constantinople were to be deemed established in that city provided they were there prior to October 30, 1918. The fact that they came there prior to this date could be proved by any means of evidence. Against this clear text, which permitted of no loophole, General de Lara, neutral member, supported the view that the mere fact that Greeks came to Constantinople before October 30, 1918, was not sufficient to prove establishment therein, but only a presumption of establishment.[19] This view occasioned the protests of the Greek delegation.

The Turkish delegation itself did not attempt to support this impossible interpretation, but asked rather that the decisions of the Sub-Commission of Constantinople, granting provisional certificates of non-exchangeability to Greeks of Constantinople who had proved to its satisfaction that they came to Constantinople prior to October 30, 1918, be not regarded as final decisions, whenever they were taken prior to the adoption of Decision XXVII by the Mixed Commission. On the assurance of Chukri Bey that the question was raised only with regard to a very small number of cases, the Greek delegation gave its consent to a reëxamination of such cases.

Decision XXVII provided that presence at Constantinople prior to October 30, 1918, could be proved "by all means of evidence" before the Mixed Commission. The Constantinople Sub-Commission, in examining the cases of Greeks of Constantinople, soon met with the opposition of the Turkish member to the admission of testimonial evidence. The Mixed Commission, when this difference was brought before it, had no difficulty in deciding, by the votes of the neutral members and the Greek delegation, that the testimony of witnesses was admissible in examining the question of establishment.[20]

Subsequently a policy of obstruction was followed by the Turkish member of the Sub-Commission of Constantinople, and the work of the Sub-Commission was seriously interrupted. During a period of nine months, ending January, 1928, 20,000 cases of native Greeks of Constantinople were exam-

[19] Procès-Verbaux, xii, 125th meet., June 16, 1927.
[20] Procès-Verbaux, xiii, 129th meet., July 25, 1927.

ined, all other cases being postponed. The Greek delegation protested against this situation, whereupon the Mixed Commission ordered the Sub-Commission to resume its work and to draft a plan for its work to be submitted to the Mixed Commission.[21] The plan was submitted to a special committee for consideration. This committee met to discuss it, but made little progress, as a number of questions of principle were raised and were submitted to the Legal Section. This Section, being unable to solve them, referred them to the general assembly of the Mixed Commission.

The Turkish delegation had in the meantime raised questions of interpretation of Decision XXVII. These questions related to the words "Greeks of Constantinople," and "actuellement qui s'y trouvaient." The Turkish argument was that the first expression meant Greeks, natives of Constantinople, and that the second implied that the persons were found in Constantinople with the intention of residing there permanently. The same delegation gave a restrictive interpretation to the provision concerning the entry in the civil registries of paragraph 4 (1) of the same decision. At Señor Rivas's proposal, it was decided to postpone decision on these questions and to have the Sub-Commission of Constantinople continue the issue of certificates of non-exchangeability. In case of opposition by a member, the certificates were to be signed by the two other members and transmitted to the Mixed Commission, where they were to be classified according to the nature of the difficulty presented. When the questions of principle should be subsequently decided, these cases would be disposed of immediately. This was indeed an ingenious way of solving the Gordian knot which had so long obstructed the work of the Sub-Commission, and credit for it, as for other solutions, is due to the indefatigable genius of Señor Rivas Vicuña.

§ 268. Greeks of Constantinople absent from the city. On the same date of March 19, 1927, another decision [22] was taken by the Mixed Commission incorporating another agree-

[21] Procès-Verbaux, 147th meet., January 5, 1928.
[22] See *infra,* § 334.

ment between the two governments. Paragraph IV of this Decision XXVIII gave power to the Greek and Turkish governments to prohibit the return to Western Thrace and Constantinople respectively of persons who left the country without a regular passport. All other persons absent from Constantinople or Western Thrace had the 'right' to return, provided they possessed the requirements for establishment in those regions as determined by Decision XXVII. This decision was against the stipulation of article 16, paragraph 2, of the Convention, which provided expressly that persons exempted from the exchange were free to return to their homes. The Turks had already at the Conference of Lausanne, at the discussions on the Declaration on Amnesty, shown their intention of prohibiting the return of certain Greeks in 'special cases.' The limitation was soon forgotten, however, and following the constitution of the Commission they disclosed their intention of forbidding reëntry to Turkey to Greeks who were absent from Constantinople, having left with passports not issued by the Angora government. One of the agreements of Angora, as will be seen, tended to give effect to this view of the Turkish government, and, in view of the protests raised by the Greeks absent from Constantinople, the neutral members refused to sanction this agreement. However, after the new Agreement of Athens of December 1, 1926, the Commission adopted the agreement as to the absent Greeks of Constantinople, as is seen in another place.[23]

In order to determine the condition of Greeks of Constantinople, absent from that city, with respect to the Convention, a committee was constituted at Athens, as an agency subordinate to the Constantinople Sub-Commission. Members of this Committee were the Consul-General of Turkey at Piraeus and an official of the Ministry of Foreign Affairs of Greece.[24]

While Decision XXVIII, paragraph 4, granted the power to the Greek and Turkish governments respectively to refuse the 'right' to return to absent persons who left Western Thrace

[23] See *infra*, § 334.
[24] Procès-Verbaux, xii, 126th meet., June 27, 1927.

or Constantinople without regular passports, it added that this did not apply to dependents of *établis* present at Constantinople or Western Thrace. That is to say, the Turkish government could not refuse the 'right' to return to wives, minor children, or unmarried daughters whose chief of family was present at Constantinople, although these dependent persons had left with irregular passports. When the Greek delegation asked that this provision be executed by allowing the children and wives of Greeks present at Constantinople to come from Greece, the Turkish delegation asked in exchange that the children and wives present at Constantinople of Greeks absent from Constantinople should leave and go to join the heads of family in Greece. There was no warrant for this proposal, but the Turkish delegation tried to frame a clever argument on the ground of reciprocity, which convinced no one. However, the neutral members asked that the discussion be postponed.[25]

The very question of regularity of passports occasioned disagreements, the Greek delegation complaining that persons possessing regular passports were denied access to Turkey. The Mixed Commission, when the question was put before it, was unable to do anything but postpone it.[26]

§ 269. Minors and married women. The Commission decided that minors were considered to be persons below eighteen years of age.[27] Also that 'exchangeable' women married to non-exchangeable persons after the coming into effect of the Convention of Lausanne were to follow the condition of their husbands. However, their properties were to be liquidated, like those of all persons subject to exchange.[28] When the mother was dead, the minor children and the daughters of age followed the condition of their father. When the father was dead, these persons followed their own condition. When the parents were divorced, the minor children followed the condition of their father in case the tribunal placed them in the care of the father. If the tribunal placed them in the care of

[25] Procès-Verbaux, xiii, 128th meet., July 21, 1927.
[26] Procès-Verbaux, xiii, 129th meet., July 25, 1927.
[27] Procès-Verbaux, August 8, 1928, Decision 46.
[28] Procès-Verbaux, August 16, 1928, Decision 47.

the mother, they followed their personal status, and the mother followed their condition unless she had contracted a new marriage, in which case the children followed the condition of their mother, unless the tribunal placed them in the care of a third person by reason of the second marriage.[29]

§ 270. **Case of the Greek Oecumenical Patriarch.** While the Permanent Court of International Justice was holding hearings on the question of the interpretation of article 2 of the Convention of Lausanne, the case of the exchangeability or non-exchangeability of the Oecumenical Patriarch Constantine was raised before the Mixed Commission. Under date of December 18, 1924, the Commission received a report from the Sub-Commission of Constantinople concerning the then Metropolitan of Derkon, Constantine Arapoglou. Although it was admitted that Constantine came to Constantinople after October 30, 1918, the Greek member of the Sub-Commission asserted that this Metropolitan, like all Greek prelates in Constantinople forming the Holy Synod, was not exchangeable. In the meantime Metropolitan Constantine was elected and became Oecumenical Patriarch at Constantinople.

The Commission, after many private discussions, adopted in January, 1925, a resolution in the following terms: [30]

"The Mixed Commission, while noting the facts contained in the report of the Sixth Sub-Commission, No. 2360, dated December 17, 1924, in regard to the question of the exchangeability of Monseigneur Constantine Arapoglou, former Metropolitan of Derkon, according to which Monseigneur Constantine, having been born in Asia Minor and having gone to Constantinople after October 30, 1918, fulfilled in his person all the conditions necessary for the purpose of exchange, holds that it is beyond its competence to take a decision in regard to the case of this prelate in view of his status as a Metropolitan." This resolution implied, as it was expressly stated, that the Mixed Commission or its agencies were to take no subsequent action.

[29] Procès-Verbaux, August 16, 1928, Decision 48.
[30] Procès-Verbaux, vii, 84th meet., January 28, 1925.

At the hearings before the Permanent Court of International Justice on the interpretation of article 2 of the Convention, Mr. Politis presented the view that, apart from any question of establishment at Constantinople, the prelates of the Orthodox Church were exempt from exchange. The Court excluded from its consideration the position of the Oecumenical Patriarchate, on the ground that it was not included among the questions placed before it for advisory opinion.

On January 30, 1925, two days after the Mixed Commission took the above decision, the Turkish authorities at Constantinople ordered Monseigneur Constantine, Oecumenical Patriarch and Archbishop of Constantinople, to leave Constantinople, and conducted him forcibly to the frontier. The Greek government, considering that this action constituted a serious infringement of the agreement of Lausanne regarding the constitution of the Patriarchate and its activities, and likewise an infringement of article 12 of the Convention concerning the Exchange of Greek and Turkish Populations, brought the question before the Council of the League at its session in March, 1925. The Turkish government refused to be represented before the Council, asserting that that body was not competent to deal with this case. Instead, it addressed a letter to the Secretary-General of the League, in which it maintained that of the two issues raised by Greece, one, that of the Patriarchate, was a purely domestic matter for Turkey; while the other, that of the exchange of Patriarch Constantine, was properly a matter for the Mixed Commission, which had already taken a decision in effect permitting the Turkish government to expel Monseigneur Constantine.[31]

At the meeting of the Council, on March 14, 1924, Mr. Caclamanos, the Greek representative, argued that the maintenance of the Patriarchate was by no means a domestic question for Turkey, in view of the discussions at the Conference of Lausanne and the solemn undertaking pronounced by Ismet Pasha at that Conference.[32] He also argued that the Mixed Commission by its decision of January 28, 1925, so far

[31] League of Nations, *Official Journal,* April, 1925, pp. 578-581.
[32] See p. 344, *supra.*

from permitting the Turkish government to expel Monseigneur Constantine, had declared itself incompetent to deal with his case, thus indicating its desire to have the question submitted to another jurisdiction. And the only proper jurisdiction in this case was the Council of the League of Nations, an organ qualified to supervise the execution of international engagements.[33]

The Council decided, after a report by Viscount Ishii, to request the Permanent Court of International Justice to give an advisory opinion on the following question:

"Do the objections to the competence of the Council raised by the Turkish Government in its letter of March 1st, which is communicated to the court, preclude the Council from being competent in the matter brought before it by the Greek Government by its telegram to the Secretary-General dated February 11, 1925?"

§ 271. Exemption of members of the Holy Synod. At the same time the Council expressed the hope that it would be possible for the question at issue to be settled by private negotiation. This hope was realized, and the Court was informed that it was no longer necessary for the Council to ask the Court to give the opinion contemplated by the previous resolution. The agreement arrived at was the following. The Turkish representative on the Mixed Commission in a letter addressed to it, a copy of which was handed to the President of the Greek delegation on the Commission, declared that he withdrew definitely the files relating to the exchangeability of the members of the Holy Synod. At the same time, the Oecumenical Patriarch Constantine having abdicated, the Holy Synod was to proceed with the election of a new Patriarch.[34] In other words, the Turkish government obtained the benefit of the *fait accompli* in connection with Monseigneur Constantine, and admitted that the Greek prelates, members of the Holy Synod, were not to be exchanged.

[33] League of Nations, *Official Journal,* April, 1925, pp. 482-484. See also the memorandum of protest of Patriarch Constantine, League of Nations, Doc. C.129.1925,VII; and Memorandum of the Greek Government, dated March 14, 1925, in League of Nations, *Official Journal,* April, 1925, pp. 637-639.

[34] See League of Nations, *Official Journal,* July, 1925, pp. 854, 895.

§ 272. Communities exempted from the Exchange. Since the Greek inhabitants of the district of Constantinople and the Moslems of Western Thrace were exempted from the exchange, it follows that the communities (including schools, churches, foundations, hospitals, etc.) of these people were not included in the exchange and that consequently their property rights were not affected. However, the Convention contained a provision which to a certain extent subjected some institutions of these communities to the exchange. This provision is the second paragraph of article 9, reading as follows:

"Property situated in the districts to which the compulsory exchange applies and belonging to religious or benevolent institutions of the communities established in a district to which the exchange does not apply, shall likewise be liquidated under the same conditions."

The second paragraph of article 9 was inserted at the proposal of the Turkish delegates at the Conference of Lausanne.[35] The Greek delegation at first refused to accept this provision, declaring that persons not subject to exchange ought not to be affected in their rights, and that the exchange concerned persons and not properties. Chukri Bey replied that such properties would give cause to conflicts, and that the communities would have great difficulty in collecting the revenues of these properties. This indicated an intention on the part of the Turkish government to subject the persons exempted from the exchange to the restrictive measures taken against them later, although the opposite was declared in article 16. The Italian delegate, Mr. Galli, brought this out when he asked what were the difficulties that the communities would meet, since free enjoyment of their liberties and of their rights of property was guaranteed to persons exempted from the exchange, Riza Nour Bey replied evasively that "the exchange ought to put an end to all possibilities of difficulties," and he added, a little bluntly, that "there was a situation of fact, and his proposal was solely inspired by the well understood interest of the communities."[36] The Greek delega-

[35] Conférence de Lausanne, *Recueil des actes,* première série, i, p. 583.

[36] *Ibid.,* p. 584. See declaration to the same effect by Riza Nour Bey, *Ibid.,* p. 597.

tion eventually had to yield to the demand of the Turks, in order to obtain concessions on other points from the Turkish delegation.[37]

§ 273. **Inhabitants of the islands of Imbros and Tenedos.** Besides the Greeks of Constantinople, there was another category of Greeks who were not subject to the compulsory exchange. These were the Greek inhabitants of the islands of Imbros and Tenedos, the two islands at the mouth of the Dardanelles which had been under the military occupation of Greece since 1912 and were returned to Turkey under the Peace Treaty of Lausanne. The exemption of these Greeks from the exchange was based not on the Convention concerning the Exchange, but on article 14, paragraph 2 of the Treaty of Lausanne, which provided as follows: "The stipulations entered into or to be entered between Greece and Turkey concerning the exchange of Greek and Turkish populations shall not be applicable to the inhabitants of the islands of Imbros and Tenedos."

A number of the inhabitants of these islands, temporarily residing abroad, were forbidden to return to their homes by the Turkish authorities. They applied to the Mixed Commission, requesting its intervention in their favor. However, the competence of the Commission to deal with these persons was challenged by the Turkish delegation, in view of the fact that the Convention concerning the Exchange and creating the Commission did not mention the inhabitants of Imbros and Tenedos.[38] The Turkish position was undoubtedly sound. In prohibiting the return of these persons, Turkey may have been violating the Declaration on Amnesty signed at Lausanne, but this was not a matter for the cognizance of the Mixed Commission.

At the census taken by the Turkish government on October 28, 1927, the population of these islands was found to be as follows: Imbros, 6762 inhabitants, of whom 3098 were males and 3664 females; Tenedos, 1631 inhabitants, of whom 763 were males and 868 females. Almost the entire population of

[37] *Ibid.*, p. 626.

[38] Procès-Verbaux, iii, 46th meet., April 1, 1924; x, 110th meet., June 17, 1926.

Imbros and the great majority of Tenedos is Greek. The above figures show that in 1927 the male population was found to be depleted in both islands.

The first paragraph of article 14 of the Treaty of Lausanne provided for a special administrative organization of these islands in order to insure local administration to the indigenous population.

§ 274. Obligatory character of the non-exchangeability. A Greek established in Constantinople raised what was termed "the question of the optional or obligatory character of the non-exchangeability" of the persons dealt with in article 2 of the Convention. He requested of the Constantinople Sub-Commission to be included in the exchange and to be granted a passport of exchangeability. His case was discussed by the Legal Section of the Mixed Commission, and it was unanimously decided that "the non-exchangeability provided for in article 2 of the Convention constituted an obligation for the persons dealt with in article 2 which they could not dispense with." [39] The terms of this decision are manifestly wrong, although the decision in substance is correct. It should simply have been said that the Sub-Commission of Constantinople had no power to consider as exchangeable a person exempted from exchange by virtue of article 2 of the Convention and to grant him a passport to go to Greece. Instructions to this effect were subsequently sent to the Sub-Commission.[40]

[39] Procès-Verbaux, ix, 106th meet., March 27, 1926.
[40] Procès-Verbaux, ix, 107th meet., April 18, 1926.

CHAPTER XXI

THE MIGRATIONS

§ 275. The plan of evacuation. The Convention concerning the Exchange of Populations provided that the compulsory exchange was to take place "as from 1st May, 1923." In view of the fact that the Treaty of Peace was not signed until July, 1923, and that the Mixed Commission was constituted and met for the first time on October 8, 1923, the two governments agreed that the exchange was to take place as from May 1, 1924. The Mixed Commission thus had a period of seven months to prepare for the transfer of populations in accordance with the Convention.

Even before the constitution of the Commission, the two governments had entered into an agreement for the immediate exchange of 8000 Greeks gathered in Samsun against an equal numbers of Moslems of the island of Lesbos. This agreement was communicated to the Commission.[1] The Greeks left

[1] Procès-Verbaux, i, 1st and 2d meets., October 8 and 9, 1923.

Samsun in the middle of November, 1923, and the Turks left Lesbos a little later.

As soon as it was constituted, the Mixed Commission, through a committee of its own, determined the methods of removal of the exchanged populations with a view to rendering the emigration as little onerous as possible to the persons concerned.

In accordance with article 16, paragraph 1, of the Convention, a plan of evacuation was adopted in advance by the Commission, with the agreement of the two governments, fixing the date on which each region in Greece and Turkey was to be evacuated by the persons subject to exchange and the ports in which these persons were to gather for the purpose of being transported to the country of their destination. The government of that country provided the ships necessary for the transportation of the emigrants and worked out its own programme with respect to the places to which these persons were to be transported and settled.

Emigrants were required to file a declaration describing the immovable property left behind which was to be liquidated by the Commission. Blanks were distributed to the emigrants in their place of residence. They filled them in and handed them to the Sub-Commissions at the ports where they boarded the steamers. A duplicate of the declaration was retained by the emigrant in order to facilitate his settlement in the new country.[2] Similar forms were distributed to former emigrants or refugees in Greece and Turkey.

Although the desire was to adapt the plan of evacuation to the plan of settlement, so that, for instance, the Moslems transported from Greece could find the houses evacuated by the Greeks in Turkey ready for their settlement, conflicts between these plans and complications in the settlement of emigrants arose.

§ 276. Supervision of the departure of emigrants. According to the plan of evacuation, the persons subject to exchange were required to leave their homes at the time appointed for each district and concentrate in the port where they were to

[2] Procès-Verbaux, i, 7th meet., October 20, 1923.

board the steamer for their transportation to the country to which they were nationally akin. For the purpose of supervising this departure of emigrants from their homes, a number of Sub-Commissions were created by the Mixed Commission.[3] They organized auxiliary committees from among the emigrants themselves for the purpose of insuring the distribution of food and other supplies to emigrants and of assisting in their concentration in the ports.

The Turkish government had insisted for some time on appointing special committees of its own for the purpose of assisting the emigrants in the ports of Saloniki, Kavala, and Candia. These committees, while receiving orders from the Turkish government, were supposed to be under the direction of the local Sub-Commissions. In fact they proved unable to coöperate with the Sub-Commissions and had to be dissolved.

Persons desirous of emigrating separately and at their own expense were given permits by the Sub-Commission to leave the country. But no permission was given to emigrants to go temporarily to the country of destination with the view of making preparations for their settlement, as was done in the case of the Greco-Bulgarian emigration. All persons departing under the Convention were provided with passports by the competent Sub-Commission.

The departure of emigrants from the ports of concentration was further assisted by the delegations of the Greek Red Cross and the Turkish Red Crescent. The sanitary conditions of the large numbers of persons concentrated in the ports inspired at times serious fears of diseases, and the efforts of the local authorities and these national organizations were greatly aided by the International League of Red Cross Societies.

§ 277. **Transportation.** The two governments contracted with shipowners for the transportation of the exchanged people, and were supposed to place at the disposal of the Commission a sufficient number of steamers for the people gathered at each port. These ports were, for Greece, Saloniki,

[3] The number and constitution of Sub-Commissions are considered *supra*, pp. 369-370.

Volo, and Kavala in Continental Greece, and Candia and Rethymno in Crete; for Turkey, Smyrna, Mersina, Chataldja, Constantinople, and Samsun. The steamers were often late in coming, and hardships resulted for the persons gathered in the ports. They had to be provided with food and shelter in public buildings and tents in open places.

The expenses of transportation were as a rule paid by the emigrants themselves. Certain reductions were allowed on the state railways of the two countries. The steamer passage of indigent persons, to a certain proportion (10% or 15%) on the number of persons exchanged from each region, was paid by the Mixed Commission.[4]

§ 278. Exemption for taxes and custom duties. The Convention provided, in article 8, that emigrants should be free to take away with them or to arrange for the transport of their movable property of every kind, without being liable on this account to the payment of any export or import duty or any other tax. This stipulation was sweeping and caused no difficulties of interpretation.

Article 16 of the same Convention prescribed that the two governments were not to impose on emigrants who had left, or were to leave, their territories any special taxes or dues. The question arose what was to be considered a 'special tax.' The Greek member of the Commission, Mr. Papas, thought that any tax that did not enter into the usual budget of a state and was limited from the point of view of time was a 'special tax.' He asserted that the tax on capital in Greece and the tax on war profits in Turkey were such taxes. Tevfic Ruchdi Bey objected that the tax on war profits was not a 'special tax.'[5] This theoretical disagreement does not seem to have caused any practical difficulties, mainly because most of the Greeks who might be liable to payment of the tax on war profits, had already left the Turkish territory.

With regard to the collection of other taxes, the Commission decided in November, 1923, that any collection of taxes should be put off until the Commission should take a

[4] Decision No. IV of the Commission, October 25, 1923; Procès-Verbaux, i, 28th meet., December 29, 1923.

[5] Procès-Verbaux, i, 20th meet., November 27, 1923.

general decision on the matter. This decision was not entirely carried out. The neutral members of the Commission made various proposals with respect to taxes, which were opposed by the Turkish delegation. At last, by a decision taken on December 29, 1923,[6] the Commission proposed to the two governments to suspend all collection of direct taxes due by the persons subject to exchange; if the two governments would not agree to cancel definitely these taxes in favor of the emigrants, they might present the lists of the taxes owed by the emigrants to the Mixed Commission at the time of the final liquidation. This proposal was accepted by the two governments, which undertook to claim recovery of the taxes at the final liquidation.[7] This suspension was extended later to indirect taxes and those owed to the districts or communes as well as to those due to the state.[8]

§ 279. Other exemptions. The Greek delegation at an early date proposed that all pecuniary penalties or fines against persons subject to exchange should be counterbalanced by the sums due to the persons against whom such fines were assessed by the government of their country of origin. The Turkish government signified its assent to this proposal in April, 1924.[9]

Greece from the time of the constitution of the Commission decided to exempt Moslems subject to exchange from military service. On the request of the Mixed Commission, Turkey reciprocated by taking a similar measure in March, 1924.[10]

§ 280. Early departure of Moslems from Greece. Although the Convention provided that the compulsory exchange was to take place as from the first of May, 1923, and this was later altered by agreement to May, 1924, the departure of emigrants began much earlier. The Greek government desired to accelerate the departure of the Moslems from Greece, pressed as it was with the question of sheltering more

[6] Decision No. XIV, taken at the 28th meeting of the Commission.
[7] Procès-Verbaux, ii, 36th meet., February 12, 1924.
[8] Procès-Verbaux, iii, 44th meet., March 18, 1924.
[9] Procès-Verbaux, iv, 48th meet., April 11, 1924.
[10] Procès-Verbaux, iii, 45th meet., March 25, 1924.

than a million homeless refugees. The Turkish government was also eager to settle the Moslems of Greece upon the lands left by the refugees, so that crops could be obtained in 1924. It was agreed, therefore, that the Moslem population of certain regions in Greece should depart before May, 1924. These regions were Eastern Macedonia (Drama, Kavala, Sari-Chaban, Pravista) and the island of Crete. Sixty Moslem families of Larissa in Thessaly and the floating population concentrated at the time in Saloniki were also included in these early removals.[11] These Moslems who were to leave Greece before May, 1924, amounted to about 150,000.

In the meantime the Greek authorities were proceeding with the settlement of more than a million refugees. They were compelled to seek shelter for them in the towns and villages of Macedonia and in the homes of Greek as well as Moslem natives. Naturally, placing under the same roof Turks native to Greece and Greeks driven out from Turkey did not conduce to peaceful cohabitation. In some places the Moslems preferred to take away their property and leave their homes. These people came together in Saloniki with the hope of departing for Turkey. By the end of October, 1923, more than 20,000 Moslems had thus gathered in Saloniki. On the other hand, the Moslems of Sari-Chaban in Eastern Macedonia, under the instigation of two former Moslem deputies in the Greek National Assembly, attacked the refugees and expelled them from their homes.[12]

These events created a situation ill adapted to the orderly exchange of the populations. The Greek government dispatched to Macedonia Mr. Canaghini, a member of the Greek delgation on the Mixed Commission, to ameliorate the housing conditions of Moslems who were not to leave Greece before May, 1924. In the meantime also Sub-Commissions were created and sent to various regions. By the middle of December the Sub-Commissions reported that the local authorities were doing everything in their power to facilitate their task. Tevfic Ruchdi Bey himself admitted that the

[11] Procès-Verbaux, i, 7th meet., October 20, 1923.
[12] Procès-Verbaux, i, 24th meet., December 14, 1923.

Turkish members of the Sub-Commissions of Drama, Kavala and Canea assured him of the satisfactory situation in their regions.[13] This time a mixed delegation of the Commission was dispatched to Macedonia to visit certain localities where there were great numbers of Moslem inhabitants in order to find out whether a partial removal could not be made with a view to improve the housing conditions of the other Moslems.[14]

The mixed delegation of the Commission, consisting of a neutral member, Mr. Ekstrand, a Greek, Mr. Pallis, and a Turk, Hamdi Bey, investigated conditions in Saloniki and in Western Macedonia (Florina, Kozani, Kailar, etc.) from December 13 to 20, 1923.[15] The report of the delegation brought out the fact that the removal from Saloniki had not been made so speedily as it should have been, by reason of delays in the arrival of the Turkish steamers. On the other hand, the delegation proposed that 50,000 Moslems should depart immediately from Western Macedonia in order to improve the situation of the remaining Moslems.

The report also disclosed that the distribution of lodgings between the Greeks and the Moslems did not conform to the Convention. A more equitable distribution in favor of the Moslems was considered possible. Moreover, the restitution of the requisitioned property of Moslems or payment for the same was found to be far from complete.

§ 281. Early departure of Greeks from Turkey. With the exception of 2500 Greeks concentrated in Samsun, it was originally decided that the Greeks should not leave Turkey before May, 1924. But in the late fall of 1923 it appeared that their situation in Asia Minor was becoming very precarious. Mr. Jackwith of the Near East Relief, in a report to Mr. Widding, neutral member of the Commission, reported that the Greeks driven to the ports of Asia Minor were in danger of suffering decimation during the winter from epidemics and starvation. Worse still was the situation of the

[13] Procès-Verbaux, i, 24th meet., December 14, 1923.
[14] Procès-Verbaux, i, 18th meet., November 21, 1923.
[15] Procès-Verbaux, i, 28th meet., December 29, 1923, and annex.

Greeks of Cilicia. The Greek delegation asked that Sub-Commissions be dispatched to the regions of Samsun and Smyrna to study the situation and advise the Commission as to the necessity of removing these populations.[16] These Sub-Commissions were also to appraise and liquidate the movable property of Greek emigrants left in Turkey in their precipitate flight, which was in the meantime being sold by the Turkish authorities.

The Commission decided then to appoint three Sub-Commissions in Turkey, at Samsun, Smyrna, and Constantinople, to prepare for the work of exchange, and to send a mixed delegation of the Commission which was to get into touch with the Angora government, it being considered impossible to investigate directly the condition of the Greek population in Turkey in view of the great distances.

This delegation, consisting of the President of the Mixed Commission, General de Lara, and of the Presidents of the Greek and Turkish delegations, Mr. Papas and Tevfic Ruchdi Bey, spent about a month and a half in Turkey, going to Angora by way of Constantinople and returning by way of Smyrna. It succeeded in obtaining the agreement of the Turkish government on certain pending major questions.[17] Among other points, an agreement was made for the partial evacuation before May 1, 1924, of the Moslems from Western Macedonia, as had been proposed by Mr. Ekstrand's delegation which had visited that region. This evacuation was to be simultaneous with the departure of 1500 Greeks from Trebizond and 16,000 Greeks from Chataldja.

§ 282. **The hastening of the departure.** By the end of January, 1924, 53,000 out of the 150,000 Moslems who were to leave Greece, according to the agreement between the two governments, before May 1, 1924, had been sent to Turkey. As more than 100,000 were still to leave before the above date, and an additional 50,000 were to be removed from Western Macedonia, the Mixed Commission considered the plan of

16 Procès-Verbaux, i, 17th meet., November 16 and 17, 1923. See also annex to 22d meet., December 7, 1923.

17 Procès-Verbaux, ii, 36th meet., February 12, 1924.

using the railway and making caravans of refugees, since the steamers were not sufficient to transport all the emigrants.[18] Removal by railway began in February, 1924, the Greek government granting a 30% reduction on fares.

The evacuation of Western Macedonia began on March 1, 1924, after a plan of evacuation was adopted by the Mixed Commission.[19] About the same time the Moslems of the Greek islands were sent to Turkey under the supervision of the Sub-Commission of Crete, which had completed the evacuation of that island.[20] The Turkish delegation now seemed determined to hasten the evacuation even of regions where the condition of the Moslems had not given room for any complaints. Thus, at its pressing demand, the Mixed Commission decided to remove before May 1, 1924, the Moslems of Thessaly, including the city of Elasson, and of the cities of Janina and Prevesa in Epirus.[21]

Although it was originally decided that the removal of the remaining Greeks in Turkey should not begin until after May 1, 1924, in fact several partial removals were made from December, 1923, on. Greeks from the interior of Asia Minor moved in hundreds towards the ports of the Black Sea, Samsun and Trebizond, and towards Mersina on the Cilician coast, and they were in such a condition of destitution that they had to be sent to Greece.

§ 283. Difficulties in the departure. The partial exchange of Moslems from Greece began by the middle of November, 1923. The difficulties caused by the concentration of Moslems in the port of Saloniki were emphasized by the arrival of great numbers of Moslems, Jugoslav subjects, who were attracted by the current of emigration to Turkey and by the hope of getting lands left by the Greek refugees. At one time the number of these Jugoslav Moslems exceeded the number of Moslems from Greece concentrated in Saloniki. The Turkish government had ordered the masters of the Turkish steam-

[18] Procès-Verbaux, ii, 35th meet., February 7, 1924.
[19] Procès-Verbaux, iii, 38th meet., February 20, 1924; 39th meet., February 22, 1924.
[20] Procès-Verbaux, iii, 38th meet., February 20, 1924.
[21] Procès-Verbaux, iii, 40th meet., February 23, 1924.

ers not to take on board Jugoslav Moslems, while the government of Belgrade was asked to forbid the exodus of Moslems towards Saloniki.[22] As the Moslems continued to emigrate from Jugoslavia, the Commission was obliged to address a communication to the League of Nations.[23]

It was planned that 150,000 Moslems should leave Greece before May, 1924. The evacuation at first was made under such satisfactory conditions and with such remarkable cooperation of local authorities that the Mixed Commission entertained a proposition of the neutral members to thank the local authorities and the government.[24] Later the occupation of Moslem houses by refugees caused the Moslems to leave their homes and hurry to Saloniki in order to reach Turkey as early as possible. It was then supposed that the above number of 150,000 might be exceeded. The Turkish delegation even in December threatened that exceptional measures would be taken against the Greeks of Constantinople for the purpose of housing the Moslem emigrants.

In the meantime the condition of the Greeks remaining in Turkey was most precarious. In the ports of the Black Sea and of Cilicia they were reduced to a state of extreme misery.[25] Many were detained in the interior of Asia Minor. Their movable property was being confiscated. They were made to travel barefoot and starving in the depth of winter for many miles to reach the ports specified for their departure, and then were ordered back again to their villages, where all their property had vanished meantime. Although whole regions were available for the settlement of the Moslem emigrants coming from Greece, these were settled in villages, towns, and homes where Greeks still lived.[26]

Persons subject to exchange were sometimes victims of attacks in the territories of the two countries. The Mixed Commission considering that it had the duty to look after

[22] Procès-Verbaux, i, 22d meet., December 7, 1923.
[23] Procès-Verbaux, i, 24th meet., December 14, 1923.
[24] Procès-Verbaux, i, 24th meet., December 14, 1923.
[25] Annex to the above meeting.
[26] See also the situation of Greeks in Mersina in Procès-Verbaux, iii, 41st meet., March 10, 1924; 42d meet., March 11, 1924; 43d meet., March 17, 1924; 47th meet., April 4, 1924.

their security, adopted a resolution and transmitted it to the two governments to the effect that persons suffering damage by attacks within their territories should be indemnified.[27]

§ 284. Final plan of departure. By May 1, 1924, the partial exchange carried out between the two countries had led to the following results: 185,278 Moslems had left Greece and 15,445 (as of May 9) Greeks had left Turkey.

On May 9 the Commission adopted the final plan of departure for Greece and Turkey. The Moslems in Greece to leave the country in the months of May, June, and July amounted to about 150,000. The departure of the remaining Greeks in Asia Minor was to be completed by the end of October, 1924. Their number, excluding the exchangeable Greeks concentrated in Constantinople, did not exceed 125,000. Most of the Greeks had already reached Greece as refugees. Those remaining in Turkey were dispersed in the interior of Asia Minor, and their concentration, in view of the distances and the lack of communications, required a long period.[28]

§ 285. Disorderly removal of Greeks from Turkey. The removal of the Greeks from Asia Minor did not take the orderly character which marked the departure of the Moslems of Greece. As the Sub-Commissions of Mersina and Samsun reported to the Mixed Commission,[29] the Turkish authorities, including higher authorities, such as governors of districts, either issued orders for the immediate and precipitate departure of the Greeks, or prevented the departure of Greeks ordered by the Sub-Commissions when these Greeks were employed on public works, such as road-building, and it was intended to profit by their services. The orders for immediate departure tended to compel the Greeks to leave behind them their movable property. Moreover, they were not admitted to the courts to collect their debts. If they were absent from their homes, although still in Turkish territory, their movable

[27] Procès-Verbaux, iv, 48th meet., April 11, 1924; 49th meet., April 17, 1924.

[28] Procès-Verbaux, iv, 52d meet., May 9, 1924.

[29] Procès-Verbaux, iv, 53d meet., May 16, 1924, and annex 3; also 54th meet., May 21, 1924.

property was often subject to seizure by the application of the Law of Abandoned Property, notwithstanding Decision XV of the Mixed Commission, which specifically aimed to render impossible such seizures.[30] Thus the Greeks who left Asia Minor after the constitution of the Mixed Commission carried with them little more than the destitute refugees that swarmed into Greece in the last months of 1922.

After the Mixed Commission transferred its seat to Constantinople in July, 1924, it was nearer to these people; yet the plan of evacuation by the Sub-Commissions was not carried out, wholesale removals of Greeks continuing. In the villages of the region of Makrikeoy, outside Constantinople, the homes of Greeks were occupied for the settlement of Turks coming from Greece, and the Greek inhabitants had to seek shelter in schools and churches. Settlement of refugees in Moslem houses in Greece certainly took place, but only in the first part of 1923, before the Convention came into force and the Commission was constituted. When the Commission took the decision that no requisitions or occupations were to be allowed after October 7, 1923, the refugees were allowed to spend the winter under tents and in sheds. The Turkish delegation, in reply to the complaints of the Greek delegation that the Convention and the decisions of the Commission were being violated, declared that it was just that the Greeks should not suffer; but that the Turks coming from Greece should also not suffer, and that the evil should be shared. The neutral members, as usual, desisted from taking part in the discussion and tried diplomatically to smooth things over.[31] This encouraged the Turks to such a degree that the neutral members had soon to feel the consequences of their lack of courage.

On July 19, 1924, the President of the Mixed Commission, Mr. Ekstrand, on being advised that certain inhabitants of Pendik, a suburb of Constantinople, had received the order to leave, made the following communication, as it appears from the minutes of the Commission:[32]

[30] Taken on March 25, 1924.
[31] Procès-Verbaux, v, 60th meet., July 19, 1924.
[32] Procès-Verbaux, v, 60th meet., July 19, 1924.

I attempted to see Hamdi Bey, president *ad interim* of the Turkish delegation. As he was busy, I spoke to Haidar Bey, to whom I furnished the information that I possessed, expressing to him my desire to communicate immediately with the Vali in order to obtain complete information. The Vali declared to me that Pendik was intended for the settlement of emigrants from Janina; as these had arrived and there was a lack of room, he had to give orders to clear half the houses occupied by Greeks.

I pointed out to him that I should have much wished that the Mixed Commission, the competent instrumentality in this matter, which had not yet decided upon the evacuation of Pendik, should have been notified. Thereupon the Vali replied to me that he had consulted with the Turkish members of the Commission and they had agreed. I asked, then, that the question be postponed for two or three days, in order that the Commission might have the necessary time to get into touch with the Angora government, but the Vali declared that he was unable to defer his measure, inasmuch as it was a *fait accompli*.

That is, the Vali decided for himself on the removal of the Greeks of Pendik, consulting the Turkish delegation on the Mixed Commission, which, behind the back of the Mixed Commission, gave its consent to a violation of decisions of the latter. The protests of the President of the Mixed Commission were met by the statement that the violation was now a *fait accompli*. As a matter of fact it was not. For, as the President stated, after his conversation with the Vali he ordered the Sub-Commission to go to Pendik and render its services to the people who were to leave their homes. The *fait accompli* was merely the order of the Vali to the Greeks to remove and not the removal itself, and yet the request of the President that the removal be postponed for two days was denied.

The President of the Mixed Commission found it necessary to telegraph to the Prime Minister, Ismet Pasha, and to the President of the Turkish delegation, who was then at Angora. The Turkish delegation, which had given its consent to the above action of the Vali, nevertheless deemed it permissible to criticize the President for sending these two telegrams without consulting the Mixed Commission. The neutral members and the Greek delegation were agreed that the incident of Pendik was a slap in the face of the Commission.

The Greek delegation subsequently agreed to the evacuation of Pendik, as well as of the villages of San Stefano, Kutchuk-Tchekmedjé and Galataria, suburbs of Constantinople. In October, 1924, the exchangeable inhabitants of Constantinople were delivered passports and left the city. By that time the work of the exchange was practically completed. A few scattered thousands were still being concentrated by the Sub-Commissions in the last months of 1924 and the first months of 1925.

But the arbitrariness on the part of the Turkish authorities and the slaps in the face of the Commission were not yet at an end.

Another case showing the attitude of the Turkish authorities is that of the compulsory transfer to Constantinople and seizure of the properties of a number of persons from Mersina. Three of these persons were Lady Chatir, 84 years old, who declared herself to be an Arab of the Greek Orthodox religion; Lady Elmadjoglou, who declared herself to be of the Catholic religion; and Lady Tahindji, wife of a Swiss national and asserting that she was not subject to exchange. The cases of these persons were all pending before the Mixed Commission, which had ordered that they be left undisturbed until their condition should be decided. However, the Vali of Mersina sent them forcibly to Constantinople to be transferred to Greece. They were not even allowed to take away their movable property, which was seized, together with their immovable property.

The President of the Mixed Commission, Mr. Widding, and the neutral member, Mr. Holstad, were obliged to protest against this arbitrary action, in view of the fundamental decision of the Commission according to which persons subject to exchange were to be allowed to go about their business undisturbed until they should be notified by the Mixed Commission that they were to leave. The Turkish delegation, after several attempts at defending the action, ended by objecting to the return of these persons to Mersina, "as this would amount to a reproach against the local government, which the Turkish delegation would never accept." [33] Thus, for the sake of saving the local authorities from a reproach, the Mixed Commission was receiving a slap in the face. It was even shown by the neutral members that, in the case of one of the above ladies, the Turkish delegation had explicitly promised that she should not be disturbed pending the examination of her case by the Mixed Commission. Invited by the neutral members to make good its promise by insuring the return of Lady Elmadjoglou to Mersina, the Turkish delegation evaded an answer.[34]

§ 286. Able-bodied Greeks detained in Turkey. Article 4 of the Convention provided that all able-bodied men belonging to the Greek population whose families had already left the Turkish territory and who were detained in Turkey were to constitute the first instalment of Greeks sent to Greece under the Convention. The Protocol annexed to the Convention also contained a promise to release such able-bodied men on the signature of the Treaty of Peace and to provide for their departure. The Treaty of Peace was signed July 24, 1923, but the Greeks above referred to had not been set free to go to Greece at the time the Mixed Commission met for the first time, in October, 1923.

When asked by the President of the Greek delegation on the Commission to inform the Commission concerning these Greeks, Tevfic Ruchdi Bey declared that the Turkish government was ready to surrender these persons and that they were at the time concentrated at Smyrna. The Commission asked that the persons in question be released immediately.[35] At the end of October they were not yet released, and Tevfic Ruchdi Bey gave assurances that they were being concentrated at Smyrna. In the meantime a delegation of the Greek Red Cross in Smyrna reported that these Greeks were suffering many hardships, and that only 100 persons were concentrated in Smyrna, out of 2500 detained there in the month

[33] Procès-Verbaux, x, 109th meet., June 5, 1926.
[34] Procès-Verbaux, x, 110th meet., June 17, 1926.
[35] Procès-Verbaux, i, 2d meet., October 9, 1923.

of September, the remainder having been dispersed in the interior of Asia Minor and subjected to forced work.

In view of this situation, the Greek delegation proposed to consider the Protocol as obsolete and non-existing, since it had not been executed, and to apply instead with regard to the persons in question the provisions of article 4 of the Convention. In such a case the Commission was to undertake to supervise their departure from Turkey. The neutral members of the Commission suggested that a Sub-Commission be sent to Smyrna to supervise the departure of the detained able-bodied Greeks. This Tevfic Ruchdi Bey opposed vigorously, giving the assurance that in two weeks they would be surrendered; [36] at the next meeting, however, he declared that the men were not released because the Convention was not yet being executed in Greece.[37] He also maintained the curious position that the detained persons in question were not included among the persons dealt with by the Convention, and that, since the Greek delegation considered the Protocol obsolete, the Commission had nothing to do with these persons, who could be released by the Turkish government whenever it thought fit to do so.

At the visit of the three Presidents to Angora in January, 1924, this question was solved, the Turkish government consenting to release immediately the able-bodied Greeks detained in Smyrna and in the interior.

§ 287. Was the exchange compulsory on the two governments? The exchange of Moslem and Greek minorities was to be compulsory, as the first article of the Convention provided. Compulsory for whom? For the population to be exchanged or for the governments? Were the two governments compelled to cause the departure of all persons subject to exchange according to the Convention, or was it simply that the persons in question were compelled to leave if the two governments so ordered? Could one of the two governments, of its own will, exempt certain persons from the exchange and permit them to stay in its territory if they wished?

[36] Procès-Verbaux, i, 13th meet., October 31, 1923.
[37] Procès-Verbaux, i, 14th meet., November 2, 1923.

The question of interpretation of the Convention in this regard arose in connection with the gypsies in Macedonia, whom the Greek authorities were willing to exempt from the exchange.[38] It was argued by the Greek delegation that the Convention was not meant to compel the two governments to exchange the two minorities, but only to give the right to each government to compel the departure of the minority.

This interpretation finds support in several provisions of the Convention. Thus, the second paragraph of article 1 stipulated that the persons exchanged were not to return to live in the country from which they departed without the authorization of the government of that country. This clearly gave each government the power to receive again the population that left its territory, and indicates that, ultimately, it rested with the power of each government to permit persons subject to exchange to remain in the country.

This question was referred to the Legal Section of the Mixed Commission, which, however, hopelessly confused the question of the interpretation of the Convention with that of its modification.[39] The neutral members as well as the Turkish delegation contended that any exception to the rules prescribed by the Convention was not possible except by agreement of the two countries approved by the Mixed Commission. The Greek delegation maintained that the question was not of an exception to the Convention, but an exception to the exchange, which might be in the power of either government if the word 'compulsory' was interpreted as referring to the population and not to the two governments. The Legal Section was again invited to interpret the word 'compulsory,' but no decision was ever reached. As in many other matters the passage of time deprived the question of a decision of all practical interest. The larger part of the gypsies had ultimately to leave Macedonia. The Greek government appears to have excepted from the exchange, of its own initiative, and

[38] Procès-Verbaux, ii, 33d meet., January 29, 1924.

[39] Procès-Verbaux, ii, 36th meet., February 13, 1924; iii, 41st meet., March 7, 1924.

by ministerial orders, Moslems to whom it felt a moral obligation on account of services rendered to Hellenism in the past.[40]

§ 288. Exchange of non-military prisoners. Article 6 of the Convention provided that prisoners in the two countries were also to be included in the exchange whenever they belonged to the two minorities concerned. Persons who had received a definite sentence of imprisonment, or a sentence which was not yet final at the time the Convention was signed, or persons against whom criminal proceedings had been begun, were to be handed over by the authorities of the prosecuting country to the authorities of the country to which they were going, in order that they might serve their sentence or be brought to trial in the latter country.

Greece passed a law on December 15, 1923, providing that Moslem prisoners subject to exchange were to be handed over to the Mixed Commission.[41] The Turkish delegation asked that prisoners be sent to Turkey at the same time as all other Moslems of the same region. It was pointed out that this could not be done, as the handing over of prisoners necessitated a special agreement between the two governments, the fulfilment of certain formalities, communication of court files, etc.

Early in the year 1924, the Commission addressed a note to the two governments asking them to organize the concentration of the prisoners in certain ports and to communicate to it complete lists with appropriate data.[42] This was done, and in June, 1924, the two governments delivered to the competent Sub-Commissions the prisoners for their transportation.[43]

§ 289. Statistics of emigrants transferred under the auspices of the Commission. The statistical data collected by the Mixed Commission give the following figures for Greeks who were transferred to Greece in the years 1923, 1924, 1925, and 1926 as subject to the exchange:

[40] See, for instance, the case of the Moslem Hafouj A. O., in the Greek legal periodical "Themis," 1930, p. 74.

[41] Procès-Verbaux, ii, 29th meet., January 4, 1924.

[42] Procès-Verbaux, ii, 33d meet., January 29, 1924; 35th meet., February 7, 1924.

[43] Procès-Verbaux, iv, 56th meet., June 12, 1924.

Through the care of the Sub-Commission of Constantinople:

In 1924	92,843	
" 1925	3,165	
" 1926	1,943	
		97,951

Through the care of the Sub-Commission of Samsun:

In 1924		38,164

Through the care of the Sub-Commission of Mersina:

In 1924	49,943	
" 1925	181	
		50,124

From Smyrna, without the intervention of the Mixed Commission:

In 1923-24		2,500

From Kirk-Kilisseh:

In 1924		1,177
Total		189,916

The statistical data for Moslems transferred from Greece to Turkey in the years 1923, 1924, and 1925 are as follows:

Through the care of the Sub-Commission of Saloniki:

In 1923	18,044	
" 1924	91,533	
		109,577

Through the care of the Sub-Commission of Rethymno (Candia):

In 1923	3,788	
" 1924	10,009	
		13,797

Through the care of the Sub-Commission of Canea:

In 1923	3,270	
" 1924	4,872	
		8,142

Through the care of the Sub-Commission of Drama:

In 1923	69	
" 1924	75,978	
		76,047

Through the care of the Sub-Commission of Kavala:

In 1923	2,184	
" 1924	43,343	
		45,527

Through the care of the Sub-Commission of Kozani:

In 1923	13	
" 1924	26,610	
		26,623

Through the care of the Sub-Commission of Kaylar:

In 1923	10	
" 1924	30,770	
		30,780
		310,493
	Reported	310,493

From Kozani and Kaylar:

In 1924		34,653

Through the care of the Sub-Commission of Goumenitza (Epirus):

In 1924	2,032	
" 1925	957	
		2,989

From Lesbos, without the intervention of the Mixed Commission		7,500
	Total	355,635

These figures do not include the few thousand people that left Greece or Turkey in the years 1923-1926 of their own initiative and by other means of transportation than those placed at the disposal of the Mixed Commission by the two governments.

§ 290. Moslems who had emigrated prior to the constitution of the Commission. The figures given above concern only the persons who were exchanged under the supervision of the Mixed Commission. Indeed, the departure and emigration of the above persons took place after November, 1923. At that time there had already emigrated reciprocally to the two countries great numbers of persons, either in an orderly manner and voluntarily, or driven out precipitately from the country of their origin and reaching the country of destination in a destitute state.[44]

The first migratory movement of Moslems from Greece took place between 1912 and 1914. After the First Balkan War some 10,000 Turks from Macedonia and the Islands left Greece

[44] See on this also Introduction, § 7.

and emigrated to Turkey. These were mainly public officials, professional men, and large landowners. Early in 1914, when the relations between Greece and Turkey were strained, a part of the Moslem population of Central and Eastern Macedonia, influenced by the vigorous propaganda of the Young Turks,[45] emigrated to Turkey to take the place of Greeks who were removed from the Aegean coast of Asia Minor. It is estimated that about 115,000 Moslems emigrated in 1914 to Turkey.[46]

Both these migratory movements of Moslems from Greece were, on the whole, orderly movements. The emigrants in almost all cases took away with them or had transported all their movable property and they either disposed by private sale or leased or rented their immovable properties. The departure was not precipitated, and no hardships were experienced by the emigrants leaving Greece. It is true that conditions in Turkey were not found to be so rosy as had been represented to them, and many went through great difficulties before they were settled in their new homes.

§ 291. **Greek emigrants from 1912 to 1923.** The migratory movement of Greeks from Turkey was almost continuous from the First Balkan War to the time the Commission was constituted, with peaks in 1914-15 and following the Greek military disaster in the fall of 1922 and spring of 1923. From 1912 to 1915 the migratory movement was in part orderly, many persons leaving Turkey of their own will to emigrate to Greece; but it was mostly conducted under moral and material pressure consequent upon the policy of the Young Turks to clear the Aegean littoral of Asia Minor and Eastern Thrace from the Greek and Armenian population, in order to settle there Moslems as a defence against foreign invasions. These Greeks were required to transfer their homes to the interior of Asia Minor, and as they saw in this step little hope of protection of life and property, they preferred instead to seek refuge in

[45] Western Thrace was at the time part of the Bulgarian territory.

[46] A. A. Pallis, *Statistical Study of Racial Migrations in Macedonia and Thrace* (in Greek) (Athens, 1925), p. 14; Racial Migrations in the Balkans during the Years 1912-1924, in *The Geographical Journal,* lxvi (1925), pp. 315-331.

Greece. As the removal from the Aegean coast and Thrace was made precipitately and to the accompaniment of acts of terrorism, most of the Greek emigrants left all their property and reached Greece destitute.

But the worst had still to come. When the Greek army retreated from its advanced positions at Eski-Shehir and Afion-Kara-Hissar in September, 1922, and fled towards the coast, it was followed by the Greek population living in all the area of the Greek occupation in Asia Minor. These people left practically everything behind except money, jewelry, and other precious things which could be carried along without difficulty. The fugitives reached the ports on the coast, where they were picked up by steamers and transported to Greece. They "invaded the country . . . in a wretched condition, starving, ill, stripped of all they had, nearly all of them mourning the loss of near relatives, a veritable human wreckage . . . After their arrival and even during their flight hunger and epidemics created gaps in their ranks . . ." [47]

Precise figures of these Greek refugees from 1912 to 1923 had not been compiled. It was believed that the refugees who swarmed into Greece after the disaster in Asia Minor numbered over a million souls. The first official census was made in 1928, when the census of all the population of Greece was taken. By that time many thousand refugees were dead from sufferings and epidemics, while many thousands had left Greece and emigrated to the United States, Egypt, France and other countries.

The census of 1928 gave the number of refugees as 1,221,849.[48] Of these 151,892 had emigrated to Greece before the Greek disaster in Asia Minor, and 1,067,957 after that event. All these refugees did not come from Turkey. 117,633 came from Bulgaria, Russia, Albania, Jugoslavia, and the Dodecanese. Taking account of the latter refugees and of the 189,916 Greeks who emigrated from Turkey under the auspices of the Mixed Commission, we must conclude that a total of 914,300 Greek emigrants from Turkey from 1912 to 1923 were

[47] League of Nations, *Greek Refugee Settlement* (Geneva, 1926), pp. 3-4.
[48] A. A. Pallis, *Collection of Principal Statistics concerning the Exchange of Populations* (in Greek) (Athens, 1929), p. 4.

found in Greece in 1928. If to these be added those who died from sufferings and epidemics as a result of the emigration, and those who left Greece to go to other countries, we may reach the total number of 1,100,000 Greek emigrants from Turkey prior to the constitution of the Commission.

CHAPTER XXII

MOVABLE PROPERTY OF EMIGRANTS

§ 292. Provisions of the Convention. The Convention concerning the Exchange of Greek and Turkish Populations in article 5 contained the general principle that "the rights of property and monetary assets of Greeks in Turkey or Moslems in Greece shall not be prejudiced in consequence of the exchange to be carried out." Article 8 undertook to define more specifically the fate of the movable property of persons to be exchanged. The emigrants "shall be free to take away with them or to arrange for the transport of their movable property of every kind." The two countries were to exempt such property from export or import duties or any other tax and were to provide the fullest facilities for transport.

It was presumed that many emigrants would not be able to take away all of their movable property. To secure their rights in such cases, the last paragraph of article 8 provided that such emigrants could leave their property behind. "In that event, the local authorities shall be required to draw up, the emigrant in question being given an opportunity to be heard, an inventory and valuation of the property left by him. Procès-verbaux containing the inventory and the valuation of the movable property left by the emigrant shall be drawn up in four copies, one of which shall be kept by the local authorities, the second transmitted to the Mixed Commission . . . to serve as the basis for the liquidation . . . , the third shall be handed to the government of the country to which the emigrant is going, and the fourth to the emigrant himself."

These provisions of the Convention remained for the most part a dead leter. The Mixed Commission has never received any such *procès-verbaux.* In particular, the transfer of the populations from Turkey took place in large measure without the intervention of the Mixed Commission. It was only in exceptional cases that the local authorities were required to draw up such *procès-verbaux.*

Moreover these provisions could not apply to the people who had emigrated prior to the constitution of the Commission, namely, between October 18, 1912, and October, 1923. With regard to these persons, it was provided by article 10 of the Convention that their movable property was to be included in the applications for liquidation together with their immovable property, and was to be liquidated by the Mixed Commission. This liquidation was to take place independently of all measures of any kind whatever which had resulted in any restriction of rights of ownership over the property in question, such as confiscation, forced sale, etc.

Emigrants could, of course, dispose freely of the movable property which they did not wish to take away or to have liquidated by the Commission as provided by the last paragraph of article 8. The Greek Refugee Settlement Commission proposed to the Mixed Commission to buy for cash the agricultural implements, cattle, and other movable property that the Moslem emigrants should desire to dispose of on their departure. This proposal was accepted by the Mixed Commission, with the reservation, insisted upon by Tevfic Ruchdi Bey, that, since Turkey was in need of horned cattle, the Refugee Settlement Commission should not buy such cattle of emigrants.[1]

[1] Procès-Verbaux, i, 20th meet., November 27, 1923.

§ 293. Abandonment of movable property by Greek refugees. Before describing the carrying out of the above provisions of the Convention, it is necessary to make two observations. First, the Greek refugees, numbering over a million, who were driven out of Turkey before the Convention entered into effect had left their homes in great haste and had taken away with them hardly any movable property, with the exception of money or valuables that could be easily carried in their precipitate flight. The provisions of the Convention with respect to movable property were of little value to them. The only thing they could hope for was the liquidation of such property by the Mixed Commission. But this hope was illusory. The Turkish authorities sold the property of refugees even before the Sub-Commissions were appointed and could supervise such sales.[2]

§ 294. Requisitions of movable property. Secondly, the influx into Greece of the masses of Greek refugees raised the question of food and clothing for them, and the government was necessarily obliged to requisition all kinds of property of the native population, whether Greek or Moslem. Hence, before the Convention entered into effect, and even later, the movable property of Moslems, which, according to the Convention, was to be respected, was seized or requisitioned by the Greek authorities.

The Mixed Commission, after certain recriminations between the two delegations, decided that "all property seized after October 7, 1923, should be restored to the owners," and "if such property had been requisitioned in favor of emigrants and could not be restored, the owners were to receive its value on the basis of the market price. The Sub-Commissions were to decide on such price in cases of dispute." [3] At the same time the Commission decided that the seized movable property of the emigrants then in the hands of the two governments should be preserved in the state in which it was, with the view of facilitating the task of liquidation. The phrase "et existant

[2] Procès-Verbaux, i, 17th meet., November 16 and 17, 1923.

[3] Decisions V and IX of the Commission, taken at the meetings of October 27 and December 7, 1923.

actuellement entre les mains des deux gouvernements" was inserted in this decision at the proposal of Tevfic Ruchdi Bey. This rendered the decision very convenient to the Turkish government, as most of the property of refugees seized by that government had already been the subject of forced sale.[5]

The decision of the Commission that no requisitions of movable property were to be allowed after October 7, 1922, was carried out in its entirety in Greece.[6] No complaint of further requisitions was brought up by the Turkish delegation. A total of 10,180,194 drachmas was paid by the Greek government to Moslem emigrants for requisitions. A further sum of three or four million drachmas remained unpaid in August, 1924, according to reports of the Sub-Commissions.[7] On the contrary, in Turkey the requisitions continued after that date. The Sub-Commissions of Mersina, Samsun, and Constantinople reported that the cattle and crops of Greeks of a value of several tens of thousands of dollars had been seized by the Turkish authorities without payment of indemnity to the emigrants.

§ 295. Definition of movable property by the Commission. The Mixed Commission defined what was movable property in the meaning of the Convention by one of its decisions: [8] "all things movable by their nature, regardless of the laws, usages, or customs according to which such things might be deemed . . . by reason of their destination, immovable." The definition did not cover "the integral parts of an immovable property, whose removal might destroy or injure wholly or in part the immovable property." This decision was occasioned by the fact that in the island of Lemnos the local authorities, following local usages, considered that seed, cattle, and agricultural implements were to be regarded as immovable property. The decision was intended to deny this view.

According to the last paragraph of the decision, the question whether a motor of a mill was movable property was to be

[5] Decision No. XIII, taken at the meeting of December 11, 1923.

[6] There have been cases where Moslems received back their cattle and were paid for the requisitions. See Procès-Verbaux, v, 65th meet., August 16, 1924.

[7] Procès-Verbaux, v, 66th meet., August 19, 1924.

[8] Decision No. XVI, taken at the 46th meeting, April 1, 1924.

decided according as its removal might or might not destroy or injure the mill.[9]

The question whether unharvested crops came under the category of movable property was raised with regard to the Greeks of Chataldja, who were allowed to sell their crops by the local authorities but later were compelled to restore the price. The Mixed Commission refused to intervene in their favor. It was, indeed, disposed to rule that the sale of unharvested crops should be allowed to emigrants, but the Turkish delegation objected, on the ground that the opposite rule was applied against the Moslem emigrants. The Sub-Commissions in Greece, being questioned on this point, denied the allegation of the Turkish delegation, which then made general statements based on personal observations.[10]

When in August, 1924, the question of seed belonging to Moslem landowners of Saloniki and their right to take it away came up before the Mixed Commission, the Greek delegation, while admitting that this was a case of movable property according to the decisions of the Commission, yet in view of the lack of reciprocity for Greeks in Turkey, maintained that the Moslems should not be allowed to take away the seed, which by virtue of special legislation constituted immovable property by destination.[11]

The Commission decided that boats and small craft of any kind were to be considered as movable property and could be taken away by the emigrants. But if such craft were burdened with a mortgage they could not be taken away unless the mortgage was paid.[12]

Gold could be taken away by the emigrants like any other property, although its export was prohibited by law. But it was feared that dangers might arise for the two countries from an excessive export of gold. It was, therefore, decided not to publish the decision allowing the taking away of gold by emigrants, while the two governments were asked to forego any

[9] Procès-Verbaux, iv, 54th meet., May 21, 1924.
[10] Procès-Verbaux, iv, 55th meet., May 27, 1924; v, 59th meet., July 12, 1924.
[11] Procès-Verbaux, iv, 55th meet., May 27, 1924; v, 59th meet., July 12, 1924.
[12] Decision No. VII, taken at the meeting of December 7, 1923.

search, unless there were indications of abuse of the liberty on the part of any emigrant.[13] Tobacco was an important item of movable property for the Moslems of Eastern Macedonia. Permission to transport was made subject to the obtaining of information from the chambers of commerce as to the actual quantity of the stocks possessed by the Moslems. Tobacco paid a large export duty in Greece, and it was feared that abuses might result from the exemption of emigrants' movable property from such duties. Besides, the export of tobacco in great quantities might have an injurious influence on the national wealth.[14]

§ 296. Material of burned buildings. The classification of the material of burned buildings as movable property was disputed. The Moslem proprietors of such buildings in Saloniki claimed the right to dispose of the loose ruins as well as of the standing ruins, which required to be torn down before they could be removed. The Greek delegation resisted these claims, in view of the fact that the Turkish government had sold to a foreign corporation the ruins of burned Greek buildings in Smyrna and thus had decided the question against the emigrants. Tevfic Ruchdi Bey admitted the analogy between the two cases.[15] The Commission subsequently decided that in both Saloniki and Smyrna ruins representing heaps of material were to be deemed movable property, and that in case they should not be sold by the emigrants before their departure they were to be included in the *procès-verbaux* provided by article 8, paragraph 4, of the Convention.[16]

§ 297. Tombstones. Moslems from Crete expressed the desire to take away as movable property the stones of family tombs. The Legal Section of the Commission doubted whether these could be considered as movable property. The Greek delegation thought that such stones might have an artistic or a moral value for the emigrants, and that they should be allowed to take them away. Tevfic Ruchdi Bey pointed out that such sentimentalism should not be encouraged, and that

[13] Decision No. VI, taken at the meeting of November 17, 1923.
[14] Procès-Verbaux, i, 6th and 9th meet., October 18 and 24, 1923.
[15] Procès-Verbaux, v, 63d meet., August 2, 1924.
[16] Procès-Verbaux, vi, 70th meet., September 15, 1924.

as these stones were embedded in the soil they ought to be considered immovable property. Mr. Widding explained that the question appeared to be practical rather than sentimental, inasmuch as the claimants intended to sell the stones. Thereupon the Commission decided to classify the tombstones as immovable property.[17]

§ 298. **Deposits in banks and moneys in safes.** Difficulties arose with regard to deposits at the banks and valuables in bankers' safes. Moratoria existed in favor of banks, and the deposits and safes were attached or seized. The Commission decided that all these impediments should be removed in view of the stipulations of the Convention. It decided that "all sums of money, stocks, or bonds, deposited by persons subject to exchange at banks, insurance companies, or other financial establishments, were to be delivered over to the interested persons." All seizures were to be cancelled. The same was to be the case with respect to the safes of emigrants, for which Tevfic Ruchdi Bey again caused the addition of the phrase "et existant actuellement." [18]

The Turkish government did not take steps for the carrying out of this decision. Complaints as to this reached the Mixed Commission repeatedly, and the neutral members called the attention of the Turkish members to this failure.[19] The Turkish delegation promised to deliver at a certain time to the Greek delegation a list of the safes seized in Smyrna, and to the interested parties certificates by which they would be enabled to receive the contents of the same.[20] Later the Commission decided to send a delegation from among its members to Smyrna to take possession of the safes of Greeks seized by the Turkish authorities, and asked the Turkish government as to the formalities to be complied with.[21] Nothing came of this.

[17] Procès-Verbaux, v, 63d meet., August 3, 1924.

[18] Decision No. X, taken at the meeting of December 11, 1923.

[19] Procès-Verbaux, ii, 32d meet., January 23, 1924; 36th meet., February 13, 1924; iii, 42d meet., March 11, 1924; 43d meet., March 14, 1924; v, 57th meet., June 18, 1924.

[20] Procès-Verbaux, iii, 46th meet., April 1, 1924.

[21] Procès-Verbaux, iv, 54th meet., May 21, 1924; v, 59th meet., July 12, 1924.

The financial establishments in Greece paid their deposits to emigrants on mere presentation by them of a certificate of the Mixed Commission or the competent Sub-Commission. On the contrary, in Turkey special governmental authorization (of the *Defter Hané*) was required for each case of paying out deposits of emigrants. The Commission asked the Turkish government to publish in its Official Journal the decision of the Mixed Commission, and to order such establishments to pay out these deposits.[22] As this was not done, the Commission repeated its letter on September 18, 1924.[23] Subsequently the Ottoman Bank of Constantinople received appropriate orders; but these were cancelled subsequently, in view of the dispute with regard to the tithe on tobacco which was alleged to have been unduly collected from Moslem emigrants by the Greek government and with regard to the interpretation of Decision X of the Mixed Commission.[24]

§ 299. Rentals and claims in movable property. Certain buildings belonging to emigrants, though not expropriated, had been taken over by the governments, which had leased them and collected the rentals. The Mixed Commission decided that these rentals should be deemed movable property of the emigrants and should be restored to them. Those who had already departed were to receive payment at the general liquidation. The sums in question were included in the applications for liquidation filed by such persons. Those who had not departed could claim the restoration of these rentals before their departure.[25]

The Commission and its sections were very busy solving individual claims for movable property left in Turkey for reasons beyond the control of persons subjected to exchange. Thus, persons subject to exchange, coproprietors with Moslems in Turkey, were not allowed to take away movable property in which they had an undivided interest; movable property

[22] Procès-Verbaux, v, 63d meet., August 2, 1924.
[23] Procès-Verbaux, vi, 70th meet., September 15, 1924; and 71st meet., September 18, 1924.
[24] See on this *infra*, § 300.
[25] Decisions X and XV, taken at the meetings of December 11, 1923, and March 25, 1924; also Procès-Verbaux, vi, 70th meet., September 15, 1924, and annex 1.

of persons subject to exchange was attached for debts owed by them and sold at auction, the remainder, after payment of such debts, being ordered deposited at the tribunal; or such persons were prevented by the authorities from taking away their property. In all such cases the Commission decided on the right of the claimants and communicated its decisions to the competent local authorities.

The Turkish authorities considered all movable property not taken away by Greek refugees as property 'left' by the emigrants in their country of origin and therefore as acquired by the state, the persons in question retaining the right to claim the value of such property in their applications for liquidation. However, it can hardly be admitted that the movable property was 'left' by the owners in the cases above enumerated, since the failure of the emigrants to take away their property was caused by legal or administrative impediments.

§ 300. Property of former emigrants. The return of money, stocks, bonds, and gold articles deposited at the banks was interrupted in 1926. A dispute arose between the two delegations as to the interpretation of Decision X of the Mixed Commission which provided for the return. According to this decision, remittance was to be made of these assets "appartenant à des personnes . . . devant émigrer ou ayant émigré de l'un ou de l'autre des deux pays." The Turkish delegation contended that the words "ayant émigré" referred only to persons who had left under the auspices of the Mixed Commission, to the exclusion of those who had departed without the intervention of the Mixed Commission. Such an interpretation excluded more than a million Greeks who left Turkey before the constitution of the Mixed Commission.

In fact, for more than two years after its adoption Decision X was broadly applied, even in Turkey, to all emigrants, without the limitation contended for by the Turkish delegation after those two years. The Turkish delegation admitted this, but maintained that it was only a gratuitous act on the part of Turkey.[26] It also asserted that the proposed broad

[26] Procès-Verbaux, xii, 127th meet., July 7, 1927.

interpretation of Decision X would be contrary to articles 8, 9, and 10 of the Convention.

The Commission, after long discussions in the competent section, decided, against the opposition of the Turkish delegation, that the expressions "devant émigrer" and "ayant émigré" in Decision X designated the same persons as those mentioned in article 3, paragraph 2, of the Convention, that is, all Greeks or Moslems who had left the Turkish or Greek territory respectively after October 18, 1912. The same decision stated that the expression "ayant déja quitté" in article 10 of the Convention designated the same persons as those mentioned in article 3, paragraph 2, under the terms "ayant émigré." [27] As a result of this decision, all money, stocks, bonds, and gold articles belonging to persons subject to exchange and deposited at banks or financial establishments were to be restored to their owners.

Additional evidence in favor of the above interpretation of the Mixed Commission is afforded by the preparatory work of the Convention. The text of article 9, as originally proposed, contained the word "volontairement" after the words "les biens meubles laissés." At Mr. Montagna's proposal this word was stricken out, for the purpose of leaving a larger liberty of interpretation to the Mixed Commission.[28]

§ 301. Conservatory sale of perishable merchandise. For a long time the Legal Section of the Mixed Commission was considering the question of the restoration of merchandise belonging to persons subject to exchange found in the hands of other persons. In the meantime such properties depreciated in value or became worthless. The Commission was thus led to take a decision for the conservatory sale of perishable merchandise.[29] By the terms of this decision the Mixed Commission was not opposed to the sale of property subject to rapid depreciation, or whose preservation was expensive, deposited with third parties, in particular with banks, insurance companies, or financial establishments, by individuals or juristic persons subject to exchange. Such sale was authorized

[27] Procès-Verbaux, xiii, 133d meet., August 11, 1927.
[28] Conférence de Lausanne, *Recueil des actes,* première sér., i, p. 583.
[29] Procès-Verbaux, ix, 106th meet., March 27, 1926.

whenever, by law or general commercial usages, it was deemed necessary for the preservation of the interests of the depositor or the depositee. Notwithstanding such sale, the character of the deposit was not modified, and the product of the sale was to remain in the hands of the depositee in lieu of the original merchandise.

§ 302. Rights *in personam* of emigrants. Article 5 of the Convention explicitly provided that rights of property and credit assets (*créances*) of emigrants were not to be prejudiced in consequence of the exchange. Under this provision the persons subject to exchange could collect debts owed them before their departure. In case the debtors should be recalcitrant, action would lie against them. But if judgment on the action was not recovered by the time the creditor was compelled to leave, were his rights in the sum ultimately recovered affected by the fact that he had then left the country?

The terms of article 5 should give a negative reply to this question. This was maintained by the Greek delegation and by the neutral members. The Turkish delegation, on the contrary, contended that the credit assets (*créances*) not collected before the departure of emigrants were movable property 'left' by the emigrants, and therefore ownership was vested in the state.

As the neutral member, Mr. Widding, pointed out, the Turkish interpretation amounted to a contention that all credit assets of persons who had emigrated were lost to those persons, which was in flagrant opposition to the terms of article 5. Mr. Holstad noted that the terms of article 8 concerning the 'taking away' or 'abandoning' of movable property could not apply to *créances,* which cannot be 'taken away' or 'abandoned,' being merely personal relations between creditor and debtor.[30]

The question remained unsolved until July, 1928, when the following decision was adopted unanimously.[31] "The money claims for sums due to 'exchanged' persons are not affected by the 'exchange' of the creditor, and his claim does

[30] Procès-Verbaux, x, 115th meet., January 25, 1927.
[31] Procès-Verbaux, 165th meet., July 26, 1928, Decision No. 44.

not enter into the liquidation of his property, whatever his date of emigration may be. He may seek the recovery of the sums due him and obtain payment by all legal means. The Mixed Commission will lend its good offices in this respect to the interested persons."

Nevertheless, creditors might, if they wished, include in the liquidation their money claim against the state whose territory they left, on condition that they applied for the same to the Mixed Cimmission before March 1, 1929.

§ 303. Pensions of exchanged persons. The pension allowances due in the two countries to state employees subject to exchange were assuredly pecuniary interests of emigrants which ought to be protected, according to the general principle of article 5 of the Convention. This article, indeed, provided that rights of property and credit assets of Greeks in Turkey or Moslems in Greece should not be prejudiced in consequence of the exchange. The Greek delegation maintained that this provision covered the case of pension allowances and imposed upon the Mixed Commission the obligation to liquidate such pensions in favor of their beneficiaries.[32] It might also be argued that these assets constituted movable property which the interested persons *ne pourraient pas emporter,* were unable to take away (article 8).

The Turkish delegation, on the contrary, insisted that the only provision applicable in the case of pensions was article 61 of the Treaty of Lausanne, of which the Convention, according to the contention of that delegation, was a part. This article dealt with pensions of persons who, as a result of the Treaty and the territorial cessions resulting therefrom, changed their nationality, and provided that "les bénéficiaires de pensions civiles et militaires turques devenus, en vertu du present Traité, ressortissants d'un État autre que la Turquie, ne pourront exercer du chef de leurs pensions aucun recours contre le Gouvernement turc."

It is not certain whether the Convention may be considered legally as a part of the Treaty of Lausanne. Even if this should be admitted, article 61 can in no way be made

[32] Procès-Verbaux, iv, 48th meet., April 11, 1924.

to apply to persons subject to exchange who changed their nationality not by reason of cession of territory under that treaty, but under the compulsory exchange carried out under the Convention.

The motive of the Turkish contention, of course, was the fact that a great number of Greeks in Turkey held public offices and were therefore entitled to pensions, whereas very few Moslems were state employees in Greece.

The Legal Section of the Commission, being unable to reach an agreement in view of the opposition of the Turkish member, proposed, on September 18, 1924, that a wish be expressed to the two governments that they should make an agreement to pay pensions to "exchanged" employees "for humanitarian reasons." [33]

§ 304. Movable property of communities. Article 8, paragraph 2, of the Convention provided that the members of communities which were to leave the territory of one of the contracting states should have the right to take away freely or to arrange for the transport of the movable property belonging to their communities. This provision, needless to say, benefited especially the Turkish communities in Greece. More than a million Greeks had left Turkey before the constitution of the Mixed Commission and under such circumstances that they were unable to take away any community property, with the exception of some icons or sacred images from churches.

Communities, in the meaning of the Convention, included "mosques [Moslem temples], tekkés [Moslem convents], meddresses [Moslem schools], churches, convents, schools, hospitals, societies, associations and juridical persons or other foundations of any nature whatever." With respect to the sums of money, deposits, stocks, and bonds belonging to orphanages and *vacoufs* in Greece and to similar foundations in Turkey, the Commission decided, at the proposal of both delegations, that the public treasuries, financial establishments, and all individuals and juristic persons possessing such funds should turn them over to the Mixed Commission or

[33] Procès-Verbaux, vi, 71st meet., September 18, 1924; vii, 82d meet., January 6, 1925.

Sub-Commissions that they might be placed at the disposal of the interested government.[34] Thus, these assets were not remitted to the mandatories or administrators of such foundations, since the latter had ceased to exist, or their purposes had become unattainable by reason of the emigration. The government in the territory of which the members of such foundations emigrated now had charge of and satisfied the needs that formed the object of the foundations, and it was right that such government should collect the assets.

It is to be noted that the Greco-Turkish Mixed Commission had no difficulty in reaching this decision. This is explained by the fact that the Greek and Turkish delegations were in agreement on this question and they formed together the majority in the Commission. On the contrary, the same question remained long undecided in the Greco-Bulgarian Mixed Commission, because of the inability of the neutral members to make a decision and the fact that the national members formed a minority in that Commission.

The archives of the communities subject to exchange were delivered to the competent Sub-Commissions by the administrators of such communities.[35]

With respect to money claims of communities and communal institutions, the Mixed Commission decided, in July, 1928, to collect them and place them at the disposal of the interested government. In case of judicial action against the debtor, that government was given authority to act through an attorney in lieu of the communities and communal institutions.[36]

[34] Procès-Verbaux, iv, 51st meet., May 2, 1924; 55th meet., June 27, 1924.
[35] Procès-Verbaux, iv, 56th meet., June 12, 1924.
[36] Procès-Verbaux, 105th meet., July 26, 1928, Decision No. 45.

CHAPTER XXIII

IMMOVABLE PROPERTY OF EMIGRANTS

§ 305. Provisions of the Convention. The Convention concerning the Exchange of Greek and Turkish Populations purported to guarantee to emigrants, in addition to other rights, payment for their immovable property which they left in their country of origin. Such property, according to article 9, as well as the movable property that the emigrants left behind, was to be liquidated. The Mixed Commission (articles 13 and 14) had power to appraise such property of all persons subject to exchange, the interested parties being heard or duly summoned. The basis for the appraisal was to be the value of the property in gold currency.

The Commission had full power to settle the methods to be followed by it as regards the appraisal and liquidation. After the liquidation, the Commission was to transmit to each proprietor a declaration stating the sum due him in respect of the property of which he had been dispossessed, and such property was to remain at the disposal of the government on whose territory it was situated. The Convention further provided that, on the basis of this declaration, the emigrant should be entitled, in principle, to receive an equivalent grant in land and property from the government of the country to which he emigrated.

All these provisions of the Convention have remained without practical effect. The Commission merely took certain decisions in preparation for this task of liquidation. Blanks were distributed to emigrants, which were filled in with the particulars of the properties left in their country of origin. And in one of the first meetings of the Commission it was decided that the appraisal of the properties was to be made on the basis of the Turkish gold pound.[1]

§ 306. Transfer of ownership to the States. The Convention provided (article 14, paragraph 1) that the property left by emigrants was to remain at the disposal of the government on whose territory it was situated. Although no explicit provision was made as to the time at which the property passed to the state, it was to be inferred from article 14 that the transfer was to take place after the Commission had appraised and liquidated the property and transmitted to the owner a declaration stating the sum due to him for such property. This provision of the Convention was not carried out, and the properties of the exchanged persons passed by gradual steps to the ownership of the two governments respectively. The Commission sanctioned this transfer by a number of its decisions,[2] the effect of which was that the persons subject to exchange lost the *jus disponendi* from the time the Convention entered into effect, and that from the time of their departure from the country of origin their properties were administered by the respective governments. Such persons continued to be in nominal possession of their properties, and consequently the revenues therefrom were due to them until the time of their dispossession. This, according to article 14, was not to take place until the moment the Mixed Commission should transmit to them a declaration stating the sum due them on the liquidation of their properties. Subsequently, a decision made in June, 1924, provided that from June 21, 1924, and from the moment the emigrants left their immovable property, this passed to the disposal of the government of the territory where it was situated. The right of the emigrants to the revenues of such properties then ceased.

[1] Procès-Verbaux, i, 7th meet., October 20, 1923.
[2] Decisions VIII, XI, and XII, of December 7 and 11, 1923.

§ 307. Joint properties and mortgages. In the case of immovable properties belonging in part to persons subject to exchange and in part to persons exempt from exchange, the Commission authorized the division of such properties according to the procedure of the law of the country where they were situated.[3] Mortgaged properties were dealt with as follows. (1) In case both the mortgagor and mortgagee were subject to exchange, their liquidation accounts were to be debited and credited respectively with the amount of the debt, while the property passed to the disposal of the state; (2) in case the mortgagor only was exchangeable, the mortgage remained in force and the debtor was to be debited with the amount of the debt in his liquidation account; (3) in case the mortgagee only was subject to exchange, he had the option either to preserve his right to recover the mortgage debt against the non-exchangeable mortgagor, or to include the amount of the mortgage debt in his application for liquidation. In the last case, the government of the country from which the mortgagee emigrated stepped into his shoes. In all the three cases above enumerated the mortgage was to be finally cancelled only on the payment of the liquidation amount.[4]

§ 308. Properties of communities. The Convention provided also for the liquidation of the immovable properties of communities. This term was made to include, according to article 8, paragraph 2, mosques (Moslem temples), tekkés (Moslem convents), meddresses (Moslem schools), churches, convents, schools, hospitals, societies, associations, and juridical persons, or other foundations of any nature whatever. In addition to the properties of communities which were established in the regions subject to exchange, properties situated in the districts to which the compulsory exchange applied and belonging to communities established in districts to which the exchange did not apply were also to be liquidated, in accordance with the second paragraph of article 9.[5]

Mandatories were appointed by the Commission, at the

[3] Procès-Verbaux, ii, 33d meet., January 29, 1924 (Decision XI *bis*); iv, 54th meet., May 21, 1924.
[4] Procès-Verbaux, iii, 42d meet., April 4, 1924.
[5] See, on this provision, *supra*, p. 417.

proposal of the respective delegations, to administer the properties of communities in the regions to which the exchange applied. These mandatories remained until the whole population subject to exchange left. As soon as the evacuation was complete, the government took over the administration of the properties.

The fourth paragraph of article 10 of the Convention provided that the Mixed Commission, when proceeding to the liquidation of *vacouf* property in Greece and of the rights and interests connected therewith, and to the liquidation of similar foundations belonging to Greeks in Turkey, was to follow the principles laid down in previous treaties with a view to fully safeguarding the rights and interests of these foundations and of the individuals interested in them. Such treaties are the Convention of Athens of November 1/14, 1913, between Greece and Turkey,[6] and the Treaty of Constantinople between Turkey and Bulgaria of September 16/29, 1913.[7] The property rights in such *vacouf* properties were complicated in the extreme, and would have challenged the ability of any Mixed Commission to verify, establish, and liquidate them. Fortunately for the Greco-Turkish Mixed Commission, it was spared this task.

§ 309. Property under seizure, confiscation, or expropriation. In addition to the properties actually owned and possessed by the emigrants before their departure, those which formed the subject of extraordinary measures in the two countries under laws or regulations passed since October 18, 1912, such as confiscation, forced sale, etc., were to be appraised and liquidated by the Mixed Commission as if the measures in question had not been applied (article 10). Further, properties expropriated since October 18, 1912, by either of the contracting countries and belonging previously to persons subject to exchange were to be reappraised by the Commission. In this case the latter was to determine the compensation due the owners for the injury through the expropriation.

[6] See article XII of this Convention in *British and Foreign State Papers,* cvii, p. 897.

[7] See article XII of this Treaty and article VIII of Annex 2 to the Treaty in *British and Foreign State Papers,* cvii, pp. 711-712, 716-717.

Moreover, the third paragraph of article 10 provided for the restoration to persons subject to exchange of the income from properties of which they had lost the enjoyment. This provision was very indefinite. The income was to be "guaranteed to them on the basis of the average yield before the war." The expression "before the war" raised difficulties of interpretation, and it was not clear whether the term "guaranteed" meant cash payment or the mere crediting of the final liquidation account of each emigrant with the amount of such income.[8] With regard to the first question, it was decided that the average yield of the properties in the five years 1909-14 should be taken as the basis for appraisal. The second question was never solved. The failure to solve it amounted practically to a rejection of the view that any actual cash payment was to be made before the completion of the liquidation.

§ 310. The problem of appraisal of immovable property. The preparatory work of the Convention betrays a naïve belief that the appraisal of the properties, their liquidation, and even the payment for them could be carried out and completed concurrently with the transfer of the populations from the two countries.[9] This accounts for the very inadequate provisions in the Convention on all these matters. The Commission, under the same naïve belief, at an early period and while the transfer of the populations was being carried out contemplated the appraisal of properties left by the emigrants and sent committees to various sections of Greece and Turkey to study the methods of appraisal that should be adopted.[10] It was at first thought, as a result of these trips for gathering information, that in Macedonia the archives of government land surveys in certain places and of the Agricultural Bank could be used for the purposes of appraisal.[11] But these data were rarely available, and any attempt to check up the declarations of emigrants on their basis would be sure to break down. In Thessaly, the appraisals, made by the government,

[8] Procès-Verbaux, i, 5th meet., October 16, 1923.

[9] Conférence de Lausanne, *Recueil des actes,* première série, i, pp. 590, 592 ff., 611, 614 ff.

[10] Procès-Verbaux, ii, 31st meet., January 11, 1924; iv, 49th meet., April 17, 1924; v, 59th meet., July 12, 1924; vii, 82d meet., January 6, 1925.

[11] Procès-Verbaux, ii, 32d meet., January 23, 1924.

of large properties which had been expropriated rendered the situation clear enough. On the contrary, in Crete and the other islands no such aids existed, and there was need of adopting some general principles.

Most of the members of the Commission seem to have wholly underestimated at that time the vastness of the problems of appraisal. An illustration is the fact that Mr. Ekstrand and Mr. Widding, the two neutral members, appeared to think that the appraisal could even be completed before the departure of the emigrants! [12] Mr. Pallis, the Greek member, more sober and experienced, gave warning that no illusions should exist on this matter, and that the appraisal was an exceedingly difficult work. His view was that the appraisal could not proceed at the same time with the exchange of populations. Tevfic Ruchdi Bey, however, agreed with the neutrals, and the Second Section of the Commission was instructed to study the matter. In fact, the removal of the populations was completed without any work of appraisal having begun at all.

The Second Section of the Commission early in 1925 reached an agreement on certain points on the question of appraisal, while several other points remained disputed. At this stage, in February, 1925, a report was submitted by this Section to the plenary assembly of the Commission, and it was proposed to enter into a discussion of this report at one of the next meetings of the Commission. A copy of the report was transmitted to the Secretariat of the League of Nations.[13] The report presented certain general ideas on appraisal; it proposed a number of resolutions concerning the appraisal of movable property; and it stated the different views of the two delegations with regard to the basis of appraisal of immovable property. In general, its effect was that individual appraisal should be undertaken only in exceptional cases, and that a lump appraisal by entire districts was more feasible and advisable. The Greek and Turkish delegations never showed

[12] Procès-Verbaux, i, 18th meet., November 21, 1923.

[13] "Rapport sur quelques Problèmes concernant l'évaluation," by Mr. Widding, dated January 15, 1925; Procès-Verbaux, vii, 85th meet., February 12, 1925.

any disposition to enter into a discussion of this report and of the question of appraisal, although invited to do so by the neutral members.[14] There was even an attempt to evade responsibility. Thus, the Minister for Foreign Affairs of Turkey, speaking in May, 1926, on the question of appraisal of the properties of the emigrants, declared that the two governments had left that question to the Mixed Commission and did not wish to interfere with its work—a declaration to which the neutral members took exception.[15]

§ 311. Appraisal and liquidation renounced. The question of appraisal and liquidation of the immovable properties of exchanged persons was subsequently entirely overshadowed by that of the properties of non-exchangeable persons, beneficiaries of the Declaration relative to Moslem properties in Greece of July 24, 1923,[16] and that of nationals of one of the two countries (Greece and Turkey) possessing properties in the other.

When Señor Rivas Vicuña became a member of the Mixed Commission, he raised for the first time the whole question of appraisal and liquidation of properties of exchanged persons. At his suggestion, the Commission adopted, in July, 1928, Decision No. 43, as follows: [17]

The Mixed Commission may apply the provisions of the Convention of Lausanne on the following conditions:

(1) The interested parties shall have a further period of six months to present their applications.

(2) The applications presented until this day, as well as those to be filed within the above period, shall be transmitted to the respective governments, which within a period of five months shall send to the Mixed Commission:

(*a*) A report on the state in which the properties in question are found.

(*b*) Their opinion on the appraisal made by the interested parties in their applications.

(*c*) Other observations suggested by these applications.

[14] Procès-Verbaux, 90th meet., March 31, 1925; viii, 94th meet., September 8, 1925; 97th meet., October 26, 1925.

[15] Procès-Verbaux, x, 108th meet., May 20, 1926.

[16] *Infra,* ch. xxiv.

[17] Procès-Verbaux, 164th meet., July 18, 1928.

(3) The Second Section of the Commission shall deal with the liquidation of the properties of persons exchanged on the basis of the above factors.

It was understood that a government which was in a position to make the communication above referred to might make it immediately without waiting for the expiration of the period provided for. The meaning of this decision was that the Commission wished to have the necessary factors to form a general appraisal of the amounts claimed by the two countries on account of the properties of the exchanged populations. It was subsequently understood [18] that the Mixed Commission, instead of communicating the applications filed by the emigrants to the two governments, would draw up lists showing the name of the applicant, the village or city where his property was situated, the number of his application, and the value claimed by him for movable and immovable property.

The Commission received no reply from either of the two governments. The neutral members were aware of the unwillingness of the governments to consider the appraisal of the properties of the exchanged persons. Referring to this matter in their comprehensive memorandum of September 12, 1928,[19] they pointed out that "unless an agreement between the two countries intervened, they were to propose the measures which the strict application of the Convention imposed." A little later, as seen in another place,[20] the Inspection Service on Appraisals began a work of classification of the applications of exchanged persons.

Both governments seemed to agree that a general set-off of mutual claims on account of the properties of exchanged persons was the only solution possible. In the abortive negotiations of 1929, referred to below,[21] this was readily agreed to. Because of the state of internal politics in the two countries, article 4 of the final Convention signed at Angora on June 10,

[18] Procès-Verbaux, 167th meet., September 4, 1928.
[19] See *infra,* § 351.
[20] See *infra,* § 357.
[21] *Ibid.*

1930, intrusted the neutral members of the Commission with the task of giving an opinion on the solution of the question of the liquidation of properties of exchanged persons. This opinion, which was agreed upon beforehand in substance, if not textually, is dated June 12, 1930, two days subsequent to the Convention of Angora.[22]

The renunciation of the application of the provisions of the Convention of Lausanne for the individual appraisal of properties of emigrants had the consequence that no emigrant was to receive a statement by the Mixed Commission as to the value placed on the property left by him in his country of origin, which statement would involve for the country to which he emigrated an obligation to make to him an equivalent grant. For this reason, a great outcry was raised in Greece by the refugees early in 1929 when it was known that a general balancing of claims was being considered. A committee of refugees had a conference with Mr. Venizelos in March, 1929, on this matter. The Greek Premier made the following statement: [23]

> The meaning of the Convention of Lausanne is that the Greek properties in Turkey and Turkish properties in Greece were to be appraised and any difference between the appraisal totals was to be collected by the state favored by such difference. However, do you think that when I signed the Convention I believed that all this would materialize?
>
> The Lausanne Convention is not really a Convention for the exchange of Greek and Moslem populations and properties, but rather a Convention for the departure of the Moslem population from Greece, because the Greeks were driven out from Turkey. That is the real fact. What the government must do for the refugees is to divide among them the existing property available in Greece.

This has the appearance of being frank and sound. But as an interpretation of the whole purpose and scope of the Convention of Lausanne it is not wholly accurate. As an *ex post facto* explanation, it is certainly convenient. We say this, of

[22] See on this *infra,* § 364.

[23] See *Atlantis,* a Greek daily newspaper published in New York, April 18, 1929.

course, without relation to the question whether the 'exchanged' Greeks received in Greece a proper indemnity for their property left in Turkey. We believe the indemnities paid them by the Greek government were equitable.[24]

[24] On the question of indemnities paid to refugees see *infra*, § 429.

CHAPTER XXIV

THE DECLARATION OF LAUSANNE AS TO MOSLEM PROPERTIES IN GREECE

§ 312. Effect of the Declaration as to Moslem Properties in Greece. The history of the signature by Greece of the Declaration of Lausanne as to Moslem Properties in Greece is given above.[1] This Declaration was in substance an annex to articles 65 and 66 of the Treaty of Lausanne, which provided for the reciprocal restoration of properties, rights, and interests of Turkish or Allied subjects respectively to the legally entitled persons, free of any charge or servitude, or the payment of the product of liquidation to such persons in case the properties, rights, or interests in question had been liquidated by the contracting countries.

The Declaration as to Moslem Properties contained provisions somewhat different from those of the above articles as regards properties of Turkish and Greek subjects. Such properties were in all cases to be restored to their owners, as were also all revenues received therefrom by the two governments. The owners could, however, apply to the Mixed Commission for the liquidation of such properties. The Mixed Commission was also to hear all claims with respect to such properties and the revenues thereof and to decide on such claims.

Although the Declaration was signed only by Greece, the last paragraph provided that it was to be executed on condition of reciprocity. In view of this, the Commission, soon after

[1] See *supra*, p. 347.

its constitution, invited the two governments to declare whether they were prepared to grant this reciprocity.[2] Indeed, this question needed to be asked only of the Turkish government, since the Greek government had signed the Declaration. However, the Greek government replied at an early date that it was ready to execute the Declaration on condition of reciprocity.[3] Turkey gave notice to the Mixed Commission on June 13, 1924, of its readiness to execute the Declaration by reciprocity.[4] The Declaration formed part of the Treaty of Lausanne and entered into effect at the same time, namely, on August 6, 1924.

§ 313. Beneficiaries of the Declaration. The definition of the persons who were entitled to the advantages of the Declaration presented difficulties in the Mixed Commission.[5] It would seem that the Declaration formed the counterpart of the Convention concerning the Exchange, so far as the persons dealt with were concerned. Under the Convention two classes of persons were included:

1. Persons subject to exchange under the provisions of articles 1 and 3, namely, Greek subjects of the Moslem religion and Turkish subjects of the Greek Orthodox religion who had been compulsorily exchanged or had left Greece or Turkey respectively after October 18, 1912.

2. Persons exempted from the exchange under article 2 of the Convention, namely, Greeks of Constantinople and Moslems of Western Thrace.

All other Greek owners of properties in Turkey and Moslem owners of properties in Greece were beneficiaries of the Declaration.[6]

Indeed, the first paragraph of the Declaration described its beneficiaries as follows: ". . . des personnes . . . qui ne sont pas visées par les dispositions de la Convention concernant l'échange des populations . . . et qui ont quitté la

[2] Procès-Verbaux, i, 5th meet., October 16, 1923.
[3] Procès-Verbaux, iii, 46th meet., April 1, 1924.
[4] Procès-Verbaux, v, 57th meet., June 18, 1924.
[5] Procès-Verbaux, iii, 46th meet., April 1, 1924; vi, 71st meet., September 18, 1924.
[6] This was rightly maintained by Tevfic Ruchdi Bey: see Procès-Verbaux, vi, 72d meet., September 23, 1924.

Grèce, y compris l'île de Crète [ou la Turquie], avant le 18 Octobre 1912 ou qui ont résidé de tout temps en dehors de la Grèce."

From the words "y compris l'île de Crète," the Greek representative on the special committee formed to examine the claims of the beneficiaries of the Declaration concluded that the Declaration concerned only Old Greece, that is, the territories over which Greek sovereignty extended prior to October 18, 1912.[7] This restrictive interpretation, though difficult to maintain, was adhered to by the President of the Greek delegation, Mr. Exintaris, who asked the views on this point of the Greek government and of Mr. Caclamanos, Minister at London, who had signed the Declaration with Mr. Venizelos. Eventually this restrictive interpretation was abandoned by the Greek delegation.[8]

The above definition of beneficiaries in the Declaration did not permit any distinction between nationals or non-nationals of each of the two countries. The only condition under which owners of properties in Greece or Turkey could claim under the Declaration was that they were Moslems or Greeks respectively, who had left the country before October 18, 1912, or had never resided therein. In this there was agreement between the two delegations.[9]

§ 314. Filing and adjudication of claims. The second paragraph of the Declaration provided that claims under it were to be filed within a period of six months from the coming into effect of the Treaty of Peace signed at Lausanne. Even before that date Moslem beneficiaries, invited by publications of the Turkish government, filed their claims with the Mixed Commission.[10] In view of the shortness of the period allowed, the two governments were asked by the Mixed Commission to compute the period of six months from December 6, 1924, the date on which the special committee began functioning. This, in effect, amounted to an extension by four months of the

[7] Procès-Verbaux, vi, 73d meet., September 30, 1924.
[8] Procès-Verbaux, vi, 74th meet., October 16, 1924, and 77th meet., November 15, 1924.
[9] Procès-Verbaux, vii, 82d meet., January 6, 1924.
[10] Procès-Verbaux, iii, 43d meet., March 14, 1924.

period provided in the Declaration. Both governments accepted the extension to June 6, 1925.[11]

The Declaration provided that the claims were to be examined as urgent business by the Mixed Commission, with a view to their adjudication within a period of one year from the date of the entering into effect of the Treaty of Lausanne. The Mixed Commission, in order to speed the work of examination, formed a committee *ad hoc* as soon as it learned of the ratification of the Treaty of Lausanne.[12] This Committee was given power to make final decisions, in case of unanimous agreement, as to applicants entitled to the benefits of the Declaration. The one-year period for the adjudication of claims expired August 6, 1925, before the work of the Committee was completed. The grant of an extension of eight months was then asked of the two governments.[13] The Turkish government granted this extension in September, 1925; [14] the Greek government was unwilling to grant further extension.

The committee *ad hoc* had examined and accepted, to July 8, 1925, 119 claims of Moslems as beneficiaries of the Declaration.[15] A list of these persons was communicated to the two governments. In the Committee these claims were recognized speedily and without opposition. When the Greek government carried out an investigation with respect to some of the claimants, it was found that some of them were really 'exchangeable' persons and not properly beneficiaries of the Declaration. The Greek government thereupon declined to consider the unanimous decisions taken by the Committee in regard to these persons as final, and reëxamined the cases of the persons who had been supplied with certificates of the Mixed Commission stating that they were beneficiaries of the Declaration as to Moslem Properties in Greece. This action occasioned a protest on the part of the Turkish delegation, in which the neutral members of the Mixed Commission joined.[16]

[11] Procès-Verbaux, vii, 82d meet., January 6, 1925; 84th meet., January 27, 1925; 89th meet., March 14, 1925.

[12] Procès-Verbaux, v, 67th meet., August 26, 1924.

[13] Procès-Verbaux, viii, 92d *bis* meet., August 5, 1925.

[14] Procès-Verbaux, viii, 95th meet., September 21, 1925.

[15] Procès-Verbaux, viii, 92d meet., July 8, 1925.

[16] Procès-Verbaux, viii, 95th meet., September 19, 1925.

The Greek law of May 25, 1925, created a commission to decide on the beneficiaries of the Declaration. It appeared later that the Ministry of Foreign Affairs was not aware of the decision of the Mixed Commission which considered the determination of the 119 cases of beneficiaries as final.[17] It was asserted that some of these claimants had been admitted as beneficiaries of the Declaration on evidence which was found subsequently by the Greek government to be false.

As a matter of fact, the admission of the 119 Moslems as beneficiaries of the Declaration was made summarily by the competent committee on the production of certificates which were erroneously taken to have an official character. When this error was discovered the procedure was modified. Lists of persons recognized as beneficiaries of the Declaration were communicated to the two governments, which could file objections to any names on the list within two months. With regard to the 119 beneficiaries already recognized by the committee, the Commission held that the decisions concerning them were to be considered final, but that they might be revised on the production of evidence by the Hellenic government showing clearly that they were erroneous.[18] It was contended by the Greek government that there was very clear proof as to 20 to 25 of these beneficiaries that they were not lawful claimants under the Declaration. Indeed, one of them had been a *mufti* in Greece after 1913, another had been a candidate for the Greek Parliament, etc. These could not claim to be Turkish nationals, since for the above offices Greek citizenship was required. And they were certainly in Greece after the date (October 18, 1912) taken as a basis for compulsory exchange.

The evidence called for by the Commission for the revision of the decisions on the above 119 claimants was presented by the Greek government in 1927, when the Agreement of Athens went into effect. However, the Turkish delegation, as will be seen, insisted that the decisions could not be revised.

With regard to the expiration of the periods fixed by the

[17] Procès-Verbaux, viii, 96th meet., October 26, 1925.
[18] Procès-Verbaux, viii, 95th, 96th, and 97th meetings.

Declaration and subsequently extended by the two governments, it should be noted that it did not affect the substance of the rights of the claimants. These periods concerned only the intervention of the Mixed Commission for the adjudication of their claims, which otherwise remained in full force and could be prosecuted directly before the state authorities and tribunals of the two countries. This view was unanimously agreed upon by the Mixed Commission.[19]

§ 315. The Declaration not carried out by Greece. The Greek government did not execute the Declaration by recognizing the 119 Moslems who were accepted as beneficiaries by the Mixed Commission and by restoring to them their properties in Greece, as the Declaration peremptorily provided. The reason for the failure of the government to restore the properties, at least of those against whom no doubt existed that they were beneficiaries, seems to be that these properties were mostly large rural estates which had been distributed by the Greek government to refugees and to rural tenants. This government appears not to have realized, until too late, what was really involved in the Declaration, and what or how many properties had to be restored under this Act. The competent Ministry, that of Agriculture, did not undertake an inquiry into the situation until a very late date. As a result, the Foreign Office and the Greek representatives who carried on negotiations with the Turkish government for the framing and later for the execution of this Declaration were insufficiently informed. Nevertheless, the insistence of the Turkish delegation at the Conference of Lausanne should have put the Greek representatives on their guard. The attitude and state of mind of the Greek government is seen in the statement of the Greek member of the Commission, Mr. Papas, in March, 1924, while the two governments were negotiating on the execution of the Declaration and the Mixed Commission was endeavoring to define its beneficiaries, that "in his opinion, the Declaration had a very limited importance." [20]

When the question of interpretation of the first paragraph

[19] Procès-Verbaux, x, 110th meet., June 19, 1926.
[20] Procès-Verbaux, iii, 46th meet., April 1, 1924.

of the Declaration arose,[21] at the end of September, 1924, the Greek delegation for a month and a half was without instructions as to the position it should finally take. The proposal by Tevfic Ruchdi Bey that the Mixed Commission should decide on this point was resisted by Mr. Exintaris, who maintained that inasmuch as the Declaration was a unilateral act, signed by the Greek delegates at the Conference of Lausanne, the Commission was incompetent to interpret it. The soundness of this view is very questionable, in view of the fact that the Mixed Commission was called upon to execute the Declaration. At the suggestion of the neutral members, Mr. Exintaris accepted their competence for the interpretation of the Declaration, when Tevfic Ruchdi Bey invited the Mixed Commission to declare that it renounced the execution of the Declaration.[22]

In January, 1925, the Mixed Commission expressed a wish to the Greek government that a part payment of 30% of the amount of revenues collected by the two governments be made forthwith to the persons whose status as beneficiaries of the Declaration and whose credit on account of revenues were indubitably proved.[23]

Nothing came of this request. In the meantime, the Greek government, confronted with the real situation as to the claims involved in the Declaration, and realizing that it was wholly unable to meet its obligations under the Declaration, since the properties had been distributed to refugees and landless farmers, sought an agreement with the Turkish government. The negotiations towards such an agreement, which would substitute for the obligation of restoration an obligation of the Greek government to purchase the properties of the beneficiaries of the Declaration, are described in another place.[24]

§ 316. Replacement of the Declaration by the Agreement of Athens. From the time the Greek government refused to extend the period for filing claims under the Declaration and for adjudicating such claims, the Declaration ceased to be of

[21] See *supra*, p. 469.
[22] Procès-Verbaux, vi, 77th meet., November 15, 1924.
[23] Procès-Verbaux, vii, 82d meet., January 5, 1924.
[24] See *infra*, § 332.

any effect. This was made clear by the neutral members, when the Turkish delegation insisted that the Declaration remained in effect after the expiration of the above periods on August 6, 1925, and argued from this in favor of their contention for excluding certain categories of Greeks from the benefits of the Declaration.[25]

The Declaration as to Moslem properties in Greece was replaced by the Agreement on Properties signed at Athens on December 1, 1926, the execution of which was undertaken by the Mixed Commission on March 19, 1927.[26] This Agreement provided, in article 16, that it was not meant to affect the provisions of the Treaty and other acts signed at Lausanne on July 24, 1923, "so far as they are not specifically dealt with by the above stipulations." The provisions of the Declaration were entirely covered by the stipulations of the Agreement. The former remained in effect, according to article 15, paragraph 2, only with respect to persons who, having Turkish or Greek nationality at the time of the coming into effect of the Treaty of Peace, had acquired subsequently a foreign nationality.

The Agreement of Athens is considered in a separate chapter. It is only necessary to say here that according to its article 13, last paragraph, the recognition of persons as beneficiaries of that Agreement was to be made by a committee *ad hoc* constituted by the Mixed Commission. It was, however, added that "cette disposition ne préjuge pas le sort des décisions déjà rendues à ce sujet."

The effect of this provision on the cases of the above mentioned 119 beneficiaries and on the principle, adopted by the Mixed Commission, that its decisions could be revised in case of manifest errors, was discussed at the 126th meeting of July 11, 1927.[27] The Greek delegation produced proof that 20 to 25 of the above 119 cases were erroneously decided, as the persons in question were in reality 'exchangeable' and not beneficiaries of the Declaration. The Turkish delegation and the neutral members thought that since no explicit provision

[25] Procès-Verbaux, 142d meet., December 20, 1927. See also *infra*, § 347.
[26] See *infra*, § 333.
[27] Procès-Verbaux, xii.

was made in the Agreement for the revision of these decisions, it should be implied that the intent of the two governments was that no revision should take place.

The Greek contention seemed sounder. It was rightly maintained that the above provision of article 13 meant only that the cases of the 119 beneficiaries were not to be submitted again to the committee *ad hoc,* like the cases of all other claimants pending before the Commission. The power of the Mixed Commission to deal with those cases, and to revise them in case of production of proof of manifest errors, remained intact. The proposal for revision rested entirely with the government concerned, and no agreement for revision between the two governments was necessary. Consequently, the lack of any provision thereon in the Agreement did not imply that the decisions could not be revised.

It will be seen that the disagreement in this matter was one of the reasons why the Agreement of Athens was not executed.[28]

[28] See *infra,* § 349.

CHAPTER XXV

TREATMENT OF THE MOSLEM MINORITY IN WESTERN THRACE AND OF THE GREEK MINORITY IN CONSTANTINOPLE

§ 317. Power of the Mixed Commission. As stated in a previous chapter,[1] the Greeks established at Constantinople and the Moslems established in Western Thrace were left out of the exchange. But there were provisions inserted in the Convention in their favor. These are in article 16, paragraph 2, as follows:

> No obstacle shall be placed in the way of the inhabitants of the districts exempted from the exchange under Article 2 exercising freely their right to remain in or return to those districts and to enjoy to the full their liberties and rights of property in Turkey and in Greece. This provision shall not be invoked as a motive for preventing the free alienation of property belonging to inhabitants of the said regions which are excepted from the exchange, or the voluntary departure of those among these inhabitants who wish to leave Turkey or Greece.

Article 18 of the Convention placed upon the two states the obligation to introduce in their respective laws such modifications as might be necessary to insure the execution of the

[1] See *supra*, p. 399.

above provision, as well as of the other provisions of the Convention. It is a question whether the Convention empowered the Commission to supervise the execution of the above provision of article 16, or whether that was merely a matter between the two governments. It is true that article 12 contained the provision that the Mixed Commission should have full power to take the measures necessitated by the execution of the Convention, and to decide all questions to which the Convention might give rise, but it would appear that this referred to the transfer of the exchanged populations, liquidation and appraisal of properties, and kindred matters.

Nevertheless, from an early date the Mixed Commission took the view that the Greek and Turkish populations excepted from the exchange were under its protection so long as it continued its work, and that thereafter they would be under the protection of the treaty stipulations concerning minorities.[2] This view was readily acquiesced in by the two governments, although at first, when the question of the return to Constantinople of Greeks temporarily absent from that city arose, the Turkish delegation on the Mixed Commission maintained that the Commission was not competent to deal with the matter, which was in the exclusive province of the Turkish Government.[3]

However, difficulties arose as regards the question of the practical means by which the Sub-Commissions in Western Thrace and at Constantinople were to secure the execution of article 16 with regard to the Greek and Turkish populations excepted from the exchange; and no agreement could be reached as to the extent to which the Mixed Commission should interfere in the treatment meted out to the populations in question.[4] The questions of rights of minorities, properly so-called, namely, liberty of movement, civil rights, etc., were agreed to be questions of the protection of minorities and outside the competence of the Sub-Commissions. The question of public order was also agreed to be outside their competence. Mr. Papas's proposal for the limitation of the competence of

[2] Procès-Verbaux, iii, 37th meet., February 19, 1924.
[3] Procès-Verbaux, i, 17th and 19th meetings, November 16 and 24, 1923.
[4] Procès-Verbaux, v, 63d meet., August 2, 1924.

Sub-Commissions to the gathering of information was perhaps unfortunate. Its motive, of course, was the desire to avoid interference in Western Thrace, but the price paid at Constantinople was somewhat heavy.[5]

§ 318. Violations of the Convention. As soon as the Commission was constituted, the question of violations of the provisions of article 16 came up. The Turkish delegation had a very legitimate complaint. The homes of the Moslem population of Western Thrace were, in many cases, seized by the Greek government for the shelter of the refugees. In 1923-24, 8245 rooms in rural houses and 5590 rooms in urban homes were so occupied. In addition, 127 mosques and Moslem schools and 667 Moslem stables and granaries were also used for the shelter of refugees. Of course, Greek homes and properties were also occupied for the same purpose. But there is little doubt that the infliction was felt more keenly by Moslems than by Greeks, if for no other reason, from the fact that no peaceful and friendly cohabitation could exist between destitute refugees who had left and lost everything in Turkey and Moslem natives whose property had enjoyed protection. If to this be added the national hatred and animosities aroused by the war and by the personal misfortunes and sufferings of the refugees, it will be easily understood that the annoyance to the Moslem population from this occupation of their properties was great. Moreover, these great masses of refugees needed food and productive occupations. The first was found by requisitions to which all the population of Western Thrace, including the Moslems, were subjected. The latter was obtained by the occupation of large rural estates of Turkish landowners, mostly absent from Western Thrace.

All this was not in conformity with article 16, according to which the Moslems of Western Thrace were to "enjoy to the full their rights of property." The explanation given by the Greeks was that Western Thrace was the first region on the way of refugees coming by land from Turkey, and that since Macedonia was filled with other refugees from Asia Minor,

[5] See, for instance, how the Turkish delegation took advantage of Mr. Papas's position, in Procès-Verbaux, v, 64th meet., August 9, 1924.

the refugees coming by land were retained in Western Thrace until Macedonia should be cleared. The measures taken in Western Thrace affected all natives, Greeks and Moslems alike. They were measures of general order, the Greeks claimed, and the only things the Moslems might justly ask were that they should not be discriminated against by suffering more than the Greek natives from the shelter of the refugees, and that an indemnity should be paid them for the loss of enjoyment of their property.

On the other side, the Greeks complained of the treatment meted out to the Greek population at Constantinople. As early as November, 1923,[6] Tevfic Ruchdi Bey asserted that the Turkish government might well forbid Greeks absent from Constantinople and excepted from the exchange to return there, and denied the right of the Mixed Commission to intervene in the matter. Later, it was complained that movable property of Greeks of Constantinople was seized by the Turkish authorities,[7] and a little later wholesale requisitions and occupations of Greek properties of that city were carried out.[8]

To the complaints of the Greek delegation the Turkish delegation replied by various assertions: first, that these measures were not in violation of article 16 of the Convention; next, that any 'mistakes' made by the local authorities would be redressed; and that, at any rate, only empty houses had been occupied. On the rejoinder of the Greek delegation that there were no empty houses in Constantinople and that the Commission had decided that no requisitions should be allowed after October 7, 1923, the Turkish members of the Commission replied that the cases were isolated, and that there was the precedent of the occupation of Turkish homes in Western Thrace for the shelter of refugees.

The latter occupation had at least the justification of the need of finding shelter for tens of thousands of refugees who had swarmed into the country. The Greeks contended that there was enough room in the homes left by 1,500,000 Greek

[6] Procès-Verbaux, i, 17th meet., November 16, 1923.
[7] Procès-Verbaux, iii, 44th meet., March 18, 1924.
[8] Procès-Verbaux, iv, 55th meet., May 27, 1924, and annexes IV and V.

refugees to house 350,000 Moslem emigrants from Greece. It is true that a number of villages in Asia Minor were destroyed during the military operations and in the flight of the Greek army, but still there was not such a dearth of homes in Turkey as to compel the Turkish authorities to occupy the homes at Constantinople of Greeks exempt from the exchange.

In the tour of inspection undertaken by the Mixed Commission in the beginning of 1924, the situation in Western Thrace and at Constantinople was investigated. Mr. Papas, the Greek member, admitted frankly that the situation in Western Thrace needed improvement, and affirmed that the Greek government contemplated the transfer of thirty to forty thousand refugees from Western Thrace to other parts of Greece to relieve the Moslem inhabitants of that region, and also the payment of indemnities to the Moslems for the requisitioning of their movable and immovable properties. Tevfic Ruchdi Bey did not consider it necessary to add anything to "this frank and loyal statement" of his Greek colleague. In fact, 12,000 refugees were removed from Western Thrace in the following few months. An additional 8500 were removed from the district of Comotini during the month of December, 1924.[9]

§ 319. Application of general laws. This did not fully satisfy the demands of the Turks. Greece in the meantime sought to extend to Western Thrace the application of the general Agrarian Law, which provided for the expropriation of large rural estates for the settlement of refugees and landless cultivators. This was declared by the Turkish delegation to be a violation of article 16 of the Convention, which provided for the free enjoyment of their properties by the Moslem inhabitants of Western Thrace. The answer of the Greek delegation was that this stipulation could not make the Moslem inhabitants a superior class above the other Greek subjects. Any general laws, limiting the rights of property of all Greek citizens with a view to carrying out general social poli-

[9] Procès-Verbaux, v, 62d meet., July 26, 1924; vii, 82d meet., January 6, 1925.

cies, could very properly be applied against Moslems as against all other citizens. This reply was accepted by the Turkish delegation, with the declaration that it would insist on certain reservations.[10] At a later meeting the Greek delegation affirmed that the Greek government did not intend to apply the Agrarian Law to Moslems in Western Thrace.[11] This seemed wise, whatever the strictly legal aspect of the question might be.

The same question of the application of general laws to the minorities came up when a Greek, not subject to exchange, was arrested by the Turkish authorities at Constantinople to be deported to Greece. He was a Turkish national, and the Turkish delegation declared that the deportation of this Greek was made in application of a general law in Turkey. The neutral member, Mr. Widding, expressed his astonishment at this deportation, as he was unaware of any modern constitution which allowed the deportation from a country of its own nationals. Mr. Pallis, a Greek member of the Commission, remarked that the municipal law could not be applied to non-exchangeable minorities, except in so far as it was not in opposition to the Convention, and that a privilege existed, in effect, in favor of such persons if the application of a general law would render impossible the enjoyment of rights secured by the Convention. Sound as this might appear, politically if not legally, it did not tally with the position the Greek delegation had taken in the application of general laws in Western Thrace. This incident may serve to show that continuity and unity in the position of the Greek delegation were sometimes lacking. Shrewd Tevfic Ruchdi Bey took note of Mr. Pallis's declaration, and undertook to ask the Governor of Constantinople to release the Greek in question.[22]

§ 320. Intervention of the Council of the League. In the meantime the treatment of the Greek population at Constantinople became worse and worse, and the Greek government brought up this question before the Council of the League of Nations in October, 1924. The Council believed that it could

[10] Procès-Verbaux, iv, 53d meet., May 16, 1924.
[11] Procès-Verbaux, iv, 54th meet., May 21, 1924.
[12] Procès-Verbaux, vi, 75th meet., October 26, 1924.

not take a decision on the treatment of these minorities until it was more fully informed, and asked the two governments to send full statementfis to the Secretary-General.[13]

On December 5, the Council received a memorandum from the Greek government on the question of the Turkish minority in Western Thrace and another from the same source on the Greek minority in Constantinople. On December 10, the Turkish government sent a long report. As these could not be distributed in time for the December session of the Council, the matter came up at its session of March, 1925. In the meantime the two governments submitted new memoranda.[14] The report of Viscount Ishii, adopted by the Council on March 13, 1925, proposed that the three neutral members of the Mixed Commission be requested to undertake, on behalf of the League of Nations, an inquiry as to the position of the two minorities as regards their rights under article 16 of the Convention concerning the Exchange of Greek and Turkish Populations.[15]

Two neutral members, Mr. Ekstrand and General de Lara, undertook to carry out the inquiry in Western Thrace. Accompanied by a Greek and a Turkish representative, they went to Thrace in the beginning of April, 1925.[16]

The neutral members completed their inquiry in Western Thrace and returned to Constantinople in May, 1925, to make a similar inquiry as to the situation of the Greek minority in that city. But they were "unable to obtain from the local authorities at Constantinople the information required for the completion" of their report, and were not in a position to send a report to the Council at its sessions of June and September, 1925.[17] Later the Secretary-General received a letter, dated December 10, 1925, from the representatives of Greece and of Turkey, informing him that the two governments were engaged in negotiations for the settlement of the questions on

[13] League of Nations, *Official Journal*, November, 1924, p. 1670.

[14] League of Nations, Doc.C.757.1924.VII; C.135.1925.VII; C.134.1925.VII; C.773.1924.I; C.773.1924.VII; C.774.1924.I; C.130.1925.I.

[15] League of Nations, *Official Journal*, April, 1925, pp. 462-463, 557-558.

[16] Procès-Verbaux, vii, 90th meet., March 31, 1925.

[17] League of Nations, *Official Journal*, July, 1925, p. 854; October, 1925, p. 1427.

which they had appealed to the Council, and that they were agreed in requesting the Council to suspend the procedure until they should again make an application to the Council.[18]

§ 321. **Report of the neutral members.** The Report prepared by the neutral members, dated November 29, 1925, was, however, communicated to the two governments. The writer had the opportunity to see this report, of which the general effect is as follows:

The investigation was limited to the following questions: right to remain in the country; right to return there; liberty to move outside the regions excepted from the exchange; free enjoyment of the right of property; right to freely dispose of property; and right to leave Turkey or Greece.

With regard to the Moslem minority in Western Thrace, the neutral members came into contact with the population; they visited all the districts and many localities; they accepted some hundreds of petitions from the hands of interested parties; and they verified the statistics and information furnished by the local Greek authorities. Concerning the rights of the Moslems to remain in the country, to return there, and to enjoy freely their liberties, the report stated that all these were fully respected. No case of expulsion was brought to the knowledge of the reporters. No case was found in which the return of a Moslem inhabitant absent from Western Thrace was prohibited by the Greek authorities. The freedom of circulation of Moslems within the territory of Greece was also entirely unrestricted. On the other hand, the right of the Moslem inhabitants to leave Greece was well recognized. The right freely to sell properties was restricted only so far as large rural estates were concerned.

The right of free and undisturbed enjoyment of their properties was the only right of the Moslem population of Western Thrace that had not been respected, a situation which dated from the autumn of 1922, the time of the first arrival of refugees in Greece. The restrictions in this connection took the form of seizures, requisitions, expropriations, and forced sharing of habitations. Cattle, cereals, agricultural implements,

[18] League of Nations, *Official Journal,* February, 1926, p. 160.

and seed were requisitioned by the Government. Building lands were expropriated for the purpose of erecting houses for the refugees.

However, the forced cohabitation in Moslem homes of Turks with Greek refugees was certainly the greatest evil suffered by the former, in view of their religious and family traditions, which made the Moslem home a place particularly unsuitable for the dwelling together of people of two different religions. This single inconvenience was so serious to the Moslem inhabitants of Western Thrace that there was a disposition among them to leave this region and go to Turkey. Added to this, there was a general feeling of uncertainty for the future, and the unpleasant realization that with the settlement of refugees in Western Thrace, the former Turkish majority became now a minority.

At the time the neutral members of the Commission made their investigation in Western Thrace (March, 1925) Moslem properties occupied by the Government for the refugees were as follows:

Rooms in Moslem houses	Schools, mosques, and *medressés*	*Stremmata* of land [19]
5927	42	22,159

These figures were a great improvement over those of the end of 1922, when the refugees swarmed into Western Thrace. At that time the number of rooms occupied was 13,833, that of schools and mosques, 127, and the area of lands 100,153 *stremmata*. The reduction in the number of rooms occupied by refugees in Moslem houses was brought about by the construction of new dwellings for the refugees, erected on land expropriated from natives of Western Thrace, including Moslems. By March, 1925, a total of 6506 houses were either constructed or in process of construction, on land of which 1896 *stremmata* had been expropriated for this purpose from Moslems. The payment of indemnities on these expropriations was progressing.

[19] A *stremma* is equivalent to about a quarter of an acre. Only lands of small rural properties are included in this figure. Large rural estates are excluded.

Large rural estates (*tsifliks*), comprising lands of an area above 300 *stremmata,* and abandoned properties were also occupied by the government. An area of 204,331 *stremmata* from a total of 467,191 classified as large rural properties were occupied. Of these 123,640 belonged to landlords present in Western Thrace, while 80,691 *stremmata* were reckoned abandoned property, that is, property not in the possession of either the owners or tenants and not otherwise used. Moreover, an area of 83,392 *stremmata* of small properties was also seized as abandoned property.

The Greek government sought through the occupation of these large and abandoned properties and the construction of new houses to set free gradually all the rooms in Moslem homes occupied by refugees. The relief of the Moslems was also sought by a transfer of refugees from Western Thrace to other parts of Greece. The number of refugees in Western Thrace, which was 150,000, at the time of the signature of the Treaty of Lausanne, was reduced to 120,000 in February, 1924, and to 85,000 in April, 1925.

In addition, a law "on indemnities due for occupations made in Western Thrace" was promulgated in Greece on January 10, 1925, which intrusted to special committees the determination of indemnities due for Moslem properties, movable or immovable, seized or occupied in Western Thrace since October, 1922, for the shelter of refugees. These committees were formed of five members each, two of which were Moslems, one a state official, and one a judge. These committees were established in January and February, 1925. The neutral members found that their work progressed satisfactorily, the bases of indemnity appearing equitable.

The second part of the report of the neutral members dealt with the Greek minority at Constantinople. The only rights secured, theoretically, to this minority by the Turkish authorities were those of remaining at Constantinople and of leaving Turkey. The "right to return" to Constantinople of non-exchangeable Greeks absent from the city was determined by the Turkish law of July 2, 1924. The effect of this law was as follows:

The Greeks who left Constantinople with a regular Turkish passport may enter Turkey freely. Those who left the city without such a passport are required to send a declaration, through the Turkish consulate of the place where they reside, to the Directorate of General Security. In case their declaration is truthful and their position as non-exchangeable is proved, they shall also be allowed to enter Turkey.

These were the provisions of the law, which seemed liberal enough. In their application the case was different. There were, roughly, 40,000 Greeks from Constantinople residing in Greece and desirous of returning to that city. A delegation of these Greeks complained to the neutral members of the Commission that, although hundreds of applications had been filed with the Turkish consulates in Greece under the above law by persons who had left Constantinople without regular passports, only five permissions to return had been granted.

The neutral members of the Commission, in order to test this allegation, asked of the Turkish authorities information on the following data: the number of applications filed by Greeks absent from Constantinople who had left the city *with* or *without* regular Turkish passports; and the number of permissions to return granted to these two categories of Greeks. The official Turkish reply, dated October 27, 1925, declared that the furnishing of these figures would require long investigations, which for the time being rendered their communication impossible. From a case before the Mixed Commission, it appeared that not only people absent from Constantinople prior to the coming into effect of the Convention, but even those who left later and with regular passports were forbidden reëntry into Turkey. This case concerned fifty persons.[20]

The right to travel within the territory of Turkey and

[20] See this case in Procès-Verbaux, ix, 101st meet., February 22, 1926. The action of the Turkish authorities in this case was not only in violation of the Convention, but also manifested bad faith towards the persons in question, who were given regular passports by the authorities of Constantinople in the summer of 1925 and were thus led to believe that they would be allowed to return. The President of the Commission proposed to address to the Turkish government the request to permit these persons to return to Turkey. The Turkish member, Chukri Bey, remarked that this would be interference; and the President, unwilling to go further, adjourned the meeting.

outside the limits of Constantinople, although theoretically unrestricted by any law, was not given effect in practice, since permission to travel was not granted to Greeks by the police of Constantinople, such permission being necessary under Turkish regulations for travel in the interior of Turkey. Thus these people were in a sense imprisoned in Constantinople.

With regard to the free enjoyment of their properties by the Greeks of Constantinople, the report stated the situation as follows:

1. Properties situated in Constantinople belonging to Greeks who were Turkish subjects and present at Constantinople remained, generally speaking, in the free enjoyment of their owners.

2. Properties situated in Constantinople belonging to Greeks who were Turkish subjects and absent from Constantinople were, as a rule, seized by the Turkish government, which sold the movable property found therein and collected all their revenues. It was reported to the neutral members that movable property on the estates of absent Greeks was sold at absurd prices.

3. Properties situated outside the zone of Constantinople and belonging to non-exchangeable Greeks of Constantinople, whether or not present in the city, were seized by the Turkish authorities for the settlement of Moslem refugees from Greece. On the inquiry of the neutral members why these measures were taken, the Turkish authorities replied that possibly mistakes had been made. The explanation was inadmissible inasmuch as all the movable and immovable property of this category had been seized by the Turkish authorities.

The right of disposing of their properties, though recognized in law, could in practice rarely be exercised by the Greeks of Constantinople. First, absent Greeks of Constantinople of course could not dispose of their properties by transfer, as these properties had been seized by the Turkish government. Second, Greeks present at Constantinople could only dispose of their property if they were recognized as non-exchangeable. In fact, out of a total of nearly 100,000 Greeks present at Constantinople, no one was officially so recognized until the end of 1925, and a few thousands only were given certificates of non-exchangeability in the following two or three years.

Sometime in August, 1925, the famous Greek Literary Club of Constantinople, whose membership was formed of Greeks from Constantinople exempt from the exchange, was dissolved by the Turkish authorities for its alleged political activity. Pretending that the property of such associations passed to the state on their dissolution, the Turkish authorities, early in September, 1925, seized the library of the Club, a most valuable and large collection, and sent the books to an "unknown destination."[21]

§ 322. Agreement of Angora. While this was the situation in the spring and summer of 1925, to which the above report of November 29, 1925, by the neutral members of the Commission referred, there was concluded in June, 1925, the Agreement of Angora, described in another place.[22] The difficulties encountered in the execution of this Agreement are also noted below. The principal of these difficulties was the refusal of the neutral members to adopt the draft decision agreed upon by the two governments, which, in particular, was in disagreement with article 16 of the Convention, concerning the rights of Greeks of Constantinople. In this connection, when a delegation of Greeks absent from Constantinople sent a memorandum on July 14, 1925, to the Mixed Commission protesting against the Agreement of Angora, a reply was sent by the Secretary-General, in the name of the Mixed Commission, to the effect that it had no power to pass judgment upon subsequent agreements entered into by the two governments the execution of which should be intrusted to it.[23]

§ 323. Continued seizures at Constantinople. In the first months of 1926, in view of the deadlock reached in the negotiations between the two governments, the Turks used again

[21] Procès-Verbaux, viii, 95th meet., September 19, 1925.
[22] See *infra,* § 331.
[23] Procès-Verbaux, viii, 93d meet., August 15, 1925.

the weapon of seizures of properties of Greeks of Constantinople as a means of compelling the Greek government to yield to the Turkish demands. As soon as a Greek left Constantinople for a trip abroad, although with a regular Turkish passport, he was considered as absent and his property was seized as 'abandoned.' The Greek delegation deluged the Mixed Commission with notes and protests relating to such seizures.[24] The Turkish delegation replied that the law on abandoned properties did not contravene the Convention, inasmuch as article 16 had not yet been interpreted by the Commission, and that, at any rate, the occupation of such properties of Greeks were reprisals for the occupation of Turkish properties in Western Thrace for the shelter of refugees.

The neutral members followed these recriminations between the two delegations without taking any position on the legal side of the questions involved. They stated that they were not in a position to declare themselves, and that article 16 of the Convention had not found an interpretation satisfactory to both parties. They also referred the notes and protests to a Section, to be buried among heaps of documents. Their constant desire was to find "a solution capable of satisfying the two interested parties." [25]

§ 324. Turkish Law of March 12, 1926. In the meantime the National Assembly of Turkey passed a law on March 12, 1926, by the terms of which the immovable property of non-exchangeable persons, seized by the Turkish government and used for the settlement of Turkish emigrants, was to be considered as in the full ownership of such emigrants. The President of the Greek delegation, Mr. Papas, on asking an explanation of this law from the Turkish Minister of Foreign Affairs, Tevfic Ruchdi Bey, received the assurance that the law did not concern at all the Greeks absent from Constantinople, although certain immovable properties of these Greeks had been used for the settlement of Turkish emigrants. This assurance of the Turkish Minister was

[24] Procès-Verbaux, ix, 99th to 106th meetings.
[25] Procès-Verbaux, ix, 103d meet., February 24, 1926.

communicated to the Mixed Commission by a note of Mr. Papas.[26]

§ 325. Improvement in Western Thrace. On February 27, 1926, in view of the repeated complaints of the Turkish delegation as to alleged violations of the Convention by the Greek authorities in Western Thrace, and the protests of the Greek delegation that, on the contrary, the situation in that region had been greatly improved by the progressive permanent settlement of the refugees in new villages and homes, it was agreed that the Sub-Commission in that region be instructed by the Mixed Commission to make a complete inquiry concerning the present condition of the Turkish population and to report to the Mixed Commission. This inquiry was not undertaken by the Sub-Commission, the Turkish member refusing to join in the investigation and alleging that he had asked instructions from the Turkish delegation on the Mixed Commission. These instructions never came, and the President of the Sub-Commission had to report on July 5, 1926, or four months later, to the Mixed Commission that the Sub-Commission was unable to comply with the instruction.[27]

A little later, the Turkish delegation, alleging that it no longer had confidence in the President of the Sub-Commission of Western Thrace, Mr. Sliben, asked that his services be dispensed with.[28] Mr. Sliben submitted his resignation. This was accepted by the Mixed Commission. The Greek delegation, however, declined to accept the principle that a neutral must go as soon as one of the two delegations declared that it no longer had confidence in him. At this time, November 17, 1926, the two governments were on the point of signing the Agreement of Athens and there was no desire to push matters to an extremity. Furthermore, Mr. Sliben had declared that, whatever the decision of the Commission should be, he would retire.

§ 326. Situation in Constantinople after the Agreement of Athens. Fresh promises of a settlement of all difficulties in Western Thrace and Constantinople were held out by the

[26] Procès-Verbaux, ix, 107th meet., April 21, 1926.
[27] Procès-Verbaux, x, 111th meet., July 15, 1926.
[28] Procès-Verbaux, x, 114th meet., November 17, 1926.

Agreement signed at Athens on December 1, 1926, and Decisions XXVII and XXVIII, adopted by the Mixed Commission on March 19, 1927, in pursuance thereof. Decision XXVIII in particular was intended to give effect to article 16 of the Convention. As is seen in another chapter,[29] the Greek government showed a clear intention of fulfilling its obligations in Western Thrace by evacuating all occupied Moslem properties and communicating to the Commission the list of properties it intended to purchase for the settlement of the refugees.

The Turkish government did not follow the example of the Greek, claiming that Greece failed to execute her obligations under the Agreement of Athens on Properties. Indeed, the Turkish government increased the restrictions upon the rights of Greeks in Constantinople in order to bring pressure on the Greek government.

At the meeting of July 18, 1928,[30] the Greek delegation called once more the attention of the Mixed Commission to the "pitiful situation" created by the Turkish government for the Greek population of Constantinople. Beside the seizures of their properties outside the zone of Constantinople, the prohibition of their journeying in the interior of Turkey or of travelling abroad, new prohibitions and difficulties were created. These Greeks were not allowed to marry, under the pretext that they had not regulated their position from the point of view of exchange. It should be recalled that only a few thousand Greeks of Constantinople had been given certificates of "non-exchangeability." No good reason appeared why Greeks who had not yet obtained such certificates should be denied the right to celebrate their marriage. This prohibition, added to that of going abroad, often created tragic situations, so the Greek delegation declared.

Persons having to leave Turkey were compelled either to go without passports or to pretend that they were exchangeable, and in both cases their properties were seized by the Turkish government. They were not permitted to transfer such

[29] See *infra*, p. 519.
[30] Procès-Verbaux, 164th meeting.

properties to third persons before their departure. In addition, Greeks, Turkish subjects, were either legally or by administrative measures precluded from engaging in certain professions or employments, which was a new reason why people should wish to leave the city at any price and to seek a gainful occupation abroad.

To these restrictions must be added the continuous effort of the Turkish authorities to exercise a pressure on the spiritual and intellectual life of the Greek population. Many Greek schools were closed, and the education in the schools remaining open was either rendered difficult by the lack of financial resources or had to be made mostly in the Turkish language.

Thus, the whole tendency of the prohibitions, restrictions, etc., on the Greek population of Constantinople was to cause this population to leave Constantinople at any price, and bring about the result that the Turkish delegation at the Conference of Lausanne had energetically sought, that is, the inclusion of the Greeks of Constantinople in the compulsory exchange.

At the above meeting of July 18, 1928, the Turkish delegation, replying to the Greek complaints, drew the attention of the Commission to the incomparably more "pitiful situation" of the Moslem population of Western Thrace who were dispossessed of their properties. This provoked the remark of the Greek delegation that if an analogy was to be sought for the occupation of Moslem properties in Thrace it was to be found in the seizure of all properties without exception of Greeks of Constantinople situated outside of Constantinople.

§ 327. **Investigation in Western Thrace in 1928.** Subsequently, the Turkish delegation, as a diversion, insisted vigorously on the transfer of the Mixed Commission to Western Thrace, so that it might be in the midst of the Moslem population of that region. It alleged that the condition of the Moslems in Western Thrace had become intolerable and that the presence of the Mixed Commission there was necessary. However, there was a Sub-Commission stationed in Western Thrace, and its reports were that the situation there was progressively improving. The Mixed Commission, unwilling to transfer its seat to Western Thrace, decided to give partial satisfaction to the Turkish demand by sending a Mixed Delegation of the Commission to make an investigation there.

This Delegation, under the chairmanship of Mr. Holstad, began its investigation in Western Thrace on November 8, 1928, and rendered its report to the Mixed Commission on December 17, 1928. The substance of this report was as follows:

The Mixed Delegation received the statements of the Moslem inhabitants of Western Thrace and also of officials of the Greek government, and made personal visits and investigations in certain localities. The conclusions of the report were that:

1. The seizure of houses and cohabitation of refugees and Moslem natives had come almost to an end.

2. The seizure of small rural properties had also been terminated wholly or in great part.

3. Rentals and other indemnities were being paid for such seizures.

4. Large rural estates occupied for the settlement of refugees were being bought from their owners by the government.

5. The National Bank of Greece had advanced large sums of money, as loans, to Moslem farmers.

The following things remained to be done by the Greek government:

1. Payment to all the Turks of rental for requisitions of houses and lands.

2. Payment to all the Turks of an indemnity for requisitions of food, livestock, and agricultural implements.

3. The appraisal of seized large rural estates not restored to their owners.

4. The restoration of properties which were not to be acquired.

All this seemed to indicate a very decisive improvement of the lot of the Moslem population in Thrace, following the progressive settlement of the refugees in this region. There were 17,000 families of such refugees in Western Thrace, settled at the time of the report in 208 villages. Of these, 103 villages were created on land belonging to the state, on large rural estates bought or requisitioned by the government, and on land of abandoned Moslem villages. The families of 52 villages were settled in Bulgarian villages whose inhabitants had emigrated to Bulgaria, and the families of 53 villages were settled on pasture land and on land of Turkish villages partially evacuated. It was the use of part of the pasture lands for the settlement of refugees that was especially resented by the Moslem population. This was an unavoidable measure. Most of this land had been little used, and the government had to see that all waste was avoided and that all the native population was satisfied with a smaller area under more intensive cultivation. This situation was created all over Greece by the settlement of the refugees.

During this investigation in Western Thrace, the Turkish delegation sought to bring before the Mixed Delegation matters which the Greek delegation considered outside the competence of the Mixed Commission. Thus, it was complained that the son of a Moslem woman was not accepted in a Moslem school by the Moslem school committee because he wore a hat instead of the traditional Turkish fez. From this it was argued that the Greek authorities were favoring the conservative element among the Moslems, which was opposed to the innovations introduced by the new rulers of Turkey. It would seem also that the Turkish members of the investigating Mixed Delegation manifested a too unrestrained activity in Western Thrace, going into the cafés of Moslem villages and questioning Moslems in the streets, with a view to extracting possible complaints against the Greek authorities and indirectly manufacturing them for presentation before the Mixed Delegation. The Greek members objected to this practice, declaring it to be 'incorrect,' and as a result the work of the Mixed Delegation had to be broken up for some time.[31]

In the opinion of a neutral, as disclosed to the present writer, the whole discussion on conditions in Western Thrace, including the visit there, was the usual sort of filibuster re-

[31] Special report by Mr. Holstad, dated December 19, 1928.

sorted to by the Turkish delegation to prevent any work being done. In his opinion, there was nothing in Western Thrace to complain of. If there was a partiality on the part of the administration in favor of the conservative element among the Moslem population, rather than in favor of the liberal element which followed the innovations of the present rulers in Turkey, this was hardly a question of minority protection, and certainly was entirely outside the competence of the Commission. The result, however, was that for six whole months after the visit to Thrace, in the neutral member's admission, "the Commission was unable to do any work, for the Turks would talk about nothing else but Thrace."

CHAPTER XXVI

NEGOTIATIONS BETWEEN THE TWO GOVERNMENTS, 1923-1926

§ 328. Failure to execute the Convention and other Acts of Lausanne. From the first meetings of the Commission, in October, 1923, the two delegations made recriminations against each other for the failure to execute the Convention. The Greeks first complained that the able-bodied men who, according to the Protocol of January 30, 1923, annexed to the Convention for exchange, were to be released by the Turkish government on the signature of the Treaty of Peace on July 24, 1923, were still detained in Asia Minor. Then the Turks complained that movable and immovable property of Moslems who were to emigrate was being seized by the Greek authorities in Macedonia and Thrace. The Greeks responded that properties of Greeks in Constantinople were being seized by the Turkish authorities contrary to the provisions of the Convention. Later, the restitution of Moslem properties provided for in the Declaration as to Moslem Properties in Greece was not carried out.

Mr. Papas, in the meeting of November 16, 1923, noted rightly that the recriminations on both sides did not much improve the situation and did not advance the prestige of the Commission. The efforts made by the two governments, he admitted, were half-hearted and had not the support of the Commission.[1] In this he spoke the whole truth. The half-heartedness of the two governments and the lack of initiative and

[1] Procès-Verbaux, i, 17th meet., November 16 and 17, 1923.

courage on the part of the Mixed Commission caused the failure to execute the Convention, as well as the subsequent agreements and the decisions of the Commission. It may be added that the second of these reasons was the most serious. For, as the two governments perceived the lack of courage on the part of the Commission, they were encouraged in their attitude. Had they been confronted from the beginning with a different attitude on the part of the Commission, doubtless they would have realized that they must change their methods.

§ 329. Inability of the Commission to secure execution. The inability of the Commission to take a courageous attitude appeared very early. In November, 1923, a flagrant violation of the decisions of the Commission was reported. The furniture of the Hotel Pera Palace in Constantinople, the property of a Greek subject to exchange, was seized for non-payment of taxes, although the Commission had decided that all collections of taxes were to be suspended. It would have been easy for the Commission to decide that this was in violation of its decisions and to invite the Turkish government to invalidate the seizure. Instead, the neutral members referred the question for solution to the Presidents of the two delegations and held back from taking a decision.[2]

The Mixed Commission had so little sense of its authority that it heard, without protest, the threat of one of the delegations to take exceptional measures in violation of the Convention.[3] By December, 1923, it became clear that the emigration of Moslems from Greece could not be made in a slow and gradual manner. One million Greek refugees had swarmed into the villages and towns of Greece and necessarily had inconvenienced the Moslem natives more than other natives. Naturally the lodging of Greek refugees with Moslem natives could not be agreeable. The latter preferred to leave for Turkey as early as possible. It seemed then that the original figure of 150,000 Moslems to leave before May, 1924, might be exceeded. The Turkish delegation then threatened that the Turkish government would forthwith take exceptional measures

[2] Procès-Verbaux, i, 20th meet., November 27, 1923 (Mr. Widding's proposal).

[3] Procès-Verbaux, i, 22d meet., December 7, 1923.

against the Greeks of Constantinople. Now, these measures were not at all made necessary by the nature of things, as was the requisition of properties or houses in Greece. Here were a million people to be fed and sheltered. In Turkey there were available not only innumerable places in Asia Minor vacated by the Greeks, but the whole of Eastern Thrace, whence 250,000 Greeks had departed, and which had not been the field of military operations. The requisitioning, therefore, at Constantinople of the homes of Greeks exempted from the exchange was entirely unjustified. It was simply intended to compel the Greeks to leave Constantinople. As no other basis could be found for compulsion, the pretext was found in the possibility of a larger emigration of Turks before May, 1924, than had been originally anticipated.

In view of this threat, Mr. Papas asked the Commission to take a position. Mr. Widding remarked that it was not possible to discuss measures which the governments were to take, since they were not yet taken. This was fallacious and absurd. Once the threatened exceptional measures were taken any decision thereon would be merely academic. When would be a better time for the Commission to act than when an open threat was addressed to it of measures to be taken against the provisions of the Convention?

On another occasion [4] the Greek delegation complained of the expulsion of the Greeks of Kaisariyeh from their homes. This took place in January, 1924, although the departure of Greeks from Asia Minor was to begin on May 1, 1924. The Turkish delegation intimated that this expulsion might be in reprisal for the act of the Greek authorities in compelling some Turkish families in Niaoussa, Macedonia, who had chosen the Turkish nationality under the Treaty of Athens of 1913, to leave the Greek territory. It was pointed out by Mr. Pallis that reprisals could not be a means of executing the Convention so long as the Mixed Commission was in being to supervise the carrying out of its stipulations, since otherwise the Commission had no reason for existence. The neutral members again refrained from taking a stand on this important issue.

[4] Procès-Verbaux, ii, 34th meet., February 1, 1924.

The Mixed Commission showed a complete incapacity to deal with situations as they arose. In March, 1924, the Sub-Commission of Mersina sent a telegram describing the sad condition of the emigrants concentrated in this city, and asking authorization to buy flour for their relief. The Turkish delegation declared that it had asked for information as to the state of these emigrants. Thereupon the Mixed Commission decided to wait for the information expected by the delegation, instead of coming forthwith to the assistance of the starving population on the ground of the information furnished by its own agency, the Sub-Commission.[5]

In several instances the President of the Mixed Commission pointed out that the Turkish authorities ignored the decisions of the Mixed Commission.[6] The Turkish delegation protested against this remark, alleging that all the decisions of the Mixed Commission were translated and communicated to the local authorities. The fact remained, the President of the Commission said, that the Sub-Commissions reported that the Governors of Turkish provinces ignored the decisions. In fact, the Greek delegation produced a list of ninety-six cases in which movable property of Greeks was seized and sold at public auction by the Turkish authorities by virtue of the law of abandoned properties, although these Greeks were in Turkish territory and Decision No. XV of the Commission expressly made this law inapplicable in such cases.[7] The Sub-Commissions continued to report that this decision was ignored by the Turkish authorities.[8]

The inability of the Commission to intervene successfully in favor of the Greeks of Constantinople is described in another place.[9] The incident of Pendik, which was called "a slap in the face of the Commission," is outlined above.[10] There were numerous meetings of the Commission where reports of the Sub-Commissions in Turkey announced violations of deci-

[5] Procès-Verbaux, iii, 41st meet., March 10, 1924.
[6] Procès-Verbaux, iv, 55th meet., May 27, 1924; v., 63d meet., August 2, 1924.
[7] Procès-Verbaux, iv, 55th meet., May 27, 1924, annexes I and II.
[8] Procès-Verbaux, v, 63d meet., August 2, 1924.
[9] See *supra,* p. 404.
[10] See *supra,* p. 431.

sions of the Commission by the Turkish authorities and where no action was taken by the Commission.[11] The latter found it impossible to devise a way to obtain the execution of its decisions for the restoration of bank deposits and strongboxes to refugees from Turkey, or of the obligation of Greece to indemnify the Moslems of Western Thrace for requisitions and occupations of their properties. There were failures on the part of both governments to execute their obligations, each failure of the one having as reason another failure on the part of the other. To this vicious circle the Commission failed to put an end.

In conclusion, it may be said without hesitation that the Mixed Commission refused to "have full powers to take measures necessitated by the execution of the Convention"; nor did it "decide all questions to which the Convention might give rise," as article 12 provided. Hardly any question of primary importance was ever decided by the Mixed Commission. Only secondary matters and details of execution were the subjects of its deliberations and resolutions. For the rest, the Commission merely recorded agreements reached between the two delegations or between the two governments. From the beginning, outside the frame of the Commission, the two governments carried on negotiations for the solution of all questions on which a disagreement was recorded in meetings of the Commission.

These negotiations, beginning in the last part of 1923, brought a definite result in the Agreement of Athens of December 1, 1926, after passing through three periods which are described hereafter.

§ 330. First period of negotiations (January-September, 1924). Following an exchange of views, it was agreed between the two governments by an exchange of notes at Angora in January, 1924, that articles 65 and 66 of the Treaty of Peace and the Declaration as to Moslem Properties in Greece were to be put into force, regardless of the fact that the Treaty had not yet come into effect.[12] Thus the two governments un-

[11] Procès-Verbaux, v, 60th meet., July 19, 1924; 61st meet., July 22, 1924.

[12] The coming into effect of the Treaty was subject to the deposit of ratifications at Paris by Great Britain, France, Italy, Japan (or three of

dertook to restore mutually to Turkish subjects in Greece and Greek subjects in Turkey their immovable properties which had become the subject of exceptional measures against enemy property during the war.

The execution of this agreement met with serious difficulties in Greece. Most of the landed estates of Turkish subjects had been used by the government for the shelter of refugees or the settlement of cultivators. Friction resulted thereupon between the two governments. Turkey resorted to reprisals in April, 1924, and ceased to restore to Greek subjects their properties in Asia Minor.[13]

The Greek government, desirous to carry out its obligation and at the same time unable to remove the refugees from the landed estates of Turkish subjects, conceived the idea of purchasing such estates. The Minister of Foreign Affairs, Mr. Roussos, made concrete proposals to this effect in May, 1924, to Tevfic Ruchdi Bey, the first Turkish delegate on the Mixed Commission, who was then going to Angora. On his return to Athens in June, 1924, Tevfic Ruchdi Bey communicated to the Greek government the consent in principle of the government of Angora to the Greek proposals. Negotiations towards the conclusion of an agreement on this basis were begun forthwith between Tevfic Ruchdi Bey and Mr. Papas, President of the Greek delegation in the Mixed Commission.

At this time, representatives of the Greeks of Constantinople who had left that city asked the Greek government that the negotiators should also consider the execution of article 16 of the Convention and their rights under it, namely, their return to Constantinople and the restoration of their properties to them. Mr. Papas succeeded in combining the two questions, and in July, 1924, two drafts were prepared: a draft agreement as to the properties of Turkish subjects in Greece and Greek subjects in Turkey, and a draft resolution to be taken by the

them) and Turkey. This did not take place until August 6, 1924. Greece deposited her ratification of the Treaty on February 11, 1924, and Turkey on March 31, 1924. See League of Nations, *Treaty Series,* xxviii, p. 12.

[13] Verbal Note of the Turkish government to the Minister of Greece at Angora, Mr. J. Politis, under date of April 14, 1924.

Mixed Commission for the execution of article 16 of the Convention.[14]

The first provided that the landed properties occupied by refugees or cultivators or indispensable for the settlement of refugees could be acquired by the Greek government on payment of an indemnity in cash. Provisions were made for the determination of this indemnity by local committees and ultimately by the Mixed Commission. All other properties were to be restored by the two governments, together with the revenues collected by them. This agreement was equitable for both parties. Greece had a clear obligation to return these properties to their owners. Her inability to do so, by reason of the settlement of refugees and peasants on these properties, transformed her original obligation into an obligation to pay an indemnity in cash.

It was agreed that the signature of this agreement was to coincide with the adoption by the Mixed Commission of the draft resolution on article 16. This provided as follows:

1. The Greek government agreed to transfer gradually from Western Thrace a sufficient number of refugees occupying the properties of Moslem inhabitants, and to establish the other refugees in properties belonging to the state or to be acquired by it. All requisitioned properties were to be evacuated and returned to the owners or their agents. The Greek government could expropriate such properties only under the conditions on which it was to purchase the properties of Turkish subjects in Greece by virtue of the above agreement; namely, the indemnity was to be fixed by local Greco-Turkish committees and ultimately by the Mixed Commission and to be paid in cash.

2. All properties, movable or immovable, seized or placed under sequestration by the two governments in Constantinople and Western Thrace by reason of the departure of the proprietors who were non-exchangeable, were to be restored to the interested persons, who had the right to dispose freely of the same.

[14] These drafts are annexed to a letter to the Greek Ministry of Foreign Affairs by Mr. Papas under date of July 4, 1924.

3. The Moslem inhabitants of Western Thrace and the Greek inhabitants of Constantinople who were not subject to exchange and were now absent from these regions had the right to return there. The return was to be made gradually. Those to go back first were the wives and children whose husbands or parents were present in the aforesaid regions and the persons owning property or having the centre of their business there. In regard to those absent persons who in the meantime had changed their nationality by complying with the laws of the country of their residence, the Mixed Commission was to submit their cases to the two governments.

4. The Moslem inhabitants of Western Thrace and the Greek inhabitants of Constantinople were to be paid an indemnity by the respective governments for the requisitions, seizures, or sales of their movable property.

The second and fourth paragraphs of this resolution need no comment. They were in conformity with the Convention. They did away, in particular, with the Turkish law on abandoned property, under which many Greek properties in Constantinople had been seized by the Turkish authorities. The third paragraph solved in favor of Greece the very important question of the 'absent' Greeks of Constantinople, over 30,000 in number, whose return to that city the Turkish government agreed to authorize, and secured to these persons the restoration of their properties. The first paragraph was wholly in favor of Turkey, but it was in conformity with article 16 of the Convention. The evacuation of the Turkish properties in Western Thrace occupied by refugees was considered possible by the Greek government at this time. In a telegram under date of February 10, 1924,[15] Mr. Caphandaris, then Prime Minister, communicated to the Governor of Thrace the decision of the government to transfer gradually 40,000 out of the 100,000 refugees of Western Thrace to other parts of Greece. Concurrently with this gradual evacuation, the government intended to purchase large Turkish properties for the settlement of the remaining refugees.

[15] This telegram was sent from the Ministry of Foreign Affairs, League of Nations Section, and bears number of registration 2049.

These two drafts were approved by the Greek government within less than a week from the date of their submission to it by Mr. Papas, subject to an agreement on the interpretation of the word 'established' (*établis*) in article 2 of the Convention and the permission to the Bank of Athens to continue its business at Constantinople.[16]

A month later, or in August, 1924, Mr. Papas and Tevfic Ruchdi Bey proceeded to Angora to obtain the approval of the Turkish government. The draft agreement met with no objections from this source. The draft resolution, on the contrary, did not seem likely to be adopted in the form in which it was drafted. In the meantime the Turkish government had promulgated the "Rules of travel in Turkey," which made such restrictions and placed such obstacles to the return of Greeks 'absent' from Constantinople that the drafting of paragraph 3 of the above resolution needed to be amended, if the Greek government was to insure permission by the Turkish government to such persons to return to Constantinople. On the other hand, the Turkish government was unwilling to pay indemnity to the Greeks of Constantinople for requisitions or seizures of movable property made during the World War and before the establishment of the Kemalist government at Constantinople. It also desired to limit the power of the Greek government to purchase lands of Moslem inhabitants in Western Thrace.

These difficulties, together with the dispute which arose about this time on the interpretation of the term 'established' in article 2 of the Convention,[17] prevented the signature of the above draft agreement and resolution. The negotiations, however, continued at Constantinople between Mr. Papas and Tevfic Ruchdi Bey, and with the assistance of the President of the Mixed Commission, Mr. Ekstrand, a new draft resolution was adopted on September 2, 1924.[18]

This new draft satisfied in certain respects the objections

[16] Telegram from the Greek Ministry of Foreign Affairs under date of July 10, 1924.
[17] See on this *supra,* p. 401.
[18] Draft annexed to Note No. 1615 of Sept. 2, 1924 by Mr. Papas, addressed to the Greek Ministry of Foreign Affairs.

formulated against the former draft by the Turkish government. The provision of the previous draft for the payment of indemnity to Greeks of Constantinople and Moslems of Western Thrace for requisitions and seizures of movable property was omitted. Since no provision to the contrary was made, the question was left open. The power of the Greek government to purchase or expropriate Moslem properties in Western Thrace was restricted. Small rural properties, not including *Tchifliks,* and urban properties could not be purchased by the Greek government except with the consent of the owners. Large rural properties might be purchased only "in so far as it was necessary to satisfy exceptional necessities and with the limitations required in order that the economic life of the native population receive no injury." The purchase was to be made by payment in cash, the amount of which was to be determined by local Greco-Turkish committees and ultimately by the Mixed Commission.

By this time the dispute on the *établis* caused the intervention of the Council of the League of Nations, described in a previous chapter,[19] and brought about the interruption of the negotiations. Mr. Papas left the Mixed Commission at the end of September, 1924, by reason of illness, and Mr. Exintaris took his place.

§ 331. Second period of negotiations (April-June, 1925). Following the interruption of the negotiations, and as a reprisal for the insistence of the Greek Delegation on its interpretation of the term *établis,* an interpretation concurred in by the three neutral members and confirmed later by the Permanent Court of International Justice, the Turkish government, in November, 1924, ordered the governors of provinces to apply in full severity the law of April, 1923, concerning the seizure of properties 'abandoned' by non-exchangeable Greeks of Constantinople. The Turkish delegation justified these measures as reprisals for the requisitions and occupations of Moslem properties in Western Thrace for the shelter of refugees.

In the beginning of November, 1924, the Turkish Prime

[19] See *supra,* p. 405.

Minister, Ismet Pasha, inquired through the Greek Minister at Angora, Mr. Politis, whether the Greek government would consent to sign the agreement for the restoration of properties of Greek and Turkish subjects, leaving the question of the execution of article 16 of the Convention to the decision of the Mixed Commission. The Greek government, naturally, refused to separate the two questions. It was deeply interested in securing permission for the 'absent' Greeks of Constantinople to return to that city. It was thought that the Turkish government would yield on this point and execute article 16 of the Convention only if Greece withheld the restoration of properties of Turkish subjects. Moreover, the Greek government now asked that a condition of reciprocity be inserted in the agreement on properties of Greek and Turkish subjects, for the case in which the Turkish government in the future should wish to expropriate or purchase properties of Greek subjects. In such case the indemnity was to be determined in the same way as that of Turkish subjects in Greece.

The Turkish government refused to accept this condition of reciprocity. Moreover, retreating from its earlier position, it now insisted on prohibiting the return to Constantinople of Greeks who had left that city without a Turkish passport or with a foreign passport. The Turkish government justified this new position on the ground that the Greek government was not undertaking to transfer from Western Thrace a definite number of refugees, as Mr. Papas had promised at an earlier stage of the negotiations.

The expulsion of the Oecumenical Patriarch Constantine once more interrupted the negotiations entirely. In the first days of April, 1925, the negotiations were again resumed at Angora, this time with the assistance of Mr. Widding, President of the Mixed Commission. The negotiations were concluded on June 21, 1925, at which date the so-called Agreement of Angora was signed by G. A. Exintaris and M. Hamdi, Presidents of the Greek and Turkish delegations respectively on the Mixed Commission.

The first part of this Agreement, concerning the properties of Turkish subjects in Greece and Greek subjects in Turkey, presented few differences from the draft prepared in July, 1924. Two essential differences constituted concessions to Greek demands. First, the payment for Turkish properties to be purchased by the Greek government was not to be paid entirely in cash, but only for the fifth of the price; for the remaining four-fifths public bonds were to be delivered to the owners, redeemable within a period of five years. Secondly, the Turkish government was not now bound to restore all the properties of Greek subjects in Turkey, but had the power to purchase such properties from their owners for the same reasons and under the same conditions as those provided for the purchase of Turkish properties by the Greek government.

The second part of that Agreement, constituting a draft of a decision to be adopted by the Mixed Commission concerning the interpretation of articles 2 and 16 of the Convention, departed widely from the draft prepared in July, 1924. To begin with, the provision that the Greek government was to transfer from Western Thrace to other parts of Greece a large part of the refugees established on Moslem properties was omitted, since the Greek government was not in a position to effect this transfer. However, the draft provided that the settlement of the refugees "should not bring any injury to the recognized rights of the Moslems of Western Thrace," which seems to have the same effect as the old provision that the settlement of refugees should be made on property belonging to the state or to be purchased by it. The draft repeated the earlier provision that the purchase of Moslem properties in Western Thrace for the settlement of refugees should be made with the limitations required "afin que la vie économique de la population indigène n'ait pas à en souffrir."

The omission from this draft of the original provision for a partial evacuation of refugees from Western Thrace was obtained by the Greek government at a heavy cost. The latter had to consent to the prohibition, in principle, of the return to Constantinople of Greeks who had left the city without regular Turkish passports. The provision to this respect in article 4 of the draft, although worded in terms of reciprocity, concerned in fact the 30,000 to 40,000 Greeks of Constantinople who left the city during the Allied occupation of 1918-22, and especially after the Greek disaster in Asia Minor. The conditions under which these people left Constantinople were described by the Allied delegates at the Conference of Lausanne and are referred to above.[20] The Greek authorities of Western Thrace had found that there were about 6000 Moslems of that region who were in the same position as the 'absent' Greeks of Constantinople, but it was well known that these Moslems were settled in the interior of Asia Minor and had no real desire of returning to Thrace.

The clause prohibiting the return of Greeks of Constantinople was rendered even more onerous to Greece by the further provisions that these persons should dispose of their properties in Turkey within a period of four years, and that the Turkish government had the power to purchase such properties under the conditions of the Agreement on Properties.

The draft provided also for the payment of rental to owners in whose properties public authorities or refugees were installed, from the time they were occupied until their evacuation. Indemnity for requisitions and seizures was to be paid by the two governments only in case such measures had taken place after notification to the League of Nations of the ratification of the Convention concerning the Exchange of Greek and Turkish populations, that is, after September 12, 1923. This provision thus left out the wholesale and enormous requisitions made in Constantinople during the World War. In fact, hardly any requisitions were made after August 24, 1923, against Greeks in Constantinople. Thus, this provision also concerned only Greece, whose authorities had made requisitions in Western Thrace after the above period.

The last matter the draft dealt with was the interpretation of the term *établis*. In this the draft appeared to accept a solution going beyond the advisory opinion of the Permanent Court of International Justice, in that it accepted as 'established' all Greeks present at Constantinople prior to October 30, 1918, and now present there, without any examination into the intention of permanency of residence. But this apparent

[20] See *supra*, pp. 349-350.

advantage in favor of Greece was in reality a hollow one, since the lack of such intention would be very difficult for the Turkish authorities to prove.

On the whole, then, it must be admitted that the Greek government displayed a very conciliatory spirit and a willingness to make real concessions in consenting to sign the above agreements. The Turkish demands were to such a large extent satisfied that one would presume that thereafter the work of winding up the economic part of the exchange of populations would meet with few serious obstacles.

At this conjuncture an unforeseen impediment arose. The neutral members of the Commission, on the return of the Greek and Turkish members to Constantinople in the last part of June, 1925, declared that they were unable to vote for the draft decision signed at Angora, in view of the fact that its provisions, and especially those concerning the execution of Article 16 of the Convention, were in disagreement with the text of the Convention. The neutral members had been long aware of the bases on which the negotiations were conducted and had never before intimated a hesitation to vote for the proposed decision. The new attitude was the result of the protests raised by the Greeks absent from Constantinople, whose right under the Convention to return to this city was now being taken away by the proposed decision.

The neutral members proposed, however, the following two solutions of the difficulty created by their refusal: (*a*) the adoption of the draft decision by a majority composed of the Greek and Turkish members, the neutrals abstaining from voting; (*b*) the presentation of the text in question as an agreement between the two governments communicated to the Mixed Commission, which was to vote unanimously for the execution of this agreement.

The new President of the Turkish delegation, Saradjoglou Chukri Bey, was ready to accept either of these two solutions. In the meantime, the government of Mr. Michalacopoulos resigned in Greece and General Pangalos formed a new ministry. The new government appeared to hesitate in view of the strong protests of the Greeks of Constantinople, who even appealed to the League of Nations against the violation of their rights under the Convention of Lausanne. The Greek delegation on the Mixed Commission, whose President was changed at this time, Mr. J. Politis taking the place of Mr. Exintaris, remained long without instructions from the government. This aroused suspicions in Turkey that the Greek government was not in reality disposed to execute the Agreement of Angora.

In September, 1925, the Ministers of Foreign Affairs of the two countries, Mr. Rentis and Tevfic Ruchdi Bey, met at Geneva and agreed upon certain slight modifications of the draft decision calculated to mitigate the impression that the text of the Convention was being modified. About this time the question of extension of the period for filing and adjudicating claims under the Declaration as to Moslem Properties in Greece came up before the Mixed Commission. The delay of the consent of the Greek government to the extension gave rise to new suspicions and misunderstandings. The Turkish government soon ordered the application of the Law concerning Reprisals against Greek subjects in Turkey and the Greeks of Constantinople.

As soon as the Greek government was informed of these developments, it authorized the Greek delegation on the Mixed Commission, on October 24, 1925, to accept the Turkish proposal and have the draft decision submitted to the Mixed Commission. With the mediation of a neutral member of the Commission, a complete agreement was reached in November, 1925. By this time the mood of the Angora government changed, and temporizing tactics were resorted to, encouraged, it is believed, by the then President of the Mixed Commission, General de Lara. This policy ended with the declaration of January 14, 1926, of the Turkish Foreign Minister to the Minister of Greece at Angora, Mr. Argyropoulos, as to the need of revising the Agreement of Angora.[21] In effect, the Turkish Government denounced this Agreement.

§ 332. Third period of negotiations (February-December, 1926). In February, 1926, Mr. Joannes Papas, then Minister

[21] Letter of the Greek Legation at Angora No. 120, under date of January 14, 1926.

of Greece at Berne, was sent to Turkey to assume the presidency of the Greek delegation on the Mixed Commission and negotiate with the Turkish government as to the execution of the Agreement of Angora. He soon reached an agreement with the Turkish Foreign Minister, Tevfic Ruchdi Bey, on the basis of putting into execution the Agreement of Angora and supplementing it with additional agreements. It was also agreed that the draft decision concerning the interpretation of articles 2 and 16 of the Convention was to be adopted by the vote of the Turkish and Greek Members of the Commission, thus doing away with the objections by the neutral members.

However, the Turkish Foreign Minister did not carry out this agreement, being influenced by the President of the Turkish delegation, Chukri Bey, who thought that the Agreement on Properties was not practical and that a new one should be made on the basis of setting off the properties of Turkish subjects in Greece against those of Greek subjects in Turkey. This idea of counterbalance, as further developed by the Turkish negotiators, involved (*a*) the purchase by the Greek government of the properties of Turkish subjects restoration of whose properties appeared impossible; (*b*) the purchase by the Turkish government of properties in regions included in the exchange belonging to Greek subjects or to Greeks considered non-exchangeable as having left Turkey before 1912.

The negotiations on this basis, carried on both at Angora and at Athens, were laborious and long, lasting for over seven months. The Turkish demands, presented and supported by Saradjoglou Chukri Bey at Athens, exceeded the original basis and were really quite without limit. Thus, they proposed to include in the set-off the Greek properties at Constantinople; to reconsider the interpretation of article 2 of the Convention, which had already been admitted in the Agreement of Angora; and to ignore that Agreement entirely. It was also insisted that the Turkish government be given the power to take possession, immediately upon the signing of the new agreements, of the properties of Greek subjects in Asia Minor and Eastern Thrace.

Gradually these various demands were abandoned by the

Turks, and a new draft agreement on properties was drawn up on September 7, 1926. In the meantime, a verbal agreement was made between the two governments that all seizures of movable and immovable property in both countries were to stop after May 31, 1926. This agreement was communicated subsequently to the Mixed Commission as concerning all persons dealt with by the Agreement of Athens as well as by the Agreement of Angora.[22] Chukri Bey, going to Angora to consult with his government, on his return presented four new demands, on which negotiations were resumed once more. The Greek government made one more concession, which satisfied the Turks and caused them to abandon all their other demands. It agreed to pay to Turkey, as soon as the Agreement was ratified, 15,000,000 drachmas for the revenues of Turkish properties.

The Greek government had proposed to revive the agreement of July, 1924, as to the return of the Greeks of Constantinople who left that city with irregular passports from 1918 to 1922. That agreement made this permission to return conditional on the transfer of 40,000 refugees from Western Thrace to other parts of Greece. In the meantime 15,000 Bulgarian emigrants left Western Thrace, and 10,000 refugees, mostly Armenians and Circassians, were transferred to other parts of Greece. The Greek authorities were prepared now to transfer 15,000 more refugees from Western Thrace, provided permission to return to Constantinople was given to the aforesaid Greeks. Saradjoglou Chukri Bey, after consulting his government, reported that the latter was unable to consent. At last, on December 1, 1926, a new Agreement was signed, together with a declaration that the Agreement of Angora remained in effect in so far as it was not opposed to the new Agreement.

All these acts were ratified in February, 1927, and the ratifications were exchanged at Athens on June 23, 1927.[23] They were communicated by identical letters of the Presidents of the two delegations to the Mixed Commission on February 17, 1927.

[22] Procès-Verbaux, xii, 126th meet., June 27, 1927.
[23] Procès-Verbaux, xii, 126th meet., June 27, 1927.

CHAPTER XXVII

THE AGREEMENTS OF ANGORA AND ATHENS

§ 333. Acts signed at Angora and Athens. At the meeting of March 19, 1927, the Mixed Commission took cognizance of the various Acts communicated to it by the two governments and intrusted to it for execution. Some of these Acts were signed at Athens on December 1, 1926, and some at Angora on June 21, 1925. The latter had not been ratified, but were now again declared to be maintained by a Declaration signed at Athens, so far as they were not replaced by the Agreement of Athens. These various Acts are as follows:

A. Agreement signed at Athens on December 1, 1926.[1]
   1. Agreement on Properties (17 articles).
   2. Annex to the Agreement.

[1] See text in League of Nations, *Treaty Series,* lxviii, pp. 12-35. This Agreement replaces B.6.

3. Final Protocol.
4. Declaration.
5. Protocol No. 1.
6. Protocol No. 2.
7. Procès-Verbal of Signature.

Supplementary

Extract from letter exchanged between Mr. Argyropoulos and Saradjoglou Chukri Bey.

B. Acts signed at Angora on June 21, 1925.

1. Protocol No. 1.
2. Protocol No. 2.
3. Draft decision to be taken by the Mixed Commission on the *établis*.
4. Draft decision to be taken by the Mixed Commission on the application of article 16 of the Convention concerning the Exchange of Greek and Turkish Populations.
5. *Procès-Verbal* of signature.
6. Agreement relating to the property of Turks in Greece and of Greeks in Turkey.

The first list of Acts concerned the properties of all Greeks and Moslems, with the exception of the exchanged persons and the persons exempt from exchange by virtue of article 2 of the Convention of Lausanne. The properties of the last, as well as their rights under article 16 of the Convention, were covered by the above Acts of the second list. The provisions of each of the above lists of Acts and the measures taken for their execution are described below.

I. Agreements of Angora and Athens as to Properties of Persons Exempted from the Exchange

§ 334. **Decisions XXVII and XXVIII.** By virtue of the Declaration signed at Athens on December 1, 1926, Protocols No. 1 and No. 2 signed at Angora on June 21, 1925, were maintained, in so far as they were not modified by the Agreement of Athens on Properties. According to the letter exchanged at Athens between Mr. Argyropoulos and Saradjoglou Chukri Bey, paragraphs 3 and 4 of the *Procès-Verbal* of signature of June 21, 1925, were to be ratified and given effect by the two governments. The draft resolution on the application of article 16 of the Convention of Exchange referred to the Agreement of Angora on Properties on June 21, 1925, with respect to the determination of the payment of indemnity to owners of properties to be expropriated. For this reason these provisions of the Agreement of Angora were to be inserted in the text of the decision to be taken by the Mixed Commission.

The two draft decisions above referred to were submitted to the vote of the Commission. The Greek and Turkish members voted for the proposed texts, while the neutral members abstained from voting and declared that, in view of the agreement between the two governments, it was not their business to express any opinion on the contents of these texts. Thus, Decisions XXVII and XXVIII were taken by the Mixed Commission.

Decision XXVII defined the persons who were to be deemed exempt from the compulsory exchange in accordance with article 2 of the Convention. On the other hand, paragraph 4 of Decision XXVIII concerned the persons absent from the regions exempted from the exchange and the conditions under which such persons were refused permission to return. These matters are considered in the chapter dealing with persons exempted from exchange.[2] The other paragraphs of Decision XXVIII dealt with the properties of persons exempted from the exchange.

With respect to properties of these persons, Decision XXVIII contained the general rule that all seizures, sequestrations, or requisitions were to be cancelled within a brief period, and that the revenues collected by the state were to be restored to the interested persons. For properties occupied by the state or by refugees and from which no revenues were received, an equitable rent was to be paid to the owners from the time of the occupation. This general rule applied to Greek properties in Constantinople.

§ 335. Moslem properties in Western Thrace. Concerning the properties of Moslem inhabitants of Western Thrace, in

[2] See *supra*, pp. 408, 411.

particular, the Commission at its meeting of March 19, 1927, took note of the declaration of the Hellenic delegation that its government was to take steps with the view to evacuating and restoring to their owners or their agents the properties of Moslems in Western Thrace within a period of nine months from the date this decision was taken, that is, by December 19, 1927.

The refugees in Western Thrace were to be settled only on land belonging to the state. The state might also acquire lands of Moslems in Western Thrace under the following conditions: (*a*) only large properties could be acquired, (*b*) and only in case of exceptional necessity, such as the settlement of refugees, (*c*) with the necessary limitations so that the development of the economic life of the Moslem population should not suffer, and (*d*) in conformity with the provisions of the Agreement of Angora of June 21, 1925, with respect to the determination of the indemnity.

The Greek government was required to indicate within a period of three months the properties which it was to acquire. Small rural properties and all urban properties, with the exception of building lands not constituting annexes to buildings, could not be acquired by the state without the consent of their proprietors.

The indemnity to be paid by the government for properties acquired by it was to be determined by a commission consisting of Greek and Turkish members in equal number, the Turkish members being designated by the majority of interested proprietors or their agents in each district. In case of equal division of votes in these commissions on the determination of the indemnity, the Mixed Commission was to decide definitively. As soon as the indemnity was fixed the Greek government was to proceed to the acquisition of the property, paying immediately one-fifth of the price in cash. For the remainder, public bonds redeemable within five years were to be delivered to the proprietors. Loans to the extent of 50% on these bonds were to be made by the National Bank of Greece.

§ 336. Movable property. With respect to movable property of non-exchangeable inhabitants of Western Thrace and

Constantinople, it was provided that such property was to be restored to proprietors or to their agents. In case such property was sold and could not be restored, an indemnity was to be paid. These provisions, however, concerned only property seized or requisitioned after the date on which notice of ratification of the Convention of Lausanne was sent to the League of Nations, that is, September 12, 1923.[3] This did not cover the exceedingly large number of seizures and requisitions of merchandise and goods from which the Greek population of Constantinople suffered during the World War. The above indemnity was to be determined by the Mixed Commission, which was also to determine the mode of payment.

§ 337. Property of persons whose return was prohibited. Article 16 of the Convention of Lausanne provided not only for the securing of the rights of property in Greece and Turkey of the non-exchangeable inhabitants of Western Thrace and Constantinople, but also for the exercising by these persons of "their right to remain or return there and to enjoy freely their liberties." Under the terms of Decision XXVIII, an important exception was made to the general rule that "no obstacle shall be raised to the free exercise by the inhabitants of the regions excepted from the exchange . . . of their right to remain or return there and to enjoy freely their liberties and rights of property in Turkey and Greece." "The Greek and Turkish governments have the power respectively to refuse the right to return to absent persons who left the country without a regular passport, respectively Greek or Turkish." Although the exception was put in terms of reciprocity, it was in fact valid only against absent Greeks of Constantinople who left that city precipitately in 1922 in the panic that followed the Greek disaster in Asia Minor.[4]

The persons whose return was not permitted retained the right to dispose of and sell freely and without special authorization, through their agents, all their movable and immovable

[3] This date was fixed by the Mixed Commission. Procès-Verbaux, xiii, 129th meet., July 25, 1927.

[4] In another place it is seen that this exception did not apply to dependents of persons properly 'established' in the regions excluded from the exchange. See *supra,* pp. 412-413.

property, which was to be restored to them. The lease of any such property rented to third persons by the government was to be terminated. The disposal or sale of such property was to be completed within a period of four years from the date of restoration. Rights *in personam* or mortgages belonging to such persons were to suffer no limitation. The two governments reserved the right to acquire the immovable property of persons whose return was prohibited, under the same conditions as to the determination of the price and payment as those under which the Greek government was empowered to acquire Moslem properties in Western Thrace. A similar indemnity was to be paid to the above persons for properties which had been sold and could not be restored, and likewise to non-exchangeable persons dwelling in the above regions for property situated in regions included in the exchange which had been sold and could not be restored. All properties of absent persons whose return was prohibited, which should not be disposed of within the above period of four years, were to be acquired by the state in the territory of which they were located. Such properties were to be appraised by the Mixed Commission and liquidated in favor of the interested parties.

§ 338. Properties outside the regions exempted from the exchange. According to article 16 of the Convention, as interpreted by paragraph 4 of Decision XXVIII of the Mixed Commission, the persons established at Constantinople and in Western Thrace were to enjoy fully their rights of property in Turkey and Greece. The properties of such persons situated outside Constantinople or Western Thrace were to be restored to the owners, unless they had been sold and could not be restored, in which case the value of such properties was to be paid them.

As early as May and June, 1927,[5] a few months after Decision XXVIII was taken by the Commission, complaints of Greeks of Constantinople reached the Mixed Commission to the effect that the Turkish authorities prohibited them from

[5] Procès-Verbaux, xii, 125th meet., June 16, 1927.

taking possession of their properties situated in towns neighboring Constantinople. The Commission agreed that such persons, on condition of retaining their establishment at Constantinople, had the right of taking possession of their properties situated outside the city. But this decision had only an academic value, as the Greeks of Constantinople were forbidden to travel outside the city.

§ 339. Execution of Decision XXVIII. The agreements comprising the texts of the two decisions considered above were ratified in February, 1927, and the ratifications were exchanged at Athens on June 23, 1927.[6] In accordance with the first article of Decision XXVII, the Greek government communicated to the Mixed Commission on June 18, 1927, a list of properties that the Greek government had decided to acquire in Western Thrace, on paying the price to the owners.[7] This list concerned only properties of Moslems of Greek nationality. Their acquisition was permitted, under Decision XXVIII, on condition that the development of the economic life of the Moslem population was not injured thereby. The Sub-Commission in Western Thrace was instructed to collect information as to whether the purchases of properties contemplated by the Greek government satisfied the above condition.[8]

On December 19, 1927, according to the same Decision XXVIII, the evacuation of immovable properties situated in Western Thrace and occupied by refugees ought to have been completed. On that date, although the evacuation was not complete,[9] it was very far along. Indeed, according to a list deposited by the Greek delegation with the Mixed Commission, the evacuation of occupied Moslem properties had progressed as follows: [10]

In 1923	there	were	8243	rural	and	5590	urban	rooms occupied
" 1925	"	"	3043	"	"	2859	"	" "
" 1926	"	"	1217	"	"	420	"	" "
On May 31, 1927	"		227	"	"	320	"	" "

[6] Procès-Verbaux, xii, 126th meet., June 27, 1927.
[7] Procès-Verbaux, xiii, 136th meet., August 25, 1927.
[8] Procès-Verbaux, xiv, 137th meet., September 15, 1927.
[9] Procès-Verbaux, 142d meet., December 20, 1927.
[10] Procès-Verbaux, 148th meet., January 16, 1928.

As regards the evacuation of mosques and schools, and stables and granaries respectively the figures were as follows:

In 1923	127	667
" 1925	42	667
" 1926	12	667
On May 31, 1927	7	69

It was pointed out by the Greek delegation that the evacuation was bound up with the question of purchase by the Greek state of properties in Western Thrace. The government had bought 47 large estates by contracts with the owners on the payment of 45,042,915 drachmas. The list of the other properties to be purchased was still in the hands of the Sub-Commission in Thrace.

On the Turkish side, practically no restorations at all were made of Greek properties in Constantinople. The justification given at first was that the Greek government had not made entire restoration and that nothing short of this was a fulfilment of the obligation of Greece. Subsequently, as was proved by the investigation carried out by the Mixed Commission in Western Thrace in November, 1928,[11] the occupation of Moslem houses and small rural properties had come almost to an end. This did not in any way cause the restoration of the Greek properties in Constantinople, nor the loosening of the strict restrictions under which the Greeks of Constantinople lived. The Turkish government refused to execute its own obligations in their favor, now alleging as a justification the failure of Greece to execute her obligations under the Agreement of Athens on Properties.

II. Agreement on Properties of December 1, 1926

§ 340. Main principles of the Agreement. The Agreement on Properties signed at Athens on December 1, 1926, was in many respects different from the previous Agreement of Angora of June 21, 1925.[12] It contained important concessions on the part of Greece and a number of secondary concessions on the part of Turkey.

[11] See *supra,* p. 492.
[12] See *supra,* pp. 506 ff.

The main principles of the Agreement of Angora were the following. With respect to the Turkish properties in Greece, it was provided:

(1) That the Greek government was to restore all such properties, with the exception of those needed by the Greek government for the settlement of refugees or peasants owning no land.

(2) That the Greek government should buy the properties which it could not restore, at prices agreed upon with the owners, or, failing such agreement, fixed by Greco-Turkish committees.

(3) That payment was to be made 20% in cash and 80% in bonds redeemable in four years.

With respect to the Greek properties in Turkey it was provided:

(1) That in principle, all such properties were to be restored to their owners.

(2) That properties which the Turkish government should feel unable to return, as necessary for the settlement of Moslem refugees, situated in any part of Turkey, including Constantinople, might be purchased under the conditions set for the purchase of Turkish properties in Greece.

The Agreement of Athens on Properties substituted for the restoration, in principle, the compulsory purchase by the state of properties in its territory occupied or needed for the purposes of the state. Thus, with regard to the Turkish properties in Greece, the Agreement provided:

(1) That the Greek government was to acquire all immovable property situated in regions subject to exchange of which the restoration was deemed impossible.

(2) That, in principle, urban properties, woods, forests, and summer pasture lands were to be restored.

With regard to the Greek properties in Turkey, it was provided:

(1) That all Greek properties at Constantinople were to be restored to their owners.

(2) That the Turkish government was to acquire all Greek properties in Asia Minor and Eastern Thrace belonging to

Greeks who left Turkey before October 18, 1912, or who had always resided outside that country, or to any Greek nationals, up to the value of the property which the Greek government might acquire.

The Agreement of Athens further introduced provisions for the appraisal of properties to be acquired by the two states by mixed appraisal committees to be created by the Mixed Commission, and it stipulated for compensation between the debts of the two states on account of such acquisition of properties. This involved the replacement of each state by the other in the payment of indemnity to the owners. Thus the Greeks were to receive payment for their properties in Turkey from the Greek government, and the Turks for their properties in Greece from the Turkish government. This permitted the two states to pay their debt to their own subjects in long-term bonds.

The main differences between the Agreements of Angora and of Athens consisted in that:

(1) Whereas the Agreement of Angora concerned only Greek subjects owning properties in Turkey and Turkish subjects owning properties in Greece, the beneficiaries of the new Agreement were of three categories:

(*a*) those (Greeks or Moslems) who had left the territory of the country (Turkey or Greece) where their properties were located before October 18, 1912;
(*b*) those (Greeks or Moslems) who had all the time resided outside the country (Turkey or Greece) where their properties were located; and
(*c*) the nationals of each country (Greece or Turkey) owning properties in the other country (Turkey or Greece).

(2) The Greek properties in Constantinople were excepted from the properties which the Turkish government could acquire, and the Turkish urban properties, forests, and summer pasture lands in Greece were to be restored.

(3) The Turkish Government could acquire Greek properties in Asia Minor and Eastern Thrace only to an amount

equal to the debt of the Greek government to Turkey from its purchase of Turkish properties in Greece.

(4) The principle of the assumption by each state of the debt of the other for such purchase of properties and of compensation for the mutual debts was established.

The Agreement of Athens replaced and comprehended the Declaration as to Moslem Properties in Greece,[13] being broader than the latter. It concerned, indeed, not only the Moslems or Greeks who had left the Greek or Turkish territory before October 18, 1912, or who had resided all the time outside Greece or Turkey, as the Declaration had done, but, in addition, all Greek or Turkish subjects owning properties in Turkey or Greece. These terms did not include (article 4, paragraph 2 of the Agreement) the persons dealt with by the Convention concerning the Exchange of Greek and Turkish Populations who, as a result of the exchange, changed their nationality and became Greek or Turkish nationals, but those who were Greek or Turkish subjects before such exchange.

§ 341. Deposit of security by Greece. It is to be noted that with regard to the balancing of the debts of the two governments, two occurrences were possible, either an equivalence between the two sums or a balance to be paid by the Greek government. The possibility of a balance payable by Turkey was excluded by the provision of article 2 that the acquisition of Greek properties by the Turkish government was to be made "up to the value of the property which the Greek government may acquire." The Turkish government wished to be secured payment in case Greece should be found a debtor in this compensation account. To satisfy this demand, Greece by article 6 of the Agreement gave as security the surplus of the revenues controlled by the International Financial Commission, not to exceed an amount of 500,000 pounds sterling. If the sum to be paid exceeded £500,000, the Greek government undertook to renew the guarantee for the remainder of the balance, which should bear interest at 6%. Indeed, as the Turkish Minister at Athens was informed by letter No. 196, under date of February 16, 1927, by the President of the In-

[13] See *infra,* p. 474.

ternational Financial Commission, the Greek government sent to the Financial Commission an irrevocable order to pay to the Turkish government from the above surplus an amount not to exceed £500,000, in case the Greek government should be found a debtor on the compensation account under the Agreement of December 1, 1926. The sum to be paid to Turkey by the International Financial Commission was to be determined by the Mixed Commission for the Exchange of Greek and Turkish Populations after the closing of the account.

§ 342. Exclusion of properties from compensation. A list of Greek nationals established at Smyrna, Mersina, and Pendik and of their immovable properties was annexed to the Agreement. These properties were situated in Smyrna (57 properties), Mersina (10 properties), and Pendik (7 properties). These properties were not to enter into the compensation account unless the Greek government should so request. Their exclusion was subject to the payment of their value by the Greek government after they were appraised. The Greek government reserved the right to exclude other properties from the compensation by advancing a sum corresponding to their value. It was agreed that any immovable property excluded from the compensation in Turkey, and therefore to be returned to the owners, should be situated in a single district easily accessible to Greek nationals, where it was believed that the resumption of economic life would render useful the possession of properties by Greeks.

§ 343. Other provisions of the Agreement. The rural and urban properties not purchased by the Greek or Turkish governments were to be restored within a month from the coming into effect of the agreement. All revenues due to Greek and Turkish subjects from their properties and dealt with by the Declaration as to Moslem Properties in Greece were to form a separate compensation account, whose balance was to be included in the general liquidation account. However, the Greek government agreed, by the Final Protocol, signed at Athens, to pay, without waiting for the ratification of the Agreement, fifteen million drachmas on account of revenues received by the Greek treasury from Turkish properties.

The fact that a person had left Turkey or Greece before October 18, 1912, or had always resided outside their limits, or that he was a national of one of these countries, with a view to his claiming under the Agreement, was to be decided, in doubtful cases, by the Mixed Commission, which was to establish for this purpose a committee *ad hoc* from among its members.

The Mixed Commission was charged with the application of the Agreement. Any important questions of principle arising in the Mixed Commission in connection with the new powers conferred upon it by the Agreement which it did not possess under previous instruments were to be submitted to the President of the Greco-Turkish Arbitral Tribunal at Constantinople for arbitration. The awards of the arbiter were to be binding.

An annex to the Agreement determined in detail the bases of appraisal of properties to be acquired by the two states. The properties were classified in three categories: urban property; rural property; and manufacturing plants, mines, and fisheries. Each piece of property was to be appraised separately after investigation on the spot. The urban and rural properties were to be appraised on the basis of the present market value. This value was to be found on the basis of (*a*) the sale price of property of the same category and of the same nature, situated in the same locality and subject to the same conditions; and (*b*) the rental of such property and of the property to be appraised. Sale prices and rentals not resulting from the operations of the law of supply and demand were not to be taken into account. Provisions were made for cases in which the ordinary bases of appraisal should not be available. For the appraisal of manufacturing plants, mines, and fisheries a special mixed technical commission was to determine the factors to be taken into consideration.[14]

§ 344. Appraisal Committees. The first thing to do in order to give effect to the Agreement was to set up the Appraisal Committees and to start the work of appraisal. On

[14] The Commission adopted the regulations for the work of appraisal by the committees on March 19, 1927. Procès-Verbaux, 116th meet., annexes XVII, XVIII.

April 7, 1927, two such Committees were created, each consisting of a neutral president and a Greek and a Turkish expert. In the fall of 1927 the Committees were increased to eight, and in July, 1928, four more Committees were created. These were distributed in the various regions in Greece and Turkey. A Greek secretary accompanied each Appraisal Committee in Greece and a Turkish secretary each Committee in Turkey.

The neutral expert was paid a salary of $350 per month. The Greek and Turkish experts received a monthly salary of $200 and a monthly indemnity of $50 when they worked in Turkey and Greece respectively. The secretary of the Committee was paid $150 per month. Transportation and travelling expenses were also paid to the experts and the secretary. These rose to unexpected heights, and the Commission had to resort to a severe checking in the fall of 1927.[15]

Although the Committees were nominally twelve in number, a much smaller number were effectively at work. By 1928 they were completely disorganized. Members were often on leave granted by the governments without the advice of the Commission. It appears that such absences were also often without any authorization.[16] As a result the efficiency of the Committees was very small. In fourteen months ending June, 1928, they had completed the appraisal of the properties of only 1000 applicants.[17] The number in Turkey was smaller than in Greece, owing to the fact that the Greek properties in Turkey were many and small and required more time for their appraisal. The end of the work did not seem near, since there were about 14,000 Greek claimants and 1500 Turkish claimants.

By the end of 1928, when about 2000 appraisals had been completed, all work was interrupted, for at this time negotiations for lump appraisal and set-off of Greek and Turkish properties were begun at Angora, and both sides were unwilling that new figures of appraisals should be available which might upset their respective arguments. From this time

[15] Circular No. 15, approved October 18, 1927.
[16] Circular No. 19 of the Mixed Commission, approved January 11, 1928.
[17] Procès-Verbaux, 158th and 159th meetings, June 21 and 28, 1928.

until July, 1929, when the negotiations were broken off, the twelve Committees remained inactive, while the two governments were paying their expenses to a total amount of about $100,000.

§ 345. How appraisals were made. In May, 1927, the Greek delegation on the Mixed Commission submitted complete lists of claimants, beneficiaries of the Agreement of Athens, with indication of properties claimed and amount of claims. The Turkish delegation merely submitted a list of 1150 claimants, without any indication as to properties and amounts claimed. The only factor given was the region in Greece where each of the claimants owned properties. The Mixed Commission communicated to each Appraisal Committee the names of the claimants, in the case of the Turkish list, and the complete data given with regard to the Greek claimants. According to the Agreement, every claim was to be appraised separately.

In the procedure for appraisal connected with the Greco-Bulgarian exchange, the Appraisal Committees had a great part of their work prepared by other agencies, as is seen in another place.[18] Here, there was no previous survey made of the properties to be appraised, no establishment of property rights, no scale of prices to be applied to various kinds of property. The Appraisal Committees had to do all the work relating to each individual piece of property.[19] The national members of the Committees could have recourse to the opinion and assistance of local agents and experts, and the Committees could ask all useful information from the local authorities. The interested proprietors or their representatives were authorized to be present at the appraisal of their properties and were heard in connection therewith, but they could not be present during the discussions of the Committee.[20]

[18] See *supra*, p. 194.

[19] With respect to buildings, the committees had to find and report their purpose, size, nature of construction, number of floors, and condition of wear and tear. With respect to rural properties, the findings concerned their nature (fields, vineyards, meadows, etc.), the area, and the unitary price. Circular No. 13, approved September 29, 1927. Survey and actual measuring of the area of properties was rarely made. Circular No. 29, approved September 11, 1928.

[20] Circular No. 7, approved July 26, 1927.

No minutes or other reports were kept by the Appraisal Committees, except a report on each individual appraisal, which was submitted to the Mixed Commission. This consisted in filling in a blank by stating the date of appraisal; the name of the interested proprietor; the district in which the property was located; the specification of properties appraised by the Committee; the amount of the appraisal; and the date of dispossession of the proprietor. This form was signed by the three members of the Committee. In case disputes arose as to the boundaries and area of properties to be appraised, both the whole of the area claimed and the uncontested part of the property were appraised and it was so stated. Any dispute as to the nationality of the proprietor or the right of property raised during the appraisal was mentioned in the appraisal report, and all documents relative thereto were annexed to it.[21]

The appraisal of each property was made by the two national members, and not by the neutral President as in the Greco-Bulgarian exchange. In case these two members agreed, the appraisal was termed unanimous. In case of disagreement between the Greek and Turkish members, two cases were considered. If the difference between the appraisals of the two experts did not exceed 25%, the neutral President of the Committee had power to determine finally the amount between the limits of the two sums named by the two members. In such case the neutral President drew up and signed the report of appraisal. If the difference was more than 25%, the case was referred to the Mixed Commission. The Greek and Turkish members in such case each submitted to the neutral President a report supporting his contention, and such reports were transmitted to the Mixed Commission, with the remarks of the neutral President.[22] These appraisals were termed 'disputed appraisals.'

The Committees were free to make the appraisal in any money that should appear convenient to them (English pound, dollar, drachma, and Turkish pound, gold or paper). The appraisal prices of each report were converted into Eng-

[21] Circulars Nos. 6 and 8, approved July 26, 1927.
[22] Circular No. 5, approved July 26, 1927.

lish pounds by the accountants of the Mixed Commission. The rate of conversion was the closing rate of the Exchange of Constantinople or Athens respectively on the date of the appraisal. In the Mixed Commission all reports of appraisal were examined by the Second Section, which in case of unanimous acceptance ratified them, and in case of difference of opinion referred them to the plenary assembly of the Mixed Commission.

In November, 1928, a Service of Inspection was created, consisting of two neutral experts, whose function was to take final decisions in the cases of 'disputed appraisals,' as it was at last realized that, since most of the appraisals made by the Committees were classified as 'disputed,' the Commission would be overwhelmed by work of appraisal for which it was entirely incompetent. This Service was also to control the work of the Appraisal Committees. However, even before the Inspectors could begin their work, the negotiations for lump appraisal and compensation began at Angora, and they were condemned to inactivity until the end of these negotiations.

§ 346. Dispute as to the bases of appraisal. While the Appraisal Committees were transmitting to the Mixed Commission their reports on individual appraisals, serious differences arose in the Mixed Commission, in particular with regard to the factors on which appraisal was to be based in the case of 'disputed appraisals' and with regard to the beneficiaries of the Agreement of Athens.

Concerning the first question, the Annex to the Agreement of December 1, 1926, provided that rural and urban properties were to be appraised on the basis of their actual market value. This value was to be ascertained from the sale price of similar properties in the same region or from the rentals of such properties. "In places," it was added, "where sales of rural immovable property have not occurred within the last three years, the basis taken shall be the prices and rents in districts where similar economic conditions prevail, or, failing such, the productivity of the property to be appraised." By productivity was to be understood the average yield of a property according to the system of cultivation ordinarily practiced in the same district.

In the appraisal by the Committees, it was often necessary to take into account the yield of rural properties. Differences of opinion then arose as to the rate of capitalization of the yield, and the weight to be given to the factor of yield as a basis of appraisal.[23] With respect to the second question, the Turkish delegation alleged that the enumeration in the Annex to the Agreement of the various factors to be taken as bases of appraisal was only illustrative, whereas the Greek delegation maintained that it was exhaustive. The latter also contended that the basic factor to be taken into consideration was the sale prices of similar properties in the district, and that if such prices were found by the Appraisal Committee to be fictitious, the factor of yield could be used as a means of controlling the reliability of sale prices. The Turkish delegation, on the contrary, urged that whenever the reliability of sale prices was suspected, such prices should be entirely discarded, and the appraisal should be based exclusively on the yield of the property. The Commission, in a circular to the Appraisal Committees,[24] had already instructed them that only in the absence of sales or leases of properties in the preceding three years, or in the case when the contracts presented were disregarded as unreliable, the provisions of article 4 of the Annex, concerning the element of yield of the property, could be applied.

On the question of the rate of capitalization of the yield, the Greek position was that the value of a large rural property should be calculated according to its revenue capitalized at the current rate of investments, and the Turkish position was that the owners should receive an indemnity insuring to them a yield equal to that they would collect from the farms. The latter view seemed opposed to the general rule of the Agreement, that properties were to be appraised on the basis of their actual market value. This seemed to indicate that the owner was not to receive an indemnity equivalent to capitalized yield, but the value which his property represented at the time

[23] Procès-Verbaux, 153d meet., March 1, 1928; 154th meet., March 3, 1928; 155th meet., March 8, 1928.

[24] Circular No. 17, approved November 3, 1927.

on the market. These differences of interpretation of the Agreement were never solved. The question was turned over to a section of the Commission, to rust away forgotten, like so many other questions. Besides, a sense of the futility of the whole work of appraisal had already begun to affect the activity of the Mixed Commission.

§ 347. Beneficiaries of the Agreement. The Committee *ad hoc,* provided for in article 13 of the Agreement, for the determination of the nationality of claimants and for establishing the fact that a person had left the Greek or Turkish territory before October 18, 1912, or had always resided outside of Greece or Turkey, was created on April 9, 1927.[25] It consisted of a Greek and Turkish member and of the Secretary-General of the Mixed Commission as chairman. This committee presented its findings to the Fifth Section of the Mixed Commission, which, if unanimous, took final decisions. Following such decisions, the Mixed Commission communicated to the two governments the lists of "beneficiaries of the Agreements of Athens."

With regard to the communication by the Mixed Commission to the two governments and to the interested parties of the names recognized as beneficiaries of the Agreement of Athens, an acute divergence arose between the two delegations. The Greeks asserted that the communication should contain the information, with regard to Greek or Turkish nationals owning properties in Turkey or Greece, that the Greek or Turkish nationality of a person was recognized by the Mixed Commission. They feared that in the absence of such a declaration on the part of the Mixed Commission the rights guaranteed by the Agreement would not be insured. Indeed, a person recognized as a beneficiary, as above, might be refused entrance into Turkey, for instance, on the ground that his Greek nationality was disputed by the Turkish authorities, so that the recognition by the Mixed Commission that he was a beneficiary of the Agreement of Athens and therefore entitled to take possession of his properties in Turkey would be without practical significance.

[25] Procès-Verbaux, xi, 119th meet.

The Turkish delegation was strongly opposed to any mention of the fact that the Commission recognized a person as a national of Turkey or Greece, although such a recognition was a necessary condition to his being recognized as a beneficiary of the Agreement. The Turkish delegation asserted that such a mention might grant to the beneficiaries broader rights than they were entitled to by virtue of the Agreement of Athens.

The Greek delegation proposed that this question be submitted to the arbitration provided for by article 4 of the Final Protocol signed at Athens on December 1, 1926. In fact, the Greek government referred the question to the arbitration of the President of the Greco-Turkish Arbitral Tribunal sitting at Constantinople. This government held the view that either of the two governments who signed the Final Protocol at Athens had the right to refer a difference to the arbiter, and it was for the latter to decide whether the question in dispute was one 'of principle' and whether "it concerned the new functions of the Mixed Commission under the Agreements," as the Protocol provided.

General de Lara expressed his surprise that the Greek government of its own initiative put the difference before the arbiter without a decision of the Commission that there was a case for arbitration. The Greek delegation pointed out that the provision of the Final Protocol for arbitration would be nullified if the final power to request it should rest with the Commission, since it could always defeat by a majority vote a proposal for arbitration supported by one of the delegations. Finally, the Commission decided unanimously that the question in dispute was "an important question of principle arising in the Mixed Commission in connection with the new powers conferred upon it," and that recourse should be had to the arbitration provided for in the Final Protocol of December 1, 1926.[26]

Subsequently, an agreement was reached between the two delegations on the form of certificates to be granted to persons recognized as beneficiaries of the Agreement of Athens. These certificates were in two forms, corresponding to the above

[26] Procès-Verbaux, xiv, 137th meet., September 15, 1927.

categories of persons who were beneficiaries of the Agreement. The one certified that a person was found to have left the territory of Greece (or Turkey) prior to October 18, 1912, or to have resided always outside Greece or Turkey; the other, that a person was found to be a national of Greece or Turkey or of a third country. Consequently the recourse to arbitration lost its occasion and was abandoned.[27]

However, this arrangement did not solve all difficulties with regard to the beneficiaries of the Agreement. Shortly thereafter an unexpected thing happened. The Turkish delegation presented an interpretation of the Agreement which nullified its advantages for Greece. Article 2 of the Agreement of Athens provided that:

> Immovable property situated in districts of Turkey, the Greek population of which has been exchanged, and belonging *to Greeks who left Turkey before October 18, 1912,* or who have always resided outside that country, *or to any Greek nationals,* shall be acquired by the Turkish Government. . . .[28]

The Turkish delegation on the Commission contended that the properties of Greeks of Turkish nationality who left Turkey prior to October 18, 1912, could not enter into the set-off or compensation account provided for in the Agreement. Also, that in order that Greek subjects might be admitted to the benefits of the Agreement they should have left Turkey prior to October 18, 1912. A neutral member told the writer that this contention was not seriously maintained by the Turks, but was rather in the nature of a filibuster. The reason for this is indicated in another place.[29] Another reason was that the Turkish delegation noted that too many Greeks were being recognized by the committee sitting on the recognition of beneficiaries of the Agreements.

The Greek government, disturbed by the spirit that this interpretation exhibited, applied to the Angora government for an explanation of its attitude. In the meantime, the neutral members in the Mixed Commission opposed the Turkish

[27] Procès-Verbaux, xiv, 140th meet., December 1, 1927.
[28] The italics are the author's.
[29] See *infra,* p. 540.

interpretation as inadmissible, in view of the clear terms of article 3 of the Agreement.[30] Because of the unyielding attitude of the Turks, the Greek delegation proposed, of its own motion, to bring the question before the arbiter provided for by the Final Protocol signed at Athens on December 1, 1926. The neutral members inclined also to the view that this dispute was a case for arbitration. The Turkish delegation, on the contrary, argued that no recourse could be had to arbitration before the Mixed Commission should decide that it was unable to find a solution to this dispute.[31] Now, as a matter of fact, there could be no such decision by the Mixed Commission, in view of the position the neutral members had constantly taken that decisions must be unanimous, notwithstanding the provision of the Convention that the Commission should decide by a majority vote.

At the proposal of the neutral members a compromise was then made. It was decided unanimously to submit to the arbitration of the President of the Greco-Turkish Arbitral Tribunal at Constantinople the following question: "Do the properties of Greeks, nationals of Turkey, who left Turkey before October 19, 1912, or had always resided outside Turkey, enter into the compensation provided for in the Agreement of Athens?" However, no steps were ever taken to submit the question to arbitration.[32]

The Commission also decided that on the question of principle concerning the conditions of recourse to arbitration under the Final Protocol above referred to, an advisory opinion should be asked of the Permanent Court of International Justice.[33] This decision was carried out.

§ 348. Advisory opinion of the Permanent Court of International Justice. On February 4, 1928, the President of the Mixed Commission wrote to the Secretary-General of the League requesting an advisory opinion from the Permanent Court on the above question.[34] The Council of the League,

[30] Procès-Verbaux, 142d and 143d meet., December 20 and 23, 1927.
[31] Procès-Verbaux, 141st meet., December 13, 1927.
[32] Memorandum of neutral members annexed to Minutes of the Meeting of September 12, 1928.
[33] Procès-Verbaux, 143d meet., December 23, 1927.
[34] League of Nations, *Official Journal,* April, 1928, pp. 454-456.

after ascertaining from the two governments that they assented to the request for an advisory opinion, decided, on June 5, 1928, to ask the Court to give an advisory opinion upon the question raised in the above letter.[35] The President of the Court fixed July 10, 1928, as the date by which the written statements of the Greek and Turkish governments were to be filed with the registry of the Court. This was complied with, and oral arguments were heard by the Court on August 6 and 7, 1928. The advisory opinion (No. 16) was handed down on August 28, 1928.[36]

The Court first reviewed the circumstances which led to the request of the Council, and, in particular, the proceedings of the Mixed Commission culminating with the application to the Council. From the review of the circumstances preceding the request, the court reached the conclusion that "the differences of opinion which have resulted in the request for an opinion relate not to the question what are the conditions to which the submission of a question to the arbitrator is subject, but to the question for whom it is to decide whether these conditions are fulfilled and by whom a question may be referred to him." [37] Thus the two questions for answer by the Court were stated as follows:

> 1. Is it for the Mixed Commission . . . to decide whether the conditions laid down by Article IV of the Final Protocol . . . are or are not fulfilled? Or is it for the arbitrator contemplated by that article to decide this?
>
> 2. The conditions laid down by the said Article IV having been fulfilled, to whom does the right of referring a question to the arbitrator contemplated by the article belong? [38]

In order to reply to these questions, the Court examined the general structure of the Mixed Commission, and found that, notwithstanding the expressions "Greek delegation" and "Turkish delegation," serving to designate in the Mixed Commission the members appointed by the two governments, each

[35] *Ibid.*, July, 1928, p. 867.
[36] Permanent Court of International Justice, *Publications,* Series B, No. 16.
[37] Opinion No. 16, p. 15.
[38] *Ibid.*, p. 16.

member of the Mixed Commission was independent and must vote individually within the Commission. The Court based its opinion on article 12, paragraph 4, of the Convention, according to which the decisions of the Mixed Commission were to be taken by a majority. Although, of course, the Convention purported to create such a Mixed Commission where each member was to act and vote individually, this was not realized in the action of the Commission, and the Court was perhaps wrong in ignoring this condition.

The Court further found that the main functions of the Commission were essentially administrative, while certain subsidiary duties were legislative or judicial in character. All these were intrusted to it with the object of facilitating the exchange of populations, and any interpretation or measure capable of impeding the work of the Commission in this domain must be regarded as contrary to the spirit of the provisions creating it. Here, again, it must be noted that the question before the Court did not relate to these duties of the Commission but to novel ones intrusted to it by another Act, the Agreement of Athens of 1926, which did not concern the exchange. However, the Court thought that the same spirit underlay this Agreement and, in general, all the instruments relating to the Mixed Commission, and that due importance should be attached to this spirit in arriving at a correct interpretation of article IV of the Final Protocol annexed to the Agreement of Athens.

From the very silence of this Article on the question by whom or when resort may be made to arbitration by the President of the Greco-Turkish Mixed Arbitral Tribunal, the Court thought that "it is possible and natural to deduce that the power to refer a matter to the arbitrator rests with the Mixed Commission when that body finds itself confronted with questions of the nature indicated." [39] Article IV contemplated "only questions arising in the course of the deliberations of the Commission." It provided for the reference of important questions of principle to a tribunal which was regarded as better qualified than the Mixed Commission to

[39] Opinion No. 16, p. 20.

decide upon the merits of such questions. The Court concluded that "the right of reference can . . . only belong to the Mixed Commission; for it is a matter of determining the extent of its own competence." It followed logically that the Commission must also decide "whether the various conditions required to make such reference possible are fulfilled." Whether a question was of principle and of importance was essentially a question of discretionary estimate, and only the Commission was in a position to decide. Once a decision of the Mixed Commission for reference of a question to the arbitrator had been taken, the arbitrator "must decide this question and he may not revert to a consideration of the question of the presence of the conditions required by Article IV of the Final Protocol." [40] Thus no "negative conflict of jurisdiction . . . between the Mixed Commission and the arbitrator" could arise, in the opinion of the Court.

The Greek position, according to which the arbitrator himself, on reference to him by either government, had the power to consider the question of the presence of the conditions required by article IV, that is, to decide of his own competence, found support in the wording of article IV, according to which the questions contemplated were to be submitted to the President of the Arbitral Tribunal "for arbitration." The Court attributed "no special importance to the use of the word 'arbitration' in the article." There could be no question of an arbitration except in the broadest sense of the expression. There were no 'parties' in a difference of opinion in the Mixed Commission, since it was composed of individual members, and a reference to the arbitrator might possibly be decided upon even if there was no difference of opinion in the Commission.

The Court thought that reference to the President of the Greco-Turkish Mixed Arbitral Tribunal was appropriate, in view of the fact that the Commission was "not necessarily the most suitable body for the settlement of legal questions of principle of some importance," and that this was why the Final Protocol conferred power to decide such questions upon

[40] Opinion No. 16, p. 22.

the President of the Mixed Tribunal. The framers of the Final Protocol may have desired "to secure a measure of consistency as between the decisions of the Mixed Commission . . . and those of the Greco-Turkish Mixed Arbitral Tribunal" in matters of liquidation.[41]

These assumptions of the Court were not all justified. Article IV of the Final Protocol spoke only of "questions of principle" and not of *legal* questions, as it certainly would have done if only the latter questions were to be referred to the arbitrator. The truth is that the provision for reference to the arbitrator was included in the Agreement of Athens in order to do away with the difficulties that had repeatedly arisen in the Mixed Commission whenever a question of principle of some importance caused a difference of opinion. The two delegations showed always an uncompromising attitude, and the neutral members very often avoided an expression of opinion and postponed indefinitely decisions on pending questions. To avoid these deadlocks seemed to be the principal consideration which inspired the adoption of article IV of the Final Protocol.

The strongest point made by the Court was this: "If . . . the right to refer a question to the arbitrator were to be attributed either to an individual member or to a group amongst the Greek or Turkish members of the Commission, or lastly to one of the States signatory to the Final Protocol, it would follow that either of these States, either directly or through members of the Mixed Commission of its nationality, could cause to be submitted . . . questions selected according to its wishes, such as, not being questions of principle and not being of any importance, should necessarily fall within the immediate jurisdiction of the Mixed Commission." [42] To this the answer may be made that the arbitrator would refuse to consider questions not presenting the conditions required by Article IV of the Final Protocol, although, as we have seen, the Permanent Court considered such refusal to be beyond his competence.[43]

[41] Opinion No. 16, p. 24.
[42] Opinion No. 16, p. 26.
[43] *Supra*, p. 33.

The Court's unanimous opinion was therefore that (1) it was "for the Mixed Commission . . . alone to decide whether the conditions enumerated in Article IV of the Final Protocol . . . are or are not fulfilled"; and (2) "the conditions contemplated by the said Article IV having been fulfilled, the right to refer a question to the arbitrator belongs to the Mixed Commission alone."

The opinion was communicated to the Council of the League of Nations, which took note of it on September 8, 1928, and ordered it communicated to the President of the Mixed Commission. In the meantime the new negotiations for the final liquidation of all pending questions were begun at Angora, and the opinion of the Court did not serve any practical purpose.

§ 349. Failure to execute the Agreement as regards restoration of properties. The work of appraisal of properties did not exhaust the Agreement of Athens of 1926. The appraisal concerned properties which should not be restored under the Agreement. All other properties were to be restored. In particular, in Greece:

1. All urban properties (lands or buildings).
2. All forests, woods, and summer pasture lands.
3. Rural properties not occupied by refugees or peasants.
4. Properties located in Western Thrace.

In Turkey:

1. Properties located in the district of Constantinople.
2. Properties elsewhere in Turkey which should be exempted from the set-off at the request of the Greek government.

Article 9 of the Agreement of Athens provided that these various properties were to be restored within one month from the coming into force of the Agreement. As no provision existed as to the time the Agreement was to come into force, the date of exchange of ratifications, June 23, 1927, was so taken. Thus, by July 23, 1927, all the above properties were to be restored, with the exception of properties in Asia Minor and Eastern Thrace not excepted from the system of set-off or compensation.

In this connection it should be noted that according to a verbal understanding reached in Athens during the time of the negotiations and communicated to the Mixed Commission on June 27, 1927,[44] the two governments undertook to stop all seizures of movable or immovable properties after May 31, 1926. This agreement concerned all persons dealt with by the Agreement of Athens. It appears that this verbal understanding was not fully carried out by the Turkish authorities, the Greek delegation protesting in several instances that the seizures continued and that Turkish refugees were being lodged in Greek buildings in Constantinople which were to be restored to the owners under the Agreement.[45]

However, in the meantime the execution of the main stipulation of the Agreement of Athens was interrupted. Both countries ordered certain restorations of properties in July, 1927, that is, within the period of one month provided for in the Agreement. At this time the dispute as to the 119 Turkish claimants of the Declaration as to Moslem Properties in Greece arose.[46] Greece, being refused a revision of the cases of those claimants who were proved to be subject to exchange and therefore should not obtain restoration of their properties, ceased from further restorations. Turkey also ceased from all further restorations.

There followed a temporary paralysis of the work of the Commission. The prevailing condition of filibuster was punctuated only by occasional outbursts of recrimination. By the end of 1927, it became clear that the provisions of the Agreement for the restoration of the properties enumerated above would not be executed. The old vicious circle of mutual recriminations was resumed in the Mixed Commission. There was again exhibited the lack of mutual confidence between the two governments. Mr. Diamantopoulos, the President of the Greek delegation, put it bluntly at a later time, on July 5, 1928: [47] "The work of restoration has not been completed

[44] Procès-Verbaux, xii, 126th meet.

[45] Procès-Verbaux, xiv, 138th meet., September 20, 1927; 152d meet., February 11, 1928; 153d meet., March 1, 1928.

[46] See *supra,* pp. 470 ff.

[47] Procès-Verbaux, 160th meeting.

in Greece. It is not just to demand of Greece the full execution of her engagements, when most of the engagements undertaken by Turkey are not executed. The restoration of the properties in Greece is certainly an important question, but this should not leave in the shade all those questions which have been awaiting solution in the Mixed Commission for a very long time." The Agreement of Athens was, after all, a whole, and moreover it could not be separated entirely from the Convention concerning the Exchange of Populations. Each government felt that it could not execute a certain obligation under the Agreement so long as it was not certain that the other government would execute another obligation under the same Agreement or under the Convention. Beside the restoration of urban and rural properties, there were pending the questions of restoration of bank deposits in Turkey, of merchandise in warehouses in Turkey, of deposits of orphanages, etc., and the question of the recognition of the *établis* of Constantinople. It was a very serious defect in the Agreement of Athens that, notwithstanding the experience of past years, it did not provide for a machinery securing the substantially automatic execution of the various provisions, so as to do away with the mutual distrust of the two governments.

An attempt was made, in negotiations between the two governments in the last months of 1927 and the first months of 1928, to find such a machinery and to provide for a general solution of all the pending questions, but this attempt failed, as is explained in another place.[48] The Mixed Commission was intrusted once more with the task of finding a solution. In June, 1928, the Commission was strengthened by the acquisition of Señor Rivas Vicuña as a neutral member. At his request, the two delegations stated before the Commission the problems needing solution and their position concerning them. He concluded [49] that there was evident correlation between the measures taken in the two countries, and pointed out that it was difficult to conceive of two countries bound by agreements yet resorting to reprisals in time of peace.

[48] See *infra,* p. 547.
[49] Procès-Verbaux, 160th meet., July 5, 1928.

§ 350. Proposals by neutral members of the Commission. Shortly thereafter,[50] while General de Lara was on leave of absence, Señor Rivas Vicuña and Mr. Holstad, the two neutral members, presented to the Commission a set of propositions and a declaration. According to these propositions, the two governments were bound to restore certain properties; with this requirement they had not fully complied. With the hope that the obligation would be executed and the measures of reprisal cancelled, the two delegations were invited to furnish to the Mixed Commission in the briefest possible time lists of the properties whose restoration was asked in Greece and Turkey respectively. The Mixed Commission would transmit the Greek list to the Turkish delegation and the Turkish list to the Greek delegation and call upon them to present information, within a month, on the following points:

(1) Which properties had been restored.

(2) The properties whose restoration was decided upon but which had not been restored.

(3) The properties which the governments were prepared to restore.

(4) The properties which the governments were unable to restore.

(5) The properties which, in their opinion, would not be subject to restoration.

These lists and observations were to be examined by a section of the Commission, which should present a report in September, 1928, to permit the Commission to take action. Another section of the Commission was to supervise the work of the two Sub-Commissions of Constantinople and Western Thrace and report thereon also in September, 1928.

The declaration deposited by the neutrals was as follows:

(1) The idea of asking the two governments that all properties seized or sequestrated be turned over to the Mixed Commission, in order that it might proceed to the restoration, constituted a solution of the difficulties. They were ready to accept this duty if intrusted with it by the two governments.

(2) The idea of making an appraisal of unrestored prop-

[50] Procès-Verbaux, 162d meet., July 12, 1928.

erties and including the value in the compensation account also constituted a solution, but it was not in accordance with the Agreements.

(3) The neutral members considered as a last solution the strict application of the Agreements. In case of failure to execute them, a government was bound to purchase the unrestored properties or to indemnify the proprietor, paying in cash in either case.

(4) For determining the value of unrestored properties and their revenues, a committee of appraisal was to be established. The national members were to be proposed by the Mortgage Banks of the two countries and designated by the delegations. The neutral member was to be chosen by the two neutral members of the Commission from a list prepared by the Economic Section of the League of Nations or from experts of Mortgage Banks of neutral countries. The opinion of the neutral member of the committee was to prevail in case of disagreement.

(5) As soon as the value of a property was determined and the right of property recognized, the Mixed Commission was to ask the interested government to place at its disposal, within a month, the amount of the appraisal.

(6) The neutral members invited the two delegations to engage themselves to accept in advance the decisions which the neutrals should propose in case no agreement was reached.

It will be seen that the effect of these propositions and declaration was to take away from the two governments, as far as possible, the execution of their obligations as between each other, and to substitute the execution of these obligations by the Mixed Commission itself, to which the means for such execution were to be supplied by the two governments.

The above proposals were adopted by the Mixed Commission at its meeting of July 14, 1928, by its Decision No. 40,[51] after the two delegations voiced their general agreement thereto. The Commission also decided to express to the two governments the request that the properties subject to restoration by virtue of the Agreement on Properties be turned over

[51] Procès-Verbaux, 163d meeting.

to the Mixed Commission with a view to their restoration to the interested parties.

Within the period provided for by the above decision, that is, before September, 1928, the lists of properties subject to restoration were presented to the Mixed Commission and transmitted by the latter to the two delegations respectively for their observations.

In September, 1928,[52] the Turkish government declared that it accepted the solution proposed by the Mixed Commission, with regard to properties subject to restoration, namely, that they should be turned over to the Mixed Commission in order that it might proceed to their restoration. The Greek government, on the contrary, accepted the other solution proposed, that all properties not restored by a government should be purchased by it and the owner be paid the value or indemnified in cash. Señor Rivas Vicuña pointed out that the two methods were not mutually exclusive. The one of the two governments might agree to place at the disposal of the Mixed Commission all seized properties and the other only the properties that it was able to restore. The restoration might be made either directly to the interested parties or by the intermediation of the Mixed Commission.

§ 351. The memorandum of two neutral members of the Commission. At this time, on September 12, 1928, the aforesaid two neutral members, Señor Rivas Vicuña and Mr. Holstad, doubtless at the initiative of the former, took the first constructive step ever attempted in the Mixed Commission. They prepared and deposited at a meeting of the Mixed Commission [53] a memorandum summing up all the problems before it and making definite proposals toward their solution. General de Lara, the third neutral member, did not sign this memorandum. He was at the time a patient at Salzo Maggiore. Knowing of the memorandum and disagreeing with certain of the proposals, he hurried from his hospital to Constantinople, arriving, however, eight days late, on September 20, 1928.[54] While congratulating his colleagues on their initia-

[52] Procès-Verbaux, 167th meet., September 4, 1928.
[53] Procès-Verbaux, 168th meeting.
[54] Procès-Verbaux, 169th meeting.

tive before the Mixed Commission, he attempted to have them change certain of their proposals, failing which he read at the next meeting, October 4, 1928,[55] a memorandum of his own, stating his divergent interpretations of matters of the past and making no definite proposals on anything. The incident caused by a declaration of General de Lara concerning his colleague, Señor Rivas Vicuña, is considered in another place.[56]

With respect to the restoration of properties provided for by the Agreement on Properties of Athens, the above memorandum of the two neutral members referred to communications made by the two governments; the Turkish, that it accepted the proposal of the neutral members to turn over to the Mixed Commission all properties to be restored; and the Greek, that properties not restored were to be purchased by the government concerned. The memorandum concluded that in case no agreement was reached on this matter within the period previously fixed by the Mixed Commission, "the neutral members would propose the solutions that the matter involves, within the powers given to the Mixed Commission by the Agreements." This was sufficiently strong language for the neutral members of the Commission, accustomed only to wait and mediate. The Presidents of both delegations left for Angora and Athens respectively to confer with their governments.

Soon afterwards, negotiations between the two governments were entered upon for the general liquidation of all questions enumerated as pending in the memorandum of Messrs. Rivas Vicuña and Holstad.

[55] Procès-Verbaux, 170th meeting.
[56] See *supra*, p. 362.

CHAPTER XXVIII

NEGOTIATIONS FOR BALANCING OF CLAIMS FOR GREEK AND TURKISH PROPERTIES

§ 352. Initiation of the new negotiations. In the preceding chapter we have seen that the execution of the Agreement signed at Athens December 1, 1926, and ratified June 23, 1927, was gradually impeded and at last wholly discontinued. The dispute with regard to the 119 claimants of the Declaration as to Moslem Properties in Greece was the main, or at least the first reason which caused the failure of the Agreement of Athens. The Greek government believed in the justice of its request that there should be a revision of the cases of the twenty to twenty-five among the 119 claimants whose admission to the benefits of the Declaration was absolutely unjust, since they came under the provisions of the Convention concerning Exchange as persons subject to exchange. The Turkish government did not see its way to accept this revision, especially in view of the fact that the 119 claimants were prominent persons in Turkey and exercised pressure on the government. The Turkish government accordingly insisted vigorously on the immediate restoration of their properties to the 119 claimants, and when the Greek government refused to yield, the work of the Mixed Commission was paralyzed by the tactics of the Turkish delegation.[1]

[1] See *supra*, p. 540.

In December, 1927, when it appeared that the work of the Mixed Commission had practically stopped, the President of the Turkish delegation proposed informally to his Greek colleague that the question of the properties covered by the Agreement of Athens should be solved once and for all by the payment to the Turkish government of the guarantee of £500,000 deposited by Greece with the International Financial Commission at Athens and by the restoration to Moslems of the urban properties as provided for in the Agreement of Athens. These proposals introduced the last period of the long negotiations between the two governments, which presented four stages.

§ 353. **First stage of negotiations.** The first stage (April-June, 1928) was described as follows by Mr. Diamantopoulos, President of the Greek delegation, at the meeting of the Mixed Commission on July 10, 1928: [2]

"The negotiations were not meant to modify the existing Agreements but rather to solve the difficulties which arose in their execution. In October, 1927, all the work of the Commission had stopped, and even the work of appraisals was in danger of paralysis. Ihsan Bey, President *ad interim* of the Turkish delegation, on his return from Angora, unofficially informed us, on behalf of the Turkish government, that the latter was not satisfied with the progress of the work. Ihsan Bey then formulated the following proposals:

"(1) Renunciation on both sides of the appraisals then in process.

"(2) Payment on the part of the Greek government to the Turkish government of the sum of £500,000, the amount of the guarantee agreed upon by the Agreement of Athens.

"(3) Departure from Constantinople, as exchangeable, of about 25,000 Greeks.

"(4) In case of acceptance of these proposals and of some other secondary ones, the dissolution of the Mixed Commission.

"This unofficial proposal was confirmed to me confiden-

[2] Procès-Verbaux, 161st meeting.

tially by Saradjoglou Chukri Bey, former President of the Turkish Delegation and now Minister of Finance.

"The Greek delegation replied that it would refer the proposal to the Greek government, but that it believed it was authorized to reject unhesitatingly the proposal to subject to exchange 25,000 Greek inhabitants of Constantinople. I pointed out that I regretted the inclusion of such a proposal, which of itself would render any agreement impossible. On January 13, 1928, Dzevad Bey, Minister of Turkey at Athens, left a memorandum with the Greek Ministry of Foreign Affairs containing the same proposals, and dealing also with the question of the liquidation of properties of the exchanged populations, for which it provided as follows: 'In this field the Mixed Commission has accomplished nothing as yet, and it may be presumed that it will not do anything. Under these conditions, that task would only serve to keep going the work of the Commission, whose maintenance is very costly, without reaching any practical result. It would be useful to study and solve this question, at the same time as that of the duration of the Commission.'

"Concerning the cessation of appraisals and the payment of £500,000, M. Michalacopoulos, the Greek Minister of Foreign Affairs, declared at the time that the Greek government had not yet studied the figures obtained by the appraisals thus far made in order to judge of the final result of the accounts. In the memorandum he saw only an indication of the error that might be made by anticipating that this result would be in favor of Turkey. He thought that the completion of the appraisals should be awaited before the Greek government should consent to any sacrifice.

"With regard to the proposal to exchange 25,000 Greeks of Constantinople, the Turkish government was willing to accept a figure to be agreed upon by the two governments. Mr. Michalacopoulos remarked that the question is settled by Decision XXVII of the Mixed Commission. He added that the Greek government could not contemplate a new examination of this question, which had been solved after the Greek government consented to an alteration in article 16 of the Convention concerning the Greeks absent from Constantinople. To accept a reconsideration of this question would be to neglect private interests whose safeguard was required by the strictest equity, and it would seriously affect public opinion. As a counter-proposal, the Greek government offered, as an alternative to the literal application of Decision XXVII of the Mixed Commission, the recognition *en bloc* as 'established' of all persons now present at Constantinople.

"Lastly, on the question of the appraisal of the properties of the exchanged populations, the Greek government proposed to submit the question to the arbitration of a neutral.

"An exchange of views with relation to these matters took place between Mr. Michalacopoulos and the Turkish Foreign Minister, Tevfic Ruchdi Bey, at their meeting in Geneva in March, 1928, and subsequently between Tevfic Ruchdi and Mr. Papas, the Greek Minister at Angora. The conversations that followed developed on several points in a satisfactory way, to such a degree that Mr. Papas found it proper to put down certain conclusions in a draft memorandum having no official character and obligating neither party.

"These points may be summed up as follows:

"(1) Lump appraisal of the properties to be balanced in the space of six months by arbitration intrusted to a neutral member of the Mixed Commission (arbitrator-liquidator) and according to a summary procedure.

"(2) A set-off of the properties which should be restored according to Article 1 of the Agreement of Athens, and which have not yet been restored.

"(3) Restoration of the properties of Greek nationals situated in Constantinople within a month from the date when the arbitrator-liquidator should be entrusted by the Mixed Commission with the above task.

"(4) Arbitration by the three neutral members of the Commission concerning the execution of Decision XXVII.

"(5) Appraisal, as speedy as possible, of the immovable properties to be acquired by the two governments by virtue of Decision XXVIII.

"(6) Liquidation of the properties of the exchanged populations by the same arbitrator-liquidator, according to the most summary procedure.

"The points of view of the two negotiators seemed to diverge less and less, when, in the course of a last meeting, the Minister of Foreign Affairs of Turkey delivered to Mr. Papas a memorandum, communicated also to the Mixed Commission, signifying that the Turkish government preferred to abide purely and simply by the strict application of the existing Agreements and by the solution of the various questions by the Mixed Commission. This was the end of the negotiations, and the Greek government had no difficulty in following the Turkish government in this way."

§ 354. Reasons for their failure. The reasons for the failure of the negotiations at this stage would appear to be two. The Greek government insisted on the solution of all pending matters by arbitration. Turkey did not feel that she could win anything by arbitration and feared that she might lose much. On the other hand, Mr. Venizelos made his appearance at this time on the political horizon in Greece, assuming once more the leadership of the Liberal party and the Premiership in Greece. The Turks preferred to watch developments in Greece before making up their minds as to what position they would take. In the meantime, they believed that they could advantageously disturb the serenity of the Greek government that would result from the elections of August, 1928, by raising an outcry as to conditions in Western Thrace.

Beginning in July, 1928, its recriminations as to Western Thrace and the alleged violations of the Convention by the Greek government, the Turkish delegation obtained at last from the Mixed Commission a decision that a mixed delegation of the Commission should proceed to Western Thrace early in October for the purpose of investigating the condition of the Moslem population. This visit was, in fact, made in November, and its interruption, following the dispute at that time between the Greek and Turkish members, is described in another place.[3]

[3] See *supra,* p. 494.

§ 355. Second stage of negotiations. In the meantime, in September, 1928, Mr. Venizelos, the head of the new government in Greece, sent a letter to Ismet Pasha suggesting that the questions pending before the Mixed Commission be decided by negotiation. Mr. Papas returned to Angora in October, 1928, with the instructions of Mr. Venizelos for new negotiations. Soon afterwards, the disputes between the Greek and Turkish members of the mixed delegation investigating in Western Thrace, and the consequent interruption of the meetings of this delegation and its return to Constantinople, delayed the negotiations, which were not seriously entered upon before the end of December, 1928.

From this time to March, 1929, the negotiations passed through their second stage. They were conducted on the basis of the Turkish proposal that the question of the set-off of Greek and Turkish properties provided for in the Agreement of Athens should be finally solved by the payment on the part of Greece of a sum of money. When negotiations began at Angora in the latter part of December, 1928, it was agreed that the lump set-off and the balance to be paid, if any, were to be determined on the basis of the appraisals already made.

§ 356. Greek and Turkish methods for lump set-off. The appraisals made by the mixed committees to November 30, 1928, in Greece and Turkey, amounted to the following figures:

In Turkey	
Unanimous appraisals of various kinds of properties	£678,525
Appraisals by the neutral members of the committees, the Greek and Turkish members disagreeing	72,914
Total	£751,439
In Greece	
Unanimous appraisals of various kinds of properties	£421,636
Appraisals by the neutral members of committees, the Greek and Turkish members disagreeing	398,160
Total	£819,796

How were these figures to be used? The Greek technical expert proposed a method which seemed scientific and certain to give results approximately correct. He proposed to use the unanimous appraisals made in both countries and extract from them for each region of Greece and Turkey 'local coefficients' or 'unitary prices' for each kind of property. These coefficients were to be applied to properties which had not yet been appraised, thus obtaining the total value of properties in Greece and Turkey.

The two governments were not on an equal footing as regards knowledge of the properties claimed by the other. The Greek delegation had already furnished to the Mixed Commission in May, 1927, when the committees of appraisal began their work, complete data as to the Greek claims, namely, the number of claimants and the number and kind of properties claimed, with an indication of the value of such property. This was a strategical mistake on the part of the Greek delegation. On the contrary, the Turkish delegation did not submit any data as to properties and values, beyond a bare list of claimants. This list contained:

Macedonia	443	claimants
Crete	384	"
Epirus	111	"
Thessaly	64	"
Thrace	108	"
Mitylene	64	"
Lemnos	10	"
Chios	37	"
Peloponnesus	2	"
Total	1223	"

The specification of each property claimed was made in Greece before the mixed committees by their Turkish members or by representatives of the claimants. Thus, at the time the negotiations began, the Greeks had no clear idea of what the Turkish claims were. Moreover, even at this stage the Greek negotiators did not see the necessity of obtaining a clear statement of the sum of the Turkish figures. Instead of this, they submitted a memorandum, setting forth detailed factors and tables concerning the Greek and Turkish properties, using in respect to the latter the statistical data of the Greek Ministry of Agriculture.

The Turkish negotiators took full advantage of these mistakes. The limit of their claims was beyond control, since verification was now rendered impossible by the desire to make a lump set-off. The Greeks would, of course, have some idea as to the accuracy of these claims, in view of their own data and estimates on Turkish properties in Greece. But, while the Turkish figures could be disputed, there was no way of checking them by previous Turkish declarations.

The memorandum mentioned above, drawn up by the Greek technical expert and presenting all the factors as to Greek and Turkish properties to be set off, gave the approximate values of these properties by the application of the coefficients found as above, in two tables which gave the following totals: [4]

	Turkish pounds	
Total value of Greek properties in Turkey......	10,144,981	
Total value of Turkish properties in Greece.....	8,498,094	
Leaving a balance in favor of Greece of.........	1,646,887	Turkish pounds

This balance of itself was sufficient to discredit in Turkish eyes the Greek method of finding the approximate values of Greek and Turkish properties to be set off. Tevfic Ruchdi Bey, the Turkish Foreign Minister, to whom Mr. Papas communicated these tables, declared that they were of no serious value, although he confessed he had not studied them.[5] Subsequently, following the visit at Angora of the Italian Foreign Minister, Signor Grandi, Tevfic Ruchdi Bey admitted that the basis proposed by the Greek expert was reasonable, but he preferred the Turkish basis based on declared values.

The Turkish system of finding the approximate values of Greek and Turkish properties to be set off attempted to find the truth in the coefficient of the difference between the values declared by the claimants and those estimated by the appraisal committees. This method was arbitrary, especially when it is recalled that the Turkish delegation had not up to that time declared as yet the values claimed by the Turkish claimants. Tevfic Ruchdi Bey declared that the coefficient of truthfulness of the claims for the Turkish properties in Greece

[4] It should be borne in mind that this refers only to properties covered by the Agreement of Athens and does not include properties of persons exchanged or of persons exempted from the exchange in Constantinople and Western Thrace.

[5] Report of Mr. Tatarakis, the Greek technical expert, to the Greek Ministry of Foreign Affairs, dated January 12, 1929.

was found to be 40% of the values declared, whereas for the Greek properties in Turkey it was 20%.

It was agreed that the two technical experts, Midhat Bey and Mr. Tatarakis, should meet for the coöperative application of the two methods.[6] The experts met on December 31. On that day and on January 2 they discussed the two methods, while Mr. Tatarakis vainly asked for the Turkish data on the properties of the Turkish claimants in Greece. At the next meeting, January 3, 1929, at the request of the Greek delegation, the Turkish expert at last presented the table of Turkish claims, containing merely figures of values and areas of properties claimed.

To questions propounded by the Greek expert it was stated that the number of Turkish claimants for the above properties was 2059. It was then remarked that the previous declarations of the Turkish delegation to the Mixed Commission put this number at 1223 claimants. The Turkish expert admitted that in the above figure of 2059 there were 306 claimants from Thrace, not included in the set-off of properties under the Agreement of Athens, whose deduction brought the number of claimants to 1753. A further deduction was made of 200 claimants from the Spinalonga region of Crete, who, as the Greek expert pointed out, could not be regarded as claimants, since their properties had been sold long before and the price deposited with the Italian consul at Candia. The number of claimants was thus reduced to 1553. It was also specified that among these claimants there were 440 who had made no declaration with regard to the value of their properties in Greece.

The value of the Turkish properties claimed as above was given by the Turkish delegation as follows:

	Turkish pounds
Macedonia	12,105,972
Thessaly	6,999,346
Epirus	2,718,584
Islands	5,154,448
Total	26,958,350

[6] Report by Mr. Tatarakis to the Greek Ministry of Foreign Affairs, dated January 12, 1929.

At this meeting of January 3, the Turkish expert declared that this table included the unanimous and disputed appraisals of properties in Greece. In reply to his inquiry, the Greek expert stated that the total value of Greek properties declared reached 52,000,000 Turkish pounds. To the remark of the Turkish expert that the lists communicated to the Mixed Commission gave a total of 39,000,000 Turkish pounds, the answer was made that this did not include 13,000,000 of properties in the city of Smyrna. Whereupon at the next meeting, January 4, 1929, the Turkish expert declared that the above figure of 26,958,350 for the Turkish properties did not include the value of properties appraised by the committees. In view of his previous declaration to the contrary, the Greek expert was decidedly surprised.

With regard to the coefficient for finding the true value from these declared values, the Turkish member, taking as a basis the unanimous appraisals, and, for the disputed appraisals, the average between the prices given by the neutral member and by the interested national member, found that this was 50% for the Turkish claims and 14% for the Greek claims. After discussion, and the reminder by the Greek expert that already Tevfic Ruchdi Bey had set the Greek coefficient at 20%, the Turkish expert admitted, first 20%, and then 25% as the Greek coefficient, which showed the lack of any real foundation for his system.

Under these conditions, the Turkish expert, applying the above coefficients, found the following:

	Turkish pounds
Total value of Turkish properties in Greece..........	16,960,834
Total value of Greek properties in Turkey..........	14,360,341
Leaving a balance in favor of the Turks of..........	2,600,493

The Turkish coefficient of 50% for Turkish claimants was reduced to 41% if based only on the unanimous appraisals, as the Greek system was based. Indeed, the Turkish delegation had found:

Unanimous appraisals of Turkish properties in Greece		£421,636
and in the disputed appraisals		
neutral prices	£398,160	
Turkish prices	721,598	
Total	£1,119,758	
and according to the Turkish view the average of these prices was $\frac{1,119,758}{2}$ or..........................		559,879
giving a total of appraisals......................		£981,515
which on the basis of the 50% coefficient named by the Turks meant a declared value of		
2 x 981,515		£1,963,030

Now the real total of appraisals, taking into account only the neutral appraisals, was £819,796 (£421,636 + £398,160), which compared to the above amount of £1,963,030 reduced the coefficient to 41%.

Indeed, the idea of reaching a sound result by taking the average between the figures of the neutral member and those of the interested national member of the appraisal committee had no basis at all. The national members had the tendency in a disputed appraisal to put the appraisal as high as they could. Sometimes the difference between the prices given by the two national members was enormous. Take, for instance, the case of the farm Koupakia in Greece, for which the Turkish member of the committee put the price of £18,220 and the neutral member that of £4960, against a claim of the owner for £178,000! Also the following appraisals of Turkish farms in Macedonia:

Farm Vichan	Neutral price	2,354,940	drachmas
	Turkish price	13,625,000	"
	Greek price	934,500	"
Farm Koula	Neutral price	183,750	"
	Turkish price	5,150,000	"
	Greek price	61,250	"
Farm Kalendra	Neutral price	346,896	"
	Turkish price	1,035,000	"
	Greek price	213,081	"
Farm Fytok	Neutral price	584,800	"
	Turkish price	5,436,000	"
	Greek price	220,500	"

It will be noted that in these appraisals the neutral prices are between two and three times higher than the Greek prices, and the Turkish prices, three, six, nine, or twenty-eight times (in the case of the farm Koula) higher than the neutral prices. Under these conditions, to take the average between the Turkish and the neutral appraisals of Turkish properties in Greece as a means of reaching the truth with regard to the value of such properties was wholly arbitrary.

With a coefficient of 41%, the total value of Turkish properties in Greece was reduced to 14,055,447 Turkish pounds, against the value of Greek properties of 14,360,391 Turkish pounds, with a difference in favor of Greece of 304,944 Turkish pounds, and this reached by applying the Turkish method.

Thus, in conclusion, the Greeks declared that under the Greek method of lump appraisal there was a balance in favor of Greece of 1,646,887, and under the Turkish method a balance of 304,944 Turkish pounds. The Turks, for their part, asserted that, on the basis of their coefficients, there was a balance in favor of Turkey of 2,600,493 Turkish pounds.

The Greek delegation had the belief that there was no basis for the Turkish figures, and that, in truth, the Greek properties were of greater value. The writer was permitted to read a confidential report, dated December 17, 1928, addressed by the Greek expert, Mr. Tatarakis, to the President of the Greek delegation, from which it appears that the Greek expert believed in the approximate accuracy of the figures gathered by him on the respective value of Greek and Turkish properties, with the exception of a small reduction with respect to the appraisal of Greek houses and stores in Turkey, most of which would probably be found by the appraisal committees ruined or dilapidated and therefore of much smaller value than that of houses already appraised in the regions visited by the Committees in Turkey. Although the Turkish properties in Greece were large estates, there were only 1553 Turkish claimants against eight times as many Greek claimants. Indeed, there were 13,500 Greek claimants. On both sides it might be difficult for many claimants to prove that they were beneficiaries of the Agreement of Athens, but the difference between the numbers of claimants from the two countries allowed for a greater proportion of false and nonproved claims on the Greek side.

Notwithstanding this situation, the Greek expert recommended reaching an agreement with the Turks, for the following reasons:

(1) The completion of the individual appraisals by the committees was impracticable. Their output was very small. Even if the work of appraisal by the committees could be completed, the difference from the two lump appraisal accounts would be 15 or 20%.

(2) With the appraisal by the committees, examination of the personal status of claimants and of the proof of ownership rights would have to go side by side. In this respect, the Greek delegation would be at a disadvantage. The interested parties had been already paid indemnities by the Greek government and were no longer interested in supplying the delegation with proof of their claims. Thus, there existed the danger that although the Greek claims were in fact greater, the Greek delegation would not be able to prove enough of them to balance the Turkish claims.

The results of the work of the technical experts were laid down in Protocols signed by them on January 5, 1929. These were submitted to the negotiators at Angora, and as on both sides there was a desire to reach an agreement, it was decided to hold this matter in abeyance while the other questions discussed in the abortive negotiations of the previous year were taken up.

§ 357. Set-off of properties of exchanged populations. The largest question, of course, was that of the lump appraisal and liquidation of the properties left in the two countries by the exchanged Greek and Turkish populations. It is sufficient to recall that as a result of the exchange upwards of a million and a quarter Greeks left their properties in Turkey, and about 400,000 Turks likewise left their properties in Greece. How were these properties to be liquidated? At the demand of the two delegations, the President of the Mixed Commission asked a report on this matter of the Inspection Service, which supervised the work of the appraisal committees in Greece and Turkey. Such a report was submitted on January 30, 1929.

It was pointed out that there were 1,022,000 applications submitted by persons subject to exchange from the two countries. These applications were filed by the exchanged persons and gave indications, not always complete, as to the properties left in the country of origin and their value. The first work to be done in order to obtain a clear idea as to these applications was to classify them, according to the region where the properties were situated, the category of property (urban or rural), and the amount of the claims. Such a classification had already begun only two months before (November, 1928) and 20,100 had been classified during this time. Accordingly, it would take eight years to classify all the applications, if the same monthly output should continue. With a substantial increase of personnel, the work could be terminated within a year.

The report considered impracticable individual appraisals for all these properties. Rejecting entirely the method practised for the appraisal of properties of non-exchangeable persons (by three experts) as extremely costly and slow, it pointed out also the impracticability of individual appraisals by a single neutral expert. It would require thirty years and a total expenditure for appraisal alone of £6,132,000 to have constantly 100 neutral experts on the task.

The method of direct individual appraisal of all properties being thus put aside, the report sought a mode of appraisal which should be as rapid as possible and give guarantees of as great approximation as possible to the real value of the properties to be liquidated. This was to be achieved by establishing regional tables of values for each category of properties, as follows. In each region in Turkey and Greece, a number of direct appraisals for various categories of properties would be undertaken by the existing appraisal committees, in which the neutral members only would decide, the national members acting merely in an advisory capacity. This would permit the finding of a relation between the amount claimed and the corresponding real value of each property. The average values for each kind of property in each region would thus be established, after account was also taken of the density of the population, the facilities of communication, and any general or local conditions affecting the value of properties. The appraisals already made for properties of non-exchangeable persons would also be taken into consideration in establishing these tables of average regional values.

The prices resulting from these tables would be applied to the properties mentioned in the applications of the exchanged persons by a competent personnel in the Mixed Commission under the supervision of the Inspection Service. Any errors involved in this method of appraisal would affect the individual claimants, but they would be counterbalanced so far as the two countries were concerned.

It is clear that this proposal for the approximate appraisal of properties of exchanged persons did not permit an immediate and lump appraisal of all properties. It merely rendered the liquidation of all individual claims a matter of accounting operations, and therefore it promised the termination of the work of appraisal in a relatively short period of time. The proposal was clearly inspired by the methods of appraisal adopted in the Greco-Bulgarian exchange. However, the negotiators at Angora in January, 1929, desired a final and immediate liquidation, and the above proposal was set aside.

The Turkish government, it might be assumed, would, in any case, never accept this method of appraisal, which, since it assumed the existence of the properties and property rights claimed by the Greek claimants, was certain to result in a balance in favor of Greece. If this assumption was accepted, it was not difficult to see that the 1,300,000 Greeks who had left Turkey would have claims of a value superior to those of 400,000 Turks who had left Greece. The assumption, however, would not hold true.

The fact was, that a very great number of Greek landed properties in Turkey would have been disputed by the Turks. According to the Turkish property law, as we have seen in another place,[7] private persons had only a right of possession in land and not of ownership. This right of possession could be lost for various reasons, among them abandonment for

[7] See *supra*, p. 180.

three years. Hundreds of thousands of Greek owners had left Turkey long before the Convention concerning Exchange came into effect, and it would take a great deal of time and argument to convince the Turks that these persons did not lose their rights in their properties by leaving Turkey to save their lives. Besides, as the persons in question had no titles or other documentary proof of their rights, it would be very difficult for them to prove their claims. In other words, practically all the legal property rights of Greeks in Turkey were based on actual possession alone, and since the latter had ceased, it was extremely difficult to prove the former.

Furthermore, there were other reasons why the Greek negotiators should fear that the claims of Greeks in Turkey might not prove to be superior to those of Turks in Greece, when it is remembered that the appraisal was to be made as of the time the committees visited the various localities and not as of the time the Greeks left Turkey. These reasons were the following. First, a part of Turkey had been the field of military operations and a great number of villages and cities inhabited by Greeks in Asia Minor had been destroyed. As soon as the Greek army was pushed out of Smyrna, Turkish revenge and hatred turned into ruins many flourishing Greek sections of cities and countryside. All Greek properties in such localities would be found in the appraisal operations to be of little or no actual value. On the contrary, the 400,000 Turks left Greece in an orderly manner and their properties were occupied by the state for the settlement of refugees and thus preserved entirely from deterioration.

Secondly, the Turkish properties in Greece, by reason of the density of the population resulting from the settlement of refugees and the general improvement of agriculture by works of communication, drainage, and irrigation would be found of much superior value to Greek properties in Asia Minor, where the sparsity of population and the general economic distress had considerably lowered the price of rural properties.

For these reasons, both parties were prepared to call square the mutual claims of their new nationals on account of real properties left in the two countries respectively.

§ 358. Properties of établis. The Greek negotiators appear to have proposed to consider the set-off of the properties of exchanged persons in connection with the other pending questions. One of them was that of the *établis* of Constantinople and in particular the restoration of their properties seized by the Turkish government. These properties were situated either within the district of Constantinople or outside it. The Turks declared forthwith that they would not restore to *établis* seized properties located outside Constantinople and in the territory included in the exchange. They were, however, ready to pay the value of such properties to their owners. The Turks were apparently unwilling to permit the economic extension of the Greeks in Asia Minor through the maintenance of such properties, and wished to restrict them to the city of Constantinople. This the Greeks well understood, and were reluctant to subscribe to what amounted to the economic death of a part of the Greek population at Constantinople. Indeed, mank Greeks in Constantinople carried on commerce in goods derived from their properties in the interior of Turkey, and for them the prohibition to own properties in the interior amounted to cutting off the roots of their business.

However, the Greek negotiators decided that the advantage of maintaining the rights of the Greeks of Constantinople was a hollow one. These properties seemed in any case lost. Either the Greeks of Constantinople would never be able or willing to penetrate into the interior and take possession of these properties, which in the meantime might have been destroyed or become impossible to identify, or the Turkish government would place all kinds of obstacles to their restoration. Therefore it was best to secure an indemnity to their owners for such properties. The Greek *établis* of Constantinople, owners of such properties, who should receive an indemnity numbered 1600 families. Their claims as declared amounted to £2,360,000.

With regard to properties of Greek *établis* located in Constantinople, it was agreed that the Turkish government would restore all such properties. There were about 1000 Greeks of Constantinople whose properties the Turks had seized. But in this connection the question again arose of the Greek *établis* of Constantinople who had left the city after the Greek disaster in Asia Minor.

There were some 30,000 to 40,000 Greeks who had left Constantinople precipitately at that time, with foreign passports or with passports issued by the Imperial Turkish government, which was still in authority in the city just before the Nationalist government occupied it. These people were usually persons who had no property to leave behind them in Constantinople, and no claims were therefore filed by these persons. However, there were sixty persons who left with imperial passports and who had very large properties in Constantinople, estimated by the Turks themselves to a total value of 300,000 Turkish gold pounds. There were also many others who had left properties located in Constantinople or outside it. The total claims of these persons were estimated by the Greeks as 2,500,000 Turkish gold pounds. All these properties were seized by the Turkish authorities as abandoned property. The Turkish government did not wish to consider the question of the restoration of these properties, while the Greek government was reluctant to abandon these claims and to have to indemnify the claimants.

§ 359. Other questions discussed. Another problem arose as to the Greek subjects whose properties, located in the district of Constantinople, were seized by the Turkish government during the war and after 1925 as reprisals for the failure to restore Turkish properties in Greece. In this connection there were three categories of claimants:

(1) 134 claimants for properties seized by the Turkish government from 1914 to 1925, with declarations of a total value of 267,873 Turkish gold pounds.

(2) 144 claimants for properties seized by the Turkish government from 1925 to 1929, with declarations of a total value of 481,470 Turkish gold pounds; and

(3) 171 claimants for properties seized in 1929 by the Turkish government, with declarations of a total value of 355,673 Turkish gold pounds.

In addition to the above questions concerning the lump

appraisal and set-off of claims of different categories of claimants in immovable properties, there were other questions on which agreement was needed. Such were the question of the Greek deposits and safes seized by the Turkish authorities, the question of rentals and revenues due to proprietors of properties seized by the two governments, the question of requisitions, etc., etc.

§ 360. Third stage of negotiations. In March, 1929, the negotiations seemed to have reached a deadlock, and it was feared that there would be no result achieved. However, after a temporary interruption, the negotiations were resumed in April, 1929, thus entering into a third stage. The basis for these negotiations was afforded by a comprehensive draft of the Turkish member of the Mixed Commission, Djemal Husni Bey, and a Greek draft drawn up at Athens in April, 1929. In May, 1929, the neutral members of the Commission were called to Angora to help in the negotiations, which had come to a standstill. Their assistance was as mediators and not as arbitrators. On the question of the Greeks who left Constantinople between 1918 and 1922, there was a legal question involved, namely, whether these persons should be allowed to return to Constantinople under the Convention. On this the opinion of the neutrals was unhesitatingly in favor of the Greek view. But the question now had degenerated into one of bargaining between the two governments, and the neutrals could do nothing. They were also asked to arbitrate on the question of the amount to be paid by the one government to the other for a general set-off, but they refused, since no basis existed on which to arbitrate. When the difference between the amounts claimed by the two governments was small, the neutrals mediated by proposing a middle amount.

After most elaborate negotiations and discussions, it appears that in June, 1929, the reciprocal claims were all reduced to certain figures. These have not been published.[8]

By July, 1929, it appears that a general agreement was reached on all matters, with the exception of the properties of

[8] However, the Greek newspaper *Hestia* of June 9, 1929, published the following note which was distributed by the Greek Ministry of Foreign

Greeks who left Constantinople with regular imperial passports. The neutral members of the Commission proposed that such persons be restored to their rights. The Turkish government refused to accept this proposal, and declared on July 15, 1929, to the neutral member, Mr. Holstad, and on July 20 to the Greek Minister at Angora, that it had decided to consider the negotiations as terminated.

This declaration brought about a very severe tension in the relations between the two governments. The Turkish papers put the responsibility on Greece and advised the government to seize all Greek properties in Constantinople. Such seizures were indeed begun shortly afterward. On July 27, the Greek government proposed that all disputed questions be referred to arbitration of one or several arbiters to be chosen by the President of the Permanent Court of International Justice

Affairs to the members of the Committee of Foreign Affairs of the National Assembly, and apparently presents the Greek view:

"By the general set-off the following properties are acquired by Greece:

Properties referred to by the Agreement of Athens and the Declaration as to Moslem Properties in Greece	7,530,000
Properties in Western Thrace: (*a*) of Turkish subjects; (*b*) of absent Moslems established in Western Thrace; (*c*) of Moslems established in Western Thrace owning properties located outside Western Thrace; and (*d*) of Moslems established in Western Thrace whose properties were seized	720,000
Total in Turkish gold pounds	8,250,000

"This amount did not include revenues collected by the Greek government and estimated at 750,000 pounds.

"On the other hand the following properties were acquired by Turkey:

Properties referred to by the Agreement of Athens and the Declaration as to Moslem Properties in Greece	10,144,961
Properties enumerated in the list annexed to the Agreement of Athens	60,000
Properties of Greeks of Constantinople who left with irregular passports (located in Constantinople and outside it)	2,000,000
Properties of *établis* of Constantinople located outside Constantinople	1,750,000
"Eventually to be added:	
Properties of Greeks of Constantinople who left with regular passports	350,000
Properties of Greeks absent from Constantinople, which had not yet been seized	100,000
Total in Turkish gold pounds	14,404,961

"This amount did not include revenues collected by the Turkish government and estimated at 5,000,000 pounds.

"These figures show an excess of value of Greek properties, including the revenues, of 10,404,961 Turkish gold pounds."

or by the President of the Swiss Confederation. The Turkish government declined,[9] arguing that the whole basis of the negotiations, as proposed by the Greek government itself, was political and not legal, and that, consequently, there was no scope for arbitration. In other words, since the whole discussion was in preparation for a bargain, it was only by mutual concessions that all the pending questions were to be settled.

§ 361. Last stage of negotiations. After an exchange of notes, in which each of the two governments insisted on its own position, the negotiations were resumed once more in November, 1929. It appears that the Italian government intervened to procure the resumption of negotiations, which were carried on both at Angora and at Athens. Concurrently, negotiations were started for improving the economic and political relations between the two governments. Through these discussions, the two countries were brought nearer to each other, and a greater spirit of conciliation permitted a slow but satisfactory progress of negotiations in the matter of mutual claims. Not only was a solution found for all questions remaining pending, but an effort was made to classify in a systematic way the various questions in the agreement and to specify all details, in order to avoid as much as possible those questions of interpretation which in the past had prevented the execution of the stipulations.

The new Convention was signed at Angora on June 10, 1930.

[9] See texts of the Greek and Turkish notes in the semi-official *Eleftheron Vima,* published in Athens under date of August 10, 1929.

CHAPTER XXIX

THE GRECO-TURKISH CONVENTION SIGNED AT ANGORA ON JUNE 10, 1930

§ 362. Nature of the Convention. The Convention proceeding from the negotiations of 1929-30 purports to settle definitively all questions arisen from the application of the previous Conventions, Declarations, Agreements, and other Acts, and Annexes thereto, referring to the exchange of Turkish and Greek populations. It consists of twelve chapters, divided into thirty-four articles. Each of the chapters deals with a particular problem. Thus, the properties of the exchangeable persons; the properties of the beneficiaries of the Declaration as to Moslem Properties in Greece; those of Turkish nationals and of Greek nationals; those of Greeks 'established' at Constantinople and of Moslems 'established' in Western Thrace; and the revenues and indemnities form the subject of the first seven chapters. The remaining chapters deal with payments by Greece, special and general provisions, arbitral clauses, and final provisions. This clear delimitation of subjects in the Convention is a distinct quality, the necessity of which was keenly felt in view of the difficulties created by the prior Acts.

§ 363. Properties of exchangeable persons. The first two articles of the Convention confirmed a condition of long standing. They provided that the immovable and movable property left by Moslem and Greek exchangeable persons in Greece and Turkey should be transferred in complete ownership to the Greek and Turkish government respectively. Article 10 of the Convention of Lausanne concerning the Exchange of Greek and Turkish Populations stipulated that such immovable and movable property was to be liquidated by the Mixed Commission, and article 14 of the same Convention indicated that such property remained in the ownership of the emigrants until the time they received payment therefore. The present Convention does away with this limitation.

While no time is fixed from which full ownership is acquired by the respective states, it should be taken that it is the date of the coming into effect of the Convention. In order to preserve a certain appearance of conformity with the original Convention, it was stipulated in article 4 of the new Convention that the neutral members of the Mixed Commission should be intrusted with the task of "rendering immediately their opinion on the solution of the question of the liquidation of properties of the exchangeable persons, including the claims for the tithe on tobaccos and the strongboxes of such persons." The two governments agreed to express their adherence to the opinion of the neutrals before the Convention should be submitted to the two Parliaments for ratification.

§ 364. Opinion of the neutral members of the Mixed Commission. The opinion of the neutral members of the Commission was rendered on June 12, 1930. After a brief historical introduction and an analysis of the provisions of the Convention of Lausanne, the opinion went on to state:

1. That the Mixed Commission had no information, even approximate, of the total number of exchangeable persons covered by the Convention of Lausanne whose properties were to be appraised and liquidated. Precise data existed only with regard to the persons transferred under the auspices of the

Mixed Commission after its constitution. The figures of emigrants from the two countries from October 18, 1912, to November, 1923, were unknown to the Commission.

2. That the Convention of Lausanne contemplated an individual appraisal of the properties of each emigrant as the basis for the final liquidation and as a basis for the indemnification of each emigrant by an equivalent property in his new country.

3. That in the plan for appraisal and liquidation worked out by a section of the Mixed Commission in April, 1924, the individual appraisal of all properties was abandoned as impossible, and instead a plan of lump and summary appraisal was proposed, which, being contrary to the provisions of the Convention, could not possibly be applied by the Commission unless an agreement should be entered into by the two states.

4. As preliminary steps to appraisal and liquidation it was necessary (*a*) that the condition of all claimants as persons subject to exchange should be recognized; this, in particular, for persons who had emigrated between October 18, 1912, and the date of the constitution of the Commission might be theoretically difficult, and was, practically, an enormous task, since the number of such persons exceeded one million; (*b*) that the property rights claimed should be verified. This would require an expert personnel, familiar with the Greek and Moslem Law of Property, and would raise an infinite number of complicated legal questions on each claim.

5. In order to proceed to appraisal an agreement was necessary with regard to the time to which the appraisal should refer. Four choices were possible: the date of dispossession of the claimant; the date of the signature of the Convention; the date of the coming into effect of the Convention; or the date the appraisal was to be made. Important consequences followed the choice of one or the other date. There were destructions of properties after dispossession of the owners and both before and after the Convention was entered into. There were revenues collected by the state from properties left by emigrants. There were to be considered an interest of the emigrant, an interest of the state where the property was located,

and an interest of the state in the territory of which the emigrant now resided. The Convention did not clearly indicate the date to which the appraisal was to refer.

6. The appraisal of movable property presented additional difficulties. The *procès-verbaux,* provided by article 8 of the Convention for movable property left by emigrants, which were to be drawn up by the local authorities at the time of the emigration of the exchanged persons, did not exist. Rarely had this provision been applied, especially in Turkey, and no *procès-verbaux* could be drawn up for persons who emigrated before the constitution of the Commission, that is, for two-thirds of the total number of exchangeable persons. Such movable property was for the most part not now in existence, and an appraisal must rely on the claims made. Such claims were very considerable, especially on the side of the Greeks, because of the manner of their flight from Turkey, the profession of the emigrants, and other reasons. From the results obtained by a partial inspection of the claims filed with the Commission, it appeared that the Greek claims for movable property represented an amount equal to 60.9% of the value of the immovable property, whereas in the Turkish claims the proportion was 4.7%. It was not possible, therefore, to determine the value of the claims for movable property for both countries by taking a proportion of the value of the claims for immovable property.

7. While the negotiations were carried on in Angora, from December, 1928, to June, 1930, the Mixed Commission's Bureau on Liquidations of exchangeable persons had examined part of the applications for liquidation. The total number of applications received was:

Turkish applications	144,169
Greek applications	450,000
Total	594,169

Of these, the Bureau had examined within a period of twenty months:

Turkish applications	73,178
Greek applications	79,697

or a total of 158,875 applications, which represent 25% of the total. This simple work of examining the applications and adding the claims required six more years to be completed with the existing personnel of the Bureau. And it was believed that there were many more applications to be filed. The only speedy and possible plan appeared to be to reduce every application by a coefficient of exaggeration. But the determination of this coefficient required collecting sufficient evidence by appraisals in different regions and for various kinds of properties. Moreover such a plan of appraisal was contrary to the provisions of the Convention of Lausanne which contemplated individual appraisals.

8. In addition to the above difficulties, there were those of the actual work of appraisal, which centred around the identification of the property to be appraised and the determination of the value. With regard to the former, the experience from the appraisal of properties of non-exchangeable persons had shown that, because of the lack of a cadastre in Greece and the obsoleteness of the one in Turkey, no official data existed. The identification of properties on the spot, especially of rural properties, was often impossible because of the emigration of the entire population of some villages, removals, the creation of new villages, the burning of towns and cities in Turkey, and the lack of assistance by the local peasants.

With regard to the determination of the value, the method of taking into account sale prices for similar properties was inapplicable for many regions in Turkey, where there was no market of lands at all. In Greece there were sales of small properties, but the contract prices were often fictitious. The method of determining the value of a property from the revenue involved two problems: (*a*) determination of the net revenue of the property, and (*b*) determination of the rate of capitalization. The first was very difficult, in view of the profound changes to which rural property especially had been subject after the war, both in Turkey and in Greece. The second had already caused long discussions in the Mixed Commission.

All these difficulties explain why, in the appraisals of properties of non-exchangeable persons made by the appraisal commitees, agreement was reached only on small properties, whereas on large properties the differences between the appraisals of the experts reached 500% or more.

The opinion, after reviewing all these facts, next called attention to the scheme urged by the report of the two Inspectors of Appraisals,[1] which was for lump appraisal and therefore not in conformity with the Convention, and to the cost of appraisal under that scheme, which would reach £1,673,050. If to this should be added the cost of ascertaining whether a claimant was entitled to claim under the Convention of Lausanne and of verifying the property rights of the claimants, the expenditure would exceed £2,000,000.

In view of all these facts, the neutral members of the Mixed Commission concluded, in their opinion, that they could not advise the two governments to proceed to the appraisal of properties as contemplated by the Convention of Lausanne. They also could not advise them to agree to a summary and lump appraisal, since this was subject to grave errors and could not give a trustworthy result. There was no basis, therefore, for finding at the present time a balance in favor of either Greece or Turkey on the general liquidation of properties of exchanged persons. The two governments were therefore advised to abandon the application of the stipulations of the Convention of Lausanne concerning the appraisal and liquidation of properties of the exchanged persons.[2]

There is no doubt that this conclusion of the opinion of the neutral members of the Mixed Commission was known to the two governments before the Convention of Angora was signed on June 10, 1930. The governments, therefore, gave notice of their adherence to the recommendations of the opinion as soon as they were communicated to them.

Only one category of the property of exchanged persons was excluded from the general set-off, namely, bank deposits

[1] See *supra,* pp. 558 ff.

[2] The sum due by the Greek government on account of the tithe on tobacco unduly paid by Moslem emigrants, and the sum due by the Turkish government for objects lost from safes left by emigrants, were also included in the general compensation.

of all kinds. All opposition by the two governments to paying out such deposits was withdrawn within fifteen days following the date of signature of the Convention of Angora. The Mixed Commission offered its good offices to the interested parties for the collection of the deposits.

§ 365. Properties of beneficiaries of the Declaration as to Moslem Properties in Greece. The second chapter of the Convention concerned the movable and immovable properties belonging to Moslems and Greeks who were beneficiaries of the Declaration as to Moslem Properties in Greece and the reciprocal declaration of the Turkish government. With regard to such properties, it was stipulated that the state in the territory of which they were located acquired them in full ownership. Thus, the previous attempts to have such properties restored to their owners, or to have the state purchase the properties from the owners, were abandoned. Such persons lost their properties both in Greece and in Turkey in favor of the Greek and Turkish states respectively. It will be recalled that beneficiaries of the Declaration were the persons who left Greece or Turkey before October 18, 1912, or who had resided all the time outside such country.

There was one exception made to the above rule. The rights of Moslem owners to whom their immovable properties had been restored and who were in effective possession and enjoyment were maintained. This exception concerned only Greece, as restorations had taken place only in that country.

§ 366. Properties of Turkish nationals in Greece. The third and fourth chapters of the Convention concerned properties of Turkish and Greek subjects who were not included in the exchange. The exchange, it will be remembered, concerned only Moslems who were Greek nationals and Greeks who were Turkish nationals. Moslems who were Turkish subjects and had properties in Greece enjoyed the protection of articles 65 and 66 of the Treaty of Lausanne, which called for the restoration of all seized property. Subsequently, the Agreement of Athens provided for the purchase of such properties by the Greek government, with certain exceptions considered above.[3] The new Convention provided here also that such immovable properties passed to the full ownership of the Greek government. Exception was made only of immovable properties which had been already restored to their owners and which were actually in their possession and enjoyment.

The movable property of Turkish subjects in Greece was left to the free disposal of the owners, with the exception of that which had been seized and liquidated subsequent to the entering into effect of the Treaty of Lausanne. This passed to the full ownership of the Greek government. All other property rights and interests were to be governed by the provisions of the Treaty of Lausanne, and, in particular, of its articles 65 and 66.

§ 367. Properties of Greek nationals in Turkey. The properties of Greek nationals situated in Turkey were divided into two categories: those situated outside the zone of Constantinople, and those within this zone, which had been excluded from the exchange.

With regard to the former, the above provisions concerning immovable and movable property of Turkish subjects in Greece were applicable, with the difference that no exception was made as to immovable properties restored to their owners. The difference is explained by the fact that no such properties had been restored. The result, therefore, was that, outside of the zone of Constantinople, all immovable property in Turkey belonging to Greek subjects passed to the Turkish state.

With regard to the immovable property of Greek subjects situated within the zone of Constantinople, which was excluded from the exchange, it was provided in article 8 that the right of property was in no way affected by the Convention. Within two months at the latest from the coming into effect of the Convention, the Greek subjects whose properties had been seized, sequestrated, or in any way occupied, were to be reinstated, either personally or through their legal representatives, in the free and complete possession of their properties. All measures against such properties were to be cancelled.

[3] See *supra,* p. 522.

For the execution of this stipulation it was necessary for the interested parties to prove their Greek citizenship. In order to make this proof free of difficulties, article 9 of the Convention contained a number of provisions. If the administrative act of seizure recited that the property in question belonged to a Greek subject, or if the Turkish title deed referred to the owner as such subject, the reinstatement of the owner in the possession of his property was not to be deferred for any reason. If any dispute should arise concerning the acquisition of the Greek or Turkish nationality under Treaties, Conventions, and Agreements, such dispute was to be settled by a decision of the neutral members of the Mixed Commission. It was understood that the 'exchangeable' persons who by virtue of the compulsory exchange acquired the Greek nationality were not included in these provisions of the Convention.

Although no provision was made in article 9 with regard to the movable property belonging to Greek subjects and situated in the zone of Constantinople, the provision of article 8 was general and applied to such property. In other words, all movable property seized and liquidated subsequent to the coming into effect of the Convention was recognized as in the full ownership of the Turkish state. All other movable property of this category was governed by articles 65 and 66 of the Treaty of Lausanne. The Greco-Turkish Mixed Arbitral Tribunal was to deal with these cases.

§ 368. Recognition of *établis* at Constantinople and in Western Thrace. Chapters V and VI of the Convention dealt with the *établis* at Constantinople and in Western Thrace respectively and their rights and properties. With regard to Greeks established at Constantinople, Turkey recognized the quality of 'established' as to all Orthodox Greeks, Turkish subjects, actually present in the zone of Constantinople and excluded from the exchange, whatever the date of their arrival at Constantinople or the place of their birth. This provision was more sweeping than that of the Agreement of Angora embodied in Decision XXVII of the Mixed Commission, in that it did not require presence at Constantinople on October 30,

1918. It was desired to do away with all necessity of evidence and formalities, and to put an end to the manifold difficulties that were presented in this connection. Besides, the Constantinople police in the meantime had pretty thoroughly cleared the city from persons subject to exchange, and there were few, if any, who would profit by this provision and obtain exemption from the exchange.

As 'established' were also recognized all persons exempt from exchange who had left Constantinople provided with passports issued by the authorities of the Turkish Republic. This provision excluded all persons who were established in Constantinople before 1918, but who had left prior to 1922, since there was no Turkish Republic before that date. These persons were deprived of the right to return to Constantinople and lost their original nationality, acquiring that of Greece.

The wives, minor children of both sexes, and unmarried daughters, though of age, whose family head was recognized as 'established' as above, had the right to join the latter at Constantinople. Widowed mothers whose sons, being of age, were recognized as 'established' were authorized to join them. The Turkish government undertook to grant all facilities for the return to Constantinople of the above persons.

On the contrary, the wives, minor children of both sexes, and unmarried daughters recognized as 'established' whose family head was not at Constantinople were not bound to quit the city. This satisfactorily ended a controversy between the Turkish and Greek delegations and the Mixed Commission, the Turks insisting that such persons were bound to quit Constantinople.

Similar provisions to those of article 10 were contained in article 14 with respect to the recognition of Moslems established in Western Thrace. The provision for the non-recognition as 'established' of persons who had left Western Thrace without being provided with passports of the Greek Republic brought about a theoretical reciprocity of terms, which, however, was not a reciprocity in fact, since there were few, if any, Moslems absent from Western Thrace and who desired to return.

The distribution of certificates of establishment to all the above categories of persons was intrusted to the neutral members of the Mixed Commission. They were empowered to adopt such procedure and formalities as they saw fit.

§ 369. Repeal of restrictive measures. Together with the recognition of the above persons as *établis,* the Convention contained provisions for insuring to such persons all their rights which had been restricted in one way or another. From the coming into effect of the Convention, and without waiting for the distribution of the certificates of *établis,* all measures which had prevented the exercise of the rights secured to the *établis* by the prior Conventions and Agreements were to be repealed. Specifically, the restrictions concerning the marriage contract, the right to acquire and sell property, the right of free movement, and all other restrictions imposed by the Turkish and Greek authorities against the *établis* were to be abolished. Again these provisions refer to restrictions imposed by the Greek as well as Turkish authorities, although none such were ever imposed by the former.

§ 370. Properties of Greeks established at Constantinople. With regard to the property of Greeks established at Constantinople, a distinction was made by the Convention between properties situated within the zone of Constantinople excluded from the exchange, and such property located outside of this zone in the other territory of Turkey. All movable and immovable property of the first category was secured to their owners free from any restrictions. All seizures or sequestrations effected on such properties were to be rescinded without any delay. On no account was the restoration of the owner or his legal representative to the full possession and enjoyment of such properties to be deferred.

On the other hand, all movable and immovable property of Greek *établis* situated outside the zone of Constantinople was transferred in full ownership to the Turkish government. This provision was in complete opposition not only to the Convention of Lausanne but also to the elementary ideas of justice. However, as will be seen, an indemnity was to be paid to these persons.

Further, all movable and immovable property situated in any part in the Turkish territory and belonging to Orthodox Greeks, Turkish subjects, exempted from the exchange, who were absent from Constantinople and whose return was prohibited, was lost to them and transferred in full ownership to the Turkish government.

§ 371. **Properties of Moslems established in Western Thrace.** The above provisions applied also to the movable and immovable property of Moslems of Western Thrace. There were, however, two other categories of Moslem properties situated in Western Thrace which passed to the ownership of the Greek government. These were:

1. The properties situated in Western Thrace which appeared on the list delivered by the Greek delegation to the Mixed Commission on June 18, 1927. This list indicated at the time the properties in Western Thrace which the Greek government had decided to acquire on paying the price to the owners. Their acquisition was permitted under Decision XXVIII of the Mixed Commission, on condition that "the development of the economic life of the Moslem population was not damaged thereby." The Mixed Commission in June, 1927, had sent this list to the Sub-Commission in Western Thrace to determine whether this condition was satisfied. Apparently the Turkish government now had no objection to the acquisition of these properties. As these properties were to pass to the Greek government, article 20 provided for an indemnity to the owners.

2. Properties, of a total area of 7000 *stremmata,* which appeared on a complementary list annexed to the Convention, provided these properties were already occupied. The owners of these properties were also to be indemnified as the previous ones.

§ 372. **Revenues, indemnities, etc.** Revenues and indemnities due to various categories of persons under the previous Conventions and Agreements were much controverted matters, on which no exact data existed, and the proof of which required extensive investigations. The Convention makes a clean slate. The two governments reciprocally renounced all such claims. However, each government undertook to settle directly with its own subjects the question of rentals and indemnities referred to by article 3 of Decision XXVIII of the Mixed Commission. These were due to *établis* at Constantinople and in Western Thrace on account of seizures and requisitions made after notice of the ratification of the Convention of Lausanne was sent to the League of Nations. Accordingly, thenceforth Greeks established at Constantinople were to look to the Turkish government alone, and not to the Mixed Commission as before, for indemnity and payment of rentals. Similarly, Moslems established in Western Thrace were to look to the Greek government only.

§ 373. Payments by the Greek government. Within a month from the coming into effect of the Convention, the Greek government was to place at the disposal of the Mixed Commission a sum of 425,000 pounds sterling. This sum was to be taken from the sum of £500,000 deposited by Greece as a security to the Turkish government under the Agreement of Athens of December 1, 1926. The Mixed Commission was to dispose of this sum as follows:

1. One hundred and fifty thousand pounds sterling were to be used to indemnify the Greeks established at Constantinople, being Turkish subjects, for the properties situated outside the zone of Constantinople which were transferred to the ownership of the Turkish government.

2. An equal amount was to be used to indemnify the Moslems established in Western Thrace, being Greek subjects, for their properties which were transferred to the ownership of the Greek government.

The distribution of these sums to the above persons was to be made by the agents of the Mixed Commission according to a summary and speedy procedure to be determined by it.

3. The balance, 125,000 pounds sterling, was to be remitted to the Turkish government by the Mixed Commission in three instalments. The first of £62,500 was to be paid within the month following the coming into effect of the Convention; the second instalment of £47,500 was to be paid as soon as the neutral members of the Commission should be convinced that

all the properties belonging to Greek subjects and situated within the zone of Constantinople had been restored to them. The last instalment of £15,000 was to be remitted to the Turkish government after the neutral members found that Turkey had carried out all its obligations under the Convention. When all these payments were completed, Greece was freed from any obligation on account of the transfer to her of the various categories of Moslem properties situated in Greece.

§ 374. **Further provisions.** Provisions were made in chapter IX of the Convention for guarantees against failure of either government to make complete restoration. From the above exposition, it appears that restorations were due, on the part of Turkey, (1) of properties of Greek subjects situated in the zone of Constantinople, and (2) of properties belonging to Greeks, Turkish subjects, established in the zone of Constantinople; and, on the part of Greece, of properties situated in Western Thrace, belonging to Moslems established in Western Thrace and not included in the list of properties referred to in article 16 of the Convention. A country required to make restoration could not acquire such property, asserting that it was impossible to make restoration, except in purely exceptional cases and after the Mixed Commission determined that circumstances rendered restoration impossible. After approval by the Mixed Commission, the property in question was to be appraised and an indemnity paid to the owner by the Mixed Commission. In case Turkey failed to restore a property to a Greek subject, a sum equal to the appraisal amount was deducted from the sum of £47,500 which was to be remitted to the Turkish government as above. In case the property of a Greek established in the zone of Constantinople was not duly restored, the value of the property was deducted from the sum of £15,000 which was to be paid to the Turkish government as third instalment. In the latter case, Turkey was required to make good the payment from this sum by remitting to the Mixed Commission the amount paid as indemnity.

The Greek government deposited with the Mixed Commission a sum of £15,000 which was to be used as a guarantee fund in the same way as the £15,000 above referred to.

Properties situated in the zone of Constantinople and in Western Thrace, and belonging to persons excluded from the exchange who had left the above regions respectively without regular passports, passed to the respective government only in case they were already occupied by such government at the time of the coming into effect of the Convention. After that date, no seizure, sequestration, or occupation could take place unless the Mixed Commission examined and approved in each case. After the termination of the work of the Mixed Commission, no further seizure, sequestration, or occupation was allowed. The Convention contained also a sweeping provision in article 33, according to which laws, decrees, regulations, legal and official interpretations, orders and circulars of any kind contrary to the stipulations of the Convention, or preventing in any way its complete execution, were entirely abolished in both countries.

§ 375. Arbitral Clauses. Chapter XI of the Convention introduced provisions whose lack had been keenly felt under the regime of the previous Conventions and Agreements. The execution of the Convention was intrusted to the Mixed Commission and its agencies. However, any difference or controversy which should arise between the Greek and Turkish delegations in the Mixed Commission with regard to the interpretation or application of the above provisions was to be definitely decided by the neutral members of the Commission. These were, in a general way, recognized by the two governments as their arbiters, and both governments bound themselves to recognize without any discussion the decisions of the arbiters.

§ 376. Observations on the Convention. The Convention of June 10, 1930, should not meet with any difficulties of interpretation and application. Its perfect clarity reduces the needs of interpretation to a minimum. The application is rendered extremely easy mainly because it confirms practically all *faits accomplis.* Almost all properties seized by the two governments are left in their ownership. The restoration of properties is applied exclusively to the regions of Western Thrace and Constantinople, where, on the whole, only isolated seizures took place. Wherever restorations are still necessary, several guarantees are provided. First, the Mixed Commission is empowered to investigate each case; then, indemnity may be paid to the owner by deducting it from the funds of the government concerned; lastly, the neutral members are given power as arbiters to solve all differences and controversies. Aside from ascertaining the restorations to be made by the two governments, the work of the Mixed Commission consists mainly in the distribution of certificates of non-exchangeability to *établis* in Western Thrace and in Constantinople, and in the distribution of indemnities to these persons for properties passing to the ownership of the respective governments. As soon as the Convention was ratified, the Commission created four committees in Constantinople and six in Western Thrace to carry out these provisions of the Convention.

Of the payment of £425,000 which Greece undertook to make to the Mixed Commission, the item of £150,000 for indemnifying Moslems in Western Thrace for properties passing to the ownership of the Greek government was a just payment. The second item of £150,000 for indemnities to Greeks in Constantinople was to be paid by Greece in the place of Turkey, to whose ownership the seized properties passed. The remainder of £125,000 was paid by Greece to Turkey as a balance in the set-off of Greek and Turkish properties of non-exchangeable persons. This sum had been fixed in the negotiations which were interrupted in July, 1929, at £150,000, and was reduced now by £25,000 in view of the agreement on the question of the Greeks absent from Constantinople. Indeed, in July, 1929, Turkey had insisted that these persons had not the right to return to Constantinople and that their properties should pass to the Turkish government without indemnity. Now, Turkey consented to give up £25,000, to which an equal amount was to be added by the Greek government, thus forming a sum of £50,000 to be used for indemnifying the Greeks who left Constantinople with irregular passports and whose properties passed to the Turkish government.

On the justice of the payment of £275,000 by Greece as above it is difficult to express an opinion. There is no doubt that Greece considered the payment unjust, as she was convinced that the properties of 1,500,000 Greeks who had left Turkey at various periods, leaving behind them their movable and immovable property, were much superior in value to the properties left by Moslems in Greece, who did not exceed 500,000. However, Greece wished to see the end of the exceedingly unpleasant and uncertain position of the Greek population of Constantinople, which was causing it to quit the city. She also wished to clear up the atmosphere of unfriendliness and tension which the economic liquidation of the exchange of populations had created for all these years. Greece hoped that, by now consenting to certain sacrifices and losses, she might receive compensation through the reëstablishment of friendly political and economic relations with Turkey.

CHAPTER XXX

FINANCES OF THE COMMISSION

§ 377. Salaries and allowances of members of the Commission.
§ 378. Salaries of personnel and other expenses.
§ 379. Payments and accounts.
§ 380. Budget of the Commission in 1924.
§ 381. Subsequent budgets.
§ 382. Total expenses of the Commission.

§ 377. Salaries and allowances of members of the Commission. The Council of the League of Nations, in appointing the three neutral members on September 17, 1923, decided that they should be entitled to receive, from the time they left their homes, and from funds provided by the two governments, a salary at the rate of £1,500 sterling per annum, in addition to necessary travelling and office expenses.[1] At one of the first meetings of the Commission, the Turkish delegation expressed the opinion that the salaries of the neutral members were "manifestly insufficient" and proposed that they be increased.[2] The Greek delegation seems to have been reluctant to have the Commission vote such increases, and proposed instead that reference should be made to the League of Nations. Mr. Ekstrand feared that the League of Nations would not be willing to reopen the question.[3] Finally it was decided to grant, in addition to the £125 per month allowed in Viscount Ishii's report, £75 per month as an allowance for quarters. The Presidents of the Greek and Turkish delegations were granted the same salary and allowance, and the other members of the Commission were granted a salary of £100 per month and an allowance for quarters of £50 per month. It was understood that the members of the two delegations were not

[1] League of Nations, *Official Journal,* November, 1923, p. 1312.
[2] Procès-Verbaux, i, 3d meet., October 10, 1923.
[3] Procès-Verbaux, i, 15th meet., November 5, 1923.

to receive full salary when the Commission was sitting in their own country.

§ 378. Salaries of personnel and other expenses. The substitutes for the neutral members and the Secretary-General of the Commission received £100 per month. The counsellors of the two delegations received £70 and the Greek and Turkish secretaries £60 per month. The other personnel of the Commission was paid as follows:

Two secretaries of the 1st class	£40	per month
" " " " 2d "	" 35	"
An archivist	" 40	"
A chief accountant	" 60	"
An auditor	" 60	"
Typists and stenographers	£8 to 40	"

The neutral Presidents of Sub-Commissions were paid at the rate of £50 per month for salary and an allowance for quarters which the Commission determined by taking into account the cost of living in the place where the Sub-Commission was located. The Greek and Turkish members of the Sub-Commissions were paid an allowance for quarters at the rate of £40 per month.

Travelling expenses were paid to members of the Mixed Commission and its personnel and to members of the Sub-Commissions for trips undertaken in the service. To cover such expenses a daily allowance was paid equal to 2% of the regular salary and allowance for quarters, plus the actual expenses of the trips.

§ 379. Payments and accounts. Because of the fluctuations of the English pound in the last part of 1923, it was decided to pay all salaries and allowances in dollars, beginning from January 1, 1924.[4]

A Financial Committee was appointed by the Commission, which dealt with all questions of the finances of the Commission and with its internal organization. This Committee decided finally on all questions concerning expenses of current administration. On all other questions it submited its resolutions to the plenary assembly of the Commission.

The accounts of the Commission were kept by a Greek

[4] Procès-Verbaux, i, 25th meet., December 18, 1923.

chief accountant and checked by a Turkish auditor. Every item of expenditure was referred to the former and all checks were countersigned by him. A quarterly financial statement was prepared by him and communicated to the two governments. Orders for payment were signed by the President of the Mixed Commission.

§ 380. **Budget of the Commission in 1924.** The first budget of the Mixed Commission, prepared for the year 1924 in December, 1923, amounted to $440,000.[5] It was, however, raised in June, 1924, to $548,436.[6] Its various items were as follows:

CHAPTER I

Monthly salaries and allowances for quarters of members of the Mixed Commission

(1) Salaries:			
5 Presidents @ $607	$ 3,035		
6 Members " 486	2,916		
3 Substitutes " 486	1,458		
4 Counsellors " 340	1,360		
(2) Allowances for quarters:			
5 Presidents @ $364	$ 1,820		
6 Members " 243	1,458		
Total	$12,047	Per yr.	$144,564

CHAPTER II

General Staff of the Mixed Commission

(3) 1 Secretary-General		$ 486		
1 Comptroller		292		
1 Chief Accountant		292		
2 First Secretaries @ $292		584		
4 Second " " 194		776		
4 Third " " 170		680		
1 Archivist		194		
1 Assistant Accountant		50		
1 Assistant Archivist		61		
5 Typists: 1 @	$ 85			
1 "	70			
1 "	58			
2 " $39	78			
		291		
1 Janitor		35		
Total		$ 3,741	Per yr.	$ 44,892

[5] Procès-Verbaux, i, 27th meet., December 28, 1923.
[6] Procès-Verbaux, v, 57th meet., June 18, 1924.

Chapter III

Rent, lighting, automobile, office furniture, etc.

(4) Rent, lighting, and heating	$ 500	
(5) Automobiles	970	
(6) Office furniture and printing	920	
(7) Telegrams, postage, and sundries	120	
Total	$ 2,510	Per yr. $ 30,120

Chapter IV

Travelling expenses and allowances, unforeseen expenses

(8) Travelling expenses and allowances	$ 2,000	
(9) Unforeseen expenses	2,000	
Total	$ 4,000	Per yr. $ 48,000

Chapter V

Sub-Commissions

(10) Salaries of Members:		
15 Presidents @ $243	$ 3,645	
Monthly allowances, 15 x $194	2,910	
30 Members @ $194	5,820	
(11) 30 Secretaries @ $61	1,830	
30 Functionaries @ $40	1,200	
(12) Office furniture and sundries	8,000	
	$23,405	Per yr. $280,860
Grand total		$548,436

§ 381. Subsequent budgets. At the end of 1924 most of the Sub-Commissions were dissolved. In the middle of 1925 there remained only the Sub-Commissions of Western Thrace and of Constantinople, which looked after the interests of the Moslems and Greeks established respectively in these two regions. The budget of the Mixed Commission was accordingly reduced in 1925 and 1926. However, in 1927 the Appraisal Committees were created to carry out the provisions of the Agreement of Athens.[7]

The budget for the six Appraisal Committees adopted in March, 1927, provided for an expenditure of $72,000 for eight months. The monthly budget for each Appraisal Committee was as follows: [8]

[7] See *supra,* p. 525.

[8] Procès-Verbaux, xi, 116th meet., March 19, 1927.

A neutral member	$ 350
A national member (Greek or Turk) working in his own country	200
A national member (Turk or Greek) working in the other country	250
A secretary	150
Travelling expenses	250
Local experts	200
Total for each Committee	$1,400 per month

In fact, the Committees were increased to twelve in the fall of 1927, and their work continued into 1929. The budget of the Commission for 1929 called for a monthly expenditure of $41,143, or a total of $493,716, which is not much below the budget for 1924.

§ 382. Total expenses of the Mixed Commission. No exact figures have been published for the expenditures of the Mixed Commission from October, 1923, when it began its work, to the present time. Taking into account the above two budgets for 1924 and 1929, and making allowances for the dismissal of personnel in 1925 and 1926 and in 1930, we may put the figure between $3,000,000 and $3,500,000 for the seven years of the work of the Commission ending October, 1930. The writer has not been able to obtain further figures of expenditure after October, 1930. At the time of writing (July, 1931) there remains little yet to be done by the Commission but it is safe to predict that the Commission will not have ended its work by the end of 1931. The expenditure of $300,000 in addition to the above until the dissolution of the Commission may undoubtedly be assumed.

This total, of course, does not represent all the cost to the two governments, for it does not cover the expenditures of the personnel of the two delegations, which were paid by the respective governments.

When it is considered how meagre have been the results obtained by the Mixed Commission during the seven years of its activity, it will be concluded that it was indeed a wasteful luxury for the two governments to maintain it for so long a time.

PART III

THE SETTLEMENT OF THE EMIGRANTS AND REFUGEES

CHAPTER XXXI

THE SETTLEMENT OF BULGARIAN EMIGRANTS AND REFUGEES [1]

§ 383. The problem of the settlement of emigrants and refugees in Bulgaria. In the first part of this study the re-

[1] The materials on which this chapter is based are chiefly contained in the *Official Journal* of the League of Nations, and particularly in the first sixteen Reports of the Commissioner of the League of Nations for the Settlement of Bulgarian Refugees, covering the period from September 15, 1926, to August 15, 1930, which have appeared in that *Journal* as follows:

Report	Number of the *Journal*	Pages
First	February, 1927	189-213
Second	April, 1927	526-535
Third	July, 1927	926-933
Fourth	October, 1927	1329-35
Fifth	February, 1928	247-253
Sixth	April, 1928	585-591
Seventh	July, 1928	1054-61
Eighth	October, 1928	1754-61
Ninth	January, 1929	183-195
Tenth	April, 1929	723-748
Eleventh	July, 1929	1207-18
Twelfth	November, 1929	1712-31
Thirteenth	June, 1930	683-694
Fourteenth	June, 1930	695-709
Fifteenth	September, 1930	1141-53
Sixteenth	November, 1930	1563-77

Our references to these Reports, which for brevity will be given in the concise form "Second Report, p. 526," etc., can readily be filled out from this table.

ciprocal emigration of minorities between Greece and Bulgaria and the liquidation of their properties were described and considered. It is now necessary to see how these emigrants were settled in their new countries. The question of the settlement of Greek emigrants from Bulgaria is inseparably connected with the larger question of the settlement of Greek refugees and emigrants from Turkey, and this is considered in the next chapter. The present chapter deals with the settlement in Bulgaria of Bulgarian emigrants and refugees from Greece and other countries.

We have seen above that the Bulgarian emigrants from Greece numbered about 96,000. While they far surpassed in number the refugees in Bulgaria from Greece, Jugoslavia, and Rumania, the problem of the settlement of the emigrants from Greece cannot be separated from the whole problem of the settlement of Bulgarian refugees.

The extent of this larger problem was first brought to the attention of the League of Nations by a letter of the Bulgarian government dated May 3, 1926, to the Secretary-General, submitted to the Council on June 10, 1926.[2] It was there stated that the Bulgarian government had on its hands some 38,000 refugee families, and that Bulgaria was unable to assimilate so large a number of refugees in a short space of time. Later, the Bulgarian government gave the number of refugees and emigrants needing assistance for settlement in Bulgaria as 220,000. The neighboring countries, Greece, Rumania, and Jugoslavia, challenged this assertion of the Bulgarian government, basing their information on official data published by the General Statistical Board of the kingdom of Bulgaria.[3] It was eventually found by the Commissioner of the League of Nations that the number to be settled did not exceed 125,000 persons or 31,271 families.[4]

The problem of the settlement of refugees in Bulgaria was different from that of Greece, where great masses arrived from

[2] League of Nations, *Official Journal,* July, 1926, pp. 884-886, 920-922, 1002-03.

[3] League of Nations, *Official Journal,* October, 1926, pp. 1243-46, 1335-38, 1343-46, 1391-94.

[4] Second Report, p. 528.

Asia Minor and Eastern Thrace in a short space of time.[5] The greater part of the refugees in need of relief in Bulgaria had been in the country for some years past, and the general problem was to confirm them in their settlements by completing and making permanent the provisional arrangements already made. Some of the refugees had settled themselves on small plots of land and erected adequate houses by their own efforts or with the assistance of the government, while others lived in huts, barns, or stables. Still others drifted toward the cities and found unskilled employment in factories and workshops. It was only needed to aid persons who had settled on lands provisionally, and to make complete arrangements for settling those refugees who were or might become agriculturists.

The Bulgarian government had not set up an adequate organization to take care of the settlement of the refugees. They were pretty much left to their own resources. Many of them drifted towards the villages of Greek emigrants from Bulgaria and settled in their properties. Settlement proceeded slowly, "mainly because of continual disputes of every sort regarding the land which it was desired to assign for this purpose. The communes, anxious to keep for themselves the available land on their own territory, did not always further the work; through political influence they sometimes succeeded in bringing it to a complete standstill. Such selfish conduct has in some localities, by preventing the satisfaction of most urgent needs, bred hostility and added to the refugees' distress." [6]

Moreover, it was observed, "many of the refugees are seriously handicapped by physical debility as a result of sickness (more especially malaria) and malnutrition. Their capacity for work has fallen considerably. . . . The infant mortality, according to the statistics collected by foreign charitable organizations, reaches in certain districts, the appalling figure of over 50 per cent." [7]

The League of Red Cross Societies carried on relief work.

[5] First Report, p. 189.
[6] Second Report, p. 529.
[7] First Report, p. 194.

At its soup kitchens more than 4000 people were fed daily; food was distributed to nearly 15,000 persons, while 4500 infants were cared for. The work of the International League of Red Cross Societies was repeatedly praised at the meetings of the Council of the League. At the meeting of March 10, 1927, M. Vandervelde, Rapporteur to the Council, pointed out that international action must necessarily be of a temporary character, and that it was for the National Red Cross of Bulgaria to take a hand in the work of assisting the refugees.[8]

§ 384. Negotiations of the Bulgarian government for a loan. In the letter referred to above, the Bulgarian government, after drawing the attention of the Council of the League to the difficult situation of the refugees, requested that a foreign loan be granted to Bulgaria, under the auspices of the League, to be used in assisting the refugees directly by advancing to them the necessary funds for the purchase of agricultural stock and implements and the erection of buildings, and in providing, by irrigation, draining, etc., suitable land for agricultural work and the establishment of the refugees.[9]

A favorable report was submitted to the Council by the Financial Committee and by the Rapporteur of the Council, M. Vandervelde, who testified, of his own experience, to the "painful and tragic impression" given him by the plight of the Bulgarian refugees. The Council adopted a resolution accepting the report of the Financial Committee, declaring its readiness to be associated with the scheme, and authorizing the President of the Council, on the recommendation of the Financial Committee, to take any necessary measures for the purpose proposed by the Committee.[10]

After some necessary agreements with the Inter-Allied Commission at Sofia and the Reparation Commission with regard to the securing of the proposed loan on certain revenues of the Bulgarian state, the President of the Council authorized the Bulgarian government to open negotiations concerning a

[8] League of Nations, *Official Journal,* April, 1927, pp. 385-386.
[9] League of Nations, *Official Journal,* July, 1926, pp. 1002-03.
[10] League of Nations, *Official Journal,* July, 1926, p. 884.

temporary advance of £400,000. These negotiations succeeded, and Bulgaria was able to obtain this sum in the form of a temporary advance from the Bank of England to the National Bank of Bulgaria. The scheme of the Financial Committee provided for the issue of a loan of two and a quarter million pounds sterling. At the meeting of the Council in September, 1926, the question of control was dealt with. The Council had approved the principle that it should have a strict and efficient control over the use of the funds and over the choice of land on which the refugees were to be established. It had also decided to enter into consultation with the representatives of states, members of the League, who were neighbors of Bulgaria, before fixing the final details of this control. These states insisted especially on the necessity of control over the use of the funds. They thought that the amount of expenditure required for the settlement of Bulgarian refugees was much less than was alleged by Bulgaria. They also challenged the figures as to the number of emigrants given by the Bulgarian government. They feared that, if left without control, the loan might have the effect of encouraging disorderly elements in Bulgaria. In particular the scheme for the construction of two railroads was objected to as having possibly a strategic character. In the end, the Financial Committee succeeded in drawing up a system of control satisfactory to all parties concerned.[11]

§ 385. Protocol for the settlement of Bulgarian refugees. This control was embodied in a draft Protocol for signature by Bulgaria. The Protocol provided for the appointment by the Council of a Commissioner, who was to report to the Council at least every three months. The proceeds of the loan were to be placed under the control of the Commissioner, and his approval was required for all the plans for establishing refugees. He was to be always free to refuse to release sums drawn from the loan if he were not sure that the sums already released had been expended in conformity with the conditions which he had authorized.[12]

[11] League of Nations, *Official Journal,* October, 1926, pp. 1243-44, 1335-38, 1391-94.

[12] League of Nations, *Official Journal,* October, 1926, pp. 1343-46.

The plan provided for certain precautions against establishing large numbers of refugees near the frontiers, and laid down a procedure by which the neighboring states would have the opportunity of taking part in the discussion of matters especially affecting their interests in the sense of Article 4 of the Covenant of the League of Nations. The question whether certain districts were suitable for the establishment of refugees, and the question of the construction of certain railways, on which depended the establishment of a considerable number of refugees, were left to be decided at a later time.[13]

The Council, on September 7, 1920, approved the report of the Financial Committee and the Protocol; it established a Commissariat, appointing M. René Charron, formerly of the General Commissariat for Hungary, as Commissioner for two years from October 31, 1926; and it expressed the hope that the loan might be successfully issued.[14]

The Protocol for the Settlement of Bulgarian Refugees was signed at Geneva by Bulgaria, September 8, 1926, and ratified November 23, 1926.[15]

§ 386. The Refugee Settlement Loan. The Refugee Settlement Loan was issued simultaneously at London and New York on December 21, 1926, with great success.[16] From it the sum of £2,247,201 8 *s.* 6 *d.* was to be used for settling the refugees. As provided by the Protocol for the Settlement of Bulgarian Refugees, the yield of the loan was paid into a special account at the National Bank of Bulgaria, which the Commissioner alone might control.

The Bulgarian government assigned to the service of the refugee loan, following a decision of the Inter-Allied Commission at Sofia which waived the Reparation first charge, the net revenue from the match monopoly and certain excise

[13] League of Nations, *Official Journal,* October, 1926, p. 1244.

[14] League of Nations, *Official Journal,* October, 1926, p. 1246.

[15] League of Nations, *Official Journal,* December, 1926, p. 1599.

[16] The loan was at 7 per cent and was to be redeemed not later than January 1, 1967. It was offered to the public at 92 per cent. The net yield amounted to £2,873,091. Of this £625,889 11*s.* 6*d.* was used to satisfy the claim of the holders of Bulgarian Treasury Bills issued in France in 1912 and 1913. See Second Report, p. 526. Again, as in the case of the Greek Refugee Loan (see *infra,* p. 637) the Great Powers did not give their consent to the Loan without extracting advantages entirely unrelated to the loan.

duties.[17] A ministerial decree of October 7, 1926, provided for the opening at the National Bank of a tied 'Assigned Reserves' account. The receipts were paid into the National Bank and all transactions in connection with this account were subject to the indorsement of the Commissioner. A law amending the Statutes of the National Bank in compliance with recommendations of the Financial Committee was passed on November 5, 1926.[18] Under the provisions of the Protocol for the Settlement of Bulgarian Refugees, the Council had undertaken to appoint Trustees to represent the interests of the bondholders of the Refugee Settlement Loan. On the proposal of the Financial Committee, three Trustees were appointed on December 10, 1926.[19]

The annual amount required for the service of the loan was about 170,000,000 leva. The receipts from the assigned reserves far exceeded this amount. The excess for the year 1929-30 was about 200%, the receipts being 515,009,911 leva.[20]

§ 387. The Bulgarian frontier zone. The Protocol provided that as a rule refugees should not be settled within a zone of 50 kilometres from the frontier between Bulgaria and the neighboring states, Greece, Jugoslavia, and Rumania. Exceptions to this rule were to be allowed on report of the Commissioner and by agreement between the Financial Committee and the representatives of the countries concerned. The Commissioner of the League of Nations did, indeed, recommend such exceptions in view of general and special considerations.[21]

The prohibited zones on the three frontiers represented approximately 57,000 square kilometres out of a total area of Bulgaria of 103,000 square kilometres. Bulgaria is poor in arable land, and the average density of population in 1920 was only 48 per square kilometre, while in cultivable regions the density reached 136. It was desired to avoid over-populating

[17] The excise duties on salt and alcohol. To these others were provisionally added by the Bulgarian government.

[18] First Report, pp. 193, 196-205.

[19] Mr. Bianchini, Sir Herbert Lawrence, and Mr. Markus Wallenberg. See League of Nations, *Official Journal,* February, 1927, p. 158.

[20] Fifteenth Report, p. 1142.

[21] First Report, pp. 181-183; Second Report, p. 515.

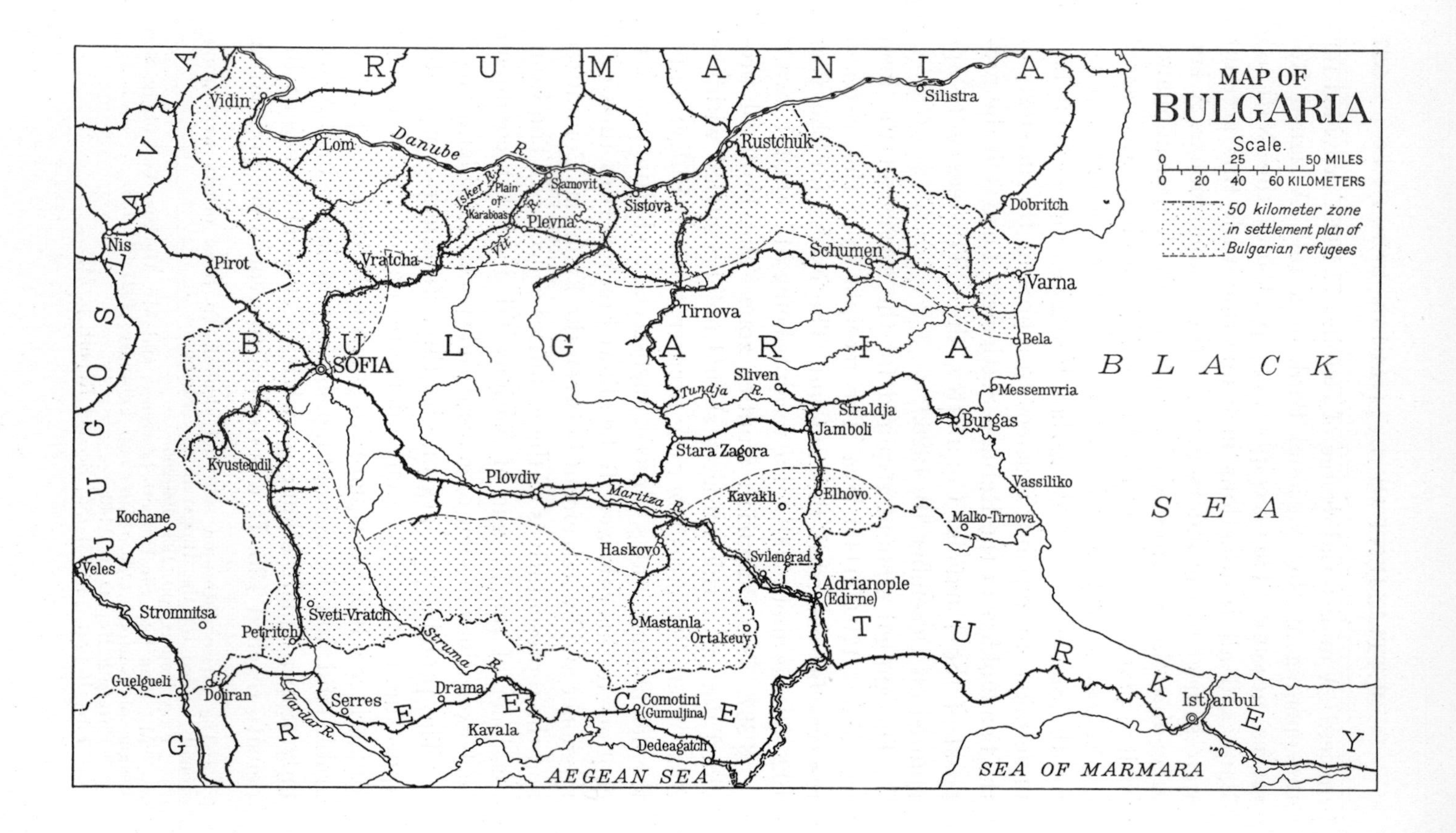
MAP OF
BULGARIA
Scale.
0 25 50 MILES
0 20 40 60 KILOMETERS
50 kilometer zone in settlement plan of Bulgarian refugees
RUMANIA
JUGOSLAVIA
BULGARIA
TURKEY
GREECE
BLACK SEA
AEGEAN SEA
SEA OF MARMARA
Danube R.
Isker R.
Vit R.
Tundja R.
Maritza R.
Struma R.
Vardar R.
Plain of Karaboas
Vidin
Lom
Samovit
Sistova
Rustchuk
Silistra
Dobritch
Varna
Bela
Schumen
Plevna
Vratcha
Nis
Pirot
SOFIA
Tirnova
Sliven
Straldja
Jamboli
Messemvria
Burgas
Stara Zagora
Plovdiv
Kyustendil
Kochane
Veles
Stromnitsa
Petritch
Sveti-Vratch
Guelgueli
Doiran
Serres
Drama
Kavala
Comotini (Gumuljina)
Dedeagatch
Mastanla
Ortakeuy
Haskovo
Kavakli
Elhovo
Svilengrad
Adrianople (Edirne)
Vassiliko
Malko-Tirnova
Istanbul

the cultivable areas. It was also necessary that refugees should be settled as far as possible on land presenting conditions similar to those under which they had lived hitherto. Many refugees had already settled within the 50-kilometre zone, and their establishment there could be completed and rendered definitive at a small cost. Any attempt to transfer them would result in waste; and, moreover, they would be unwilling to leave.

With regard especially to the Rumanian frontier zone,[22] there was the Danube, for over 400 kilometres without a bridge, which formed a natural boundary of over two kilometres in average breadth. Over 3000 refugee families had settled in the zone, and two-thirds of them had already installed themselves in such a manner that they needed little help for their definitive settlement. Moreover, a considerable amount of arable land was available in the zone between Lom and Sistova, a distance of about 170 kilometres.[23]

In the Greek frontier zone from Nevrokop on the west to the Maritza on the east the zone included about 6000 refugee families. For a considerable distance the frontier runs along the crest of a mountain chain the summits of which are 1000 to 2000 metres high.[24] In the region of Mastanla, north of Western Thrace, only one road crossed the frontier. It was a very sparsely populated region. In the Ortakeuy and Svilengrad section, farther east, several roads crossed the frontier. These regions were suitable for the intensive cultivation of tobacco and other crops. There were in this part of the zone large arable areas, calculated at over 100,000 decares. By reason of the fertility of the soil, it was estimated that 15 decares could be allowed to each family and would be sufficient to maintain it. The part of the district of Svilengrad on the left of the Maritza, which, although within the 50-kilometre zone,

[22] See map on page 598.

[23] Lom is on the Danube, sixty miles below the point where the frontiers of Bulgaria, Jugoslavia, and Rumania meet; Sistova is a like distance from the point where the frontiers between Bulgaria and Rumania turns from the Danube to the southeast.

[24] These mountains are Dospat Dagh, Kushlar Dagh, Kartal Dagh, Tokatjik Dagh. From Kutchuk Derbend to the Maritza the mountains are not high.

touched the Greek frontier only for a few kilometres, was extremely fertile, suitable for the rearing of silkworms and comprising a considerable amount of vacant arable land. It was proposed to settle in this area 2828 families, 1114 of which were to be new settlements. Colonel Siefvert, of the Swedish army, who was assisting in the reorganization of the frontier guards on the Greco-Bulgarian frontier, remarked that while formerly in the Ortakeuy district Bulgarian refugees from Greece used to make incursions into Greek territory, and professional brigands still committed occasional outrages on both sides of the border, the Svilengrad region was much quieter, largely because the Maritza formed a barrier difficult to cross and easy to guard.[25]

In the Jugoslavian frontier zone, between Vidin on the north and Petritch on the south, about 4000 refugee families were installed at a distance of less than 50 kilometres from the boundary. Of these, 2500 families were still in a very precarious situation. Little available land was included in this zone, therefore no special exception was asked with respect to it.[26]

§ 388. Settlements allowed in the frontier zone. After several conferences, an agreement was reached between the Financial Committee, representatives of the countries concerned, and the Commissioner of the League of Nations, as to settlements within the 50-kilometre frontier zone. As a result, the Council adopted a resolution on December 7, 1926,[27] which maintained the principle of the 50-kilometre zone, but provided for the following exceptions.

(1) Refugees less than 50 kilometres from the frontiers, living under material conditions which could not be considered satisfactory, should be provided with land for their settlement elsewhere than in the zone, in so far as the Commissioner should find it possible.

(2) Refugees of Rumanian origin might be settled in the zone between Lom and Sistova-Bela, as far south of the Danube as possible. To this district might be transferred

[25] Second Report, p. 515.
[26] First Report, pp. 182-183.
[27] League of Nations, *Official Journal,* February, 1927, pp. 122, 174, 187.

refugees living in the 50-kilometre zone along the land frontier between Bulgaria and Rumania.

(3) In the district of Mastanla, bordering the Greek frontier to the north of Comotini, owing to the natural obstacles which separated this district from Thrace, new settlements were allowed at a distance of more than 10 kilometres from the frontier, with the exception that refugees of Greek origin could not be settled at a distance of less than 15 kilometres from the frontier, and with the qualification that the density of the settlements should decrease as the limit of 10 kilometres was approached.

(4) As regards the districts of Ortakeuy and Svilengrad, bordering on the eastern parts of Western Thrace, the question of an exception was reserved. The Commissioner was instructed to study the possibility of settling in areas away from these districts refugees from the neighboring parts of Thrace living in these districts under unsatisfactory conditions and close to the frontier. The Commissioner reported again on this question at the session of the Council in March, 1927.[28] On the proposal of the Financial Committee, the Council adopted a resolution allowing no exception to the rule against new establishment of refugees within the 50-kilometre zone in the district of Ortakeuy and in the part of the district of Svilengrad on the right of the Maritza. A number of families already installed there under unsatisfactory conditions were to be transferred elsewhere. As regards the part of the district of Svilengrad on the left of the Maritza, which is only contiguous with the Greek frontier for a few kilometres and for the rest marches on the Turkish frontier, new establishments might be made, but no family coming from any part of Greece was to be settled at a distance less than 10 kilometres from the Greek frontier.

§ 389. The general plan of settlement. When the Council of the League in September, 1926, appointed the Commissioner for the Settlement of Refugees in Bulgaria, it was understood and was provided in the Protocol (article VII, paragraph 1) that a general plan of settlement should be

[28] League of Nations, *Official Journal,* April, 1927, pp. 385, 511.

drawn up as soon as possible, so that the work could be carried on speedily and systematically.

In the meantime a programme of urgent work was to be executed to provide for the more pressing needs before the winter, and in particular to distribute seed for the autumn sowings in order to secure a first crop the next year. This was made possible by the advance of £400,000 by the Bank of England, which was repaid later from the yield of the loan. Seed was distributed to about 3000 families.[29]

At the same time the necessary information was collected for the drawing up of a general plan of settlement. As already stated, prior to the intervention of the League no adequate organization for this purpose was in existence in Bulgaria. In accordance with article VI of the Protocol, the Bulgarian Law for the Settlement of Refugees of December 14, 1926,[30] set up an organization which was to be the sole authority responsible for the settlement of refugees. Mr. Sarafoff, a banker and former General Manager of Railways, was appointed by the Bulgarian government as Director-General.

In his second report to the Council of the League, covering the period from November 15, 1926, to February 15, 1927,[31] the Commissioner, M. Charron, announced that the general plan of settlement was ready, after the General Directorate had succeeded in collecting the necessary information and statistics. The plan included a census of the families in need of relief; the definition of the relief to be granted to each family; the amount of land available and the work to be done in preparing it; lastly, an approximate estimate of the cost of settlement under each of these items. The plan was to be published in Bulgaria, with the name of each family in need of relief and the place where the family was to be settled. Thus every refugee would know where he was to be installed, how he was to be installed, what facilities for work would be provided, and what were his rights and obligations.

The summary of the plan was as follows. The number of families to be assisted reached 31,271, not including 372 fam-

[29] First Report, pp. 189-191.
[30] First Report, pp. 205-213; Second Report, pp. 532-535.
[31] Second Report, pp. 526-535.

ilies the settlement of which was still under consideration. The Mixed Commission for the Greco-Bulgarian Emigration had found that each family consisted, on the average, of three persons. By reckoning each of the above 31,271 families as containing four persons on the average, we have a total of 125,084 persons.

There existed 15,262 houses available for refugees, of which 2068 were in need of repair. The estimated cost of repair amounted to 14,616,000 leva. It was expected that 16,019 new houses would be built at an expenditure of 480,-270,000 leva. The type of houses to be constructed was similar to the ordinary Bulgarian type. An expenditure of 40,000 leva for a house was estimated which was not consistent with the estimated total expenditure for house-building just given. The agricultural material to be distributed to refugees was to comprise 23,257 ploughs, 7645 harrows, and 19,758 carts, of a total estimated cost of 138,904,600 leva. To a number of refugees fishing tackle was to be distributed, at a total cost of 7,000,000 leva, and to others live stock, 28,564 head, for which the expenditure was estimated at 171,384,000 leva.

The total area of land included in the plan was about 1,750,000 decares (432,425 acres). This land was at the disposal of the Agrarian Fund [32] of the government. Part of this total area could not be utilized, either because its preparation would be too costly or because of its situation. The remainder also needed preparation in the way of surveying, clearing, deforestration, etc., and the draining of marshes in the district of Burgas and along the banks of the Danube. The expenditure on this account was estimated at 408,917,331 leva.

§ 390. The land question and the allocation of holdings. The land question was of vital importance. The first concern of the Bulgarian refugee was to obtain possession of land rather than of a house. "Love of the soil is responsible to a large exent for this sentiment, but it is also undoubtedly due

[32] This was formed from expropriated large land estates, lands owned by the National Bank and the Agricultural Bank, government and communal lands, etc. See Leo Pasvolsky, *Bulgaria's Economic Position.* Washington, 1930, p. 206.

to a feeling of confidence that they can, by the work of their own hands, support both themselves and their families."

The object of the settlement plan was "the formation of small agricultural holdings in adequate plots of arable land belonging to the Bulgarian Government." The basis, then, of the plan was the allocation of land to refugees. Only after the refugee was granted permanent possession of land could a house be built for him and material or live stock supplied to him.

The Geneva Protocol for the Settlement (article VIII) provided that at least 1,320,000 decares of land suitable for agricultural settlement, exclusive of pasture land, the unencumbered property of the Bulgarian Government, were to be provided for the settlement of refugees. On August 1, 1927, the Government had clear title only to 309,431 decares.[33] Of these, 280,000 decares belonged to Greek emigrants who had left Bulgaria. There was litigation affecting lands of an area of 1,400,000 decares. The communes, in a selfish spirit, resisted the attempts of the government to take away unoccupied or vacant land for the purpose of settlement of refugees. In many places there was no land register or land survey record which could be used for purposes of reference and for the avoidance of lengthy litigation. Moreover, side by side with the settlement of refugees, the government was allocating land to native peasants. All land intended for allocation under both schemes was held by the organization in charge of the latter work, which supplied the Refugee Settlement Commission with land for the settlement of the refugees. A transfer once made under the Refugee Settlement scheme might be called in question at a later time. Government agencies sometimes prevented refugees from sowing lands granted them by other government agencies. This state of affairs gave rise to strongly unpleasant feelings between the refugees and the local inhabitants.[34]

The total of 1,750,000 decares of land included in the settlement plan by the Bulgarian government really consisted

[33] Fourth Report, p. 1332.
[34] League of Nations, *Official Journal,* January, 1929, p. 186.

in a list showing only the communes and categories (meadows, fields, marshland, etc.) to which the land belonged. No topographical documents in regard to this area existed. In order to allocate land it was necessary to identify it on the spot and establish its boundaries. The measuring and dividing up of the land was intrusted to the Bulgarian Geographical Institute. Surveying parties were formed and the agencies of the General Directorate for the Settlement of Refugees distributed the plots of land as they became available. The work of the Institute was carried on amid innumerable difficulties, including lack of means of communication and the more or less active hostility of the local peasants. Later, a private group of engineers was employed to do surveying work. Great difficulties arose with respect to property left by the Greek emigrants. The local inhabitants had shown an inclination to take possession of such land. The Mixed Commission on Greco-Bulgarian Emigration helped matters by placing at the disposal of the General Directorate the details relating to the property of emigrants. Thus it has been possible to identify the lands and to oust illegal occupants. This involved great loss of time, since each case required separate consideration and the boundaries of an exceedingly large number of small plots must be fixed. Bulgarian peasants preferred to have small plots of land scattered in various parts of the village rather than single large parcels of land. The reason was that in many parts of Bulgaria the crops were often destroyed by floods and hail, especially at the end of the season, and the peasants had noted from experience that only parts of a village might suffer from storms. Of course the best thing would have been to have an adequate system of insurance, but this was still unknown in the country.

In addition, much uncultivated land required mechanical ploughing before it could be worked by the refugees. It was either stiff clay soil, a lighter clay soil containing roots and covered with heather or oak scrub, or clayey soil, covered with shrubs and coarse scrub.[35] It required either powerful tractors to break it up for cultivation, or special machinery to break

[35] Fourth Report, p. 1332.

up the soil to a sufficient depth to allow of the removal of the roots. Contracts were entered into by the General Directorate with private owners for the mechanical ploughing of lands in various localities. Refugees also were given advances for the clearing of forest or heath land by their own effort.

The sixteenth report of the Commissioner of the League of Nations, covering four years of the work of settlement to August 15, 1930, gives the following table showing the allocation of land.[36]

Department	Land surveyed (decares)	Land allotted (decares)	Number of families	Average area allotted (decares)
Burgas	549,393	486,586	11,767	41.35
Varna	68,625	61,098	1,555	39.29
Vidin	8,929	8,929	282	31.66
Petritch	120,663	111,023	4,962	22.37
Vratcha	22,621	21,872	639	34.17
Plovdiv	24,505	23,971	1,290	18.58
Plevna	18,761	17,201	517	33.27
Rustchuk	49,108	32,449	860	37.73
Stara Zagora	14,051	12,886	395	32.62
Tirnovo	17,111	17,012	455	37.39
Haskovo	156,876	131,729	3,012	43.73
Schumen	41,364	39,360	1,136	34.65
Mastanla	82,356	52,579	1,472	35.72
Total	1,174,363	1,016,695	28,342	35.87

By August, 1930, the survey operations had been almost completed. Plans were drawn up for each plot, which were attached to the deeds of ownership handed to the refugees.[37] The final appraisal of the land distributed was begun in May, 1929, by the Land Valuation Committee. The land was divided for purposes of appraisal into five categories according to quality. The value differed also according to the geographical situation, the local value of the land, proximity to markets, and means of transport. The general average was 700 leva per decare, which was a very moderate figure.[38]

§ 391. Construction of buildings. It was originally estimated that 16,000 new houses would have to be erected for

[36] Sixteenth Report, p. 1566.
[37] *Ibid.*
[38] Thirteenth Report, p. 686.

the settlement of refugee families. After about two and a half years, or by May 15, 1929, only 1831 houses had been built and 2854 more were contracted for.[39] There were several reasons for the slowness of the work.

As a very large number of refugees were settled in villages of the district of Burgas or of other districts, often at the rate of two or three families in each village, no building programme of a large scope could be carried out in each locality. Materials had to be transported to each village for these scattered undertakings under very inadequate conditions of transport. Besides, work on a large scale was beyond the capacity of local contractors. The market for building timber proved limited. In some cases contractors had to obtain supplies from Rumania for work under construction in the extreme south of Bulgaria. The Commissioner was justified in deploring the fact that "abundant local resources were not more judiciously exploited." [40] Moreover, the building programme was necessarily dependent on the allocation of land. Naturally, houses could be built only after lands were granted to refugees to secure their livelihood.

For agricultural holdings a house is insufficient for the needs of the peasant without a shed or a stable for housing cattle and storing crops. The construction of such buildings could be left to be done by the refugees themselves, but it was felt that their construction by the General Directorate would be preferable from the point of view of the preservation of the cattle, of hygienic considerations, and of the general appearance of the new quarters. Refugees asked, generally, for sheds and stables in addition to the houses.

The general method of construction was by private contractors on the acceptance of tenders by the General Directorate. To make up for the failure of builders to fulfil their

[39] To these must be added the following:

Sheds		Byres	
Completed	Contracted for	Completed	Contracted for
1444	2107	1441	2556

Eleventh Report, p. 1209.

[40] Ninth Report, pp. 185-186.

contracts, the experiment of construction on a monopoly basis by the General Directorate was applied on a small scale. In a very few cases the refugees received cash advances and themselves made the necessary arrangements regarding the work and the supply of material.

At the end of the season of 1927, on the basis of contracts concluded until that time, the available cost of a house was about 29,453 leva or £43. The total cost, including shed and byre, then reached 44,200 leva. By May, 1929, the increase in the cost of labor and materials raised this cost to 66,000 to 68,000 leva, or about £100.[41]

As the erection of buildings by the General Directorate progressed slowly, many refugees built their own houses. In the meantime the Mixed Commission on Greco-Bulgarian Emigration made payments to emigrants from Greece, and the latter were able to finance the construction. By August 15, 1930, there were applications for 9769 houses instead of the originally estimated 16,000. The number of houses built by the above date reached 4465 and 4282 were in process of construction, while 1022 were still to be built. In addition, the total of sheds and byres built reached 3383 and 3908 respectively, while 2890 more sheds and 3193 more byres had been contracted for.[42]

§ 392. Distribution of seed, cattle, and supplies. To refugees who were being settled and who possessed no land prior to their settlement, seed was distributed. Until August 15, 1930, a total of 10,170,577 kilogrammes of seed was distributed, of a value of 65,189,112 leva.[43]

The agricultural holdings were also provided with cattle. The General Directorate purchased cattle at fairs and markets in Bulgaria, the refugees themselves often choosing them, under the superintendence of the departmental veterinary surgeons. Oxen, cows, buffalos, and horses were supplied. These animals were chiefly used for ploughing. The land assigned to refugees had remained waste for many years and needed to be intensively worked. Besides, the live-stock were utilized as draught

[41] Eleventh Report, p. 1209.
[42] Sixteenth Report, p. 1565.
[43] *Ibid.*

animals.[44] By August 15, 1930, the total number distributed was:

	Number	Value in leva
Horses and mules	5,943	53,352,887
Oxen and cows	12,183	71,763,110
Buffaloes	2,520	15,445,551

The total value reached 140,561,548 leva.[45]

Supplies necessary for refugees was also allotted by the General Directorate, such as carts, wagons, ploughs, harrows, and fishing gear. Carts, wagons, and harrows were supplied by the Bulgarian craftsmen. The ploughs were purchased abroad after tenders had been invited. It appears, however, that modern ploughs, although carefully selected in view of local conditions in Bulgaria, aroused no great enthusiasm among the refugees, who seemed to prefer the wooden ploughs made by themselves. The Commissioner noted that "this is by no means an isolated example of the hostility of the Bulgarian peasant to modern agricultural methods." [46]

The Black Sea fisheries belonged before 1924 to the Greek coastal population, and Greeks were practically the only people who engaged in that industry. The Directorate made an effort to interest the refugees in fishing. It appears that the results, in the region of Messemvria at least, proved quite successful.[47] A total of 219 refugee families engaged in fishing in the small Black Sea ports. For farm material, fishing gear was substituted in the case of these refugees, that is, herring nets, drag-nets, tunny nets, boats, and sailing boats. By August 15, 1930, the General Directorate had allotted various supplies as follows:

		Value in leva
Implements		
Ploughs:	7,698	10,363,413
Harrows:	2,533	1,658,578
Carts:	8,951	43,662,858
Fishing tackle		
Nets:	27	6,160,610
Boats:	64	
Motor boats:	3	
Total		61,845,489 [48]

[44] Third Report, p. 927; Fifth Report, p. 248.
[45] Sixteenth Report, p. 1565.
[46] Twelfth Report, p. 1714.
[47] *Ibid.*
[48] Sixteenth Report, p. 1565.

§ 393. **Campaign against malaria and syphilis.** A large number of refugees, about one-half of the whole, were settled in the district of Burgas, the great port of Bulgaria on the Black Sea. This district was not subject to the restrictions of the forbidden zone, and a large area of land was available there as a result of the emigration of the Greek minority. It included 333 villages. The plan called for the settlement of from two to thirty families in 248 of these villages; from thirty to one hundred families in 50 villages; and more than one hundred refugee families in each of twenty other villages. By August 15, 1930, 11,767 refugee families were settled on 486,586 decares of land in this district.

This region was full of marshes, and malaria was particularly rife. Many refugees were "horrified at the idea of settling in districts where they would be in danger of infection and death." The Health Section of the League of Nations sent there the Dutch Professor Swellengrebel, a member of the League Malaria Commission, who, after an exhaustive study of the subject, arrived at practical conclusions regarding medical assistance and the destruction of the larvae. The campaign against malaria was deemed to be one of the aspects of the refugee settlement. A great amount of quinine was acquired by the General Directorate and distributed to refugees. The Burgas Malariological Institute made laudable and successful efforts for putting down malaria. By means of propaganda in the schools, by posters, lectures, etc., by the distribution of quinine, regularization of small ponds and streams, filling up ditches, etc., confidence was established among the refugees in the district of Burgas. The Rockefeller Foundation also agreed to take part in the anti-malaria campaign. Its centre of work was the district of Petritch near the meeting-point of the Greco-Jugoslav-Bulgarian boundaries. The Commissariat's financial contribution consisted in maintaining six doctors and an anti-larval detachment and in supplying 251 kilogrammes of quinine annually. Later an anti-malaria centre was created by the Commissariat at Sveti-Vratch, north of Petritch. A total expenditure of 13,000,000 leva was contemplated, distributed over a period of three years ending December 31, 1929.[49]

At a later time, the Commissioner found that in certain districts of the province of Burgas, where there were large colonies of refugees, syphilis was present in a very acute form, having spread to a dangerous extent. At the request of the Bulgarian government, Dr. Mackenzie of the Health Section of the Secretariat of the League made a tour of inspection in the Vassiliko district, and preparatory measures were immediately taken with a view to drawing up a definite scheme. It was found that the population of districts officially recognized as infected exceeded 200,000. Five research parties were to begin medical investigations as soon as possible, and a course for training the staff was to be organized at Sofia by the Bulgarian Department of Public Health.[50]

§ 394. Drainage work. Also, the work of draining certain places was undertaken, as a means of destroying the larvae and as a supplement to agronomical work. The Bulgarian Ministry of Agriculture planned for the draining of several marshes. These plans were submitted to an expert of the Italian Government, Mr. Fornari, whose report was to the effect that they were inadequate and their cost would exceed the estimates.[51] The Commissioner, therefore, went carefully in this matter. Contracts for draining the two marshes of Messemvria and Straldja, of an area of 11,000 and 17,000 decares respectively, were concluded with Bulgarian contractors. Work began in the autumn of 1928. The estimated expenditure amounted to 12,636,000 and 15,075,000 leva.[52] The progress under these contracts was slow, and new arrangements were made in 1930 for the draining of the Straldja marsh.[53]

[49] Fifth Report, pp. 251-252; Sixth Report, p. 589; Seventh Report, p. 1060; Eighth Report, pp. 1759-60; Ninth Report, p. 188; Tenth Report, pp. 727-728; Twelfth Report, p. 1718; Thirteenth Report, p. 687; Fourteenth Report, p. 698; Fifteenth Report, p. 1145; Sixteenth Report, p. 1567.

[50] Thirteenth Report, pp. 687-688.

[51] Third Report, pp. 929-930; Fourth Report, pp. 1332-33; Fifth Report, p. 251; Sixth Report, p. 588.

[52] Ninth Report, p. 187; Tenth Report, p. 727.

[53] Thirteenth Report, pp. 686-687; Fifteenth Report, p. 1145; Sixteenth Report, p. 1567.

Of the same nature was the construction of a dike for the protection of the low-lying plain of Karaboas, which had been already begun by the Bulgarian government at its own expense. A satisfactory arrangement was made early in 1929 in respect to this work, which was intended to save from floods an area of arable land extending 24 kilometres along the banks of the Danube between the rivers Isker and Vit.[54] The work was put in the hands of the Compulsory Labor Organization, which operates under the law of Bulgaria whereby all able-bodied citizens are obliged, on reaching a certain age, to work for the state for a specific time.[55] The work was begun in July, 1929, with 2500 workmen. It was estimated that 170,000 decares of land would be reclaimed, 85,000 of which were to be utilized for the settlement of 2000 families. The land was of exceptionally high quality, giving in certain drained areas two crops a year. It was hoped that the work could be completed by February, 1931.[56]

§ 395. Means of communication and water supply. As is stated above, the settlement plan provided for the construction of a railway from Rakowsky to Mastanla in the centre of Southern Bulgaria. The governments of Jugoslavia, Rumania, and, especially, Greece made reservations in regard to this part of the plan, considering that the railway might have a strategic importance. The Inter-Allied Military Commission of Control at Sofia expressed the opinion that the proposed railway line could be used, like any other railway line, for the transport of troops and their supplies; but that none of the facilities mentioned in the scheme of equipment was designed exclusively for military use.[57] Eventually the construction was allowed.

The work on the railway line was carried out partly by the Bulgarian Railway Administration and partly, when work of special skill was involved, by contract. The section Rakowsky-Hascovo (23 kilometres) was opened to general

[54] Eighth Report, p. 1759; Tenth Report, p. 727.
[55] Ninth Report, p. 187.
[56] Twelfth Report, p. 1717; Fifteenth Report, p. 1145; Sixteenth Report, p. 1566.
[57] Third Report, pp. 931, 933.

traffic in December, 1927. The section Hascovo-Knijovnic (18 kilometres) was opened for traffic in December, 1928. The piercing of a tunnel 1120 metres long on this railway was completed in July, 1929.[58]

In certain parts of the centres where refugees were settled, the construction of roads was undertaken by the government. As some of these works were at a standstill, owing to lack of budgetary resources, the General Directorate for the Settlement of Refugees participated in the construction with the help of the loan funds. The Commissioner at first decided that only a section of the Vasiliko-Burgas road along the Black Sea coast, the completion of which was urgent in connection with the settlement of a large number of refugees in that district, should be constructed with the aid of the loan funds. Later, the question was reconsidered by the Commissioner, and the completion of two other roads in the district of Burgas with the aid of the loan funds was authorized: from Malko Tirnovo to Burgas and between Elhovo and Kavakli. These roads were completed in 1929. Two other roads were constructed in the same section by the Bulgarian government, so that at the end of 1929 the refugee colonies between Burgas, Vasiliko, and Malko Tirnovo possessed good roads, which were much needed for this region rich in forests. In the fall of 1928 the utilization of the loan for the completion of still another road, from Varna to Bela, was authorized by the Commissioner.[59]

As in the case of the Greek refugee settlement, in Bulgaria also a very serious difficulty to cope with in the creation of new colonies was the absence of available drinking water. In certain villages, peasants used for drinking the stagnant water of ponds. The inhabitants of other villages had to transport water from long distances. The Commissioner, in order to strengthen the new colonies and facilitate the success of isolated settlements in old villages, allocated a part of the funds to the supply of drinking water. A great number of

[58] Fifth Report, p. 251; Ninth Report, p. 187; Tenth Report, p. 727; Eleventh Report, p. 1210; Twelfth Report, p. 1717.

[59] Fourth Report, p. 1334; Sixth Report, p. 589; Ninth Report, p. 187; Thirteenth Report, p. 687.

pumping stations were thus set up and the plans included canalization and distribution works.[60]

§ 396. **Obligations of the refugees.** Refugees were charged with the cost of buildings, supplies, seed, cattle, etc., granted to them by the General Directorate. A Committee appraised the land allotted to them, and the value was charged against the refugees. The interest charges and the manner in which the refugees were to refund the cost of the relief granted them were set forth in articles 54 and 55 of the Law for the Settlement of Refugees. They were liable to the payment of interest on the value of their lands, houses, seed, live-stock, and material, at a rate equal to that of the loan, with the addition of one per cent to form a fund to provide against bad debts and of one-half per cent to remunerate the Agricultural Bank for its services, i.e., a rate of 8½%.

The payment of interest was to begin at the end of a period of two years reckoned from the date of signature of the contracts. As to the refunding of the capital, the value of the seed was to be paid during the third year; the value of the live-stock and material, in five yearly payments, beginning in the fourth year; the value of the houses in fifteen yearly payments, beginning in the ninth year; the value of the land, also beginning in the ninth year, and continuing for not longer than the period of amortization of the loan. Article 62 of the aforesaid law permitted refugees to anticipate payments in discharge of their liabilities. Such anticipatory payments amounted to 972,631 leva on May 1, 1928. Bulgarian emigrants from Greece who had received Bulgarian state bonds in payment for property left behind in Greece were to deliver these bonds in payment for the land assigned to them, being credited with their full face value.[61]

§ 397. **Expenditure for the settlement of refugees.** In accordance with article VII of the Protocol for the Settlement of Bulgarian Refugees, annual accounts of the expenditure of the loan were drawn up under the direction of the Commissioner and submitted through him to the Council of the

[60] Twelfth Report, pp. 1716-17; Fourteenth Report, p. 697.
[61] Second Report, pp. 210-211; Third Report, p. 534; Seventh Report, p. 1060.

League of Nations. The statement of December 31, 1929, which covers a period of three years and four months, showed that from the total of 985,064,310 leva placed at the disposal of the General Directorate a sum of 953,750,468.97 leva had been expended.

This had been disposed of as follows:

	Leva
Preparation of land (surveying, ploughing, clearing)...	50,199,841.40
Distribution of seed, live-stock and agricultural material	242,442,128.19
Buildings	270,143,888
Draining of marshes	15,680,692.69
Means of communication	229,955,020.49
Health work	9,858,835
Laying out of villages	617,434
Settlement expenses not yet accounted for	106,195,364.25
General expenses	28,657,468.95
Total	953,750,468.97 [62]

It is interesting to note that the general expenses as compared with total expenditure were only 3 per cent.

On January 31, 1930, the amounts released by the Commissioner and placed at the disposal of the Directorate General and the Bulgarian government amounted to 1,013,824,302 leva. At the time there remained still from the amount of the loan the following sums:

£586,263 16 *s.* 7 *d.* deposited in London
$611,526.54 " " New York, and
Leva 115,360,970 deposited with the National Bank of Bulgaria [63]

§ 398. Results of the settlement. The conditions of the problem of the settlement of refugees in Bulgaria, as dealt with above, complicated the work in view of the fact that many individual cases had to be considered. The execution of the plan of settlement has progressed much more slowly than was anticipated. The difficulties encountered are described in the reports of the Commissioner of the League of Nations. In this study sixteen of these reports covering the period from September 15, 1926, to August 15, 1930, were considered.[64] It was expected that only a little work would remain for the year 1931, such as the draining of the marshes,

[62] Fourteenth Report, p. 699.
[63] *Ibid.*, p. 707.
[64] See p. 591, note 1, for a list of these reports.

the construction of the railway, and the building of houses in the Karaboas district.[65]

The numerous advance repayments made by the refugees on the expenditure for settlement would seem to indicate the success of the refugee colonies. The Commissioner noted also the dogged perseverance and the capacity for hard work that are qualities of the Bulgarian people.[66] Success also was due to the fact that "the soil of Bulgaria is, generally speaking, highly fertile, and the various climatic zones make it possible to cultivate the different products of the soil satisfactorily in the different parts of the country." [67]

The work of the settlement of Bulgarian refugees had many important results. A humanitarian purpose was achieved by the relief granted to people in distress. An international aim was fulfilled by the wiping out of the main causes of dissatisfaction among people who had furnished recruits for the comitadji bands that made frequent incursions in the neighboring countries. The internal situation of Bulgaria was improved from the point of view of the troubles and hostile feelings at first existing between refugees and the local inhabitants. Lastly, the economic condition of Bulgaria was vastly ameliorated through the works of communication and health and the extension of the cultivated area. It was reported in 1928 that the area under cereals in Bulgaria increased as follows between 1926 and 1928:

1926	23,280,000	decares
1927	24,000,000	"
1928	24,496,000	"

that is, an increase of over 1,200,000 decares was noted within the space of two years.[68]

Very remarkable, in particular, is the great change that the settlement and the work done in connection with it had in the important section of Bulgaria on the Black Sea coast. Following the health work, the construction of roads, and the building of colonies, desolate areas which were repugnant to

[65] Fifteenth Report, p. 1143.
[66] Tenth Report, p. 724.
[67] Twelfth Report, p. 1714.
[68] Eighth Report, p. 1756.

refugees in 1926 became highly productive and densely populated regions in 1929.[69]

In the year 1929 Bulgaria suffered from the world crisis which affected the Eastern European agricultural countries. Agricultural production had remained stagnant and even diminished, owing to lack of credit facilities and to increasing difficulty in finding outlet. The striking fact was also noted that Bulgaria imported great amounts of cereals and vegetable seeds. This import jumped from 27,155,000 leva in 1928 to 340,806,000 in 1929. 50,000 tons of wheat, with a value of more than 300,000,000 leva, were imported from Jugoslavia. Apparently inadequate organization of marketing and distribution, and speculation, which maintained an artificial price level in Bulgaria, were liable for this increase in imports.[70] In 1930 the situation improved considerably. There was an increase in cereal production, which in the case of wheat reached 662,500 tons, or 73%, over the production of 1929. For the first seven months of 1930 exports exceeded imports by 786,231,000 leva, whereas in the corresponding period of 1929 the value of exports was 1,372,770,000 leva less than the value of imports. The exportable surplus of grain for 1930 was expected to be at least double that of the preceding year; but it was doubtful whether this could be disposed of at reasonable figures, in view of the depressed condition of grain prices.[71, 72]

[69] Twelfth Report, p. 1718.
[70] Fourteenth Report, pp. 704-705.
[71] Sixteenth Report, pp. 1572-73.
[72] On the general economic condition of Bulgaria see the excellent study of Leo Pasvolsky, *Bulgaria's Economic Position*. Washington, 1930. Pp. 409.

CHAPTER XXXII

THE GREEK REFUGEES SETTLEMENT

§ 399. The preliminary work of Dr. Nansen. The first to call attention to the desperate plight of the Greek refugees and to appeal for international help was Dr. Fritjof Nansen, the High Commissioner of the League of Nations for Russian Refugees at Constantinople. On September 18, 1922, President Edwards presented to the Third Assembly of the League a letter from Dr. Nansen, requesting permission to utilize the organization of the High Commissariat for Refugees in Constantinople for administering relief to the many thousands of Greek and Armenian refugees who had arrived there from Smyrna and Broussa. This letter was promptly considered by the Fifth Committee, and on the next day, on the report of that Committee, the Assembly adopted a resolution authorizing the above utilization of the Russian Refugee Organization and inviting the Council to consider placing a sum at the disposal of Dr. Nansen from the item "Unforeseen Expenditure" of the budget of the League.[1] The Council decided to put at the disposal of Dr. Nansen the sum of 100,000 Swiss francs.[2] Great Britain came forward with an offer of £50,000 on the condition that a similar amount should be contributed by other countries.[3] The problem at that time, as Dr. Nansen stated it, was to get the refugees away, if it were necessary, from Smyrna to some Greek island and to provide a shipload of flour to feed them for a period of fourteen days, until it would be decided what more could be done.[4]

Dr. Nansen sped to Constantinople, and, on October 11, 1922, sent a telegram to the Secretary-General of the League, informing him that the refugee problem was far more serious even than that presented to the Assembly. He found that

[1] League of Nations, *Records of the Third Assembly, Plenary Meetings,* i, pp. 123-125, 137-142.

[2] League of Nations, *Official Journal,* November, 1922, pp. 1195-96.

[3] League of Nations, *Records of the Third Assembly, Plenary Meetings,* i, pp. 226-231, 378.

By September 30, 1922, the following additional contributions had been paid or promised:

Canada	£5000	New Zealand	£1000	Spain	£2000
Norway	1000	Denmark	1000		
Sweden	1000	Greece	5000		

Later Japan contributed £1036, Brazil £1000, and Switzerland £625. The Polish government made a gift of thirty large military tents for the accommodation of refugees, and the Belgian government provided 1000 tents and 1000 blankets. See League of Nations, *Official Journal,* January, 1923, p. 126.

[4] League of Nations, *Records of the Third Assembly Plenary Meetings,* i, pp. 228-229. The Assembly adopted a resolution, proposed by Sir James Allen, the delegate of New Zealand, to the effect that "its members will at once place the situation before their respective governments, recommending an immediate and adequate financial contribution to Dr. Nansen's organization." *Ibid.,* p. 231. It also adopted a resolution expressing "the unanimous wish of the Assembly for an early restoration of peace." *Ibid.,* pp. 295-296.

there were probably no fewer than 750,000 refugees, the greater part of whom were women and children, scattered over every part of Greece, Thrace, and the Islands. "The evacuation of the refugees from Asia Minor was carried out with admirable thoroughness and efficiency, and undoubtedly saved innumerable lives." He spoke of the help given by the Greek government and the relief agencies to keep the refugees alive, but he thought that further help on a large scale was needed if a great catastrophe was to be avoided. He concluded with an urgent appeal to the public opinion of the world for its fullest support.[5, 6]

In November, 1922, Dr. Nansen returned to Geneva and reported, in the first place, with regard to his negotiations with the two governments for the reciprocal emigration of the racial minorities of the two countries. These are described above.[7] He then described the situation of the refugees in Greece and Asia Minor as he had investigated it during the month of October.[8]

The situation of the Turkish population of Asia Minor, although undoubtedly serious, could, according to Dr. Nansen, be taken care of by the Turkish authorities without great assistance from outside. Certain urgent measures of relief had been already taken for these people. The refugees in Greece numbered not less than 900,000, 50,000 among these being Armenians. One-third of the refugees were from Eastern Thrace and the remainder from Asia Minor. Most of the former left their homes after the Armistice of Mudania and were in comparatively good condition. They had some movable property and some money. "The refugees from Asia Minor, on the other hand, have left their homes with such precipitation that they had no other possessions of any kind than the light summer clothes which they wear. They urgently require not only shelter but also winter clothing and blankets to enable them to face the severity of the coming winter; they

[5] League of Nations, *Official Journal,* November, 1922, p. 1141.

[6] Mention should be made here of the wonderful assistance and relief work of the American National Red Cross and the American Near East Relief. See as to this, Charles B. Eddy, *Greece and the Greek Refugees,* p. 53.

[7] See *supra,* p. 338.

[8] See League of Nations, *Official Journal,* January, 1923, pp. 133-136.

are also without any money with which to supply themselves with food."

The Greek government, he went on to say, "has made great efforts to distribute these refugees throughout the country in such a way as to permit of their absorption by the local population." The American Red Cross was performing a great work by bringing help in the form of food and other direct relief. But Dr. Nansen pointed out the great need of shelter and clothing, and the serious risk of epidemics, which threatened not only Greece but the whole of Southern Europe. After mentioning the great efforts of the Greek government "to deal with the situation and to deal with it upon constructive lines," and calling to mind that the problem was not merely one of immediate relief but of settling the refugees and absorbing them into the economic life of Greece, Dr. Nansen proposed that an international loan, made, perhaps, through the advice of the League of Nations, should be provided for.

Lastly, he called attention to the report that 250,000 more Greek and 100,000 Armenian refugees from Asia Minor were moving towards the coast to take refuge in Europe, as destitute as the other refugees from Asia Minor, that is to say, with nothing but the clothes they wore. He declared that if this exodus should take place, the consequences would be grave in the extreme, and ended with the impassionate plea: "I cannot too strongly insist that the support and the assistance of the world at large will be necessary to cope with these desperate problems."

§ 400. The proposal for a Refugee Settlement Loan. At the session of the Council in February, 1923, Dr. Nansen presented a new report describing the relief work carried out until that time. The condition of the refugees had become steadily and universally worse. Vast numbers of refugees were "still only fed on famine rations." A series of feeding camps were organized in Western Thrace, where 10,000 refugees were being fed. The appeal to the world at large was finding response. Fourteen hundred crates of clothes had been received. But the Macedonian winter had caused intense suffering among the refugees, and great numbers had died from illness caused by exposure. The Council voted to set aside 50,000 Swiss francs from the item "Unforeseen Expenses" of the League budget, in order to enable Dr. Nansen to fulfil the various administrative engagements which he had assumed. At the same time the Greek government, through Mr. Politis, put forward as its own proposal the suggestion of Dr. Nansen for an international loan to Greece for the settlement of the refugees. The Council referred the proposal of Mr. Politis to the Financial Committee of the League for examination and report.[9] At the next meeting of the Council, in April, 1923, a Sub-Committee was appointed, consisting of the British, French, and Italian members of the Council, with authority to invite the Greek government to add a fourth member. This Sub-Committee was to receive the reports of the Financial Committee, which was examining the practicability of floating a loan on the basis of the securities which Greece could offer.[10] The High Commissariat of Refugees was to prepare a general plan for enabling refugees to be settled in Greece on a self-supporting basis.[11]

In the meantime the great catastrophe that had threatened the refugees was averted by the very generous help of relief societies, especially the American relief societies. The Americans during the last months of 1922 and the first half of 1923 were feeding from 500,000 to 850,000 people. At the same time a representative of the United States, Colonel Logan, was assisting the Sub-Committee appointed by the Council to consider the scheme for the settlement of the refugees. The Council, at the session of July, 1923, adopted a resolution declaring that the securities offered by the Greek government appeared to be suitable as a basis for the negotiation of a loan. If the Greek government succeeded in arranging a loan for the settlement of the refugees, the Council would be willing to assist in organizing the administration of the funds produced by the loan.[12]

[9] League of Nations, *Official Journal,* March, 1923, pp. 234-235, 383-386.
[10] With regard to the negotiations for the loan see also Henri Morgenthau, *I was sent to Athens,* New York, 1929, pp. 175 ff.
[11] *Ibid.,* June, 1923, pp. 602-603, 696-703.
[12] League of Nations, *Official Journal,* August, 1923, pp. 903-904, 1014-15.

§ 401. Protocol for the Settlement of Refugees. The Sub-Committee approved a Protocol and Organic Statutes in connection with the refugees settlement scheme, and these were approved by the Council at its meeting in September, 1923.[13] The Protocol, entitled "Protocol Relating to the Settlement of Refugees in Greece and the Creation for this Purpose of a Refugees Settlement Commission," was signed by the representative of Greece, Mr. A. Michalacopoulos, on September 29, 1923.[14] It consisted of fourteen articles, the effect of which was the following:

The Greek government undertook to establish a Refugees Settlement Commission,[15] to possess the constitution, capacity, and functions set forth in the Organic Statutes annexed to the Protocol and forming an integral part thereof. The municipal law of Greece was to be brought into agreement with the Statutes and was not to be modified subsequently without the consent of the Council. The government was to assign to the Commission at least 500,000 hectares of land suitable, in the opinion of the Commission, for the settlement of refugees. This land was to be held by the Commission as its absolute property. According to the amendment of the Protocol adopted in September, 1924, land not included in the minimum of 500,000 hectares might be subject to ordinary servitudes and to obligations arising out of rights acquired by tenants on shares and similar holders. The Commission could settle refugees also (*a*) on land of Moslems subject to exchange, even before the Greek government became *de jure* owner thereof; (*b*) on land requisitioned by the government or in process of expropriation; (*c*) on land taken on lease by the Greek government, when the lease was perpetual and it was transferred to the Commission; or (*d*) on land of which the government was not the owner, but in respect of which

[13] *Ibid.*, November, 1923, pp. 1356-57.

[14] *Ibid.*, pp. 1506-10. At the close of the first year of the work of the Refugees Settlement Commission experience pointed to the desirability of certain modifications in the Protocol and the Statutes. These were adopted in September, 1924, as proposed by the Greek Government. *Ibid.*, November, 1924, pp. 1308, 1558 ff.

[15] After a short time this title became "Refugee Settlement Commission" in common usage and even in the reports of the Commission.

the Commission considered that it had acquired sufficient rights to insure a permanent settlement.

Any advances which had been obtained by the National Bank of Greece for the purpose of the establishment of refugees in productive work in Greece were to be forthwith placed at the disposal of the Commission. Originally the Protocol provided that the Greek government was to raise a loan or loans to the amount of not less than three million and not more than six million English pounds, of which one million at least was to be subscribed by Greek banks or financial groups. By the amendment of the Protocol in 1924, the maximum of the loans to be raised was increased to £10,000,000, of which one-fourth was to be subscribed by Greek banks or financial groups. The whole proceeds of the loans were to be placed directly under the disposal of the Commission.

The service of the loans was to be assured by the International Financial Commission established in Greece since 1898, from certain revenues or surplus revenues which were to be assigned to or held by that Commission.[16] It also was to be a first charge upon the property and income of the Refugees Settlement Commission. The Greek government undertook not to create any charges on its revenues by way of security for any loans not intended for productive purposes or for carrying out its obligations under the Treaties of Peace. For such cases the Greek government could create a charge of inferior rank upon the revenues or surplus revenues assigned to the Refugee Loan. As regards other revenues, the Greek government was to create no charges, unless the International Financial Commission should recognize that the yield of the revenues assigned to the Refugee Loan was not endangered thereby. The government also undertook to secure as soon as possible an equilibrium between the ordinary receipts and the expenses of the state.

[16] These revenues were the following: (1) the monopolies of New Greece, i.e., salt, matches, cards, and cigarette paper; (2) the customs receipts received at the customs of Canea, Candia, Samos, Chios, Mitylene, and Syra; (3) the tobacco duty in New Greece; (4) the stamp duty in New Greece; (5) the duty on alcohol in the whole of Greece; and (6) any surplus of the revenues already assigned to the Financial Commission, subject always to existing charges on such revenues.

The Refugees Settlement Commission was to be exempt from all taxes and charges in respect of all its operations and property. The government was to pay to the Commission each year the total sum at which the occupiers of lands held by the Commission were assessed for taxation, until the loans raised for the settlement of refugees should be completely refunded. The reimbursement of advances made to refugees by the Commission was to have priority over taxation or any other claim.

The Greek government undertook to facilitate any inquiries which the Council of the League might direct into the activities of the Commission, and to give effect to the decisions of the Council so far as they required action by the Greek government. The obligations of the government under the Protocol were to cease as soon as the Refugees Settlement Commission should have been dissolved and the loans should have been repaid in full. The interpretation of the Protocol belonged to the Council. The English text (the French also being original) was considered the authentic text. The Protocol was to enter into effect on the deposit of the ratification by the Greek government.

§ 402. Organic Statutes of the Refugees Settlement Commission. The Organic Statutes of the Greek Refugees Settlement Commission, consisting of twenty-three articles, were signed on September 29 by the representative of Greece.[17] The Commission was to be established in Greece as a legal person, competent to sue and to be sued in its own name, to hold and alienate property of all kinds, and, in general, to perform any acts which could be performed by a corporation possessing full legal personality under the law of Greece.

The Commission was to enter upon its functions as soon as its members were appointed. These were four: two appointed by the Greek government with the approval of the Council of the League; one appointed by the Council; and the fourth member, the Chairman, who was to be a national

[17] See text, League of Nations, *Official Journal,* November, 1923, pp. 1508-10.

of the United States of America and a person representative of relief organizations, appointed in such method as the Council should from time to time determine. The last two members were to enjoy diplomatic privileges and immunities in Greece. These members could only be replaced by the Council, whereas the Greek government could replace the members appointed by it with the consent of the Council. The salaries of the two members appointed by the Greek government were to be fixed by that government; those of the two others were to be fixed by the Council. These salaries were to be paid out of the funds of the Commission, but the Greek government was to refund to the Commission the amount of the two salaries fixed by the Council.

Any vacancy in the Commission not filled by the competent authorities could be filled by the Council until such time as the competent appointing authority should act. In the event of temporary absence, the absent member should designate a substitute who should have the right to vote, failing which the Chairman had power to designate such a substitute. In the absence of the Chairman, the chair should be taken by the member appointed by the Council. The presence of three members or their substitutes, including always the two members not appointed by the Greek government, was necessary to form a quorum and validate decisions of the Commission.

The Commission was to take decisions by a majority vote of the members present at the meeting, the Chairman having a second vote in case of equal division of votes. The Commission was to establish its own rules of procedure. The Chairman was to sign all documents and be responsible for the execution of the decisions of the Commission. The necessary personnel for the discharge of its functions should be appointed by the Commission. All expenses of the Commission were to be paid out of the funds at its disposal or out of its income.

The functions of the Commission were, by means of the lands assigned to it, the funds at its disposal, and its own income, to promote the establishment of refugees in productive work upon the land or otherwise in Greece. Thus the Commission was concerned only with the establishment of refugees and not with their relief: this establishment was limited to productive work, and it was further limited to settlement in Greece. Nevertheless, the Commission, when it established suburbs or villages, was authorized to make disbursements, of a general or social nature (such as hospitals or schools) as might serve to promote the development of these settlements and improve the sanitary conditions of the population. The lands were to be applied to the settlement of refugees as tenants or owners, but they could also be sold to other than refugees, provided the sums raised thereby were paid into a special account and applied to the redemption of the settlement loans. The Commission should sell land if such sale became necessary to meet any deficit in the service of the loan.

Quarterly reports were to be communicated by the Commission to the Greek government and to the Council of the League. The latter should have the right to consider the reports and to take such action thereon as it might consider proper. It could also conduct inquiries into the manner in which the Commission was discharging its functions. The Council could dissolve the Commission when, in its opinion, the latter's services were no longer required, subject to the establishment of arrangements approved by representatives of the lenders, until the loans were fully repaid. After the dissolution of the Commission and the repayment of the loans, the balance of all assets of the Commission were to become the absolute property of the Greek state.

The opinion of the Council was to be accepted in the event of any difference as to the interpretation of the Statutes. The English text (the French being original also) was the authentic text. The Statutes were to be ratified by the Greek government.

Greece promulgated the Decree-Law of December 17, 1923, with a view to the application of the Protocol and Organic Statutes. The Protocol and Organic Statutes were ratified by the Greek government on June 7, 1924. The amendments of

September 19, 1924, were ratified on December 4, 1924.[18] As several questions remained to be settled between the Commission and the Greek government, the Agreement of January 25, 1925, was signed by them, including certain changes in the Decree-Law of 1923. An important provision of this Agreement was that creating a Mixed Board, composed of representatives of the Ministries of Agriculture and Public Welfare, the refugees, and the Settlement Commission, whose business was to follow closely the work of colonization, to give advice to the Commission, and to serve as a connecting body between the government, the refugees, and public opinion.

§ 403. Membership of the Commission. On September 29, 1923, the Council of the League of Nations appointed Sir John Campbell as League member on the Commission for two years at a salary of £1000 per annum, and Mr. Henry Morgenthau, on the nomination of the Near East Relief, as Chairman of the Commission for two years, at a salary of £2500 per annum. It also approved the appointment of Mr. Etienne Delta and Mr. Pericles Argyropoulos, nominated by the Greek government, as members of the Commission.[19]

Mr. Morgenthau resigned his post in December, 1924, and was temporarily replaced by Dr. Alfred Bonzon, and permanently by Mr. Charles P. Howland on February 7, 1925.[20] The latter resigned in September, 1926, and was replaced by Mr. Charles B. Eddy as from October 15, 1926,[21] Sir John Campbell resigned his position as member of the Commission on January 15, 1927. He had held this post for more than three years and had formed a valuable element of permanence and stability in the work. In his place Sir John Hope Simpson was appointed from January 16, 1927.[22] Sir John had already served in the Commission as a substitute member.

One of the Greek members, Mr. Argyropoulos, resigned in

[18] League of Nations, *Treaty Series,* xxx, pp. 413-419.
[19] League of Nations, *Official Journal,* November, 1923, p. 1357.
[20] League of Nations, *Official Journal,* February, 1925, p. 156; April, 1925, pp. 437-438, 514.
[21] League of Nations, *Official Journal,* October, 1926, pp. 1237-38.
[22] League of Nations, *Official Journal,* February, 1927, pp. 140, 158, 173.

August, 1924, and was replaced by Mr. Theodore Eustathopoulos.[23] A year later, in August, 1925, both Greek members, Mr. Delta and Mr. Eustathopoulos, resigned, and Mr. Alexander Pallis and Mr. Achilles Lambros were appointed in their stead on September 10, 1925.[24]

During the temporary absences of the Chairman and the member appointed by the Council of the League of Nations, Sir Robert Graves, Dr. Alfred Bonzon, Colonel Cunliffe-Owen, Dr. Bert Hodge Hill, Mr. Royall Tyler, and Sir John Hope Simpson filled their places. The Greek members were replaced during their absences by Messrs. Miltiades Negreponte, J. Damala, and D. Tantalides.

Mr. Adossidis was appointed Secretary-General of the Commission on August 23, 1924.

§ 404. The organization of the Commission. The Commission met first at Saloniki on November 11, 1923. It considered that it was unnecessary to make an entirely fresh start, and that the greater part of the machinery in being could be usefully taken over and could continue to be operated under the aegis of the Commission, inasmuch as it had accomplished a successful work until that time.[25]

Three central departments were thus organized: financial, urban, and agricultural. The first was formed of officials and accountants lent to the Commission by the National Bank of Greece and other personnel engaged by the Commission. It had as its function to control and check all financial transactions of the Commission. The urban department concerned itself with the formation of urban settlements for refugees. Its personnel was partly loaned by the Ministries of Public Welfare and Public Health and partly engaged by the Commission. The agricultural department dealt with the settlement of refugees in agricultural settlements. Its staff was

[23] League of Nations, *Official Journal,* October, 1924, p. 1348.

[24] *Ibid.,* October, 1925, p. 1360. Mr. Pallis resigned his post in the Commission in October, 1926, and his place was filled temporarily by Mr. Alexander Paspati. But Mr. Pallis a little later withdrew his resignation and resumed his duties.

[25] See Report of the Refugee Settlement Commission of February 25, 1924, in League of Nations, *Official Journal,* April, 1924, pp. 585-590. See also League of Nations, *Greek Refugee Settlement* (Geneva, 1926), pp. 9-11.

either appointed by the Commission or taken from the Ministry of Agriculture. The latter had already the following services engaged in agricultural settlement: (1) the Section of Colonization at the Ministry; (2) the Directorate-General of Colonization of Macedonia; (3) the Directorate of Colonization of Thrace; and (4) the Colonization Bureaus of Epirus, Attica and Boeotia, Etolia and Acarnania, and Crete.

The Agricultural Colonization Department at the headquarters of the Commission at Athens directed the settlement all over Greece. However, in Macedonia there was organized a General Directorate of Colonization, with a General Director and three Directors for Central, Eastern, and Western Macedonia. These Directors administered fourteen colonization bureaus. Each of these bureaus was directed by an agricultural expert, who supervised the operations of twenty-five agricultural superintendents (*epimelitae*). Each superintendent administered an area which contained approximately 250 refugee families.[26]

A colonization department was also organized in Western Thrace with five bureaus. In other parts of Greece the refugees were so scattered that no local colonization bureaus were organized. These were replaced by the district agricultural experts of each prefecture. However, an Inspector of Colonization was appointed where a large number of refugees were established. He inspected four bureaus and supervised the district agriculturists. Each head of a bureau was assisted by the necessary staff and an accountant.

All this organization was established by the Greek government before the Commission took up its duties. Only slight modifications were made by the Commission. To the thirty-five government colonization bureaus the Commission added two others in Patras and Argos. The personnel were mostly government employees. The Commission added to them technical experts, engineers, hydraulic experts, and accountants. All were of Greek nationality and many were recruited from among the refugees. Only three foreign officials were employed by the Commission in the first years of its work. It was rightly

[26] League of Nations, *Official Journal*, April, 1924, p. 587.

thought that "Greece should be left to perform a Greek task, not only out of feeling for the country, but because there was confidence in the capacity of Greek officials when well guided."

At the time the Commission was performing its task, Greece was carrying out a plan of agrarian reform in favor of native tenant-farmers. The personnel of the Commission conducted the two works. This shows again the wisdom of the Commission in using the government staff for the settlement work. It eliminated possible conflicts and friction between the two tasks and rendered the work of the Commission easier through the training and experience of the personnel of the administration.

The Commission also established an Observation Service, composed of functionaries directly under its employ, whose duty was to follow the working of the existing machinery, to inform the Commission of the progress of the work, and to point out abuses or suggest improvements of the administration, and, in general, to keep the Commission in contact with the actual facts.

The movement of staff from 1924, when the work of the Commission began, to 1930, when the Commission was dissolved, was as follows: [27]

	Employees
End of 1924	784
Year 1925 (end of)	1822
1926	1829
1927	1755
1928	2042
1929 (first quarter)	2003
1930 (beginning of)	1416

As the dissolution of the Commission was already agreed upon in 1929, the strength of the staff diminished rapidly from the second quarter of 1929.

Approximately one-half of the staff was engaged in the services of the Directorate-General of Macedonia, since this was the region where the refugees were settled most thickly. Out of 2003 employees at the end of the first quarter of 1929, 1010 formed the strength of the Directorate-General of Macedonia, and 398 of the Directorate of Thrace.

[27] See Twenty-Seventh Quarterly Report of the Commission, August 21, 1930, in League of Nations, *Official Journal,* November, 1930, pp. 1469-89.

§ 405. Legal status of the Commission. No precise legal definition of the status of the Commission was contained in the Protocol for Refugee Settlement and the Organic Statutes. The Protocol provided (Article I) that the Commission was "to possess the constitution, capacity and functions set out in the Organic Statutes." Article II of the Organic Statutes provided that the Commission was "established as a legal person . . . to perform any acts which can be performed by a corporation possessing full legal personality under the law of Greece." While this indicated that the Commission had merely corporate powers under Greek law, Article III of the Statutes added: "The Refugee Settlement Commission shall not be dependent upon any Greek executive or administrative authority, but shall be completely autonomous in the exercise of its functions." Thus the Commission was independent of executive or administrative control in Greece, although not of legal control. However, the Commission's actions were subject to review by the Council of the League of Nations to which the Commission was bound to submit quarterly reports on its work. In May, 1925, difficulties arose between the Greek government and the Commission relating to the procedure under which certain Greek officials in the service of the Commission had been prosecuted. The government began judicial proceedings against certain higher officials of the Commission (the Director-General of Colonization in Macedonia and two of his chief engineers), in which inquiries were undertaken as to the profitable or unprofitable nature of the contracts or agreements concluded by the Commission. This considerably hampered the work of the Commission for some time.[28] A feeling of unrest was produced among the general body of officials engaged in the work of establishing the refugees in Macedonia. A question of interpretation of the provisions of the Protocol and the Organic Statutes was raised, and the mediation of the Council of the League was sought in September, 1925. The Greek government was obliged to take certain measures with the view of securing the progress of the

[28] Seventh Quarterly Report of the Commission, in League of Nations, *Official Journal,* November, 1925, pp. 1673-78. See on this, Charles B. Eddy, *Greece and the Greek Refugees,* pp. 79 ff.

work, and the Commission undertook to present reports to the Greek government monthly.[29]

The Decree of December 2, 1925, promulgated by the Greek government, provided that no judicial proceedings could in future be instituted against persons employed by the Commission except at the instance of the Commission or the Minister of Justice. The Decree was declared applicable to cases in progress, and as a result the criminal charges against the three officials of the Commission were withdrawn. The government at first asked of the Commission not to reinstate these officials in their posts in Macedonia; but it did not insist on this demand, and the officials resumed their duties.[30]

§ 406. The First Refugee Loan. When the Refugees Settlement Commission started work in Greece in November, 1923, the Greek government was at the end of its resources. It had spent about 550,000,000 drachmas, or £2,000,000, until that time for the establishment of refugees. Through the National Bank it assumed obligations to the amount of £100,000 for the supply of seed, lumber, etc., without any funds to meet them, but in confidence that the League would aid to raise the refugee loan. The Bank of England had advanced to the National Bank of Greece in August, 1923, a sum of £1,000,000 to be repaid from the loan. But the loan was not immediately forthcoming.

In vain the Greek representative reminded the Council at the session of March, 1924, that the assets set aside under the Protocol afforded a complete guarantee for the loan.[31] Greece was passing then through a series of successive cabinet changes, and the Council recognized that the provision of resources "will be impossible unless political developments in Greece in the immediate future are such as to offer a prospect of order and economic stability and the consequent improvement in the foreign credit of the country." The Sub-Committee of the Council of the League on the Greek Refugees was authorized "to take such decisions in relation to the settlement scheme" as it might consider useful.[32]

[29] League of Nations, *Official Journal,* October, 1925, p. 1360.
[30] *Ibid.,* February, 1926, p. 322; April, 1926, p. 554.
[31] League of Nations, *Official Journal,* April, 1924, p. 509.
[32] *Ibid.,* p. 510.

In May, 1924, a second advance of £1,000,000 was made by the Bank of England to the National Bank of Greece, on the understanding that the settlement work under the Protocol would be continued. At this time the Sub-Committee of the Council of the League on the Greek Refugees met at London and decided to continue the work of the Refugees Settlement Commission.[33]

In September of the same year [34] the Chairman of the Commission, Mr. Morgenthau, appeared before the Council of the League, and made an address which may be considered a guarded expression of impatience that the Council was not proceeding with due speed in the matter of the Greek loan. He declared that in order to stabilize Greece and to take care of all the refugees a sum of £10,000,000 was needed, of which Greece was prepared to supply one-fourth. He believed that the security given was ample and proper, and that the Greek government was stable. He asked the Council to investigate the situation through the Financial Committee of the League and to put its stamp of approval on the desire of Greece to raise the loan of £10,000,000.

The amendments to the Refugees Settlement Protocol of 1923, adopted in September, 1924, authorized the issue of a loan up to £10,000,000. The Sub-Committee of the Council of the League found from estimates given it from an authorized source that the revenues assigned by the Greek government had a yield of 700,000,000 drachmas per year, and that the land which was to constitute a guarantee for the loan represented a value of about £10,000,000.

Encouraged by the support of the League, the Greek government entered into negotiations in London for the floating of the loan. These resulted in the signature of contracts in December, 1924, with Hambros Bank, Limited, in London, Speyer & Co.'s Bank of New York, and the National Bank of Greece. These contracts provided for the issue of a seven per cent loan of £12,300,000, face amount, of which £7,500,000 were to be issued in London, £2,500,000 at Athens and £2,300,-

[33] League of Nations, *Official Journal,* July, 1924, pp. 911-912.
[34] League of Nations, *Official Journal,* October, 1924, pp. 1299-1302.

000 (in dollars) in New York. The issue took place at the rate of 88. Deducting, however, the British stamp duty of 2% and the expenses of issue and commission of Banks of 5%, the net produce was 81 per cent. Thus the nominal interest of 7% rose finally to 8.71%. This is a tragi-comic commentary on the high-sounding discussion of the Refugee Loan as a humanitarian and philanthropic work! [35] Greece could probably have raised such a loan without the intervention of the League. A loan bearing such interest naturally proved entirely successful, the sum required of the public being covered five and a half times at Athens and nearly twenty times in London, and entirely subscribed by Speyer & Co. in New York. The net proceeds of the loan were £9,970,016 6 *s.* 9 *d.*

At the session of the Council of the League in September, 1925, the chairman of the Refugees Settlement Commission reported that the assigned revenues for the service of all Greek foreign loans controlled by the International Financial Commission, which handles the service of the Greek foreign debt, amounted to more than double the amount necessary for the service of these loans.[36] In the year 1926 the revenues assigned to the Refugee Loan yielded more than six times the sum required for interest and ordinary redemption.[37] In 1927 the yield of the revenues exceeded by more than eleven times the sum required for interest and redemption.[38] The annuities paid by the refugees on the price of lands ceded to them were devoted to an 'extraordinary amortization' of the loan. For this indefinite amount a fixed sum of £60,000 was substituted in 1930, as is seen in another place.[39] This amortization, added to the ordinary redemption of ½%, will have the result that the loan will be paid in 30 years instead of in 40. The annual service of the loan thus approaches 10%. It is indeed remarkable that a loan intended to help the pro-

[35] See A. Andreades et al., *Les effets économiques et sociaux de la guerre en Grèce* (*Publications de la Dotation Carnegie*), p. 101.

[36] League of Nations, *Official Journal,* October, 1925, pp. 1359-60.

[37] Thirteenth Quarterly Report of the Commission, in League of Nations, *Official Journal,* April, 1927, p. 520. The sum required for interest and redemption being 359,588,152 drachmas, the assigned revenues yielded 2,143,-332,004 drachmas.

[38] League of Nations, *Official Journal,* April, 1928, p. 482.

[39] See *infra,* § 431 *in fine*.

ductive and mainly agricultural work of the refugees should be charged with an annual service of 10%.

§ 407. The Second Refugee Loan. By the middle of 1926 the Commission had settled in Greece 622,865 refugees, of whom 550,635 were rural and 72,230 urban. The work was not yet finished. The following further expenditure was deemed necessary:

A. For the extension of existing settlement	£2,200,000
B. For the settlement of 8,000 new rural families	800,000
C. For " " " 20,000 " urban "	2,000,000

The existing settlements needed improvement and further equipment if they were to become really productive. Dwellings left by Moslems or Bulgarians and occupied by refugees were in a state of dilapidation; settlers in mountainous districts needed herds and flocks, as the tilling of the barren soil did not afford to these people a livelihood; marshes in the neighborhood of refugee villages should be drained to safeguard the settlers from malaria; a land register should be drawn up for the final distribution of the lands to refugees. New rural families could not be settled without finding new land. Already there was a great shortage of land. The average holding of a refugee family did not exceed 3½ hectares, or 8 2/3 acres, of both cultivable and non-cultivable land. Certain refugee families continued living in crowded and deplorable conditions in towns.

The suggestion that a new loan be granted for the completion of the work of the Commission was advanced both by the Greek government and the Refugee Settlement Commission to the Financial Committee of the League and to the Council in June, 1926.[40] As a change of government had taken place in Greece, consideration of the future of the settlement work was postponed until later.[41] The Financial Committee of the League was not disposed to consider the possibility of a second refugee loan until full information on the financial situation of Greece could be obtained, and in March, 1927,

[40] League of Nations, *Official Journal,* July, 1926, pp. 865, 920, 924-927.
[41] *Ibid.,* October, 1926, pp. 1237-38, 1335.

requested the Secretariat of the League to collect as full information as possible.[42]

Mr. Avenol of the Secretariat, on behalf of the Financial Committee, went to Greece and collected the essential facts on the spot, with the assistance of the Greek government. A detailed and precise report was prepared by him. The Financial Committee, accepting the view of the Greek government that the work of completing the refugee settlement was bound up with the reform of the finances of the Greek Republic, advised that a loan of £9,000,000 was necessary. For the urgent work of refugee settlement £3,000,000 was considered sufficient. The budget of recent years had left deficits, and the arrears due in 1927 amounted to about £3,000,000. For the stabilization of the drachma on a gold exchange basis and the strengthening of the National Bank of Greece, it was felt that another £3,000,000 was needed.[43]

A scheme for currency and banking reforms in Greece had to be drawn up before the Council would give its final approval to the issue of the proposed loan. This scheme was proposed and approved by the Council at its session of September, 1927.[44] The Protocol embodying this scheme was signed by the Greek government on September 15, 1927.

As this loan was to be guaranteed by certain revenues assigned to its service, provision was made that the International Financial Commission at Athens should continue to control the surplus revenues and apply them to the service of the new loan. The consent of the three governments represented on this Commission (British, French and Italian) was required for this purpose, and a draft declaration for signature by these governments was appended to the Protocol, as on the occasion of the first Refugee Loan of 1924. All kinds of concessions were extracted from Greece for signing this declaration and making possible the issuance of the loan. Among others, the Greek government had to put aside from the loan 150,000,000 drachmas in order to pay in gold for large rural estates of English, French, and Italian proprietors, which

[42] League of Nations, *Official Journal,* April, 1927, pp. 383, 510.
[43] *Ibid.,* July, 1927, pp. 796, 921-922, 926.
[44] *Ibid.,* pp. 1134-35, 1302-03, 1306-08.

were expropriated, like those of Greek proprietors, under the Agrarian Reform Law. These foreigners were thus paid fourteen times the price paid to Greek proprietors. Moreover, the French government refused to give its consent until the accounts between Greece and France were settled. Very laborious negotiations had then to be carried on, which terminated December 8, 1927, when the French, British, and Italian representatives signed at Geneva the above declaration.[45]

Thus the way was open for the issue of the Stabilization Loan. This was issued at London and New York, in accordance with contracts signed on January 30, 1928, with Hambros Bank, Limited, and Erlangers, and Speyer & Co., the National City Bank of New York and the National City Company of New York respectively. The loan was over-subscribed many times with great rapidity. Under the above two agreements the net yield of the loans issued in London and New York amounted to £6,500,000. A further loan of £2,500,000 ($12,167,000) was granted to Greece by the American government under the terms of the settlement of the Greek war debt to the United States.

The loan of the American government was granted at par at 4 per cent interest, and was to be repaid in twenty years in half-yearly instalments. The loan of £6,500,000 was issued at 86 per cent[46] at 6 per cent interest and was redeemable in forty years.[47] The whole of the American loan of £2,500,000 was turned over to the Refugee Settlement Commission for its work of settlement. This loan at par and at 4 per cent could indeed properly be considered a refugee settlement loan, and the moderation of its terms serves only to enhance the enormity of the interest on the first international Refugee Loan. The sum of £500,000 only was paid to the Commission from the loan of £6,500,000, thus making a total of £3,000,000 for

[45] League of Nations, *Official Journal*, February, 1928, pp. 167-168, 242.

[46] The loan was issued at 91, but its net produce was 86, the difference of 5 pounds being caused by the British stamp duty of 2% and the bank commission, etc., of 3%. The nominal value of the loan subscribed through the Banks was £7,500,000.

[47] The real interest amounted to 7.05%, which is an improvement over the 8.71% real interest of the loan of 1924.

the settlement work, in accordance with the Protocol of September 15, 1927.[48]

The loan of the United States government did not become available until May, 1929.[49] The sum of £500,000 turned over to the Commission in the spring of 1928 could not enable the Commission to continue its work further than September, 1928. For this reason the President of the Financial Committee of the League, in accordance with article VII, paragraph 1 of the Protocol of 1927, authorized an advance of £500,000 from the unused proceeds of the 1928 Stabilization Loan at the rate of £100,000 per month from October 1, 1928. A further sum of £500,000 from the same source was promised as soon as required. Thus the Commission was able to distribute among its services supplementary credits for the execution of its programme.[50]

§ 408. Settlement programme of the Commission. No general settlement plan was drawn up by the Commission. The general lines, however, of the settlement scheme proposed by the High Commissioner, Dr. Nansen, and the Greek government were approved and followed by the Commission. The Greek government had promised to assign to the Commission an area of land unencumbered and suitable for the settlement of refugees of not less than 500,000 hectares, or 1,235,500 acres. On this land the Commission was to settle refugees on a self-supporting basis; it was also to furnish productive work to other refugees who could not be settled on the land.

When the Commission assembled for the first time in Saloniki in November, 1923, it found a situation which could not be altered, and a beginning of the settlement of the refugees which it was wise to continue rather than to upset.[51] Thus, the great bulk of the refugees were to be settled in Macedonia, because this was the part of Greece with the great-

[48] League of Nations, *Official Journal,* April, 1928, pp. 373, 463, 494-495.

[49] The United States Congress adjourned in May, 1928, without consenting to ratification of the Agreement with Greece. It met again in December, 1928, and gave its consent in January, 1929.

[50] League of Nations, *Official Journal,* July, 1928, pp. 919-920, 1030-31, 1044-48.

[51] On the settlement work carried out by the Greek government, see Hadjopoulos, *Die Flüchtlingsfrage in Griechenland* (Athens, 1929); also Protonotarios, *The Refugee Problem* (in Greek) (Athens, 1929), pp. 69 ff.

est potentialities for settlement purposes. The largest part of the Moslems to leave Greece under the Convention of Lausanne came from Macedonia. There were large areas of uncultivated but arable land, and, if certain important irrigation work could be carried out, a vast and fertile area could be made available for refugee settlement. Moreover, work for the installation of the urban population had already begun. Contracts had been passed for the construction of buildings and materials had been ordered. In fact, this beginning of the settlement of the refugees had been accomplished with much success, and the Commission found that the Greek government and the Greek people had "grappled with this colossal problem in a manner worthy of the highest praise." [52] Of the 120,000 agricultural refugee families included in the estimates at the end of 1923, 72,581 families had been settled provisionally by the Greek government on agrarian holdings. Of these 66,920 were in Macedonia and 5661 in old Greece. In addition, there were 12,000 families accommodated in Moslem houses in Western Thrace. The government had also built 5023 houses and used 50,000 houses belonging to exchangeable Turks from Macedonia.

Consequently, the Commission decided to assume responsibility for the continuation of the work begun. As it was handicapped by the lack of the whole amount of funds provided for in the Protocol, it could not work out a general scheme. With £160,000 placed at its disposal by the National Bank of Greece, it assumed responsibility for the payment for materials already ordered by the Greek government. It had at its further disposal until the loan should be contracted only £1,000,000 advanced by the Bank of England in September, 1923. Two possible alternatives were before the Commission for the allocation of this sum: either to fully equip and settle a small number of refugees, who would then be able to stand on their feet without any further help; or to spread the available funds among a large number of refugees, which would permit them a partial settlement and a starting in

[52] See First Quarterly Report of the Commission, in League of Nations, *Official Journal,* April, 1924, p. 586. See also statement by Mr. Howland before the Council of the League, *ibid.,* October, 1925, p. 1359.

productive work. The second alternative was chosen. This may theoretically appear to have been not a happy choice, as a partial settlement was no settlement and consequently uneconomical; but it probably was the only practical choice under the circumstances.[53]

In May, 1924, the Bank of England advanced a second million English pounds to the Refugee Commission. The National Bank of Greece also made further advances, which at the end of 1924 reached the sum of £1,700,000. These advances helped to maintain the work of settlement uninterrupted. Thus 62,583 rural families were settled during 1924 by the Commission. Also 11,359 houses were built, and animals, seed, carts, and ploughs were distributed.[54]

The first instalment of the loan of £10,000,000 concluded in December, 1924, in London was placed at the disposal of the Commission in January, 1925. From that time the Commission was able to draw up the programme of its work. The balance of the loan, amounting to £6,274,543, after the repayment of the advances by the Bank of England and the National Bank of Greece to the amount of £3,700,000, was allocated as follows: £800,000 was kept as a reserve fund; a sum of £1,380,000 was devoted to the urban settlement; the remainder was appropriated for agricultural settlements. In its main lines, the work of agricultural settlement followed the practice of the preceding years, with the aim of establishing rural families on a definitive and self-supporting basis on land assigned by the Commission, with the necessary agricultural implements, cattle, and seed.

Urban colonization presented greater difficulties. Until the end of 1924, the Commission was "forced to devote its resources to completing work already begun and in many cases proceeded with to a considerable extent (districts in Athens, Piraeus, Eleusis, Volo, and Edessa) under the pressure of urgent needs in the early days of the influx." [55] Much of

[53] Fifth Quarterly Report, February 25, 1925, in League of Nations, *Official Journal,* April, 1925, p. 504.
[54] League of Nations, *Official Journal,* April, 1925, p. 504.
[55] See Fifth Quarterly Report of the Commission, in League of Nations, *Official Journal,* April, 1925, p. 511.

this work had been carried out by the Refugee Relief Fund, a Greek organization. With the resources of the loan at its disposal, the Commission considered the whole problem of settling urban refugees.

It first decided to undertake no constructional work in the large centres: Athens, Piraeus, Saloniki, and Patras. These cities had already absorbed large masses of refugees, and it was feared that further concentration there would be fraught with economic and social dangers for Greece. Moreover, it was deemed wise to coördinate the work of urban and agricultural settlement, since it had been noted that the creation of new agricultural settlements in a certain region had the effect of increasing the capacity of absorption of towns in that region.[56]

The urban settlement included the construction of new quarters; the improvement of existing quarters by providing them with public services and carrying out works of general utility; the leasing of houses and shops to refugees; and the granting of facilities of payment to refugees who wished to become owners of houses and shops occupied by them.[57] At the same time it was decided to make a certain number of professional grants, intended to help artisans and small shopkeepers living among the agricultural groups, as well as fishermen settled by the Commission at different points on the coast to carry on their trade.

By the end of 1926 the main work of agricultural settlement was completed. This is considered in detail below. The following years were devoted by the Commission not to the creation of new colonies or to the settlement of additional families, but to the strengthening of existing settlements. Thus the Commission filled "the gap between the amount actually expended for each family and the amount which normally should have been expended." [58]

Article VI of the Protocol of 1927 provided that one-third of the yield of the Stabilization Loan, or three million pounds sterling, was to be employed for the settlement of Greek

[56] *Ibid.*, pp. 511-512.
[57] *Ibid.*, p. 512.
[58] Twenty-First Quarterly Report of the Commission, in League of Nations, *Official Journal,* April, 1929, p. 5.

refugees. Besides the purposes described in the Protocol of 1923-24 and Statutes, the Refugee Settlement Commission could employ this loan for other purposes connected with promoting the establishment of refugees in productive work, subject to approval by the Council of the League on the proposal of the Commission.

The Council in March, 1928, soon after the loan became available, on the proposal of the Commission and after agreement with the Greek government, gave authority for the sums of £150,000, £100,000, and £29,000 to be allocated respectively to the construction of certain roads and bridges in Macedonia, the promotion of the domestic carpet industry, and village arts and crafts among refugees.[59]

The fact that the whole credit of three millions was not available from the beginning of 1928 prevented the Commission from embarking upon the execution of its programme. Work was generally slowed down, while the organization of the Commission was kept at full strength, occasioning heavy administrative expenses.[60]

§ 409. Number of refugees. One of the most difficult questions with which the Commission had to cope was the lack of precise statistics on the number of refugees whose settlement it had to undertake. This was due "in particular, to the fact that waves of refugees have flooded the country from time to time without passing through the hands of the official organizations, have dispersed to different parts of the country and since then have frequently moved from one place to another." [61] All provisional figures were constantly upset by the influx of new refugees.

A first census of the refugees was made in April, 1923, before the Commission began its work in Greece. Their number was estimated to be 847,931. Subsequently refugees continued to pour into Greece from Turkey, Bulgaria, and Russia, and as the refugees, especially in the cities, were absorbed among the natives, no definite figure could be found. The

[59] League of Nations, *Official Journal,* April, 1928, pp. 373, 463.

[60] *Ibid.,* January, 1929, p. 198.

[61] Eighth Quarterly Report of the Commission in League of Nations, *Official Journal,* February, 1926, p. 324.

real strength of the refugee population was only found at the general census of the population in Greece on May 15, 1928. The refugees were found to number 1,221,849 souls, of whom 1,069,957 swarmed into Greece after the disaster in Asia Minor, and 151,892 sought refuge in Greece at various times after the Balkan Wars and before the evacuation of Asia Minor by the Greek army.[62]

According to their place of origin the refugees were classified as follows: [63]

From Turkey:		
Asia Minor	626,954	
Eastern Thrace	256,635	
Pontus	182,169	
Constantinople	38,458	
		1,104,216
From Bulgaria		49,027
From Russia:		
Caucasus	47,091	
Other parts of Russia	11,435	58,526
From other countries:		
Albania	2,186	
Serbia	5,250	
Dodecanesus	561	
Other countries	2,083	10,080
		1,221,849

Not all these refugees were cared for by the Commission. A part of them were able to settle themselves in Greece before the Commission began its work. Another part came to Greece with sufficient resources to take care of themselves and not to depend on the advances of the Commission. A last part, perhaps 50,000, left the country again, some of them being Armenians and going to Soviet Armenia, and some Greeks leaving to rejoin families in Greek foreign colonies in Egypt, France, and the United States.

By the end of 1925 the Commission had installed on land

[62] Mr. Charles B. Eddy believes that the figure of 1,221,849 seems for many reasons an understatement and that the figure of 1,300,000 is nearer the truth. See *Greece and the Greek Refugees,* pp. 52, 248. This number represents the refugees found in Greece in 1928 and does not take account of the deaths and emigrations from Greece between 1922 and 1928.

[63] A. A. Pallis, *Collection of Statistics concerning the Exchange of Populations* (in Greek) (Athens, 1929), p. 4. Mr. Pallis was a member of the Refugee Settlement Commission.

granted by the Greek government 147,333 rural families, or 550,635 persons, as follows:

In Macedonia	116,391 families	or 429,990	persons
In Thrace	16,274 "	" 65,915	"
In other regions	14,668 "	" 54,730	"

In the following years these numbers were continuously changing. Many families left the country for urban centres, either because they did not belong to the agricultural class or could not adapt themselves to country life, or because they preferred to enroll themselves among the urban settlers and take advantage of the indemnity granted them by the state. Thus on December 1, 1927, the families settled in rural sections were as follows:

In Macedonia	112,111 families
In Thrace	16,757 "
In other provinces	14,144 "
Total	143,012 families or 551,468 persons

On the other hand, the urban population settled by the Commission in the refugee quarters of the suburbs of Athens, Piraeus, and of some twenty urban centres in Macedonia and Thrace numbered 72,230 persons.

Thus the total number of refugees cared for by the Commission by the end of 1927 reached 623,698 persons, or nearly one-half of the total number of 1,221,849 refugees in Greece. Account must be taken also of a total of 2167 families or 8688 persons settled by the Greek state, independently of the Commission, before December 31, 1928, in Old Greece, Epirus, and the Islands. At that time a minimum of 8000 agricultural families and 20,000 urban families were in need of settlement. In the meantime, of course, great numbers of refugees had been established, either by their own efforts or with the assistance of the Government. These included upwards of 200,000 necessitous urban refugees, who, as they could not be settled on an immediately productive basis, remained outside the province of the Commission.

§ 410. Classes and characteristics of refugees. The refugees were people of different classes. Most of them, perhaps, came from small or large towns on the coast or the interior of

Thrace and Asia Minor, and represented such occupations and professions as commerce, industry and banking, retail trading, shipbuilding, teaching, medicine, law, journalism, etc. With these were many artisans and craftsmen and workers of all categories. The remainder were cultivators, shepherds, and fishermen.[64]

The urban element probably outnumbered the rural.[65] However, on their arrival the refugees were settled by the government according to the necessities of shelter, sometimes without due attention to their class. Thus some agriculturists swelled the ranks of urban refugees in the towns, while many urban refugees were sent to villages to till the soil. As productive employment in the towns was scarce, many town refugees had to be settled in rural settlements.

With regard to the characteristics and traits of the refugees coming from various regions, this extract from the *Greek Refugee Settlement* [66] is worth quoting:

> Among these brothers by race, there is a complete identity of feeling, aspirations, and national and religious traditions, but, having lived in different countries and districts, they differ in character, temperament, and mentality and show striking individuality.
>
> Among those of a certain degree of education and among the townspeople in general, these differences frequently become blurred or even disappear. Among men fashioned in the same mould by town life or frequent travel, which in the long run efface marks of their origin, contrasts appear less striking than among the inhabitants of the countryside.
>
> Among the Greeks of Asia Minor, for example, there are some who, having lived more immediately beneath the yoke in distant provinces of the interior and in the midst of Turks and Kurds, have the characteristics of Asiatic peoples. They are backward, submissive, and timid. Some of them have adopted the language of the conquerors and speak Turkish.
>
> Others, like the Cappadocians, coming from the very heart of Anatolia, represent a serious and reflective type, hard-working and energetic, enterprising and practical.

[64] *Greek Refugee Settlement,* pp. 13-16.
[65] *Ibid.,* p. 15.
[66] *Ibid.,* pp. 20-22.

Others again, like the Greeks of the coast or from the valley of the Lower Meander, are true Ionians in their individualism, their gaiety, energy, suppleness of mind, their adaptability, their great powers of assimilation, their love of change, their talkativeness and their carping spirit.

Elsewhere we find in the same district (Greeks from Cilicia and the Propontis) the Anatolian type and the southern type together.

Entering the Pontus, a district with its own individual note, we find, according as we go east or west, towards the coast or into the interior, the most dissimilar specimens, from the rough, heavy, and dull-witted type to the subtlest of Greeks.

The mountainous provinces and the high plateaux of the Pontus breed a race of men of austere morals, who have retained all the combative ardour and the warlike virtues of their ancestor, the mediaeval hero, Digenis Acritas. The women are pleasing, gifted with courage and vigour, and work even harder in the fields than in their homes.

The Pontians of these parts are regarded as the truest of the Hellenes. Their imposing height, the purity of their features and language, give proof of their descent. They speak a Greek rich in vowel sounds, while classical expressions and Homeric phrases are common in their speech.

The refugees from the Caucasus are closely related to them, but display different characteristics. The descendants of Pontians who emigrated into the Russian Caucasus during the 19th century, they are of two quite different origins. Those from the Kars district are industrious, energetic, and supple-minded; the rest come from the Chaka area (Tiflis) and are less civilized than the others.

The Thracian peasant, shepherd or farmer is a quiet, reflective man, slow and serious and of regular habits; he gives that impression of stability and solid strength which is typical of those attached to the soil. He reasons sedately and coolly, chewing his ideas slowly. Hard-working and of great endurance and tenacity, he is thrifty and takes thought for the morrow. He forms a conservative and somewhat stolid element, living under an almost patriarchal régime.

His brother from Bulgaria also represents the true peasant type, who lives by the soil and for the soil. His chief qualities are initiative, power of assimilation, devotion to work, energy, and capacity to save; he is more developed than the Thracian of Eastern Thrace. He constitutes a progressive factor and a rural element of the first class.

§ 411. The land for refugee settlement. The area of 500,000 hectares to be assigned by the Greek government to the Commission was of three categories: (*a*) land belonging to the state; (*b*) land vacated by Turks subject to exchange under the Convention of Lausanne; and (*c*) land which was to be expropriated by the Greek government by virtue of the agrarian reform laws. The total area of lands of the first category that the Greek government was in a position to assign to the Commission by the end of 1923 did not exceed 50,000 hectares. Lands to be vacated by Moslems were probably of a total area of 350,000 hectares. The balance of 100,000 hectares was to be obtained from a vigorous application of the agrarian laws and a speedy expropriation of large rural properties.

The Agrarian Reform Law, passed on October 3, 1924, adopted this vigorous system. As a rule, owners of large estates subject to expropriation were permitted to retain 30 hectares, the remainder being distributed to native tenants and to refugees. By the end of 1924[67] the land assigned to the Commission for the settlement of refugees was as follows:

	Total area granted	Cultivable land
Macedonia	420,000 hectares	241,457 hectares
Thrace	10,000 "	10,000 "
Old Greece, Epirus, and the Islands	49,487 "	33,542 "
	479,487	284,999

There was an increasing shortage of land, which sometimes led to trouble between native cultivators and refugees, or between several groups of refugees desirous of obtaining the same land.

With the progressive application of expropriation under the Agrarian Reform Law, the area of cultivable land placed at the disposal of the Commission increased. At the end of 1925 this area reached 448,486 hectares, and at the end of 1927 the figures were as follows:

	Cultivable land, hectares	Non-cultivable, hectares	Total
Macedonia	388,760	277,353	616,112
Thrace	66,170	65,090	131,261
Other provinces	44,092	21,127	65,219
Total	499,022	313,570	812,592

[67] League of Nations, *Official Journal,* 1925, pp. 509-510.

Lastly, the final statistics in the summer of 1929 showed the total area of land ceded to the Commission for settlement purposes as:

Cultivable land, hectares	Non-cultivable, hectares	Total
525,741	335,268	861,010

The Decree-Law of May 15, 1926, transferred to the Commission the legal title in the lands assigned to it, of which it had until then only the possession.

The value of the rural property assigned by the Greek government to the Commission was estimated by the former, on the basis of the market price—that is, the average selling price of small estates—of at least 2000 drachmas per *stremma,* of a total of about 10,515,000,000 drachmas or about £30,000,000. This amount, of course, could never be realized at an actual sale of the land by the creditors, and the figure must be taken with a grain of salt. The Commission did not sell the land to refugees at the market price, but rather nearer the rate fixed by the Assessment Committees which applied the agrarian reform laws. As will be seen below, this rate was fixed at 400 drachmas per *stremma* by the Agreement of March 27, 1930, between the government and the Commission.[68] At this price the value of 525,741 hectares of cultivated land made over to the Commission was 2,102,964,000 drachmas or (at 350 drachmas to the pound) about £6,000,000.

The urban property made over to the Commission included the land for the erection of urban houses and the houses erected by the Public Relief Fund, a state department. Taking as a basis the price at which the Commission sold this property to the refugees, the total value of this property was about 141,706,440 drachmas, or £404,875, at the rate of 350 drachmas to the pound.

For some time the Greek government contemplated the possibility of creating a Refugees Bank, to which buildings of exchangeable Moslems and land not transferred to the Refugee Settlement Commission was to be transferred. This project was abandoned. Instead, by a convention with the

[68] See *infra,* § 430.

National Bank of Greece, concluded on May 5, 1925, the Greek state transferred to the Bank all its rights over urban real property belonging to exchangeable Moslems, as well as over all agricultural properties which were not legally surrendered for colonization purposes, including the estates planted with olives, grape vines, and other shrub cultivations, which the Bank employed for the establishment of specialist refugee cultivators.

The land distributed to refugees was insufficient.[69] The draining of the lakes of Ardjan and Amatovo in Macedonia was expected to set free an area of about 100,000 *stremmata* of land. The project of draining the two valleys of the Struma and the Axios, from which some 1,500,000 *stremmata* are to be reclaimed, is considered below.

The legal status of land ceded by the government to the Commission and allocated by the latter to refugees was finally determined by legislative measures in 1930. One of these laws provided that refugees settled on such land were not to be longer molested by any claims, the judicial authorities being bound to refuse to hear any petition or any action against the settler's right of possession. Right of possession was to be established by a simple attestation on the part of bureaus of the Commission. The Commission at the same time issued title-deeds of possession to refugees whose land was finally allocated. The final title-deeds of ownership were not to be granted until the debts to the Commission were paid.

Another legislative measure passed in 1930 regulated finally the vexing question of irregular transactions by which lands of Moslems emigrating from Greece were purchased by natives, despite the prohibition of such transactions ever since 1913. Purchasers of such land had been in possession for years, and it was not possible to disregard the interests and rights created in the meantime. By this law, as a rule such transactions concerning small agricultural holdings were declared valid. To safeguard the Commission from any difficulties which might arise through this validation of transac-

[69] See *infra*, p. 654, as to the size of family holdings.

tions in regard to parts of estates already colonized, a provision was devised for exchanges of land.

§ 412. **Topographical service and Cadaster.** Greece had no survey of lands or cadaster, and the distribution of lots to refugees was at first made in a temporary way, pending an exact fixing of boundaries. For the purpose of final distribution and fixing of the debt of each refugee, it was necessary to have maps of the villages showing the individual lots and also to make an appraisal of lands of different qualities. The Commission entertained proposals of topographical societies for surveys from aeroplanes. This was deemed too costly.[70] Instead, a technical service was appointed to make polygonic plans of the whole of the properties of the villages, in which the limits of each individual property would then be marked.

The number of surveying parties increased gradually, as in the beginning no expert staff was available and one had to be formed by special training. The thirty-eight surveying parties in the first quarter of 1927 were increased to eighty-one for Macedonia and sixteen for Thrace in the summer of 1928. At the same time a number of parties started work in Old Greece.[71]

As a result, the surveying work progressed gradually, after the slow output in the first years. By the middle of 1926 only 30,000 hectares of land had been surveyed. By the end of 1928 the survey had covered a total of 1,129,140 hectares. On August 1, 1930, the figures were as follows:

In Macedonia	1,067,100
In Thrace	147,000
In other provinces	47,026
	1,261,126

These figures, as is clear, include not only the lands distributed to refugees, but also lands of natives.

At the same time the work of distribution of the individual lots granted to each refugee was under way. The work lagged, not only by reason of the lack of sufficient technical

[70] However, the mountainous district of Karajova was topographically studied by means of air photographs with satisfactory results.

[71] See Nineteenth Quarterly Report, in League of Nations, *Official Journal*, October, 1928, pp. 1694-95.

staff, but for other reasons also. Many lands allotted to refugees were bordered by lands belonging to natives or to foreign nationals or by large estates expropriated by the state which were not yet appraised.[72] This complicated the matter of distribution. The Commission had proposed a general and radical solution, the effacement of all boundaries and the redistribution of the land of each village. This would have the further advantage of regrouping properties which were too much parcelled out. However, no such measure was adopted. By the end of 1928 a total of 180,410 hectares had been distributed by the service of the Commission. On August 1, 1930, the figures were as follows:

In Macedonia	378,100	hectares distributed
In Thrace	13,500	" "
In other provinces	19,747	" "
Total	411,347	" "

It was expected that by the end of 1931 the cadaster of the Commission and the distribution among the refugees might be completed. A sum of £100,000 was set apart for the cadaster by the Commission.

The method of distribution adopted was ingenious. In the first place the village was divided into categories of land by a commission constituted in the same way as that which dealt with claims by native cultivators. When the village had been thus divided, the refugee community was called upon to form itself into groups of ten to twelve families who desired to have contiguous lots. Each category was then divided into the same number of portions as that of groups so formed. The head man of each group then drew by lot the portion falling to the group, and in this portion each family drew by lot the bit of land which it would receive for its holding. In this manner it was impossible for any family to allege, or to believe, that favor had been shown to any family in the distribution.[73]

It was often noted that when the survey had been com-

[72] Twentieth Quarterly Report, in League of Nations, *Official Journal*, January, 1929, p. 201.

[73] Twenty-Sixth Quarterly Report, in League of Nations, *Official Journal*, June, 1930, p. 716.

pleted and the land finally distributed to each refugee family, the cultivation of the soil was more intensive and the production greater. This is easy to understand. The settlers were unwilling to work hard on a piece of land that they were not certain would remain theirs at the final distribution.[74]

§ 413. The agricultural settlement. The most of the agricultural settlement of refugees was effected in Macedonia and Western Thrace where there were large areas of vacant land, and where great numbers of Moslems and Bulgarians left Greece by virtue of the Conventions of Lausanne and Neuilly. On a much smaller scale, colonization also took place in Epirus and Crete where the Commission found land left by the exchangeable Moslems. In the other regions of Greece few agricultural colonies were created. There was no land available in these regions except in Thessaly and Euboea, where large rural estates were expropriated in favor of native tenants on shares and little land could be found for refugees. In these regions the few colonies that were created devoted themselves to the development of special cultures, such as arboriculture, sericulture, and viticulture.

The agricultural colonization proceeded on the basis of group settlement. Even before the constitution of the Commission, the Greek Decree-Law of July 6, 1923, for the regulation of colonization required that the settlement should be made by legally constituted groups. Individual settlements were authorized only in exceptional circumstances. The group was constituted by the association of a number of families who appointed a council to represent the group, and by the deposit of the statutes with a local magistrate.

The ideal sort of settlement was to regroup together the refugees coming from each village in Turkey and to create their new colony in a place presenting the same climatic, geographic, and soil conditions as their place of origin. This was achieved gradually to a great extent. It tended to permit the refugees to recreate the community life, broken up by the exodus, with the least possible difficulties and handicaps.

[74] Fourteenth Quarterly Report, in League of Nations, *Official Journal*, July, 1927, p. 942.

However, this ideal was not or could not always be realized. The precipitated flight from Asia Minor had separated the village folk. Their sheltering on their arrival in Greece was of necessity done hurriedly and without consideration of their place of origin. For this reason a great many groups settled in rural colonies were not homogeneous, but included refugees from various places of origin.

Representatives of the groups, after making a tour of several provinces, chose the land on which they desired to be settled. They communicated this choice to the Ministry of Agriculture, which either accepted or rejected it. Competition between various groups in this matter was often keen, and the intervention of politicians, usually from among the refugees, who had been appropriately called in Greece 'fathers of refugees,' made the allocation of lands to the various groups not always in accordance with the requirements of the future communities.

The group at last reached its destination, and the government official delivered the land to the council of the group by an act signed by them and by him. Shares were allotted provisionally to each family, taking as a basis, in general, a family of four members, and adding or subtracting from the basal allotment for families of more or fewer persons.

The family share differed in the various places according to the nature of the cultivation, the quality of the soil, the value of the product, and the number of families of each group. In Western Macedonia and Thrace the family share of lands for cereal cultivation varied between 20 and 60 *stremmata,* with an average of 35 *stremmata* (3½ hectares or 8 2/3 acres). In Thessaly the family holdings were a little larger and in Epirus a little smaller. In the valley of the Maritsa, where the soil is very fertile, the family lot did not exceed 15 *stremmata.* In the tobacco districts in Macedonia and Thrace the shares per family varied between 9 and 20 *stremmata.* In the vegetable gardens and orchards in Macedonia and Old Greece an average of 10 *stremmata* was allotted to each family. In Crete the small fields were accompanied by small plots of vegetable garden and of vineyard and a number of olive trees. A certain amount of pasture land was granted to families engaged in cereal cultivation. To the cattle-breeding groups settled in the mountainous districts of Macedonia and Thrace an area of 80 to 100 *stremmata* for pasturage was granted to each family, with a small field. The value of family allotments differed naturally from place to place, varying between 30,000 and 80,000 drachmas, or about £85 to £225. For the settlement of each agricultural family after the allotment of land to it, there would have been required, as the Commission found, one horse, two oxen, a subsistence allowance, seed, harness, forage, plough, other implements, and a cart, of a total value of about 40,000 drachmas. The Commission, being compelled to settle the greatest possible number of refugees without delay, provided only one ploughing animal per family, and one cart for four families. It had to spend a part of its funds for public utility works, which were necessary for the solidity of the settlements. The average expenditure for each agricultural family has been further affected by the expenditures of the state, amounting to £1,688,150 from its budgets of 1922 to 1927 on agricultural settlement, which supplied some of the needs of the refugees. In addition, most of the refugees from Eastern Thrace and from Bulgaria were able to take away their ploughing animals, seed, and agricultural implements, and the Commission did not have to supply these.

As a general rule, the allotments made to each refugee family were small, and they were not always sufficient to its needs. For the time being this was not without its advantages. As there was no alternative, refugees had to adopt intensive methods of cultivation. The settlers found it necessary to be instructed in modern agriculture and were eager to listen to the experts of the Commission and of the government. The remarkable progress in agriculture in Greece, described below, received its impetus from the smallness of the holdings.

The refugee population in the colonies has proved very prolific in recent years, the birth rate in 1928 rising to 45 per thousand, while the death rate was only 12 per thousand. This fact increases the serious problem of the shortage of land. The large drainage works undertaken in the valleys of the Axios and the Struma are expected to alleviate this problem with a new supply of 1,500,000 *stremmata* of fertile land.

The settlement of agricultural refugees came practically to an end in 1927 and was definitely discontinued in 1928. At the end of 1928 a new, though small, influx of agricultural refugees occurred. These were Greeks of Pontus, who in 1922 sought refuge in the Caucasus, where they cultivated tobacco. The Greek government, being repeatedly requested by these people to permit them to come to Greece, allowed one thousand of them who had relations in Greece to immigrate.[75] They were settled mostly in Thrace and in the district of Kateriri at the foot of Mount Olympus, where they continued to cultivate tobacco.

By the end of June, 1928, the results of the work of the Commission were presented in its nineteenth Report.[76] The villages which had sprung up could be divided into three categories:

(1) Prosperous colonies which were solidly established. These represented nearly one-third of the settlements, and included many settled by Thracians and Pontians.

(2) Colonies not yet fully established, which still needed support and had to be watched. They represented about forty per cent of the settlements, and many of them were occupied by settlers from certain districts of Asia Minor who were not hereditarily predisposed to rapid progress. The efforts made by these settlers were not always in proportion to the resources furnished to them. In general they had not the saving spirit; rejoicings and merry-makings were frequent, and expenditure on luxuries took an increasing toll from their scanty means.

(3) The remainder, representing less than one-third of the settlers, were the unsuccessful colonies whose wretched aspect was the token of a hard and precarious existence. These included many of the mountain colonies and some of the vil-

[75] League of Nations, *Official Journal,* November, 1929, p. 1739.
[76] League of Nations, *Official Journal,* October, 1928, pp. 1683-1707.

lages in the plains. The lands granted them were poor, or the settlers were unfitted for agricultural work or were lacking in energy, and unable to oppose ill fortune. These settlers had still to fight against hunger, and lived a hand-to-mouth existence.

The last two categories of colonies presented continuous problems of an individualized sort to the Commission. As its report stated: "One settler seeks to obtain a further loan, another needs seed or forage; a draught or plough animal has died and must be replaced; or a man has fallen sick or lost his live-stock in an epidemic. Our offices are not always able to comply with these requests for fear of exceeding the financial limits which have been assigned to them and to which they must keep in order to provide for earlier or more pressing needs." The delay in obtaining the proceeds of the second Refugee Loan prevented the Commission from satisfying the more urgent needs and eliminating many tragedies.

In 1929 and 1930 the main task of the Commission was to meet the most urgent requirements of the settlements already created and to strengthen them by works of public utility, such as water supply, irrigation, agricultural and veterinary stations, mechanical cultivation, bridges, roads, etc.[77] In this respect the Commission gave a very liberal interpretation to the clause of the Protocol which required that expenditure was only to be incurred for productive works. By the end of 1929 the condition of the former unprosperous districts was much improved. Many of them were well on the road to prosperity. Significant in this connection was the case of the large district of Chalcidice, which in 1926 seemed likely to be abandoned altogether, and had become in 1929 "a flourishing centre of production."

In the first years of colonization the country districts lost a number of settlers who went to swell the forces of the workers in the large towns and cities. There resulted an overcrowding and unemployment in the towns which was fraught with social and economic dangers. However, the gradual and

[77] Twenty-Third Quarterly Report, in League of Nations, *Official Journal,* November, 1929, p. 1739.

relative prosperity of the rural districts later exercised an increasing attraction for persons capable of cultivating the soil, and there was a movement towards the country in 1928 and 1929. By the end of this year it seemed as if the agricultural settlement had reached a degree of stability.[78]

The only colonies which remained in an unsatisfactory condition were those of the mountainous frontier districts in Macedonia and Thrace. In these districts, where the soil is poor and unfit for cultivation, a pastoral population was settled, coming mainly from the Pontus. This population, 20,000 strong, formed 123 mountain colonies on the Macedonian frontier, while 12,000 more formed 131 colonies on the Thracian frontier. They received from the state originally the requisite amount of pastural land, some live-stock, and, whenever possible, a field. The severe winter and the incursions of the comitadjis in the first years of colonization did much damage to the live-stock of these settlers and caused some to migrate to the plains. Those who remained experienced great difficulties in communicating with the plains, as there was a complete lack of roads.

In view of the danger of the complete abandonment of these colonies, which possessed a national importance as the homes of a sturdy and warlike race of men, the government promulgated a special law, No. 4124 of April 23, 1929, to remedy the situation. A sum of 120,000,000 drachmas was provided for the reënforcement of these colonies. Two central Commissions were created in Macedonia and Thrace, which took decisions on reports by Sub-Commissions that visited the colonies and examined the situation on the spot. The settlers were furnished with additional supplies and were exempted from taxation. Works of public utility, such as roads, water supply, irrigation, sanitation, and the erection of schools and churches were carried out.

Sir John Campbell, Vice-Chairman of the Commission from January, 1924, to January, 1927, had returned to England and came back to Greece in May, 1929. He visited Macedonia and Thrace. His impressions of the work which had been accom-

[78] *Ibid.*

plished are contained in a report published in the League of Nations *Official Journal* for June, 1930, as follows: [79]

The aspect of the country has entirely changed. Everywhere, one sees the cheerful red roofs of the colonization settlements. Where formerly vast uncultivated plains stretched, there are now flourishing villages, full of bustling activity, and showing obvious signs of comfort, and in many cases of prosperity. The whole countryside is awake, and alive with new life. The refugees are working with admirable energy and courage. . . . All the indices of progress are apparent: new constructions made by the refugees themselves, important increases in their live stock, improvements to their dwellings, the cultivation of new and higher-yielding varieties, the use of improved methods of cultivation, the adornment of their houses. Excellent schools have been, and are being, built; . . . churches have been constructed, water supplies arranged for; in several cases, important minor irrigation projects have been carried to completion.

Sir John speaks of competent foreign observers who paid their tribute of admiration to the sterling qualities of the refugees, their questing and eager spirit, their confident outlook toward the future. "The refugees . . . have shown a spirit of progress—a readiness to adopt new methods, to try new crops, to adopt new varieties." "It is no exaggeration to say that, when visiting the refugee quarters in the majority of the towns in Macedonia and Thrace, one steps from the seventeenth to the twentieth century." The refugees are taking deeper and deeper root in the soil. It is significant to note that "these results are due, in the first place, to the courage, the energy, the capacity for work, the receptivity to new ideas, which characterize the mass of the refugees."

Professor Jacques Ancel wrote in the *Europe Centrale* of Prague of October 5, 1929: [80]

It is not in books that the vitality of a people may be studied. For several years now I have visited the Balkan countries during the summer, and I am able to mark, at every stage, the progress

[79] P. 712.

[80] Quoted in the Twenty-Fifth Report of the Commission, League of Nations, *Official Journal,* June, 1930, p. 714.

made. . . . Those miserable Turkish hamlets, nothing but hovels of mud and straw lying in the midst of an uncultivated plain or of unhealthy marshes, are now replaced by large cheerful villages on the hillside, with their little, white, red-roofed houses built alongside broad streets. All around, one sees sheaves of maize, fields of tobacco, with their tiny mauve flowers, . . . orchards with wonderful apples, and vines. . . . What a miracle! And this has been accomplished by the refugees in six years, aided by the Greek Government and the League of Nations. . . . Florina has become a magnificent orchard, with European varieties of trees flourishing in it. Karadjova, at the foot of the gigantic mountains of the Greco-Serbian frontier, is now a forest of mulberry trees. . . . The country round Salonika, which was formerly pasture for sheep, . . . is now transformed into orchards and vineyards. . . .

The rapid development of the various branches of agricultural life has resulted in such an abundance of products that in certain parts it bordered on over-production in 1929.[81] This has been followed by the sale of the produce at too low a price.

§ 414. **Agricultural production by refugees.** The production of cereals was that in which the refugees most generally engaged. Greece often suffers from drought. The Commission and the government, in an effort to make the settlements successful, undertook to instruct the refugees in the intensive cultivation of their fields, which would eliminate, at least in part, the dangers of drought. Seventy experimental and demonstration fields were established in Macedonia. Experiments were there made with the most suitable kinds of grain and their acclimatization. Several varieties of foreign and native wheat were tried. The experiments with the Australian wheat Canberra, among others, proved very successful. This wheat ripens in Greece before the period in which the burning *livas* wind destroys the harvest. In Chalcidice especially this seed yielded fifteen to twenty-five fold, and at Serres as much as twenty fold.[82]

In the experimental fields, the number of which continued

[81] *Ibid.*

[82] Experiments were also made with the Italian varieties, Cologna and Arditti.

to increase, the refugees themselves undertaking their cultivation, experiments were also made with new plants introduced for the first time in Macedonia, such as clover, sugar beet and forage beet-root, millet, castor oil plants, etc. Assisted and instructed by specialists of the Commission, the refugees carried on cultivation according to the most modern principles. The use of chemical manure went on steadily increasing. An Improvement Station created by the Ministry of Agriculture at Larissa was placed at the disposal of the Commission and transferred to Saloniki. Experiments in the cultivation of winter wheat were also undertaken on experimental plots at Saloniki and Florina.

The results of this effort appear in the following figures. From 1923 to 1928 the cultivated area of the whole of Greece gradually and continuously increased from 12,690,281 to 15,901,486 *stremmata,* an increase of 3,211,207 *stremmata,* or 25% of the area cultivated in 1923. The production of cereals showed the following development in tons: [83]

Crops	1922	1923	1924	1925	1926	1927 & 1928
wheat, barley, maslin, maize, oats, rye	639,811	624,120	544,729	772,152	850,565	over 1,000,000

With respect to wheat alone, the production increased as follows:

1922..................	245,540 tons
1923..................	238,992 "
1924..................	210,226 "
1925..................	305,411 "
1926..................	337,552 "
1927..................	438,342 "
1928..................	450,200 " [84]

Besides the culture of cereals, vine-growing assumed a great importance with the refugees. The Greek immigrants from Bulgaria were expert vine-growers. Hundreds of thousands of slips from Bulgaria and other countries were introduced. Nurseries were established in various places. Many plantations were laid out on uncultivated land and gave a considerable yield. In Thrace, owing to the phylloxera and other bad conditions, the vineyards had practically disappeared. A programme for the rehabilitation of the vine-

[83] League of Nations, *Official Journal,* October, 1928, p. 1691.
[84] *Ibid.,* p. 1692.

growing industry was worked out, based upon a minute study of the soil and of the varieties suitable for introduction. The execution of this programme was attended with complete success.[85]

Cotton and hemp were other branches of cultivation developed chiefly by the refugees. Market gardening received such an extension that for the first time it became a significant cultivation in Greece. Arboriculture was also encouraged by the distribution of fruit trees to refugees and the creation of stations. Five large stations were established in Macedonia, two in Thrace, one in Epirus, and one in Old Greece. Besides, 88 model orchards were established in Macedonia. Bee-keeping could not, at first, be developed, owing to the absence of honey-yielding flowers at certain seasons of the year. The Commission received a gift of seed of various melliferous plants from Switzerland. Then it began distributing thousands of hives to refugees.

There were among the refugees experienced silkworm breeders. Of these a colony of 550 families was established by the Commission on the Gulf of Nauplia. The sum of 32,000,000 drachmas was assigned for this purpose. 6500 *stremmata* were planted with mulberry trees. The Commission thus helped to reëstablish an ancient industry of the Peloponnesus, where in the Middle Ages the breeding of silkworms was very widespread. In Thrace and Macedonia, where conditions were favorable, some millions of mulberry trees were distributed. A large silkworm nursery was constructed according to the most modern methods at Ardea, in the frontier district of Karadjova in Macedonia. It was to benefit the local breeders, who were grouped in a federation composed of refugees and natives. Similar nurseries were created in other parts of Greece.[86]

Aside from cereals, the most important single branch of cultivation in which the refugees engaged was the growing of tobacco. Two-thirds of the total tobacco production for 1926 in Greece was produced by the refugees. The production in

[85] *Ibid.*
[86] *Ibid.*

1922, the year when the refugees arrived, amounted for the whole of Greece to 25,306,656 kilogrammes. Since then production more than doubled and tripled:

1924	50,096,125	kilogrammes
1925	65,462,009	"
1926	54,724,849	"
1927	61,709,013	"
1928	54,180,250	"
1929	85,944,990	" [87]

The export figures for tobacco are:

1924	41,832,923	kilogrammes of the value of	£ 6,821,236
1925	42,219,525	" " " " "	9,500,513
1926	55,324,172	" " " " "	8,838,981
1927	53,460,304	" " " " "	10,786,974

Thanks to the refugees, the production of tobacco increased, and from its export a sum of £18,000,000, exceeding in amount the two Refugee Loans, was brought into the country during the four years 1924-27. Not only did the refugees increase the quantity of tobacco produced, they also introduced new qualities, the finest varieties of Oriental tobacco and those most highly reputed for their aroma and flavor.

The tobacco industry has also its dark side. Expenses of cultivation of the finer qualities, handling costs and heavy taxes raise the price of tobacco. Greek tobacco, especially, when not of the finest quality, competes at a disadvantage in foreign markets with the tobacco of neighboring countries where the prices are lower. In addition, the tobacco industry has created in Greece a labor problem of a disquieting character. In 1928 there were 40,000 tobacco workers in the whole of Greece, about half of whom were refugees. The superabundance of labor contributed to the severity of the labor crisis. However, the power of the labor unions kept wages at a disproportionately high level. The producers, ill equipped to resist the buyers, sell at the prices dictated by them and forced downward by the labor troubles. The Commission took steps to concentrate the tobacco from Western Thrace at Xanthi, in order to insure its handling and sale by the refugee cooperative societies.[88]

[87] *Ibid.*, October, 1928, p. 1693; June, 1930, p. 717.
[88] *Ibid.*, October, 1928, pp. 1693-94.

Greece abounds in mountains and pasture lands, and the breeding of stock has always been an important industry. The Commission helped to preserve and develop this industry. Several stud farms were established in Macedonia and Thrace for horses, donkeys, bulls, and pigs. Arab and Hungarian sires, Cyprus asses, Jersey bulls, Brittany cows, Yorkshire pigs, Rhode Island Red and Plymouth Rock fowls were introduced at these farms and other zoötechnical stations. At the same time veterinary services were installed in various parts of Greece, and a microbiological laboratory was established in Saloniki. Two large model farms at Florina and Saloniki, and smaller stations at Langada, Verria, Yannitsa, Grevena, and Nevoliani continued the work of the improvement of live stock. Permanent improvement could not be expected without the extensive cultivation of plants for fodder, hitherto unknown in Greece. Seed for such plants was distributed to refugees. On the other hand, the limitation of pasture lands induced the owners of stock to undertake the cultivation of forage plants with which to supplement the lack of pasture.[89] The stock of the nomad shepherds has been reduced by 50% through the bringing under the plough of the large pastures. This loss, however, was more than compensated for by the fact that large numbers of refugees commenced breeding animals both large and small. The acquisition of such animals by refugees until December 31, 1928, is shown in the following table:

	Cattle	Other animals
Distributed by the Commission	81,245	77,354
Distributed by the state	70,695	54,776
Acquired by the refugees	213,324	569,227
	365,264	701,357

§ 415. **Mechanical cultivation.** Much of the land in Macedonia and Thrace had remained uncultivated for many years. To make these soils available for immediate cultivation, motor tractors and ploughs were necessary to break up the sod. In Macedonia to the end of 1929 a total of 270,155 *stremmata* had been broken up by 47 tractors of the Direction of Coloni-

[89] League of Nations, *Official Journal,* June, 1930, p. 718.

zation. The effect of deep ploughing has been to create vineyards in the Saloniki plain and in Chalcidice from land where nothing had grown within human memory but briars and thistles. Furthermore, the yield of cereals was considerably increased by tractor cultivation of the impoverished soil. The breaking up of land was also carried on in Epirus, Thessaly, and Achaia.

Agricultural machinery was furnished by the Commission to individuals or groups or to agricultural associations. The machinery distributed consisted especially of seed-sorters, reapers and reapers-and-binders, threshers, seed-drills, etc. As a rule the cost was paid by the Commission, the peasants undertaking to repay it in from two to five years. The demands for such machinery increased gradually. At first the machinery belonging to agricultural associations was operated, supervised, and repaired by experts of the Commission. Its mechanics and drivers trained others, and the use seemed certain to become common.

The service of mechanical cultivation was transferred to the Ministry of Agriculture at the end of December, 1930. The service consisted of 150 technical employees, well trained and disciplined.[90]

§ 416. **Drainage and irrigation work.** In the middle of 1928 a contract for a loan of $75,000,000 was concluded between the Greek government and foreign capitalists, for the financing of public utility works which were closely connected with the task of the Commission. The contract for this loan was cancelled, but the government found means from other sources to carry out the contracts for the works. These works comprised road construction and important drainage and irrigation undertakings. Already, in 1926, the drainage of the valley of Axios was begun. The Struma (Strymon) was another river whose course was to be regulated for the purpose of recovering, in combination with the drainage of Lakes Boutkovo and Achinos and the marshes of Philippi, an area of 1,600,000 *stremmata* of very fertile land. In the plains of Serres and Drama, watered by the Struma, the Commission

[90] League of Nations, *Official Journal,* June, 1930, p. 718.

had established many large settlements, all of which were to benefit by these works.

It was calculated that the execution of the work would absorb a sum of $15,000,000. On an area of 1,600,000 *stremmata* to be reclaimed, the cost per *stremma* of drained land would amount to less than 1000 drachmas, which was a sum that could easily be paid from the produce.[91]

The reclamation of land by these works would cause the disappearance of marshes and help the fight against the malaria which sapped the energy and force of the cultivators. Agricultural production would become more secure, because of the fertility of the soil and the elimination of the floods which for centuries had carried away the produce of the fields.

In the beginning of 1929, the Commission was engaged in carrying out drainage work in Macedonia at the Saloniki agricultural station (1000 *stremmata*) and on the land belonging to the colony of Vangueni in the district of Edessa (1000 *stremmata*); and at Mudania in Chalcidice (500 *stremmata*). At Ptolemaïs (Kojani) the large marsh of Sari-Ghiol (25,000 *stremmata*) was also to be reclaimed. Embankments were being constructed to protect 15,000 *stremmata* belonging to the colony of Nea Gallipoli from floods, and irrigation works were begun at Obar (45,000 *stremmata*).[92]

The importance of the work of drainage of the valley of the Axios will be understood when it will be taken into consideration that this included the following:

1. The drainage and canalization of Lakes Ardjan and Amatovo, the water being taken to the river Axios.

2. Correction of the course of the Axios from Voemitsa to the Saloniki-Monastir railway.

3. Correction and deviation of the Axios from the Saloniki-Monastir railway to the sea.

4. Correction of the course of the river Gallicos.

5. The drainage of Lake Yannitsa through a navigable canal to the sea, utilizing the bed of the river Ludia (Karasmak).

[91] League of Nations, *Official Journal,* January, 1929, p. 202.
[92] League of Nations, *Official Journal,* July, 1929, p. 1189.

6. The construction of a peripheric canal east of Lake Yannitsa, linking up the waters of all the tributaries and diverting them to the river Aliakmon.

7. Correction of the course of the Aliakmon from the ravine to the sea, including protective dikes and deviations.

8. The study and construction of an irrigation system for the plain of Saloniki.

It was estimated that all this work might be completed by 1935. The contracting company hoped to recover 442,000 *stremmata* for cultivation. The experts of the Commission estimated that the area would not exceed 370,000 *stremmata,* and found evidence of the presence of alkaline soil, which is unsuitable for cultivation.

The work in the plain of the Struma (Strymon) was intended to regulate the course of this river. The Struma rises south of Sofia and debouches into the Gulf of Orphano, collecting throughout its course water from an area of 17,300 square kilometres. It emerges into Greek territory from the gorge of Rupel on the Bulgarian-Greek frontier, flowing 3000-4000 cubic metres per second. Its length in the plain of Serres is 110 kilometres. This plain has an area of 1,180,000 *stremmata,* and is crossed lengthwise by the river, which at the south-east end of the plain forms Lake Achinos, with an area varying from 110,000 to 140,000 *stremmata,* according to the level of the water. The river passes out of the lake through the gorge of Amphipolis, and after a course of 10 kilometres empties into the Gulf of Orphano. The Struma carries down an enormous quantity of débris and a very fine silt, which it deposits in its course across the plain, thereby overflowing and raising its banks. It frequently changes its bed, and invades fertile cultivated areas and many villages.

The other main waterway of the Serres plain is the Belitsa drainage canal, which collects all the waters descending to the plain from the mountains in the northeast and also the waters overflowing from the Struma. The bed of the Belitsa has no embankments, therefore the water running into it overflows and forms a series of marshes. In addition, from the mountains surrounding the plain in every direction there descend rapid torrents carrying large quantities of débris, mainly sand and pebbles, which cover part of the cultivated land.

This is the condition of the waterways of this plain which it is desired to remedy. Out of 1,180,000 *stremmata,* the area of the Serres plain, only 437,000 are not liable to be flooded, 290,000 consist of permanent marshes and lakes, 283,000 are periodically flooded, and 170,000 are so saturated as to be unusable for cultivation. The area of the plain of Drama which would come within the scope of drainage work is 380,000 *stremmata,* of which 117,000 at present are mud banks and another 43,000 are periodically flooded.

The main problem for the hydraulic works in the valley is to determine where to place the débris carried down by the Struma. A solution which found much favor was to construct in the plain of Serres a lake in which to collect the débris, the river being diverted there through one of its former branches. At the southeast corner of the lake a weir could be built, enabling the flow of the river to be fixed at 500 cubic metres of water per second. From this point on the former bed of the river, provided with strong embankments, would be used, and the river would cross Lake Achinos from end to end by a drainage canal.[93]

An area of over 1,000,000 *stremmata* was to be reclaimed through this regulation of the course of the Struma, the Belitsa canal, and other minor waterways.

§ 417. Water supply for rural colonies. The Commission often established colonies at places where land was available for cultivation although there was no water supply. In the first years of settlement the refugees suffered greatly on this account, being compelled to transport water for their use from distant points. The Commission proceeded to provide water for these villages, either by causing borings to be made whenever water was believed to exist underground or by building aqueducts. At the end of October, 1929, the amount of work done was as follows:

Aqueducts	474	of a total	length	of	750 kilometres
Artesian wells	508	" "	depth	"	23,430 metres
Ordinary wells	648	" "	"	"	7,856 "

[93] League of Nations, *Official Journal,* November, 1929, pp. 1743-44.

The problem of water supply was not solved in all colonies at the time the Commission reached the end of its work.[94]

§ 418. **Agricultural housing.** When the Commission got to work in 1924 it had at its disposal two categories of rural buildings for the settlement of refugees: (*a*) houses of Moslems and Bulgarians who left or were leaving Greece under the Conventions of Neuilly and Lausanne; and (*b*) houses built by the Colonization Service of the Greek government from 1922 to 1924. The Commission supplied the further needs by causing thousands of additional rural buildings to be erected, especially in places where new colonies were established. In the beginning the Commission followed the system employed by the state, which consisted in advancing to shelterless refugees sums of money to enable them to erect their own houses by supplying their own labor to a large extent. This system gave good results only in Thrace. For the most part the Commission adopted the system of building by small local firms of contractors or of employing the refugees established in each village as workmen under the superintendence of the technical service of the Commission. Contracts were also made with building societies.[95]

The houses built in the first years by the Commission were usually of two rooms and a small hall. They were monotonous both as regards the lay-out of the streets and the type of the house. The refugee whose condition improved after the first years of privations and sufferings was not particularly enraptured with these homes, and after 1928 the Commission had to introduce a certain variety and make houses of three rooms instead of two. The standard price of two-room houses was £100 or 37,000 drachmas. The larger houses cost 52,000 drachmas. In Thrace, where the refugees built their own houses, not only was their price much below that at which dwellings were built by building companies, but the houses presented a variety, a picturesqueness, and a special individuality.

A few thousand rural buildings were erected by the Commission in the regions of Greece other than Macedonia and

[94] League of Nations, *Official Journal,* June, 1930, p. 716.

[95] Sixth Quarterly Report of the Commission, in League of Nations, *Official Journal,* 1925, p. 1056.

Thrace. By the end of 1929 a total of 10,048 houses had been constructed in Old Greece, Epirus, and the Islands. In addition, 3,981 houses of Bulgarian and Moslem emigrants were repaired by the Commission for the use of refugees.

In Macedonia and Thrace the situation at the end of October, 1929, was as follows:

Houses constructed by the Commission	54,780
Houses left by the exchange of Turks and the emigration of Bulgarians	54,027
Houses in course of construction or to be constructed	2,485
Total	111,292

These did not enable the Commission to make provision for all the refugees established in these two regions, who numbered about 130,000 families. In a number of the houses two or three families were settled under undesirable conditions. Furthermore, at least 10,000 of the houses left by Moslem emigrants were in ruinous condition and in dire need of repairs to be made really inhabitable. Lastly, a minimum of 12,600 houses were still required to house the rural families who were still sheltered in huts and makeshift quarters.[96]

It is a general desire with the Greek to have his child educated. This explains the fact that rural refugees, even before they were settled in their new colony, sent "anxious requests" to the Commission for a school building. As a rule the Commission was unable to comply with such requests. However, the Commission provided the material and the refugees the labor for about 400 school buildings. In some villages one of the available buildings was turned into a school. The greatest number of colonies built their own schools, either without outside assistance or with the financial aid of the Government.

§ 419. **Agricultural associations.** The settlement of rural refugees gave impetus to the coöperative idea in agriculture in Greece. Almost one-fourth of the rural associations in existence in Greece in 1929 were formed by refugee associations, and a great number were also associations of refugees and natives together. At the end of 1927 there were already 656

[96] League of Nations, *Official Journal,* June, 1930, p. 715.

refugee associations in Macedonia, with a total membership of 44,815, and 234 in Thrace, with 13,258 members. These organizations were mostly associations for lending, buying, and selling, with limited liability. About 100 were unlimited in liability. They effected purchases of farm implements and sales of their products. They erected barns and coöperative stores.[97]

The National Bank of Greece, which until 1929 was practically the only bank which dealt in rural credit, had loaned as follows in 1928 to individual farmers and to rural coöperative associations:

	Number	Loans in drachmas
Native farmers	46,185	271,910,906
Native associations	2,327	750,338,890
Refugee farmers	24,603	63,780,797
Refugee associations	983	259,445,860
	3,310	1,345,476,453

It is to be noted that in this total of loans made in 1928, the arrears amounted in March, 1929, to 32,150,000 drachmas, or 2.39 per cent. The arrears were due to the considerable damage suffered by the crops and to sales at a loss.[98]

Two of the most interesting accomplishments of rural associations must be mentioned. One is that of the coöperative societies of the tobacco growers of Xanthi, which united for the operation in common of the warehousing, sale, and manipulation of tobacco, and for defence against the combination of commercial companies which tried to set the price of tobacco at a figure satisfactory to themselves. As a result of the above union of the societies, the tobacco of their members was sold at more than double the price set by the companies.

Another of the successful experiments was the large silkworm nursery of Ardea in the valley of the Karadjova, for the storing of 130,000 silkworm cocoons. The Commission advanced 700,000 drachmas to a local federation of producers composed of natives and refugees for the construction of an up-to-date building of four stories. The building was also to serve for the storing of local tobacco, the tobacco harvest not

[97] *Ibid.*, October, 1928, pp. 1696-97.
[98] League of Nations, *Official Journal*, July, 1929, pp. 1190-91.

coinciding with the production of cocoons. The ground floor was to be used for storing red pepper, one of the principal products of the district.[99]

§ 420. **The urban settlement.** When the Commission began its functions in 1924 it found that the Greek government was already applying a general scheme for urban settlement of refugees, which consisted mainly of building urban dwellings for the refugees in or near the cities or towns where it was hoped that they would be able to find and engage in gainful occupations. This work was intrusted by the Greek government to an autonomous administration, the Relief Fund, and it was continued by it and by the Ministry of Relief after May, 1925. The Commission originally did not include the urban settlement in its work. Later, by agreement with the government, the Commission undertook to improve and extend the urban quarters started by the former.

When an estimate of the number of urban refugees was made in 1927 the following numbers were given: [100]

1. Athens and Piraeus district,	about	75,000	families	or	300,000 persons
2. Macedonia and Thrace,	"	75,000	"	"	300,000 "
3. Old Greece and Islands,	"	25,000	"	"	100,000 "

The city of Saloniki, it was supposed, alone contained 170,000 refugees.[101] Thus it was thought that 60% of the town refugees were concentrated in the three largest cities of Greece, Athens, Piraeus, and Saloniki. The concentration in these three cities is explained by the fact that at the time the refugees swarmed into Greece, in the autumn of 1922, they afforded the greatest number of convenient shelters, such as theatres, schools, churches, warehouses, and requisitioned houses, and ready materials for the erection of temporary barracks; and also by the expectation of the government that most of the town refugees must ultimately be settled near the

[99] Twenty-Third Quarterly Report, *ibid.*, November, 1929, p. 1741.
[100] Fourteenth Quarterly Report, *ibid.*, July, 1927, pp. 947-948.
[101] The Sixteenth Quarterly Report, in League of Nations, *Official Journal*, February, 1928, pp. 236-237, based on census returns, gives the number of urban refugees as 615,000. The difference was due chiefly to the fact that in the earlier figures the number of refugees in Saloniki had been vastly overestimated.

large cities, where it was hoped that industry and commerce would provide gainful work.

The condition of the refugees was, indeed, so tragic in the first two years, 1922 and 1923, that the need of affording to town refugees healthy living quarters in order to reduce the appalling mortality among them led every other consideration. The Commission, when adopting its programme for urban settlement in the beginning of 1925, bound as it was by the provision of the Geneva Protocol that the funds of the loan should be devoted to productive work, was confronted with two solutions as to the urban refugees. One was to make them cultivators and settle them on the land. It was realized that the older persons would find it very difficult to become successful cultivators of the soil. The new generation might easily adapt itself to agriculture. However, many families had lost their young men in the wars or in the exodus from Asia Minor. A census taken by the Commission in June, 1926, in the four refugee quarters in the outskirts of Athens showed that while male and female refugees below 16 years of age were about equal in numbers, the inequality between the numbers of the two sexes after the age of sixteen was very great. Thus, of a total of 42,204 refugees above sixteen in the above quarters, 16,029 only were males against 26,175 females, or 62% against 38% in favor of the so-called weaker sex. Moreover, the available land in Greece was restricted in area, and it was not advisable to deprive the farming refugee populations of a part of such land for an experimental settlement of town refugees.

The other solution was to provide the urban refugees with urban trades. This could not be accomplished in a brief period. For one thing, the callings in which the town refugees had been engaged in their place of origin were well represented in Greece. In fact, the small traders, artisans, and shopkeepers in Greece, before the influx of the refugees, were already too numerous in the small towns and the larger cities. It was only by the creation of new industries, or the multiplication of gainful occupations in new centres developed by the changed economic conditions, the course of commerce, the increase of agricultural production, the development of a mercantile marine, drainage and irrigation work, etc., that the settlement of the town refugees could ultimately be accomplished. All this was too complicated a problem, and one in the solution of which the Commission could not use the resources of the loan on a productive basis. Everything was as yet speculative and uncertain.

The Commission, accordingly, preferred, after lending financial support to certain outstanding arts and crafts of the refugees which promised an assured return for the money lent, to limit its work on urban settlement to the construction of urban buildings of a permanent character which could be let or sold. This construction was mainly made in the large cities, Athens, Piraeus, and Saloniki, where already the Greek government had begun new urban quarters. It was also believed that the first two cities were places in which new industries were most likely to be established and to absorb the refugees, while Saloniki, as centre of the most important agricultural district of Greece, promised to afford gainful work to a great number of refugees. However, the Commission erected urban quarters in many other cities and towns all over Greece, where conditions were deemed favorable to such settlement, or where a beginning of settlement was found in the buildings left by the Bulgarian emigrants and the Moslem exchangeables.

In the first years of its work, the Commission turned its attention mainly to rural colonization. It appropriated only one-tenth of the first Refugee Loan to urban settlement. It was only in August, 1927, before the second loan was obtained, that a systematic investigation into the condition of the urban refugees and their needs was made. These refugees were then classified as follows:

1. Those who lived in houses which were in good condition and fulfilled all the requirements of permanent dwellings. 39,450 families belonged to this class.

2. Those who lived in houses which would be fit for habitation for a certain time. 26,288 families were of this class.

3. Those who were still sheltered under bad conditions, for instance, in churches, warehouses, houses in ruinous condition,

or houses scandalously overcrowded. No less than 35,667 families belonged to this class.

4. Those who lived in private houses, either as tenants or as proprietors, outside the quarters inhabited exclusively by refugees. Not all of these made declarations. The number of 23,077 families was deemed to be only about one-half of the real number.[102]

At the completion of this investigation, the Commission decided that the task was, first, to build homes for the 35,667 families who were still sheltered under bad conditions, and then to ameliorate the condition of the second class above referred to.

At the end of 1929, the urban houses built in various parts of Greece by the Commission were as follows: [103]

	Quarters	Houses
Continental Greece	26	14,857
Peloponnesus	12	1,232
Islands	14	1,086
Macedonia	41	3,953
Thrace	32	6,215
Total	125	27,343

To this total must be added 22,337 dwellings constructed by the state in quarters scattered over most of the towns in Greece before the Commission took up the work of urban settlement, and several thousands built by the government subsequently. The work of properly sheltering all the town refugees will undoubtedly still require a number of years.

Until 1929 the houses built by the Commission and the government were single or double houses. At that time the construction of apartment houses was contemplated, in view of the fact that the new quarters spread over so large an area as to increase considerably the expenses of the municipalities. The refugees, however, did not appear to welcome the institution of the horizontal ownership of apartments to render it possible for them to purchase the dwellings.

[102] League of Nations, *Official Journal,* February, 1928, pp. 236-237.

[103] Twenty-Seventh Quarterly Report, August 21, 1930, in League of Nations, *Official Journal,* November, 1930, p. 1481.

Urban dwellings were mostly constructed by building companies under contracts made with the Commission, and their price differed according to the size from 30,000 to 190,000 drachmas, or $400 to $2500. By the end of 1929 the Refugee Settlement Commission had expended 798,402,532 drachmas in urban settlement, while an additional 98,885,818 had been spent by the Relief Fund before the urban quarters were handed over to the Commission. The total amount of 897,-288,350 drachmas is distributed as follows from the point of view of the purposes to which it was appropriated:

Building	762,695,100
Works of general utility	71,783,068
Maintenance, administration, survey, and salaries of technical staff	62,810,184 [104]

Parallel with this work of sheltering the refugees were their efforts to obtain the means of subsistence. There were two ways in which the Greek government tried to help these efforts. First, it began public works of all kinds in all parts of Greece. Great numbers of laborers among the refugees thus found gainful employment. Moreover, it succeeded in obtaining from the National Bank of Greece, which created a special department for this purpose, the grant of vocational loans to small laborers and artisans among the refugees. Between July and December 31, 1925, the National Bank advanced the sum of 138,000,000 drachmas to 21,886 refugee tradesmen. These advances have been repaid remarkably well. These refugee Greeks, with their alertness, industry, and persistence, and aided by this direct help, have been able to reëstablish their business or calling.

According to the reports of the Commission, aside from this assistance, and the support of all kinds they received from the Greek people, the refugees relied mainly on their own labor and intelligence. "During three years at least, the urban refugees, urged by some strange instinct, were continually on the move. There are very few urban families which have not flitted again and again from one large town to another in order to see with their own eyes the possibilities offered by

[104] League of Nations, *Official Journal,* November, 1930, p. 1481.

each locality visited. . . . Gradually families have sorted themselves out in such a way that each is now settled in the locality it considers most suitable. The process is terminated, and what neither the State nor any form of management could have accomplished when the refugees were arriving in Greece, namely, the selection for each category of the locality in which it would be most likely to settle down without difficulty, has been achieved by the refugees themselves." The excessive growth of urban centres had certainly many disadvantages. But excess of urban population has always been a characteristic of Hellenism in Turkey, where the Greeks have for centuries congregated in the great cities in Thrace and Asia Minor, the powerful centres of intellectual or social life.[105]

In one of its reports the Commission described the condition of the urban refugees in the summer of 1928, distinguishing them into three classes, as follows: [106]

1. Refugees who were able to make for themselves an enviable or even brilliant position in trade, industry, banking, or the liberal professions in Greece. Most of these had brought parts of their fortunes from Turkey, but some had arrived in Greece without capital.

2. The second and most numerous class of refugees had been able to build up a new life in Greece by dint of hard work, perseverance, energy, good sense, or ingenuity, and had a comfortable existence or a modest livelihood.

3. A third class, less numerous than the second, but larger than the first, comprised those refugees who were still in an undesirable condition. They were of two categories: (*a*) those who in their country of origin occupied a good social and economic position, but, owing to repeated ill-luck or unsuccess, had been unable to establish themselves in their adopted country, keeping up, perhaps, a decent appearance at the price of privations of all sorts; and (*b*) working-class people, small shopkeepers, artisans, laborers, or unemployed, who were vegetating or living a hand-to-mouth existence. They represented

[105] Nineteenth Quarterly Report, in League of Nations, *Official Journal*, October, 1928, p. 1705.

[106] *Ibid.*, pp. 1703-04.

the misfits that accumulate and ferment in large urban centres.

In the next two years the situation of this third class of town refugees appears to have improved, as the writer was able to learn on his visit to Greece. The large public works (roads, drainage, etc.) to which a new impetus was given by the government of Mr. Venizelos, provided work for great numbers of refugees. It is the class of middlemen and of small traders that seems to be the most severely suffering in the large cities, such as Saloniki.

The first class of urban refugees above referred to needs a number of remarks. It includes a large percentage of people who have nothing in common with the hungry and destitute refugees who swarmed into the villages and towns of Greece. They were inhabitants of Constantinople and its neighborhood, Smyrna, Aivali, and other great centres in Turkey, where they were leaders in liberal professions, in banking, shipping, commerce, and industry. These persons brought to Greece not only their great abilities in their respective callings, and especially their long tradition and experience in organization and international commerce, but also their capital. Although no data exist as to the amount of the capital thus imported into Greece, it must have been very large, if we may judge from the great development that followed immediately after the coming of these people into Greece in the great centres of the country, such as Athens, Piraeus, Saloniki, etc., and from the economic depression in Turkey occasioned by their departure.

Great as have been the effects of the importation of this capital into Greece, especially in the years of stress and difficulties after the military disaster in Asia Minor, the influence of this class of refugees in reorganizing and invigorating the economic life of the people has been greater still. The men of business in Old Greece were distinctly provincial in outlook, and their capacity to compete in the international market was limited. The refugee bankers, shipowners, and merchants, who had held in their hands most of the foreign trade of Turkey, were much superior to the ordinary merchant or banker of Old Greece. Furthermore, they brought into Greece not only their experience and capital, but also a body of employees and specialists.

The result was that in the large centres a new spirit permeated the economic life of Greece, and that a short space of time saw the rise and development of new industries, which used to advantage the raw materials produced in the country, such as wool, cotton, fruits, tobacco, etc. Thus, to mention only two examples, the production of woollen stuffs and fabrics jumped from 1,700,000 yards in 1922 to 2,600,000 in 1925, and the production of cement from 37,000 tons to 60,000 in the same year. Special mention must be made of the carpet industry, arts and crafts, and fisheries.

§ 421. Oriental carpets. The peasants in Old Greece possessed from time immemorial the domestic art of making carpets from the wool of their flocks. But these were of an inferior type, totally different from the famous Oriental carpets of knotted points made on a high warp. Thus the Oriental carpet industry was transplanted to Greece only with the coming of the refugees, when it took root both in rural colonies and in urban centres. About 11,000 specialist refugee women workers were occupied in 1928 in the manufacture of carpets, employing 5600 looms with an annual production exceeding 250,000 square metres or 300,000 square yards. A sum of £100,000 from the supplementary second Refugee Loan was devoted by the Commission to encouraging the carpet industry.[107] The main centre of the industry is the quarter of Ionia in the Athenian suburbs. The qualities manufactured in Greece are the six chief products of Anatolia, Uchak, Giordès, Pergames, Sparta, Sivas, and a new quality, Seldjuk, specially manufactured for the American market. The carpet, although an industrial product, is also an artistic product in the composition of the design and the combination of tones.

The government created in 1929 an autonomous "Greek Carpet-making Organization," with the purpose of protecting the production and encouraging the sale of carpets. The organization was granted special rights as regards collecting its

[107] Nineteenth Quarterly Report, in League of Nations, *Official Journal,* October, 1928, p. 1701.

advances and loans. A special tax on raw materials (wool and cotton yarn) was paid into account of the Organization.[108]

§ 422. **Arts and crafts.** With the view of providing work for urban refugees and taking advantage of the traditional abilities of refugees, the Commission devoted the sum of £12,320 4*s*. 7 *d*. to encouraging certain domestic arts and crafts. For centuries past, the Pontians have been renowned for the manufacture of copper articles, the inhabitants of Ionian cities and the Dardanelles for pottery, and the Caucasians for leather and silver objects. On the other hand, women refugees were experienced in weaving fine silk tissues or woollen rugs. The sum allocated by the Commission served to organize the production and marketing of these different products.[109]

When the Commission was wound up, a Corporation was created to take up the Arts and Crafts service, so that the work could be continued and further developed. This service included especially the following industries: [110]

(1) The Kiutahia pottery. This industry, a specialty of the village of that name in Asia Minor, is derived from Persian art. The refugee artisans tried to revive this art, the secret of which they possessed, having handed it down as a cherished tradition from father to son. After many unsuccessful attempts, the industry reached in 1929 a stage where great artistic and commercial progress appeared likely. A loan of 600,000 drachmas was granted by the Commission.

(2) Fancy materials and embroideries. These industries were established in various localities in Greece. Thus, in Crete the domestic industry of woven materials, with designs and characteristics of its own, had begun to decline. This has been revived and reorganized by private enterprise, not as formerly to produce goods of the ordinary class, but to meet the gradually increasing demand for articles of luxury. As a result of a loan of 100,000 drachmas from the Commission, the organization of the 'Double Axe,' the Minoan emblem, spread among the inhabitants of the urban districts of Crete.

[108] League of Nations, *Official Journal,* July, 1929, pp. 1193-94; June, 1930, pp. 726-727.

[109] League of Nations, *Official Journal,* October, 1928, p. 1701.

[110] *Ibid.,* November, 1929, pp. 1747-48.

A similar undertaking has been established at Zante, with the aid of 125,000 drachmas from the Commission, refugee labor being employed. At Saloniki and Florina loans were granted to weavers from Broussa who had the tradition of the manufacture of the beautiful fabrics of that district. At Athens a loan of 150,000 drachmas was granted to the Diacosmitiki Decoration Company, established by refugees from Smyrna.

(3) The silk-working industry was steadily growing in Macedonia, and a loan of 500,000 drachmas was advanced by the Commission.

(4) Workshops at Athens. Silverware and chased and enamelled articles were formerly important industries in Epirus and Northern Macedonia. The bazaars of Janina and Kastoria were famed for such articles. Today there are still clever artisans, but the market is shrinking. The refugees brought a very similar art from the interior of Asia Minor. A loan of 150,000 drachmas was advanced for a workshop for *objets d'art,* silver work, and enamel ware, and another of 100,000 for a workshop for pure enamel ware, both of which have been established by refugees.

§ 423. **Fisheries.** At certain points along the coast, in particular the coast of the Peninsula of Chalcidice, in the channel of the Euripos between Euboea and the mainland, and on the coast of Attica, the Commission established refugee fishing villages. In these were settled seafaring and fishing folk, mostly from the Bosphorus and the Princes' Islands. In addition to a dwelling and a small shop, and ground for a vineyard, orchard, or vegetable garden, nets and sail, steam, or motor-driven boats were acquired by these settlers, usually in groups of six or eight heads of families. They were, in general, skilled in the harvests of the sea; they located fishing grounds and introduced new fishing appliances into Greece. They thus gave a new stimulus to fishing in Greece, where pisci culture was badly neglected, and the local fishermen employed most primitive methods. Although complete statistics are lacking, in the Gulf of Euboea alone 390,000 more kilogrammes were caught in 1923 than in 1922.[111]

[111] *Greek Refugee Settlement,* pp. 186-187.

§ 424. Works of public health and general utility. The liberal interpretation by the Commission of the clause of the Geneva Protocol providing that expenditure was only to be incurred for productive work is shown by the fact that the Commission incurred expenditure for certain major works, the return from which it would be difficult to calculate, but the necessity of which is apparent if the settlement of the refugees was to have a sound and permanent basis. These works are the improvement of public health and of communications.

§ 425. Public health improvement. Macedonia and Thrace were two provinces of Greece where malaria played havoc. Marshes abounded all over these regions. Refugees suffered from malaria even more than from any other of the ills visited upon them since they were driven from their homes. At first great use was made of quinine as a prophylactic. The American Red Cross despatched whole tons of it to keep the refugees in health.[112] More substantial and radical means were soon put into execution, such as schemes of drainage and precautions against mosquitoes. The whole sanitary situation in the regions where refugees were established was precarious during the first years.

The Commission decided from the beginning of 1925 to take the sanitary conditions in hand more vigorously than before. It adopted a scheme for the establishment of dispensaries in small agricultural centres to which a certain number of neighboring villages were affiliated. The inhabitants of these villages had the right to the services of a doctor appointed by the Commission, to medicines, and to the distribution of quinine. A payment was fixed for medicines and quinine, but families known to be without means received them free. The cost of setting up these dispensaries and of the doctors' and pharmacists' salaries was debited to each refugee individually in equal shares.[113]

[112] League of Nations, *Official Journal,* April, 1924, p. 588; *ibid.,* April, 1925, p. 511.

[113] Sixth Quarterly Report of the Commission, in League of Nations, *Official Journal,* August, 1925, p. 1056. Some of these dispensaries were subsequently bought by the refugee colonies.

The effect of these measures was most encouraging. In the first nine months of 1925, in Macedonia, among a population of 413,804 settled refugees the average death rate was 19 per thousand per annum, while the average birth rate for the same population over the same period was 29 per thousand. In Thrace, among a population of 63,572 settled refugees, the average rates were 20 for deaths and 30 for births. The situation as to malaria had appreciably improved. In the three worst months, July, August, and September, the number of cases of malaria treated by the service of the Commission in Macedonia was 25,733, with only 100 deaths.[114]

In Chalcidice successful experiments were made with the use of Schweinfurth-green for destroying the anopheles mosquito. From the month of March onwards a territory of about one thousand *stremmata* of marsh was treated every ten days by spraying the surface of the stagnant water with Schweinfurth-green, the effect of which was to destroy the larvae and prevent new cases of malaria. In 1928 a nursery of eucalyptus plants was laid down. This species grows rapidly in wet soil and possesses antimiasmatic properties which are valuable against malaria.

By an agreement of the Commission with the General Staff of the Army, squads of engineers coöperated with the services of the Commission for the execution of minor sanitary works.[115]

Marshlands of great extent and most dangerous swamps were found in Macedonia in the districts watered by the rivers Axios, Strymon and Haliakmon and near certain lakes. These were great malaria centres and their clearance and drainage would considerably improve the hygienic conditions of the districts. But the Commission did not feel that it could undertake a work of such a scope and left it to the Greek government.[116]

When, at the end of 1929, the Commission turned over to the government the Health Service established by it in Mace-

[114] Eighth Quarterly Report of the Commission, in League of Nations, *Official Journal,* February, 1926, p. 328.
[115] League of Nations, *Official Journal,* April, 1926, p. 558. .
[116] *Ibid.,* July, 1927, p. 944.

donia, the service comprised 59 dispensaries and 145 medical officers and chemists. At that time Greece had drawn up, with the aid of the health officers whom the League of Nations had sent to Greece, a scheme for a national service of public health. Most of the 59 dispensaries had their own premises, which contained, besides the examination and waiting rooms, comfortable quarters for the medical officers, the pharmacists, and their families.

By the end of 1929 the birth rate among the refugees was 45.7 per thousand and the death rate 12.6.

The malaria and other hardships had occasioned another danger to health. The Refugee Settlement Commission noted the prevalence of tuberculosis among the refugees in its Report to the Council dated February 17, 1928. Relations were then established between the Commission and the Health Organization of the League of Nations, with the hope that the latter might render assistance to the Commission and the Greek government in dealing with this situation.[117] An anti-tuberculosis programme for Greece was outlined in May, 1928, in a report by Professor Léon Bernard, which was supported by a memorandum by Dr. Copanaris, Director of the Public Health Service in Greece. The Medical Director of the League, Dr. L. Rajchman, was requested to study a detailed plan for carrying out this programme. The programme advocated the establishment of dispensaries, hospital accommodation, and organization for the protection of children, and notably the setting up of villages for the reception of tuberculosis cases and their families.[118]

A microbiological laboratory was founded in 1928 in Saloniki, which was to collaborate with the Pasteur Institute at Athens in preparing vaccines, sera, and anti-tuberculosis vaccine B. C. G.[119]

§ 426. Improvement of communications. In some districts there was such a complete absence of roads as to impede the utilization of fertile regions otherwise suitable for the settlement of refugees. Two of these districts, in particular, re-

[117] League of Nations, *Official Journal,* April, 1928, pp. 463,486.
[118] *Ibid.,* July, 1928, p. 970; October, 1928, p. 1700.
[119] *Ibid.,* October, 1928, p. 1699.

ceived the attention of the Commission, namely, the district of Ossenitza and Bukia, to the northeast of the river Nestos, and the district of Grevena in Western Macedonia. In the first, 1600 families were settled by the Commission to 1927. With better communications a further 3000 families could be settled there.[120]

Whenever it was possible to remedy the situation at small expense, the Commission authorized its services in Macedonia to have local roads and bridges constructed by the communes. Thirty-one bridges were thus constructed in Macedonia. On the other hand, six piers were constructed in fishing villages along the coast.[121]

An inspection tour in the winter of 1927-28 was made to ascertain the reasons for the failure of colonization in a part of the district of Drama, north of the river Nestos and close to the Bulgarian frontier. Out of about 2000 families that the Commission had established there, 1000 only had remained. The soil and climate were very favorable for the colonization, but the district was isolated from social and commercial centres. The road from Drama to this district was in very bad condition, and there was no bridge over the Nestos, except one used only for railway traffic. The difficulties of communication raised the prices of commodities excessively. For these reasons the settlers left this fertile region and descended to the plain of Drama. It could not be doubted that the region was naturally so advantageous that more than 10,000 families could be settled there.[122]

In accordance with the provisions of the new Protocol of 1927, authorizing the supplementary loan of £3,000,000 for the work of settlement, and with the authorization of the Council of the League, in March, 1928, the sum of 52,500,000 drachmas, or £150,000, was provided for the construction of two sections of road and a bridge in the above region.[123]

[120] Fourteenth Quarterly Report of the Commission, in League of Nations, *Official Journal,* July, 1927, p. 946.

[121] League of Nations, *Official Journal,* October, 1928, p. 1700.

[122] Seventeenth Report of the Commission, in League of Nations, *Official Journal,* April, 1928, pp. 482-483.

[123] Eighteenth Report of the Commission, in League of Nations, *Official Journal,* July, 1928, p. 1048; Nineteenth Report, *ibid.,* October, 1928, p. 1700.

§ 427. Use of the funds by the Commission. The balance-sheet of the Commission on June 30, 1930, six and a half years after the beginning of its work, was as follows: [124]

	£	s.	d.	£	s.	d.
Liabilities						
Proceeds of the 7% 1924 Loan				9,970,016	6	9
Proceeds of the 6% 1926 Loan				499,759	17	0
Proceeds of the 4% 1929 Loan				2,503,278	16	1
Receipts (interest, tithe, etc.)				805,084	10	1
Bonds paid in by refugees against their debts				365,215	0	0
Various liabilities				211,477	1	5
Various *per contra* accounts				384,314	14	1
				£14,739,146	5	5
Assets						
Balance available at the Bank and cash				790,368	5	3
Bonds deposited				365,215	0	0
Receivable advances				11,023	0	5
Expenditure:	£	s.	d.			
Agricultural settlement	10,422,931	16	2			
Urban settlement	2,011,458	7	3			
Arts and crafts	12,320	4	7			
Carpet industry	100,000	0	0			
Central administration	230,024	4	6			
Furniture and fittings	26,753	2	9			
Service for the compensation of agricultural refugees	12,135	7	11			
				£12,815,623	3	2
Sums applied for the ordinary service of the 7% 1924 loan				216,593	2	1
Sums applied for the extraordinary amortisation of the 7% 1924 loan				156,009	0	5
Various *per contra* accounts				384,314	14	1
				£14,739,146	5	5

The Commission placed credits for purposes of colonization at the disposal of its three Directorates as follows from January 1, 1924, to December 31, 1929: [125]

	Drachmas	
Directorate-General of Macedonia	2,405,098,463	or 73 %
Directorate of Thrace	385,105,069	or 11.7%
Directorate of Old Greece, Epirus, and the Islands	502,898,918	or 15.3%
Total	3,293,102,450	

This amount is equal to about £9,408,864, at the rate of 350 drachmas per pound sterling, which is about the average of the rate of conversion of drachmas to pounds sterling since the constitution of the Commission.

[124] League of Nations, *Official Journal,* November, 1930, pp. 1487-89.
[125] *Ibid.,* pp. 1474-76.

The expenditure for colonization includes payments made on behalf of the rural refugees for cattle, houses, agricultural implements, cadastral survey, works of general utility, public health, cost of administration, etc.

On the other hand, the Commission expended for urban establishment 798,402,532 drachmas. This sum and in addition 98,885,818 drachmas spent by the Relief Fund of the Greek government was distributed as follows:

	Drachmas	
Old Greece and the Islands	572,519,717	or 63.8%
Macedonia	121,652,877	or 13.6%
Thrace	203,115,756	or 22.6%
Total	897,288,350	or £2,563,681

Thus less money was spent in urban establishment in Macedonia than in the other regions, whereas Macedonia absorbed most of the credits for purposes of colonization.

In another place the organization and staff of the Commission are described. Their cost, which may be termed the 'general expenses' of the Commission, has been somewhat high. In the first three years, 1924-26, when the work of settlement was in its full swing, the general expenses of the Commission were moderate, their proportion to the total expenditure being 8.36 per cent.[126] During the latter part of 1926 and 1927 the Commission was uncertain whether a new loan would be forthcoming for the completion of the settlement, and was, accordingly, very cautious in expending its funds. However, in anticipation of the conclusion of the supplementary plan, it maintained its complete organization intact. This raised the proportion of general expenses to a very high figure. Thus, the budget of 1927 called for the following expenditure: [127]

	£
1. General expenses	305,831
2. Urban and rural settlement, fresh credits	507,433
3. Balance of 1926 credits	537,556

[126] The total expenditure at the end of 1926 was £8,609,647 9 *s.* 7 *d.*, and the general expenses £664,112. See Thirteenth Quarterly Report, in League of Nations, *Official Journal,* April, 1927, pp. 517-518.

[127] Fourteenth Quarterly Report of the Commission, in League of Nations, *Official Journal,* 1927, p. 935.

Or, of a total of £1,350,820, the general expenses formed 22.64 per cent. In 1928 and the first half of 1929, while the supplementary loan was being expended, the proportion of general expenses was reduced to a little over 10%. Although no figures have been published as to the general expenses for the whole period from 1924 to 1930, it would seem that the proportion to the general cost of settlement was well over 10%. It is known that the proportion of the cost of the provincial administration to the cost of colonization in the three Directorates was as follows:

		Total cost of colonization	Cost of administration	%
Macedonia	Dr.	2,405,098,463	270,296,996	11.23
Thrace	"	385,105,069	42,081,534	10.9
Old Greece, Epirus, and the Islands	"	502,898,918	39,844,921	7.9 [128]

The Commission heard many criticisms on the question of general expenses from several quarters. In one of its reports [129] the Commission defended the high proportion of general expenses on the ground of its non-permanent character and the necessity of a numerous staff to hear and decide the numberless questions arising because of the hurried settlement of the refugees. Moreover, as the work of the Commission was being terminated, its expenses were more and more becoming overhead. It would seem that the character of the Commission, a sort of government in itself, rendered inevitable a high percentage of general expenses.

§ 428. Sums spent by the Greek Government. Besides the proceeds of the two loans expended by the Commission for the refugee settlement, the Greek government devoted part of its budgetary resources to the satisfaction of the urgent needs of the refugees both before and after the Commission began its work. The expenditure by the Greek government from April 1, 1922, to December 31, 1926, was as follows:

[128] See Twenty-Seventh Quarterly Report, August 21, 1930, in League of Nations, *Official Journal,* November, 1930, pp. 1474-76. The low percentage of general expenses in the third Directorate is explained by the fact that the organization and staff under it were of much less importance than in the two other Directorates.

[129] Twenty-First Quarterly Report, in League of Nations, *Official Journal,* April, 1929, p. 705.

Financial year	Assistance, Transportation, Housing, etc.	Settlement	Total
1922-23	£ 831,775	£ 228,210	£1,059,985
1923-24	847,980	667,405	1,515,385
1924-25	1,356,125	363,850	1,719,975
1925-26	1,194,040	67,000	1,261,040
Second half of 1926	387,250	342,105	729,355
Total	£4,617,170	£1,668,570	£6,285,740 [130]

To this amount must be added £438,515 which the state expended for the maintenance of orphans, who, for the most part, are refugee children. The government, moreover, has spent various sums since 1927 which in great part are destined for the improvement of the condition of the refugees, but which are so mixed with sums expended for the benefit of natives that no accurate figures can be given.

§ 429. **Indemnification of refugees and emigrants.** We have seen above [131] how the Greek emigrants from Bulgaria were paid by orders of the Mixed Greco-Bulgarian Commission following the liquidation of their properties. The Greek emigrants and refugees from Turkey could not expect a payment of the same kind, since no liquidation of their properties was undertaken by the Mixed Greco-Turkish Commission. In fact, as seen above,[132] following the Angora Convention of June 30, 1930, the neutral members of this Commission handed down an advisory opinion to the effect that no liquidation be undertaken of the properties of the exchanged populations. There remained, however, a moral obligation for each government, Greek and Turkish, to indemnify the exchangeable populations in view of the provisions, especially, of article 14 of the Convention of Lausanne: "The emigrant shall in principle be entitled to receive in the country to which he emigrates, as representing the sums due to him,

[130] These figures are given by Mr. Pallis, a member of the Refugee Settlement Commission, in his *Collection of Principal Statistics concerning the Exchange of Populations* (in Greek) (Athens, 1929), p. 6. On the other hand, Mr. Tsouderos, Vice-President of the National Bank of Greece, in his study, *The Indemnification of Exchangeables* (in Greek) (Athens, 1927), p. 6, gives the figures of expenditure of the Greek government from 1912 to the end of 1926 on account of the refugees for assistance, shelter, and settlement as a total of 2,240,019,318 drachmas, or £16,866,595.

[131] See *supra,* p. 299.

[132] See *supra,* p. 572.

property of a value equal to and of the same nature as that which he has left behind."

Since the appraisal and liquidation of properties was abandoned, the above provision of article 14 taken out of the other provisions of the Convention to which it was related, could only mean that the Greek refugees should divide among themselves the fund constituted by the property left in Greece by the Moslem emigrants. The larger part of this fund, namely, the agricultural lands in general and the rural buildings left by the Moslems, was assigned to the Refugee Settlement Commission by the government in accordance with the Geneva Protocol of 1923. How this part of the fund was used to indemnify the rural refugees shall be seen below.

The other part, consisting chiefly of urban premises, was turned over by the Greek government to the National Bank of Greece by an agreement dated May 5, 1925, which provided for the liquidation of this property for the benefit of urban refugees and emigrants.[133] The value of the latter property was estimated at over four billion drachmas.[134] The National Bank of Greece was authorized to issue bonds to the value of three billion drachmas, to be secured on the value of the above property, which was to be sold at auction by degrees. The interest of the bonds at 8% was guaranteed by the state. The refugees received these bonds "on account of" their claims, assessed as hereinafter explained, one-fifth in cash and four-fifths in bonds, in compensation for their properties left in Turkey. The bonds were redeemable at par in proportion as the property was sold by the bank.

The assessment of claims of refugees was made as follows. Special commissions, composed of refugee natives of the same district as the claimants, appraised the value of the property abandoned in Turkey. A superior council, composed of government officials and representatives of refugees, revised such

[133] League of Nations, *Official Journal,* April, 1927, p. 519. See on the question of indemnities to refugees, Tsouderos, *The Indemnification of Exchangeables* (in Greek), (Athens, 1927). Protonotarios, *The Refugee Problem* (in Greek) (Athens, 1929). See also Eddy, *Greece and the Greek Refugees,* pp. 264 ff.

[134] Some 56,000 estates were turned over to the National Bank of Greece; of these 40,000 were urban estates and the rest rural.

assessments as were found to be exaggerated. To September 30, 1927, a total of 141,249 claims were recognized, representing a total value of 93,908,589 Turkish pounds gold, or an average of 665 Turkish pounds gold per beneficiary. The National Bank paid to each beneficiary a sum in bonds representing a certain percentage of the sum awarded, on the basis of a scale determined by a vote of the National Assembly of April 3, 1925. The average sum actually paid by the Bank was 32,648 drachmas or 91.2 Turkish pounds gold. The relative soundness of this financial plan was upset by the fact that payments were made to refugees before determination of the total of claims. On September 30, 1927, about 120,000 claims were still in suspense, and the sum still to be awarded was estimated at about 42,000,000 Turkish pounds gold. To compensate these claimants on the same scale as the others, a sum of about 5,400,000 Turkish pounds gold, or 1,800,000,000 drachmas, was required.[135] This was provided by a further transfer of estates by the Greek government to the National Bank of Greece. A new convention with this bank, under date of April 14, 1928, authorized the issue of further 8% bonds for an amount of 3,000,000,000 drachmas. These bonds had no equivalent property behind them and the government had to pledge its revenues to their service.

An attempt was made in 1928 after Mr. Venizelos came into power to reduce the interest of all these bonds allotted to refugees from 8% to 6% in order to alleviate the burden of the government. This attempt failed in view of the hostility of the refugees to this measure. However, a compromise was reached under which the interest of 8% was maintained for all bonds issued to refugees while the interest of bonds authorized but not issued was reduced to 6%.

On July 31, 1929, the situation with regard to payments in bonds was as follows: [136]

8 per cent bonds outstanding	Dr. 3,727,760,000
6 per cent bonds authorized	" 1,650,000,000
Total	Dr. 5,377,760,000
On the other hand, cash payments to the end of 1929 represented a total of	Dr. 1,223,626,841

135 League of Nations, *Official Journal,* February, 1928, p. 233.
136 Eddy, *Greece and the Greek Refugees,* p. 266.

The Greek government proposed that the Commission should accept the bonds issued to urban refugees in settlement of their debts to the Commission. They were to be received on a provisional account, and when they were redeemed, their equivalent in sterling was to be placed finally to the credit of the refugee debtor; also the interest of the bonds was to be credited to the refugee. The Commission accepted this proposal, which, as is clear, had many advantages for the refugees and for the Commission.[137]

The rural refugees received their indemnity for properties left in Turkey in a similar way, although in this case, as practically all were settled by the Commission or by the government, the indemnity was granted by way of compensation or set-off between the indemnity and the settlement debts of the refugees. The scheme for this compensation formed first the subject of an agreement between the Commission and the Ministry of Agriculture, which was signed on November 7, 1927.[138] However, this was never carried into effect, and was replaced by the agreements of 1930, which are considered below.[139]

§ 430. Repayments by the refugees. The refugees began to make repayments to the Commission on their debts in 1925. The system of collection was organized on the basis of the gradual transformation of the rural colonies into coöperative societies. Under the Decree of June 6, 1923, these colonies formed legal persons, whose members were jointly and severally responsible for their debts. These groups later became coöperative societies based upon the principle of collective responsibility. No rigid system for repayments by agricultural refugees was made. No fixed annuity in proportion to their debts was asked of the refugees, but a sum fixed on a very variable basis, taking into account the economic situation of each colony.[140]

Of the payments made by the refugees, 75% of the pay-

[137] Thirteenth Quarterly Report of the Commission, in League of Nations, *Official Journal,* April, 1927, p. 520.

[138] Sixteenth Report in League of Nations, *Official Journal,* February, 1928, p. 233.

[139] See *infra,* § 430.

[140] League of Nations, *Official Journal,* April, 1927, p. 519.

ments on account of capital constituted the extraordinary amortization and the rest was used for settlement. The following table shows the repayments by refugees.

	Regular amortization paid by the Greek government	Payments by refugees	Extraordinary amortization
1925	£459,948	£ 26,465	£16,124
1926	919,708	81,074	60,847
1927	914,852	148,284	24,114
1928	911,702	157,291	15,029

A number of refugees made payments higher than those required of them.[141] However, the return from urban settlements caused much anxiety to the Commission. The refugees were reluctant to pay for the houses occupied by them, asserting that these had been given them by the government as a compensation for losses incurred in connection with their real property in Turkey. They were, however, willing to pay, if the Commission, instead of charging rent, would accept annual payments from the refugees for the purchase of the houses. The Commission, concurring in this view, assessed the houses at their cost price and offered them for sale, fixing the period for payment at fifteen years and the rate of interest and amortization at 8 per cent. At first this plan had little success.

The Greek government soon paid compensation to the urban refugees. This brought them some relief; it satisfied their demands against the government and permitted them to begin to meet their annuities.[142] From the beginning of the year 1927 payments by the refugees showed a considerable increase, a clear sign of their increasing prosperity. This was true of agricultural as well as urban refugees.[143]

In anticipation of the dissolution of the Commission at the end of 1930, a convention was signed at Geneva between the Greek government and the Refugee Settlement Commission on January 24, 1930.[144] This Convention stipulated, in

[141] Twelfth Quarterly Report of the Commission, in League of Nations, *Official Journal,* February, 1927, p. 230.

[142] Thirteenth Quarterly Report of the Commission, in League of Nations, *Official Journal,* April, 1927, p. 519.

[143] Fourteenth Quarterly Report of the Commission, in League of Nations, *Official Journal,* July, 1927, pp. 939-940.

[144] League of Nations, *Official Journal,* June, 1930, pp. 730-735.

particular, in articles 9 to 15, the way in which the debts of refugees were to be settled.

As regards agricultural refugees, the debit side of the account of each refugee was formed by:

(*a*) The amount or value of all advances, in cash or in kind, made to him by the Commission, and of debts due the Greek government which had been transferred to the Commission;
(*b*) The value of the agricultural lot which he had received;
(*c*) The value of the house supplied and of the land appurtenant thereto;
(*d*) An amount for interest on the debt due.

On the credit side there were entered:

(*a*) All payments made to the Commission on account of the debt and also all amounts equivalent to the nominal value of any bonds deposited by the refugee concerned as security for his debt;
(*b*) The portion of the indemnity adjudged by the Greek government payable to him and to dependent members of his family in respect of the property which he and the said dependent members formerly possessed in Turkey.

The amount shown on the debit side, after deduction of the credit account, was the debt due by the refugee to the Commission. If the balance was in favor of the refugee, it was to be liquidated by the Greek government.

As regards urban refugees, on the debit side of the account were entered:

(*a*) The amount or value of all advances in cash or in kind, and the value of the house, if any, supplied by the Commission, including additional charges to cover the cost of general administration, transport, and other expenses;
(*b*) The value of the lot which the refugee had received;
(*c*) An amount for interest on the debt due.

On the credit side were to be included all payments made to the Commission on account of the debt, and also all amounts equivalent to the nominal value of any bonds deposited by the refugee concerned as security for the payment of his debt.

As regards refugees to whom 'professional loans' had been granted, and agricultural refugees other than those exchanged under the Convention of Lausanne,[145] the debit side of their account was formed as that of agricultural refugees and the credit side as that of urban refugees.

The debts due to the Refugee Settlement Commission by the agricultural refugees were to be collected by the Agricultural Bank of Greece and the debts due by the urban refugees were to be collected by the National Bank of Greece or the Bank of Greece.

On March 27, 1930, a further agreement was reached between the Commission and the government, as follows: [146]

1. The balance of the debts of the agricultural refugees was to be repaid in fifteen years from January 1, 1931. Interest was to be charged only as from January 1, 1931.

2. The rate of interest on these debts was reduced from 8 per cent, which the Commission had required until 1930, to 3 per cent.

3. The rate of interest on arrears was fixed at 8 per cent.

4. Interest was not to be charged on sums due by agricultural refugees prior to January 1, 1931. All payments made to that date were to be credited in the capital account.

5. The agricultural refugees were not to be charged with the administrative expenses of the Refugee Settlement Commission.

6. The agricultural refugees were to be debited with the value of the land they had received at an average price of 400 drachmas per *stremma* of cultivable land (10 *stremmata* = 1 hectare = 2.471 acres).

[145] These were, in particular, emigrants from Bulgaria, Greek citizens who left Turkey although not subject to exchange, and Greek refugees from Russia.

[146] League of Nations, *Official Journal*, August, 1930, p. 983.

The price of 400 drachmas represented the average price at which the state indemnified the proprietors in Greece whose land had been expropriated under the provisions of the Agrarian Law.

It could be foreseen that the total of the indemnities due to the agricultural refugees for property they possessed in Turkey would reach £8,500,000. The total of the refugees' debts, after deduction of the indemnities, was calculated to amount to approximately £8,500,000. The total of agricultural refugees settled by the Commission being 145,000 families, the average debt of each family appeared to be £56 10 *s.* It was then calculated that the annual sum to be paid toward the liquidation of the debt, under the new conditions, reached per family about £4 10 *s.*

The law authorizing the Greek government to ratify the Convention, as thus modified, and to issue decrees to settle all questions which, under the terms of the Convention itself, require legislative approval, was passed by the Chamber of Deputies on April 12, 1930.[147] It is clear from the above that the Greek government undertook to shoulder the greater part of the burden of the refugee loans and the settlement expenditure, thus relieving the rural refugees from a substantial part of their obligations. The extension of these measures to the urban refugees was also considered in the latter part of 1930 by the Greek government.[148]

§ 431. Final liquidation of the Refugee Settlement Commission. Early in 1929, the Commission reported to the League [149] that its final liquidation could take place in the second half of 1930, since its funds would soon be exhausted and there was no question of obtaining new funds. It was proposed that its winding up would be divided into three periods.[150] In the second half of 1929 the extraordinary services established by the Commission which were to be taken over and maintained by the government should be transferred

[147] *Ibid.*

[148] See on all this the Twenty-Sixth and Twenty-Seventh Quarterly Reports of the Commission, in League of Nations, *Official Journal,* August, 1930, pp. 977-983; November, 1930, pp. 1469-89.

[149] League of Nations, *Official Journal,* July, 1929, pp. 1015, 1185-86.

[150] *Ibid.,* pp. 1186-87.

to it. Similarly the permanent services handed over to the Commission would automatically return to the government. These services, extraordinary and permanent, were:

(1) The health service established by the Commission in Macedonia.
(2) The agricultural and veterinary services, with the model farms and stud farms.
(3) The rural syndicates' supervisory service.
(4) The mechanical cultivation service.
(5) The irrigation service.

The Greek government had granted considerable credit to the Department of Agriculture as a stimulus to agriculture, and the turning over to that Department of the above agricultural services of the Commission was well advised.

In the second period, starting at the beginning of 1930, the special services involved by the work of colonization were to be wound up. These services were:

(1) Supply, stock, and warehouse services, which could be wound up soon after the credits for refugees' supplies had been exhausted.
(2) Engineer service for the erection of houses on the farms.
(3) Water-supply service, i.e., wells and aqueducts.
(4) Urban department and its dependencies.
(5) Staff and records.

The last-named service could not be completely done away with until all the work was finished.

The third period was to coincide with the second half of 1930, and would mark the complete liquidation of the Commission. There were three services, however, the work of which could not be completed by the end of 1930. These were the cadastral service, the accounting service, and the collections service. The part of the cadastral work concerning the distribution of land and the granting of legal titles to colonists' plots had progressed slowly, because of the difficulties related elsewhere. It is clear also that the accounting service could not be abolished so long as the refugee debt collections of the Commission continued.

At the time the Commission proposed to wind up its services, the Greek Chamber passed a series of legislative measures designed to give a fresh impetus to agriculture in all its branches. In particular, a general Directorate of Agriculture was established, at the head of which was placed Mr. Joannes Caramanos, who as Director-General of Colonization in Macedonia had helped in the settlement work of the Commission and was now to continue and complete that work after the dissolution of the Commission.[151] Further, the Agrarian Bank of Greece was founded and began its work with ample resources to come to the aid of agricultural production of all kinds through short and long term loans to individual farmers and to agricultural coöperative societies.[152]

On May, 1930,[153] the Council of the League approved the Convention signed on January 24, 1930,[154] between the Greek government and the Refugee Settlement Commission, which was intended to contain the provisions that would make it possible for the Commission to be dissolved on December 31, 1930.

Under this Convention, the Commission transferred to the Greek government all property, real and personal, possessed by it, and all its rights and claims of every kind. By this transfer, the Greek government stands in the place of the Commission and assumes the discharge of all obligations binding the Commission. The property thus turned over includes the agricultural, veterinary, and allied services; the various stations, nurseries, model farms, etc.; the dispensaries, sanitation, and water-supply services, hospitals, stocks of medicines, etc.; all records of a public character, maps, etc.

As security for the performance by the Greek government of its obligations in regard to the service of the Refugee Loan of 1924, the above transfer was made subject to a first charge

151 League of Nations, *Official Journal,* July, 1929, pp. 1188-89.
152 *Ibid.,* November, 1929, pp. 1742-43.
153 *Ibid.,* June, 1930, p. 520.
154 *Ibid.,* June, 1930, pp. 730-735.

upon all immovable properties belonging to the Commission, which was to remain until the Refugee Loan of 1924 had been paid in full. However, refugees paying their debts in full are entitled to receive title deeds to their lands and houses free from any mortgage charge.

From the collections made as above [155] by the Agricultural Bank and the National Bank of Greece or the Bank of Greece respectively a sum of £30,000 (£26,000 by the first and £4,000 by the last two) is to be paid each six months commencing on April 20, 1931. Any deficiency in these sums is to be paid by the Greek government. An irrevocable mandate, communicated to the International Financial Commission by the Greek government, authorizes it to pay any such deficit from the proceeds of the pledged revenues in its possession. This sum of £30,000 is to be applied to the extraordinary amortization of the Refugee Loan of 1924 by redeeming bonds of this loan by half-yearly drawings at par. This redemption is not to reduce the amount of the fixed half-yearly payments due for the ordinary service of the loan.

§ 432. General remarks on the settlement. In the previous pages, the gradual establishment of the rural colonists and the town refugees has been described. The increase and improvement in agricultural production of all kinds, the development and creation of new industries and arts and crafts through the refugees, the initiation of fundamental measures for the improvement of public health have also been noted.

Without any doubt, the outstanding feature in the settlement of the refugees is the great stimulus given to progress as a result of the pressing demand upon the Greek people to shelter, provide with work, and render productive the great masses of refugees that swarmed into Greece. This stimulus, coming as it did on the morrow of a terrible defeat, served not only to repel dismay and demoralization from the hearts of the Greek people and to restore confidence, but also to give the state and the citizens new ideals, with the strength and the determined desire for peace, concentrated effort, and hard work.

[155] See *supra,* p. 695.

It is difficult to forecast the political effect of the movement of populations in the Near East. It may be said here, however, that whatever the future may keep in store, whether the Greek people solve their problems with great or small success, the one thing that is certain, the thing that will remain, is the change in the attitude of the Greek people towards their problems, the greater courage, the greater energy, the greater efficiency, the greater confidence springing up in their hearts.

Another important consequence of the Greek refugee settlement is the definite Hellenization of Greek Macedonia, and the end of the disturbances and ethnic conflicts that have marred life, order, and progress in many sections of this unhappy region in the past. The large Moslem population and a great part of the Bulgarian having evacuated Greek Macedonia under the Conventions, the region is now almost wholly Greek, and the war of races in Greek Macedonia is at an end. An ethnographical map, annexed to the publication of the League of Nations on the settlement of the refugees,[156] gives in numbers and colors the situation of Macedonia in 1912 before the Balkan wars and in 1926 after the refugee colonization. Here is the summary given:

	1912		*1926*	
	Population	%	Population	%
Greeks	513,000	42.6	1,341,000	88.8
Moslems	475,000	39.4	2,000 [157]	0.1
Bulgarians	119,000	9.9	77,000	5.1
Miscellaneous	98,000	8.1	91,000	6.0
	1,205,000	100	1,511,000	100

With regard to the whole of Greece, the ethnological changes wrought by the refugee settlement are shown in the following table: [158]

[156] *Greek Refugee Settlement* (Geneva, 1926). See also map on p. 701. The black dots on the map indicate settlements of refugees.

[157] The Moslems referred to here are those of Albanian origin who were exempted from the compulsory exchange.

[158] Taken from A. A. Pallis, *Collection of Principal Statistics concerning the Exchange of Populations and Settlement of Refugees* (in Greek) (Athens, 1929), p. 11.

See growth of Greece in map on p. 702 which forms a Greek stamp issued on the Centenary of her independence (1930).

MAP OF
GREECE
SHOWING
REFUGEE SETTLEMENTS
Scale
0 25 50 MILES
0 20 40 60 KILOMETERS
Refugee settlements
ALBANIA
JUGOSLAVIA
BULGARIA
TURKEY
GREECE
AEGEAN SEA
Adrianople
Mastanla
Nevrokop
Petritch
Strumnitsa
Prelip
Monastir
Lake Ochrida
Lake Presba
Florina
Langadia
Koritza
Kastoria
Kailaria
Nabussa
Edessa
Verria
Kozani
Grevena
Doiran
Guelgueli
Demir Hissar
Serres
Xanthi
Comotini
(Gumuljina)
Dedimotica
Alexandroupolis
(Dedeagatch)
Maritza
Kavala
Thasos
Samothraki
Imbros
Salonaki
CHALKIDIKI
Lemnos
Yanina
Corfu
Trikkala
Larissa
Volo
Mytilene
Skyros
Euboea
Levkas
Agrinion
Missolonghi
Cephalonia
Khalkis
Chios
Patras
Megara
Athens
Piraeus
Corinth
Andros
Tinos
Nicaria
Zante
Argos
Tripolis
Kyparissia
Sparta
Kalamata
Paros
Naxos
Milo
Cythera
Canea
Rethymno
Candia
CRETE

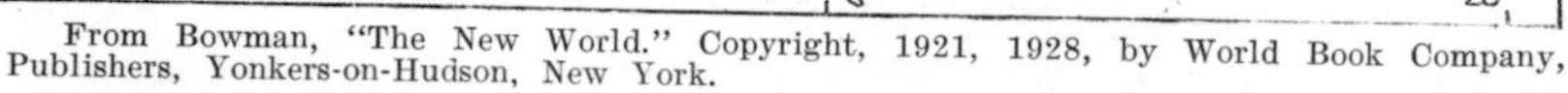
From Bowman, "The New World." Copyright, 1921, 1928, by World Book Company, Publishers, Yonkers-on-Hudson, New York.

Nationalities	1920 Number	%	1928 Number	%
Greeks	4,470,000	80.75	5,822,000	93.83
Turks	770,000 *	13.91	103,000 **	1.66
Bulgarians	139,000	2.51	82,000	1.32
Albanians	18,000	0.32	20,000 ***	0.32
Jews	65,000 ****	1.17	70,000	1.13
Armenians	1,000	0.02	35,000	0.56
Foreign citizens ...	73,000	1.32	73,000	1.18
Total	5,536,000	100	6,205,000 [159]	100

* Including 300,000 Turks of Eastern Thrace, which in 1920 was occupied by Greece.

** Now only in Western Thrace.

*** Found almost exclusively in the district of Tsamouria in Northern Epirus.

**** It includes only Jews of Saloniki.

[159] The area of Greece is now 130,199 sq. km. against 63,211 in 1912. The density of population is 47.66 per sq. km. against 41.64 in 1912.

From the social and cultural point of view the settlement of the refugees had many important consequences. The overcrowding of the cities with a working population brought with it the social ills naturally attendant: increase of crime, a certain amount of pauperism, a lowering of public morals.[160] On the other hand, the gradual absorption of the refugees into the life of the native population creates daily phenomena similar to the fusion of ideas, traditions, and characteristics in America which are considered in the Conclusion of this study.

While, undoubtedly, the success of the refugee settlement is due primarily to "the courage, effort, and energy of the refugees," it is impossible not to notice the intelligence and devotion, the admirable and enlightened activity displayed by the Refugee Settlement Commission in the work. The Commission supplied and remedied the defects of the governmental action in the first years of the colonization, when the Greek government, by reason of its instability and the military domination, was greatly handicapped by political and other considerations in carrying out an objective and really scientific work of settlement. The Commission worked out definite plans and programmes of settlement and carried them out with the assistance of a staff which, even when inadequate, acted with sufficient independence and efficiency. It interpreted the Geneva Protocol liberally, and helped to preserve and maintain colonies which after their foundation might have been ruined for lack of proper assistance. It contributed to the study and improvement of the agricultural resources in the country; it encouraged the creative initiative of its technical experts; and it singled out employees able to occupy positions of major responsibility and directing activity. In all this it created a tradition, and in its dissolution it left to the government a well trained and expert staff which will be of great value to Greece.

The benefits of the refugee settlement were obtained by the Greek people at the cost of great financial sacrifices. In addition, indeed, to the total amount of £15,382,450 of the

[160] See on this A. Deimezis, *Situation sociale crèce en Grèce à la suite de l'échange des populations* (Paris, 1927).

Refugee Loans contracted abroad in 1924 and 1928 (representing, indeed, an effective amount of only £13,000,000 received by Greece), the Greek government contracted a number of internal loans in order to pay indemnities to refugees in Greece for properties possessed by them in Bulgaria and Turkey. These loans are five:

	Drachmas
(1) Loan of 1923 for indemnification of the Greek emigrants from Bulgaria, issued at par at 6%	600,000,000
(2) Loan of 1926 for indemnities to urban refugees, issued at par at 8%	3,000,000,000
(3) A similar loan of 1926	500,000,000
(4) A similar loan of 1928	2,500,000,000
(5) A loan of 1927 for indemnities to Greek subjects, refugees from Turkey, issued at par at 8%	800,000,000
Total Drachmas	7,400,000,000

On the loan above numbered (4), the interest was reduced to 6% for bonds not yet distributed on November 2, 1928. Mention also must be made of the annual sum of 59,751,735 drachmas, due to Bulgaria for thirty years from 1929, for the amortization of 850,000,000 drachmas, representing the difference between the value of the properties of Bulgarian and Greek emigrants.

If to the service of these loans be added the indemnities due by the Greek government for the properties of Greek or foreign landowners, expropriated to be distributed among the refugees, the burden upon the Greek budget for the settlement of the refugees reaches the neighborhood of £3,000,000 yearly.[161] This will be a heavy burden to the Greek people for many years to come.

[161] See A. A. Pallis, *Collection of Principal Statistics concerning the Exchange of Populations and Settlement of Refugees* (Athens, 1929), p. 6.

CHAPTER XXXIII

THE SETTLEMENT OF THE TURKISH EMIGRANTS

§ 433. The problem of the settlement of Turkish emigrants. While Bulgaria and Greece were making great efforts to settle in their respective territories the refugees and emigrants who arrived in continuous waves, Turkey was receiving the Moslems of Greece who were compelled to leave Greece under the Convention of Lausanne of 1923. As we have seen, these Moslem emigrants amounted to 388,146 persons. They left Greece, in a more or less orderly manner, under the auspices of the Mixed Commission created under the provisions of the Convention of Lausanne. Few, if any, left their movable property behind, except when such property, especially cereals and cattle, was sometimes requisitioned by the Greek government for the purpose of providing the refugees with necessary supplies. Moreover, Turkey, generally speaking, had sufficient room to settle the refugees. For one thing, there was Eastern Thrace, which had been evacuated by from 180,000 to 200,000 Greeks in a peaceful manner. Eastern Thrace had not been a field of military operations in recent years and might well absorb an equal number of Moslem emigrants. Again, upward of 1,000,000 Greeks had been driven from or emigrated from Asia Minor, and their homes and lands could well provide room for the remaining 200,000 Moslem emigrants. There was, of course, much destruction in the part of this territory where the Greeks and Turks had fought, but this certainly did not affect the whole of Asia

Minor. More serious was the fact that the Turkish population itself, in a spirit of vengeance against whatever was Greek, had followed the expulsion of the Greeks with the destruction of their properties. On the whole, however, the problem of settlement of the Moslem emigrants was much simpler in Turkey than the similar problem in Greece and Bulgaria.

However, Turkey, handicapped by a wrong tradition and a lack of financial resources, grappled with the problem of settlement in an inadequate way. The wrong tradition came from the manner in which previous migratory movements to Turkey had been dealt with. Turkey has been in a sense a country of refugees and emigrants for practically a whole century. With the successive emancipations of subject peoples, the Moslem inhabitants of territories lost to Turkey, especially public officers and rich landowners, often left their country of origin and emigrated to seek refuge in the territories remaining to the Turkish Empire. This migratory movement became more important after the first Balkan War of 1912. It is estimated that about 10,000 Moslems from Macedonia left before the advancing armies of the Balkan states in that year, and a further 50,000 Moslems removed from Western Thrace in 1913, when the region was occupied by Bulgaria, either of their own free will or in consequence of the Convention of November, 1913, above referred to,[1] for the reciprocal emigration of the frontier populations of Bulgaria and Turkey. In 1914, under the influence of the propaganda of the Young Turks, at least 100,000 Moslems emigrated from Greek Macedonia to Eastern Thrace and the coast of Asia Minor, to take the place left by the departed and expelled Greeks and Armenians. There were also the migrations of populations, tribal for the most part, on the eastern and southern frontiers of Turkey.

It appears that prior to 1913 no government organization was ever set up in Turkey to provide for the installation and settlement of the successive waves of refugees and emigrants. They were, in general, left to their resources. If the imperial administration interested itself at all, it was to en-

[1] See *supra*, p. 18.

courage them to help themselves by the primitive and convenient method of turning Christian owners out of their properties and taking their place. In 1913, for the first time, an organization was created called the Department of Settlement and Tribes. Its purpose was to assist in the establishment of refugees and to control the movements of the Arab and Kurdish tribes in the eastern provinces. This Department does not seem to have improved the previous method of settlement of Moslem refugees, except that it systematized the deportation of Greeks and Armenians, and thereby rendered the work of replacement of Christians by the Moslem emigrants much easier.

After the Treaty of Lausanne and the Convention concerning the Compulsory Exchange of Greek and Turkish Populations, the Republican Turkish government was under the necessity of providing for the settlement of a large number of Moslem emigrants who were compelled to leave Greece in the fall of 1923 and later. This was a serious problem. It was desired not merely to establish these people wherever there was room for them, but to settle them on a productive basis and in a manner that would provide for the cultivation of the lands left vacant by the Greek refugees and for the replacement of the latter in productive work and professional occupations in Turkey. How did the Republican government grapple with this important problem of securing the continuation of the economic life of the country? [2]

§ 434. Organization of the work of settlement. A law adopted on November 8, 1923, created a Ministry of Reconstruction, Exchange, and Settlement. To the head of this Ministry sweeping powers were given to take decisions on questions concerning the settlement of refugees and to use for this purpose all state employees and the military and police authorities. A Director in each vilayet [3] and a number of Inspectors locally supervised the work of settlement.

[2] The writer applied for information in answer to this question to various sources in Turkey, meeting with little success, as there is no general information collected and available. The data and tables given here were supplied to the writer through the kindness of Hazim Atif, Esq., of Constantinople, to whom he wishes to express his indebtedness.

[3] A territorial administrative division similar to the French department.

The work of this Ministry gave little satisfaction, since it caused conflicts of authorities and proved too costly in its administration. On December 11, 1924, a more modest plan was adopted. A Department of Settlement was created in the Ministry of the Interior, with a Director-General at its head and Directors of Settlement in each vilayet. A number of Inspectors were appointed at first, but these were dismissed in 1926, as soon as the greater part of the settlement work was completed. In 1929 a section was added to this Department to take care of the settlement of the Kurdish tribes.

There is no general plan published giving the main lines of the settlement work carried out. It appears that on their arrival from Greece the Moslem emigrants were transported to the places which were chosen for their settlement. All emigrants were installed in villages and properties left by the Greek refugees. In this respect the problem has been easy enough, as there was more than sufficient vacant room to place the emigrants. Land also was abundant, and every new settler was granted sufficient land to secure his livelihood. In numerous villages, in the part of Asia Minor which had been the field of military operations, many houses had been destroyed by war or burned down by the armies. Both armies shared in the responsibility for this destruction. In such places the Turkish government had to build new rural dwellings for the Moslem emigrants.

The emigrants were also granted agricultural implements by the state and seed to raise crops, whenever they were unable to acquire such from their own resources. Artisans were granted a small capital to give them a start. All debts of emigrants to the state were payable by instalments in twenty years, beginning with the second year from the date of signing an 'obligation' in the amount of the debt. It was provided that the value of the property left in Greece by each emigrant was to be deducted from the amount of the 'obligation.'

§ 435. Expenditure on settlement. The following table shows the expenditure of the Turkish government on account of the settlement of the emigrants from 1923 to 1928.

Year	Total expenditure in Turkish pounds (paper)
1923	798,737.08
1924	4,952,208.83
1925	1,326,849.08
1926	473,877.62
1927	1,292,970.99
1928	496,944.79

Or a total of 9,341,588.39 Turkish pounds paper, equal to about $4,670,794, or less than a million pounds sterling.

This is less than one-twentieth of the expenditure incurred by the Greek government in the settlement of Greek refugees three times as numerous, and only one-half the expenditure of the Bulgarian government in the settlement of Bulgarian refugees one-fourth as many in number. With regard to the items to which the expenditures of the Turkish government refer, there are available statistics only for the years 1925 to 1928, as shown on following page, in Turkish pounds paper.

It will be noted that building and repairs and aid in farm settlement by the distribution of seed, cattle, implements, etc., have been the largest items of expense. No general expenses are indicated for the years subsequent to 1925. Those for this year seem exceedingly high, reaching 44% of the total settlement expenditures for 1925. The Department of Settlement in the Ministry of the Interior had its separate budget after 1926. This department was concerned not only with the settlement of the Moslem emigrants from Greece, but also with that of other refugees and tribes in the eastern part of Turkey. The budget of this department for the years 1926 to 1929 was as follows:

Year	Turkish pounds (paper)
1926	1,206,353
1927	2,575,859
1928	1,025,433
1929	1,460,690

§ 436. Total number of persons settled. Although no exact statistics exist of the emigrants and refugees who entered Turkey from Greece, Jugoslavia, Bulgaria, Rumania, Soviet Russia, etc., the Turkish Department of Statistics has pub-

Expenditures	1925	1926	1927	1928	Totals
Transportation	47,970.84	26,054.34	168,555.61	117,880.63	594,461.42
Food supplies	343,758.15	5,765.40	132,714.80	53,832.11	536,070.55
Fuel	4,414.85	2,686.02	8,909.34	......	16,010.21
Medical treatment	......	30.60	20.50	......	51.10
Expenses of allotment of land and buildings	165,369.84	82,761.64	106,704.10	29,865.30	384,700.88
Building and repairs	......	69,881.25	445,547.55	206,827.30	722,256.10
Seed, cattle, and implements	......	286,698.28	430,519.09	88,539.45	805,756.82
Assistance to artisans	158,317.57	......	......	......	158,317.57
Harness animals	11,738.06	......	......	......	11,738.06
General expenses	595,279.77	......	......	......	595,279.77
Totals	1,326,849.08	473,877.62	1,292,970.99	496,944.79	

lished two tables concerning the people settled from the year 1921 to the year 1928 in Turkey. The first table, showing the number of emigrants and refugees settled in Turkey, is as follows:

Year	Males	Females	Total
1921	5,488	5,591	11,079
1922	5,189	4,904	10,093
1923	25,553	25,136	50,689
1924	120,322	115,092	235,414
1925	28,353	28,170	56,523
1926	18,481	16,570	35,051
1927	15,557	16,656	32,213
1928	15,603	16,656	32,259
Totals	234,546	228,988	463,534

In the total of 463,534 [4] persons the greatest part is represented by the Moslem emigrants from Greece. Their number is given by the Mixed Commission for the Exchange of Greek and Turkish Populations as 388,146. Adding to this number a few thousand people who left Greece of their own initiative and by other means of transportation than those placed at their disposal by the Turkish government, we may reach possibly the number of 400,000 as Moslem emigrants from Greece from 1921 to 1928. The remaining 63,534 are Moslem emigrants or refugees from other countries.

§ 437. **Regions of settlement.** The second table published by the department of statistics shows the regions in which Moslem emigrants and refugees were settled. This is as follows:

Names of Vilayets	Males	Females	Total
Adana	4,153	4,287	8,440
Afyon Kara Hissar	541	504	1,045
Aksaray	1,726	1,560	3,286
Amasya	1,917	1,927	3,844
Ankara	878	773	1,651
Antalya	2,428	2,492	4,920
Artvin	24	22	46
Aydin	3,387	3,243	6,630
Balikesir	18,445	18,729	37,174
Bayazit	1,532	1,324	2,856
Bilecik	2,154	2,307	4,461
Bitlis	1,604	2,026	3,630

[4] The official census of 1927 places the number of persons settled at 434,079, but this includes only persons "exchanged under conventions." See République Turque, Office Central de Statistique, *Annuaire statistique,* i, (Angora, 1928), pp. 36 ff.

Names of Vilayets	Males	Females	Total
Bolu	95	99	194
Burdur	234	214	448
Bursa	17,393	17,060	34,453
Djebel Bereket	1,578	1,366	2,944
Chanakkale	5,802	5,836	11,638
Chankiri		none	
Chorum	825	750	1,570
Denizli	1,382	1,346	2,728
Diarbekir	255	229	484
Edirné	24,931	24,510	49,441
Elaziz	1,175	949	2,124
Erzingan	55	61	116
Erzerum	492	603	1,095
Eskishehir	1,303	1,264	2,567
Giresun	321	302	623
Gümüshane	381	430	811
Gaziayintap	660	670	1,330
Hakari	176	134	310
Itchel	528	509	1,037
Izmir	15,788	15,714	31,502
Isparta	603	572	1,175
Istanbul	17,448	19,039	36,487
Kars	1,286	1,226	2,512
Kastamonu	464	378	842
Kayseri	3,794	3,486	7,280
Kirklareli	18,011	15,108	33,119
Kirshehir	94	99	193
Kocaeli	14,307	13,380	27,687
Konya	2,751	2,798	5,549
Kutahya	1,017	864	1,881
Malatya	42	34	76
Manisa	6,978	6,851	13,829
Mardin	103	97	200
Marash	603	540	1,143
Mersin	1,675	1,655	3,330
Mugla	2,488	2,480	4,968
Nigde	8,107	7,595	15,702
Ordu	583	665	1,248
Rize		none	
Samsun	11,761	10,907	22,668
Siirt		none	
Sinope	638	551	1,189
Sivas	3,580	3,959	7,539
Shebin Kara Hisar	3,122	2,757	5,879
Tekirdag	16,563	17,165	33,728
Trebizond	246	158	404
Tokat	4,455	3,763	8,218
Urfa	189	101	290
Van	150	125	275
Yozgat	688	747	1,635
Zongudalk	637	648	1,285
Totals	234,546	228,988	463,534

From this table it appears that the largest settlements of Moslem emigrants were made in the following vilayets: [5]

[5] See on this map on page 716.

Balikesir
Bursa
Chanakkalé
Edirné
Izmir
Istanbul
Kirklareli
Kocacli
Manisa
Nigde
Samsun
and Tekirdag

Substantial settlements were also made in the following vilayets:

Adana
Antalya
Aydin
Bilecik
Kayseri
Konya
Mugla
Sivas
Shebin Kara Hisar
and Tokat

In the rest of the vilayets the number of emigrants settled did not exceed 4,000, and in many of them it was only a few hundred.

If the above two groups of vilayets are considered, it will be noted that they are those of Eastern Thrace and of the coast of Asia Minor. The four vilayets of Eastern Thrace, i.e., Istanbul (Constantinople), Kirklareli, Edirné (Adrianople), and Tekirdag (Rodosto) absorbed by themselves 152,770 Moslem emigrants, that is, 38% of the total number of the Moslems who left Greece.

In the vilayets on the Aegean coast of Asia Minor and on the Sea of Marmora, i.e., Kocacli (Ismid), Bursa (Broussa), Balikesir, Chanakkale, Ismir, (Smyrna), Aidin, Manisa (Maghnissa), Mugla (Moughla), a total of 167,891 emigrants were settled. These form about 42% of the Moslem emigrants from Greece.

Thus these two regions absorbed together 80% of the Moslem emigrants from Greece.[6] Another 10% was settled in the vilayets on the Mediterranean, Antalya (Adalia), Ichel (Selefké), Mersin (Mersina), Adana, and Djebel Bereket, and in the vilayet of Samsun on the Black Sea coast.

These settlements have only in part replaced the Greek population living in Turkey before the war. Although precise statistics of this population are not available, the existing estimates being subject to all kinds of doubts, it would appear

[6] Or 69% of the total of 463,534 emigrants and refugees settled between 1921 and 1928 in Turkey.

from official censuses[7] of the Turkish Empire that at least 600,000 Greeks lived before 1914 in Eastern Thrace, including Constantinople. In this part of the Turkish territory 152,770 Moslem emigrants were settled between 1921 and 1928.[7a]

The Greeks living in Asia Minor in 1914 numbered above 1,600,000 people.[8] They were replaced only by 310,000 Moslem emigrants after 1921.

From the above it also appears that the great majority of the Moslem emigrants were settled in the districts where the Greek population was established before the war. But the lack of a settlement programme and adequate organization caused serious errors and consequent economic losses in the distribution of the emigrants. Thus, tobacco cultivators among the Moslem emigrants from Eastern Macedonia were settled in vine districts along the mountain slopes of the coast of Asia Minor. These settlers destroyed the vineyards and turned them into tobacco fields, only to learn through experience the costly lesson that tobacco could not be grown in those districts.

Moreover, no effort was made to select from the emigrants and distribute properly the few thousand artisans, merchants, small traders, workers, and professional men, so as to fill the enormous gaps left by the Greek refugees. Indeed, nearly 90% of the Moslem emigrants from Greece were cultivators, and the remaining 10% of non-agricultural population followed the destiny of the majority.

§ 438. Results of the settlement. It is very difficult to draw precise and definite conclusions as to the results of the settlement of the emigrants in Turkey. Had the Turkish government been able to dispose of larger financial resources and to spend greater sums of money in placing the emigrants on a really productive basis, it is probable that the consequences of the partial depopulation of Turkey through the exodus of its Greek population might have been felt less severely. The

[7] See Antoniades, *Le développement économique de la Thrace* (Athens, 1922), pp. 13, 193, 197.

[7a] There remain, of course, still in Constantinople the Greeks exempt from exchange who have now dwindled to about 100,000 people.

[8] Mr. Pallis (in *Les Effets—économiques et sociaux de la guerre en Grèce*, by A. Andreades et autres) estimates the Greek population of Asia Minor at 1,684,000. See also *supra*, p. 14.

assistance of about one million Turkish pounds granted by the Turkish government towards the settlement of 463,534 emigrants and refugees, i.e., an expenditure of a little over £2 per person, was too meagre to be of any real effect.

People and authorities in Turkey are quite unanimous in believing that the economic life of the country has suffered severely as a result of the exodus of the Greek population, and that it has not been substantially helped by the settlement of the Moslem emigrants. Some industries seemed irreparably damaged, such as the carpet industry, fig packing, the olive oil industry, etc. The foreign trade was also severely hurt. Imports and exports were paralyzed for the time and have scarcely begun to recover. The emigration deprived Turkey of those Greek merchants who alone carried on the foreign trade of the country; and it has been hard to make new connections with foreign countries, inasmuch as the Greeks who left transferred their place of business and their connections to their new establishments in Greece, especially at Piraeus, Volo, and Saloniki.

The Turkish government could not, of course, seek foreign financial assistance for the settlement of emigrants, as this would be contrary to the fundamental principle of the new Turkish state, the complete political and economic independence of the nation. In the minds of the new Turkish rulers it was far better that the emigrants should suffer for a number of years, while they were struggling to stand on their feet and to achieve an independent and productive existence, than to have the future of the nation mortgaged by an appeal to foreign financial assistance. The small productivity of the emigrants, and the general slow rhythm of economic life, caused by the limited resources of the state and the general impoverishment occasioned by long continued wars, will postpone the time of economic prosperity in Turkey. At any rate, its rulers have saved the country from financial bondage to foreign countries and from heavy mortgages on the future. In the meantime, the government proceeds with its general programme of educating the people and imbuing them with the spirit of progress. It hopes in this way to render really pro-

economic progress, namely, communications. The government attacked this evil with great energy. Besides the laying out of a number of railways, it built in the year 1927 alone a total of 2,316,392 kilometres of new or extended roads, and repaired 1,893,314 kilometres additional.[11]

After the severe paralysis of economic life that followed the exodus of the Greek refugees, there appeared a distinct improvement with the gradual settlement of the Moslem refugees. The *Annuaire Statistique* [12] gives the figures for the foreign commerce for the years 1923-26 as follows in Turkish pounds (paper):

Year	Imports	Exports
1923	144,788,671	84,651,190
1924	193,611,048	158,867,958
1925	242,314,138	193,119,453
1926	234,591,722	187,742,801

Turkey will not be able to reach real prosperity until she obtains a favorable trade balance, since she has no invisible credit items to render her economic balance favorable. In view of the limited production and the small volume of exports, the movement of shipping has remained of small importance. This movement has been:

1924	70,302	vessels	of	total	tonnage	14,643,089
1925	85,734	"	"	"	"	22,594,895
1926	78,632	"	"	"	"	24,840,499
1927	68,747	"	"	"	"	23,727,846

The financial limitations of the government are shown by the figures of budgetary receipts and expenses:

	Turkish pounds	
Year	Receipts	Expenses
1924	129,214,610	117,993,800
1925	153,046,854	246,405,491
1926	190,158,854	193,559,769
1927	194,580,554	194,454,619
1928	207,173,199	207,169,888

A very substantial part of the budget expenditures are devoted by the state to the defence of the country. Turkey,

[11] The difficulties in this respect of Turkey may be understood by considering the relief of Anatolia as shown in the map on page 717.

[12] République Turque, Office Central de Statistique, *Annuaire statistique*, i, p. 103.

after all its territorial losses in the Balkan Wars and the World War, still has a total land frontier of 2418 kilometres with Greece, Bulgaria, Russia, Persia, Irak, and Syria to protect, in addition to 3455 miles of maritime frontier. Peace, therefore, is for Turkey a vital necessity.

CONCLUSION

In the preceding pages an attempt has been made to describe the reciprocal emigration of national minorities between Greece and Bulgaria and the compulsory exchange of Greek and Turkish populations, and to show the work accomplished in the settlement of these uprooted people in their new countries. It has been seen that the Conventions of Neuilly and Lausanne, which adopted for the first time in history these solutions of the problem of minorities and attempted to regulate the liquidation of the properties and the indemnification of the emigrants, failed entirely of their real purpose, which was that "of furnishing promptly to those who emigrated under their terms, the necessary financial means to begin life in the country of destination." [1] The Mixed Commissions established under these Conventions proved a failure. The Greco-Turkish Mixed Commission did not even attempt to liquidate the properties and pay any indemnities to the exchanged populations. It was only long after the departure of the emigrants that the Greco-Bulgarian Mixed Commission was able to liquidate their properties and pay them a partial indemnity in cash, while the balance of the indemnity was paid in bonds which at times depreciated as much as thirty to fifty per cent. In the case both of the Greco-Bulgarian emigration and of the Greco-Turkish exchange, it was necessary for the governments concerned to come to the assistance of the immigrating minorities and to supplement the Conventions by their own action. The fact is, of course, that large numbers of the minorities exchanged, and, in the case of the Greek minority in Turkey, the great majority, had already been driven out from their country of origin before the conventions were entered into and the Mixed Commissions were created. These refugees had to be taken care of by the country

[1] Charles B. Eddy, *Greece and the Greek Refugees* (London, 1931), p. 227.

of their kinsfolk in which they sought asylum. Assistance could not be given as fully and as promptly as the conditions required, and although in the course of time great sacrifices were made by each country to install and settle its immigrant kin, the sufferings of the refugees were many and severe. Many thousands perished, and time has not yet repaired the losses or assuaged the sorrows of the survivors. The result of all this is that the experiment in international relations forming the subject matter of this volume can hardly be described as a real agreement for the reciprocal exchange of minorities. Both conventions, and especially that of Lausanne, proved to be agreements confirming accomplished facts. It may be of service, however, to inquire whether the plan of an exchange of minorities was really sound and whether it has, at least, a character of permanency.

The reciprocal emigration of the Greek and Bulgarian minorities is on a different footing from the exchange of Turkish and Greek populations. Voluntary in theory, it became, in fact, to a great extent compulsory. It was early evident that if carried out as a voluntary emigration it would be a failure. Few were prepared to avail themselves of the Convention voluntarily. There was serious doubt whether the Convention would effect any important results, except in the case of those who had emigrated prior to its coming into effect and who could not hope to return to their country of origin. Only when emigration was made practically compulsory did the Convention become a factor of real significance.

The Greco-Bulgarian emigration affected only a small proportion of the population of the countries concerned. Although practically the entire Greek minority in Bulgaria moved to Greece, it did not exceed 46,000. About two-thirds of the Bulgarian minority in Greece, 96,000, emigrated to Bulgaria. That more than a third of the Bulgarian minority has remained in Greece indicates a partial failure of the Convention, unless it be assumed that those who remain intend to give their moral allegiance to the Greek state. The truth rather is that these people are of an agrarian or pastoral stock, and love the soil they live on too much to abandon it. Both minorities were mostly rural and agricultural. They were assisted in their settlement by the governments concerned and by the League organizations. The two populations were interchanged without disturbing the economic equilibrium in either country. They took each other's place in the general economy of each nation. If Greece received fewer Greeks than she lost Bulgarians, the vacuum was more than readily filled by the Greek refugees from Turkey. The surplus of Bulgarian immigrants in Bulgaria was placed upon new lands reclaimed from uncultivated soil. By and large, the reciprocal emigration not only did not disturb economic life, but gave it a new stimulus through the assistance of the institutions created to supervise the installation of the new settlers and through the generous indemnities paid to emigrants. It was, indeed, admitted in the Mixed Greco-Bulgarian Commission, by the neutrals as well as by the national members, that the later emigrants were often impelled by economic motives. The Commission gave such high prices for emigrants' property that persons of a dubious nationality claimed the benefits of the Convention concerning Reciprocal Emigration in order to have their properties liquidated by the Mixed Commission.[2]

Politically, also, the exchange of Greek and Bulgarian minorities had a good result. The Convention concerning Reciprocal Emigration to a large extent regularized a migratory movement which had already been carried out. At the end of the War, many thousand exiles from the minorities in Greece or Bulgaria did not transfer their moral allegiance from their old to their new government. Remaining in the state of refugees, they formed elements of disorder and caused friction between the two states. These have for the most part availed themselves of the Convention and become firmly established in their new country. On the other hand, the exchange has practically eliminated the problem of protection of minorities between the two countries, while it has brought about in the territory of each an ethnical homogeneity conducive to a greater stability. Although, it is true, 77,000 Bulgarians still remain in Macedonia, these live far from the frontier, their

[2] Commission Mixte, *Procès-Verbaux,* 546th meet., May 3, 1930, pp. 2 ff.

conduct is above reproach, their rights are protected, and they do not constitute an element of instability.

That the exchange of the Greek and Bulgarian minorities has a character of permanency is not disputed. There is no reason why these rural emigrants, now firmly settled in their new homes and fields, should seek to uproot themselves yet once more in order to return to their old seats. Indeed, one of the questions disturbing Greco-Bulgarian relations at the present time is the request for the liquidation of the properties of 6000 Bulgarian emigrants, now settled in Bulgaria, who failed to file declarations at the proper time, but who do not wish to return to Greece.

This particular question will probably be associated as a matter for negotiation and arbitration with the counter claims of Greece for damage done in Western Thrace by Bulgarians during the war and for damages done in 1906 in the anti-Greek riots at Anhialo, and with the demand of Greece for the restoration of the right of a Greek company to exploit the great Dospat forest in Bulgaria under a concession made before the war. Negotiations for submitting all these disputes to arbitration have now been carried on for the last year, and it is expected that a formula will be found satisfying both countries.

The major dispute today between Greece and Bulgaria is the demand of the latter country for an access to the Aegean Sea. This question is outside the province of this book. It may only be said, that if the Bulgarian government had really decided to give up the idea of a territorial acquisition, and to restrict itself to an economic outlet, which alone was promised her by the Treaty of Neuilly [3] and the Treaty of Sèvres concerning Thrace,[4] the matter would have been solved long ago. Greece has gone a long way towards meeting the demand of Bulgaria for an outlet by offering her a port under Bulgarian administration in Dedeagatch, which would be connected with Bulgarian territory by the railway placed under an inter-

[3] Treaty of Peace with Bulgaria signed at Neuilly, November 27, 1919, art. 48, § 3.

[4] Treaty concerning Thrace signed at Sèvres on Aug. 10, 1920, and put into effect by Protocol XVI signed at Lausanne, July 24, 1923, arts. 4-16.

national administration. As an alternative, a free port at Saloniki similar to that granted to Jugoslavia was offered to Bulgaria. The latter would be more advantageous, as it would connect Sofia with the Aegean by the quickest route, while it would bring about a connection between the Greek and Bulgarian railways above Demir Issar (Siderocastron) by way of Petritch, the lack of which today seems an absurdity.[5]

On the whole, it seems that the exchange of minorities between Greece and Bulgaria has cleared the relations between the two countries of many troublesome matters, and that a better atmosphere is being slowly created between them. A spirit of mutual confidence, of course, is not yet there; yet one may easily perceive the gradual disappearance of the feelings of hatred and contempt, and the growth of mutual respect between the two countries, as they now more and more turn their attention to economic matters of common interest.

The exchange of Greek and Turkish populations is a matter that can be less easily evaluated. It affected nearly two million people. The populations were compelled to leave their homes and transfer themselves to the country to which they were nationally akin. In the great majority of cases in Turkey, and in a few cases in Greece, the movement of the populations took the character of a widespread exodus of people leaving everything behind them and reaching their new country destitute and starving. The sufferings of the Greek population driven out from Turkey within the space of a few weeks were cruel beyond measure. Tens of thousands of Greeks perished in this flight from Turkey and as a result of it. Practically, the emigration of the Greek population from Turkey was completed when the Convention concerning the exchange was entered into at Lausanne. Was the exchange of populations the only solution possible at Lausanne?

The answer is not easy to give. Events are too fresh to allow of complete analysis. The minutes of the meetings at

[5] Cf. Leo Pasvolsky, *Bulgaria's Economic Position,* Washington, 1930, p. 289. The author points out the considerable importance Greece is recently acquiring as a market for Bulgaria's exports. At the present time the connection of Sofia with Saloniki is made indirectly through Jugoslavia by way of Nish.

Lausanne do not tell the whole story. So much as is known from Greek official documents shows that the Greek government was too much concerned with the actual problem of installation of a million and a half refugees to give full consideration to the other questions involved. Immediate necessities seem in its mind to have obscured other solutions. The government feared that if the principle of voluntary exchange should be adopted, few, if any, Moslems would leave Greece, whereas hundreds of thousands of Greeks would be unable to return to Turkey, and the bargain would be a fool's bargain. Little, if anything, is known of the views of the Turkish government at the time. The writer has gathered from conversations at Istanbul and Angora the impression that no final decision was taken to insist at Lausanne upon the compulsory exchange of the Greek and Turkish minorities. Indeed, the Turks are ready to declare that they only accepted the compulsory exchange of populations on the proposal of Mr. Venizelos. It is certain, however, that the Turks would have been reluctant to permit the return to Turkey of great numbers of refugees. Probably they would have insisted on certain conditions for such return. There is no evidence, however, that the Turks would have definitively refused to allow the return to Turkey of the great majority of the Greek refugees. Yet no attempt was made at Lausanne to find another solution than that actually adopted. Would it not have been possible, for instance, to agree on an exchange, perhaps compulsory, limited to the Greeks of Eastern Thrace and the Moslems of Western Thrace, that is, the inhabitants of the region where there was a land frontier between the two countries? The inference is strong that the Greek government, when the discussions began at Lausanne, had based a decision to favor a compulsory exchange upon an assumption which is not proven, namely, that the Turks would not permit the return to Turkey of any of the refugees.

Now that the exchange of the Greek and Turkish populations is an accomplished fact, it is easy to discover advantages and to praise the results. It may be asserted that as a result of the exchange the problem of the protection of minorities between the two countries has disappeared, to the great advantage of peaceful relations between the two countries and of greater stability. This is undoubtedly true, yet it must be recalled that the compulsory exchange allowed of two exceptions, and that the Greek minority is retained in Constantinople and the Moslem minority in Western Thrace. There have also remained in Greece Moslems who are Turkish subjects, and in Turkey Greeks who are Hellenic subjects. Indeed, the protection of the rights of these two classes of people has been a matter of constant controversies between the two countries from the morrow of the Conference of Lausanne to but a few months ago. Even today, after the Convention of Angora of 1930, the Greeks of Constantinople are not as yet treated in the same way as Turkish citizens. They are deprived of political and civil rights, they are hampered by discriminating and vexatious restrictions and burdens, their schools and other institutions are threatened with economic destruction.

It may also be asserted that as a result of the exchange the two nations acquired an ethnical homogeneity which is a source of both strength and stability to them. This is particularly true in the case of Greece, which has been able to Hellenize completely its northern provinces, in particular, Macedonia. Moreover, with the settlement of refugees in Greece with the aid of the League of Nations and the Greek Refugee Commission, a new development was given to agriculture and industry, from which the country is deriving great benefits and because of which it is making marked progress.

This is quite true, indeed, yet one may be permitted to make some observations. One is that the Moslem minority in Northern Greece was not a troublesome minority. It enjoyed an equal protection of the law with the Greek majority. The Moslems who had remained in Greece and had not emigrated from 1912 to 1914 had really transferred both their legal and moral allegiance to Greece. It was a population speaking, as a rule, Greek, and having many common traits with the native Greeks. The two populations lived peacefully and harmoniously side by side.

A second observation is that it is quite certain that the economic development and progress of the northern provinces, as well as of the whole of Greece, would have taken place after 1922, even though no systematic installation of refugees had taken place. It must be remembered that ever since Greece had acquired the new provinces in 1912, she had been engaged almost continuously in war operations which did not permit her to turn her attention to the development of the resources of these provinces. At the end of the war with Turkey in 1922, Greece would, in any case, undoubtedly have sought to develop her agriculture and industry and natural resources and to improve communications and public services, all much neglected during the previous decade.

It is, of course, true that the coming of the refugees, and the great need of setting them at productive work, accelerated greatly the pace of development of the northern provinces of Greece; but this acceleration was achieved at great sacrifices. This leads to the third observation that should be made. The figures mentioned in another place [6] show that, as a result of the financial cost of the settlement of the refugees, the whole Greek people is overburdened with the service of costly foreign and domestic loans. Unless production is increased sufficiently in Greece to alleviate the situation, the burden of taxation will be a great handicap to any further development. Today everything is taxed to its capacity. In the meantime the government proceeds with its extensive programme of so-called productive works, such as new roads, new railways, and the Strymon drainage works. These are, of course, means of increasing the productivity of the country, but whether production will increase fast enough to supply the means for meeting the service of the foreign loans expended in these works is somewhat a matter of conjecture.

Lastly, it may be noted that, if the settlement of refugees had as a result a great development of the rural sections of Greece, on the other side it caused dangerous and unhealthy growth of the cities and towns. A poverty-stricken and unemployed or inadequately employed urban population has grown

[6] See *supra*, p. 704.

up in the outskirts of the Greek cities. The class of middlemen, small artisans, and small traders has been multiplied, with a resulting catastrophic decline in its economic status.

On the other side of the picture, Turkey has not fared any better as a result of driving out the Greek population. The new Turkish rulers thought that the exchange was the best way of satisfying their legitimate desire of preventing the Greek minority from becoming a weapon in the hands of foreign governments and from being utilized for subversive purposes. Kemal Pasha and his party had in mind the revolts and unrest of subject populations that have so long punctuated the history of the Turkish Empire. However, they failed to read that history correctly. It was not the fault of the minorities in Turkey that they had felt no moral allegiance to the Turkish state and had sought to cut themselves loose from the Empire during the last hundred years. It was rather the fact that the Empire, intellectually bankrupt, made no effort to satisfy the legitimate demands of the minorities. Moreover, the theocratic conception of the Turkish state, which resulted in leaving the non-Moslem races out of the purview of the Turkish law, had helped to maintain in them a separate national consciousness. Wise and patient effort on the part of the rulers, and Kemal's introduction into Turkey of Western ideas and laws, might have rendered it possible for the Greek minority to acquire a new loyalty to the new Turkish state.

As a result of the exchange, Turkey received only 500,000 Moslems from Greece, against almost 2,000,000 Greeks that she had lost since 1912. She experienced for years something like an economic paralysis. She is still in a transitory period. The departure of the Greeks upset the economic situation, not only by the partial depopulation of certain regions of Turkey, but also by the disappearance of a productive class which could not be easily replaced. Turkey is filling up at a slow pace the gaps left by the refugees in industry, banking, shipping, and professional occupations.

Another factor which has upset the economic situation for the time being is that a fundamental part of Kemal's programme is the development of Anatolia. In the old times Anatolia was a neglected part of the Empire. All its reserves were accumulated in Constantinople, to be spent in extravagance and stupid luxury. At the present time Constantinople, and with it Eastern Thrace, is neglected in favor of Anatolia, on whose development most of the resources of the state are expended.

However, Anatolia is still a riddle, for its secret is its people. Will the Kemalist government be able to spread its new ideas and awaken the conservative and backward Anatolian peasant? If not, the economic difficulties of Turkey will continue. Here we find one more reason to regret, for Turkey's sake, that the Greeks were driven out from Anatolia. They have left the country too sparsely populated. Of course, it is a great happiness for a state to have abundance of land and Turkey is on that account a happy country. But viewed from the effect on its people today there is too much land, there is not much inducement for the application of modern methods of agriculture. Moreover, Turkey lost in the Greeks the element of the population best fitted to take hold of the new ideas and to help the government in its ambitions for economic development.

The above reasons indicate why Turkey is still contending against great difficulties in the economic and financial fields. This is despite the fact that the Treaty of Lausanne emancipated Turkey from her old economic shackles: the privileges of foreigners in the matter of taxation; the restrictions in the raising of customs tariffs; the international administration of revenues. Turkey has contracted no loan since the war. This may be due to the fear of economic bondage and to the unwillingness to grant guarantees to foreign capital. But it is also due to the fact that the wise rulers of Turkey are unwilling to finance their schemes for public works with foreign loans when they are not certain that an increase of production by the people will supply the means for the service of such loans.

The exchange of Greek and Turkish populations thus appears to have been a solution adopted at a time when the minds of men were not yet free from the feelings aroused by war, and when racial animosity and the hostility of the majority towards the minority were at a high pitch. Only wise statesmanship and great foresight could have avoided the surgical operation adopted to heal the age-long ills involved in the existence of the national minorities in Greece and Turkey.

Ismet Pasha, the Turkish Premier, was sincere when he admitted in a press interview in July, 1930, after the signature of the Treaty of Angora with the Greek government: "Asia Minor, the Islands, and Greece supplement each other from all points of view. The Aegean unites Greece and Turkey and satisfies their mutual needs. The interest and the intelligence of the two nations dictate to them to be friends if they wish to prosper. . . . We have always prized the services which our former Christian fellow-citizens accomplished for us in the field of exports and international trade. The general economy of Constantinople has suffered as much from the absence of the non-Moslem Turkish citizens as from the interruption of the Russian trade."

It was not merely producers that Turkey lost by the departure of the Greeks. The Greek population that left Asia Minor had been settled there for over two thousand years, and still retained a higher degree of culture than was visible on the surface. Although under the corrupt administration of the Turkish Empire there had been a selection of the unfit rather than of the fittest among the Greeks in the struggle for survival, there were great cultural forces still preserved, which under favorable conditions might have expanded and brought about a flourishing civilization. The Greeks of Asia Minor drew their cultural inspiration not primarily from Athens, but from Constantinople and from the West. They had great schools, an educational system in many respects superior to that of old Greece, a poetry and literature of their own; and they cultivated arts and crafts, long handed down, which had been lost in Greece proper.

When Mustafa Kemal and the New Turks decided to destroy the Islamic and theocratic state and launched their programme for the Westernization of their country, they could have found in the Greeks, who had long been in cultural contact with the West, the best help for the realization of their views. The new ideas could have found their most effective carriers in the Greeks, and their spread among the Anatolian peasantry would have been a less difficult problem.

The loss in this respect to Turkey was a distinct gain to Greece. Indeed, the restoration of the unity of Hellenism within a continuous free land constitutes a historical fact of great significance. It is analogous to a similar event in the first centuries of the Byzantine Empire and to a lesser extent to one in the last part of the 6th Century B. C. In the former case, the Greeks of the post-Alexandrian colonization, under the pressure of the Persians and Saracens, retreated towards the centre of the Empire, to Constantinople and the surrounding provinces. They formed the ruling class, the aristocracy of the Lower Empire, to which they gave their language and their culture, a culture formed from Greek and Asiatic elements. In the other case, the Persian conquest after 544 B. C. of Ionia drove great numbers of Greeks away. Rather than accept the yoke, the inhabitants of certain cities left the country either collectively or isolated. The Ionian emigrants—merchants, mariners, artists, poets and thinkers—carried their higher culture to Greece proper where civilization, after the Dorian invasion, was at its dawn. The result was an interinfluence of Eastern and Western traditions and ideas and the development of Greek civilization.[7]

The new uprooting of Greeks from their ancient strongholds in Asia Minor and Thrace is a similar contraction of Hellenism. There is much evidence that it will have the cultural effects of the previous one. The mixing of the two stocks of Greeks and the mutual influence of their traditions and ideas has, to begin with, accelerated a movement which had its chief beginnings in the early nineties of the last century. This, the movement of reaction against the conscious efforts of Greeks in the past to Westernize their country and to imitate as much as possible Western models, requires a word of explanation.

[7] See A. Jardè, *La formation du peuple grec,* Paris, 1925, Part III, ch. 2.

In Greece, during the century of her revived independent life, the past has been a heavy weight upon the present. She has had too many memories. The shadow of the glory of the ancient Greek civilization has thwarted all the efforts of modern Greeks at creativeness. They have long overlooked the truth that they are more closely the descendants of Byzantine Greeks than of the ancients. This is easy to understand.

The political freedom of Greece was brought about under the inspiration of the dream and ideal of reviving the Golden Age of Pericles. Modern Greece was born in the land which was the cradle of the classic civilization. The men who constituted the leaders of Greece in the past century were Byzantine Greeks, descendants of those who, through all the thousand years' history of the Byzantine Empire, preserved and cultivated the ideal of the old Greek civilization. Moreover, the foreign lovers of Greece were almost always lovers of her past, and led the Greeks to look also to the past. Greeks also observed, as Professor Carathéodory has put it,[8] that their ancient civilization had been taken over by Western Europe, which was now its depository. They thought that by absorbing Western civilization they would reach more quickly their ultimate goal, the revival of their old civilization. This fact accounts for the conscious efforts of Greeks to Westernize their country. In this effort, the true and historical mission of Greece, that of blending together East and West, of absorbing Eastern and Western ideas, tendencies, and elements and giving them a new shape, the mission which had been realized again and again in the past, was forgotten by modern Greeks.

But the inevitable reaction set in. It began in the early nineties, through the work of a very small but chosen circle of writers, statesmen, and poets. Theirs was a movement of return to the 'people,' of studying its cultural forces, and of helping their unfolding and development for the creation of a Greek culture. Their voice had no echo in their generation, but their words acquired a prophetic meaning for the new generation, which listened to them under the influence of two events. In 1912-13 Greece exhibited an immense vitality in

[8] In a talk with the present writer in 1928.

the Balkan Wars, which added to Greece Southern Macedonia, Epirus, the Aegean Islands, and Crete. Instantly a feeling of self-confidence and a desire for self-assertion were manifested. Greeks turned their attention to the living forces of the people, which had been neglected to that time. On the other hand, the Greeks of the new provinces retained to a great extent the old Byzantine traditions, formed from Greek and Asiatic elements, and there resulted a first mixing of two stocks of Greeks with a reciprocation of cultural forces and traditions. With the coming of the refugees the so-called 'popular movement' became predominant. There resulted a melting pot of the ideas, tendencies, and traditions of the two stocks, so long separated, yet possessing a community of national feelings and aspirations and of religious traditions. A most remarkable phenomenon of this process that may be instanced is that of intellectual decentralization. Until the beginning of this century the cultural centre of all Greece was Athens. There was only one university, that of Athens. All literary life, all periodicals and books emanated from Athens. Much of this came from Western Europe. Little was genuine Greek, for Greece was little known to the leaders in the intellectual life. Today the picture is very different. There is a new university in Saloniki and two colleges on the Islands. There is a very active literary life in many cities in Crete, Thessaly, Peloponnesus, and Macedonia. There is a decentralization of the cultural movement, or rather a movement for the creation of various centres. Moreover, literary creation today more and more springs directly from the people and soil of Greece.

The above seems a fair analysis of the consequences of the exchange of the Greek and Turkish minorities. There is one further question to consider, namely, whether the exchange of Greek and Turkish populations has a character of permanency. That the exchanged Moslem population will not return to Greece may be taken for granted, chiefly for the reason that, this population being rural, it could not find any available lands in densely populated Greece. The same probably cannot be said of the Greeks who left Turkey. It seems very difficult to imagine that a movement which began with the dawn of Greek history and carried the Greeks to the shores of Asia Minor will be now stopped forever. Moreover, it has been noted above that the supply of land in Greece is insufficient, many rural refugees having been allocated an area of cultivated soil hardly adequate to their maintenance; and that the urban refugees are overcrowded, and can with great difficulty be absorbed by gainful occupations. Taking into account the high birth-rate among the refugees, it will not be long before a real problem of the disposal of surplus population will arise in Greece. Turkey, on the other hand, is a sparsely populated country. Only three-fourths of her cultivable land is in use. Her natural resources still remain to be developed. Her industry and commerce are in need of recruits. The Turkish government is still reluctant to open the doors to those who would help in developing the country. Will it long resist the nature of things? Will not the Greeks once more cross the Aegean and build their workshops and their exchanges on the shores of Ionia and Pontus? [8]

Greece may, however, hope that the Turkish Government will delay granting permission to the old Greek refugees to settle permanently in Turkey anew. For these people will require some time yet in order to acquire new roots in Greece. In the meantime the Greek people expect to continue the work of developing the country's resources, modernizing and intensifying agriculture, and creating new industries so that an abundant population may find productive employment. Greece may ill afford to neglect building up a strong and prosperous population, especially in her northern provinces. Her security, as well as her hopes of a Greek civilization depend on that. When this is accomplished, an emigration to the shores of Turkey, in pursuit of commerce and gainful occupations, will redound to the benefit of both neighboring countries.

[8] The *New York Times* published on November 11, 1931, a dispatch from Istanbul to the effect that the Foreign Minister telegraphed to all Turkish consuls authorizing them to issue visas to exchanged Greeks desiring to revisit Turkey. Such visas authorized a limited stay in Turkey.

Madness and hatred destroyed the peaceful life of innocent people who wished only to be left undisturbed. Slow and patient labor and mutual tolerance and understanding will be required to recreate that life. It will call for great and determined effort on the part of the responsible leaders if peace and mutual confidence are to be assured in this tempestuous part of the world. Naturally it is difficult to visualize the establishment of a stable peace in this region so long as much of the rest of the world, including some of the greatest and most civilized peoples, maintain only an armed peace. Greece, at last, is doing her part. Her leaders, in the face of one million refugees who were driven from their homes less than a decade ago and who have suffered too recently and too intensely to forget, miss no opportunity to preach mutual respect, coöperation, and understanding. They declare again and again that Greece is satisfied with her present frontiers and is determined to live in peace with all her neighbors. The people are taught to forget the old nationalist ideals and to be animated by the new ideals of internal reconstruction and of the creation of a new civilization. If the response of Turkey and Bulgaria to this new spirit of Greece is still faint, there is reason to believe that it will be reciprocated in the near future. Already the relations between Greece and Turkey have reached a high degree of cordiality which is due to the efforts of Turkey just as much as of Greece. If Bulgaria is somewhat behind, the reason is that she has not been able as yet to rid herself of the influences exerted by the Macedonian Revolutionary Committee.

The First Balkan Conference of October, 1930, meeting with the view of bringing about a political rapprochement of the Balkan peoples, was as successful as could be wished. Among other resolutions, it adopted one warmly approving the idea of a Balkan Union of independent nations. But though this may still be far off, there were other resolutions which struck a more realistic note. One recommended various measures for bringing about intellectual relations between these peoples who in the past have all but ignored each other; and other resolutions urged economic coöperation, the development of inter-Balkan communications, and common social improvement.[9]

The present relations of these nations are still in a state in which the stormy, bloody, and ungenerous yesterday weighs heavily against the promises, the hopes, and the needs of tomorrow. It is certain, however, that the political and religious jealousies of the past are giving way before new economic forces, now more than ever before essential to the life and happiness of the Balkan peoples. It is these irresistible forces which in the end may secure peace between these countries, that in so many respects constitute an economic unity.

[9] The Second Balkan Conference met on October, 1931, at Istanbul. Real progress was made on inter-Balkan communications and the marketing of such products as cereals and tobacco. A resolution was adopted to form an inter-Balkan chamber of commerce and industry at Istanbul. A special committee was appointed to elaborate a non-aggression compact with particular reference to the rights of minorities.

APPENDICES

APPENDIX I

CONVENTION BETWEEN GREECE AND BULGARIA RESPECTING RECIPROCAL EMIGRATION

Original text from League of Nations, *Treaty Series*, i, pp. 68-72, and the same, *Protection of Linguistic, Racial, and Religious Minorities* (Geneva, 1927), pp. 103-105. English translation in both these places.

CONVENTION ENTRE LA GRÈCE ET LA BULGARIE RELATIVE À L'ÉMIGRATION RECIPROQUE, SIGNÉE À NEUILLY-SUR-SEINE, LE 27 NOVEMBRE, 1919

Ainsi qu'il est prévu à l'article 56, alinéa 2 du Traité de paix avec la Bulgarie conclu le 27 novembre 1919 et conformément à la décision des Principales Puissances alliées et associées en date du 27 novembre 1919 et ainsi concue:

"Vu l'article 56, alinéa 2 du Traité de paix avec la Bulgarie, les Principales Puissances alliées et associées jugent opportun que l'émigration réciproque et volontaire des minorités ethniques, de religion ou de langue en Grèce et en Bulgarie, soient réglées par une Convention conclue entre ces deux Puissances dans les termes arrêtés à la date de ce jour."

Les Plénipotentiaires soussignés de la Grèce, d'une part,

Et de la Bulgarie d'autre part,

Après échange de leurs pleins pouvoirs, respectivement reconnus en bonne et due forme, sont convenus des dispositions suivantes:

Article Premier

Les Hautes Parties Contractantes reconnaissent à leurs ressortissants appartenant à des minorités ethniques, de religion ou de langue, le droit d'émigrer librement dans leurs territoires respectifs.

Article 2

Les Hautes Parties Contractantes s'engagent à faciliter, par tous les moyens dont elles disposent, l'exercice du droit prévu à l'article 1er, et à n'apporter directement ou indirectement aucune entrave à la liberté d'émigration, nonobstant les lois ou règlements contraires, qui, à cet égard, seront réputés sans effet.

En particulier, l'exercice du droit d'émigration ne portera pas atteinte aux droits pécuniaires des émigrants, tels que ces droits se trouvent constitués au moment de l'émigration.

Article 3

Il ne pourra être apporté aucun obstacle au départ d'un émigrant volontaire pour quelque cause que ce soit, sauf en cas de condamnation définitive à une peine afflictive pour infraction de droit commun. En cas de condamnation non encore définitive ou de poursuite pénale de droit commun contre un émigrant, ce dernier sera livré aux autorités du pays où il se rend, par les autorités du pays poursuivant, afin qu'il soit jugé.

Article 4

Le droit d'émigration volontaire appartient à toute personne âgée de plus de 18 ans. Il pourra être exercé dans un délai de deux ans à partir de la constitution de la Commission mixte prévue à l'article 8, au moyen d'une déclaration devant ladite Commission ou devant ses Représentants. La déclaration d'émigration du mari impliquera celle de la femme; la déclaration d'émigration des parents ou des tuteurs impliquera celle de leurs enfants ou pupilles âgés de moins de 18 ans.

Article 5

Les émigrants perdront la nationalité du pays qu'ils abandonnent, dès l'instant où ils l'auront quitté, et ils acquerront celle du pays de destination, des leur arrivée sur le territoire de ce pays.

Article 6

Les personnes qui, en exécution des dispositions précédentes, exerceront le droit d'émigration, seront libres d'emporter avec elles ou de faire transporter leurs biens meubles de toute nature, sans qu'il leur soit imposé de ce chef aucun droit, soit de sortie, soit d'entrée.

De même, au cas où le droit d'émigration serait exercé par des membres de Communautés (y compris les églises, couvents, écoles, hôpitaux ou fondations de quelque nature que ce soit), qui, de ce chef, devront être dissoutes, la Commission mixte prévue à l'article 8 déterminera si, et dans quelles conditions, ces membres auront la faculté d'emporter librement ou de faire transporter les biens meubles qui appartiennent à ces communautés.

Article 7

Les biens immobiliers, ruraux ou urbains, appartenant aux émigrants volontaires ou aux communautés visées à l'article 6, seront liquidés conformément aux dispositions ci-après, par la Commission mixte prévue à l'article 9.

Article 8

Dans un délai de trois mois, à partir de la mise en vigueur de la présente Convention, il sera créé une Commission mixte, composée d'un membre nommé par chacun des États contractants intéressés et d'un nombre égal de membres d'une autre nationalité, parmi lesquels le président sera choisi et qui seront nommés par le Conseil de la Société des Nations.

Article 9

La Commission mixte aura pour attributions, de surveiller et faciliter l'émigration volontaire prévue par la présente Convention et de liquider les immeubles des émigrants.

Elle fixera les modalités de l'émigration et de la liquidation des biens immobiliers.

D'une façon générale, la Commission mixte aura tous pouvoirs de prendre les mesures que nécessitera l'exécution de la présente Convention et de décider toutes les questions, auxquelles cette Convention pourrait donner lieu.

Les décisions de la Commission mixte seront prises à la majorité des voix, la voix du Président étant prépondérante, en cas de partage.

Article 10

La Commission mixte aura tout pouvoir pour faire procéder à l'estimation des biens immobiliers, les intéressés étant entendus ou ayant été dûment convoqués pour être entendus.

Le Gouvernement du pays où la liquidation aura eu lieu, devra verser à la Commission mixte, dans les conditions à fixer par celle-ci et pour être remis aux ayants droit, le montant de la valeur des biens immobiliers liquidés, qui resteront la propriété dudit Gouvernement.

Article 11

Des fonds seront avancés à la Commission mixte par les États intéressés, en vue de faciliter l'émigration et dans les conditions fixées par ladite Commission. Celleci avancera aux émigrants, dans la mesure des fonds disponibles, la valeur de leurs biens immobiliers.

Article 12

Les personnes qui, avant la mise en vigueur de la présente Convention, auraient quitté le territoire d'un des États contractants et se seraient déjà établies sur le territoire de l'État, dont elles relèvent au point de vue ethnique, de la religion ou de la langue, auront droit à la valeur des biens laissés par elles dans le pays qu'elles ont quitté, telle que cette valeur résultera de la liquidation qui en sera faite par la Commission mixte.

Article 13

Les frais d'entretien et de fonctionnement de la Commission mixte et de ses organes seront supportés par les Gouvernements intéressés dans des proportions à déterminer par la Commission.

Article 14

La présente Convention ne porte pas atteinte aux droits qui seraient reconnus aux intéressés par les dispositions des Traités ou Conventions conclus ou à conclure pour le réglement des affaires actuelles.

Article 15

Les Hautes Parties Contractantes s'engagent à apporter à leur législation respective les modifications qui seraient nécessaires pour assurer l'éxecution de la présente Convention.

Article 16

Dans le délai d'un an à dater de sa mise en vigueur, la présente Convention sera ouverte à l'adhésion des États ayant une frontière commune avec l'un des États signataires.

Cette adhésion sera signifiée, par la voie diplomatique, au Gouvernement de la République française et par celui-ci aux États signataires ou adhérents ainsi qu'à la Commission mixte. Elle portera effet quinze jours après la signification au Gouvernement français.

La présente Convention sera ratifiée et les ratifications seront respectivement déposées à Paris par les Puissances signataires en même temps que leurs ratifications du Traité de paix signé à Neuilly-sur-Seine, le 27 novembre 1919. Elle entrera en vigueur en même temps que ledit Traité de paix entrera en vigueur entre la Grèce et la Bulgarie.

Fait à Neuilly-sur-Seine, le vingt-sept novembre mil neuf cent dix neuf, en un seul exemplaire qui restera déposé dans les Archives du Gouvernement de la République française et dont les expéditions authentiques seront remises à chacune des Puissances signataires.

Eleftherios Veniselos,
N. Politis,
Al. Stamboliiski.

APPENDIX II

RULES ON THE RECIPROCAL AND VOLUNTARY EMIGRATION OF GREEK AND BULGARIAN MINORITIES

Original text from the unpublished document placed at the disposal of the writer by the Mixed Commission.

RÉGLEMENT

SUR

L'ÉMIGRATION RÉCIPROQUE ET VOLONTAIRE DES MINORITÉS GRECQUES ET BULGARES,

ÉLABORÉ

PAR

LA COMMISSION MIXTE d'ÉMIGRATION GRÉCO-BULGARE

Première Partie

Section Première—Dispositions Générales

Article premier

La liberté d'émigration et l'exercice des autres droits découlant de la Convention seront assurés par la Commission Mixte et ses organes.

Article 2

Sont organes de la Commission Mixte: les Sous-Commissions et les agents que la Commission Mixte nommera éventuellement.

Sous-Commissions [1]

Article 3

La Commission Mixte créera des Sous-Commissions auxquelles elle déléguéra une partie de ses attributions comme il est indiqué ci-dessous.

[1] These intermediate headings in heavy-faced type are written as side-headings in the manuscript. We have assigned them their present position as equally clear and more economical of space.

Ces Sous-Commissions seront composées de: un Président et deux Membres, nommés par la Commission Mixte. Le Président sera de nationalité étrangère aux deux pays intéressés. La nomination des deux Membres, Bulgare et Grec, sera faite par la Commission Mixte sur présentation des Délégués respectifs.

Auprès de chaque Sous-Commission il y aura un Secrétaire, nommé par la Commission Mixte, qui assistera aux séances sans voix délibérative.

Le personnel subalterne des Sous-Commissions sera également nommé par la Commission Mixte.

Droits et devoirs des Sous-Commissions

Article 4

Les Sous-Commissions décideront en premier ressort, conformément au présent Règlement et aux instructions qu'elles recevront de la Commission Mixte, toutes les questions se rapportant à des cas concrets d'émigration de membres appartenant à l'une des deux minorités et domiciliés dans leur circonscription. Elles pourront être saisies de ces cas, soit par la Commission Mixte, soit par un des Sous-Commissaires agissant de son propre mouvement ou sur demande des autorités respectives, soit par les intéressés ou leurs mandataires.

Les Sous-Commissions délivreront les feuilles de route, les certificats d'exemption de douane, les permis de voyage à prix réduits ou graduits, etc.

Article 5

Les Sous-Commissions feront, suivant la procédure fixée plus loin, une première évaluation des biens immobiliers que les émigrants et émigrés désireront faire liquider par la Commission Mixte.

Les protocoles d'évaluation dressés par les Sous-Commissions seront soumis à la Commission Mixte, qui fixera définitivement le prix de liquidation.

Article 6

Toutes les autres décisions des Sous-Commissions sont également sujettes à révision par la Commission Mixte en cas de recours ou par la propre initiative de celle-ci.

Section II

Conditions Requises Pour Être Admis à se Prévaloir de la Convention

Article 7

Sont admis à se prévaloir de la Convention:

a. Les ressortissants de chacun des deux Pays, Grèce et Bulgarie, agés de plus de 18 ans, appartenant soit à la minorité bulgare de Grèce, soit à la minorité grecque de Bulgarie, et qui veulent émigrer vers le pays auquel les rattachent leurs affinités ethniques;

b. Les personnes qui ont quitté les territoires actuellement grecs ou bulgares pour s'établir sur les territoires actuellement bulgares ou grecs à la condition:

1) que leur mouvement d'émigration ait pris place entre le 18 Décembre 1900 et le 18 Décembre 1920;

2) que, au moment de leur départ, elles aient appartenu à la minorité ethnique grecque ou bulgare du pays qu'elles quittaient, et qu'elles aient donc eu, à ce moment, la sujétion nationale de ce pays (bulgare et ottomane, s'il s'agit d'émigrés grecs, grecque ou ottomane, s'il s'agit d'émigrés bulgares);

3) qu'elles aient, depuis leur émigration, soit conservé leur sujétion ancienne, soit acquis la sujétion du pays vers lequel elles ont émigré, à l'exclusion de toute autre sujétion;

c. Les Communautés (églises, couvents, écoles, hôpitaux, ou fondations de quelque nature que ce soit) qui, comme personnes morales, remplissent, au point de vue de nationalité et émigration, les mêmes conditions que les personnes physiques définies dans les litteras a et b ci-dessus.

Remarque I. Si une personne qui était domiciliée en un endroit des territoires ottomans, entre les dates spécifiées au littera b ci-dessus, était simultanément propriétaire de biens immobiliers situés en une ou plusieurs autres localités de l'Empire Ottoman, et si, depuis lors, le lieu de situation des biens et le lieu de son domicile ancien on cessé d'appartenir à un même pays, cette personne pourra, en ce qui concerne le restitution ou la liquidation de chacun desdits biens, revendiquer les mêmes droits que si elle avait été effectivement domiciliée au lieu de situation de chacun d'eux.

Remarque II. Au cas où existerait un doute sur le fait de savoir si la date d'émigration d'une personne voulant se prévaloir de la Convention est antérieure ou postérieure au 18 Décembre 1900, mais où cette personne pourrait établir d'une façon certaine qu'elle avait la disposition de ses biens après le 18 Décembre 1900, elle profitera du bénéfice du doute sur la date exacte do son émigration.

Article 8

Les personnes désireuses d'obtenir le bénéfice de la Convention et d'user du droit d'émigration volontaire devront exercer celui-ci au moyen d'une déclaration faite à la Commission Mixte, ou à une des Sous-Commissions *avant le 31 Aout 1924*, dans les formes prévues dans les articles 32 à 34 du présent Règlement.

La déclaration d'émigration du mari impliquera celle de la femme; la déclaration des parents ou des tuteurs impliquera celle de leurs enfants ou pupilles âgés de moins de 18 ans. Par contre, les enfants agés de plus de 18 ans, qui voudront émigrer, devront remettre eux-mêmes une déclaration, indépendamment de celle éventuellement remise par le père de famille.

Le droit pour les tuteurs de remettre des déclarations d'émigrations pour leurs pupilles âgés de moins de 18 ans, comme il est dit ci-dessus, existe alors même que le statut personnel desdits tuteurs ne les autoriserait pas à se prévaloir eux-mêmes de la Convention.

La déclaration d'émigration doit exprimer la décision définitive de l'émigrant de quitter le pays d'origine pour s'installer dans le pays d'affinités ethniques, étant donné qu'elle constitue un acte solennel et irrévocable. Toutefois, ce n'est que deux mois après qu'auront été effectuées les publications visées à l'alinéa 4 de l'article 19, que la déclaration sera devenue irrévocable. Jusqu'à cette date, les personnes ayant remis une déclaration d'émigration pourront annuler celle-ci en notifiant leur volonté nouvelle, soit par lettre recommandée répondant aux conditions exigées par l'article 18, soit par une lettre remise contre reçu à la Sous-Commission à laquelle ils auront eu déposé leur déclaration d'émigration.

Section III

Droits et Obligations

Droits reconnus aux personnes se prévalant de la Convention et obligations leur incombant.

A. Emigrants futurs

Article 9

Les personnes désignés à l'article 7 sous le littera a, ont le droit d'émigrer dans le pays d'affinités ethniques sans qu'aucune entrave d'aucune espèce puisse être opposée à l'exercise de ce droit.

Font seuls exception, les condamnés à une peine afflictive pour infraction de droit commun, si la condamnation dont ils ont été frappés est définitive.

ARTICLE 10

Aucune pression, directe ou indirecte, ne pourra être exercée par qui que ce soit en vue d'empêcher une personne, appartenant à la minorité grecque ou bulgare, d'émigrer si elle désire, ni en vue d'amener une pareille personne à émigrer si elle ne le désire pas elle-même. La Commission Mixte ainsi que les Sous-Commissions et ses autres représentants veilleront à l'exercice libre et volontaire du droit d'émigration.

ARTICLE 11

Les candidats-émigrants qui ont fait une déclaration d'émigration seront tenus de quitter leur pays d'origine dans un délai de trois mois prenant cours à la liquidation de tous leurs biens ou à l'enrégistrement de la vente de ceux-ci, ou, s'ils ne sont pas propriétaires, à l'en régistrement de leur déclaration d'émigration.

Ils perdront la nationalité du pays qu'ils abandonnent dès l'instant où ils l'auront quitté et ils acquerront celle du pays de destination dès leur arrivée sur son territoire. La Commission Mixte veillera, s'il y a lieu, à ce que l'émigrant soit effectivement rayé du rôle des habitants du pays qu'il quitte, et inscrit au rôle des habitants du pays où il se rend.

Facilités de voyage

ARTICLE 12

Les Sous-Commissions délivreront gratuitement aux candidats-émigrants des feuilles de route pour se rendre dans leur pays de destination. Ces feuilles de route tiendront lieu de passeports pour le voyage en vue duquel elles seront libellées.

En vue de la délivrance de ces feuilles de route, le candidat-émigrant devra présenter à la Sous-Commission respective un certificat des Autorités Financières établissant qu'il a payé ses impôts.

Les indigents sont dispensés de l'obligation de présenter un certificat de payement d'impôts, s'ils présentent un certificat de la commune établissant leur indigence.

Ne peuvent être considérés comme indigents, même s'ils présentent un certificat, les émigrants qui demandent la liquidation de biens immobiliers, qu'elle qu'en soit l'importance.

Aux personnes qui désireraient se rendre dans le pays de destination afin d'y faire choix d'une propriété ou d'y préparer leur installation, il pourra être accordé une feuille de route, sur présentation de leur part d'un certificat des autorités policières, établissant qu'il n'y a pas de raisons d'empêchement à ce voyage.

ARTICLE 13

Les indigents auront droit au transport gratuit par chemin de fer, pour eux et les membres de leur familles, ainsi que pour 50 kilos de bagage par personne.

La qualité d'indigent sera établie par devant la Commission Mixte ou les Sous-Commission au moyen de certificats délivrés par les Communes comme il est dit à l'article 12, alinéa 3.

Biens meubles des émigrants

ARTICLE 14

Les émigrants sont libres d'emporter avec eux, ou de faire transporter leurs meubles de toute nature sans qu'il leur soit imposé de ce chef aucun droit, soit de sortie, soit d'entrée.

Le mobilier de maison, les ustensiles de ménage, les hardes et effets, les instruments d'agriculture et de métiers, le bétail et les troupeaux quel' émigrant a entretenus généralement, sont considérés comme meubles.

Les marchandises et tous produits que l'émigrant a généralement destinés à la vente sont considérés comme ayant fait partie du fonds de commerce ou d'industrie et exclus de l'exemption des droits de sortie et d'entrée, et des reductions de tarif.

Les vivres pour l'entretien de la famille de l'émigrant cultivateur, jusqu'à la prochaine récolte, ainsi que les semences qui pourraient lui être nécessaires pour cette récolte, jouissent de l'exemption des droits de sortie et d'entrée et des réduction de tarif.

Biens immobiliers des émigrants

(i) Vente sans intervention de la Commission Mixte

ARTICLE 15

Les candidats-émigrants qui auront déposé leur déclaration d'émigration ont le droit de vendre eux-mêmes directement ou par fondée de pouvoirs, jusqu'à la date du 31 Août 1924, les biens immobiliers qu'ils possèdent dans le pays qu'ils quittent, cela indépendamment des interdictions d'ordre général qui s'opposeraient aux transactions de ce genre.

Ils sont exonérés des droits d'enrégistrement de la vente de leurs propriétés.

ARTICLE 16

Dans le cas où un candidat-émigrant qui aura déposé sa déclaration d'émigration n'aura pas vendu, luimême ou par mandataire, tous ses biens immobiliers avant le 31 Août 1924, les biens non encore vendus seront liquidés d'office par la Commission Mixte, sous les conditions d'évaluation et de payement qui figurent aux Articles 18, 19, 20 et 21 ci-dessous.

Toutefois, la Commission Mixte pourra accorder aux candidats-émigrants des délais à valoir à partir du 31 Août 1924 leur permettant d'achever les ventes qu'ils auront entreprises et qu'ils n'auront pu parfaire à raison des formalités à accomplir.

(ii) Liquidation par la Commission Mixte

ARTICLE 17

Tout candidat-émigrant a le droit de demander la liquidation de ses beins immeubles par les soins de la Commission Mixte. Cette liquidation sera faite sans frais pour lui.

ARTICLE 18

Les biens à liquider par la Commission Mixte seront évalués, suivant la procédure fixée plus loin, par la Commission Mixte et ses représentants.

La base d'estimation des propriétés sera la valeur réelle de celles-ci à l'époque de la liquidation,—dans l'état où elles seront trouvées,—et non la valeur dépréciée que ces propriétés pourraient éventuellement avoir du fait de cette liquidation projetée.

Exception, en ce qui concerne l'état des biens, est faite pour les propriétés englobées dans les travaux publics depuis le 4 Octobre 1920, et qui seront considérées à l'état où elles se trouvaient au moment de l'expropriation et évaluées au prix du jour de l'estimation par la Commission Mixte.

ARTICLE 19

Le prix des immeubles liquidés, tel qu'il aura été fixé par la Commission Mixte, sera payé à l'ayant-droit par les soins de celle-ci, partie en argent comptant, partie en obligations nominatives spécialement émises à cet effet par les deux Gouvernements.

Le montant de la fraction payée en argent comptant pourra varier d'après la situation de l'émigrant et l'état des fonds spéciaux immédiatement disponibles. Il sera en ordre général de l'importance de 10% de la valeur des biens liquidés.

Les obligations seront productives d'intérêt. Elles seront des fonds d'État, couverts par les garanties supplémentaires nécessaires pour rendre possible à l'émigrant la mobilization immédiate de ces titres, dans son pays de destination, en vue de son installation nouvelle.

Dès qu'auront été arrêtées les modalités détaillées de ces payements, ainsi que les dispositions prises en vue de faciliter l'emploi ou l'escompte des obligations dans le pays de destination, la Commission Mixte les portera à la connaissance des intéressés et leur fera connaître, en même temps, les éléments qui seront pris en considération pour les évaluations visées à l'article précédent. Elle donnera à cette communication la même publicité qu'au présent Règlement.

ARTICLE 20

Aucun candidat-émigrant ne peut être obligé de quitter le pays ou être dépossédé de ses biens avant d'avoir reçu le payement intégral de ceux-ci, dans les formes prévues à l'article précédent.

ARTICLE 21

Après le payement du prix, les biens liquidés par la Commission Mixte sont acquis à l'État sur le territoire duquel ils sont sis et sur les fonds duquel ils ont été payés.

B. Émigrés

ARTICLE 22

Sont 'émigrés' aux termes de ce règlement, les personnes déterminées à l'article 7, littera b, et qui auraient remis à la Commission Mixte, ou a ses représentants, une déclaration établissant leur désir de se prévaloir de la Convention d'Émigration. (Formulaire No. 1, annexé au présent Règlement.)

ARTICLE 23

Les émigrés qui auraient déposé leur déclaration d'émigration seront rayés des listes des habitants du pays d'origine et inscrits—

s'ils ne l'ont pas été déjà—parmi les habitants du pays d'adoption, dont ils acquerront ainsi tous les droits des nationaux. L'épouse et les enfants âgés de moins de 18 ans suivront la sujétion du mari ou des parents.

Facilités de voyage

Article 24

Les émigrés qui auront déposé leur déclaration seront autorisés à faire un ou plusieurs voyages dans le pays quitté en vue d'y chercher leurs familles ou d'y mettre leurs affaires en ordre. A cet effet, des feuilles de route leur seront délivrés par la Commission Mixte ou ses représentants après renseignement sur leur personne auprès des autorités de l'un et de l'autre pays.

Article 25

Les membres de la famille d'un émigré restés dans le pays d'origine jouissent de toutes les facilités de voyage et de transport accordées aux émigrants futurs.

Biens meubles des émigrés

Article 26

Les émigrés auront le droit de chercher, ou de faire transporter, les biens meubles qu'ils ont laissés dans leur pays d'origine sans qu'il puisse leur être imposé pour ces biens aucun droit de sortie ou d'entrée.

Article 27

Les biens meubles qui leur ont été confisqués ou saisis pour des raisons autres que de droit commun et qui se trouvent encore entre les mains des autorités, leur seront remis sans qu'il leur puisse être réclamé aucun droit de garde ou autre.

Les biens meubles qui auraient été vendus ou employés par les autorités depuis le 4 Octobre 1920, et au sujet desquels il existe des preuves écrites, seront remboursés aux ayants-droits par la Commission Mixte au prix encaissé par le Fisc—s'ils ont été vendus, à un prix que la Commission Mixte fixera d'après les prix de l'époque de consommation—s'ils ont été employés.

Les facilités et franchises fixées aux Articles 13 et 14 sont accordées également aux émigrés et à leurs familles.

Biens immeubles des émigrés

ARTICLE 28

Les émigrés qui auront déposé leur déclaration sont tenus de vendre avant le 31 Aout 1924, ou de faire liquider par la Commission Mixte, tous les biens immobiliers qu'ils ont laissés dans le pays d'origine. Les règles fixées pour la vente et la liquidation des biens des émigrants seront appliquées également aux biens des émigrés (Voir Articles 15-21).

Levée des mesures d'exception

ARTICLE 29

Sont levées toutes les mesures d'exception qu'elles aient été prises en base de lois, règlements, circulaires ou autrement, frappant les biens des personnes de la minorité respectivement grecque ou bulgare, qui ont quitté le pays d'origine et qui se trouvent établies sur le territoire de l'État dont elles relèvant ethniquement.

Les personnes ci-dessous désignées ont le droit, indépendamment de la remise ou non d'une déclaration d'émigration définitive, de reprendre leurs biens, que ceux-ci aient été considérés ou non comme confisqués, séquestrés, abandonnés, etc., et d'en disposer librement jusqu'au 31 Août 1924 en les faisant fructifier, en les aliénant, etc., sous réserve des restrictions fixées plus loin.

Dans le cas où ces biens ont été sous le coup d'une confiscation ou placés sous séquestre, les propriétaires ont droit au revenu touché par l'État ou par le séquestre depuis le jour de la confiscation, ou mise sous séquestre, jusqu'à la restitution des biens à leurs ayants-droits. Ces revenus seront versés par l'entremise de la Commission Mixte.

Les propriétaires de biens confisqués ou séquestrés ont droit à une indemnité pour les endommagements que leurs propriétées auraient subis, postérieurement au 4 Octobre 1920 par le fait ou par suite de la négligence des autorités chargées de la gestion et de la garde de ces biens. Les intéressés auront à prouver que les endommagements ont eu lieu postérieurement au 4 Octobre 1920 et qu'il y a eu réellement, de la part des autorités en question, de la négligence ayant produit des effets tels que: destruction d'immeubles, de vignes, plantations, etc., au vu et au su de la population ou des autorités—, non payement de primes d'assurances alors que les revenus produits par l'immeuble permettaient de les couvrir, etc., etc.

Dans le cas où les biens ont été utilisés par des réfugiés sans que ceux-ci aient payé de loyer, il n'est dû aucune indemnité au propriétaire.

Les biens immeubles appartenant aux personnes définies à l'article 7 littera b. qui ont été expropriés après le 4 Octobre 1920, *pour cause d'utilité publique ou sociale,* pourront, sur la demande des intéressés, faire l'objet d'une re-évaluation par la Commission Mixte en base de leur ancien état et de leur valeur au moment de la nouvelle évaluation. Dans ce cas le prix déjà payé sera défalqué du prix qui résultera de la liquidation par la Commission Mixte.

Restrictions

Article 30

Les restrictions suivantes sont approvées au droit de libre disposition des biens visés par l'article précédent:

1. Dans le cas où les biens ont été utilisés pour l'installation de réfugiés, les propriétaires n'auront pas droit à la restitution, mais seulement à la contrevaleur de ces biens, telle qu'elle sera déterminée lors de la liquidation par la Commission Mixte.

2. Dans le cas où une propriété serait l'objet d'un contrat de location, dont le terme dépasse le 1er Juillet 1925 et qui ne contient pas de clause résiliatoire, la Commission Mixte ou les Sous-Commissions prendront les mesures nécessaires pour remédier à cette situation, l'indemnisation pour l'avenir de qui de droit étant à charge de l'État.

3. Dans le cas où il se produit une contestation entre l'émigré et une tierce personne relativement à la reprise des biens par le premier, la Sous-Commission entendra les deux parties.

Si les droits dont se prévaut la tierce personne sont des droits réels qu'elle aurait acquis sur les biens après leur saisie par l'État Hellénique ou Bulgare, après occupation des dits biens par celui-ci, et si la Commission Mixte ou le Tribunal Helléneque ou Bulgare, saisi par elle, constate l'existence de ces droits, l'émigré propriétaire aura droit seulement à la valeur du bien telle qu'elle aura été fixée par la Commission Mixte.

Si les droits dont se prévaut la tierce personne n'ont pas été acquis dans les conditions spécifiées dans l'alinéa ci-dessus, mais si la Commission Mixte juge que ce sont des droits réels en base de la loi commune, elle renverra les parties devant les tribunaux: sinon elle demandera aux autorités la restitution à l'émigré du bien qui lui appartient.

Ne seront pas considérés comme créant des droits réels en base de la loi commune: a) des titres crées ou émis par les Commissions Ottomanes ayant appliqué la loi sur l'Emvalul-Metrouké; b) des donations ou des opérations d'achat, mais celles-ci réelles ou à tel prix que l'opération ne constitue au fond qu'un don déguisé; c) la prescription sauf sans le cas où la Commission Mixte constate que le propriétaire émigré a quitté son pays pour des raisons personnelles indépendamment de tout mouvement d'émigration forcée ou en masse.

4. Dans le cas où une tierce personne qui a possédé sans juste titre la propriété d'un émigré, pendant l'absence de ce dernier, y a apporté des améliorations sensibles consistant en bâtisses, plantations, etc., la Commission Mixte, appelée à liquider l'immeuble, sur la demande de l'émigré, en procédant à l'estimation, fixera la part revenant à chacun dans la valeur de la propriété.

Si l'émigré ne s'adresse pas à la Commission Mixte pour la liquidation de la propriété, la contestation entre ce dernier et le possesseur ci-dessus visé devra être portée par devant les tribunaux.

Article 31

Les personnes qui n'auront pas remis de déclaration d'émigration définitive avant le 31 Août 1924 n'auront plus, à partir de cette date, de droits constitués auprès de la Commission Mixte; elles ne pourront plus demander l'intervention de celle-ci en vue de la sauvegarde d'aucun droit. Néanmoins, les transactions qu'elles auront faites de leurs biens jusqu'à cette date seront valablement faites et définitives.

Deuxième Partie

Section IV

Procédure

A. Procédure Concernant les Émigrants

Déclaration d'émigration

Article 32

Toute personne âgée de plus de 18 ans, appartenant à l'une des minorités ethniques grecque ou bulgare, et désirant émigrer dans le pays d'affinités ethniques, en base de la Convention d'Émigration Réciproque, doit remettre à la Commission Mixte ou à une des Sous-Commissions avant le 18 Décembre 1922, une déclaration d'émigration dans les formes décrites à l'article 33 accompagnée du certificat de minorité ethnique défini à l'article 34.

ARTICLE 33

Des formulaires imprimés de 'déclaration d'émigration' du modèle No. 1 A, joint en annexe au présent Règlement, seront mis à la disposition des candidats-émigrants, notamment dans les bureaux de la Commission Mixte et des Sous-Commissions. Les intéressés pourront en demander personnellement, ou par lettre, ou par tout autre moyen.

Les formulaires portent un questionnaire trilingue, en français, bulgare et grec.

La déclaration d'émigration devra être rédigée sur un semblable formulaire, conformément au questionnaire, et indifféremment en français, en grec ou en bulgare, au choix de l'intéressé.

La déclaration devra etre signée et datée.

Les illettrés pourront faire rédiger leurs déclarations par d'autres personnes, mais en présence de deux témoins sachant lire et écrire, qui devront y apposer leur signature et y mentionner leur adresse.

La déclaration dûment remplie et signée comme il est dit ci-dessus, et accompagnée du certificat de minorité ethnique défini à l'article 34, devra être remise par le déclarant à la Sous-Commission, sur le zone d'action de laquelle il a son domicile.

Il sera également loisible au déclarant de ne pas porter sa déclaration personnellement mais de l'envoyer à ladite Sous-Commission; toutefois dans ce cas sa signature,—ou celles des témoins s'il est illettré,—devront avoir été légalisées par le Maire de la Commune de son domicile.

REMARQUE I. Jusqu'à ce que les Sous-Commissions soient constituées, les candidats-émigrants pourront adresser leurs déclarations à la Commission elle-même. Ils pourront le faire également après la constitution des Sous-Commissions, mais cela seulement dans le cas où ils habitent près du siège de la Commission Mixte ou qu'ils doutent à quelle Sous-Commission ils doivent s'adresser.

REMARQUE II. En cas de doute sur l'authenticité de la signature d'une déclaration, la Sous-Commission procédera à une enquête.

REMARQUE III. Tout candidat qui se présentera personnellement aux bureaux de la Sous-Commission, muni de son certificat de minorité ethnique, pourra demander au Sécrétariat qu'un des employés remplisse pour lui le formulaire de déclaration. Il devra toutefois signer lui-même. Dans le cas où il ne sait signer, une autre personne pourra signer pour lui devant l'employés même, mais dans ce cas il devra être fait mention de la qualité d'illettré du déclarant et la déclaration devra porter la signature du témoin.

Certificat de minorité ethnique

ARTICLE 34

Tout candidat-émigrant, pour être admis à remettre sa déclaration d'émigration, devra établir qu'il appartient à la minorité ethnique grecque ou bulgare du pays dont il veut émigrer.

A cette fin, il devra se munir d'un certificat de minorité ethnique (du modèle No. II A, joint en annexe au présent Règlement) qui lui délivrera gratuitement le Maire de la Commune de son domicile.

Ce certificat devra obligatoirement être annexé à la déclaration d'émigration.

Dans le cas où l'autorité communale refuserait de délivrer un pareil certificat, le candidat-émigrant pourra saisir de son cas la Sous-Commission de son ressort. Celle-ci fera une enquête. Si la conclusion de cette enquête est favorable à l'intéressé, la Sous-Commission pourra le dispenser de l'obligation de présenter un certificat de minorité ethnique, en mentionnant cette dispense en marge de la déclaration.

Feuille de route

ARTICLE 35

Toute demande, en vue de l'obtention des feuilles de route prévues à l'article 12, devra être fait par écrit.

Elle devra contenir des renseignements détaillés sur les personnes qui désirent se déplacer ainsi que sur le but de leur voyage.

A la demande devra être joint, en plus des certificats prévus à l'article 12, un certificat de minorité ethnique, à moins que cette dernière pièce n'ait déjà été déposée à la Sous-Commission.

Exemption des droits de douane

ARTICLE 36

Tout candidat-émigrant désirant obtenir les réductions de tarif de chemin de fer et l'exemption de droits de douane prévus aux articles 12 et 14 devra adresser à la Sous-Commission de son domicile une demande indiquant les noms et l'âge des membres de sa famille qui vont se déplacer et la liste détaillée des objets mobiliers qu'il désire transporter dans l'autre pays.

Après vérification, la Sous-Commission lui délivrera les pièces nécessaires.

Demandes en liquidation

ARTICLE 37

Tout candidat-émigrant qui désire faire liquider par la Commission Mixte une ou plusieurs propriétés immobilières devra manifester cette volonté avant le 31 Août 1924, par la remise d'une 'demande en liquidation' faite dans les formes spécifiés ci-dessous:

Toute 'demande en liquidation' devra être faite suivant un formulaire modèle No. III A joint en annexe au présent Règlement. Le dit formulaire pourra être rempli, au choix de l'intéressé: en bulgare, en grec ou en français.

Toute demande en liquidation pourra être remise soit en même temps que la déclaration d'émigration, soit postérieurement à celle-ci, mais avant le 31 Août 1924.

Toute demande en liquidation remise postérieurement à la déclaration d'émigration devra nécessairement mentionner la date et le No. d'enregistrement de la déclaration d'émigration.

Les conditions imposées par l'article 33 relativement à la signature et la légalisation de signature et à la destination pour la déclaration d'émigration sont également de rigueur pour la demande en liquidation.

Il pourra être remis par un même candidat-émigrant, un même jour ou à des dates différentes, plusiers demandes en liquidation à condition qu'elles se rapportent à des biens différents.

ARTICLE 38

Dans le cas où, à la date du 31 Août 1924, un candidat-émigrant n'aura pas, soit vendu lui-même ses biens immobiliers, soit demandé leur liquidation, la Sous-Commission pourra, sur la demande d'un de ses Membres, procéder d'office à l'évaluation des biens immobiliers restés en la propriété de l'émigrant, mais cela après avoir convoqué celui-ci comme il est indiqué à l'article 43.

Affichage des demandes en liquidation

ARTICLE 39

Dès la réception de la demande en liquidation d'un bien, la Sous-Commission fera afficher, à la Mairie du village où ce bien est situé, un avis au public.

Cet avis indiquera que telle personne, candidat-émigrant, demande liquidation de tel bien, que toute personne qui aurait des objections à formuler contre cette liquidation parcequ'elle croirait avoir des droits légalement constitués sur la propriété en question, sera admise à les faire valoir, par écrit, par devant la Sous-Commission avant l'expiration du trentième jour, à dater de l'affichage de l'avis faute de quoi il sera procédé à la liquidation.

Pourtant les Sous-Commission pourront admettre les tiers intéressés à défendre leurs droits oralement au jour de l'évaluation des biens, même si ceux-ci n'ont pas présenté des objections par écrit dans le délai fixé, mais cela seulement si elles estiment qu'il y a des motifs suffisants pour justifier cette exception.

Article 40

Des déclarations d'émigration, les notifications de retrait de déclaration, ainsi que les demandes en liquidation seront enregistrées dans des livres spéciaux.

Toute personne qui aura remis l'un ou l'autre de ces actes pourra en demander personnellement un reçu qui indiquera le numéro et la date d'enregistrement.

Évaluation par les Sous-Commissions

Article 41

Après avoir reçu un certain nombre de déclarations, les Sous-Commissions élaboreront un plan d'ensemble pour l'évaluation des propriétés dont la liquidation par la Commission Mixte des demandée.

Pour l'élaboration de ce plan elles tiendront compte de l'utilité qu'il y a pour les candidats à ce que la Sous-Commission se rende sur place pour procéder à l'évaluation des biens à liquider. Le plan sera donc élaboré en base de la situation géographique des localités où il y aura des biens à liquider et des moyens de communication.

L'évaluation des biens peu importants dans les endroits éloignés pourra se faire dans la localité la plus voisine où la Sous-Commission aura à se rendre.

Article 42

Le plan de mouvement des Sous-Commissions sera porté à la connaissance du public aussitôt élaboré. En outre, chaque Sous-Commission informera les Maires, trente jours à l'avance, si possible, de la date à laquelle elle se rendra dans leur commune, afin que les intéressés en soient prévenus.

Les Maires des Communes qui ne seront pas visités seront informés de la localité et de la date à laquelle aura lieu l'évaluation des biens de leurs administrés candidats-émigrants.

Convocation des candidats-émigrants

Article 43

Les Sous-Commissions citeront par devant elles, par lettre, envoyée directement ou par l'entremise des maires, tout candidat-émigrant qui aurait demandé la liquidation de ses biens par la Commission, lui faisant connaitre l'endroit et le jour où il doit se présenter pour être entendu.

Dans le cas où le candidat-émigrant aura indiqué dans sa déclaration une adresse spéciale, toutes les communications lui seront faits à cette adresse.

Dans le cas où l'émigrant cité ne se présente pas, l'évaluation pourra se faire en son absence.

Droit de représentation

Article 44

Les candidats-émigrants peuvent se présenter personnellement ou se faire représenter par mandataire muni d'un plein pouvoir soit notarié, soit sous seingprivé, mais celui-ci de la même écriture que le texte de la déclaration et portant légalisation de la signature par le maire de la localité où le candidat est domicilié.

Tout candidat peut indiquer dans sa déclaration une personne qui le représentera par devant la Commission Mixte ou les Sous-Commissions. Dans ce cas c'est cette personne qui sera citée en lieu et place de candidat-émigrant. La désignation d'un représentant peut se faire également dans cheque demande en liquidation, mais en ce cas le représentant ne sera qualifié que pour l'évaluation des biens que concerne la demande.

Toutefois, aucun payement, soit en espèces, soit en obligations, ne pourra être fait à quelqu'un d'autre qu'à l'émigrant lui-même, ou à un mandataire muni d'une procuration notariée mentionnant explicitement qu'il peut toucher le payement.

Remarque: Tout candidat-émigrant qui s'éloigne ou qui se trouve éloigné des territoires des deux pays est tenu de se faire représenter en se conformant aux règles fixées pour la représentation facultative.

ARTICLE 45

Peuvent être mandataires: les parents ou amis du candidat-émigrant, indépendamment du sexe, les gérants de leurs propriétés et les avocats inscrits à l'un des barreaux de l'un ou l'autre des deux pays, indifféremment. Sont écartées d'office toutes personnes qui, sans être avocats inscrits, feraient profession de représentants d'émigrants ou qui chercheraient à réaliser des profits personnels par cette représentation.

ARTICLE 46

Pour toute communication avec la Commission Mixte ou les Sous-Commissions, écrite ou verbale, les candidats-émigrants ou leurs représentants peuvent faire usage d'une des trois langues citées à l'article 33 (Grec, Bulgare ou Français).

Toutefois, si les candidats se font représenter par des avocats, ceux-ci sont tenus de faire toutes les communications en français uniquement.

Preuves de la propriété

ARTICLE 47

Les candidats-émigrants devront établir par devant les Sous-Commissions leurs droits de propriété sur les biens dont ils demandent la liquidation.

ARTICLE 48

Les droits de propriété peuvent être établis par l'un des moyens suivants:

a) par un titre en règle répondant aux exigences de la loi du lieu de situation des biens;

b) pour les territoires nouvellement acquis (depuis 1912) par un titre ou copie authentique de titre répondant aux exigences de la loi Ottomane accompagné d'une traduction dans l'une des deux langues grecque ou bulgare, celle-ci légalisée par le Ministère respectif des Affaires Etrangères, ou faite au préalable en Français par un employé spécial auprès de la Commission Mixte. Cette dernière traduction ne pourra servir qu'auprès de la Commission Mixte et des Sous-Commission;

c) par des 'hudgets' et jugements des tribunaux;

d) par des quittances de payement d'impôts délivrées par les autorités Ottomanes, pour les territoires nouvellement acquis, et soutenus par le témoignage de deux personnes de la commune où sont situés les biens;

e) par le témoignage de deux habitants de la commune où sont situés les biens, qui déclareront, sous serment, devant le juge de paix de leur domicile, que les biens appartiennent aux candidats. Le Procès-Verbal dressé par le juge de paix à cette occasion sera produit devant la Sous-Commission du lieu de situation des biens;

f) par le témoignage de trois habitants de la commune en présence du Maire (ou son adjoint) ou d'un habitant désigné à cet effet par le Conseil Communal comme il est indiqué à l'article 50;

g) par d'anciennes pièces ayant date certaine et émanant d'autorités ou d'administrations nationales;

h) par le témoignage sous serment d'anciens habitants de la commune dans le cas où il s'agit de biens situés dans des endroits que l'ancienne population a abandonnés postérieurement à 1900 en connexité avec des événements politiques.

Audiences publiques des Sous-Commissions

Article 49

Après avoir présenté devant la Sous-Commission, en audience publique, les preuves de droit de propriété, les candidats-émigrants exposeront comme ils établissent le prix qu'ils réclament et, dans le cas ou ils se basent sur les prix obtenus dernièrement pour des biens similaires, ils en fourniront les preuves et présenteront les témoins qu'ils demandent à la Sous-Commission d'entendre.

Article 50

Aucun témoignage ne pourra être entendu qu'en présence du maire (ou son adjoint) ou d'un représentant désigné par le Conseil Communal pour assister aux audiences de la Sous-Commission.

Le représentant de la commune ne peut pas être choisi parmi les candidats-émigrants.

Dans le cas où tout le village émigré, le représentant de la Commune devra être choisi par le Conseil Communal parmi les habitants d'un village voisin de la même commune et, si la majorité même de la commune émigré, il devra être choisi par le conseil départemental parmi les notables d'une des communes voisines.

Les représentants des communes recevront de la Sous-Commission une indemnité journalière que celle-ci fixera, d'après le cas.

Décisions des Sous-Commissions

Article 51

Après avoir entendu le candidat-émigrant et ses témoins et pris connaissance des pièces écrites, la Sous-Commission se retirera et entendra à huis clos l'avis du représentant communal aussi bien sur les faits allégués et l'honorabilité des témoins que sur les prétentions du candidat-émigrant. Puis, en dehors de la présence du représentant communal, elle procèdera à une évaluation des biens à liquider en base des données qu'elle possède elle-même ou de celle qui lui ont été fournies par l'intéressé et par le représentant communal, ou par un agent chargé de recueillir des renseignements, cela en toute conscience et sans être liée par les dépositions ou avis quelconques qui ne seront considérés que comme des éléments d'appréciation destineés à former la conviction des membres de la Sous-Commission. Dans le cas où la Sous-Commission juge utile de procéder à un nouvel examen sur les lieux, elle pourra surseoir à la décision en fixant le jour et l'heure pour cet examen et en donnant connaissance à l'intéressé. Dans le cas où ce nouvel examen n'est pas jugé utile, la Sous-Commission se prononcera sans délai.

Article 52

Les décisions des Sous-Commission seront prises à la majorité des voix. Dans le cas où il est impossible d'obtenir une majorité, le Président aura voix prépondérante.

Article 53

Un procès-verbal sera dressé pour cheque évaluation contenant une description complète du bien, les prétentions de l'intéressé, la nature des preuves de propriété, les noms et qualités des témoins entendus, s'il y en a, et la décision de la Sous-Commission.

Les décisions ne seront pas motivées excepté dans le cas où elles auront été prises par la voix prépondérante du Président.

Article 54

Copie du procès-verbal sera communiqué au candidat-émigrant. Cette copie devra porter un résumé de la décision dans une langue connue par le candidat-émigrant, excepté dans le cas où il se fait représenter par un avocat.

Le délai de 30 jours fixé à l'article 39 pour la présentation des objections, prendra cours du jour de cette communication.

ARTICLE 55

Une liste des prix auxquels la Sous-Commission a évalué les divers biens sera affichée dans ses bureaux dans les communes de situation des biens, au fur et à mesure des évaluations.

Recours à la Commission Mixte

ARTICLE 56

Toutes les décisions des Sous-Commissions portant évaluation de biens à liquider-par la Commission Mixte seront soumises à celle-ci pour les suites qu'elle donnera comme il est indiqué plus loin.

ARTICLE 57

Tout candidat-émigrant aura droit de déposer ou d'envoyer, dans le délai de trente jours à dater de la communication de la décision, au bureau de la Sous-Commission respective, pour être transmises à la Commission Mixte, les 'objections' qu'il a à formuler contre la décision de la Sous-Commission. Les tiers intéressés seront également admis à soumettre des objections par écrit dans le même délai.

ARTICLE 58

Les membres des Sous-Commissions pourront, au cours du délai fixé à l'article précédent, déposer aux bureaux de la Sous-Commission une 'notice' contenant leurs vues particulières s'ils jugent nécessaire de les faire connaître à la Commission Mixte.

ARTICLE 59

Trente jours après la communication au candidat-émigrant de la décision de la Sous-Commission, le Secrétaire de la Sous-Commission constituera un dossier relatif à l'évaluation des biens que cette décision concerne. Ce dossier contiendra:

1) la demande en liquidation et la déclaration d'émigration, si celle-ci n'a pas été envoyée à une autre occasion;

2) le procès-verbal relatif à l'évaluation par la Sous-Commission;

3) les notices des membres de la Sous-Commission, s'il y en a;

4) les objections du candidat-émigrant, s'il y en a, ou une mention du Secrétariat s'il n'y a pas de pareilles objections;

5) les objections éventuelles des tiers intéressés;

6) les titres de propriété ou copies authentiques, si le candidat-émigrant possédait de pareils titres, ainsi que toute autre pièce présentée à la Sous-Commission ou bien une mention de la manière dont le droit de propriété a été établi, dans le cas où des documents écrits n'ont pu être produits devant la Sous-Commission;

7) un certificat du notaire ou autre autorité compétente établissant que le bien est franc d'hypothèque ou saisi;

8) un certificat de la Banque Nationale et de la Banque Agricole du pays de situation des biens à liquider, établissant que l'ayant-droit n'a pas de dettes vis-à-vis de ces banques;

9) un certificat du percepteur des finances établissant que les impôts ont été payés.

Liquidation par la Commission Mixte

Article 60

Le dossier constitué comme il est indiqué à l'article précédent sera transmis au Secrétariat de la Commission Mixte qui, après enregistrement, portera le cas au 'rôle des liquidations' dans l'ordre des entrées des dossiers. Toutefois, s'il existe des raisons très importantes en faveur de la liquidation plus rapide d'un cas particulier, le Président de la Commission Mixte pourra disposer que cette liquidation soit faite en dehors du rôle.

Le rôle des liquidations sera affiché au Secrétariat de la Commission Mixte et des Sous-Commissions. C'est là que pourront le constituer les intéressés qui désireront en avoir connaissance.

Article 61

Toute procédure par devant la Commission Mixte est écrite. Les intéressés ne peuvent demander à être entendus oralement.

Article 62

Les décisions de la Commission Mixte sont définitives. Aucun recours n'est ouvert à leur sujet.

Article 63

Des extraits des décisions seront communiqués au Gouvernement, sur le territoire duquel les biens liquidés sont situés, et à l'intéressé. Les extraits pour l'intéressé pourront se rapporter à la liquidation de biens différents appartenant au même propriétaire.

ARTICLE 64

Après la décision de liquidation, la Commission Mixte fera tenir à l'ayant-droit le prix du bien liquidé dans les formes prévues à l'article 19.

Après ce payement, l'émigrant perd tout droit sur les biens liquidés, ceux-ci étant devenus la propriété de l'État sur les fonds duquel ils ont été payés.

ARTICLE 65

Le délai de troit mois, fixé à l'article 11, dans lequel l'émigrant doit quitter le pays d'origine, prend cours à dater du jour où il aura reçu, dans les formes fixées à l'article 19, le payement intégral de tous les biens soumis à liquidation.

B. PROCÉDURE POUR LES ÉMIGRÉS

Reprise des biens immobiliers

ARTICLE 66

Les émigrés désirant jouir du droit qui leur est accordé par l'article 29, alinéa 2, peuvent, indépendamment de toute remise d'une déclaration d'émigration, suivre la procédure suivante:

1) L'intéressé se fera délivrer, par le Maire de la Commune de son domicile actuel un certificat de minorité ethnique conforme au Modèle 2. B. annexé au présent Règlement.

2) Il remettra ou adressera à la Sous-Commission de son domicile (ou à la Commission Mixte) une demande sur formulaire Modèle No. 4 (voir en annexe au présent Règlement) si il joindra à cette demande le certificat Modèle 2.B. mentionné ci-dessus.

3) La Sous-Commission compétente, après examen, lui délivrera, s'il y a lieu, un certificat Modèle No. 5 (voir en annexe au présent Règlement) constatant qu'il remplit les conditions requises par l'article 7, littera b.

Muni de ces certificats, l'émigré s'adressera, directement ou par mandataire, aux autorités administratives du lieu de situation de ses biens, qui lui feront la remise desdits biens, avec faculté d'en disposer librement jusqu'au 31 Août 1924.

4) Si une contestation s'élève entre l'émigré et les autorités administratives locales, ou entre lui et des tiers, relativement à des droits de propriété sur les biens qu'il revendique, il pourra recourir à la Sous-Commission du lieu de situation de ses biens, dans

les formes préscrites aux articles 72 à 74. La Sous-Commission examinera les droit de l'émigré à la lumière des articles 29 et 30.

Remarque: Tout émigré qui aura, conformément à l'article 67, remis une déclaration d'émigration,—accompagnée du certificat de minorité ethnique Modèle II. B.—et une demande en liquidation pour un bien, sera dispensé pour ce bien, des formalités de la procédure ci-dessus.

Déclaration d'émigration

Article 67

Les personnes définies à l'article 7 littera b doivent, si elles désirent jouir des avantages de la Convention et être considérées comme ayant définitivement émigré, remettre à la Sous-Commission de leur domicile ou à la Commission Mixte, avant le 31 Août 1924, une déclaration d'émigration, suivant le formulaire Modèle No. I.B. accompagnée d'un certificat de minorité ethnique Modèle No. 2.B. délivré par le Maire de la Commune de leur domicile actuel. Les préscriptions des articles 33 et 34 relatives à la déclaration d'émigration Modèle No. I.A. et au certificat No. 2.A. s'appliquent également à la déclaration Modèle No. I.B. et au certificat No. 2.B.

Liquidation par la Commission Mixte

Article 68

La procédure pour la liquidation des biens des émigrés est identique à celle pour les biens des émigrants futurs, le formulaire Modéle No. III.A. mentionné à l'alinéa 2 de l'article 37, étant remplacé par le modèle No. III.B. joint en annexe au présent Règlement.

Toutefois, pour éviter que, en vue de défendre leurs intérêts à la liquidation de leurs biens, beaucoup d'émigrés ne doivent effectuer un voyage dont les difficultés et le coût seraient hors de proportion avec la valeur du bien à liquider, les facilités les plus grandes seront données aux émigrés pour se faire représenter par mandataires, de façon individuelle ou collectives.

La Commission Mixte et les Sous-Commission rechercheront les moyens propres à permettre aux réfugiés des localités qu'a abandonnées une grande partie de la population, d'établir la distribution ancienne des terres, les limites de chaque propriété et les droits de chacun. Elles s'efforceront de faciliter à ces réfugiés l'organisation de représentations collectives.

Remarque I: L'État de guerres en Grèce, tant qu'il se prolongera, suspend l'application du principe de la convocation personnelle obligatoire de tout émigré pour la liquidation de ses biens.

Pendant cette période, les Sous-Commission ne pourront convoquer en Grèce, pour y assister aux liquidations, que ceux des émigrés dont elles jugeront la présence indispensable. En cas de contestation relative à cette nécessité, la Commission Mixte sera seule juge, en dernier ressort.

Les émigrés convoqués dans ces conditions devront passer la frontière, à l'aller et au retour, au poste frontière qui leur aura été désigné dans la convocation. Ils ne pourront se déplacer en Grèce que suivant les itinéraires qui leur auront été fixés par les Sous-Commissions et qui auront été notifiés par celles-ci aux autorités de police Hellénique.. La durée de leur séjour en territoire Hellénique ne pourra pas excéder celle fixée par la Sous-Commission, celle-ci ne pouvant dépasser deux mois.

Les émigrés dont la Sous-Commission compétente n'aura pas jugé la présence à la liquidation indispensable et qui n'auraient pas encore designé un mandataire seront invités par elle, soit à désigner un mandataire individuel, soit à confier la défense de leurs intérêts à l'une des représentations collectives prévues ci-dessus.

Remarque II: Les intérêts matériels des émigrés, dans les liquidations, ne devront pas souffrir des restrictions apportées, par suite de l'état de guerre en Grèce, à la présentation personnelle par eux de leurs titres de propriété.

Restitution des revenus

Article 69

Les personnes définies à l'article 7, littera b, et qui, conformément à l'article 29, alinéa 3, ont droit aux revenus touchés par l'État, devront introduire auprès de la Commission Mixte ou des Sous-Commissions 'une demande en restitution des revenus' contenant: specifications des biens pour lesquels l'État à touché des revenus avec le lieu de situation et la nature du bien, le montant des revenus, dans le cas où ils le connaissent, ou l'importance approximative de ces revenus, dans le cas où ils ne connaissent pas le chiffre exact; désignation de l'administration qui a encaissé ou a pu encaisser les revenus, ainsi que tout renseignement qu'ils croiraient utiles pour les recherches et vérifications.

Indemnités pour endommagements

ARTICLE 70

Les personnes qui ont droit à une indemnité en vertu de l'article 29, alinéa 4, devront introduire auprès de la Commission Mixte ou des Sous-Commissions une 'demande en dédommagement' contenant: spécification des biens endommagés; désignation de l'administration sous la garde de laquelle ces biens se trouvaient; description des dommages subis; date à laquelle ils ont été subis et par le fait de qui; évaluation des dommages et indication des preuves relatives à l'époque où les biens ont été endommagés.

Facilités de voyage et de transport

ARTICLE 71

En vue de jouir des facilités prévues aux articles 24, 25 et 26, les émigrés devront procéder comme il est indiqué aux articles 35 et 36 concernant les candidats-émigrants.

C. DISPOSITIONS GÉNÉRALES

ARTICLE 72

Toute réclamation dont les candidats-émigrants et émigrés voudraient saisir la Commission Mixte ou les Sous-Comissions et se rapportant à leurs biens mobiliers et immobiliers ou aux facilités de voyage, doit faire l'objet d'une demande écrite.

ARTICLE 73

Toute demande, requête ou lettre adressée à la Commission Mixte ou aux Sous-Commissions doit nécessairement contenir des données suffisantes sur la personne et le domicile du requérant et sur le cas dans lequel il se trouve. Ainsi s'il s'agit d'un émigré ou candidat-émigrant qui a déjà remis une déclaration d'émigration ou introduit une demande en reprise des biens, il doit s'y référer en donnant la date et le numéro d'enregistrement de la déclaration ou de la demande.

Recours aux Sous-Commissions et à la Commission Mixte

ARTICLE 74

Les émigrés peuvent à tout moment s'adresser directement ou par l'entremise de l'un des Sous-Commissaires aux Sous-Commissions respectives, pour demander leur appui s'ils se croient lésés dans des droits découlant pour eux de la Convention et du présent Règlement.

Les Sous-Commissions examineront leurs réclamations et, si elles les trouvent justifiées, elles prendront les mesures qu'elles jugeront opportunes.

Dans le cas où les intéressés ne recevraient pas satisfaction, ils pourront recourir à la Commission Mixte en lui adressant une demande écrite par l'intermédiaire des Sous-Commissions.

Article 75

Les requêtes, demandes, certificats, copies de documents et toutes autres pièces de n'importe quelle nature adressées ou destinées à la Commission Mixte ou aux Sous-Commissions, ou émanant d'elles, sont libres de toutes taxes et droits y compris le droit de timbre. Sont exceptées les pièces émanant des tribunaux des deux pays.

Article dernier

La Commission Mixte complètera ultérieurement le présent Règlement par la communication annoncée à l'article 19, ainsi que par toute autre communication qu'elle jugerait nécessaire.

Les additions et modifications éventuelles qui seraient ainsi apportées au présent Règlement, recevront la même publicité que lui.

Fait à Athènes, le 6 Mars 1922.

A. C. Corfe,
M. de Roover,
G. Tzorbazoglu,
V. Robeff.

APPENDIX III

PLAN GOVERNING THE PAYMENTS TO BE MADE BY BULGARIA AND GREECE

Original text from the unpublished document placed at the disposal of the writer by the Mixed Commission.

PLAN

REGISSANT LES PAYEMENTS À EFFECTUER PAR LA BULGARIE ET LA GRÈCE

ADOPTÉ LE 8 DÉCEMBRE 1922, EN EXÉCUTION DE LA CONVENTION GRÉCO-BULGARE SUR L'ÉMIGRATION RÉCIPROQUE ET VOLONTAIRE DES MINORITÉS ETHNIQUES SIGNÉ À NEUILLY-SUR-SEINE, LE 27, XI, 1919.

ARTICLE PREMIER

Le présent acte a pour objet de régir les payements incombant aux Gouvernements Bulgare et Grec, vis-à-vis des émigrants,[1] en exécution de la Convention d'Emigration Réciproque de Neuilly, et de régler les exportations de fonds, de l'un vers l'autre Pays, corrélatives à l'application de ladite Convention.

ARTICLE 2

Les payements dûs aux émigrants par chacune des deux Hautes Parties, en exécution de la Convention Gréco-Bulgare d'Émigration, comprennent:

en ordre principal: le payement de la valeur actuelle de leurs biens immobiliers liquidés par la Commission Mixte, évaluée par celle-ci conformément à l'article 18 du Règlement d'Émigration;

[1] Dans le présent document, le terme 'émigrants' couvre aussi bien les émigrés se prévalant de l'article 12 de la Convention d'Émigration que les émigrants futurs se prévalant des autres stipulations de cet acte.

en ordre secondaire: la restitution de certains revenus, loyers et prix de ventes, perçus par le Fisc, et le payement de certaines indemnités,—conformément aux articles 27 et 29 du Règlement d'Émigration.

Ces créances, évaluées dans la monnaie légale du Pays de situation des biens, seront aussitôt converties en créances en Dollars. La conversion étant faite au cours du jour ou à un cours moyen qu'aura déterminé la Commission Mixte. Les sommes ainsi libellées en Dollars seront dûes et payées aux ayant-droits dans les conditions et les monnaies déterminées dans les articles 4 à 11 et 13 à 17 ci-dessous.

Fonds exportables

ARTICLE 3

Les fonds dont l'exportation de l'un vere l'autre Pays est autorisée et reglée par le présent acte, comprennent:

1. Pour les émigrants sous le régime de la Convention: les sommes qui leur sont acquises comme avance au comptant conformément à l'article 5, ou comme prix de vente directe de leurs biens immobiliers, ou comme économies personnelles;

2. Pour les réfugiés qui ne se prévalent pas de la Convention d'Émigration mais qui ont obtenu la restitution de leurs propriétés sises dans leur pays d'origine: les sommes qui leur zont acquises comme prix de vente de ces propriétés.

Organisation générale des payements

ARTICLE 4

Cos exportations de fonds se feront dans les conditions prescrites à l'article 12.

Les payements prévus à l'article 2 seront faits à tout ayant-droit; partie au comptant, partie à terme.

L'importance relative de la partie payée comptant et la partie payée à terme pourra varier d'après la situation de l'ayant-droit et l'état de fonds spéciaux immédiatement disponibles.

Le montant payé comptant sera, en ordre général, de l'importance de dix pour cent du montant des sommes.

Les payements comptant seront faits comme il est dit à l'article 5.

Les payements à terme seront faits suivant le mécanisme décrit aux articles 6 et suivants.

Payements comptant

ARTICLE 5

Les payements au comptant seront faits par prélèvement sur les fonds *ad hoc* prévus ou à prévoir aux budgets bulgare et grec pour les exercices 1922-1923 à 1925-1926.

Tout payement comptant sera fait en un chèque émis par la Commission Mixte sur la Banque Nationale du pays de situation du bien et libellé en Dollars. Ce chèque sera accompagné d'un bordereau délivré par la Commission Mixte, indiquant, suivant les besoins de l'émigrant, en quelle monnaie (Drachmes ou Levas en proportion déterminée de l'une et l'autre), ledit chèque sera payable.

Le change sera fait au cours du jour où le titulaire remettra son chèque à la Banque Nationale de l'une et l'autre pays, ce cours étant calculé d'après ceux du chèque sur New-York à Athènes et Sofia.

Subrogation mutuelle des Gouvernements pour les payements à terme

ARTICLE 6

Chacun des Gouvernements se substitue, en bloc, à l'autre Gouvernement dans le service des payements à terme dûs par celui-ci, et simultanément, en contre-partie, il est subrogé aux droits qu'ont vis-à-vis de cet autre Gouvernement, les émigrants créanciers dont il assume le payement.

ARTICLE 7

Par suite des substitutions et subrogations prévues à l'article précédent, la créance de chaque émigrant sur le Gouvernement dont il quitte le territoire est convertie en une créance sur le Gouvernement dont il devient sujet; simultanément, chaque Gouvernement devient crèditeur de l'autre Gouvernement pour le montant total de la dette à terms de celui-ci.

Les comptes créditeur et débiteur ainsi créés entre les deux Gouvernements se balançant partiellement, l'ensemble de la dette à terme des deux Gouvernements vis-à-vis de l'ensemble des émigrants créanciers se compose en dernière analyse de:

1. Une dette propre de chacun des Gouvernements vis-à-vis de ses nauveaux nationaux, ces dettes étant toutes deux égales à

la créance de celui des deux groupes d'émigrants dont la créance est la plus petite;

2. Une dette de l'un des Gouvernements vis-à-vis de l'autre Gouvernement et une dette identique de ce dernier Gouvernement vis-à-vis de ses nouveaux nationaux, le montant de cette dette étant égal à la différence des créances des deux groupes d'émigrants.

ARTICLE 8

Des deux dettes dont est ainsi chargé celui des deux Gouvernements dont la dette totale est la plus grande, une priorité est reconnue à celle de la catégorie 2 de l'article 7.

Mécanisme général des payements à terme

ARTICLE 9

Les payements à terme seront faits aux ayants-droits, au moment de la liquidation de leurs propriétés, en 'titres provisoires' décrits à l'article 10, lesquels 'titres provisoires' seront ultérieurement, comme il est dit à l'article 14, payés ou consolidés sous la forme de 'titres définitifs' décrits à l'article 15.

Les comptes créditeur et débiteur entre les deux Gouvernements, subséquents à l'émission des 'titres provisoires,' feront mensuellement l'objet d'un règlement provisoire conformément à l'article 11, et ils seront définitivement soldés comme il est dit aux articles 16 et 17.

Les propriétés liquidées seront, à dater de leur payement en 'titres provisoires' jusqu'au moment de la consolidation des dettes à terme créées par l'émission de ces titres, gérées comme il est dit à l'article 19.

Pendant la période des liquidations, les exportations des fonds prévues à l'article 3 se feront par le fonctionnement du compte-change créé en vertu de l'article 12. Ce compte fera mensuellement l'objet du règlement provisoire prévu à l'article 12, et il sera définitivement solidés, après la clôture des liquidations, comme il est dit aux articles 16 et 18.

'Titres provisoires'

ARTICLE 10

Les 'titres provisoires' qui seront remis aux émigrants au moment de la liquidation de leurs propriétés et en attendant la délivrance des 'titres définitifs' prévus à l'article 15, seront libellés comme un engagement du pays d'installation de l'émigrant.

Ils seront remis aux ayants-droits à l'intervention de la Commission Mixte. Celle-ci tiendra compte des 'titres provisoires' ainsi émis par chacun des Gouvernements.

Ces 'titres provisoires' seront productifs d'intérêt au taux de 6% l'an, à dater du jour où l'émigrant aura perdu définitivement la jouissance du bien en payement duquel ils auront été émis, ce jour étant fixé par la Commission Mixte dans chaque cas particulier.

Les intérêts seront payables semestriellement.

Les 'titres provisoires' auront pouvoir libératoire pour certaines catégories de payements à faire par l'émigré détenteur au Gouvernement émetteur. Ils pourront notamment être donnés en payement de propriétés que les titulaires voudraient acquérir du Gouvernement sur les territoires desquels ils s'installent, que ces propriétés entrent ou non dans la constitution du fonds créé en vertu de l'article 19. Ils pourront notamment aussi, pour leur valeur nominale, être donnés comme cautionnement pour tous contracts passés ou à passer avec le Gouvernement émetteur.

La forme des 'titres provisoires' à émettre par chacun des Gouvernements et le détail des privilèges dont ils jouiront dans leur pays d'émission, seront établis par des accords directs entre chacun des Gouvernements et la Commission Mixte. Ils seront conçus de manière à mettre l'émigrant à l'abri des pertes au change entre le moment de l'évaluation de sa propriété et le moment du réemploi de son titre de payement. Ils devront également comprendre de grandes facilités pour l'obtention d'avance sur titres ou escompte des titres.

Les 'titres provisoires' seront garantis par:

I. Les engagements pris par les deux Hautes Parties notamment aux articles 14 et 17 du présent acte:

II. Les garanties constituées en vertu de l'article 19.

Comptes-liquidations et 'bons provisoires'

ARTICLE 11

Au début de chaque mois, la Commission Mixte établira le montant des 'titres provisoires' émis, sur sa demande, pendant le mois écoulé, par chacun des Gouvernements.

Chaque Gouvernement étant créditeur de l'autre Gouvernement

pour ce montant, la Commission Mixte établira la balance pour le mois écoulé des comptes créditeur et débiteur ainsi créés entre les deux Gouvernements.

Pour le montant de cette balance, l'État débiteur remettra à l'État créditeur par l'entremise de la Commission Mixte, un 'bon provisoire.'

Ces 'bons provisoires' seront libellés en Dollars et productifs d'intérêt au taux de 6% l'an.

Ils porteront l'engagement du Gouvernement émetteur de les payer ou les consolider comme il est dit aux articles 16 et 17.

Compte-change et 'reconnaissances provisoires'

ARTICLE 12

Pendant toute la période des liquidations par la Commission Mixte, des facilités de change seront accordées aux personnes mentionnées à l'article 3 pour leur permettre d'exporter vers leur pays de destination les fonds visés dans le même article.

En vue de l'octroi de ces facilités de change, les Banques Nationales de Grèce et de Bulgarie s'ouvriront mutuellement un crédit en Dollars dont il sera usé comme il est dit ci-dessous.

Les émigrants et réfugiés Bulgares désireux d'exporter leurs fonds de Grèce en Bulgarie, verseront ceux-ci en Drachmes à la Banque Nationale de Grèce en accompagnant leur versement d'un certificat de la Commission Mixte attestant leur qualité et indiquant l'origine des fonds déposés. La Banque Nationale de Grèce leur remettra un chèque en Dollars sur la Banque Nationale de Bulgarie, le change étant fait au prix moyen entre ses cours d'achat et de vente du jour, et ledit chèque étant payable par la Banque Nationale de Bulgarie en Levas au prix moyen entre ses cours d'achat et de vente du jour de la présentation.

Il sera agi de la même manière par la Banque Nationale de Bulgarie en ce qui concerne les émigrants et réfugiés Grecs.

Au début de chaque mois, les deux Banques dresseront un état de débits et crédits mutuels, en Dollars, résultant des opérations du mois écoulé. La Banque dont le solde sera créditeur un title de 'reconnaissance provisoire' du montant de ce solde.

Ces 'reconnaissances provisoires' seront libellées en Dollars et productives d'intérêt à 6% l'an.

Elles porteront l'engagement de la Banque émettrice de les payer ou les consolider comme il est dit aux articles 16 et 18.

Clôture des comptes provisoires

ARTICLE 13

Lorsqu'auront été terminées l'évaluation par la Commission Mixte de tous les biens immobiliers à liquider et l'émission de tous les 'titres provisoires' nécessaires à leur payement, la Commission Mixte déclarera clôs les comptes ouverts en vertu de l'article 10.

Elle notifiera ce fait aux deux Gouvernements et aux deux Banques Nationales et les invitera à clôturer avant le 20 du mois suivant, les comptes ouverts en vertu des articles 11 et 12, par l'émission d'un dernier 'bon provisoire' et celle d'une dernière 'reconnaissance provisoire.'

Elle les invitera simultanément à liquider ou consolider les dettes à leur charge, chacun en ce qui le concerne, dans un délai de trois mois prenant cours à la date fixée à l'alinéa précédent, et dans les conditions fixées aux articles 14, 16, 17 et 18.

Consolidation des 'titres provisoires,' 'titres definitifs'

ARTICLE 14

Lorsqu'il aura été saisi par la Commission Mixte conformément à l'article 13 de la demande de payement ou de consolidation de ses 'titres provisoires,' chaque Gouvernement devra:

Soit payer comptant la contrevaleur de ces titres;

Soit affecter au service de la dette représentée par eux, dans le délai de trois mois prévu à l'article précédent, des revenus certains et suffisants qui seront placés sous le contrôle d'un organisme financier international. Dans ces cas, aussitôt les affectations faites, la Commission Mixte fera remplacer les 'titres provisoires' par les 'titres définitifs' du type décrit à l'article 15, ou elle fera transformer les 'titres provisoires' en 'titres définitifs' par l'apposition des écritures prévues à l'alinéa 5 de l'article 15.

ARTICLE 15

Les 'titres définitifs' mentionnés à l'article 14, représentatifs des payements à terme aux émigrants, seront productifs d'intérêt à 6% l'an, et amortissables à dater du 1er Juillet 1926, en un nombre d'années restreint et ne dépassant pas 12 ans.

Leur service sera assuré par une annuité garantie comme il est dit à l'article 14.

Ils jouiront de tous les privilèges reconnus aux 'titres provisoires.' à l'exception des garanties prévues au dernier alinéa de l'article 10.

Ils seront couverts par les garanties prévues à l'article 14.

Leur texte mentionnera explicitement les garanties affectées à leur service.

La forme des 'titres définitifs' à émettre par chacun des Gouvernements, leur durée d'amortissement et le détail des privilèges dont ils jouiront dans leur pays d'émission seront établis, tout comme pour les 'titres provisoires,' par des accords directs entre chacun des Gouvernements et la Commission Mixte.

Compensation entre les 'bons provisoires' et les 'reconnaissances provisoires'

Article 16

Dès la notification prévue à l'article 13, la Commission Mixte établira les totaux des crédits et des débits constitués entre les deux Gouvernements par les 'bons provisoires,' prévus à l'article 11, et les intérêts capitalisés de ces bons.

Elle établira, entre ces débits et crédits, une compensation d'où résultera le débit de l'un des Gouvernements envers l'autre au titre du compte-liquidations. Simultanément, la Commission Mixte établira, d'accord avec les deux Banques Nationales, les totaux des crédits et débits constitués entre les Banques par les 'reconnaissances provisoires,' prévues à l'article 12, et les intérêts capitalisés de ces titres.

Si, en suite de ces opérations, l'un des Pays est débiteur envers l'autre au titre du compte-liquidations pendant entre les Gouvernements et simultanément créditeur envers lui au titre du compte-change pendant entre les Banques Nationales, une compensation sera établie entre ces deux comptes.

De cette compensation résultera le débit final de l'un des Gouvernements envers l'autre ou de l'une des Banques Nationales envers l'autre.

Cette opération de compensation aura pour corolaire un réglement direct à intervenir entre chaque Gouvernement et sa propre Banque Nationale pour le montant ayant fait l'objet de la Compensation de Pays à Pays.

Les dettes qui subsisteront, de l'un à l'autre Gouvernement ou de l'une à l'autre Banque Nationale, après les opérations de compensation, seront payées ou consolidées comme il est dit aux articles

17 et 18, sans qu'il puisse être imposé, par la Partie débitrice, une compensation quelconque entre ces dettes et tout autre compte pendant entre les deux Pays.

Règlement des dettes entre Gouvernements au titre du compte-liquidations. 'Obligations'

ARTICLE 17

Pour consolider la dette qui subsistera éventuellement de l'un envers l'autre Gouvernement au titre du compte-liquidations, après les opérations de compensation décrites à l'article 16, le Gouvernement débiteur devra, dans le délai de trois mois prévu à l'article 13, remettre le montant de cette dette au Gouvernement créditeur en 'obligations' du type décrit ci-dessous ou en petit nombre d'annuités suivant toute autre méthode qu'agréeraient les deux Parties à l'intervention de la Commission Mixte.

Les 'obligations' prévues à l'alinéa ci-dessus seront des titres au porteur, libellés en Dollars, productifs d'intérêt à 6% l'an, amortissables en six années à dater du 1er Juillet 1926, au pair et par tirage au sort.

Elles seront payables, principal et intérêt, en chèque sur New-York.

Les intérêts seront payables semestriellement les 1er Janvier et 1er Juillet de chaque année.

Leur service sera assuré par une annuité constante en Dollars, garantie par des revenus suffisants que le Gouvernement émetteur devra affecter à ce service, sous le contrôle d'un organisme financier international.

Si, après la date prévue à l'article 13 alinéa 2, et avant l'amortissement intégral des 'obligations' émises par lui en vertu du présent article, le Gouvernement débiteur conclut un emprunt extérieur destiné à la consolidation de sa dette flottante, il sera tenu d'effectuer, sur le produit de cet emprunt, l'amortissement anticipé desdites 'obligations.'

Règlement des dettes entre Banques Nationales au titre du compte-change

ARTICLE 18

La dette qui subsistera éventuellement de l'une envers l'autre Banque Nationale au titre du compte change prévu à l'article 12 après les opérations de compensations décrites à l'article 16, sera payée, par la Banque débitrice à la Banque créditrice, dans le délai de trois mois prévu à l'article 13 en traites libellées en Dollars, portant intérêt à 6% l'an, et dont le délai de payement n'excédera pas trois mois.

Fonds de garantie

ARTICLE 19

Les propriétés liquidées seront gérées, depuis leur payement en 'titres provisoires' jusqu'au moment de la consolidation des dettes à terme créées par l'émission de ces titres, comme il est dit ci-dessous.

Il sera créé, dans chacun des deux Pays, un fonds qui comprendra toutes les propriétés liquidées par la Commission Mixte.

Chaque fonds sera géré par une administration spéciale, fonctionnant sous le contrôle de la Commission Mixte, et conformément à un statut qui sera élaboré ultérieurement, dans chaque Pays, par accord entre le Gouvernement et la Commission Mixte.

Les Gouvernements respectifs auront la jouissance des biens qui constituent les fonds, mais ils ne pourront les aliéner que dans les conditions suivantes:

> Le Gouvernement qui désirera aliéner un bien immobilier entrant dans la constitution du fonds de garantie, devra verser, à l'administration du fonds, dans les conditions qui auront été déterminées ultérieurement, le prix de cet immeuble tel qu'il aura été fixé lors de la liquidation par la Commission Mixte, ou tel autre prix agrée par celle-ci. Dans le cas où l'acheteur de l'immeuble est un émigrant se prévalant de l'article 10, alinéa 5, le versement à faire par le Gouvernement au fonds de garantie pourra être fait au moyen des titres provisoires par lesquels l'acheteur a payé l'immeuble.
>
> Les propriétés ainsi aliénées cesseront définitivement d'appartenir aux fonds de garantie.

Dans les cas où l'un des Gouvernements ne satisferait pas entièrement aux obligations qui lui incombent pour la consolidation de sa dette à terme, conformément aux articles 14, 16, 17 et 18, la Commission Mixte poursuivra directement la réalisation des biens qui constituent, jusqu'à concurrence de la somme dont le payement n'aura pas été assuré, ou elle transférera à une organisation existante, ou qu'elle créera, la gestion du fonds et la réalisation eventuelle des biens, à charge pour cette organisation de faire le service de la dette non encore consolidée.

Au contraire, dès que l'un des Gouvernements aura payé ou consolidé intégralement sa dette à terme conformément aux articles 14 et 17, la Commission Mixte lévera le contrôle sur le fonds garantissant cette dette; ce Gouvernement pourra alors disposer librement des biens qui auront constitué le fonds.

Si l'un des Gouvernements desire acquérir la pleine propriété de tout ou partie des immeubles liquidés par la Commission Mixte sur son territoire, des leur payement en 'titres provisoires' ou alors qu'ils font partie du fonds de garantie, il pourra offrir à la Commission Mixte de remplacer la garantie que constitueraient ces immeubles en tant que partie du fonds par ces garanties au moins équivalantes, la Commission Mixte étant compétente de juger si les garanties ainsi offertes sont suffisantes et de rejeter la substitution en cas contraire.

APPENDIX IV

FINANCIAL AGREEMENT BETWEEN BULGARIA AND GREECE

Original text from League of Nations, *Treaty Series,* lxxxvii, pp. 200-208. English translation in the same place, pp. 201-209, also in League of Nations, *Official Journal,* February, 1928, pp. 244-245.

ACCORD FINANCIER ENTRE LA BULGARIE ET LA GRÈCE, CONCERNANT LA PROCÉDURE SELON LAQUELLE LES POPULATIONS ÉCHANGÉES SERONT INDEMNISÉES, ET LE RÈGLEMENT DES DETTES INCOMBANT DE CE FAIT AUX DEUX GOUVERNEMENTS. SIGNÉ A GENÈVE, LE 9 DÉCEMBRE 1927.

Vu la Convention relative à l'émigration réciproque, signée à Neuilly-sur-Seine, le 27 novembre 1919:

Vu le "Plan de paiements" adopté le 8 décembre 1922;

Considérant que le président de la Commission mixte prévue par ladite convention a été consulté et qu'il a exprimé un avis conforme:

Les représentants soussignés de la Bulgarie et de la Grèce sont convenus de ce qui suit:

Aux lieu et place des dispositions actuelles de l'article 9, paragraphes 2, 3 et 4, et des articles 11-19 du "Plan de paiements" du 8 décembre 1922, les dispositions suivantes prendront effet:

Article premier

Les titres définitifs envisagés par le "Plan de paiements" auront la forme de titres, numérotés consecutivement, libellés en leva ou en drachmes (suivant le cas), nets de tous impôts bulgares ou helléniques (suivant le cas), portant intérêt à 6% l'an, l'intérêt étant payable semestriellement le 1er janvier et le 1er juillet et remboursables au moyen d'un fonds d'amortissement, ainsi qu'il est prévu ci-dessous, ce fonds d'amortissement commençant à fonctionnèr le 1er juillet 1928. Le texte des titres définitifs à émettre par chacun des gouvernements sera identique et fixé par voie d'accord direct entre chacun des gouvernements et la Commission Mixte.

Les deux gouvernements s'engagent—aussi longtemps qu'il existera des titres non remboursés de ces émissions pour chaque semestre à partir du 1er juillet 1928,—à consacrer à l'achat de titres, en vue de leur annulation, une somme équivalant à un soixantième de la valeur nominale du total de tous les titres émis (y compris les titres provisoires non encore échangés contre des titres définitifs).

A cette fin, un titre sera considéré comme ayant été "émis" un mois après la date à laquelle la Commission mixte aura notifié aux organismes compétents des deux gouvernements le nom de l'ayant droit et le montant qui lui est dû.

Pour autant que les titres nécessaires ne pourront être achetés ou dans tous les cas si leur prix sur le marché est au-dessus du pair, il sera procédé au tirage de titres pour remboursement aupair. Les tirages seront effectués par les directions respectives des Dettes publiques. Les achats et les tirages pour les fonds d'amortissement seront effectués par la Banque nationale de Bulgarie et par la Banque d'émission de Grèce respectivement, et les sommes semestriellement affectés au fonds d'amortissement seront transférées auxdites banques par le gouvernement intéressé, le 1er janvier et le 1er juillet respectivement, au cours de chaque année à partir du 1er juillet 1928. S'il est nécessaire de procéder à un tirage, les tirages devront avoir lieu au plus tard un mois avant la fin du semestre en question, c'est-à-dire que les premiers tirages ne s'effectueraient pas plus tard que le 1er décembre 1928, pour remboursement au pair le 1er janvier 1929. Les renseignements concernant tous les titres sortis au tirage seront publiés dans le *Journal Officiel* et affichés dans toutes les succursales de la Banque d'émission du pays intéressé.

Les banques devront notifier à la Commission mixte et au Conseil de la Société des Nations, à la fin de chaque semestre, les montants versés pour les intérêts sur les titres, les montants reçus par eux pour le fonds d'amortissement et les sommes qui auront été affectées par elles au remboursement *a*) par achats, et *b*) par tirages.

Chacun des deux gouvernements aura, en outre, le droit de rembourser au pair, à un moment quelconque, moyennant préavis d'un mois, la totalité ou toute fraction additionnelle (déterminée par voie de tirage) des titres émis en sa propre monnaie. En ce cas, les sommes nécessaires pour les versements semestriels au fonds d'amortissement seront réduites suivant le rapport existant entre la valeur nominale des titres remboursés et la valeur nominale du montant total des titres émis.

Les titres et leurs coupons seront exonérés de tous impôts, taxes, redevances et charges quelconques, présents ou futurs, dans le pays d'émission et seront acceptées dans ledit pays, pour leur valeur nominale, comme cautionnement pour tous contrats passés avec l'État.

Les deux gouvernements s'engagent par le présent accord à obtenir sans délai toutes autorisations législatives nécessaires pour assurer l'inscription annuelle au budget ordinaire de l'État des sommes requises pour le service des émissions susmentionnées.

ARTICLE 2

Dès que les deux gouvernements auront approuvé le présent accord, l'émission des titres provisoires cessera et les titres provisoires existants seront échangés, aussi rapidement que possible, contre des titres définitifs.

ARTICLE 3

Tous les titres provisoires qu'il serait nécessaire d'émettre après le 1er janvier 1928 seront libellés suivant les nouvelles formules qui figurent aux annexes I et II.

ARTICLE 4

Le 31 décembre 1927 et à la fin de chaque semestre ultérieur, jusqu'à la mise en application de l'article 5, la Commission mixte fixera, d'accord avec le Ministère des Finances de chaque pays, la valeur nominale totale des titres (y compris les titres provisoires) émis (suivant la définition figurant à l'alinéa 3 de l'article 1 ci-dessus).

La Commission mixte confrontera les totaux ainsi émis en leva et en drachmes respectivement, en convertissant la monnaie du pays débiteur au cours moyen, sur le pays créancier qui a été pratiqué pendant le dernier des six mois en question.

Le gouvernement qui, à la suite de cette comparaison, se trouvera alors débiteur de l'autre gouvernement, devra immédiatement (et en tout cas, au plus tard un mois après la fin du semestre), verser au gouvernement créancier, dans la monnaie dudit gouvernement, une somme représentant l'intérêt semestriel afférent au montant des titres équivalant à sa dette, ainsi que l'amortissement dû, le cas échéant, sur ces titres. Pour le premier règlement, tous les intérêts antérieurement versés ou dus seront compris dans le calcul.

Il incombera à la Commission mixte d'obtenir rapidement des deux Ministères des Finances les renseignements nécessaires pour établir la comparaison susmentionnée; les deux gouvernements s'engagent, par le présent accord, à donner à la Commission ou à ses représentants toutes facilités pour obtenir lesdits renseignements; ils s'engagent, en outre, à prendre eux-mêmes toutes les mesures administratives nécessaires pour assurer que tous les renseignements indispensables seront promptement accessibles.

Article 5

Dès que tous les 'titres définitifs' (ou un nombre de ces titres suffisant pour justifier, de l'avis de la Commission mixte, cette mesure) auront été émis suivant le définition figurant à l'alinéa 3 de l'article 1 ci-dessus, la Commission mixte fixera le total, sous réserve, le cas échéant, de rectification ultérieure, du solde dû par l'État débiteur (calculé comme il est dit à l'article précédent). La Commission mixte calculera le service semestriel (intérêt et amortissement) afférent au total ci-dessus et l'État débiteur remettra à une banque neutre, que le Conseil de la Société des Nations désignera comme son mandataire, des effets portant respectivement la date du 15 décembre et du 15 juin, à raison d'un effet pour chaque versement semestriel (intérêts et fonds d'amortissement, à savoir un soixantième chaque semestre pendant trente ans). Ces effets seront payables dans la monnaie du pays créancier. Le mandataire présentera ces effets, lors de leur échéance, à l'État débiteur et remettra les sommes reçues au gouvernement créancier, de façon que les sommes dues parviennent au gouvernement créancier au moins trois jours pleins avant le 1er janvier et le 1er juillet respectivement. Le gouvernement débiteur payera les frais et charges du mandataire pour ce service.

Article 6

Les organisations de la Société des Nations, chargées dans les deux pays de l'établissement des réfugiés, prendront des arrangements avec les gouvernements respectifs pour accepter des réfugiés au pair, à titre de règlement de certaines sommes dues par ces derniers aux organisations d'établissement, les titres provisoires et définitifs émis par les gouvernements respectifs.

Article 7

Les fonctions incombant à la Commission mixte en vertu du présent accord peuvent être transférées à toute autre personne ou organisation qui pourra être approuvée à cet effet par le Conseil de la Société des Nations, si celui-ci en décide ainsi à un moment quelconque.

Article 8

Tout différend relatif à l'interprétation du présent accord sera tranché par le Conseil de la Société des Nations, qui prendra sa décision à la majorités des voix.

Article 9

Le présent accord sera soumis, pour ce qui concerne la Société des Nations, à l'acceptation du Conseil.

Article 10

Le présent accord sera ratifié et les ratifications seront déposées au Secrétariat de la Société des Nations.

Fait à Genève, le 9 décembre 1927, en un seul exemplaire qui restera déposé au Secrétariat de la Société des Nations et sera, par lui, enregistré aussitôt que possible.

Pour la Bulgarie:
Wl. Molloff,
Ministre des Finances.
Pour la Grèce:
C. Caphandaris,
Ministre des Finances.

Le Président de la Commission mixte:
James de Reynier.

APPENDIX V

CONVENTION CONCERNING THE EXCHANGE OF GREEK AND TURKISH POPULATIONS

Original text from League of Nations, *Treaty Series,* xxxii, pp. 76-86, and France, Ministère des Affaires Étrangères, *Documents diplomatiques: Conférence de Lausanne* (Paris, 1923), ii, pp. 116-122. The text is also given in Conférence de Lausanne, *Recueil des actes* (Paris, 1923), première série, i, pp. 320-324, while both the French text and an English translation may be found in Great Britain, *Parliamentary Papers, Turkey No. 1 (1923), Lausanne Conference* (London, 1923), pp. 817-827. The text in the *Treaty Series* is also accompanied by an English translation.

CONVENTION CONCERNANT L'ÉCHANGE DES POPULATIONS GRECQUES ET TURQUES, ET PROTOCOLE, SIGNÉS À LAUSANNE, LE 30 JANVIER 1923

Le Gouvernement de la Grande Assemblée Nationale de Turquie et le Gouvernement hellénique sont convenus des dispositions suivantes:

Article premier

Il sera procédé dès le 1er mai 1923 à l'échange obligatoire des ressortissants turcs de religion grecque-orthodoxe établis sur les territoires turcs et des ressortissants grecs de religion musulmane établis sur les territoires grecs.

Ces personnes ne pourront venir se réétablir en Turquie ou, respectivement, en Grèce, sans l'autorisation du Gouvernement turc ou, respectivement, du Gouvernement hellénique.

Article 2

Ne seront pas compris dans l'échange prévu a l'Article premier:

a) Les habitants grecs de Constantinople;

b) Les habitants musulmans de la Thrace occidentale.

Seront considérés comme habitants grecs de Constantinople tous les Grecs déjà établis avant le 30 octobre 1918 dans les circonscriptions de la Préfecture de la Ville de Constantinople, telles qu'elles sont délimitées par la loi de 1912.

Seront considérés comme habitants musulmans de la Thrace occidentale tous les musulmans établis dans la région à l'Est de la ligne-frontière établie en 1913 par le Traité de Bucarest.

Article 3

Les Grecs et les musulmans, ayant déjà quitté depuis le 18 octobre 1912 les territoires dont les habitants grecs et turcs doivent être respectivement échangés, seront considérés comme compris dans l'échange prévu dans l'Article premier.

L'expression "émigrant" dans la présente Convention comprend toutes les personnes physiques et morales devant émigrer ou ayant émigré depuis le 18 octobre 1912.

Article 4

Tous les hommes valides appartenant à la population grecque dont les familles ont déjà quitté le territoire turc et qui sont actuellement retenus en Turquie, constitueront le premier contingent de Grecs à envoyer en Grèce conformément à la présente Convention.

Article 5

Sous réserve des stipulations des Articles 9 et 10 de la présente Convention, aucune atteinte ne sera portée aux droits de propriété et créances des Grecs de la Turquie, ou des musulmans de la Grèce, par suite de l'échange à effectuer en vertu de la présente Convention.

Article 6

Il ne pourra être apporté aucun obstacle, pour quelque cause que ce soit, au départ d'une personne appartenant aux populations à échanger. En cas de condamnation définitive à une peine afflictive et en cas de condamnation non encore définitive ou de poursuite pénale contre un émigrant, ce dernier sera livré, par les autorités du pays poursuivant, aux autorités du pays òu il se rend, afin qu'il purge sa peine ou qu'il soit jugé.

Article 7

Les émigrants perdront la nationalité du pays qu'ils abandonnent, et ils acquerront celle du pays de destination dès leur arrivée sur le territoire de ce pays.

Les émigrés qui auraient déjà quitté l'un ou l'autre des deux pays et qui n'auraient pas encore acquis leur nouvelle nationalité, acquerront cette nationalité à la date de la signature de la présente Convention.

ARTICLE 8

Les émigrants seront libres d'emporter avec eux ou de faire transporter leurs biens meubles de toute nature sans qu'il leur soit imposé de ce chef aucun droit, soit de sortie, soit d'entrée, ni aucune autre taxe.

De même, les membres de toute communauté (y compris le personnel des mosquées, tekkés, medressés, églises, couvents, écoles, hôpitaux, sociétés, associations et personnes morales, ou autres fondations de quelque nature que ce soit), qui doit quitter le territoire d'un des États contractants en vertu de la présente Convention, auront le droit d'emporter librement ou de faire transporter les biens meubles appartenant à leurs communautés.

Les plus grandes facilités de transport seront fournies par les autorités des deux pays, sur la recommandation de la Commission mixte prévue dans l'Article 11.

Les émigrants qui ne pourraient pas emporter tout ou une partie de leurs biens meubles pourront les laisser sur place. Dans ce cas, les autorités locales seront tenues d'établir contradictoirement avec l'émigrant l'inventire et la valeur des biens meubles laissés par lui. Les procès-verbaux contenant l'inventaire et la valeur des biens meubles laissés par l'émigrant seront dressés en quatre exemplaires, dont l'un sera conservé par les autorités locales, le second sera remis à la Commission mixte prévue à l'Article 11 pour servir de base à la liquidation prévue à l'Article 9, le troisième exemplaire sera remis au Gouvernement du pays d'immigration et le quatrième à l'émigrant.

ARTICLE 9

Les biens immobiliers, ruraux ou urbains, appartenant aux émigrants, aux communautés visées à l'Article 8, ainsi que les biens meubles laissés par ces émigrants ou communautés, seront liquidés, conformément aux dispositions ci-après, par la Commission mixte prévue à l'Article 11.

Les biens situés dans les régions soumises à l'échange obligatoire et appartenant aux institutions religieuses ou de bienfaisance des communautés établies dans une région non soumise à l'échange, devront également être liquidés dans les mêmes conditions.

Article 10

La liquidation des biens mobiliers et immobiliers appartenant aux personnes ayant déjà quitté les territoires des Hautes Parties contractantes et considérées en vertu de l'Article 3 de la présente Convention comme rentrant dans l'échange des populations, sera effectuée conformément à l'Article 9 et indépendamment de toutes les mesures de quelque caractère que ce soit qui, conformément aux lois établies et aux règlements de toute nature édictés depuis le 18 octobre 1912 en Grèce et en Turquie ou de toute autre manière, ont eu pour résultat une restriction quelconque du droit de propriété sur ces biens, telles que confiscation, vente forcée et autres. Dans le cas où des biens visés au présent Article ainsi qu'à l'Article 9 auraient été frappés d'une mesure de cette nature, leur valeur sera fixée par la Commission prévue à l'Article 11, comme si les mesures en question n'avaient pas été appliquées.

En ce qui concerne les biens expropriés, la Commission Mixte procédera à une nouvelle évaluation de ces biens expropriés depuis le 18 octobre 1912, qui appartenaient aux personnes soumises à l'échange dans les deux pays and qui sont situés dans les territoires soumis à l'échange. La Commission fixera en faveur des propriétaires une compensation qui réparera le préjudice qu'elle constatera. Le montant de cette compensation sera porté au crédit de ces propriétaires et au débit du Gouvernement sur le territoire duquel se trouvent les immeubles expropriés.

Au cas où les personnes visées aux Articles 8 et 9 n'auraient pas touché le revenu des biens de la jouissance desquels elles auraient été privées d'une manière ou d'une autre, la restitution de la valeur de ces revenus leur sera assurée sur la base du rendement moyen d'avant-guerre, suivant les modalités à fixer par la Commission Mixte.

En procédant à la liquidation des biens Wakoufs en Grèce et des droits et intérêts en découlant, ainsi que des fondations analogues appartenant aux Grecs en Turquie, la Commission Mixte prévue à l'Article 11 s'inspirera des principes consacrés dans les Traités antérieurs, dans le but de faire valoir pleinement les droits et intérêts de ces fondations et des particuliers qui y sont intéressés.

La Commission Mixte prévue à l'Article 11 sera chargée d'appliquer ces stipulations.

Article 11

Dans un délai d'un mois à partir de l'entrée en vigueur de la présente Convention, il sera créé une Commission Mixte résidant en Turquie ou en Grèce et composée de quatre membres pour chacune des Hautes Parties contractantes et de trois membres choisis par le Conseil de la Société des Nations parmi les ressortissants des Puissances n'ayant pas participé à la guerre de 1914-1918. La présidence de la Commission sera assumée à tour de rôle par chacun de ces trois membres neutres.

La Commission Mixte aura le droit de constituer, dans les localités où il lui paraîtra nécessaire, des Sous-Commissions travaillant sous ses ordres, et composées chacune d'un membre turc, d'un membre grec, et d'un Président neutre qui sera désigné par la Commission Mixte. La Commission Mixte déterminera les pouvoirs à déléguer aux Sous-Commissions.

Article 12

La Commission Mixte aura pour attributions de surveiller et faciliter l'émigration prévue par la présente Convention et de procéder à la liquidation des biens mobiliers et immobiliers prévue aux Articles 9 et 10.

Elle fixera les modalités de l'émigration et celles de la liquidation ci-dessus visée.

D'une façon générale, la Commission Mixte aura tous pouvoirs de prendre les mesures que nécessitera l'exécution de la présente Convention et de décider toutes les questions auxquelles cette Convention pourrait donner lieu.

Les décisions de la Commission Mixte seront prises à la majorité des voix.

Toutes les contestations relatives aux biens, droits et intérêts à liquider seront réglées définitivement par elle.

Article 13

La Commission Mixte aura tout pouvoir pour faire procéder à l'estimation des biens mobiliers et immobiliers qui doivent être liquidés en vertu de la présente Convention, les intéressés étant entendus ou ayant été dûment convoqués pour être entendus.

La base de l'estimation des biens qui doivent être liquidés sera la valeur de ces biens en monnaie d'or.

Article 14

La Commission remettra au propriétaire intéressé une déclaration constatant la somme qui lui est due du chef des biens dont il a été dépossédé, biens qui resteront à la disposition du Gouvernement sur le territoire duquel ils sont situés.

Les montants dus sur la base de ces déclarations constitueront une dette du Gouvernement du pays où la liquidation aura eu lieu envers le Gouvernement dont relève l'émigrant. Celui-ci devra en principe recevoir, dans le pays où il émigre, en représentation des sommes qui lui sont dues, des biens d'égale valeur et de même nature que ceux qu'il aura abandonnés.

Tous les six mois, on établira un compte des sommes dues par les Gouvernements respectifs sur la base des déclarations émises comme ci-dessus.

A la liquidation finale, s'il y a équivalence entre les montants respectivement dus, les comptes y relatifs seront compensés. Si l'un des Gouvernements reste débiteur envers l'autre après compensation, le solde débiteur sera payé au comptant. Si le Gouvernement débiteur demande des délais pour ce paiement, la Commission pourra les lui accorder, pourvu que la somme due soit payée au maximum dans trois annuités. La Commission fixera les intérêts à payer pendant ces délais.

Si la somme à payer est assez importante et nécessite des délais plus longs, le Gouvernement débiteur payera au comptant une somme à déterminer par la Commission Mixte jusqu'à concurrence de 20% du montant dû et émettra pour le solde des titres d'emprunt portant un intérêt à fixer par la Commission Mixte, amortissable dans un délai maximum de 20 ans. Le Gouvernement débiteur affectera au service de cet emprunt des gages agréés par la Commission, gages qui seront gérés et dont les revenus seront encaissés par la Commission Internationale en Grèce et par le Conseil de la Dette Publique à Constantinople. A défaut d'accord sur ces gages, il appartiendra au Conseil de la Société des Nations de fixer ceux-ci.

Article 15

En vue de faciliter l'émigration, des fonds seront avancés à la Commission Mixte par les États intéressés, dans les conditions fixées par ladite Commission.

Article 16

Les Gouvernements de la Turquie et de la Grèce se mettront d'accord avec la Commission Mixte prévue à l'Article 11 sur toutes les questions relatives aux notifications à faire aux personnes devant quitter leurs territoires en vertu de la présente Convention et aux ports sur lesquels ces personnes doivent se diriger pour être transportées à leurs pays de destination.

Les Hautes Parties Contractantes s'engagent mutuellement à se qu'aucune pression directe ou indirecte ne soit exercée sur les populations qui doivent être échangées pour leur faire quitter leurs foyers ou se dessaisir de leurs biens avant la date fixée pour leur départ. Elle s'engagent également à ne soumettre les émigrants, ayant quitté ou qui doivent quitter le pays, à aucun impôt ou taxe extraordinaire. Aucune entrave ne sera apportée au libre exercice par les habitants des régions exceptées de l'échange en vertu de l'Article 2, de leur droit d'y rester ou d'y rentrer et de jouir librement de leurs libertés et de leurs droits de propriété en Turquie et en Grèce. Cette disposition ne sera pas invoquée comme motif pour empêcher la libre aliénation des biens appartenant aux habitants desdites régions exceptées de l'échange et le départ volontaire de ceux de ces habitants qui désirent quitter la Turquie ou la Grèce.

Article 17

Les frais d'entretien et de fonctionnement de la Commission Mixte et de ses organes seront supportés par les Gouvernements intéressés dans des proportions à déterminer par la Commission.

Article 18

Les Hautes Parties Contractantes s'engagent à apporter à leur législation respective les modifications qui seraient nécessaires pour assurer l'exécution de la présente Convention.

Article 19

La présente Convention aura même force et valeur, au regard des Hautes Parties ici contractantes, que si elle figurait dans le Traité de Paix qui sera conclu avec la Turquie. Elle entrera en vigueur immédiatement après la ratification dudit Traité par les deux Hautes Parties Contractantes.

En foi de quoi, les Plénipotentiaires soussignés, dont les pleins pouvoirs ont été respectivement reconnus en bonne et due forme, ont signé la présente Convention.

Fait à Lausanne, le trente janvier mil neuf cent vingt-trois, en triple exemplaire, dont un sera remis au Gouvernement hellénique et un au Gouvernement de la Grande Assemblée nationale de Turquie, et dont le troisième sera déposé aux archives du Gouvernement de la République Française, qui en délivrera des copies authentiques aux autres Puissances signataires du Traité de Paix avec la Turquie.

E. K. VENISELOS.
D. CACLAMANOS.

ISMET.
DR. RIZA NOUR.
HASSAN.

PROTOCOLE

Les Plénipotentiaires turcs soussignés, dûment autorisés, déclarent que, sans attendre la mise en vigueur de la Convention conclue avec la Grèce, en date de ce jour, relativement à l'échange des populations grecques et turques, et par dérogation à l'Article 1er de cette Convention, le Gouvernement turc, dès la signature du Traité de Paix, libérera les hommes valides visés à l'Article 4 de ladite Convention et assurera leur départ.

Fait en triple examplaire à Lausanne, le trente janvier mil neuf cent vingt-trois.

ISMET.
DR. RIZA NOUR.
HASSAN.

APPENDIX VI

DECLARATION AS TO MOSLEM PROPERTIES IN GREECE

Original text from Conférence de Lausanne, *Recueil des actes* (Paris, 1923), deuxième série, ii, pp. 115-116.

In later publications this is sometimes referred to by error as the "Ninth Declaration." The confusion results from the arrangement of the volume, mentioned above, in which the Declaration was printed. The volume contains the eighteen Acts of the Conference of Lausanne, numbered consecutively from first to last, being (I) the Treaty, (II-VI) Conventions, (VII) an Agreement, (VIII-XI) Declarations, (XII-XVII) Protocols, and (XVIII) the Final Act. Thus in the contents and in the heading we have "IX. Déclaration relative aux propriétés musulmanes," etc., which might, perhaps, properly be spoken of as a 'Ninth Act,' but is in no sense a 'Ninth Declaration.'

DÉCLARATION RELATIVE AUX PROPRIÉTÉS MUSULMANES EN GRÈCE SIGNÉE LE 24 JUILLET 1923

Les soussignés, agissant en vertu de leurs pleins pouvoirs, déclarent, au nom du Gouvernement hellénique, qu'aucune atteinte ne sera portée aux droits de propriété des personnes musulmanes, qui ne sont pas visées par les dispositions de la Convention concernant l'échange des populations signée à Lausanne le 30 janvier 1923, et qui ont quitté la Grèce, y compris l'île de Crète, avant le 18 octobre 1912 ou qui ont résidé de tout temps en dehors de la Grèce. Elles garderont le droit de disposer librement de leurs propriétés.

Toutes les dispositions et mesures qui auraient été prises ou appliquées à titre exceptionnel à l'égard des biens desdits musulmans, seront levées. Au cas où les revenus de ces biens auraient été encaissés par le Gouvernement ou les autorités helléniques, sans avoir été jusqu'ici restitués ou avoir fait l'objet d'arrangements spéciaux entre le Gouvernement et les intéressés, ces revenus seront versés entre les mains des propriétaires. Toutes réclamations relatives aux revenus en question ainsi que toutes réclamations résultant du fait que ces personnes prétendraient avoir été lésées dans leurs droits par l'application inégale des mesures d'ordre général, seront décidées par la Commission prévue dans la Convention susmentionnée, à la condition toutefois que ces réclamations soient formulées dans un délai de six mois à partir de la mise en vigueur du Traité de Paix signé en date de ce jour. Lesdites réclamations seront examinées d'urgence par la Commission, afin de pouvoir être décidées dans un délai d'un an au plus tard à partir de la mise en vigueur du dit Traité.

Vu les difficultés d'ordre pratique, qui pourraient se présenter pour les personnes susvisées en ce qui concerne le droit de libre disposition de leurs biens à cause de leur absence, le Gouvernement hellénique admet qu'elles pourront profiter, si elles le veulent, des bons offices de la Commission mixte précitée pour aliéner leurs propriétés. Il demeure entendu qu'en ce cas l'intervention de la Commission mixte ne comportera pour le Gouvernement hellénique aucune obligation d'acheter les propriétés en question et que la tâche de la Commission se bornera à en faciliter l'aliénation.

Il demeure entendu que la présente Déclaration est faite sou condition de réciprocité en faveur des propriétaires grecs ayant quitté la Turquie avant le 18 octobre 1912 ou ayant habité de tout temps en dehors de la Turquie.

Fait à Lausanne, le 24 juillet 1923.

E. K. Venizelos.
D. Caclamanos.

APPENDIX VII

AGREEMENT OF ATHENS

Original text from League of Nations, *Treaty Series,* lxviii, pp. 12-34. English translation, *ibid.,* pp. 13-35. The courtesy of the Mixed Commission has supplied the writer with the exchange of letters and a part of the *Procès-Verbal* of Signature, omitted from the edition in the *Treaty Series.*

This is sometimes called the Agreement on Properties.

ACCORD ENTRE LA GRÈCE ET LA TURQUIE EN VUE DE FACILITER L'APPLICATION DE CERTAINES DISPOSITIONS DU TRAITÉ DE LAUSANNE ET DE LA DECLARATION N° IX ANNEXÉE À CE TRAITÉ. SIGNÉ À ATHÈNES, le 1er DÉCEMBRE 1926.

Le Président de la République hellénique et le Président de la République turque, animés du désir d'aplanir les difficultés surgies relativement à l'application de certaines dispositions du Traité de Paix de Lausanne et de la Déclaration N° IX annexée à ce traité, ont décidé de conclure un accord en vue de faciliter l'application desdites stipulations du traité et nommé à cet effet leurs plénipotentiaires, savoir:

Le Président de la République hellénique:

Son Excellence Monsieur P. Argyropoulos, ministre des Affaires Étrangères;

Le Président de la République turque:

Son Excellence Monsieur Saradjoglou Chukri Bey, président de la Délégation turque à la Commission mixte pour l'échange des populations grecques et turques,

Lesquels, après avoir échangé leurs pleins pouvoirs, trouves en bonne et due forme, sont convenus des dispositions qui suivent:

ARTICLE PREMIER

Les biens immeubles situés dans les régions de Grèce soumises à l'échange et appartenant aux musulmans qui ont quitté ces régions avant le 18 octobre 1912 ou résidé de tout temps en dehors de la Grèce, ainsi qu'à tous ressortissants turcs, seront acquis par le Gouvernement hellénique aux conditions prévues par les articles 5 et 6, si la restitution aux propriétaires en est impossible en raison de leur occupation par des immigrés ou des paysans.

Les biens urbains bâtis ou non bâtis, de même que les bois et forêts et les pâturages d'été, seront rendus, en principe, à leurs propriétaires.

Article 2

Les biens immeubles sis dans les régions de Turquie dont la population grecque a été échangée et appartenant à des grecs ayant quitté la Turquie avant le 18 octobre 1912, ou résidé de tout temps en dehors de ce pays, ainsi qu'à tous ressortissants hellènes, seront acquis par le Gouvernement turc aux conditions fixées dans les articles 5 et 6 et jusqu'à concurrence de la valeur des biens qu'aura acquis le Gouvernement hellénique.

Article 3

La mesure prévue par les articles qui précèdent s'applique aussi aux mines et aux pêcheries que peuvent posséder les personnes visées par ces mêmes dispositions.

Article 4

Les termes "musulman," "grec," "ressortissant hellène" et "ressortissant turc," employés dans les articles 1 et 2, désignent aussi bien les personnes physiques que les personnes morales.

Les termes "ressortissant hellène" et "ressortissant turc" ne visent pas les personnes régies par la Convention concernant l'échange des populations grecques et turques.

Article 5

Les biens à acquérir par les deux Hautes Parties contractantes, conformément aux prescriptions ci-dessus, seront évalués suivant les principes posés dans l'annexe ci-jointe.

Les intéressés auront le droit d'assister à l'évaluation de leurs biens, soit personnellement, soit par fondé de pouvoirs en vertu de procurations individuelles ou collectives.

Article 6

Les travaux d'évaluation terminés, les montants respectivement dûs seront compensés. S'il n'y a pas d'équivalence entre ces montants, le solde sera payé au comptant par le Gouvernement hellénique, qui affecte à cet effet les excédents des revenus soumis au contrôle de la Commission financière internationale jusqu'à concurrence de 500.000 livres sterling.

Au cas où la somme dûe dépasserait les prévisions ci-dessus, le

Gouvernement hellénique s'engage à renouveler, après le premier versement, la garantie donnée conformément à l'alinéa précédent, pour le restant du solde, qui portera un intérêt de 6%.

Si, la compensation faite, l'un des deux Gouvernements se trouve en possession de biens restés en dehors de la liquidation, toutes questions relatives à l'obligation de restituer lesdits biens, notamment celles d'indemnité pour restitution tardive ou de garanties éventuelles, seront décidées par la Commission mixte.

Article 7

En vue de restreindre l'application du système de compensation ci-dessus prévu, le Gouvernement hellénique aura la faculté de conclure des arrangements spéciaux avec les propriétaires turcs qui voudraient lui vendre leurs immeubles sis en Grèce. Cependant, au cas où de tels achats auront été conclus avant la détermination du prix moyen régional des biens par la Commission mixte et à un prix inférieur de plus de 35% à cette moyenne, le propriétaire aura droit à la différence entre le prix obtenu et la moyenne régionale diminuée de 35%. Une estimation du bien vendu sera faite, en cas de nécessité, par la Commission mixte sur la demande du propriétaire. La différence de prix sera portés au compte de liquidation générale.

Le Gouvernement hellénique se réserve également la faculté de payer au comptant le prix d'estimation de tout bien à acquérir par lui, en l'éliminant du compte de compensation. Le payement sera fait au Gouvernement turc.

Article 8

Les biens se trouvant en la possession du propriétaire hellène actuellement établi dans les régions soumises à la compensation et dont la liste est annexée au présent accord, ne peuvent pas être saisis avant leur estimation. Ils n'entreront dans la compensation que sur la demande éventuelle du Gouvernement hellénique. L'exclusion de ces biens de la compensation donnera lieu, après leur estimation, à un versement du Gouvernement hellénique correspondant à leur valeur et à valoir sur la dette à compenser de ce gouvernement.

Le Gouvernement hellénique se réserve la faculté de faire excepter de la compensation tous autres biens visés par l'article 2 en avançant, un mois après leur estimation, une somme correspondant à leur valeur et à valoir sur sa dette à compenser.

L'intention du Gouvernement hellénique d'user de cette faculté doit être exprimée quinze jours après l'estimation au plus tard.

Au cas, toutefois, où un bien aurait été affecté à ce jour à un but d'utilité générale, il ne pourra être excepté de la compensation sans l'acquiescement du Gouvernement turc.

Article 9

Les propriétés rurales et urbaines restées en dehors de l'application de la mesure prévue dans l'article premier, de même que celles situées dans la région de Grèce exceptée de l'échange, seront restituées à leurs propriétaires, libres de toutes charges, dans un délai d'un mois à partir de la mise en vigueur du présent accord.

Seront également restitués à leurs propriétaires dans le même délai et libres de toutes charges les biens appartenant aux personnes visées par l'article 2 et situés dans les parties de Turquie où l'échange des populations n'a pas été appliqué.

En ce qui concerne les biens situés en Asie-Mineure et en Thrace orientale, leur restitution éventuelle aura lieu dans les mêmes conditions, au fur et à mesure de leur exception de la compensation.

La restitution d'un bien rural doit être intégrale. Néanmoins, un bien peut être restitué partiellement si le propriétaire n'en considère pas la division comme préjudiciable à ses intérêts. Les biens ruraux visés au second alinéa de l'article premier peuvent dans tous les cas être restitués indépendamment du domaine dont ils feraient partie.

Les propriétaires qui seront rentrés en possession de leurs biens, conformément aux dispositions ci-dessus, auront le droit d'en disposer librement et sans aucune entrave.

Article 10

Toutes dispositions ou mesures prises à titre exceptionnel, soit avant, soit après la mise en vigueur du Traité de Paix de Lausanne, par l'un ou l'autre des deux gouvernements, à l'égard des propriétés visées dans l'article précédent ou à l'égard de la fortune mobilière des ressortissants respectifs, seront levées dès la mise en vigueur du présent accord.

Article 11

Les Hautes Parties contractantes conviennent de faire bénéficier réciproquement du présent accord les propriétaires dont les biens ont été frappés d'expropriation dans les pays respectifs, soit avant, soit après la mise en vigueur du Traité de Paix de Lausanne.

Les biens expropriés, ainsi que ceux confisqués ou frappés d'une mesure exceptionnelle à ce jour, seront évalués, conformément à l'annexe ci-jointe comme si les mesures en question n'avaient pas été appliquées. La restitution éventuelle de biens de cette catégorie aux ayants-droit aura lieu dans les conditions fixées par l'article 9.

Article 12

Les revenus dont le versement aux propriétaires est prévu par le paragraphe 2 de la Déclaration N° IX annexée au Traité de Paix de Lausanne, formeront un compte de compensation distinct dont le solde sera porté au compte de liquidation générale.

Des règles identiques régiront les revenus afférents à tous autres biens visés par le présent accord.

Il demeure entendu que, sauf arrangement spécial entre les deux gouvernements, toutes difficultés pouvant surgir à propos de ces revenus seront tranchées par la Commission mixte.

Article 13

Le fait, par les personnes visées dans les articles 1 et 2, d'avoir quitté respectivement les territoires hellénique et turc avant le 18 octobre 1912, ou d'avoir résidé de tout temps en dehors de ces territoires, pourra être établi par tous les moyens de preuve. Dans les cas douteux, cette preuve sera faite par-devant la Commission mixte.

La nationalité d'une personne ne fera pas l'objet d'un examen si elle a été reconnue antérieurement par les autorités du pays où sont situés les immeubles à compenser ou à restituer.

Toutes contestations relatives à la nationalité seront résolues par la Commission mixte, sans préjudice des décisions qui pourront être rendues incidemment par le Tribunal arbitral gréco-turc sur des recours précédemment exercés par les intéressés en conformité des traités.

L'enquête réclamée par l'application des premier et troisième alinéas ci-dessus sera faite dorénavant par un comité *ad hoc* créé au sein de la Commission mixte. Cette disposition ne préjuge pas le sort des décisions déjà rendues à ce sujet.

Article 14

La Commission mixte d'échange des populations grecques et turques sera chargée de l'application du présent accord.

La Commission mixte constituera les équipes d'évaluation nécessaires dont chacune sera composée d'un expert turc, d'un expert hellène et d'un chef ressortissant d'une Puissance tierce.

Article 15

Les dispositions du présent accord n'ont d'application qu'à l'égard des ressortissants des Hautes Parties contractantes.

Il est cependant bien entendu que les personnes qui ayant, au moment de la mise en vigueur du Traité de Paix de Lausanne, la qualité de sujet turc ou de sujet hellène, ont acquis postérieurement une nationalité étrangère, conservent tous les droits assurés par les articles 65 et 66 du dit Traité de Paix et par la Déclaration N° IX annexée à ce Traité.

Article 16

Le présent accord visant le mode d'exécution de certains engagements découlant des Traités et autres Actes signés à Lausanne le 24 juillet 1923, ne porte aucune atteinte aux dispositions desdits instruments internationaux qui ne sont pas spécialement visées par les stipulations ci-dessus.

Les principes admis pour l'estimation des biens visés par le présent accord ne préjugent pas les bases sur lesquelles s'effectuera l'evaluation des biens laissés dans les pays respectifs par les personnes soumises à l'échange.

Article 17

Le présent accord sera ratifié. Les ratifications seront échangées à Athènes dans le plus bref délai.

En foi de quoi, les plénipotentiaires susnommés ont signé le présent accord.

Fait à Athènes, le premier décembre mil neuf cent vingt-six, en deux exemplaires.

P. A. Argyropoulos.
Saradjoglou Chukri.

Liste d'immeubles appartenant à des ressortissants hellènes établis à Smyrne, Mersine et Pendik et se trouvant en possession de leurs propriétaires

A. Smyrne.

1. Marie Petrou Sassou et Eugénie P. Sassou: Une maison, rue Lazarre 88.

2. Ignatius Jean Sclavos, Pauline St. Sclavou et Marie D. Anastassaki: Une maison.

3. Nic. Vassiliou Glytsos: Une maison, rue Messoudjié 125.

4. Nicolas Spyr. Dragonas: Quatre maisons avec un jardin, rue Hendek 22, 24, 26, 28.

5. Calliopi Jean Kaouri: Une maison, rue Binbachi Serafedine 28.

6. Dimitri Divaris: Une maison, rue Caracol 5.

7. Pauline Alex. Varibati: Une maison, rue Henkiam 40.

8. Antonia Georges Kaloumenou: Une maison, rue Méidam 40.

9. Thomais Themist. Stylianopoulou: Une maison, rue Banka 1.

10. Lucie Polycarpou Psalti: Une maison avec un magasin, rue Tozlou 24.

11. Pierre Jean Armao: Une maison, rue Banca 44.

12. Constantin Ath. Stamatiadis, Theophane Const. Stamatiadis et Jacques Ath. Stamatiadis: Une Usine (moulin), Quartier du cimetière. Une maison.

13. Dr. Eustache Jean Halkiopoulos: Les 4/7 d'une maison, rue Birindji: Cordon 638.

14. Athina J. Halkiopoulos: Une maison, rue Parali Kiopru 129.

15. Antoine Pierre Guizi: Une maison, rue Hadji Bekir 23.

16. Jacques Abraam Benghiat: Maison, Haviar Hamami 45.

17. Irène Georges Corfiatou: Maison avec jardin, rue Tramway 769.

18. Judas Abraam: Maison, rue Tocandi 2.

19. Marie Veuve Nicolas Foscolo: Deux maisons et un jardin, 28 rue Tchaciroglou, et Osman Zadé 12.

20. Marie Th. Palamari, née J. Halkiopoulos: Maison, rue Ikindji Cordon 487.

21. Eriphile Panay. Kastritsou: Maison, rue Donan Madji 23.

22. Catherine Const. Vitali, née Corinthiou: Maison, rue Hendik 67.

23. Marie Veuve Jean Vitali: Maison, rue Dermendji 4.

24. Catherine Veuve Nic. Foscolo: Maison, rue Donan Madji Nazli 12.

25. Catherine Fr. Alberti: Maison, rue Sevda.

26. Dr. Raphaël V. Corrès: Maison, rue Saadoulah 21.

27. Marie Fr. Prélorenzo: Maison, rue Carakol 46.

28. Georges Pavlou Vitali: Maison, rue Mouadess Mezar 5.

29. Pierre Const. Zallone: Maison, rue Inkiam 16.

30. Victoria Georges Prindizi: Maison, rue Scarayinou 80.

31. Polycarpos Ant. Caloumenos: Maison, rue Mouradié 40.

32. Emilie Jean Caloumenos: Le quart de 3 maisons, rue Mouradié et Sélimié 20,7 et 9.

33. Steph. Polyc. Dermon: Une maison avec un magasin, rue Station.

34. Antoine Vinc. Damolino: Maison et jardin, rue Mazgema 27.

35. Antoinette Joseph Collaro: Maison 115, Mortakia.

36. Marie J. Fr. Gambéli, née V. Haviara: Maison, rue Henkiam 27.

37. Joseph, Adèle, Marius Gambéli et Marie Psalti: Maison, Donam Madji.

38. François Gambéli: Maison, rue Donam Madji 41.

39. Olympia Veuve Jean Pestemadjoglou: Maison, rue Gazel 22.

40. Jean Nikiph. Vitali et Marie Vitali: Maison, rue Osman Zadé.

41. Philippe Léonard Vitali: Maison, rue Caracol 33.

42. Marguerite Exarhou, née Corsini: Maison, rue Acdenis 25.

43. Héritiers de Sophoclis Adamopoulos: Trois maisons, rue Vassil 18, Caracol 52 et Gomma 16.

44. Sophie Joseph Armacola: Deux maisons, rue Caracol 23,25.

45. Rozita C. Zira, née Boretti: Maison, rue Sayesté 31.

46. Marie Xenopoulo, née Batista: Maison, rue Esref Pacha 6.

47. Marie Michel Leshopoulou: Maison, rue Siahi 33.

48. Calisea Zallone: Maison, Yenikislar 47.

49. Vassilia Mologari, née Zamofta: Maison, rue Souzan 3.

50. Mme. Baldji: Maison.

51. M. Djavelopoulos: Maison.

52. (Rayé.)

53. Rocos Galinos: Une maison.

54. Marie Rigou: Une maison.

55. Paul Savopoulos: Une maison.

56. Cather. Vitali: La moitié d'une maison.

57. N. Leftméris: Un immeuble.

B. Mersine.

1. André C. Mavromati: Quatre magasins et un dépôt (Quartier Mahmoudié). Une maison (Résidence du Vali). Une maison et cinq magasins (Quartier Chypre). Plusieurs magasins (Quartier Chypre). Une maison en pierre (Banque de Salonique).

2. Georges C. Mavromati: Un han, sis à Adana.

3. Héritiers de Constantin Mavromati: Un champ sis à You-

mourtalik. Maison à deux étages (près de l'Église orthodoxe). Maison sise à côté de la précédente. Maison sise à côté de la précédente. Maison à deux étages sise à Tarsos (Kouzou Kalé).

4. Héritiers de Christopoulos Dembas: Maison à deux étages et à 19 pièces sise à Tarsos. Dépôt en pierre sis à Tarsos. Jardin d'arbres fruitiers (60 str.) sur la route de Tarsos à Mersine. Terrain de 2274 p^2, sis à Tarsos près de la gare. Trois maisons sises à Giozhané. Jardin sis Giozhané (70 str.). La moitié d'une usine de cotonnades.

5. Grégoire Carayoryi: Terrain de 400 p^2 (marché de Mersine). Jardins dans la ville de Mersine (9 str.). Champ cultivable près de Mersine (29 str.). Champ cultivable près de Mersine (25 str.).

6. David Antoniadis: Maison sise près de la gare.

7. Europi D. Mathioudi: Maison de deux étages sise à Adana (Kourou Kioprou). Une vigne. Plusieurs champs et terrains.

8. H. Veuve Barouti: Maison en pierre et terrain de 1000 p. à Mersine. Terrain de 1800 p. sis à Mersine.

9. Héritiers de André Nicolaïdis: Maison à un étage avec jardin de 700 p^2 à Mersine. Maison de campagne avec jardin de 1 str. (Foundouk Pounar). Maison à un étage à Mersine (Kiooproussou Mahali).

10. Emmanuel Argyriadis: Maison à un étage à Mersine (Bachtassi Mahali). Maison à deux étages près de l'église arabe.

C. Pendik.

1. Dimitri Lambriadis: Une maison.
2. Nicolas J. Vassilopoulo: Une maison.
3. Timoléon Picmaléon: Une maison.
4. Anguéliki Xenaki: Une maison.
5. Dimitri Aristidou: Une maison.
6. Victoria Koutéli: Une maison.
7. Aristidi Riga: Une maison.

P. A. Argyropoulos.
Saradjoglou Chukri.

N.B.—D'après les informations du Gouvernement hellénique, la valeur des biens ci-dessus mentionnés ne dépasserait pas de beaucoup la somme de 60.000 livres sterling.

P. A. Argyropoulos.
Saradjoglou Chukri.

Annexe

1. L'estimation des biens sera faite selon les principles ci-dessous:

Les biens seront classés en trois catégories:

A.—Propriétés urbaines comprenant:

a) Les habitations, magasins et autres bâtiments;

b) Les terrains de construction.

B.—Propriétés rurales comprenant:

a) les champs et prairies;

b) les vignobles, vergers, figuiers, oliviers, noisetiers, jardins potagers et autres;

c) les pâturages;

d) les bâtiments ruraux;

e) les forêts.

C.—Usines, fabriques, mines et pêcheries.

2. L'estimation de ces biens sera faite isolément pour chaque bien, après enquête sur place.

Les biens urbains et ruraux seront évalués sur la base de leur valeur marchande actuelle. Pour établir cette valeur, on se basera sur ces données:

a) les prix de vente des biens de même catégorie et de même genre se trouvant dans la même localité et dans les mêmes conditions.

b) les loyers de ces biens et du bien à évaluer.

3. Les prix de vente et les loyers arbitrairement fixés et s'écartant de ceux fournis par la loi de l'offre et de la demande ne seront pas pris en considération. Tels seraient les loyers et les prix de vente influencés par la loi sur le moratorium ou arrêtés sans le libre consentement du propriétaire.

Seront par contre prises en considération les ventes non visées par des lois et mesures restrictives et légalement conclues sans obtention d'une autorisation spéciale. Les prix de vente de biens ruraux de petite superficie ne constitueront cependant qu'une base indicative pour l'estimation d'immeubles d'étendue plus considérable.

4. Dans les localités où des ventes d'immeubles ruraux n'auraient pas eu lieu dans les trois dernières années, on se basera sur les prix et loyers des régions se trouvant dans des conditions économiques analogues ou, à défaut, sur la productivité des biens à

estimer. On entend par productivité le rendement moyen d'une propriété d'après le système de culture (semis, rotation, jachère, intensité) employé d'ordinaire dans les propriétés de même genre dans la même région.

S'il s'agit de petites propriétés paysannes on se basera sur les systèmes de culture employés dans la région dans des conditions normales.

5. Les bâtiments ruraux ne seront estimés séparément que s'ils représentent un capital indépendant du capital de l'exploitation agricole. Par exemple, seront estimées les habitations des propriétaires et les installations d'industries rurales (moulins, laiterie, caves).

N'entreront pas dans l'estimation spéciale les écuries, les dépôts, les habitations des ouvriers ou des métayers, les installations d'arrosage, etc. Pour l'estimation de constructions rurales dans les localités où les bases du prix marchand ou du loyer feraient défaut, on se basera sur les prix des bâtiments situés dans la ville la plus proche, en tenant compte d'une diminution due à l'éloignement de cette ville.

Les terres affectées actuellement au jardinage ou à d'autres exploitations agricoles, seront évaluées comme terrains de constructions, si elles sont comprises dans le plan des villes et faubourgs.

6. Dans l'estimation des propriétés rurales on ne prendra pas en considération les constructions qui auraient été faites après la dépossession du propriétaire.

7. Dans les localités où il existe un nombre considérable de bâtiments à évaluer se trouvant dans des conditions identiques, on pourra procéder à l'éstimation globale de ces biens, en estimant quelques-uns de ces bâtiments seulement et en comparant la valeur actuelle avec celle inscrite dans les régistres de l'impôt foncier.

Au cas où cette comparaison présenterait un certain écart, on établira un coéfficient à appliquer à tous les bâtiment du même type situés dans la même localité et dans les mêmes conditions.

8. Si le prix d'estimation d'une habitation ou d'un bâtiment à compenser en Turquie est de plus de 10% inférieur à la valeur inscrite sur les registres dressés consécutivement à la loi du 5 février 1328 relative à l'enregistrement des biens immobiliers, le Gouvernement turc aura la faculté de faire excepter ces biens de la compensation ou de les acquérir au prix porté sur les dits registres diminué de 10%.

De même, si le prix d'estimation d'un terrain de construction ou d'un bien rural est de plus de 50% inférieur au prix d'avant guerre, le Gouvernement turc aura la faculté de la faire excepter de la compensation ou de l'acquérir à la moitié du prix d'avant guerre.

9. En ce qui concerne spécialement les biens situés en Thrace orientale et dans la presqu'île de Vourla, seront appliquées les dispositions suivantes:

Si le prix d'estimation d'une habitation ou d'un bâtiment est de plus de 10% au-dessous de la valeur inscrite sur les registres dressés consécutivement à la loi turque du 5 février 1328, le Gouvernement hellénique aura la faculté de le faire excepter de la compensation en exprimant son intention à ce sujet dans un délai maximum d'un mois.

Il en sera de même des terrains de construction et des biens ruraux dont le prix d'estimation serait de plus de 50% inférieur au prix d'avant-guerre.

La valeur des biens qui seraient ainsi exceptés de la compensation fera l'objet d'un compte spécial qui sera réglé par priorité dans un délai maximum d'un mois et en sus des sommes à verser, s'il y a lieu, par le Gouvernement héllénique à titre de solde débiteur de la compensation.

10. Les forêts seront estimées d'après leur capacité de rendement, en tenant compte de leur éloignement des centres de communications.

11. L'estimation des terrains à bâtir des zones incendiées de Salonique et de Smyrne sera faite sur la base des prix actuels de ces terrains, les prix moyens obtenus par les ventes aux enchères dans chaque secteur étant considérés, à titre indicatif, comme base de cette estimation.

12. Pour l'estimation des usines, fabriques, mines et pêcheries, on prendra comme base des éléments spéciaux à déterminer par une commission composée de deux techniciens nommés par chacune des deux Hautes Parties et d'un troisième choisi d'un commun accord parmi les ressortissants d'un pays neutre.

Fait à Athènes, en double exemplaire, le 1er décembre 1926.

P. A. Argyropoulos.
Saradjoglou Chukri.

Protocole Final

I

Les deux gouvernements s'engagent à prendre les dispositions nécessaires afin que la ratification de l'accord ne soit pas différée au delà du mois de janvier prochain.

Les soussignés conviennent cependant de ce qui suit:

a) Les articles 9, 10 et 13 de l'accord seront mis en vigueur aussitôt après sa signature.

b) La Commission mixte pourra procéder avant la ratification de l'accord à la constitution des équipes prévues par l'article 14, ainsi qu'à tous travaux préliminaires de l'estimation.

c) Les deux gouvernements se réservent d'examiner ensemble l'opportunité de faire commencer, sous certaines conditions, l'estimation des biens se trouvant en leur possession dans quelques localités avant l'échange des ratifications.

d) Il sera versé au Gouvernement turc par le Gouvernement hellénique, sans attendre la ratification, une somme de quinze millions de drachmes à valoir sur les revenus des biens turcs encaissés par le fisc hellénique. Le Gouvernement hellénique aura cependant la faculté de reporter ultérieurement cette somme au compte des paiements qu'il aura à faire en exécution de l'article 8 de l'accord.

II

Les biens visés par l'article 2 de l'accord ne devant entrer en compensation que jusqu'à concurrence de la valeur des biens que le Gouvernement hellénique acquerra suivant l'article premier, il est entendu que les immeubles qui, restés éventuellement en dehors de la compensation en Turquie, devraient être rendus à leurs propriétaires, seront situés dans une seule région d'accès facile pour les ressortissants hellènes.

III

Toutes sommes adjugées par des décisions définitives du Tribunal arbitral gréco-turc dans des matières rentrant dans la sphère d'application des articles 65 et 66 du Traité de Paix de Lausanne, pris en combinaison avec les dispositions de l'accord conclu ce jour, seront portées au compte de compensation et liquidation prévu dans l'article 6 dudit accord, tant que le compte en question n'aura pas été clos.

IV

Les questions de principe présentant quelque importance et qui pourraient surgir au sein de la Commission mixte à l'occasion des attributions nouvelles que lui confère l'accord signé ce jour et qu'elle n'avait pas à la conclusion de ce dernier sur la base des actes antérieurs fixant sa compétence, seront soumises à l'arbitrage du président du Tribunal arbitral gréco-turc, siégeant à Constantinople. Les sentences de l'arbitre seront obligatoires.

V

Les deux Hautes Parties contractantes sont d'accord pour déclarer que, conformément à l'article 6 de la Convention relative à l'établissement et à la compétence judiciaire signée le 24 juillet 1923, et sous réserve des dispositions de l'Accord signé en date de ce jour, aucun ressortissant turc en Grèce et aucun ressortissant hellène en Turquie ne pourra être exproprié de ses biens que pour cause légalement reconnue d'utilité publique et moyennant une juste et préalable indemnité.

VI

Le présent acte fait partie intégrante de l'accord signé ce jour à Athènes et sera ratifié en même temps que ce dernier.

En foi de quoi les plénipotentiaires respectifs ont signé le présent protocole.

Fait à Athènes en double exemplaire le 1er décembre 1926.

P. A. Argyropoulos.
Saradjoglou Chukri.

Déclaration

I

Les soussignés, agissant en vertu de leurs pleins pouvoirs, déclarent, au nom de leurs gouvernements respectifs, que l'accord conclu à Athènes en date de ce jour remplace un des actes signés à Angora, le 21 juin 1925 l'Accord relatif aux biens des Turcs en Grèce et des Hellènes en Turquie.

II

Les Protocoles sous N[os] I et II signés à ladite date à Angora, ainsi que l'acte dit "Procès-verbal de signature," dont maintenus dans la mesure où ils ne sont pas modifiés par le nouvel accord.

Il est cependant bien entendu que le premier paragraphe du protocole sous N° II est maintenu intact.

III

Les dispositions arrêtées à Angora le 21 juin 1925 en vue de l'application des articles 2 et 16 de la Convention signée à Lausanne le 30 janvier 1923, seront soumises à la Commission mixte pour revêtir la forme de résolution de cette commission dans l'intervalle qui doit s'écouler entre la ratification de l'accord par les pouvoirs compétents des deux pays et l'échange des instruments de ratification.

Etant donné que l'acte contenant les disposition relatives à l'article 16 précité se réfère à l'Accord signé à Angora le 21 juin 1925, quant au mode de fixation et de payement de l'indemnité à allouer aux propriétaires des immeubles à exproprier, il est entendu que les clauses de cet ancien accord réglant les points dont il s'agit seront intercalées, dans le texte de la résolution y relative de la Commission mixte.

Il est également bien entendu qu'en attendant les résolutions de la Commission mixte, il ne sera procédé de part et d'autre à aucune mesure ou acte quelconque pouvant aggraver l'état de choses actuel, soit au point de vue de la situation personnelle des individus visés par les dites résolutions, soit à celui de leurs biens et intérêts.

IV

En ce qui concerne l'évaluation de propriétés qui, d'après l'article IV, alinéa 4, de la résolution interprétative de l'article 16 de la Convention du 30 janvier 1923, doit être éventuellement faite à l'expiration de quatre ans après la mise en vigueur de la dite résolution, par les soins de la Commission mixte, il est convenu que les deux gouvernements auront recours pour faire remplir cette mission, au cas où la Commission mixte viendrait à terminer sa tâche dans l'intervalle, à une commission composée d'un membre turc, d'un membre hellène et d'un président ressortissant d'une Puissance demeurée neutre pendant la guerre de 1914 à 1918, lequel sera choisi d'un commun accord ou, en cas de divergence, par la Cour fédérale suisse, si elle y consent.

En foi de quoi les plénipotentiaires respectifs, dont les plein pouvoirs ont été reconnus en bonne et due forme, ont signé la présente déclaration qui fait partie intégrante de l'accord signé ce jour à Athènes et sera ratifiée en même temps que ce dernier.

Fait à Athènes en double exemplaire le 1er décembre 1928.

P. A. Argyropoulos.
Djevad.

Protocole N° I

Le terme "personne morale" mentionné dans l'accord relatif aux biens signé aujourd'hui comprend l'Union et Progrès, les Sociétés commerciales, industrielles et financières, y compris les sociétés de transport et d'assurance, ainsi qui toutes autres associations et personnes morales.

Les actes de procuration présentés par les fondés de pouvoir des propriétaires des biens, dont la restitution est prévue dans le susdit accord, seront légalisés le plus promptement possible par les gouvernements respectifs, la légalisation ne se rapportant qu'à la signature ou au sceau apposé sur ces actes. Tout vérification concernant la nationalité du propriétaire ou le fait par lui d'avoir quitté la Grèce avant le 18 octobre 1912, ou d'avoir résidé de tout temps en dehors de la Grèce, sera faite indépendemment de la légalisation des dits actes de procuration.

En ce qui concerne la "Liste civile," les deux gouvernements sont d'accord pour soumettre cette question à un arbitrage, ou bien pour la résoudre ultérieurement par des négociations directes.

Fait à Angora, en double exemplaire, le 21 juin 1925.

G. A. Exintaris.
M. Hamdi.

Protocole N° II

Tous les musulmans ayant quitté depuis le 18 octobre 1912 les territoires de la Grèce, dont les habitants musulmans doivent être échangés, sont compris dans l'échange par application de l'article 3 de la Convention de Lausanne, nonobstant toutes formalités qu'ils aient pu remplir en exécution de traités ou conventions alors existants et notamment l'option en faveur de la nationalité turque qu'ils aient pu exercer en conformité du traité d'Athènes.

Toutefois, les personnes qui, ayant quitté les territoires susmentionnés avant la dite date du 18 octobre 1912, mais qui seraient rendus, depuis cette date, dans leurs pays d'origine pour y faire un court séjour, sans l'intention de s'y fixer à nouveau, ni conserver leur ancienne nationalité hellénique, ne rentrent pas dans les dispositions de l'alinéa précédent.

Le fait de s'être muni après l'année 1918 d'un passeport hellénique pour se rendre en Grèce dans les conditions qui précèdent ne constitue pas en soi une preuve que les intéressés ont conservé la nationalité hellénique, à moins d'être corroboré par d'autres faits, tels que d'avoir séjourné dans le pays pendant plus d'une année, y avoir participé à la vie politique comme électeur ou éligible, accepté des fonctions ou charges publiques, procédé à l'achat ou la vente d'immeubles en qualité de ressortissant hellène, ainsi que d'avoir esté en justice ou figuré, en cette même qualité, dans un acte authentique notarié ou administratif.

Fait à Angora, en double exemplaire, le 21 juin 1925.

G. A. Exintaris.
M. Hamdi.

Procès-Verbal de Signature

Désireux de faciliter la mise à exécution de l'accord relatif aux biens des ressortissants turcs, sis en Grèce, et des ressortissants hellènes, sis en Turquie, signé ce jour entre le Gouvernement hellénique et le Gouvernement turc, et d'éviter, dans toute la mesure du possible, des difficultés d'application et d'interprétation du dit accord, ainsi que du Protocole relatif à l'interprétation du terme "personnes morales" signé le même jour entre les deux Gouvernements et de la résolution à prendre par la Commission mixte concernant l'application de l'article 16 de la Convention sur l'Échange des Populations turques et grecques, laquelle d'un commun accord des deux Gouvernements turc et hellénique sera soumise à la Commission mixte E.P. aux fins d'être revêtue de la forme de résolution de la dite Commission, les Plénipotentiaires soussignés des deux Gouvernements susmentionés ont convenu de ce qui suit:

I

Les Gouvernements turc et hellénique s'engagent à soumettre l'accord relatif aux biens susindiqués à la ratification de leur Parlement respectif aussitôt que faire se pourra.

En attendant cette ratification et en prévision d'un retard éventuel dans celle-ci, ils s'engagent:

1. A payer en leur totalité les revenus encaissés aux ayants-

droit, tels qu'ils sont prévus par l'accord sur les biens dans l'espace d'un an à partir de la signature de cet accord.

2. A échanger dans un délai de deux mois également à partir de la signature du même accord, la liste des biens que chacun des deux Etats voudra acquérir.

Pour ce qui est des biens non compris dans les listes précitées, ils seront restitués à leurs propriétaires dans un délai de 4 mois à partir de l'échange des listes en question. Toutefois les biens ainsi restitués ne pourront être éventuellement aliénés par leurs propriétaires qu'après la ratification de l'accord par les deux Parlements turc et grec.

II

Dans le but de faciliter la politique économique des deux pays il est convenu d'étendre également le droit d'acquisition de biens immobiliers conféré aux deux Gouvernements signataires pour l'accord susmentionné aux mines que peuvent posséder les ressortissants de chacun des deux États sur le territoire de l'autre et qui pourront être acquiquises par les Gouvernements en question suivant les modes et conditions prévus par l'accord.

III

Il est entendu que le protocole N° 1 relatif à l'interprétation du terme "personnes morales" ne concerne en aucune façon les différents biens Vakoufs situés sur le territoire hellénique et relevant du ci-devant ministère de l'Evkaf, la question ne se posant pas à leur sujet, attendu qu'elle a été définitivement tranchée par la Convention sur l'échange des populations grecques et turques. Il va de soi que le protocole susmentionné ne concerne pas non plus les biens de toute nature appartenant aux communautés visées dans les articles 8 et 9 de ladite convention sur l'échange qui prescrit leur mode de liquidation.

IV

Les deux gouvernements s'engagent à entrer en pourparlers, après l'expiration du délai de six mois prévu dans l'article 4 de la résolution à prendre par la Commission mixte concernant l'application de l'article 16 de la Convention de Lausanne, pour la remise des listes des personnes dont le retour sera autorisé aux fins de règlement du statut personnel des personnes visées dans ledit article et qui ne bénéficieraient pas du droit de retour. Toutefois, il est d'ores et déjà entendu que ce règlement ne pourra en aucun cas avoir pour effet de porter une atteinte ni une déchéance quelconque dans les droits patrimoniaux en général et, plus spécialement, dans les droits de succession desdites personnes.

Fait à Angora, en double exemplaire, le 21 juin 1925.

G. A. EXINTARIS.
M. HAMDI.

EXTRAIT DE LA LETTRE ÉCHANGÉE ENTRE LL. EE. MM. ARGYROPOULOS ET SARADJOGLOU CHUKRI BEY

Athènes, le 1er Décembre 1926.

Monsieur le Ministre,

J'ai l'honneur d'accuser réception de la lettre que vous avez bien voulu m'adresser en date de ce jour et qui est ainsi conçue:

Monsieur le Délégué,

....

....

3) Les deux derniers paragraphes sou Nos III et IV du "Procès-verbal de signature" du 21 juin 1925 qui ont trait à la Convention d'Echange sont les seules dispositions de cet acte qui, n'ayant pas été modifiées, doivent être soumises à la ratification des pouvoirs compétents dans les deux pays.

Veuillez agréer, Monsieur le Délégué, les assurances de ma haute considération.

Je m'empresse de déclarer à mon tour que je suis entièrement d'accord avec vous sur les trois points qui précèdent.

Veuillez agréer, Monsieur le Ministre, les assurances de ma haute considération.

SARADJOGLOU CHUKRI.

LETTRE DE GARANTIE DU PRÉSIDENT DE LA COMMISSION FINANCIÈRE INTERNATIONALE EN GRÈCE AU MINISTRE DE TURQUIE À ATHÈNES

Athènes, le 16 Février 1927.

No 196.

Monsieur le Ministre,

J'ai l'honneur de vous informer que la Commission Financière Internationale a reçu du Gouvernement Hellénique le mandat ir-

Article 3

Toutes oppositions faites par les deux Gouvernements sur les dépôts de toute nature, actuellement existant auprès des Banques, seront levées dans les quinze jours, suivant la date de la signature de la présente Convention et lesdits dépôts seront restitués à leurs ayants-droit, la Commission Mixte pouvant à cet effet prêter, le cas échéant, ses bons offices aux intéressés.

Article 4

Les deux Gouvernements confient aux trois Membres neutres de la Commission Mixte d'Échange le soin d'émettre immédiatement leur avis sur la solution de la question de la liquidation des biens des échangeables parmi lesquels sont comprises les réclamations sur la dîme des tabacs et les coffresforts au sujet des échangeables.

Ils s'engagent à faire connaître leur adhésion dans le plus bref délai et avant de soumettre le présent accord à la ratification.

Chapitre II

BIENS DES BÉNÉFICIAIRES DE LA DÉCLARATION IX

Article 5

Les biens meubles et immeubles appartenant aux Musulmans, bénéficiaires de la Déclaration IX passent, en toute propriété, au Gouvernement hellénique, exception faite des biens immeubles qui ont été restitués à leurs propriétaires et qui se trouvant effectivement en leur possession et jouissance.

Article 6

Les biens meubles et immeubles appartenant aux Grecs, bénéficiaires de la Déclaration IX, passent, en toute propriété, au Gouvernement turc.

Chapitre III

BIENS DES RESSORTISSANTS TURCS

Article 7

Les biens immeubles appartenant aux Musulmans, ressortissants turcs, situés en Grèce, passent, en toute propriété, au Gouvernement hellénique, exception faite des biens immeubles qui ont été restitués à leurs propriétaires et qui se trouvent effectivement en leur possession et jouissance.

Passent également en la propriété du Gouvernement hellénique les meubles des ressortissants turcs saisis et liquidés postérieurement à la mise en vigueur du Traité de Lausanne.

Il demeure entendu que les meubles existant dans les immeubles qui passent en la propriété du Gouvernement hellénique, en vertu de l'alinéa 1, seront laissés à la libre disposition de leurs propriétaires.

Tous autres biens, droits et intérêts, non visés spécialement dans les alinéas précédents du présent article, continueront à être régis par les dispositions y relatives du Traité de Lausanne et notamment celles contenues dans les articles 65 et 66 dudit Traité.

CHAPITRE IV

BIENS DES RESSORTISSANTS HELLÈNES

ARTICLE 8

Les biens immeubles appartenant aux ressortissants hellènes et situés hors de la zone d'Istanbul exceptés de l'échange passent, en toute propriété, au Gouvernement turc.

Passent également en la propriété du Gouvernement turc les meubles des ressortissants hellènes saisis et liquidés postérieurement à la mise en vigueur du Traité de Lausanne.

Il demeure entendu que les meubles existant dans les immeubles qui passent en la propriété du Gouvernement turc, en vertu de l'alinéa 1, seront laissés à la libre disposition de leurs propriétaires.

Tous autres biens, droits et intérêts, non visés spécialement dans les alinéas précédents du présent article, continueront à être régis par les dispositions y relatives du Traité de Lausanne et notamment celles contenues dans les articles 65 et 66 dudit Traité.

ARTICLE 9

Le droit de propriété des ressortissants hellènes sur leurs biens immeubles situés dans la zone d'Istanbul, exceptés de l'échange, n'est, en aucune façon, affecté par les dispositions de la présente Convention.

Dans les deux mois au plus tard à partir de la mise en vigueur de la présente Convention, les ressortissants hellènes dont les biens immeubles ont été frappes d'une mesure de saisie, séquestre ou occupation quelconque, seront rentrés, personnellement ou par l'intermédiaire de leurs représentants légaux, dans la libre et pleine possession de leurs biens et toute mesure de la susdite nature sera immédiatement levée.

Si les mesures ci-devant énoncées ont été prises en raison de la nationalité hellénique du propriétaire et dans le cas où la nationalité hellénique figure dans le titre de propriété émanant du Cadastre du pays, la levée de ces mesures ainsi que la réintégration du propriétaire dans la libre et pleine possession et jouissance de ces biens ne pourront être différées à aucun titre.

Toutes les contestations relatives aux conditions suivant lesquelles la nationalité hellénique ou turque aurait pu être acquise en conformité des Traités, Conventions et Accords en vigueur entre les deux Pays seront définitivement tranchées par décision des Membres neutres de la Commission Mixte.

Au surplus, les deux Parties Contractantes sont entièrement d'accord pour reconnaître que les dispositions de cette Convention, notamment l'article 12, ne doivent recevoir aucune interprétation susceptible d'augmenter ou de diminuer le nombre des ressortissants hellènes dont les biens se trouvent dans la région d'Istanbul, excepté de l'échange, tels qu'ils sont définis par les stipulations contractuelles autres que la présente Convention.

Il demeure entendu que la nationalité hellénique reconnue aux échangeables n'est d'effet pour ce qui concerne la restitution d'immeubles prévue dans la présente Convention.

Les décisions qui pourraient être prises par les Membres Neutres de la Commission Mixte en exécution des dispositions contenues dans cet article, ne pourrent être opposables à quiconque à propos de toute autre litige qui viendrait à surgir en dehors de la sphère d'application des dispositions de la présente Convention.

CHAPITRE V

BIENS DES ÉTABLIS D'ISTANBUL

ARTICLE 10

La Turquie reconnaît la qualité d' 'établis' à tous les Grecs orthodoxes, ressortissants turcs actuellement présents dans la zone d'Istanbul exceptée de l'échange, quels que soient la date de leur arrivée à Istanbul et le lieu de leur naissance.

Cette même qualité d' 'établis' est reconnue aux personnes non échangeables ayant quitté Istanbul, munies de passeports émanant des autorités de la République turque.

Les femmes, enfants mineurs des deux sexes et filles non mariées, même majeures, dont le chef de famille est reconnu établi aux termes des alinéas précédents de cet article ont le droit de rejoindre leur chef de famille à Istanbul. Les mères veuves dont le fils majeur est reconnu établi dans les conditions ci-dessus sont également autorisées à le rejoindre à Istanbul.

Toutes facilités seront accordées par le Gouvernement turc pour le retour dans la zone d'Istanbul exceptée de l'échange, des personnes visées dans les alinéas précédents.

Les femmes, enfants mineurs des deux sexes et filles non mariées même majeures, reconnus établis aux termes de l'alinéa du présent article et dont le chef de famille se trouve actuellement hors d'Istanbul, ne seront pas tenues de quitter l'endroit de leur séjour.

La distribution des certificats d'établis à toutes les catégories de personnes désignées ci-dessus est confiée aux Membres neutres de la Commission Mixte, suivant telles forme et procédure qu'il leur appartient d'adopter.

ARTICLE 11

Toutes les mesures qui ont entravé l'exercice des droits garantis aux établis par les Conventions et Accords conclus, notamment celles concernant le droit de contracter mariage, le droit d'acquérir et de vendre des propriétés, le droit de libre circulation, ainsi que toutes autres restrictions ordonnées par les autorités turques à l'égard des personnes visées dans l'article précédent, seront levées dès la mise en vigueur de la Présente Convention sans attendre la distribution des certificats d'établis, prévue dans le dernier alinéa de l'article précédent.

ARTICLE 12

Les biens meubles et immeubles ci-dessous énoncés passent en toute propriété au Gouvernement turc:

1°) Les biens meubles et immeubles sis en Turquie, appartenant aux Grecs orthodoxes, ressortissants turcs, non-échangeables, ayant quitté la zone d'Istanbul, exceptés de l'échange et privés du droit de retour aux termes de l'article 28 de la présente Convention.

2°) Les biens meubles et immeubles sis hors de la zone d'Istanbul, exceptés de l'échange, appartenant aux établis grecs présents dans la zone d'Istanbul ou aux personnes bénéficiant du droit de retour aux termes de l'article 10 de la présente Convention.

Article 13

Le droit de propriété des établis grecs présents dans la zone d'Istanbul, exceptés de l'échange ainsi que des personnes bénéficiant du droit de retour aux termes de l'article 10 de la présente Convention sur leurs biens meubles et immeubles sis dans la zone d'Istanbul exceptés de l'échange n'est en aucun sens affecté par les dispositions de la présente Convention.

Tous saisie ou séquestre opérés sur les biens mentionnés dans l'alinéa précédent de cet article seront levés sans aucun retard; la réintégration du propriétaire ou de son représentant légal dans la libre et pleine possession et jouissance de ces biens ne pouvant être différés à aucun titre.

CHAPITRE VI

BIENS DES ÉTABLIS MUSULMANS DE LA THRACE OCCIDENTALE

Article 14

La Grèce reconnaît la qualité d'établis à tous les Musulmans, ressortissants hellènes, actuellement présents dans la zone de la Thrace Occidentale exceptée de l'échange quels que soient la date de leur arrivée en Thrace Occidentale et le lieu de naissance.

Cette même qualité d' 'établis' est reconnue aux personnes non-échangeables ayant quitté la Thrace Occidentale munies de passeports émanant des autorités de la République hellénique.

Les femmes, enfants mineurs des deux sexes et filles mariées, même majeures, dont le chef de famille est reconnu aux termes des alinéas précédents de cet article, ont le droit de rejoindre leur chef de famille en Thrace Occidentale. Les mères veuves dont le fils majeur est reconnu établi dans les conditions ci-dessus sont également autorisées à le rejoindre en Thrace Occidentale.

Toutes facilités seront accordées par le Gouvernement hellénique pour le retour dans la zone de la Thrace occidentale exceptée de l'échange des personnes visées dans les alinéas précédents.

Les femmes, enfants mineurs des deux sexes et filles non mariées même majeures aux termes de l'alinéa du présent article et dont le chef de famille se trouve actuellement hors de la Thrace Occidentale, ne seront pas tenus de quitter l'endroit de leur séjour.

La distribution des certificats d'établis à toutes les catégories de personnes désignées ci-dessus est confiée aux Membres neutres de la Commission Mixte, suivant telles forme et procédure qu'il leur appartient d'adopter.

ARTICLE 15

Toutes les mesures qui ont entravé l'exercice des droits garanti aux établis par les Conventions et Accords conclus, notamment celles concernant le droit de contracter mariage, le droit d'acquérir et de vendre des propriétés, le droit de libre circulation ainsi que toutes autres restrictions ordonnées par les autorités helléniques à l'égard des personnes visées dans l'article précédent, seront levées dès la mise en vigueur de la présente Convention sans attendre la distribution des certificats d'établis prévue dans le dernier alinéa de l'article précédent.

ARTICLE 16

Les biens meubles et immeubles ci-dessous énoncés passent en toute propriété au Gouvernement hellénique:

1°) Les meubles et immeubles sis en Grèce appartenant aux Musulmans, ressortissants hellènes, non-échangeables, ayant quitté la zone de la Thrace Occidentale exceptée de l'échange et privés du droit de retour aux termes de l'article 28 de la présente Convention.

2°) Les biens meubles et immeubles sis hors de la zone de la Thrace Occidentale exceptée de l'échange et appartenant aux établis musulmans présents dans cette même zone de la Thrace Occidentale ou aux personnes bénéficiant du droit de retour aux termes de l'article 14 de la présente Convention.

3°) Les biens sis en Thrace Occidentale et figurant sur la liste remise par la Délégation hellénique à la Commission Mixte en date du 18 juin 1927.

4°) Les propriétés d'une étendue totale de 7000 stremmas qui figurent sur une autre liste complémentaire ci-jointe, pour autant que ces terres se trouvent déjà occupées.

ARTICLE 17

Sous réserve des dispositions contenues dans les alinéas 3 et 4 de l'article 16, le droit de propriété des établis musulmans présents dans la zone de la Thrace Occidentale exceptée de l'échange, ainsi que des personnes bénéficiant du droit de retour aux termes de l'article 14 de la présente Convention sur leurs biens meubles et immeubles sis dans la zone de la Thrace Occidentale exceptée de l'échange, n'est en aucun sens affecté par les dispositions de la présente Convention.

Tous saisie ou sequestre opérés sur les biens mentionnés dans l'alinéa précédent de cet article seront levés sans aucun retard la réintégration du propriétaire ou de son représentant légal dans la libre et pleine possession et jouissance de ses biens ne pouvant être différée à aucun titre.

CHAPITRE VII

REVENUS OU LEURS EQUIVALENTS, INDEMNITÉS

ARTICLE 18

Les deux Gouvernements renoncent réciproquement à toutes réclamations du chef des revenus ou leurs équivalents dûs pour l'occupation des biens appartenant à l'une quelconque des catégories ci-dessus énoncées (Chapitre 2, 3, 4, 5 et 6).

ARTICLE 19

Il incombera aux deux Gouvernements de régler directement avec leurs propres ressortissants la question de loyers et autres indemnités dues en vertu de l'article 3 de la décision 28 de la Commission Mixte.

CHAPITRE VIII

VERSEMENT DES SOMMES ET INDEMNISATIONS

ARTICLE 20

Le Gouvernement hellénique mettra à la disposition de la Commission Mixte dans le mois qui suivra la mise en vigueur de la présente Convention une somme de quatre cent vingt cinq mille (425.000) Livres sterling.

De cette somme la Commission Mixte affectera:

a) Cent cinquante mille (150.000) Livres sterling on vue d'indemniser par ses soins, les établis grecs ressortissants turcs présents à Istanbul ainsi que les personnes bénéfiant du droit de retour aux termes de l'article 10 de la présente Convention, pour les biens qu'ils possèdent hors de la zone d'Istanbul exceptée de l'échange.

b) Cent cinquante mille (150.000) Livres Sterling en vue d'indemniser par ses soins les établis musulmans ressortissants Hellènes dont les biens passent en la propriété du Gouvernement hellénique en vertu de l'article 16 de la présente Convention. La distribution des sommes destinées pour l'indemnisation des personnes visées ci-dessus par les alinéas 1 et 2 du présent article sera opérée par les organes de la Commission Mixte suivant une procédure sommaire et rapide qui sera fixée par elle.

Le solde s'élevant à Cent vingt cinq mille (125.000) Livres Sterling sera remis au Gouvernement Turc par la Commission Mixte, en trois versements. Le premier versement s'élevant à Soixante deux mille cinq cents (62.500) Livres Sterling sera effectué dans le mois qui suivra la mise en vigueur de la présente Convention; le deuxième versement s'élevant à Quarante sept mille cinq cents (47.500) Livres sterling aura lieu dès que les Membres Neutres de la Commission Mixte estimeront que toutes les propriétés appartenant aux ressortissants hellènes ont été restituées en conformité de l'article 9 de la présente Convention; le troisième et le dernier versement s'élevant à Quinze mille (15.00) Livres Sterling après constatation par les Membres Neutres de la Commission Mixte de l'exécution intégrale de toutes les charges et obligations incombant à la Turquie aux termes de la présente Convention.

A la suite du paiement des sommes dues par la Grèce en exécution des dispositions contenues dans le présent article la Grèce est libérée de toutes obligations résultant du fait de l'acquisition des propriétés, consenties à son profit aux termes de la présente Convention.

Article 21

La somme de Quatre cent vingt cinq mille (425.000) Livres Sterling que le Gouvernement Hellénique s'engage à mettre à la disposition de la Commission Mixte en vertu de l'article précédent et la somme de Quinze mille (15.000) Livres Sterling prévue dans le quatrième alinéa de l'article 22 de la présente Convention seront prélevées sur le montant de la somme de Cinq cent mille (500.000) Livres Sterling, cédée en garantie par la Grèce au Gouvernement Turc en conformité de l'article 6 de l'accord d'Athènes du ler décembre 1926 toutes formalités de rétrocession et remboursement à la Grèce du reliquat Soixante mille (60.000) Livres Sterling lui revenant devant être accomplies sans retard par les deux Gouvernements.

CHAPITRE IX

DISPOSITIONS SPÉCIALES

ARTICLE 22

En cas d'impossibilité de restitution d'un immeuble appartenant à l'une des catégories mentionnées dans les Chapitres 4, 5 et 6 de la présente Convention, les Gouvernements des Pays de la situation des immeubles ne pourront respectivement s'en rendre acquéreurs que dans des cas purement exceptionnels et après constatation par la Commission Mixte des circonstances rendant la restitution impossible. Après approbation de chaque cas par elle, la Commission Mixte procédera à l'évaluation du bien en question et indemnisera son propriétaire comme suit:

S'il s'agit d'un immeuble appartenant à un ressortissant Hellène, une somme égale au montant de l'estimation de l'immeuble sera prélevée, pour être payée à l'ayant-droit, sur le fond des quarante sept mille cinq cents (47.500) Livres Sterling se trouvant en la possession de la Commission Mixte et devant être versée au Gouvernement Turc dans les conditions prescrites à l'article 20 de la présente Convention.

S'il s'agit d'un immeuble appartenant à un établi Grec le prélèvement aura lieu sur le fond de quinze mille (15.000) Livres Sterling se trouvant entre les mains de la Commission Mixte pour être versé au Gouvernement Turc selon les prescriptions de l'article 20 susmentionné.

Le Gouvernement Hellénique s'engage à verser entre les mains de la Commission Mixte une somme de quinze mille (15.000) Livres Sterling à prélever selon les conditions prévues à l'article 21 de cette Convention qui sera destinée à indemniser le cas échéant les propriétaires des biens appartenant aux établis Musulmans de la Thrace Occidentale et dont l'acquisition serait autorisée conformément aux conditions et modalités prévues dans l'alinéa 1er du présent article.

ARTICLE 23

Les fonds mentionnés dans les alinéas 3 et 4 de l'article précédent étant constitués en garantie de l'exécution intégrale des clauses et disposition contenues dans la présente Convention, lesdits fonds devront être reconstitués sur demande des Membres Neutres de la Commission Mixte après chaque prélèvement effectué conformément aux prescriptions contenues dans l'article précédent, au moyen d'un versement qui sera égale au montant prélevé.

Chaque Gouvernement aura droit à se faire restituer le fond de quinze mille (15.000) Livres Sterling lui appartenant après constatation par les Membres Neutres de la Commission Mixte de l'exécution intégrale de toutes les charges et obligations lui incombant en vertu de la présente Convention.

Article 24

Sous réserve des dispositions de l'article 22 de la présente Convention le Gouvernement Turc est libéré de toutes les obligations résultant du fait de l'acquisition des propriétés consentie à son profit aux termes des dispositions de la présente Convention.

Article 25

Au cas où des immeubles visés aux articles 12 al. 1 et 16 al. 1 de la présente Convention n'auraient pas été éventuellement occupés par les Gouvernements respectifs, à la date de la mise en vigueur de la présente Convention, il ne pourra être procédé à leur saisie, séquestre ou occupation qu'après examen et approbation préalables de chaque cas par la Commission Mixte.

Aucune saisie, séquestre ou occupation ne pourra être fait après la clôture des travaux de la Commission Mixte.

Article 26

A la demande des intéressés et sous réserve des dispositions du droit commun et de celles relatives aux biens passant en la propriété du Gouvernement Hellénique et du Gouvernement Turc, les autorités cadastrales dans les deux pays sont tenues de procéder sans retard à toutes les formalités nécessaires, non accomplies jusqu'à ce jour, pour le transfert des biens sis respectivement à Istambul et en Thrace Occidentale et revenant soit à des ressortissants hellènes soit à des ressortissants turcs se trouvant en la possession effective de leurs biens, soit à des établis Grecs ou Musulmans, à la suite d'un héritage laissé par un non-échangeable.

CHAPITRE X

DISPOSITIONS GÉNÉRALES

ARTICLE 27

Le mot Istambul figurant dans la présente Convention désigne la ville de Constantinople telle qu'elle est indiquée à l'article 2 de la Convention sur l'échange des populations grecques et turques signée à Lausanne le 30 janvier 1923.

Les expressions bénéficiaires de la Déclaration IX, ressortissants turcs, ressortissants hellènes, établis grecs d'Istambul, établis musulmans de la Thrace Occidentale, sont applicables aux personnes physiques aussi bien qu'aux personnes morales.

ARTICLE 28

Sont privés du droit de retour, dans le sens de la présente Convention, les Grecs orthodoxes ressortissants turcs non-échangeables actuellement absents et ayant quitté Istambul sans être munis de passeports émanant des autorités de la République Turque, de même que les Musulmans ressortissants hellènes non-échangeables actuellement absents et ayant quitté la Thrace Occidentale sans être munis de passeports émanant des autorités de la République Hellénique.

Les deux Gouvernements déclarent reconnaître respectivement la nationalité hellénique aux Grecs ressortissants Turcs d'Istambul privés de droit de retour conformément à l'alinéa précédent et aux Grecs bénéficiaires de la Déclaration IX, et la nationalité turque aux Musulmans ressortissants Hellènes de la Thrace Occidentale, privés de droit de retour conformément à l'alinéa précédent et aux Musulmans bénéficiaires de la Déclaration IX.

Les personnes en question n'encourent, dans leurs pays d'origine, aucune déchéance du fait de ce changement de nationalité, notamment en ce qui concerne leurs droits patrimoniaux quelconques, le droit de succession, le droit d'ester en justice, etc. Le changement de nationalité de ces personnes entraine le changement de la nationalité de leurs femmes et enfants présents à Istambul ou en Thrace Occidentale, à moins que la loi nationale de chaque pays ne s'y oppose.

ARTICLE 29

Sous réserve des disposition de droit commun et de celles de l'article 25 de la présente Convention, il ne sera procédé à l'avenir à aucune saisie ou mesures restrictives quelconques à l'égard des biens dont la propriété n'aura pas été transférée à l'un des deux Gouvernements en vertu de la présente Convention, et leurs propriétaires seront libres de jouir et disposer de leurs biens et de les administrer comme bon leur semble.

ARTICLE 30

Les termes actuellement et effectivement figurant dans la présente Convention se rapportent à la situation de fait existant à la date du 1er août 1929.

CHAPITRE XI

CLAUSES ARBITRALES

ARTICLE 31

L'application de la présente Convention est confiée par les deux Gouvernements à la Commission Mixte, qui constituera à cet effet les organes nécessaires.

ARTICLE 32

Les deux Gouvernements reconnaissant d'une manière générale la qualité d'arbitre à MM. les Membres Neutres de la Commission Mixte, dans tout différent qui pourrait surgir à l'avenir au sein de cette Commission relativement à l'interprétation et à l'application de la présente Convention, s'engagent d'ores et déjà à reconnaître sans discussion leurs décisions.

Tout différend ou litige qui pourrait survenir entre les deux Délégations Turque et Hellénique dans le domaine de l'application de la présente Convention sera ainsi définitivement résolu par les Membres Neutres de la Commission Mixte.

CHAPITRE XII

DISPOSITIONS FINALES

ARTICLE 33

Les lois, décrets, règlements, interprétations légales et officielles ou ordonnances et circulaires de toute sorte contraires aux dispositions contenues dans la présente Convention ou empêchant d'une manière quelconque son exécution intégrale sont abolis de plein droit dans les deux pays.

ARTICLE 34

La présente Convention sera ratifiée prenant ainsi force de loi dans les deux pays.

Toutes publications ou notifications requises par la législation des Pays respectifs seront faites pour sa mise en exécution immédiate.

L'échange des ratifications se fera à Athènes.

Ankara, le 10 juin 1930.

BIBLIOGRAPHY

The main sources for this study have been the unpublished *Procès-Verbaux* of the Mixed Commissions established under the Convention of Neuilly of 1919 concerning the Reciprocal and Voluntary Emigration of national minorities between Greece and Bulgaria and the Convention of Lausanne of 1923 concerning the exchange of Greek and Turkish populations. In addition to the *Procès-Verbaux* several other printed and unprinted reports, memoranda, documents, etc., of the Mixed Commissions and of governments and committees have been used by the writer. These are referred to in footnotes.

Several of the documents most important for our purpose are printed as appendices in the immediately preceding pages of the present volume. The *Official Journal* of the League of Nations is an important source of information with regard to the execution of the two Conventions considered in this study. References to its volumes from 1921 to 1930 are found in the notes.

Publications dealing with various aspects or parts of the subject of this study are the following:

ANDREADES, A., et autres. *Les Effets économiques et sociaux de la guerre en Grèce.* Yale University Press, 1929.

ANCEL, JACQUES. *La Macédoine, son evolution contemporaine.* Paris, 1930, Pp. 352.

DEIMEZIS, A. *Situation sociale créée en Grèce à la suite de l'échange des populations.* Paris, 1927. Pp. 83.

DEVEDJI, ALEXANDRE. *L'échange obligatoire des minorités grecques et turques en vertu de la Convention de Lausanne du 30 Janvier 1923.* Paris, 1929.

EDDY, CHARLES B. *Greece and the Greek Refugees.* London, 1931. Pp. 280.

GOUNARAKI, P. N. *An Address on the Treaty of Lausanne and in particular on the Convention concerning the Exchange of Populations* (in Greek), Athens, 1927. Pp. 39.

HADJOPULOS, ANGELOS. *Die Flüchtlingsfrage in Griechenland.* Athens, 1927. Pp. 150.

HOWLAND, CHARLES B. "Greece and the Greeks," "Greece and the Refugees." *Foreign Affairs,* April and July, 1926.

KIOSSEOGLOU, TH. P. *L'échange forcé des minorités d'après le Traité de Lausanne.* Nancy, 1926. Pp. 215.

League of Nations. *Greek Refugee Settlement.* Geneva, 1926. Pp. 216.

MEARS, E. C. *Greece Today.* Stanford University Press, 1929.

MORGENTHAU, H. *I was Sent to Athens.* New York, 1929. Pp. 327.

PALLIS, A. A. *Collection of Reciprocal Statistics concerning the Exchange of Populations and the Refugee Settlement with Analysis and Interpretation* (multigraphed—in Greek). Athens, 1929. Pp. 42.

————. "The Exchange of Populations in the Balkans." *The Nineteenth Century and After,* xcvii (1925), pp. 376-383.

————. "Racial Migrations in the Balkans during the years 1912-1924." *The Geographical Journal,* xlvi (1925), pp. 315-331.

PASVOLSKY, L. *Bulgaria's Economic Position.* The Brookings Institution, Washington, 1930. Pp. xiii, 409.

PROTONOTARIOS, A. B. *The Refugee Problem* (in Greek). Athens, 1929. Pp. 185.

SÉFÉRIADES, STÉLIO. "L'échange des populations." Académie de Droit International, *Recueil des cours,* 1928, iv, pp. 311-437.

Streit, Georg. *Der Lausanner Vertrag und der griechisch-türkische Bevölkerungsaustausch.* Berlin, 1929.

Tenekidis. "Les status des minorités et l'échange obligatoire des populations Grèco-Turques." *Revue générale de droit international public,* 1924.

Theotoka, M. G. *The Treaty Rights of Greeks in Turkey and of Turks in Greece* (in Greek). Athens, 1928. Pp. 19.

Tsouderos, E. I. *The Indemnification of the Exchangeables* (in Greek). Athens, 1927. Pp. 112.

Wurfbain, André. *L'échange Grèco-Bulgare des minorités ethniques.* Lausanne, 1930. Pp. 217.